Researching Cyber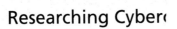

Anita Lavorgna · Thomas J. Holt
Editors

Researching Cybercrimes

Methodologies, Ethics, and Critical Approaches

Editors
Anita Lavorgna
Department of Sociology, Social Policy
and Criminology
University of Southampton
Southampton, UK

Thomas J. Holt
School of Criminal Justice
Michigan State University
East Lansing, MI, USA

ISBN 978-3-030-74836-4   ISBN 978-3-030-74837-1   (eBook)
https://doi.org/10.1007/978-3-030-74837-1

Cover design by eStudioCalamar

This Palgrave Macmillan imprint is published by the registered company Springer Nature Switzerland AG
The registered company address is: Gewerbestrasse 11, 6330 Cham, Switzerland

Preface

The wealth of data that is readily available online, whether through text-based or more image-driven social media platforms, presents substantial opportunities for researchers to investigate and assess a number of online behaviours like dating and political expression, along with deviant and criminal acts that are facilitated in part by technology.

In cyberspace, textual, visual or meta-data from content can be collected manually by researchers or through the use of automated programmes and tools. There is no real standard or consistent processes for the collection of online data, creating substantive variations in the practices researchers adopt. The data may then be analysed through qualitative or quantitative means informed by the researchers' experiences with and understanding of automated tools and hand coding strategies. Some of these approaches closely resemble long standing social science research methods, such as the use of interview protocols administered via Skype or instant messaging. Others often require innovative approaches that need cross-disciplinary knowledge of computational methods more common to computer science.

Additionally, ethical standards required to collect these data are still under development and vary by place. The guidelines used in traditional research methods may be inadequate to respond to the challenges and possibilities presented by online research, especially in a sensitive area such as cybercrimes.

It is not surprising that the unique and dynamic characteristics of online spaces demand multi- and inter-disciplinary methodological approaches. These conditions mean that certain approaches may be less effective, as there is generally poor communication within and across the social and technical sciences. The different lexicon and analytical frameworks applied may be viewed as incompatible, challenging the ability of researchers to collaborate or understand one another's research agendas. These issues can be exacerbated in cross-national contexts because of linguistic and cultural differences that may be present.

The absence of consensus regarding online methodologies and ethical standards is an issue that severely complicates academic research in the cybercrime arena. Thus, there is both an opportunity for and responsibility among researchers to develop a common language around online data use, including its ethical collection, the limitations and benefits of collection, and techniques for analysis. Such information is largely absent in any single textbook or edited volume to date, making it difficult to find a uniform set of insights into the nature of online data and its use in practice.

This edited book proposes to address this gap in the literature by offering a single volume that provides a state-of-the-art collection on the critical use of online data throughout its three parts (*Knowledge production and research datafication in cybercrime research*; *Methodologies and strategies for cybercrime research*; and *Geographies and cultures of ethics in cybercrime research*). This work will also provide a review of the ethics associated with the use of online data sources across various parts of the globe. The authors are drawn from multiple disciplines and nations, providing unique insights into the value and challenges evident in online data use for cybercrime scholarship.

By the end of the book, we hope you will be fascinated—as we are—by the possibilities cyberspace offers to the research community to further our understanding of complex societal issues. Also, we hope this book encourages a discussion on the importance of cross-disciplinary collaboration, which is at times complicated, but nonetheless increasingly necessary to meet the challenges of much cybercrime research.

Southampton, UK   Anita Lavorgna
East Lansing, USA   Thomas J. Holt

Acknowledgements

Thanks to my inspiring co-editor Tom, and to Dave and Russell among the others, to drag me, with their work, into the fascinating world of cybercrime research. And to all the contributors for making the preparation of this book a pleasant effort.

In these increasingly challenging times for early career researchers, international researchers and—more in general—researchers, my graduate students are a constant reminder of what academia can and should be. This book is for you.

—Anita Lavorgna

I would like to thank my co-editor, Anita, for all of her efforts with this work from start to finish. It would not have been possible without her dedication. I would also like to thank all of the contributors for this book for sharing their views and insights.

—Thomas J. Holt

Contents

Editors and Contributors

About the Editors

Anita Lavorgna is Associate Professor of Criminology at the University of Southampton (UK). Anita has an international research track record on and expertise in interdisciplinary research drawing together criminology, socio-legal studies and web science. She has worked extensively on cybercrime, serious and organised crime, and online social harms. Among her more recent publications are the textbook *Cybercrimes: Critical Issues in a Global Context* and the books *Medical Misinformation and Social Harm in Non-Science Based Health Practices: A Multidisciplinary Perspective* and *Information pollution as social harm: Investigating the digital drift of medical misinformation in a time of crisis*.

Thomas J. Holt is a Professor in the School of Criminal Justice at Michigan State University whose research focuses on cybercrime, cyberterrorism and the policy response to these phenomena. His work has appeared in a range of academic journals in criminology and criminal justice. Additionally, Dr. Holt has authored multiple textbooks and edited volumes in cybercrime. He is also the co-editor for the Studies on Cybercrime and Cybersecurity series (Palgrave). In addition, he regularly teaches courses in cybercrime, cyberwarfare and terrorism at the undergraduate and graduate level.

Contributors

Kacy Amory began the Criminology Ph.D. program in Fall of 2018 after completing her M.A. in Criminology from George Washington University and B.A. in Psychology from Old Dominion University. Her research interests include gender and crime, social media use, public perceptions of crime and online victimization.

Omar Arauza is a Graduate of the Department of Justice Studies programme at San Jose State University. His interests include rehabilitative justice and prosecutorial discretion. He is currently researching crime sentiments in media and works in expungement and peer-support-based re-entry services.

Mark Berry is a Lecturer of Criminology at Royal Holloway, University of London. His work focuses on drug markets and the use of technology in criminal activity. He earned his doctorate at Cardiff University where he was a Dawes scholar.

Russell Brewer is a Senior Lecturer in Criminology at the University of Adelaide. His research interests include cybercrime, youth delinquency, crime prevention and policing. He has published his research findings through several leading publication outlets, holds multiple nationally competitive grants, and has been called upon by government agencies both domestically and abroad to advise on policy.

George W. Burruss is an Associate Professor in and the Associate Department Chair of the Department of Criminology at the University of South Florida. He is also affiliated with Cyber Florida, the Center for Cybersecurity at the University of South Florida. He also serves as editor-in-chief for the *Journal of Crime & Justice*. His main research interests focus on criminal justice organizations and cybercrime. He received his doctorate in Criminology and Criminal Justice from the University of Missouri St. Louis.

Fabian Campbell-West is a Computer Scientist working in applied data science for startup companies. He specialises in data analytics for cybersecurity and computer vision applications. He has worked on diverse interdisciplinary criminology projects from monitoring websites for evidence of human trafficking; reviewing cybercrime forums performing automated analysis; and tracking pedestrian movements to help suicide prevention. As co-founder of Digitect he provides consultancy in software and data for open source intelligence and cybersecurity. He is also co-founder and Chief Technology Officer at Liopa, a venture capital-backed startup that uses artificial intelligence to provide automated lip reading as a service.

Helena Carrapico is Jean Monnet Chair in European Integration and Associate Professor in Criminology and International Relations at Northumbria University, where she is also Director of Research. Her research focuses on European Union Justice and Home Affairs governance, namely organised crime and cybercrime policies. She has published extensively on European internal security topics in journals such as the *Journal of Common Market Studies*; the *Journal of European Integration*; *European Foreign Affairs Review*; *Crime, Law and Social Change*; *European Security*; and *Global Crime*. Her most recent book *Brexit and Internal Security: Political and legal concerns in the context of the future UK–EU relationship* was published with Palgrave Macmillan in 2019.

Francisco J. Castro-Toledo is Assistant Professor of Criminal Law and Criminology at the Universidad Miguel Hernández in Elche, researcher at the CRÍMINA centre for the study and prevention of crime and CEO and co-founder of Plus Ethics. His current research interests focus on research designs in crime sciences, epistemology in social sciences and ethical analysis applied to criminological research. He has participated in more than fifteen international and national research projects on security and crime prevention. He has participated in some of the most important criminological and security conferences and has published in high impact scientific journals.

Lennon Yao-Chung Chang is a Senior Lecturer in Criminology in the School of Social Sciences, Monash University. He is a co-founder and vice-chairman of the Asia Pacific Association of Technology and Society. He is the Project Director of Strengthening Cyber capacity and Raising Cyber Awareness in the Indo-Pacific Region: Australia and Myanmar. He authored *Cybercrime in the Greater China Region: Regulatory Responses and Crime Prevention* (Edward Elgar, 2012). Together with Myanmar National Cyber Security Centre and Kenerllix, he initiated and founded "CyberBayKin", a cyberawareness campaign in Myanmar. Dr. Chang is particularly interested in the regulation and governance of cyberspace in the Asia-Pacific region.

Steven M. Chermak is a Professor in the School of Criminal Justice and studies firearms violence, school violence, terrorism and cybercrimes. He is a member of the DHS Center of Excellence (COE), NCITE and a past member of two other COEs, CAOE and START. He has been the PI for many projects funded by the National Institute of Justice and the Department of Homeland Security, including projects that examine the offending pathways of hate crime offenders and terrorists, and another that tests the application of life course theories to school shooters. He has been a central role in creating three open source databases, including the Extremist Crime Database (ECDB), the School Shooting Database (SSDB), and the CyberTerrorism Database (CTDB).

Yi Ting Chua is a Research Associate at the University of Cambridge, Cambridge Cybercrime Centre. Her research centres around the role of the Internet in criminal offending and is shaped primarily by the increasing role of technology and cyberspace in criminal and deviant behaviours. Her current work spans across three research areas: (1) individuals' pathway into cybercrime; (2) impact of social networks and structures on the evolution of subcultural values, beliefs, and behaviours; and (3) countermeasures against cybercrime.

Cassandra Cross is an Associate Professor in the School of Justice, Queensland University of Technology. In 2011, while working for the

Queensland Police Service, she was awarded a Churchill Fellowship to examine the prevention and support of online fraud victims worldwide. Since taking up her position at QUT in 2012, she has continued her research into fraud, publishing over 60 outputs across the policing, prevention, and victim support aspects of fraud. Further, she has been awarded over AUD$1.3million in funding, largely to drive her research in this area. She is co-author (with Professor Mark Button) of the book *Cyber frauds, scams and their victims* published by Routledge in 2017.

Bart Custers is a Full Professor of Law and Data Science and director of eLaw, the Center for Law and Digital Technologies at Leiden University, The Netherlands. He has a background in both law and physics and is an expert in the area of law and digital technologies, including topics like profiling, big data, privacy, discrimination, cybercrime, technology in policing and artificial intelligence. Professor Custers published seven books and over a hundred articles in academic and professional journals.

Felipe Cardoso Moreira de Oliveira is a Lawyer and a University Lecturer, teaching Criminal Procedure, Criminal Law and Criminology at *Pontifícia Universidade Católica do Rio Grande do Sul* (RS-Brazil) School of Law. He has a Master degree in Criminal Sciences and a Ph.D. in Law from PUCRS (RS-Brazil). He has founded the *Instituto Transdisciplinar de Estudos Criminais*—ITEC, in Porto Alegre (RS-Brazil).

Benjamin Farrand is Reader in Law & Emerging Technologies at Newcastle University. His research focuses on the law and politics of technology regulation in areas of uncertainty, including topics such as regulatory approaches to neuroprosthetic and stem-cell research, the combating of disinformation and extremist populist discourses on social media, and the sale of counterfeit goods online. He has published research in these areas in journals such as *European Security; Crime, Law and Social Change*; the *Journal of European Integration*; and the *Oxford Journal of Legal Studies*. He is also currently a coordinator of the UACES Research Network "Communicating Europe", which looks at the role of political communication in shaping areas of European Union politics and policy, including in the field of cybersecurity.

Joshua D. Freilich is a Professor in the Criminal Justice Department at John Jay College, and a Creator and co-Director of three open source database studies: U.S. Extremist Crime Database (ECDB), U.S. School Shooting Database (SSDB) and the Extremist Cyber Crime Database (ECCD). He is a member of the DHS Center of Excellence (COE), NCITE and a past member of two other COEs, CAOE and START. Freilich's research has been funded by DHS and NIJ and focuses on the causes of and responses to bias crimes, terrorism, cyberterrorism and targeted mass violence; open source research methods and measurement issues; and criminology theory, especially situational crime prevention.

Nicholas Gibbs is Ph.D. Candidate at Northumbria University, Newcastle upon Tyne. His thesis concerns the consumption and supply of image and performance enhancing drugs and the intersection of social media, contemporary gym culture and late-capitalist subjectivity. He values interdisciplinary collaboration as well as emerging research methodologies, including connective ethnography and visual methods.

Emily Ann Greene-Colozzi is a Doctoral Candidate in the criminal justice program at John Jay College of Criminal Justice. She has been a research assistant and project manager on several open source databases, including the U.S. School Shooting Database (SSDB) and the Extremist Cyber Crime Database (ECCD). Her dissertation investigates the application of Situational Crime Prevention to public mass shooting incidents and is supported by the National Institute of Justice Graduate Research Fellowship.

Rajeev V. Gundur is a Lecturer of criminology at Flinders University. He is based at the Centre for Crime Policy and Research. He uses novel methodological approaches to solve data collection obstacles in his work. He focuses on illicit markets, prison gangs and cybercrime.

Alexandra Hall is Associate Professor in Criminology at Northumbria University, Newcastle upon Tyne. She is an interdisciplinary criminologist whose research integrates approaches from criminology, sociology and political economy. She is the co-author of *Fake Meds Online* (Palgrave Macmillan) and *Fake Goods, Real Money* (Policy Press).

Tahlia Hart is a Ph.D. Candidate at Flinders University. Her research examines how young people engage in deception within online settings. Her interests include juvenile delinquency and cybercrime, in particular how youth initiate and maintain relationships online.

C. Jordan Howell is an Assistant Professor at the University of Texas at El Paso. He has published several papers in theoretical criminology, and his main research interest is cybercrime. Currently, Jordan's work focuses on cybercrime intervention using experimental designs and developing analytic strategies capable of predicting cybercrime involvement.

Jack Hughes is a Ph.D. Student at the University of Cambridge. His research interests are within the intersection of cybersecurity, cybercrime and interpretable machine learning. His Ph.D. work is based around analytical techniques for cybercrime pathways within underground discussion platforms.

Alice Hutchings is a University Lecturer in the Security Group at the Computer Laboratory, University of Cambridge. She is also Deputy-Director of the Cambridge Cybercrime Centre, an interdisciplinary initiative combining expertise from computer science, criminology and law. Specialising in cybercrime, she bridges the gap between criminology and computer science. Generally, her research interests include understanding cybercrime offenders, cybercrime events, and the prevention and disruption of online crime.

Ashton Kingdon is a Ph.D. Candidate in Web Science at the University of Southampton and a Doctoral Fellow at the Centre for Analysis of the Radical Right. Her research is interdisciplinary, combining criminology, history and computer science to examine the ways in which far right extremists utilise technology for recruitment and radicalisation, while giving equal weight to the subcultural elements of the users of this technology.

Edward R. Kleemans is Full Professor at the VU School of Criminology, Faculty of Law, Vrije Universiteit Amsterdam, the Netherlands (Full Professor in Serious and Organized Crime and Criminal Justice). He is Vice-Dean / Director of Research of the Faculty of Law and conducts research into organised crime and cybercrime activities and the interaction between offenders and the criminal justice system (including policing issues).

E. Rutger Leukfeldt is Senior Researcher Cybercrime at the Netherlands Institute for the Study of Crime and Law Enforcement (NSCR) and Academic Director of Centre of Expertise Cybersecurity of the Hague University of Applied Sciences. His work focuses on the human factor in cybercrime and cybersecurity.

James Martin is Associate Professor and Director of Criminology at Swinburne University of Technology. James' research expertise is in cryptomarkets and the dark web trade in illicit drugs. He has conducted both qualitative and quantitative research in this field, and is author of two books on the dark web drugs trade—*Drugs on the Darknet: How Cryptomarkets are Transforming the Global Trade in Illicit Drugs* (2014) and *Cryptomarkets: A Research Companion* (2020) (the latter co-authored with Jack Cunliffe and Rasmus Munksgaard).

Ashley A. Mattheis is a Ph.D. Candidate in the Department of Communication at the University of North Carolina at Chapel Hill. She is also a Doctoral Fellow with the Centre for Analysis of the Radical Right (CARR), an Associate Fellow with the Global Network on Extremism and Technology (GNET), and a Fellow at the Institute for Research on Male Supremacism. Her work brings together Cultural and Media Studies, feminist theory and rhetorical criticism to explore the effects of digital propaganda and the use of gendered discourses by extremist cultures online.

Ruth McAlister is a Lecturer in Criminology at Ulster University. She specialises in cybercrime offending, victimisation and the policing of cyberspace primarily through utilising webscraping, open source intelligence techniques and social network analysis. Her research has examined hacking forums, online recruitment for the purposes of human trafficking, online child sexual abuse and animal rights extremism. She has worked with a range of UK law enforcement agencies examining how digital technology has impacted on criminal activities pertaining to serious and organised crime, investigating how organised networks evolve, diversify and function within cyberspace in order that strategies can be developed to disrupt their criminal activity.

Stuart E. Middleton is a Lecturer in Computer Science within the Department of Computer Science at the University of Southampton, UK. His research work focuses on the Artificial Intelligence areas of Natural Language Processing, Information Extraction and Machine Learning. Stuart has led UK Government, DSTL, Innovate UK and FP7/H2020 projects, served on international conference and workshop steering committees and has been an invited AI expert to government agencies including the UK Cabinet Office Ministerial Roundtable for "use of AI in policing".

Fernando Miró-Llinares is Full Professor of Criminal Law and Criminology at the Universidad Miguel Hernández de Elche (UMH) and Director of the CRIMINA centre for the study and prevention of crime at the same university. He is the author of multiple high impact publications on cybercrime, environmental criminology, crime trends, artificial intelligence and criminal policy, regulatory compliance or criminal law, among others. He has been the principal researcher in more than 30 international and national projects and research contracts on security and the analysis, prevention and mitigation of crime. He is also currently co-founder of Plus Ethics, a UMH spin-off dedicated to ethical and legal support in international R+D, and president of the Spanish Society of Criminological Research.

Souvik Mukherjee is a Doctoral Candidate at West Bengal National University of Juridical Sciences, Kolkata (WBNUJS). He currently serves as Research Associate at the Centre For Regulatory Studies, Governance and Public Policy (CRSGPP), WBNUJS. Before venturing into the academia, Mr. Mukherjee practised law before Delhi High Court, Districts Courts at Delhi, Consumer Forums at Delhi and Kolkata, Alipore Judges Court, Kolkata. Mr. Mukherjee has taught in Goa, India and Kolkata, India from 2017 till 2019, and imparted lectures on several subjects on Public Law.

Tully O'Neill is a Digital Criminologist and Feminist Scholar living and working on the stolen land of the Wurundjeri people of the Koolin

Nation, also known as Melbourne, Australia. Tully's research interests are concerned sexual violence, how digital technologies facilitate informal justice, as well as digital ethics and methodologies.

Elena Pavan is Senior Assistant Professor at the Department of Sociology and Social Research of the University of Trento. Her main research interests pertain to the nexus between digital media and social movements particularly in the field of gender-related mobilisations. In her work, she combines network analysis, digital methods and big data approaches to unveil the implications of digital media use in contemporary mobilisation processes. Her work has been published in international journals such as *Global Networks, Policy and Society, Mobilization, Social Movement Studies, Information Communication and Society, Social Media+Society*. More than anything, she likes drinking coffee at dawn listening to the news on the radio.

Robert C. Perkins is a Doctoral Student in the Department of Criminal Justice and Criminology at Georgia State University and a graduate research assistant for the Evidence-Based Cybersecurity Research Group. He received his Bachelor of Arts in both criminology and psychology from the University of South Florida (USF) in 2017 and a Master of Arts in criminology from USF in 2020. His research encompasses cybercrime and other forms of technologically facilitated criminal behaviour.

Brian Pickering is a Senior Research Fellow in the School of Electronics and Computer Science, University of Southampton, carrying out research into online behaviours and the acceptance of technology. Using mainly qualitative research methods, he investigates trust relationships and online group formation. Further, as part of application and technology evaluation, he focuses on how potential adopters and users create narratives with technology embedded as a predictor of technology acceptance rather than more traditional models in domains from healthcare to cybersecurity.

Silke Roth is Professor of Sociology in the Department of Sociology, Social Policy and Criminology at the University of Southampton (UK) and Chair of the Faculty Research Ethics Committee of the Faculty of Social Sciences. She is the author of *Paradoxes of Aid Work* and is particularly interested in questions of solidarity, inclusion and exclusion. This includes a critical assessment of the impact of information and communication technologies (ICT) on aid relationships (ICT for development/ICT4D, digital humanitarianism).

Lisa Sugiura is a Principal Lecturer in Criminology and Cybercrime at the Institute of Criminal Justice Studies at the University of Portsmouth, Themes Strategic Innovation Fellow (TRIF), and the Deputy Director of the Cybercrime Awareness Clinic. Her research focuses on online deviance, and technology facilitated gender-based abuse and sexual violence. She has published on topics including the online pharmaceutical trade, phishing, online research ethics and rape culture online. Her research projects which include funding from the National Cyber Security Centre (NCSC) and the Home Office involve the language of cybersexism, victims of computer misuse, the use of technologies to assist marginalised women into employment, and extremist and misogynistic behaviours in incel communities.

Dean Taodang is a Graduate of Flinders University. His honours project used open source data to evaluate scams during the Australian Bushfires and COVID-19.

Pamela Ugwudike is Associate Professor of Criminology at the University of Southampton, a Fellow of the Alan Turing Institute, and Co-Editor-in-Chief of *Criminology and Criminal Justice Journal* (with Dr. Anita Lavorgna and Professor Lorine Gelsthorpe). Dr. Ugwudike is currently researching AI ethics and accountability, with a focus on data bias and the implications for justice. Her current research project is funded by the Alan Turing Institute.

Craig Webber is Associate Professor in Criminology within Sociology at the University of Southampton, carrying out research into the intersection of criminological, sociological and psychological insights on cybercrime, youth crime and criminological theory. Dr. Webber has been a key member of the Web Science Institute at the University of Southampton since its inception. Dr. Webber has written on various aspects of cybercrime including online fraud called carding and hacktivism.

Bryce Westlake is an Associate Professor in the Department of Justice Studies at San Jose State University. He developed one of the first in-person digital forensic curriculums in the USA. His current research focuses on the development of automated tools for detecting and analysing child sexual abuse media on the Surface and Dark Web, and the testing and validating of digital forensic investigation tools.

Marleen Weulen Kranenbarg is an assistant professor at Vrije Universiteit (VU University) Amsterdam, The Netherlands. Her research mostly focuses on cyber-dependent criminals. She recently received a prestigious personal grant to study life course, cultural and situational factors that lead to non-criminal (ethical) hacking. Marleen is also a research fellow of the NSCR (Netherlands Institute for the Study of Crime and Law Enforcement), board member of the ESC Cybercrime Working Group and part of the steering committee of the IIRCC (International Interdisciplinary Research Consortium on Cybercrime).

List of Figures

List of Tables

Part I

Knowledge Production and Research Datafication in Cybercrime Research

Anita Lavorgna and Thomas J. Holt

Introduction to Part I

An increasing number of criminal or deviant behaviours have an online component, even simple text messages between drug dealers on disposable cell phones can be used for tracking and triangulation in physical space. At the same time, "cybercrime research" is often still regarded as a specialist area, struggling to find its place in an academic and educational context of traditionally distinct disciplines—*in primis*criminology and computer science. This approach is anachronistic as it is essential to meet the societal and technological (or, even better, socio-technical) challenges that cybercrimes pose through cross-disciplinary approaches.

We need to look at current and emerging issues from different angles to promote security while preserving our individual rights and the public good in the digital age. To that end, this book brings together scholars from criminology, sociology, law, political sciences and computer sciences with a particular emphasis on critical analyses of cybercrimes—here broadly intended as all those criminal, deviant or otherwise harmful behaviours that are enabled or significantly facilitated by cyberspace and cybercrime research. The first part of this book aims at facilitating cross-disciplinary dialogue with the hope of aiding people from different backgrounds to speak a more common language, so as to facilitate collaboration among different bodies of expertise, each with their scopes, theoretical and methodological frameworks, and standards.

In Chapter 1, Anita Lavorgna discusses the epistemological dimensions of current online research, recognising how a different understanding of what is scientific "knowledge", and how it is produced, lies at the basis of the difficulties towards multi- and interdisciplinary collaborations in cybercrime research. Different disciplines, notably from the social and the computer sciences, often struggle in understanding each other's language, theoretical and methodological frameworks, and standards which may vary considerably. These difficulties can be overcome by adopting a pragmatic approach, of the utmost importance to advance research in this field.

Chapter 2, by Benjamin Farrand and Helena Carrapico, shifts the focus from epistemology to ontology, and on the social construction of cybercrimes: What drives policymakers to decide that an issue in cyberspace is a "crime" issue, and what type of response is most suited to that issue? The authors will use the European Union as a case study to discuss the political nature of framing cybercrimes as a specific form of insecurity, which leads those nations to be ultimately ill-equipped to counter them.

In Chapter 3, Ruth McAlister and Fabian Campbell-West discuss the importance for criminologists to develop "cyber skills" and familiarise themselves with emerging methodological approaches to better understand criminal behaviour in cyberspace and implement evidence-based prevention measures. They offer practical suggestions on how techniques exploited in other fields, such as software engineering and data science, can assist social scientists to process large datasets, and quickly test and share ideas.

This section of the book concludes by offering critical analysis of the current and upcoming challenges of research datafication, which are driven by much cybercrime research. In Chapter 4, Bart Custers discusses the ways that both the availability and usability of data in cybercrime research is rapidly increasing, together with the tools for big data analytics. As a consequence, the strong focus on such quantitative, data-driven approaches leave out sufficient room for nuances and interpretation, creating challenges for methodological, practical and ethical perspectives. As Pamela Ugwudike argues in Chapter 5, this increased epistemological function of data-driven approaches can cause important social harms—an issue that unfortunately has received insufficient attention in cybercrime research so far.

These chapters also provide an important framing for the remaining sections of the book. The authors highlight broad issues that are explored in depth in Part II and III of the volume, which focuses on research methods and ethical issues, respectively.

1

Epistemologies of Cyberspace: Notes for Interdisciplinary Research

Anita Lavorgna

Introduction

Researching, teaching and even tackling cybercrimes are increasingly becoming a specialist area of expertise, with its own jargon and sometimes its own mythology. These endeavors are bringing together disciplinary contexts that were traditionally very distinct, and continue to be often delimited by frames that, if not sufficiently unhinged, might be limiting our ability to study and address many forms of cybercrimes. Indeed, we are embedded in education and research systems that mostly are based on, and often reward (in publications, or more generally in career advancement), strict disciplinary boundaries, even if both researchers and professionals need to work from different angles to identify patterns, promote good behaviors or preserve security in

A. Lavorgna (✉)
University of Southampton, Southampton, UK
e-mail: a.lavorgna@soton.ac.uk

5

cyberspace. Indeed, cybercrime and cybersecurity are topics that inherently require a cross-disciplinary approach: both technical knowledge and the capacity to contextualize them into broader complex societal challenges are needed, and both are essential to progress while maintaining our individual rights and the public good in the digital age (Lavorgna, 2020a, 2020b). This is why, especially in very recent years, there is increasing attention toward approaches that draw on intellectual and methodological insights from different disciplines. While promising, these approaches are not easy to be implemented, as they require different disciplines and professions to make a serious effort in understanding each other's language, theoretical and methodological frameworks and standards—which may vary considerably. Furthermore, epistemologies at the very basis of different disciplines are at times, at least apparently, not well aligned, making it difficult to fully integrate them.

Epistemology can be narrowly defined as the study of knowledge and justified belief; in a broader sense, it has to do with the creation and dissemination of knowledge in a certain area of inquiry. This chapter stems from the recognition that criminology and computer sciences, which are the disciplines leading research on cybercrimes, traditionally have a different understanding of what are the necessary and sufficient conditions of knowledge, its sources and its limits, and what makes justified beliefs justified—all questions epistemology is concerned with (Steup, 2005). This issue has practical implications hindering effective cross-disciplinary communication, as a different "language" when it comes to epistemology reflects on a different way of thinking, a different way to create meaning (Vamos, 2010).

Background

Epistemologies of Science

At the core of this epistemological issue, is the answer to the question "what is it to be scientific"—an answer that is still object of a lot of pushing and pulling among disciplines and cultures on about just how far the "scientific" blanket can reach (see Gellner, 1984). Science is characterized by having a relatively objective, consensual evaluation of explicit criteria and accepted procedures (even if scientific criteria and procedures are neither stable nor perfectly unequivocal, as stressed in Joseph & Sullivan, 1975). Many different categorizations of theories of sciences have been proposed, all characterized by some common features such as accurate observation, testing, shared and rigorous conceptual models and paradigms, and the avoidance for circular arguments or transcendence (Gellner, 1984).

Simplifying a lot for the sake of this discussion and the necessary brevity of this chapter, from an epistemological point of view we can recognize three main research traditions: logical or empirical *positivism* (positing an objective reality which we can observe and measure, in line with quantitative approaches), *constructivism* (which is skeptical of universal truth, and is more aligned with qualitative approaches trying to illuminate the subjective nature of the world) and *pragmatism* (which simply sees method as a means to capture useful data, as we generally find in mixed methods research approaches trying the best combination of methods to answer a research question) (Wheeldon & Ahlberg, 2012; Wheeldon et al., 2014).

In a more paradigmatic sense, a definition of what makes something "scientific" is needed to define whether, and to what extent, the social sciences (which in large part include criminology) and the computer sciences are scientific themselves in creating knowledge. This issue matters because in our modern society the notion of "scientific" is linked to the notions of validation, legitimation and authority (Gellner, 1984), in a context where the popular understanding of "scientific" is closely linked to a conception of research method that is modeled on positivism and the natural sciences (Cassidy, 2014; Hagège et al., 2007; Sala, 2013). In order to support advancements in cybercrime research, a preliminary step is therefore needed to unpack the epistemological differences among our key disciplines, so to facilitate mutual understanding.

Two Cultures of Debate

Computer science started to develop its own epistemological status, as separate from the one developed by its precursor mathematics, when the academic discipline of computer science (as well as software development) started to become an independent subject, toward the late 1960s. Traditionally, it has been accepted that computer science is to be considered partially a mathematical discipline, partially a branch of engineering and partially as a natural sciences discipline, as it makes use of methods and approaches of all the three of them (Turner & Angius, 2000; Tedre & Sutinen, 2008). As summarized by Turner and Angius (2000), at the basis of the design, specification, programming, verification, implementation and testing of human-made computing systems, indeed, there are assumptions about the nature of these systems: when we stress the mathematical component of the discipline, we assume that programs are mathematical entities to be dealt with through the deductive reasoning provided by the formal methods of theoretical computer science (Vamos, 2010). When we stress the engineering aspects, we emphasize computer science's ability to managing the complexity of computer systems and evaluating their reliability (DeMillo et al., 1979). Finally, when we stress the natural sciences component of the discipline (interestingly, the only one simply labeled the "scientific" one by Turner and Angius), we recognize that computer science makes use of both deductive and inductive probabilistic reasoning to examine computer systems, as it often relies on both formal methods and empirical testing (Denning, 2005).

In addition, ad hoc epistemologies have been proposed. Computational epistemology, for instance, is emerging as a field dealing with question such as how and to what extent we can learn things about the world by performing computations, and what are the standards of rigor for research based on computer modeling (Bankes et al., 2002). Rugai (2013) defined it as a new cross-disciplinary field including a set of admissible methods and the essential likeness of induction (via logical reliability) and deduction. All these various approaches, however, stem consistently from logical and empirical positivism.

Also the *social sciences* (and criminology as a social science), which are based on systematic, disciplined and verifiable methods of acquiring knowledge, rely on many (at times very different) approaches (Sala, 2013), so it is difficult to make them converge toward a one-size-fits-all philosophy. Nonetheless, it needs to be recognized that according to many of these views and most notably those which can be led back to the constructivist and the pragmatic approaches, the aim is not to reveal the true nature of reality or search for eternal truths; rather, scientific work is done in the context of actual human problems and defined research questions, recognizing that all the things considered relevant for answering these are considered relevant from some actor's point of view (Kivinen & Piiroinen, 2004). Especially for constructivists, the research effort does not aim at ultimate laws, but rather at offering relevant meanings through interpretation (Hayward & Young, 2004).

While some aspects of social life are indeed quantifiable or observable with (semi)experimental precision, others are not; nonetheless, the *corpus* of cumulative knowledge that well-trained researchers on the subject bring forward is undeniable, and so is the impact on our cognitive world (Gellner, 1984). Additionally, even if in the social sciences it is not uncommon to have diverging schools of thought—as different explanations are offered to certain issues, different weights assigned to certain variables, and even different agendas are advocated—the construction of knowledge is not arbitrary, but backed by a community of practice: Knowledge becomes a social enterprise, and some propositions are better supported than others because there are shared rules and practices allowing members of a scholarly community to tell the difference (Kuhn, 1962/1970; Polbsy, 1998). Furthermore, even if the laws of social life differ according to time and place, at the core of the strategy of science there is a choice of puzzles to be investigated and the criticism of tentative and provisional attempts to solve them (Popper, 1957/1991, 1994/1996a, 1994/1996b). Objectivity in the social sciences is hence situated in a more communal and intersubjective sense, meaning that it is the social result of mutual criticism, competition (of individual scientists and of schools of thoughts), critical tradition and peer review (Cibangu, 2012; Jarvie, 1986).

It should be noted, however, that toward and even within the social sciences there has been a long-standing diatribe between those claiming that the study of man and society can be scientific only in a sense radically different than in, for instance, the natural sciences, and those suggesting that social scientists could/should turn into "genuine scientists" by taking a more positivistic turn (as discussed, for instance, in Gellner, 1984). The idea that the social sciences should resemble the natural sciences is still present (consider, for instance, the creation of a "crime science," see Laycock, 2012), even if this has been long critiqued (Winch, 2007). For instance, it has been claimed that the social sciences should not suffer the so-called physics envy (Mills, 1959), creating a false sense of mathematical precision through quantification to seem more rigorous, in a dangerous push toward reductionism, as many research arenas in the social sciences are by their very nature "contested, blurred, ambiguous, and unsuited for quantification" (Hayward & Young, 2004, p. 114). In criminology, the partial change in paradigm in the discipline has been connected to the influence that crime control industry has upon academic criminology, with its demands for quantification to bring forwards its various "wars" (against drugs, terrorism… and now cybercrime) rather than debating the very nature of these battles (Hayward & Young, 2004). As already underlined by Wheeldon and colleagues (2014), in this debate we cannot avoid mentioning issues of "career concerns": In a very competitive career environment as the one in academia, quantitative approaches seem to offer a preferred route to publication in some of the top peer-reviewed journals, creating an incentive (especially for early career researchers) to "invest" in certain positivistic approaches, potentially self-perpetuating a bias toward different, but still scientific, approaches.

To overcome this diatribe, which could be summed-up as constructivism vs positivism, some argue for a third road—pragmatism. Wheeldon and colleagues (2014), for instance, call for the need to reject "the siren song of universalism via logical positivism" (p. 117); a step which requires being aware of different epistemological and ontological starting points but also being ready to accept—with methodological modesty—equal footing of different research traditions and a more fluid understanding of research processes. As stressed by criminologists such as Agnew (2011) and Maruna (2010), using mixed methods is a way to allow to address the shortcomings of both quantitative and qualitative research, while taking the best from both worlds.

Bridging the Divide

The Road Forward: Multidisciplinary and Interdisciplinary Pathways

Bridging or otherwise overcoming the divide between these different epistemological traditions, and hence creating a common language to understand what is "proper" scientific research when it comes to investigating cyberspace (and, for what matters for the scope of this book, to investigate cybercrimes), has been de facto occurring in recent years following three different pathways: a computer science-led path, a criminology/social sciences-led path, and a third path comprising a few attempts to promote genuinely interdisciplinary programs of study and research.

Debates on whether there is an emerging "science" of cybersecurity (Hatleback, 2018; Kott, 2014; Maxion, 2011) with proper principles and methods emerged over the past decade, generally stemming from the computer sciences. These discussions, however, are problematic as they tend to depart from a very narrow, positivistic view of what scientific research is. Hatleback (2018)—for instance—prefers to define cybersecurity as a "protoscience," meaning that it is in a stage of development coming before the transition to fully-fledged science as currently in cybersecurity error-free measurement and a rigorous experimental methodology are not always available yet (as if the only alternative would be to downgrade cybersecurity to pseudoscience).

From within the social sciences, there has been increased awareness on the importance of improving methodological approaches through interactive mechanisms that combine human and machine capabilities (Bankes et al., 2002; Islam et al., 2019), if only to make good use of the availability to new "big" data sources available through cyberspace. Indeed, social scientists have increasingly to deal with a corpus of big data, which are often attributed quantification and patterns-revealing functions offering social scientists new tools to expand their sociological (or criminological) imagination (Burrows & Savage, 2014). In criminology, for instance, computer science methods can be used to identify, among other things, emerging patterns, crime generators and attractors, and online crimes; the notion of "computational criminology" has been suggested to subsume a range of approaches making use of computational power to further research on crime and deviancy (Brantingham, 2011), especially in cyberspace (see also Chapters 3, 10 and 11).

Here, the epistemological shift is in the sense that much of computational social sciences has standards of rigor based on inductive and abductive logic, which are generally defined in terms of falsifiability and reproducibility (Popper, 1994/1996a; Bankes et al., 2002). At times, models can be experimentally validated for a predictive outcome, but even if predictive modeling tends to have a bias toward positivistic stances, the standards of rigor differ from positivist ones; in most cases, predictive accuracy is not possible, even if models can still be very useful for doing good science and informing policy (Bankes et al., 2002). In any case, the shift encourages leaning toward an epistemological approach claiming objectivity and accuracy (by somehow "measuring" society), with the risk to downplay the role of constructivist (interpretative and critical) approaches in furthering knowledge (Fuchs, 2019), and in enabling us to adopt a more critical standpoint asking for biases within big data (as well as the context of its creation and use) to be better acknowledged (Boyd & Crawford, 2012; Davidson et al., 2019; see also Chapters 4 and 5). Furthermore, we should not forget that "big data" can be precious not only for quantitative but also for qualitative analyses; for these latter, the challenge is to retain the distinctive attention to nuanced context and detail that is proper of rigorous qualitative research (so-called big qualitative data, Davidson et al., 2019).

The two approaches briefly discussed so far are certainly deserving in furthering research agendas by expanding computer science and criminological imagination and promoting some sort of cross-disciplinary effort. However, they still largely draw on distinct intellectual and methodological insights from different disciplines, which tend to work independently one alongside each other (*multidisciplinarity*), even if sometimes "borrowing" specific methodological approaches.

To further support the advancements in cybercrime research, the next step should be to encourage harmonization and synthesis of different disciplinary approaches into a coherent whole (*interdisciplinarity*). The ground in this direction has been probably best laid in the emerging context of web sciences and similar socio-technical approaches embracing pragmatism. Halford and colleagues (2018), for instance, reflect on the use of social media data, which offer important new avenues for research but that need to be dealt with critically (especially as regards potential biases and unknown provenance of some data). They argue for the need of a socio-technical approach, needed to support methodologically informed social media research. After all, to borrow their words, "harvesting data is one thing, but understanding these data is quite another" (p. 3342). Data—certainly cyberspace data, as cyberspace is a pervasive space allowing a dynamic interaction with information (Bricken, 1991)—are socially constructed; they do not exist in the wild and are not discovered, but they are rather constructed as objects/subjects of knowledge (Halford et al., 2018; Manovich, 2001). It is necessary to recognize in full the complexities of cybercrimes as socio-technical phenomena; the technical and social domains should be integrated (Gloria & Erickson, 2010), and potential biases in both the study of social phenomena and the technology involved in those studies should be explicitly acknowledged, discussed and pragmatically minimized, rather than engaging in epistemological fights. In this context, mixed methods (quantitative and qualitative, online and offline) are welcomed as a way to enable us to make social claim on social media data (Halford et al., 2018).

In working with cyberspace (as a data source or analytical resource), social scientists have a toolbox of non-positivistic methods comprising both approaches that have been traditionally central to the evolution of their discipline (such as ethnography, see, for instance, Chapters 14 and 24) and more innovative methods (such as visual methods, see, for instance, Chapter 15) (Halford et al., 2013), which are precious resources to build knowledge, researching cyberspace (and, in our case, researching crime and deviancy in cyberspace). In genuine interdisciplinary research, these methods retain a proper space, as positivistic and constructivist standpoints can work together pragmatically, utilizing a broad range of complementary methodologies to garner deeper insights, depending on the specific research questions. As stressed already by Halford and colleagues (2013), this interdisciplinary effort also requires recognizing that reality transcends the disciplinary pigeonholing of knowledge—which depends on social and political struggles for identity, power and resources, as there is no "natural" division of knowledge and expertise.

Socio-Technical Approaches in Cybercrime Research: Examples of Interdisciplinarity

Research focusing on cyberspace is particularly suitable to interdisciplinary collaboration because of the methodological challenges it entails (see, among others, Berendt et al., 2020; Halford et al., 2018; Tinati et al., 2012, 2014a, 2014b). Interdisciplinarity has become a buzzword in many research endeavors and is boosted in some countries by funding bodies within and beyond the social sciences. Such calls do not always give rise to truly interdisciplinary projects. When investigating crime, deviance or—more broadly—social harms in cyberspace, interdisciplinary research is not yet common, even if it is increasing (see Payne & Hadzhidimova, 2020) and if there are notable exceptions (see, for instance, the book edited by Holt [2017]).

This section offers a couple of recent examples of interdisciplinary efforts stemming from some research projects I recently led, that were grounded on the use of iterative socio-technical frameworks based on a cross-disciplinary incremental feedback system.

In the context of the "FloraGuard" project, we studied online forums around internet-facilitated illegal trades of endangered species bringing together computer science, criminology and conservation science expertise (Lavorgna et al., 2020a). A common problem in analyzing online forums and marketplaces with cybercrime activity is that often there is only a small subset of relevant posts, hiding in plain sight among a long tail of irrelevant, legitimate discussion posts. Hence, relevant posts can be time consuming to find and extract, often requiring specialist domain knowledge to select search terms and wider exploration of connected posts, profiles and external sites to understand the context in which behaviors occur. In developing a socio-technical artificial intelligence (AI) approach to information extraction from the long tail of relevant online forums, we developed a highly iterative strategy, taking entities of interest (e.g., endangered plant species, suspects, locations) identified by a criminologist and using them to direct computer science tools including crawling, searching and information extraction over many steps until an acceptable resulting intelligence package was achieved (see Middleton et al., 2020, and Chapter 11 of this book), helping to reduce the volume of posts for in-depth, qualitative analysis. In gathering relevant information from large crawls, constructivist approaches (i.e., in-depth qualitative textual and visual analysis to identify among other things suspect trades, subcultural features, framing of conservation-related matters and techniques of neutralization) were used alongside positivistic elements (i.e., the use of two experiments over a one-week period each, where posts from 100's of authors were manually browsed to identify a limited number of ground truth suspects who were probably engaging in illegal trade activity and their connected entities; the datasets were then processed using topic modeling and named entity directed graph visualization methods; the mean recall of ground truth entities per species, averaged across the number of suspects, was then calculated, demonstrating how named entity directed graph visualization consistently outperformed topic modeling for discovering connected entities in the long tail of online forums and marketplaces) (Middleton et al., 2020). The pragmatic approach adopted and the continuous cross-disciplinary conversations allowed us to discuss in detail issues of AI trustworthiness and to promote it through the incremental feedback system used, as the qualitative insight and specialized human knowledge mitigated any excessive generalization or streamlining introduced by the automation of the data gathering and analysis processes (Lavorgna et al., 2020b; Middleton et al., 2020).

A second example of the approach is provided with reference to a study on the online propagation of potentially harmful medical misinformation through social media (Lavorgna & Carr, 2021). This study combined criminological and computer science expertise to unpack the complex social dynamics surrounding the Twitter presence of providers of non-science-based anti-cancer treatments and their active supporters. Both the dataset and the analytical strategies were developed through a continuous incremental feedback system: In data crawling and preparation, biases were minimized through a system of blacklisting refined with subject-specific manual analysis. While social media analytics have allowed us to explore the existence of structural relationships among actors involved in relevant discourses in the Twittersphere (showing, among other things, the lack of a proper community of interest, and rather the existence of transient collectives clustering around specific and popular discussions, themes or actors in the social network—hence questioning the presence of a deviant subculture), qualitative content analysis "zooming in" into popular tweets and users recognized the presence of a shared system of values, political beliefs and possibly also lifestyle and cultural preferences, and patterns in building successful health misinformation—with implications for harm reduction through the creation of better tailored awareness-raising efforts.

Conclusions

In this chapter, we have seen how in researching cybercrimes, depending on our different disciplinary background and/or methodological preferences, we tend to be bound to a certain way to understand what is knowledge, and what type of knowledge is "good enough" to be considered valid, legitimate and authoritative. For most of us, epistemological issues are closely embedded in our research routines to the point that we tend to keep them implicit in our reasoning and in defining research designs. However, in the effort to facilitate and foster effective cross-disciplinary communication and collaboration, it is good to remind ourselves that there are different cultures of debates, and that meaning and knowledge can be created also in ways we might be less familiar with. This short contribution focused on social sciences/criminology and computer science, but there are many more disciplines with a lot to say on cybercrimes—psychology, economics, law and moral philosophy among the many.

Collaboration and when possible integration of multiple disciplines is not an easy task, as they come with different epistemologies, but also with different histories and languages (Gloria & Erickson, 2010; Halford et al., 2013; Smart et al., 2019). Even if monodisciplinary endeavors maintain their descriptive, explanatory or heuristic value, multi- and interdisciplinary efforts are increasingly needed to deal with technical challenges, big data availability and complex social issues, first and foremost in cyberspace. Nowadays, social scientists are probably not the main actors in studying society and defining the nature itself of social knowledge (Burrows & Savage, 2014), and similarly criminologists are not the only or possibly the main actors studying crime and deviance. Nonetheless, they still are in a good position to do this, as they have the subject-knowledge, critical skills and methodological tools that are still of great value in unpacking social, behavioral and organizational dynamics in cyberspace. Disciplines such as criminology have inherently an adaptive potential (Zedner, 2007), but they need to become more open toward new forms of cross-disciplinary collaboration, to maintain their relevance.

It is also worth remembering that epistemic cultures are not monolithic, and neither the computer sciences nor the social sciences and criminology are a coherent, fixed ensemble of paradigms and methods (Sala, 2013)—how knowledge is built evolves in time, and there are epistemological debates within disciplines that might be seen as unitary from the outside. Hence, it is not surprising that interactions between the computer sciences and the strands of criminology more inclined to positivistic methods might be, or look, easier. Nonetheless, communication and collaboration should be fostered also and especially with those strands stemming from different and apparently conflicting epistemological traditions, as this allows to look at research problems truly from different perspectives, and possibly to mitigate oversights and biases.

Developing sensitivity toward the importance of interdisciplinarity is also needed to try and improve the long-established institutional structures based on a rigid division among disciplines, and that make interdisciplinary endeavors harder to carry out in practice. Research has shown, for instance, that interdisciplinary publishing is likely to suffer a "productivity penalty" (Leahey et al., 2017), and that, in order to be effective, it necessitates not only of a good composition of the research team, but also of subject editors who are familiar with the interdisciplinary merits of a specific project, and reviewers who are open minded about interdisciplinary efforts (Pohl et al., 2015)—something that is not always available within the ranks of traditional, top (and, indeed, disciplinary) journals. If a cross-disciplinary mind, willing to engage in cross-disciplinary discussions can certainly support advancements in cybercrime research at the micro-level, broader systemic changes are needed to foster these research endeavors.

References

Agnew, R. (2011). *Toward a unified Criminology: Integrating assumptions about crime, people, and society.* New York University Press.

Bankes, S., Lempert, R., & Popper, S. (2002). Making computational social science effective: Epistemology, methodology, and technology. *Social Science Computer Review, 20*(4), 377–388.

Berendt, B., Gandon F., Halford S., Hall, W., Hendler, J., Kindr-Kurlanda, K., Ntoutsi, E., & Staab, S. (2020). *Web futures: Inclusive, intelligent, sustainable.* The 2020 Manifesto for Web Science. Available at: https://www.webscience. org/wp-content/uploads/sites/117/2020/07/main.pdf.

Boyd, D., & Crawford, K. (2012). Critical questions for big data. *Information, Communication & Society, 15*(5), 662–679.

Brantingham, P. L. (2011). *Computational criminology.* Intelligence and Security Infomatics Conference, Athens.

Bricken, W. (1991). A formal foundation for cyberspace. *Proceedings of Virtual Reality '91,* San Francisco.

Burrows, R., & Savage, M. (2014). After the crisis? Big data and the methodological challenges of empirical sociology. *Big Data & Society, 1*(1).

Cassidy, A. (2014). Commutating the social sciences. A specific challenge? In M. Bucchi & B. Trench (Eds.), *Routledge handbook of public communication of science and technology.* Routledge.

Cibangu, S. K. (2012). Karl Popper and the social sciences. In A. Lopez-Varela (Ed.), *Social sciences and cultural studies—Issues of language, public opinion and welfare.* InTech.

Davidson, E., Edwards, R., Jamieson, L., & Weller, S. (2019). Big data, qualitative style: A breadth-and-depth method for working with large amounts of secondary qualitative data. *Quality & Quantity, 53,* 363–376.

De Millo, R. A., Lipton, R. J., & Perlis, A. J. (1979). Social processes and proofs of theorems and programs. *Communications of the ACM, 22*(5), 271–281.

Denning, P. J. (2005). Is computer science science? *Communications of the ACM, 48*(4), 27–31.

Fuchs, C. (2019). What is critical digital social research? Five reflections on the study of digital society. *Journal of Digital Social Research, 1*(1), 10–16.

Gellner, E. (1984). The scientific status of the social sciences. *International Social Science Journal, 36*, 567–586.

M. J. K. T. Gloria, & J. S. Erickson. (2010). *Studying cybercrime: Raising questions about objectivity and bias.* ACM. Available at: http://tw.rpi.edu/media/2014/10/22/706d/Cybercrime_WkspWS2014_Gloria.pdf.

Hagège, H., Dartnell, C., & Sallantin, J. (2007). Positivism against constructivism: A network game to learn epistemology. In V. Corruble, M. Takeda, & E. Suzuki (Eds.), *Discovery science. DS 2007.* Lecture Notes in Computer Science (Vol. 4755). Springer.

Halford, S., Pope, C., & Weal, M. (2013). Digital futures? Sociological challenges and opportunities in the emergent Semantic Web. *Sociology, 47*(1), 173–189.

Halford, S., Weal, M., Tinati, R., Carr, L., & Pope, C. (2018). Understanding the production and circulation of social media data: Towards methodological principles and praxis. *New Media & Society, 20*(9), 3341–3358.

Hatleback, E. (2018). The protoscience of cybersecurity. *The Journal of Defense Modeling and Simulation: Applications, Methodology, Technology, 51*(1), 5–12.

Hayward, K. J., & Young, J. (2004). Cultural Criminology: Some notes on the script. *Theoretical Criminology, 8*(3), 259–273.

Holt, T. J. (Ed.). (2017). *Cybercrime through interdisciplinary lens.* Routledge.

Islam, T., Becker, I., Posner, R., Ekblom, P., McGuire, M., Borrion, H., & Li, S. (2019) A socio-technical and co-evolutionary framework for reducing human-related risks in cyber security and cybercrime ecosystems. In G. Wang, M. Bhuiyan, S. De Capitani di Vimercati, & Y. Ren (Eds.), *Dependability in sensor, cloud, and big data systems and applications: Communications in computer and information science* (Vol. 1123). Springer.

Jarvie, I. C. (1986). Popper on the difference between the natural and the social sciences. *Thinking about society: Theory and practice: Boston Studies in the Philosophy of Science* (Vol. 93). Springer.

Joseph, B. D., & Sullivan, T. A. (1975). Sociology of science. *Annual Review of Sociology, 1*(1), 203–222.

Kivinen, O., & Piiroinen, T. (2004). The relevance of ontological commitments in social sciences: Realist and pragmatist viewpoints. *Journal for the Theory of Social Behaviour, 34*(3), 231–248.

Kott, A. (2014). Towards fundamental science of cyber security In R. E. Pino (Ed.), *Network science and cybersecurity*. Springer.

Kuhn, T. S. (1962/1970). *The structure of scientific revolutions*. University Chicago Press.

Lavorgna, A. (2020a). Studying and addressing (cyber)crimes beyond traditional boundaries. *Macmillan International Higher Education Blog*. Available at: https://www.macmillanihe.com/blog/post/addressing-cybercrimes-anita-lavorgna/.

Lavorgna, A. (2020b). *Cybercrimes: Critical issues in a global context*. Palgrave Macmillan.

Lavorgna, A., Middleton, S. E., Whitehead, D., & Cowell, C. (2020a). *FloraGuard: Tackling the illegal trade in endangered plants*. Project report. Royal Botanic Gardens.

Lavorgna, A., Middleton, S. E., Pickering, B., & Neumann, G. (2020b). FloraGuard: Tackling the online trade in endangered plants through a cross-disciplinary ICT-enabled methodology. *Journal of Contemporary Criminal Justice* (online first).

Lavorgna, A., & Carr, L. (2021). Tweets and quacks: Network and content analyses of providers of non-science-based anti-cancer treatments and their supporters on Twitter. *Sage Open*.

Laycock, G. (2012). Defining crime science. In M. J. Smith & N. Tilley (Eds.), *Crime science: New approaches to preventing and detecting crime*. Routledge.

Leahey, E., Beckman, C. M., & Stanko, T. L. (2017). Prominent but less productive: The impact of interdisciplinarity on scientists' research. *Administrative Science Quarterly, 62*, 105–139.

Manovich, L. (2001). *Software takes command*. Bloomsbury.

Maruna, S. (2010). Mixed method research in Criminology: Why not go both ways? In A. Piquero & D. Weisburd (Eds.), *Handbook of quantitative Criminology*. Springer.

Maxion, R. (2011). Making experiments dependable. In C. Jone & J. L. Lloyd (Eds.), *Dependable and historic computing: Essays dedicated to Brian Randell on the occasion of his 75th birthday*. Springer.

Middleton, S., Lavorgna, A., Neumann, G., & Whitehead, D. (2020). *Information extraction form the long tale. A socio-technical approach for criminology investigations into the online illegal plant trade*. WebSci'20 STAIDDC workshop.

Mills, W. (1959). *The sociological imagination.* Oxford University Press.

Payne, B. K., & Hadzhidimova, L. (2020). Disciplinary and interdisciplinary trends in cybercrime research: An examination. *International Journal of Cyber Criminology, 14*(1), 81–105.

Polbsy, N. W. (1998). Social sciences and scientific change: A note on Thomas S. Kuhn's Contribution. *Annual Review of Political Science, 1,* 199–210.

Pohl, C., Wuelser, G., Bebi, P., Bugmann, H., Buttler, A., Elkin, C., Grêt-Regamey, A., Hirschi, C., Le, Q. B., Peringer, A., Rigling, A., Seidl, R., & Huber, R. (2015). How to successfully publish interdisciplinary research: Learning from an Ecology and society special feature. *Ecology and Society, 20*(2), 23.

Popper, R. K. (1957/1991). *The poverty of historicism.* Routledge.

Popper, R. K. (1994/1996a). *The myth of framework: In defence of science and rationality.* Routledge.

Popper, R. K. (1994/1996b). *In search of a better world: Lectures and essays from thirty years.* Routledge.

Rugai, N. (2013). *Computational Epistemology: From reality to wisdom* (Second ed.). Lulu Press.

Sala, R. (2013). One, two, or three cultures? Humanities versus the natural and social sciences in modern Germany. *Journal of Knowledge Economy, 4,* 83–97.

Smart, P., Ming-chin, M., O'Hara, K., Carr, L., & Hall, W. (2019). *Geopolitical drivers of personal data: The four horsemen of the datapocalypse.* University of Southampton.

Steup, M. (2005). *Epistemology.* Stanford Encyclopaedia of Philosophy.

Tedre, M., & Sutinen, E. (2008). Three traditions of computing: What educators should know. *Computer Science Education, 18*(3), 153–170.

Tinati, R., Halford, S., Carr, L., & Pope, C. (2012). Mixing methods and theory to explore web activity (pp. 308–316). In *Proceedings of the 2012 ACM conference on Web Science.*

Tinati, R., Halford, S., Carr, L., & Pope, C. (2014a). Big data: Methodological challenges and approaches for sociological analysis. *Sociology, 48*(4), 663–681.

Tinati, R., Philippe, O., Pope, C., Carr, L., & Halford, S. (2014b). Challenging social media analytics: Web science perspectives. In *Proceedings of the 2014 ACM conference on Web Science* (pp. 177–181).

Turner, R., & Angius, N. (2020). The philosophy of Computer Science. In E. N. Zalta (Ed.), *The Stanford encyclopedia of philosophy.*

Vamos, T. (2010). *Knowledge and computing: Computer Epistemology and constructive skepticism.* Central European University Press.

Wheeldon, J., & Ahlberg, M. (2012). *Visualizing social science research: Maps, methods, and meaning.* Sage.

Wheeldon, J., Heidt, J., & Dooley, B. (2014). The trouble(s) with unification: Debating assumptions, methods, and expertise in criminology. *Journal of Theoretical and Philosophical Criminology, 6,* 111–128.

Winch, P. (2007). *The idea of a social science and its relation to philosophy.* Routledge.

Zedner, L. (2007). Pre-crime and post-criminology. *Theoretical Criminology, 11*(2), 261–281.

2

The How and Why of Cybercrime: The EU as a Case Study of the Role of Ideas, Interests, and Institutions as Drivers of a Security-Governance Approach

Benjamin Farrand and Helena Carrapico

Introduction

Cybercrime is often thought of (perhaps unsurprisingly) as a preoccupation of doctrinal law, criminology, and technology, as a form of activity occurring at the nexus of these distinct areas of study. What can be overlooked through this approach, however, is the inherently political nature of *what* constitutes a "cybercrime," *how* that is determined, and *why* a particular approach to that activity is pursued. Crime is conceptualized within a framework in which culture, social, and economic contexts all play a part in the problematization of a particular form of

B. Farrand (✉)
Newcastle University, Newcastle upon Tyne, UK
e-mail: ben.farrand@ncl.ac.uk

H. Carrapico
Northumbria University, Newcastle upon Tyne, UK
e-mail: helena.farrand-carrapico@northumbria.ac.uk

© The Author(s), under exclusive license to Springer Nature
Switzerland AG 2021
A. Lavorgna and T. J. Holt (eds.), *Researching Cybercrimes*,
https://doi.org/10.1007/978-3-030-74837-1_2

conduct, and the responses to that "crime" are equally influenced by these factors. The purpose of this chapter is to explore this in more detail, uncovering the "why" and "how" of cybercrime policies in the European Union (EU), as a case study used to demonstrate the importance of the security-governance approach in understanding current cybercrime developments.

In particular, this chapter contextualizes the "security governance approach" to cybercrime adopted by the EU by identifying the ideas, interests, and institutions that have served as drivers for this type of response to illicit activities that goes beyond a consideration of "crime" to complement a much broader agenda within the Area of Freedom, Security, and Justice. As the distinctions between crime, information warfare, and other "hybrid threats" blur, as indeed do the lines between "state" and "non-state" in terms of both the perpetrators and victims of these attacks, a restrictive approach to notions of crime appear ineffective in the online environment.

This chapter is structured as follows: the first section provides background and context for the EU's approach to cybercrime. The second section expands upon this context, demonstrating the ideas, interests, and institutions that have served to adapt, challenge, and broaden the EU's approach, highlighting the changing nature of threats online, before drawing conclusions for the study of cybercrime as a politically contested and contestable area of EU security governance.

Background

Cybercrime is ranked among the most important threats to EU security and stability. As clearly outlined in its 2020–2025 Security Union Strategy, the perceived continuous rise of cybercrime is presented as a challenge to the good functioning of European societies' infrastructures, the values that those societies are based on, and the well-being of citizens (European Commission, 2020a). As described by Margaritis Schinas, the Vice-President of the European Commission:

Fighting cybercrime is a key part of our work towards building a Union that protects its citizens. Cybercriminals know no borders. This is why we will continue to support cooperation and exchange of information between law enforcement authorities and make sure they have the right tools and skills to address the challenges of the digital age. (European Commission, 2020b)

The understanding of cybercrime's impacts as having become pervasive has been the result of the perceived risks associated with the proliferation of new technologies, such as portable and wearable technological devices, the increased technological dependency of Europe (both of which creates new vulnerabilities and opportunities for criminal activity), and the facilitated access to cybercrime products and services as part of a thriving illegal economy. Its impact is seen as transversal to all sectors of societal activity, from the safety of our homes to the good functioning of hospitals, with the blurring lines between the physical and the digital world leading to a multiplication of effects. The recent examples of cyberattacks attempting to capitalize on the COVID-19 pandemic and its acceleration of the shift to digital home working and digital services illustrate particularly well the disruption that cybercrime can create at a societal level (*The Guardian*, 2020).

The idea that daily life has become susceptible to a wide range of cyberattacks has also become widespread among the European population, which has expressed concern over the frequency and severity of cybercrime risks and the existence of insufficient measures. According to the 2020 security Eurobarometer, only half of the European population believes that they are well informed about the risks posed by cybercrime, and a third has been the victim of fraudulent e-mails, or phone calls. It is also worth noting that 93% of all respondents have changed the way they use the internet as a result of their security concerns over cybercrime (European Commission, 2020c).

These societal and institutional concerns have been translated into a rapidly expanding policy field characterized by the introduction of legislative measures, preventative programs, and instruments, the fostering of general awareness, and the development of improved cooperation mechanisms at EU level. Over the past 15 years, in particular, it has become a crucial policy field within the EU's Area of Freedom, Security, and Justice. This boom in practitioner and policy-making activity has often been captured in the academic literature by disciplines such as Law (Clough, 2015; de Arimatéia da Cruz, 2020; Fahey, 2014; Gercke, 2009), International Relations (Carrapico & Farrand, 2018; Christou, 2015), and to a lesser extent Criminology (Wall, 2007; Wall & Williams, 2013). The approach to the topic, however, has often tended to be limited to reflections on legislative developments and on the nature of the threat caused by cybercrime, with the political ideas shaping this policy field not being sufficiently considered. The present chapter argues that it is not possible to fully understand the response of the EU to cybercrime without identifying the internal political dynamics of the field, in particular the role of the actors that are present in the field, their ideas, and their interests. Therefore, the chapter takes the social constructivist view that policy responses should not be understood as a neutral and unproblematic reaction to external phenomena, but rather as the result of actors' perceptions of a problem and framing of solutions, which are themselves embedded in a wider institutional and policy background (Kingdon, 1984; Wendt, 1999).

Critical Perspectives on Cybercrime as a Political Issue

Phase 1: Foundations of EU Cybercrime Policy

The EU is something of a latecomer to the cybercrime policy field. By the time it began to develop an interest in taking action in the mid-1990s, the Council of Europe had already proposed the creation of a separate category for computer crime in the mid-1970s (Schjolberg, 2008), and the Organization for Economic Cooperation and Development (OECD) and the Group of Eight (G8) had suggested the harmonization of European computer crime legislations in the mid-1980s (Deflem & Shutt, 2006). At national level, the USA had already regulated unauthorized access to computers and computer networks in the Comprehensive Crime Control Act of 1984, and the Computer Fraud and Abuse Act of 1986 (Computer Crime and Intellectual Property Section Criminal Division, 2007). The UK had taken the same step with its Computer Misuse Act in 1990.

This delay, however, should not be understood as a lack of interest in the field, but rather as an absence of competence in the area of security, given that the European Community (EC) was not able to develop security-related policies until the introduction of the Justice and Home Affairs Pillar by the Treaty of Maastricht. The lack of legal competence also explains the reason why the first EC initiatives in this field were related to economic interests, rather than security ones. As can be seen from the 1985 White Paper on Completing the Internal Market, the 1993 White Paper on Growth, Competitiveness, and Employment, and the 1994 Bangemann Report, the European Community's initial approach to cybercrime was the highlighting of the importance of protecting data, hardware, and software explicitly in the development of the Internal Market (European Commission, 1985, 1993; European Commission and Bangemann Group, 1994). The ideas underlining this approach were the centrality of free trade in bringing prosperity to European Member States, as well as the European Community's desired role in regulating healthy market competition (European Commission, 1985). In this context, computer-related crime was understood as threatening the completion of the Internal Market, with information technologies being presented as a two-edged sword: if on the one hand, technological advancement provided the necessary basis for economic and social development, on the other hand, it also contained the potential to disrupt that same development (European Commission, 1993; European Commission and Bangemann Group, 1994). The EU's interests in cybercrime as an area for potential regulation were therefore initially based on concerns over the economic impacts of the facilitation of "old" crimes such as identify theft and the unauthorized access to information that could be facilitated by "new" technologies (Computer Crime and Intellectual Property Section Criminal Division, 2007). Furthermore, if Member States adopted diverging regulatory approaches to the digital world, criminals might take advantage of legal loopholes, such as the differences in legal definitions and sentences. Such concerns led the European Commission to call for more systematic studies regarding the impact of cybercrime on a wider number of European Union activities.

The transition from an economic understanding of the concept of cybercrime to a security one started to take place at the end of the 1990s, based on the growing perception that there was more than market stability and development at stake. The European Commission's 1998 COMCRIME report on computer crime highlighted the impact on information infrastructures and revealed the extent of their vulnerability, in particular that of computer networks (Kierkegaard, 2007): "computer crime has developed into a major threat of todays' information society. The spreading of computer technology into almost all areas of life as well as the interconnection of computers by international computer networks has made computer crime more diverse, more dangerous, and internationally present" (Sieber, 1998, p. 3). The view that the ramifications of cybercrime were going beyond the market was also started to be present in other security-related policies and instruments, such as the Action Plan to Combat organized Crime and the: "Technological innovations such as the Internet and electronic banking turn out to be extremely convenient vehicles either for committing crime or for transferring the resulting profits into seemingly licit activities" (Council of the European Union, 1997, p. 1). This connection of cybercrime with other areas of the Justice and Home Affairs Pillar is, however, not surprising given not only the growing awareness of how technology abuse could impact other areas of society, but also the European Commission's desire to reinforce its competence in internal security, which was based on the perception that the EU was best positioned to support Member States' coordination in Justice and Home Affairs.

On the basis of the COMCRIME report, the European Commission proposed that action should be taken to further explore the impact of cybercrime on other areas of internal security, as well as to accelerate the cooperation efforts between Member States in order to more effectively address this problem. The Commission's initiative resulted in cybercrime being recognized for the first time as a security threat in the European Council Tampere conclusions in 1999, which stated that action should be taken in tackling "high tech" crimes, which also included the sexual exploitation of children online, through common action aimed at coordinating definitions for these crimes (European Council, 1999, para. 48). It also opened the door for the creation of security-specific instruments related to cybercrime, such as the 1999 Safer Internet Action Plan (European Parliament and Council of the European Union, 1999).

Phase 2: Institutionalization and Expansion, with Lingering Problems

The proposals that followed the Tampere Conclusions formed part of the *eEurope 2002* action plan, which made it clear that the concerns regarding crime in this area, were predominantly associated with ensuring the proper functioning of the internal market through the provision of a safe and secure Internet (Council of the European Union, 2000). In line with the action plan, the Commission produced another report on improving the security of Information Infrastructures and combating computer-related crime, again predominantly arguing that this was necessary in order to ensure that the EU was well-placed to benefit from the economic advantages that the use of the Internet by commercial operators could provide (European Commission, 2000, p. 2). While the facilitation of the sexual exploitation of minors through the Internet was explicitly acknowledged as a subject that needed to be immediately addressed, the main driver of the proposals in the field of cybercrime was predominantly economic, but framed in terms of economic security (European Commission, 2000, p. 3). This phase of EU cybercrime development resulted in the passing of the Council Framework Decisions on combating the sexual exploitation of children and child pornography (2004/68/JHA) and attacks against information systems (2005/222/JHA). These Framework Decisions were subsequently updated and transformed into Directives, Directives 2011/93/EU and Directive 2013/40/EU, respectively. This period also saw the beginning of an approach to European "cybersecurity" as distinct from cybercrime, and the beginning of the agencification of the field (see for example Levi-Faur, 2012), with the establishment of cybersecurity focused EU agencies such as the European Network and Information

Security Agency, or ENISA, in 2004. ENISA's creation was based in the idea that there was a need for greater levels of coherence and coordination in the EU's approach to cybersecurity, which could be facilitated through the cooperation between national authorities and private cybersecurity professionals, with ENISA acting as both an information hub and a center for the development of best practices. The success of ENISA has led to a gradual expansion of its mandate, budget, and operational capacity under subsequent revisions to legislation, the most recent of which was completed in 2019 under Regulation 2019/881.

The understanding of a need for greater coherence in combating cybercrime was highlighted in 2007 with the publication of the Communication on the fight against cybercrime (European Commission, 2007). The key focus of this particular Communication was the perception that there was a lack of coherence in the approaches of the Member States toward the issue of cybercrime, as well as a lack of cooperation between national authorities (2007, p. 4). While the focus of cybercrime policies remains based in a concern over economic costs of criminal activity, the approach at this time was not the establishment of new offenses or harmonizing legislation, but instead measures to improve understanding of the phenomenon and increasing cooperation between national authorities, and more importantly between national authorities and the private sector in order to effectively combat online crimes (Carrapico & Farrand, 2017). Central to this effort was the creation of Europol's European Cyber Crime Centre (or EC3) unit in 2012 (European Commission, 2012). At a broader level, however, this period of cybercrime development is marked by the drawing together of issues of crime, security, and defense in the context of the AFSJ through the publication of the EU's Cyber Security Strategy (for commentary, see Carrapico & Barrinha, 2018; European Commission and High Representative of the European Union for Foreign Affairs and Security Policy, 2013). The EU Cyber Security Strategy underscored the perception on the part of the EU that the concepts of crime and security are inextricably linked, insofar as "resilience" is central to both (European Commission and High Representative of the European Union for Foreign Affairs and Security Policy, 2013, pp. 5–6). Resilience, which was discussed in the context of resilience from cyberattacks specifically in a 2010 Communication on the EU's internal security strategy (European Commission, 2010, pp. 9–10), is understood as a more holistic approach to security, which "does not refer to the absence of danger but rather the ability of a system [...] to reorganize to rebound from a potentially catastrophic event" (Dunn Cavelty, 2013, p. 6). In this respects, the interests of the EU in ensuring resilience are best ensured through a process of "Europeanisation through standardization" in which cooperation between technical experts and national authorities results in the development of robust security best practices, using the EU's agencies such as ENISA to coordinate action (Cantero Gamito, 2018). Furthermore, the private sector operators of digital services are brought into the regulatory network, the rationale for their inclusion in both policy formation and security provision being based on a perception of shared risk as the result of this interdependence that incentivizes cooperation (Ballou et al., 2016; Christensen & Petersen, 2017). In this understanding of security, cybercrime and cybersecurity are not distinct policy fields with their own separate legislative and policy regimes, but instead part of a complex tapestry of interconnected and interdependent laws, policies, institutions, and actors. Researching this area of activity therefore requires going beyond the specific laws applicable to online criminal activity to consider the broader security and defense frameworks that represent the other two pillars of the EU's general approach to online security.

It must be stated, however, that the problems of lack of cooperation and incoherence continue in this field (Barrinha, 2020; Carrapico & Farrand, 2016), much to the EU's consternation. Despite the focus on increased coherence and cooperation that served as the basis for the new institutional structures within Europol as EC3 and through the creation of ENISA as the EU's Cybersecurity Agency, recent initiatives have indicated that problems remain with the EU's cybercrime framework. In 2019, the EU launched infringement proceedings against 23 Member States for a failure to correctly transpose the Directive on combating child sexual abuse, and four Member States for failing to correctly transpose the Directive on attacks against information systems (European Commission, 2019a, p. 12), indicating that the creation of a coherent European approach to these specific forms of cybercrime has not yet been successful. Cross-border cooperation also appears to remain an issue, with the Commission noting in its 2020 Security Union Strategy that access to evidence, police cooperation, and improving law enforcement capacities in digital investigations could all be improved, proposing coordination between the Commission, ENISA, and Europol on a cybercrime "rapid alert system" that could be used to facilitate speedy exchange of information and investigation in the event of significant cyber-incidents (see European Commission, 2020a, pp. 10–13). However, these coordination efforts are becoming even more difficult in light of the developments apparent in the third phase of cybercrime law and policy, in which we see a further convergence between issues of crime, security, and defense, as well as a blurring of the lines between economically and politically motivated cyberattacks, as well as the lines between private and public perpetrators of such attacks.

Phase 3: Cybercrime, Hybrid Threats, and the Blurring of Cybersecurity

Convergence and blurring are the watchwords of the latest phase of cybersecurity developments. In the European Agenda on Security, published in 2015, we can see a continuation of the idea that increased coordination and coherence of policies in this field are required, and in particular, a more "joined-up inter-agency and cross-sectoral approach" (European Commission, 2015, p. 4) and a "need to bring together all internal and external dimensions of security" (European Commission, 2015, p. 4). Furthermore, the three identified areas of focus are those of terrorism, organized crime, and cybercrime, with the recognition that "they are clearly interlinked and cross-border threats" (European Commission, 2015, p. 13). In its approach to cybercrime, the European Agenda on Security treats the subject as one aspect of a multi-faceted security threat, in which cybersecurity is the first line of defense against cybercrime, which could include attacks on critical information infrastructures powering an electricity grid (for example) by an organized crime group using ransomware in order to demand money, a terrorist organization in order to cause a serious incident, or a state entity to destabilize a neighboring power. For this reason, increased coordination between EC3, ENISA, and other agencies was highlighted as a key objective, reinforcing the idea of cybercrime only being effectively tackled through increased agencification and public–private cooperation (European Commission, 2015, p. 20). Following this initiative, the EU implemented Directive 2016/1148 on Network and Information Systems (NIS) security, increasing national authority and private security coordination, as well as requiring private providers of NIS to ensure the protection of their networks and disclose potential breaches.

Since 2016 in particular, however, the emphasis of EU policies and actions in this field has focused on the nature of cyberthreats as being of a "hybrid" form where the lines between economic and political motivations, as well as between public and private perpetrators, begin to blur. With an emphasis placed upon the use of conventional and unconventional methods, including diplomatic, military, economic and technological means to achieve specific objectives while remaining below the threshold of formally declared warfare (European Commission and High Representative of the Union for Foreign Affairs and Security Policy, 2016, p. 2), we have entered a particularly contentious period for cybercrime policies, where the nature, means, and perpetrators of actions online make legislating (and indeed, researching) cyber*crime* as a distinct field increasingly difficult. In the Hybrid Threats Communication, the Commission and High Representative indicated that the resilience approach to cybersecurity allows parties to detect, withstand and respond to attacks and cybercrimes, "which can counter hybrid threats" (2016, pp. 14–15). This is reflective of an understanding that Russia is an active proponent of "information warfare" as well more "traditional" forms of cyberattack such as DDoS attacks and malicious code, as a means of exerting control throughout Eastern Europe (Bachmann & Gunneriusson, 2015), and was particularly active in sewing disinformation during its incursion into Ukraine (Treverton et al., 2018). Disinformation is identified in the Hybrid Threats Communication as a new challenge for the EU, which raises concerns over actors using it "to radicalize individuals, destabilize society and control the political narrative" (2016, p. 4). Disinformation is presented by the Commission as being a source of rising instability in the EU, as well as presenting threats for effective policy-making in fields such as health and climate change (European Commission, 2018a), but is not explicitly framed in "crime" terms, despite being identified as a clear security threat. Measures intended to tackle it have focused on measures such as encouraging social media platforms to deprioritize disinformation stories and identify bots used to spread falsehoods, as well as promoting fact-checking and transparency initiatives (European Commission, 2018b). However, the active spread of disinformation online is not categorized as a cybercrime. There are academics that consider that given the harms to the victims of disinformation, as well as the broader social harms, including it within the sphere of criminal activity would be beneficial (see also Bossetta, 2018 on the links to cybercrime; Buchanan & Benson, 2019). Instead, EU efforts have focused on non-legal measures to control the spread of disinformation, although they have not discounted active regulation of social mediaplatforms should they prove unwilling or unable to mitigate this cyber-enabled threat (European Commission, 2019b).

The interrelation of disinformation with other security threats that make it a key focus of current cybersecurity policies is made even more evident by the COVID-19 pandemic, with conspiracy theories regarding the origin of SARS-COV-2 (the virus that causes the COVID-19 disease) as well as promoting anti-vaccine positions have been referred to by the Commission as an "infodemic" (European Commission, 2020d, p. 15). Disinformation, despite not being classified as "criminal" activity, is nevertheless linked to cybercrime more broadly, including by Europol (Europol, 2020) and in the Commission's 20th Security Union Progress Report, where it was included in a list of contemporary threats— "terrorism, organized crime, cyberattacks, disinformation" (European Commission, 2019a, p. 1). It is also worth considering that in the July 2020 Communication on the EU Security Union Strategy, which sets out the security objectives of the EU for 2020–2025, tackling cybercrime and hybrid threats including disinformation are listed as key priorities in ensuring effective cybersecurity (European Commission, 2020a, pp. 3–4). Yet if disinformation is a potential source of real harm to democracy, health, and security, why is the intentional dissemination of it not considered criminal activity?

The answer to this, it could be argued, is inherently political, and linked back to the ideas, interests, and institutions that act as drivers of EU cybercrime law-making, and in this respect, is equally applicable to efforts to create a Regulation pertaining to the dissemination of terrorist content online (European Commission, 2018c). While both the spread of disinformation and content glorifying or promoting terrorism in such a way as to further radicalization efforts are both explicitly framed as security threats, and that it is clearly in the interests of the EU to suppress such content, active regulation of this content comes into conflict with competing ideas and interests that have shaped the EU's institutions. In particular, both disinformation and terrorist material are forms of *expression* of ideas or opinions. For this reason, efforts to tackle this content can potentially result in conflicts with the right to freedom of expression under Article 10 of the European Convention on Human Rights and Article 11 of the Charter of Fundamental Rights of the EU, as stated in the Code of Practice on disinformation (European Commission, 2018b, p. 3) and the Proposal for the Regulation on terrorist content online (European Commission, 2018c, p. 2). There has been considerable academic discussion of how difficult these issues are to regulate due to the potential conflicts with human rights (Bechtold, 2020; see for example Klompmaker, 2019; Marsden et al., 2020; Pielemeier, 2020), which has resulted so far in a limited approach to how disinformation is treated in law, and delays to the approval of the proposed Regulation. Given these complexities, both in terms of the relation between these areas and other areas of law not explicitly in the domain of cybercrime, such as human rights laws relating to expression, as well as the broader security frameworks and interests of the EU, it is essential that researchers seeking to better understand the evolution of this field are aware of the way in which cybercrime specifically fits into the EU's approach to cybersecurity as an essential dimension of the AFSJ more generally.

Conclusion

This chapter explored the ideas, interests, and actors active in EU cybercrime policy, to illustrate the need to take into account the political context in which the cybercrime legal and policy framework is developed. As mentioned in the background section, the existing academic literature has often tended to analyze the different dimensions of the phenomena of cybercrime as separate and distinct issues, and accordingly, the adequacy of legal and policy responses without however problematizing the relation between the problem and the response. The chapter instead advocates that cybercrime is not its own distinct legal or policy domain, and cannot be separated from the broader cybersecurity framework, which is marked by a convergence between crime, security, and defense. Due to this conceptual and practical blurring, the study of cybercrime must take place at the intersection between disciplines in order for a more holistic and contextualized understanding of current law and policy changes. If cybersecurity is a puzzle, then the different disciplines studying the field are the pieces that help to build the bigger picture; a study of cybercrime that comes from a purely legal perspective, and only looks at those hard legally binding instruments tackling the dissemination of child abuse material and attacks against information systems, will only provide a partial image of the broad array of developments in the field that while not explicitly categorized as criminal law instruments, nevertheless contribute to the combating of online crimes.

That combating harmful activities online is becoming increasingly complex and politically contested is part of the reason why both legislating and studying this field in isolation are incredibly difficult. Whereas in the first phase it would be possible to treat cybercrime and its related instruments as separate and distinct from other online concerns, with the expansion and development of a concept of "cybersecurity" in the second phase, where greater coherence between systems of law, policy, soft mechanisms, and agencies resulted in a need for greater policy coherence, many of the results were focused upon setting up institutions and networks, rather than imposing penalties. Furthermore, the focus on security as resilience has meant an increased emphasis on prevention before the fact, rather than criminal investigation afterward, which an approach that focuses only upon laws may miss. With the third phase, in which the lines between public and private, economically motivated and politically instigated all blur, and the nature of the actions politically sensitive to the extent that explicit criminalization is difficult to achieve or justify, then a broader, holistic approach that looks at these developments in the context of a joined-up approach to the AFSJ may be more beneficial for the cyber-researcher than one that focuses in on one area of development specifically. This of course does not entail that all researchers need to be interdisciplinary champions, taking approaches from law, criminology, international relations, sociology, and computer science at the same time—instead, it requires that researchers with an interest in cybercrime are aware of these other disciplines and their findings, and how they can be made relevant to their own work.

References

Bachmann, S. D., & Gunneriusson, H. (2015). Russia's hybrid warfare in the East: The integral nature of the information sphere military matters. *Georgetown Journal of International Affairs, 16*, 198–211.

Ballou, T., Allen, J., & Francis, K. (2016). Hands-off approach or effective partnership? *Journal of Information Warfare, 15*, 44–59.

Barrinha, A. (2020). European security in cyberspace. In A. Calcara, R. Csernatoni, & C. Lavallée (Eds.), *Emerging security technologies and EU governance: Actors, practices and processes*. Routledge.

Bechtold, E. (2020). Terrorism, the internet, and the threat to freedom of expression: The regulation of digital intermediaries in Europe and the United States. *Journal of Media Law, 12*, 13–46.

Bossetta, M. (2018). The weaponization of social media: Spear phishing and cyberattack on democracy. *Journal of International Affairs, 71*, 97–106.

Buchanan, T., & Benson, V. (2019). Spreading disinformation on Facebook: Do trust in message source, risk propensity, or personality affect the organic reach of "fake news"? *Social Media + Society, 5*, 1–9.

Cantero Gamito, M. (2018). Europeanization through standardization: ICT and telecommunications. *Yearbook of European Law, 37*, 395–423.

Carrapico, H., & Barrinha, A. (2018). European Union cyber security as an emerging research and policy field. *European Politics and Society, 19,* 299–303.

Carrapico, H., & Farrand, B. (2018). Cyber crime as a fragmented policy field in the context of the area of freedom, security and justice. In A. Ripoll Servent & F. Trauner (Eds.), *The Routledge handbook of justice and home affairs research, Routledge Handbook Series.* Routledge.

Carrapico, H., & Farrand, B. (2017). Dialogue, partnership and empowerment for network and information security: The changing role of the private sector from objects of regulation to regulation shapers. *Crime, Law and Social Change, 67,* 245–263.

Carrapico, H., & Farrand, B. (2016). The European Union's fight against cybercrime: Policy, legal and practical challenges. In M. Fletcher, E. Herlin-Karnell & C. Matera (Eds.), *The European Union as an area of freedom, security and justice.* Routledge.

Christensen, K. K., & Petersen, K. L. (2017). Public–private partnerships on cyber security: A practice of loyalty. *International Affairs, 93,* 1435–1452.

Christou, G. (2015). *Cybersecurity in the European Union: Resilience and adaptability in governance policy.* AIAA. Houndmills.

Clough, J. (2015). *Principles of cybercrime.* Cambridge University Press.

Computer Crime and Intellectual Property Section Criminal Division. (2007). *Prosecuting computer crimes.* Office of Legal Education Executive Office for United States Attorneys.

Council of the European Union. (2000). *eEurope 2002—An information society for all.* Brussels.

Council of the European Union. (1997). *Action plan to combat organised crime* (No. C251/1–15.8.97). Official Journal of the European Communities.

de Arimatéia da Cruz, J. (2020). The legislative framework of the European Union (EU) convention on cybercrime. In T. J. Holt & A. M. Bossler (Eds.), *The Palgrave handbook of international cybercrime and cyberdeviance.* Springer.

Deflem, M., & Shutt, E. (2006). Law enforcement and computer security threats and measures. In H. Bidgodi (Ed.), *Handbook of information security, information warfare, social, legal, and international issues, and security foundations.* Wiley.

Dunn Cavelty, M. (2013). *A resilient Europe for an open, safe and secure cyberspace* (No. 23). Swedish Institute of International Affairs.

European Commission. (1985). *White paper: Completing the internal market* (No. COM(85) 310 final). European Commission, Brussels.

European Commission. (1993). *Growth, competitiveness, employment: The challenges and ways forward into the 21st century—White paper* (No. COM(93)700 final).

European Commission. (2000). *Creating a safer information society by improving the security of information infrastructures and combating computer-related crime* (No. COM(2000) 890).

European Commission. (2007). *Towards a general policy on the fight against cyber crime* (No. COM(2007) 267).

European Commission. (2010). *The EU internal security strategy in action: Five steps towards a more secure Europe* (No. COM(2010) 673 final).

European Commission. (2012). *Tackling crime in our digital age: Establishing a European cybercrime centre* (No. COM(2012) 140).

European Commission. (2015). *The European agenda on security* (No. COM(2015) 185).

European Commission. (2018a). *Tackling online disinformation: A European approach* (No. COM(2018) 236).

European Commission. (2018b). *EU code of practice on online disinformation.*

European Commission. (2018c). *Proposal for a regulation on preventing the dissemination of terrorist content online* (No. COM(2018) 640).

European Commission. (2019a). *Twentieth progress report towards an effective and genuine Security Union* (No. COM(2019) 552).

European Commission. (2019b). *Code of practice on disinformation: First annual reports.*

European Commission. (2020a). *Communication on the EU security union strategy* (No. COM(2020) 605.

European Commission. (2020b). *Cybercrime: New survey shows Europeans feel better informed but remain concerned.* Accessible at: https://ec.europa.eu/commission/commissioners/2019-2024/schinas/announcements/cybercrime-new-survey-shows-europeans-feel-better-informed-remain-concerned_en.

European Commission. (2020c). *Special Eurobarometer 499—European's attitudes towards cyber security.*

European Commission. (2020d). *Europe's moment: Repair and prepare for the next generation* (No. COM(2020) 456 final).

European Commission, Bangemann Group. (1994). *Europe and the global information society: Recommendations of the high-level group on the information society to the Corfu European Council* (No. S.2/94). Brussels.

European Commission and High Representative of the European Union for Foreign Affairs and Security Policy. (2013). *Cybersecurity strategy of the European Union: An open, safe and secure cyberspace* (No. JOIN(2013) 1). Brussels.

European Commission and High Representative of the Union for Foreign Affairs and Security Policy. (2016). *Joint framework on countering hybrid threats* (No. JOIN(2016) 18).

European Council. (1999). *Tampere European Council conclusions.* Tampere.

European Parliament and Council of the European Union. (1999). Decision No. 276/1999/EC of the European Parliament and of the Council of 25 January 1999 adopting a multiannual Community action plan on promoting safer use of the Internet by combating illegal and harmful content on global networks.

Europol. (2020). *Catching the virus: Cybercrime, disinformation and the COVID-19 pandemic.* Accessible at: https://www.europol.europa.eu/publications-doc uments/catching-virus-cybercrime-disinformation-and-covid-19-pandemic.

Fahey, E. (2014). The EU's cybercrime and cyber-security rulemaking: Mapping the internal and external dimensions of EU security. *European Journal of Risk Regulation, 5,* 46.

Gercke, M. (2009). Europe's legal approaches to cybercrime. *ERA Forum, 10,* 409–420.

Kierkegaard, S. M. (2007). EU tackles cyber crime. In L. J. Janczewski & A. M. Colarik (Eds.), *Cyber warfare and cyber terrorism.* IGI Global.

Kingdon, J. W. (1984). *Agendas, alternatives, and public policies.* Harper Collins.

Klompmaker, N. (2019). Censor them at any cost: A social and legal assessment of enhanced action against terrorist content online scientific. *Amsterdam L.F. 11,* 3–29.

Levi-Faur, D. (2012). Regulatory networks and regulatory agencification: Towards a single European regulatory space. In B. Rittberger & A. Wonka (Eds.), *Agency governance in the EU.* Routledge.

Marsden, C., Meyer, T., & Brown, I. (2020). Platform values and democratic elections: How can the law regulate digital disinformation? *Computer Law & Security Review, 36,* 105373.

Pielemeier, J. (2020). Disentangling disinformation: What makes regulating disinformation so difficult? Symposium: News, disinformation, and social media responsibility. *Utah Law Review, 2020,* 917–940.

Schjolberg, S. (2008). *The history of global harmonization on cybercrime legislation—The road to Geneva.* Cyber Crime Law. Accessible at: https://cyberc rimelaw.net/documents/cybercrime_history.pdf.

Sabbagh, D. (2020). Covid-related cybercrime drives attacks on UK to record number. *The Guardian*. Accessible at: https://www.theguardian.com/techno logy/2020/nov/03/covid-related-cybercrime-drives-attacks-on-uk-to-record-number.

Sieber, U. (1998). *Legal aspects of computer-related crime in the information society: Prepared for the European Commission*. University of Würzburg. Accessible at: https://www.law.tuwien.ac.at/sieber.pdf.

Treverton, G. F., Thvedt, A., Chen, A. R., Lee, K., & McCue, M. (2018). *Addressing hybrid threats*. Center for Asymmetric Threat Studies; The European Centre of Excellence for Countering Hybrid Threats, Swedish Defence University.

Wall, D.S. (2007). *Cybercrime: The transformation of crime in the information age*. Polity Press.

Wall, D. S., & Williams, M. L. (2013). Policing cybercrime: Networked and social media technologies and the challenges for policing. *Policing and Society, 23*, 409–412.

Wendt, A. (1999). *Social theory of international politics*. Cambridge University Press.

3

Programming the Criminologist: Developing Cyber Skills to Investigate Cybercrime

Ruth McAlister and Fabian Campbell-West

Introduction

The modern World Wide Web went live to a global public on August 6, 1991 (Leiner et al., 2009) and today vast swaths of society have become increasingly dependent on digital technology, with most people connecting to the internet for business, study, or pleasure in their daily lives through a range of digital technologies. The rapid pace at which large parts of the world have become connected is evident when we consider in the early 1990s approximately 15 million people were connected to the internet (IWS, 2020) which at this time was largely an information and retrieval tool. In 2020 over 4.9 billion users are

R. McAlister (✉)
School of Applied Social and Policy Sciences, Ulster University, Northern Ireland, UK
e-mail: r.mcalister@ulster.ac.uk

F. Campbell-West
Queen's University Belfast, Belfast, UK

© The Author(s), under exclusive license to Springer Nature Switzerland AG 2021
A. Lavorgna and T. J. Holt (eds.), *Researching Cybercrimes*,
https://doi.org/10.1007/978-3-030-74837-1_3

43

connected to the internet (IWS, 2020) utilizing the now fully immersive, and transformative social arena that is interwoven into society. Not only has connectivity spread rapidly, but technical capabilities of digital tools and speed with which they can transmit data. The criminological study of cybercrime has likewise rapidly expanded. Examining this scholarship alongside developments in computing, communications, and other digital technologies reveals the influence of key technological progress in relation to cybercrime research.

In terms of tracing the history of such research, the early 1990s were typically concerned with understanding "computer" crime, while in the late 1990s to 2000s the shift became focused on "cybercrime" research (Stratton et al., 2017). This scholarship not only takes place on the surface, or open web (the web we use every day with standard search engines), but also on the dark web (first introduced in 2000), where content is not available via standard search engines (Baravalle et al., 2017). Not all content on the dark web is necessarily illicit or illegal, but it is here that you will find illegal websites selling weapons, drugs, fake identity documents, stolen credit card data, and those that host extreme adult pornography, or indecent child abuse imagery (Alnabulsi & Islam, 2018; Cubitt et al., 2020; Martin, 2014; McAlister & Monaghan, 2020; Pastrana et al., 2018; Weimann, 2016).

A growing focus of cybercrime research has sought to understand the nature, trust, and patterns of online criminal networks (Holt, 2013; Lavorgna et al., 2020; Motoyama et al., 2012; Pete et al., 2020; Tavabi et al., 2019). However, it has been argued that criminological engagement with cybercrime has been largely inward-looking and lacking a critical and interdisciplinary engagement with other disciplines, such as computer science and software engineering (Stratton et al., 2017), meaning that much potential of the internet for crime research remains untapped (van Gelder & Van Daele, 2014). Given that the online world is such a rich crime site for criminologists it is important that we think in a more technical manner, diversify skills and really embrace interdisciplinarity in order that cybercrime research can truly become *digital* research. As such, this chapter will chart how a criminologist can begin to develop cyber skills in order to advance a new generation of scholarship on cybercrime. In so doing do it will encourage a way of thinking about problems that uses elements of software engineering and data science to empower criminological research.

Background

Before discussing how criminologists could think differently about researching cybercrime, it is important to go back to the beginning and briefly discuss what we mean by criminology. There are many theories, methods, and schools of thought that come under the broad rubric of criminology, with criminologists interested generally in crime and its control, including, but not limited to criminal justice processes, crime trends, offending behavior, and victimization. Since the field's genesis in the early twentieth century, methodological procedures have tended to be quite traditional, with an inclination within the discipline to adhere to particular research traditions: survey data, official statistics, interviews, ethnographies, and observational data (Kleck et al., 2006; van Gelder & Van Deale, 2014). While there is no evidence yet of a paradigmatic shift within criminology, there is some evidence of greater interdisciplinarity with other subject areas such as computer science and software engineering. Chan and Bennett Moses (2017) observe some engagement with big data research with projects investigating social media data analysis, and an increasing uptake of computer modeling/algorithms as a predictive tool in police and criminal justice decision making. While this is welcoming, they suggest that "criminologists and, indeed, social scientists more broadly must increasingly 'share the podium' and collaborate with technical experts to further progress this field" (Chan & Bennett Moses, 2017, p. 25).

The proliferation of open-source software, open-access journals, and different social media platforms means that activities that were once niche and specialized are now democratized. It has never been easier to learn new digital skills, but with that comes increased expectations on diversity of skills. It is no longer possible to remain in a silo, with academic funding sources requiring cross-disciplinary and applied projects.

Fig. 3.1 Workflow for a digital criminologist

Depending on academic training or work experience, people view, solve, and communicate problems differently. Though people are not easily assigned single labels, for the purpose of this chapter we will consider three different viewpoints:

- A software engineer will think about getting hold of data, manipulating it according to some automated process and outputting it as quickly as possible;
- A data scientist will transform, condense, and model data to extract concrete information;
- A criminologist will scrutinize information and use domain knowledge to make decisions.

These viewpoints fit naturally together in a single workflow to take observations from the real world and inferring new facts and intelligence (see Fig. 3.1).

This chapter will introduce ways of thinking and tools that can be used by criminologists to help them progress efficiently. Readers familiar with this subject can find more advanced discussions in Chapters 8 and 10–13.

Software Engineering for Criminologists

A software engineer solves problems by writing computer code to perform a set of actions. This is useful to a criminologist for many reasons, including:

- Running long and complex steps repeatedly and consistently;
- Being able to share methodology with colleagues and partners;

- Executing programs multiple times, to either confirm correct results or to try multiple different random elements (hypotheses).

Being able to share not only results but also data and methodology will increase the impact of an author's work and therefore increase citations and other measures of dissemination.

A key aspect of good software engineering is his/her writing to be understood. There are many ways to achieve this including:

- Designing software and producing documents to help communicate that design;
- Structuring code in units to make it easier to understand;
- Writing comments in code to indicate goal and motivation.

Comments are simply natural language text placed in a computer program to inform a human reader *what* is being attempted and *why*. The code itself is the *how*. The computer will ignore comments and focus on the code itself. When starting programming people often think "no one else will read this" and "I will remember what this does." The latter statement is a spectacularly common fallacy. You may come across a relatively recent trend advocating "self-documenting code." This has its place, but it is important when starting out to build the discipline of making comments for yourself if nothing else. Returning to code you wrote six months ago and smiling because you left yourself notes is a very positive thing.

Software programs will typically take information as input, process it in some way, and then output new information. Some examples are:

- A web crawler may take as an input URLs of websites and output downloaded pages;
- A translation program may take as an input a list of sentences in one language and output those sentences in another language;
- A semantic analysis program may take as an input a short piece of text, such as a social media post, and output if that text was positive, negative, or neutral.

Learning to write good software takes time and dedication, but that is all you need. The best way to learn to write software is to just start writing software. To get started use the official documentation for your chosen language and computing platform. A comprehensive guide to getting started with Python, for example, is available at the official website (www.python.org).

A useful thought process for a (digital) criminologist to follow for a given project is:

- What is the overall problem I'm trying to solve?
- What data or information do I have?
- What do I need to do with this information?
- What does success look like?
- What are the main entities ("things") in my data?
- How can I simplify the problem into smaller pieces?
- Repeat 1–6 for each piece
- Write new or find existing programs to solve each piece
- Join everything together.

Sometimes it is very difficult to write programs to do each piece of work. However, there is often an advantage to writing programs for the rest of pieces to reduce the overall amount of work that needs done. Software programs can help you focus on the main task that requires your time and attention, by reliably and automatically performing processing tasks on peripheral tasks.

A Software Engineer's Toolkit

Programming Language(s)

There are many programming languages available and all have pros and cons. There is no single *best* language for all situations. A programming language is like a tool, where one needs to choose the most appropriate one for the job. Some blogs and opinion pieces online will attempt to make arguments that you *have* to learn language X but that is not the case. Choose one language at first and commit to it.

A language the authors recommend for a beginner is Python (https://www.python.org/). It has been designed to be simple and clear. It is also free and there is a large community of people who can help with whatever problem you are working on. There are also a variety of high-quality books and learning materials available with the content being continually updated (Matthes, 2019; Ramalho, 2015; Shaw, 2017). More advanced techniques include the use of design patterns, which are known and accepted solutions to common problems (Freeman & Robson, 2020). If you want to choose a different language, there are several things to consider:

- What is it you want to achieve? If you want to run a program once and get results then a beginner-friendly language that lets you get started quickly is helpful.
- How long has the language been around? There are several relatively new languages that are appealing to experienced software engineers, but older languages may be more stable and have better documentation and support.
- How easy is it to get started? Is it simple to install? Is the documentation good?
- How regularly is the language updated? Is there still an active community around the language?
- What are your long-term goals? If you're dedicating time and effort to learn a language you want to maximize the return on investment.
- What are your peers in your area of research using? If you want to share your research findings it may be more impactful to follow colleagues in the field.

You can use a similar decision-making process that you would for a spoken language. Learning Latin would be interesting and rewarding, but learning English or Spanish is more useful for most people.

Source Code Editor / Integrated Development Environment (IDE)

When starting out with a language a good editor or IDE can help you get started more easily. The authors recommend PyCharm Community Edition for Python development (https://www.jetbrains.com/pycharm/). An IDE can offer assistance while writing programs by highlighting errors in syntax, offering suggestions to improve your code, and pointing to errors that occur when the program runs.

Version control

When writing papers and documents you may find yourself in the situation where you have several versions of a document like

- My Paper v1
- My Paper v2
- My Paper v2b
- My Paper v3 FINAL.

This is a form of manual version control which is very fragile. Anyone who has had to merge tracked changes from multiple colleagues into a single document knows the challenges associated with having several slightly different copies of the same document!

Software engineers use version control systems to help mitigate these problems. Once you become comfortable with programming it is worth investing time learning for many reasons:

- It becomes easier to track the history of your own work;
- It is easier to collaborate with other colleagues on the same programs;
- It becomes trivial to share your work with peers.

You may have read academic papers who share source code and materials online and they use version control systems to do this. Two popular ones are GitHub (https://github.com/) and GitLab (https://about.git lab.com/). These are commercial services built on top of open-source technology called *git*. Git has become the de-facto standard for version control and is the best system to learn. There is an excellent online book and tutorial videos official git website (https://git-scm.com/doc).

Databases

Databases are a large topic and there are many excellent books on the subject for beginners and experts alike. Readers who are new to the topic can read (Beaulieu, 2020; Beighley, 2007). As a brief introduction, people use the word database to refer to two main things:

- A management system for holding database records. The management system allows authenticated access, ensures data coherence, performs maintenance to keep the system in optimal condition, backups to help ensure data integrity.
- Database records themselves. A table is a collection of structured data with beneficial properties.

There are different types of database, but the most common type is *relational*. Relational databases store data in structures called relations or tables. A database table is conceptually the same as a table you would find in a document, with each row called a database entry/record/tuple and each column called a field.

A database table often denotes an entity, either real or conceptual; or a relationship between entities. Database designs are often visualized using entity-relationship diagrams, which show how different entities interact with each other. Figure 3.2 is an example of an entity-relationship diagram for a database about a cybercrime forum. You can read this diagram as follows:

- An Author creates 0 or more Threads. A Thread is created by exactly 1 Author.
- A Thread contains 1 or more Posts. A Post belongs to exactly 1 Thread.
- An Author writes 1 or more Posts. A Post is written by exactly 1 Author.

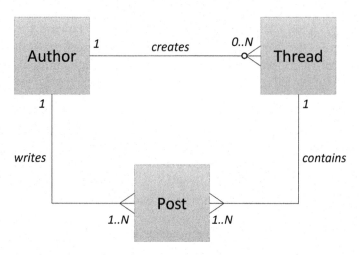

Fig. 3.2 Entity-relationship diagram for threads, posts, and authors on a cybercrime forum

Where to Look for More Help

When learning a new topic, particularly one that has matured, a recent book is a good way to get started quickly. There are many online resources to get up-to-date help and support with problems. The first place to check is the official documentation for the topic you are working on. Web searches for specific topics or errors often lead to community forums, documentation, or tutorial videos that can help with a solution. One of the most reputable and popular websites for support is Stack Overflow (https://stackoverflow.com/).

Data Science for Criminologists

Data science is related to software engineering, albeit with a different emphasis on the pieces of work. Many of the conceptual skills are the same, including attention to detail and breaking a problem down into smaller sub-problems. A key goal in data science is to clean and arrange data to either learn from it or infer some new information. Data scientists often use software programs, either bespoke for the task at hand, such as a translation program; or general tools that can perform many tasks, such as a spreadsheet program (Godsey, 2017).

Some simple data analysis can be to calculate statistics about data. This can help you understand where the value lies in your data sets. More advanced data science is to apply previously trained algorithms to the data to extract information or make inferences (Geron, 2019). An example would be translating between languages or estimating the sentiment of a piece of text.

A useful data workflow for a criminologist is as follows:

- Collect your data in raw form;
- Organize data into a structured format;
- Clean data ready for analysis:

  - Remove bad records;
  - Detect and remove (or mark) duplicates;
  - Fill in missing gaps to make later steps easier;

- Extract features—such as user names, key measurements, or dates;
- Calculate statistics or decisions based on the features—such as date ranges, occurrences of a particular key term;
- Filter data based on metrics—select the data you are interested in, or discard the data that's less relevant;
- Visualize results—tabulate complex data or plot numeric data;
- Repeat earlier stages as required, refining at each iteration.

You will not always need to do every step in the workflow. Sometimes you will be given clean data, sometimes you need to iterate parts of the process as you learn more about the problem. You can adapt this workflow to suit your needs, but the overall steps are the same.

A Data Scientist's Toolkit

Software Tools

Programming languages with large software libraries for performing statistical and machine learning operations, such as *scikit-learn* and *pandas* in Python (Geron, 2019). Statistical software, including visualization packages and spreadsheets, can be invaluable for quantitative analysis and communicating results.

Data Cleaning

Making sure data is coherent and high quality is an often overlooked and certainly less glamorous side of data science. However, making sure data is organized and errors have been removed will simplify the later stages considerably (McCallum, 2012).

Consider a few examples:

- A web scraper pulling data from a website fails to detect some information about one of the fields;
- Human error in data entry means a field is missing or contains a typo;
- Data collated from USA and European sources has dates in different formats;
- Open-source information from social media contains different time zones.

The key goal of data cleaning is to ensure that later analysis steps can continue. Some records may need to be removed if the data cannot be fixed. In some cases, incorrect or missing information can be ignored. In other instances, the data can be fixed by either interpolating values or mapping to a standard format.

Structuring, Filtering, and Clustering Data

Once data has been cleaned the next stage is to prepare it for analysis. Some data will need to be reviewed by a domain expert, but often there are ways to simplify the data to make this easier. Three stages to consider are:

- Structuring;
- Filtering;
- Clustering.

Structuring is grouping elements of data into related objects, often real-world entities. To use the database example earlier, a *forum post* has an author, a date and content; an *author* has a username, a join date, and other biographical data. Data structuring is often highly correlated with database design. In many cases the data may be structured explicitly, but sometimes there are many ways to do it. Do not let concern over the "best" structure stop you from moving forward. The key thing is to decide on a structure consciously that makes sense to you as the domain expert.

Filtering is a way of selecting elements from a data set based on some criteria. A simple example of this is to use dates. For example, "show all the cases from a law enforcement agency between March and December 2020." Structured data can usually be filtered very easily. Filtering helps remove irrelevant data for the task at hand.

Clustering is a process of grouping elements together based on some criteria. How to cluster the data may be obvious, such as grouping all cases to a particular investigator; or it may be more complex, such as grouping all cases based on the geographical region that was covered. Clustering can use mathematical models to calculate optimal boundaries between elements in your data (Geron, 2019).

Data Visualization

One of the most satisfying parts of data science is visualizing the results. This is an opportunity to think of creative ways to illustrate the data, which will depend heavily on what kind of data you have. Effective visualizations will highlight the conclusion being inferred. Graphical plots are more appealing than tables, but sometimes a table is the best way to communicate your message. Data scientists will focus on the key message they wish to convey and state this message as the title of their graphs or tables.

More information and examples on visualization can be found in Chapters 11 and 13.

An Example of Applied Digital Criminology

For a criminology researcher, the amount of data available online can seem insurmountable, with the volume of data exceeding the limits of conventional manual analysis, yet at the same time the data is too rich and important to ignore. The skills described in this chapter have outlined different ways of thinking about digital criminological analysis by adapting best practice processes from software engineering and data science. Digital skills can help a criminologist filter out irrelevant data and focus on the critical thinking and decision making to advance empirical research in this field (see also Chapters 10 and 11).

There are countless opportunities for a digital criminologist to embrace big data due to advancements in technology, such as with smartphones, GPS data, wearable technology, and Internet of Things (IoT) devices. For the purpose of this brief introductory chapter, however, we wish to explore how using digital procedures mentioned previously here can be applied to an online underground forum.

Online underground sites, such as hacking forums which will be discussed in the example, tend to bring together individuals interested in cybercrime and illicit monetizing techniques (Holt, 2007; Motoyama et al., 2012; Tavabi et al., 2019). The underground economy attracts a variety of actors, from those who trade in malicious goods and services, to those deemed more inexperienced to avail of tools to launch cyber-attacks. Identifying the evolution of these actors is useful from a criminological perspective in order to help develop programs to deter the activity, and of course to boost cyber security by understanding better discussions and tools being deployed.

Online forums can hold a rich amount of user-generated material with some forums having thousands of users, potentially posting in hundreds of threads. This text is usually structured clearly around topics/themes of the forum with threads of text considered as relatively authentic natural data. The sheer amount of data, however, means that employing "traditional" manual approaches to data analysis would take an inordinate amount of time to the point where the process may not even be feasible.

The following example shows how digital skills and processes were used by an interdisciplinary team analyzing suspected criminal activity on hacking forums. The project team wanted to understand the dynamics of people interacting on a cybercrime forum which had an excess of 500 k posts. The key goals were to understand if people were engaging in criminal activity, how prevalent the activity was, and who the main contributors were.

From the criminologist view, it was necessary to read the posts and infer details from the wording used. The forum was too large to read manually, so the following process was devised:

- *Software engineering process.* What is the problem we are trying to solve? Extract data from this forum and put it in a database. The data is mostly text, with some dates and numbers. Key steps are:
  - Scrape the website to build a database of sub-forums, threads, posts, and authors;
  - Identify the thread information, the first author, subsequent posts, and their authors;
  - Extract each bit of information, use automatic translation tools to convert the post text into English, and store in a database.

- *Data science process.* Use preliminary data analysis to get broad statistics about the forum:
  - How many posts per thread?

- What is the average number of posts per thread?
- How many unique authors were involved in a thread?
- How many posts did an author make (maximum, average)?
- Calculate metrics to judge the quality of the forum;
- Using these statistics filter threads with only 1 post (i.e., there is no discussion) and spam posts that are duplicates;
- Use keyword searching to find threads with specific discussion topics.

- *Criminologist process.*

  - Look at the statistics for each forum;
  - Judge if there is evidence of information sharing and dialogue between multiple people;
  - Review the contents of the posts to determine the type of conversation;
  - Based on the analysis, decide whether the forum is worth pursuing in more detail or if another forum must be found.

The result of this process is a curated list of hundreds of posts automatically filtered from 500 k, which the criminologist can then analyze in detail. Note that the step 3 above is arguably the most important, but all the other steps make it possible and tractable. Using software engineering and data science tools the criminologist can very rapidly get insight using their domain knowledge.

A digital criminologist sees these steps as one workflow, but they use elements traditionally used in software engineering and data science disciplines. The authors have used this process to review the hundreds of thousands of posts across five web forums in only a few days.

Conclusion

The avenues for digital criminological research presented here are intended both to encompass and to expand substantially the traditional focus of cybercrime scholarship. At the same time, they represent an enticement and a provocation for continued development of the field which embraces the plethora of data available online. A software engineer or a data scientist is able to gather, clean, and organize data into a coherent structure. A criminologist is able to interpret, cross-reference, infer, and theorize from this data. A software engineer alone lacks the insight to use the information for maximal value. A criminologist alone may have to systematically work through large volumes of bad quality data to find the valuable information. Combining both sets of skills uses the strengths of each to solve the problem quickly, accurately, and effectively.

In this chapter, we have presented a way of thinking. It is very rare to find diverse skills in a single person, so it is best to focus on doing *something* rather than doing it *perfectly*. Using digital skills can accelerate criminological analysis, freeing researchers to focus on their domain rather than on mundane mechanical details. In other words, modern digital criminology is about using computers to empower researchers: adopting a more technical approach as outlined in this chapter ensures that the discipline of criminology benefits from an increased awareness, acceptance, and use of digital analysis which is central given how integral technology is to our daily lives, and those of criminals.

References

Alnabulsi, H., & Islam, R. (2018). *Identification of illegal forum activities inside the Dark Net* (pp. 22–29). International Conference on Machine Learning and Data Engineering (iCMLDE), Sydney, Australia.

Baravalle, A., Sanchez Lopez, M., & Wee Lee, S. (2017). *Mining the Dark Web: Drugs and fake ids.* 2016 IEEE 16th International Conference on Data Mining Workshops (ICDMW) Institute of Electrical and Electronics Engineers (IEEE). https://doi.org/10.1109/ICDMW.2016.0056.

Beaulieu, A. (2020). *Learning SQL: Generate, manipulate, and retrieve data* (3rd ed.). O'Reilly Media.

Beighley, L. (2007). *Head first SQL: Your brain on SQL.* A Learner's Guide. O'Reilly Media.

Chan, J., & Bennet Moses, L. (2017). Is Big Data challenging Criminology? *Theoretical Criminology, 20*(1), 21–39.

Cubitt, T. I. C., Wooden, K. R., & Roberts, K. A. (2020). A machine learning analysis of serious misconduct among Australian police. *Crime Science, 9*(22), 1–13.

Freeman, E., & Robson, E. (2020). *Head first design patterns: A brain-friendly guide: Building extensible and maintainable object-oriented software* (2nd ed.). O'Reilly Media.

Geron, A. (2019). *Hands-on machine learning with Scikit-Learn, Keras, and TensorFlow: Concepts, tools, and techniques to build intelligent systems* (2nd ed.). O'Reilly Media.

Godsey, B. (2017). *Think like a data scientist: Tackle the data science process step-by-step*. Manning Publications.

Holt, T. J. (2007). Subcultural evolution? Examining the influence of on- and off-line experiences on deviant subcultures. *Deviant Behavior, 28*(2), 171–198.

Holt, T. J. (2013). Examining the forces shaping cybercrime markets online. *Social Science Computer Review, 31*(2), 165–177.

Internet World Stats. (2020). *IWS usage and population statistics*. Available at: https://www.internetworldstats.com/.

Kleck, G., Tark, J., & Bellows, J. J. (2006). What methods are most frequently used in research in criminology and criminal justice? *Journal of Criminal Justice, 34*(2), 147–152.

Lavorgna, A., Middleton, S., Pickering, B., & Neumann, G. (2020). FloraGuard: Tackling the online illegal trade in endangered plants through a cross-cutting disciplinary ICT-enabled methodology. *Journal of Contemporary Criminal Justice, 36*(3), 1–23.

Leiner, B. M., Cerf, V. G., Clark, D. D., Kahn, R. E., Kleinrock, L., Lynch, D. C., Postel, J., Roberts, L. G., & Wolff, S. (2009). A brief history of the Internet. *ACM SIGCOMM Computer Communication Review, 39*(5), 22–31.

Martin, J. (2014). Lost on Silk Road. Online drug distribution and the "cryptomarket". *Criminology and Criminal Justice, 14*(3), 363–388.

Matthes, E. (2019). *Python crash course: A hands-on, project-based introduction to programming paperback* (2nd ed.). No Starch Press.

McAlister, R., & Monaghan, R. (2020). Animal rights extremism and the internet. In M. Littler & B. Lee (Eds.), *Digital extremisms: Readings in violence, radicalisation and extremism in the online space*. MacMillan.

McCallum, Q. E. (2012). *Bad data handbook: Cleaning up the data so you can get back to work*. O'Reilly Media.

Motoyama, M., Mccoy, D. Levchenko, K., Savage, S., & Voelker, G. (2012). *An analysis of underground forums.* https://doi.org/10.1145/2068816.206 8824.

Pastrana S., Hutchings A., Caines A., & Buttery P. (2018). Characterizing eve: Analysing cybercrime actors in a large underground forum. In M. Bailey, T. Holz, M. Stamatogiannakis, & S. Ioannidis (Eds.), *Research in attacks, intrusions, and defenses. RAID 2018.* Lecture Notes in Computer Science, Vol 11050. Springer, Cham. https://doi.org/10.1007/978-3-030-00470-5_1.

Pete, I., Hughes, J. Chua Y. T. & Bada, M. (2020). A social network analysis and comparison of six dark web forums (pp. 484–493). *2020 IEEE European Symposium on Security and Privacy Workshops (EuroS&PW)*, Genoa, Italy. https://doi.org/10.1109/EuroSPW51379.2020.0007.

Python Software Foundation. (2020). *Beginners guide.* Available at: https://wiki.python.org/moin/BeginnersGuide.

Ramalho, L. (2015). *Fluent Python: Clear concise, and effective programming.* O'Reilly Media.

Shaw, Z. (2017). *Learn Python 3 the hard way* (4th ed.). Addison-Wesley Professional.

Stratton, G., Powell, A., & Cameron, R. (2017). Crime and justice in a digital Society. Towards a digital Criminology? *International Journal for Crime Justice and Social Democracy, 6*(2), 17–33.

Tavabi, N., Bartley, N. Abeliuk, A., Sandeep, S., Ferrara, E. & Lerman, K. (2019). Characterizing activity on the deep and dark web. *Companion Proceedings of the 2019 World Wide Web Conference*, 206–213. https://doi.org/10.1145/3308560.3316502.

van Gelder, J., & Van Daele, S. (2014). Innovative data collection methods in criminological research: Editorial introduction. *Crime Science, 3*, 6.

Weimann, G. (2016). Going dark: Terrorism on the dark web. *Studies in Conflict and Terrorism, 39*(3), 195–207.

4

Profiling and Predictions: Challenges in Cybercrime Research Datafication

Bart Custers

Introduction

Due to its online nature, each form of cybercrime typically leaves digital traces. Such data can be useful for criminal investigations, but also for cybercrime researchers. When large amounts of data, such as data on the characteristics, actions, behavior and whereabouts of suspects, witnesses, and victims, or data on *modi operandi* is available in digital formats, for instance, in police records, court cases, and other sources, it becomes possible to search for patterns in these datasets. Such patterns may reveal novel and unexpected insights from the raw data.

In order to keep at least some control and overview over such large amounts of data, new data analytics tools have been developed, such as data mining and machine learning, that allow for automated data

B. Custers (✉)
Leiden University, Leiden, Netherlands
e-mail: b.h.m.custers@law.leidenuniv.nl

© The Author(s), under exclusive license to Springer Nature
Switzerland AG 2021
A. Lavorgna and T. J. Holt (eds.), *Researching Cybercrimes*,
https://doi.org/10.1007/978-3-030-74837-1_4

analyses. Such techniques, categorized in supervised learning and unsupervised learning, may result in profiles, which are a characteristic or a collection of characteristics of people. This can concern individual profiles, such as for terrorists or serial murderers (Chifflet, 2014), or group profiles, such as risk profiles for aggression or violence (Harcourt, 2007; Schauer, 2003). All patterns discovered, particularly profiles, may contribute to making predictions, for instance, on who committed a crime, who may intend to commit a crime, which people are at increased risk of becoming crime victims, at which locations crime is more likely to happen, and so on.

The automated data analyses, and the profiling and predictions that may result from it, provide tremendous opportunities to gain new criminological insights. Furthermore, this can be done much faster and at a significantly larger scale than when human researchers have to go through these large amounts of data. At the same time, however, a strong focus on such quantitative, data-driven research methods may involve some challenges from methodological, practical, and ethical perspectives. This chapter will examine these challenges of big data research in cybercrime, particularly challenges related to profiling and privacy.

Big Data in Cybercrime Research

Automated Data Analyses

A traditional approach in criminology is to use a hypothesis-driven or theory-driven approach, in which a hypothesis is formulated on the basis of existing theory that is verified or falsified with relevant data, that sometimes has to be collected first. With the exponential increase of available data, very large amounts of data are available nowadays, allowing for a different approach, namely a *data-driven approach*. In this approach, comparable to explorative data analysis, the focus is not on specific hypotheses, trying to get confirmation or rejection of what is expected, but on looking at what the data are telling. Particularly when researching cybercrime this may be relevant, since due to its online nature, each form of cybercrime typically leaves digital traces, resulting in useful research data.

The very large amounts of data are often referred to as big data (see also Chapters 10 and 11), but big data is not only defined by its sheer volume, many terabytes, or even petabytes of data (Gandomi & Haider, 2015). Other challenging characteristics include its velocity, i.e., the fact that many data are real time or nearly real time, and variety, i.e., the fact that the data comes in many types and formats, such as text, numbers, images, videos, and sound (Laney, 2001).

Very large amounts of data usually do not allow for finding patterns via human intuition or overview. For that reason, many different tools for automated data analytics, usually based on algorithms, have been developed that can be used to disclose hidden patterns in large datasets (Calders & Custers, 2013). Typically, machine learning and data mining are such tools, of which many different forms exist, that allow for the automated extraction of patterns from large datasets, a process usually referred to as knowledge discovery in databases (KDD) (Fayyad et al., 1996). Data mining is an automated analysis of data, using mathematical algorithms in order to find new patterns and relations in data. Machine learning is the way in which computer algorithms improve themselves automatically through experience, i.e., on training data. Both these and other tools allow machines to show intelligence, which is why they are also important in the field of artificial intelligence (see also Chapter 12).

The use of these tools for automated data analyses may yield new knowledge extracted from the data (Adriaans & Zantinge, 1996). This knowledge usually consists of disclosing patterns and relationships in the data, sometimes novel and unexpected. What kind of patterns may be discovered depends on the types of tools used. These tools can be distinguished in supervised and unsupervised learning techniques (Bloch, 2019). The most important types of tools are regression, classification, and clustering tools. Classification is a supervised technique that requires the availability of pre-existing classes or categories, whereas regression and clustering are unsupervised techniques, with regression aiming to describe particular trends or regularities in the data and clustering aiming to build models by dividing datasets into clusters of homogeneous data records.

Profiling and Predictions

Regression, classification, and clustering techniques can all be used for profiling, i.e., the process of ascribing one or more characteristics (attributes) to individuals or groups of people (Custers, 2013; Hildebrandt & Gutwirth, 2008). Such profiles may contain typical attributes and forms of stereotyping offenders, suspects, witnesses, and victims. For instance, it may reveal that money mules are used in laundering cybercrime profits are typically from Eastern European countries (UNODC, 2014) or that people with low self-control and people participating in online forums are at increased risk of becoming consumer fraud victims (van Wilsem, 2011), or that people generally find it hard to assess which online protections actually safeguard them against online fraud (Jansen & Leukfeldt, 2016).

Risk profiles may not only relate to people or groups of people, but also to objects and locations of crimes. For instance, in the fight against cyberterrorism, risk profiles for critical infrastructure are commonly used to make threat assessments (Brown et al., 2006). Typical examples of profiling crime locations are heat maps for crime mapping (Khan et al., 2019; Weisburd & McEwen, 2015). Such information is often subsequently used for patrolling strategies (Mastrobuoni, 2017), a typical example of predictive policing (Ferguson, 2019).

Apart from the usefulness of risk profiles in preventing crime or identifying suspects, risk profiles are also commonly used on parole and probation assessments (Dressel & Farid, 2018; Hudson & Bramhall, 2005; Wright et al., 1984). Based on personality characteristics and characteristics of the crimes committed, risks can be assessed. A key element in this is predicting recidivism (Skeem & Lowenkamp, 2020). Typically, when models for such assessments are based on large amounts of data, this can yield more objective parole and probation decisions, pushing back any personal opinions, prejudice or subjective notions of the decision-maker that may play a role, or at least further inform decision-makers (Ball, 2011).

Another area in which profiling and predictions may be relevant is assessing evidence in courts (Vlek et al., 2015). When courts have to decide whether a suspect is guilty, there may be probabilities to deal with.

Typical examples are matches for fingerprints or DNA. The methods used are usually good but not perfect, meaning there may be false positives (the test result shows a match, but in reality there is no match) or false negatives (the test result shows no match, but in reality there is a match). In cybercrime, fingerprints and DNA are usually not part of the evidence that needs to be assessed in courtrooms, but similar issues may apply to identifying suspects. For instance, how likely is it that a suspect has used a particular computer from which malware was sent, or how likely is it that a particular e-mail or IP address belongs to a suspect. Courts are supposed to take such probabilities into account when determining guilt, but this is not an easy task. This brings in assessment problems that humans, including judges or juries, may have when dealing with probabilities and risks, including the so-called prosecutor's fallacy and the defense attorney's fallacy (Thompson & Schuman, 1987).

Challenges

The use of profiling and predictions brings along several challenges. Here we discuss three categories of challenges, i.e., methodological, practical, and ethical challenges. The methodological challenges focus on the creation of profiles and prediction models, the practical challenges focus on the use or usability of profiles and predictions, and the ethical challenges focus on any moral or societal concerns profiles and predictions may cause.

Methodological Challenges

From a methodological perspective, there are several challenges that the use of profiles and predictions may pose when researching cybercrime. These methodological challenges can be related to the data collection and preparation, to the profiling process, or to making any predictions.

It can be hard to collect data for cybercrime research. Although there should be data on each cybercrime, as it always leaves digital traces, it can be hard to locate and access such data. Data may be located on servers in other countries. Governments and private companies (such as hosting providers) may not be willing to provide data for various reasons. Apart from jurisdictional issues, there may also be language issues. But even before making any data requests, an initial problem may already be on which door to knock, as it may not be clear who has the relevant data. On top of this, obviously cybercriminals do not want their data to be disclosed and may have taken measures to prevent this, such as encrypting the data, splitting data over many different locations (e.g., in cloud computing), or deleting data to the extent they are able to do so.

If research data is available, another issue may be that the data is from different sources and in different formats. Any data that is to be used in automated analysis may need some form of preparation before it can be processed. Typical pre-processing techniques include discretization, missing value imputation, dimensionality reduction, and feature extraction and construction (Calders & Custers, 2013). Also the velocity of data (e.g., real time, streaming) may require specific tools.

The advantage of using large amounts of data is that typical issues normally encountered in sampling do not occur. Using big data analytics, all data can be used ('N = All' according to Mayer-Schönberger & Cukier, 2013), without any need for sampling. So questions on the representativeness of a sample and questions on minimum sample sizes can easily be avoided.

However, the profiling process can yield other challenges. In essence, profiling is a form of building models, and if done automatically, it can result in too few or too many patterns. This can easily be compared with using online search engines like Google or Yahoo: ideally, any search yields 3–5 answers, but if there are zero or a few thousand search results, this is undesirable. Apart from too many results, it may also be problematic that some results are non-novel or trivial. For instance, any correlation between size and weight of people may not be remarkable, nor is finding that people driving under influence are over 16 years old.

Another challenge is that of overfitting (Mooney & Pejaver, 2018). Overfitting is the production of a model or profile that corresponds too closely with the dataset or the people in it. If the model is as detailed as the number of people in the dataset, it is not a generalization. The model then contains more parameters than justified by the dataset. This may typically occur if datasets are too small, models too detailed, or both.

This makes clear that the choice of automated data analytics tools needs careful consideration before getting started. Some tools may be a better choice than others, depending on the data and the intended goals of any automated analysis. It could be argued that, if in doubt about the right choice of tools, several tools can be used (subsequently or in parallel), but this may significantly add up the required computing power and times required. Also, using more tools may yield (many) more results.

Practical Challenges

Although the use of profiles and predictions can be very valuable in many aspects when researching cybercrime, there can also be practical challenges regarding their usefulness and effectiveness. Perhaps the most important challenge is that profiles and predictions are never absolutely correct. They are models with a limited accuracy. Even though that accuracy can in some cases be very high, it is never perfect. Therefore, there may be reliability issues (Custers, 2003). Typically, each profile may yield false positives and false negatives when it is applied.

False positives are people in a profile, that should not actually be in the profile. For instance, when a profile shows that ransomware campaigns are ran by Eastern European cybercriminals, it does not mean that all Eastern European cybercriminals run ransomware campaigns. False negatives are the opposite, namely people that are not in a profile, that should actually be in the profile. In the same example, it would be cybercriminals from other countries than those in Eastern Europe running ransomware campaigns.

Limited accuracy can lead to incorrect conclusions, which may result in ethical issues like bias, prejudice, and discrimination toward particular groups of people (see next subsection). From a practical perspective, the main challenge is to determine which levels of accuracy are acceptable. This may depend on the context. For instance, in advertising, profiles that increase outreach to target groups with only a few percent already can make a huge difference. However, in most criminal law and criminology contexts, accuracy has to be high to avoid stereotyping, incorrect generalizations, and false accusations. For instance, when people are denied boarding a plane because they (incorrectly) match a terrorist profile, this may cause significant unnecessary trouble. In practical contexts, like law enforcement and criminal investigations, accuracy also needs to be high in order to be effective.

This leads to another practical challenge, namely that profiles can quickly become outdated. To illustrate this, suppose a risk profile is created suggesting that terrorists are young males with black beards wearing a djellaba. Apart from the fact this profile would be too general and inaccurate to be practical (and could be considered discrimination), actual terrorist could easily avoid matching this profile by shaving their beard and wearing something different. In fact, terrorist groups have even reverted to training female terrorists, to avoid such profiles (Jacques & Taylor, 2009). Apart from people adjusting their behavior, another reason why criminological profiles may 'run empty' and therefore become less effective is because people get caught. For instance, if a profile shows that people trafficking drugs wear white tennis socks under their suit and this profile turns out to be effective, border police may catch them. Once in prison, these people will no longer turn up in border controls, rendering the profile ineffective for border police after some time.

In order to deal with outdated profiles (and predictions based on them), it is imperative that profiles are continuously updated. Since building profiles is based on data and data analytics tools, it means that both the datasets and the tools for analysis need to be revised from time to time. In practice, many organizations tend to focus on building profiles, but have limited attention for updating them, which may result in tunnel vision and low-quality profiles and predictions. From a research perspective, it would be good to add expiry dates to profiles (or at least qualify limited validity), perhaps similar to confidence intervals in statistical data.

Since automated data analysis is data-driven, the focus is on statistical relationships. These may be indicative for causal relationships, but obviously not all statistical relations are causal relations. A data-driven approach may reveal novel patterns, which can be highly interesting, but focuses less on theory and causality. For this, additional work, using other research methods, may be necessary.

From a practical perspective, profiles based on a combination of automated data analytics and human expertise seem to be the most effective. Introducing expert knowledge into data analytics can be helpful to avoid too many or non-novel profiles, but too much expect knowledge may result in looking for assumed patterns in the data rather than looking at what the data is telling. Obviously, it can be challenging to find the right balance here.

A common phenomenon is that data-driven models are built on large numbers of parameters, but that does not always guarantee better results for accurate profiles and predictions. A typical example in this respect may be COMPAS, the decision support tool used by US courts to assess recidivism. Research has shown that despite COMPAS's collection of 137 features, the same accuracy can be achieved with a simple linear classifier with only two features (Dressel & Farid, 2018). In addition, COMPAS is no more accurate or fair than predictions made by people with little or no criminal justice expertise.

The use of profiles and predictions can also be challenging in courts. Whereas in criminal investigations, reasonable suspicion or probable cause may be sufficient to act, in courts convictions have to be beyond reasonable doubt. Reasonable suspicion and probable cause may be based (at least partially) on statistical evidence and, as such, can by their nature go hand in hand with probabilities. However, when dealing with evidence, particularly if the criterion of beyond reasonable doubt has to be met, there is obviously friction with statistical concepts like probabilities. Unless accuracy is very high, risk profiles may not weigh heavily as actual evidence when convicting suspects.

Ethical Challenges

Generally speaking, all datasets, particularly large datasets, contain errors. Parts of the data may be incorrect or incomplete. Furthermore, data may be biased, for instance due to the ways in which is it collected. Obviously, this may reduce the accuracy of profiles and predictions (according to the adage garbage in = garbage out). Apart from accuracy issues discussed above, this may also lead to ethical issues regarding equal treatment, privacy, and fairness that will be discussed here.

A typical example of bias is data collector bias (Berk, 1983), which is also common in criminological datasets. In most countries law regulates that the police can only collect data on suspects and convicted criminals (consider, for instance, EU Directive 2016/680 regulating the use of personal data in criminal law for all EU member states). This already creates a bias, as no data on non-suspects is available. If, for instance, the goal is to find profiles for perpetrators, this can only be done by contrasting characteristics of suspects and non-suspects, which is difficult if no data is available on the latter group.

This may also lead to self-fulfilling prophecies. A typical example of this may occur when surveillance of law enforcement agencies focuses on neighborhoods with ethnic minorities. The probable result of such a policy would be that law enforcement databases get filled with people from these ethnic minorities. This is a form of selective sampling. When these law enforcement databases are subsequently used to find patterns on which people are more prone to show criminal behavior, it may not be surprising to discover that people from these ethnic minorities may be profiled as showing increased levels of criminal behavior. However, since the data was biased, this is a mere self-fulfilling prophecy.

A related issue here is that some of the data analytics tools may be self-reinforcing, resulting in the amplification and further entrenchment of patterns. These effects may amplify existing bias and inequality in datasets when deriving profiles from it, undermine democracy, and further push people into categories that are hard to break out (O'Neil, 2016).

In fact, the data analytics tools may be biased themselves, in the way they are designed (Barocas & Selbst, 2016; Hutchinson, 2016) or by the training data provided to them. For instance, face recognition software still struggles to recognize black faces: even top performing facial recognition systems misidentify blacks at rates five to ten times higher than they do whites (Simonite, 2019).

All this may have profound impact from an ethical perspective. Any kind of bias in datasets or the design and use of data analytics tools may propagate and even amplify prejudice and discrimination. Although the use of profiles and predictions may avoid prejudice and discrimination of law enforcement on the ground (i.e., using evidence-based objective profiles may neutralize personal preferences and misjudgments), this will not work if the profiles are prejudiced and discriminating themselves.

Even without errors and bias, discrimination may be an issue when using profiles. For instance, particular attributes may appear in risk profiles that are not acceptable or even violating antidiscrimination laws, particularly when these criteria are used for decision making. This may concern particularly sensitive attributes like religion, political preferences, sexual preferences, criminal records, and gender. Research has shown that even when these sensitive attributes are not included in the datasets, they may appear by proxy (Calders et al., 2013). A typical example of such indirectly discriminating profiling is so-called redlining, in which characteristics are ascribed to people on the basis of their zip codes, whereas zip codes may be a strong indicator for someone's ethnic background. There are discrimination-aware data mining tools that can be used to avoid these discrimination issues (Zliobaite & Custers, 2016).

Apart from discrimination issues, the use of profiling and predictions can also be highly invasive for personal privacy. Typically, these methods can be very helpful in predicting characteristics of people they are not willing to disclose (Custers, 2012). For instance, Kosinski et al. (2013) show that, based on Facebook likes for movies, music, games, comments, etc., reliable predictions can be made about a person's gender, ethnic background, sexual orientation, religion, happiness, substance abuse, parental divorce, intelligence, etc. Furthermore, big data analyses may even predict attributes of people that they do not even know, such as their life expectancy, their risk to attract cancer, and so on. When trying to predict whether people will become criminals becomes more and more sophisticated, this may get close to dystopian perspectives like depicted in the 2002 movie Minority Report. Nevertheless, predictive policing is currently changing law enforcement (Ferguson, 2019).

It is often suggested that preserving privacy can be achieved by properly anonymizing datasets. However, removing key attributes such as name, address, and social security number of data subjects is insufficient to guarantee privacy; it is often still possible to uniquely identify particular persons or entities from the data, for instance by combining different attributes (Ohm, 2010).

The use of profiles may also yield chilling effects in society (Büchi et al., 2019). When particular profiles have become publicly known, people may want to avoid matching unfavorable profiles. This may not only concern criminals, but people in general if they do not want to be associated with particular groups. Also the fact that data is being collected on them and the fact people may be monitored may affect their behavior. To the extent this prevents people from committing crimes, this may be ok, but when it affects their rights and freedoms, it may be worrisome.

Profiles can be discriminating or privacy-invasive, but they can also be unfair in other ways (La Fors et al., 2019). Typically, profiles and predictions used in a law enforcement context can indicate increased likeliness for particular (groups of) people to commit crimes or having committed a specific crime. Such risk profiles can be considered accusatory and stigmatizing, in the sense that they cast suspicion on specific groups of people. For these groups of people, it may be hard to defend themselves against such practices for several reasons. For instance, it may not be clear on which data the profiles were built, the tools for analysis may be complex and therefore hard to challenge, and the subsequent decision-making processes are not always transparent. For these reasons, the use of profiles for such decision-making processes has been likened with the novel The Trial by Franz Kafka, in which the protagonist is arrested by government officials without knowing on the bases of which accusation, evidence, or underlying information (Solove, 2004).

Also the right to a fair trial can be under pressure. If a profile indicates increased crime risks for particular people, it may influence any existing unprejudiced, open-minded perspectives of law enforcement officers and judges and juries in courts. Apart from discrimination and stigmatization issues discussed above, profiles and predictions may put the presumption of innocence under pressure. Instead of assuming a person is innocent until proven guilty, assessors primed with such profiles may start off with bias and prejudice, even unintentionally and unaware of this.

Conclusions

Profiling and predictions can be very strong, useful, and effective tools in researching cybercrime. Based on all kinds of available data, criminological profiles can be built, for instance, on who committed a crime, who may intend to commit a crime, which people are at increased risk of becoming crime victims, at which locations crime is more likely to happen, and so on. Given the sometimes very large amounts of data, big data analytics (e.g., data mining, machine learning) is increasingly applied for the automated finding of hidden patterns. When applied to prospective characteristics, profiles may also be used as predictions. This may reveal novel patterns in datasets that can be highly interesting.

In this chapter, challenges of big data research in cybercrime, particularly with regard to profiling and predictions, were mapped. Three categories of challenges were identified: methodological, practical, and ethical challenges. The methodological challenges focus on the creation of profiles and prediction models, the practical challenges focus the use or usability of profiles and predictions, and the ethical challenges focus on any moral or societal concerns profiles and predictions may cause.

Methodological challenges can be related to the data collection and preparation, to the profiling process, or to making any predictions. Data collection can be hard due to an international context (e.g., due to unwillingness to share data) or due to technology (e.g., encryption, cloud computing). Data preparation can be complicated due to the large volumes, velocity (e.g., streaming data), and variety (e.g., different formats). The profiling process is in essence a delicate modeling process, which caveats like overfitting and finding merely non-novel, trivial results.

Practical challenges include the accuracy of profiles and predictions, which if limited can considerably reduce their usefulness and effectiveness. Limited accuracy can cause false positives and negatives, stereotyping, incorrect generalizations, and, in a law enforcement context, even false accusations. Profiles need to be updated continuously, as they can become outdated quickly. Since data-driven approaches focus on statistical relations, additional work may be needed for establishing causal relations and further development of criminological theories. Introducing human intuition and expert knowledge may significantly enhance the usefulness and effectiveness of profiles and predictions and reduce overly complex models. In courts, evidence criteria like 'beyond reasonable doubt' can be in tension with statistical concepts like probabilities and error margins.

Ethical challenges when dealing with profiles and predictions typically are equal treatment, privacy, and fairness issues. These can be caused by bias in the data or data analysis tools, which may propagate and even amplify existing prejudices. People may be pushed into categories that are hard to break out. If the profiles are based on particularly sensitive attributes, this may be considered discrimination or stigmatization. If data analytics are used to predict characteristics of people they are not willing to disclose, this may interfere with their privacy. Profiles may also yield chilling effects, if people want to avoid matching less favorable profiles. Fairness as a value can also get under pressure when the use of profiles and subsequent decisions is not transparent, making it hard for people to defend themselves. This may even interfere with the presumption of innocence in practice.

Altogether, it can be concluded that the use of profiles and predictions can be very valuable in law enforcement and criminology, particularly in cybercrime research. At the same time there are many caveats. On the one hand, this means that these new approaches and methods do not invalidate or set aside existing tools, but essentially are an addition to the criminologist's toolbox, providing new research opportunities. On the other hand, this means that these new tools should only be used after careful consideration and preparation, assessing their pros and cons before deciding they are the most appropriate tools to use in a given context. If not applied in the right way, profiles and predictions are better not used at all.

References

Adriaans, P., & Zantinge, D. (1996). *Data mining*. Addison Wesley Longman.

Ball, W. D. (2011). Normative elements of parole risk. 22 *Stanford Law & Policy Review, 395*.

Barocas, S., & Selbst, A. D. (2016). Big Data's disparate impact. 104 *California Law Review, 671*.

Berk, R. A. (1983). An introduction to sample selection bias in sociological data. *American Sociological Review, 48*(3), 386–398.

Bloch, D.A. (2019). *Machine learning: Models and algorithms*. Quantitative Analytics.

Brown, G., Carlyle, M., Salmeron, J., & Wood, K. (2006). Defending critical infrastructure. *Interfaces, 36*(6), 530–544.

Büchi, M., Fosch Villaronga, E., Lutz, Chr., Tamò-Larrieux, A., Velidi, S. & Viljoen, S. (2019). *Chilling effects of profiling activities: Mapping the issues*. Available at: https://ssrn.com/abstract=3379275.

Calders, T., & Custers, B. H. M. (2013). What is data mining and how does it work? In B. H. M. Custers, T. Calders, B. Schermer, & T. Zarsky (Eds.), *Discrimination and privacy in the information society*. Springer.

Calders, T., Karim, A., Kamiran, F., Ali, W., & Zhang, X. (2013). Controlling attribute effect in linear regression (pp. 71–80). In *Proceedings of 13th IEEE ICDM*.

Custers, B. H. M. (2003). *Effects of unreliable group profiling by means of data mining*. In G. Grieser, Y. Tanaka, & A. Yamamoto (Eds.), *Lecture notes in artificial Intelligence, Proceedings of the 6th International Conference on Discovery Science (DS 2003)*, (Vol. 2843). Springer-Verlag.

Custers, B. H. M. (2012). Predicting data that people refuse to disclose. How data mining predictions challenge informational self-determination. *Privacy Observatory Magazine*, p. 3.

Custers, B. H. M. (2013). Data dilemmas in the information society. In B. H. M. Custers, T. Calders, B. Schermer, T. & Zarsky (Eds.), *Discrimination and privacy in the information society*. Springer.

Chifflet, P. (2014). Questioning the validity of criminal profiling: An evidence-based approach. *Australian & New Zealand Journal of Criminology*. https://doi.org/10.1177/0004865814530732.

Dressel, J., & Farid, H. (2018). The accuracy, fairness and limits of predicting recidivism. *Science Advances, 4*(1).

Fayyad, U. M., Piatetsky-Shapiro, G., & Smyth, P. (1996). The KDD process for extracting useful knowledge from volumes of data. *Communications of the ACM*, *39*(11).

Ferguson, A.G. (2019). Predictive policing theory. In T. R. Lave & E. J. Miller (Eds.), *The Cambridge handbook of policing in the United States*. Cambridge University Press.

Gandomi, A., & Haider, M. (2015). Beyond the hype: Big data concepts, methods and analytics. *International Journal of Information Management*, *35*, 137–144.

Harcourt, B.E. (2007). *Against prediction: Profiling, policing and punishing in an actuarial age*. Chicago University Press.

Hildebrandt, M., & Gutwirth, S. (2008). *Profiling the European citizen*. Springer.

Hudson, B., & Bramhall, G. (2005). Assessing the "Other": Constructions of "Asainness" in risk assessments by probation officers. *The British Journal of Criminology*, *45*(5), 721–740.

Hutchinson, Y. (2016, August 23). Biased by design. *MIT Technology Review*.

Jacques, K., & Taylor, P. J. (2009). Female terrorism: A review. *Terrorism and Political Violence*, *21*(3), 499–515.

Jansen, J., & Leukfeldt, E. R. (2016). Phishing and malware attacks on online banking customers in the Netherlands: A qualitative analysis of factors leading to victimization. *International Journal of Cyber Criminology*, *10*(1), 79–91.

Khan, M., Azhar, R. & Rauf, A. (2019). *Hotspot analysis of crimes using GIS: A case study of district Abbottabad*. Available at: https://ssrn.com/abstract=331 2540.

Kosinski, M., Stillwell, D., & Graepel, T. (2013). Private traits and attributes are predictable from digital records of human behaviour. In *Proceedings of the National Academy of Sciences* (PNAS). Available at: www.pnas.org/con tent/early/2013/03/06/1218772110.

La Fors, K., Custers, B. H. M., & Keymolen, E. (2019). Reassessing values for emerging big data technologies: Integrating design-based and application-based approaches. *Ethics and Information Technology*, *21*(3), 209–226.

Laney, D. (2001). *3D data management: Controlling data volume, velocity and variety*. Gartner. META Group.

Mastrobuoni, G. (2017). Crime is terribly revealing: Information technology and police productivity. *Review of Economic Studies* (online first).

Mayer-Schönberger, V., & Cukier, K. (2013). *Big data: A revolution that will transform how we live, work and think*. Harcourt Publishing Company.

Mitchell, T. M. (1999). Machine learning and data mining. *Communications of the ACM, 42*(11).

Mooney, S. J., & Pejaver, V. (2018). Big data in public health: Terminology, machine learning, and privacy. *Annual Review of Public Health, 39,* 95–112. https://doi.org/10.1146/annurev-publhealth-040617-014208.

Ohm, P. (2010). Broken promises of privacy: Responding to the surprising failure of anonymization. *UCLA Law Review, 57,* 1701.

O'Neil, C. (2016). *Weapons of math destruction; How big data increases inequality and threatens democracy.* Crown

Schauer, F. (2003). *Profiles, probabilities and stereotypes.* Harvard University Press.

Simonite, T. (2019, July 22). The best algorithms struggle to recognize black faces equally. *Wired.*

Skeem, J., & Lowenkamp, C. (2020). Using algorithms to address trade-offs inherent in predicting recidivism. *Behavioral Sciences & the Law, 38,* 259–278.

Solove, D. (2004). *The digital person; Technology and privacy in the information age.* New York University Press.

Thompson, W. C., & Schuman, E. L. (1987). Interpretation of statistical evidence in criminal trials: The prosecutor's fallacy and the defense attorney's fallacy. *Law and Human Behavior, 11,* 167–187.

UNODC. (2014). *Basic manual on the detection and investigation of the laundering of crime proceeds using virtual currencies.* Available at: https://www.imolin.org/pdf/imolin/FULL10-UNODCVirtualCurrencies_final.pdf.

van Wilsem, J. A. (2011). Bought it, but never got it: Assessing risk factors for online consumer fraud victimization. *European Sociological Review, 29*(2), 168–178.

Vlek, C., Prakken, H., Renooij, S. & Verheij, B. (2015). Constructing and understanding bayesian networks for legal evidence with scenario schemes (pp. 128–137). In *Proceedings of the 15th International Conference on Artificial Intelligence and Law.* ACM Press.

Weisburd, D. L., McEwen, T. (2015). *Introduction: Crime mapping and crime prevention.* Available at: https://ssrn.com/abstract=2629850.

Wright, K. N., Clear, T. R., & Dickson, P. (1984). Universal applicability of probation risk-assessment instruments. *Criminology, 22,* 113–134.

Zliobaite, I., & Custers, B. (2016). Using sensitive personal data may be necessary for avoiding discrimination in datadriven decision models. *Artificial Intelligence and Law, 24,* 183201.

5

Data-Driven Technologies in Justice Systems: Intersections of Power, Data Configurations, and Knowledge Production

Pamela Ugwudike

Introduction

Criminal justice systems across advanced liberal jurisdictions are increasingly using data-driven predictive algorithms, also known as risk assessment tools, to predict recidivism rates and inform adjudications in relation to the severity of penal interventions, probation revocation investigations, parole hearings, and other procedures that can deprive individuals of their rights, privileges, and freedoms. Beyond penal systems, the predictive algorithms are influencing decision making in policing contexts (Bennet Moses & Chan, 2016) and court settings (Kehl et al., 2017). Added to their role in decisions that impact directly on citizen's rights and freedoms, the technologies are emerging as powerful knowledge producers, capable of fomenting what can be conceptualized as digitized epistemic domination (see also Ugwudike, 2020). This form

P. Ugwudike (✉)
University of Southampton, Southampton, UK
e-mail: P.Ugwudike@soton.ac.uk

© The Author(s), under exclusive license to Springer Nature
Switzerland AG 2021
A. Lavorgna and T. J. Holt (eds.), *Researching Cybercrimes*,
https://doi.org/10.1007/978-3-030-74837-1_5

of domination manifests itself as the power and ability of influential state and non-state actors to create data-driven algorithms whose inferences from patterns in datasets inform key discourses that evolve into knowledge about risk and the efficient management of groups labeled as risky.

There is however a dearth of criminological scholarship on the data configurations that can undermine the quality of algorithmic outputs (predictions) and the knowledge they produce. Yet, of "big data" analytics is proliferating across industry and academe where criminologists, data scientists, software developers and programmers, technology vendors, policymakers, and others are increasingly deploying "big data" analytics including the extraction and analysis of sometimes linked datasets retrieved from an ever-increasing array of commercial, open source, administrative, and other sources. These actors are creating models that rely on large-scale data for predictive criminal justice, cyberspace research, and other applications. However, critical scholars from diverse disciplines are increasingly highlighting a number of data-related issues that are typically ignored during "big data" analytics (Andrejevic, 2018; Chan & Bennett Moses, 2017; Kitchin, 2014a; Lyon, 2014; Završnik, 2019). Examples include bias, privacy and rights violations, as well as transparency and accountability concerns (Andrejevic, 2018; Chan & Bennett Moses, 2017; Kitchin, 2014a; Lyon, 2014; Završnik, 2019). Additional problems primarily relate to flawed epistemological assumptions which rest on several myths such as the supposed representativeness of big data, the idea that such datasets are devoid of human bias and lack context specificity (Kitchin 2014a; Završnik, 2019). These epistemological fallacies conflate big data with unadulterated "knowledge" and ignore their political and ideological basises. However, as Crawford (2013) notes in a discussion about data bases and algorithmic outputs, data and datasets are not objective; they are creations of human design. Empirical research also shows that big data analytics for tasks such as predictive policing can be political, imbued as it is with subjective logics that are reconfiguring the ontological foundations of crime and deviance (Kaufmann et al., 2019).

In criminological scholarship specifically, the few existing studies on data-related harms as they apply to the creation and deployment of data-driven technologies in justice systems have drawn attention to problems such as, (1) questionable data provenance and quality (Hannah-Moffat, 2018), and (2) the capacity of predictors (risk factors) and recidivism constructs derived from criminal justice datasets such as arrest and prosecution data, to operate as proxies for social categories, particularly race (Ugwudike, 2020) and socioeconomic status (van Eijk, 2016).[1] A consequence of these data-related issues is that the algorithms can cause harm by exposing affected populations to unnecessarily excessive surveillance and control, while entrenching historical stereotypes and even creating "new epistemologies" or truth claims (see also Kitchin, 2014a). In the United Kingdom, these problems have been recognized by many, including legal institutions and human rights organizations, amidst calls for the legal and ethical regulation of data-driven algorithms (Amnesty International, 2017; Centre for Data Ethics and Innovation (CDEI)/Rovastos et al., 2020; House of Commons Science and Technology Committee, 2018; Law Society, 2019). Yet, with few exceptions (e.g., Benjamin 2019; Ugwudike 2020), the harms arising from applications of data-driven algorithms in the justice system have been undertheorized within criminological scholarship.

Influenced by Bourdieu's (1994) position that the conventional social scientific construction of the object of inquiry should be challenged and expanded, this chapter seeks to refract the criminological lens toward considerations of algorithmic harms. To achieve its objectives, the paper provides an empirical example of the generic, data-driven predictive algorithms proliferating across justice systems. It demonstrates how the data on which the tools rely for prediction can over-predict the risks posed by minorities and socially marginal groups, in the process creating forms of knowledge that equate risk with race and socioeconomic marginality. In its analysis of the epistemological function of the technologies and the consequent harms, this chapter draws on Foucault's (1977) perspective

---

[1] The commonly used predictors include: criminal history such arrests and deficiencies in education and employment (see for example, Desmarais et al., 2016; Hamilton, 2015). Examples of typical recidivism variables are number of arrests and incidents of institutional misconduct (Desmarais & Singh, 2013).

on the nexus of power and knowledge production, and the diffusion of epistemic power in advanced liberal jurisdictions.

The Proliferation of Data-Driven Algorithms

The knowledge produced by data-driven algorithms is being used by institutions and organizations across the world to structure decision making, with potentially life-changing consequences for affected populations. Within the public and private sectors, the algorithms are informing the decisions made by employers (Ajunwa et al., 2016), social security agencies (Eubanks, 2018), and healthcare services (Ledford, 2019), to name a few of many examples. But a fast-growing scholarship on the nature and implications of the technologies has emerged and is detailing the data-related problems that can generate flawed algorithmic outputs. In the specific context of algorithmic decision making, an additional data-related issue pertains primarily to the classic *garbage in, garbage out problem*. As Lum and Isaac (2016, p. 19) rightly note in their critical analysis of predictive policing algorithms: "Every student who has taken a course on statistics or data analysis has heard the old adage 'garbage in garbage out'". Reiterating this point, Oswald et al. (2018, p. 12) observe in their analysis of risk prediction tools applied by police services that "algorithms will only be as good as the data available". In the book *Race After Technology*, Benjamin (2019) also makes it clear that the algorithms applied in many institutional contexts rely on flawed "data that have been produced through histories of exclusion and discrimination" such as racially biased arrest data. Reinforcing this stance, Eubanks (2018) notes that the algorithms that welfare services in a number of countries use to personalize decisions about social security payments are relying on biased "big data" and risk factors that are prompting the algorithms to flag up some of the most vulnerable welfare recipients as potential perpetrators of social security fraud. Eubanks (2018) goes on to describe this process as the "automation of poverty" that is fueling the emergence of a "digital poorhouse". In the same vein, O'Neill (2016) and Noble (2018) have, in their seminal texts, explained how search engine algorithms rely on unrepresentative data to generate results which reproduce existing racial, gender, and other biases and accompanying structural inequalities. Noble (2018) describes the algorithms as "algorithms of oppression" and O'Neill (2016) conceptualizes them as "weapons of math destruction". Other scholars have shown how the use of unrepresentative datasets derived mainly from white male populations render certain algorithms unsuitable for minorities and women. Biometric algorithms such as those used by law enforcement for facial recognition represent an example and have been found to misidentify minorities, particularly black women (Raji et al., 2020). Big data analytics in general, whether deployed for cybersecurity research or law enforcement, can encounter this problem of unrepresentativeness and poor generalizability.

Re-orientating Cybercrime Research and Policy

Despite the growing corpus of research on algorithmic harms, criminological scholarship on cybercrime has paid insufficient attention to the harms that can emerge from applications of data-driven predictive algorithms in justice systems. This chapter seeks to broaden and reorientate current scholarship on cybercrime, by demonstrating that such harms also constitute fitting objects of criminological inquiry. The chapter is inspired by Bourdieu's (1994) view that social scientists should expand social scientific construction of the object of inquiry by constructing their own objects of enquiry. If not, they risk perpetuating the pre-constructed objects that embody the motivations, preferences, and interests of dominant knowledge producers. Bourdieu (1994) maintains that the entrenchment of pre-defined objects of inquiry within social science and policy discourse represents the exercise of symbolic power since the objects convey meanings that maintain structural inequalities (Bourdieu, 1994; Wacquant, 2008). Therefore, this contribution reconstructs the object by expanding the focus of criminological enquiry to include the harms that can emerge from data-driven technologies applied in justice systems. In doing so, it recasts the harms as fitting targets of criminological enquiry and broader regulation.

In particular, the chapter focuses on the predictive algorithms also known as risk assessment tools, now informing penal governance. It shows how the algorithms operate as mechanisms of penal governance through their knowledge producing powers. But as the aforementioned scholarship shows, there are data harms that call into question the judiciousness of viewing algorithmic outputs as sources of unbiased or objective knowledge.

To elucidate the role of the technologies as knowledge producers and the accompanying harms, the chapter also draws on Foucauldian theorizations of the epistemic power of discourse. In his analysis of the exercise of power in postmodern societies and the links to penal governance, Foucault (1977) argued that the human science disciplines including criminology and psychology were able to exercise power through discourse. This discourse then morphed into accepted knowledge of normative behavior and the characteristics of deviant individuals deserving of surveillance, discipline, and control (Ugwudike, 2015). For Foucault (1977), the ability of the disciplines to exercise such power, albeit through epidemic domination, demonstrates the decentralization of power that occurred in the shift toward industrial capitalism and the rise of the modern prison. In his view, "the disciplines became the arbiters of normality" bolstered by the justice system of that period (see also Ugwudike, 2015). Risk technologies have furthered this diffusion of power given their ability to exert digitized epistemic domination over normative constructions of risk and risk-focused penal control.

Predictive Algorithms in Justice Systems

We have already seen that data-related problems can influence algorithmic outputs (predictions) and call into question their epistemic potential. In this section, the chapter uses the example of the theory-driven generic, risk prediction algorithms that are commonly applied in justice systems across several western jurisdictions to illustrate several algorithmic harms requiring criminological and policy attention. In particular, this example demonstrates how the algorithms dominate knowledge production concerning risk despite the data-oriented problems that render the knowledge they produce capable of causing penal and social harms.

This work focuses on the theory-driven algorithms inspired by the "what works" model of practice that emerged from the 1980s onwards across Western jurisdictions such as the United Kingdom, the United States, Canada, and Australia. The model is also known as the Risk, Need, Responsivity (RNR) model of effective practice and it emerged from meta-analytic reviews of mainly North American research literature on criminal justice interventions, and small-scale studies in the United Kingdom (Andrews et al., 1990; McGuire, 1995). As a model of practice that emerged from research, it has been consistently depicted at policy level as central to "evidence-based" effective practice. Indeed, In England and Wales in the mid-1990s, the RNR model heavily influenced the Labour Government's policy on offender rehabilitation. In 1998, two Home Office publications documented the development of offender behavior programs (OBPs) based on the model. The documents *Strategies for effective offender supervision* (Underdown, 1998) and *The evidence-based practice guide* (Chapman & Hough, 1998) revealed the New Labour government's plans to develop pathfinder programs informed by the model. Another document by Goldblatt and Lewis (1998) summarized several research reports which contributed to the development of the Crime Reduction Programme (CRP) which was instituted in 1999 to pilot the model and then roll it out nationally over the early 2000s. In 2005, a review by Harper and Chitty (2005) updated Goldblatt and Lewis's (1998) review and reinforced the New Labour government's commitment to the RNR model.

From the 1990s to date, the development and application of risk assessment and prediction tools has remained central to the policy implementation of the model (HMPPS & MOJ, 2019; Home Office, 1999; National Offender Management Service (NPS), 2016). Proponents of the model have, however, long emphasized that the purpose of risk assessment is not to categorize people as dangerous and eligible for punitive interventions and incapacitation. Instead, its aim should be to determine an individual's needs in order to allocate them to interventions that are suitable for addressing their change-related and welfare needs (Bonta &

Andrews, 2007). As Bonta and Andrews (2007, p. 7) note, the purpose of risk assessment is not to differentiate "low risk from high risk offenders so that the high-risk offender can be controlled through incapacitation or strict monitoring". Nevertheless, this seems to have been largely ignored and the tools have become the means through which individuals are allocated risk scores and categories which determine levels of penal control (for instance, HMPPS & MOJ, 2019).

The tools emerged initially as actuarial tools which were designed to predict risk by comparing an individual's attributes (attitudes and circumstances) with weighted predictor and recidivism variables. Some of the tools predict risk using regression models and data from criminal justice populations (Berk & Bleich, 2013), for example administrative datasets such as police arrest data. With the advent of the digital age, advanced variants of the technologies have emerged, with some possessing Machine Learning capabilities and able to use complex algorithms to detect patterns in data and predict risk (Brennan & Oliver, 2013). The algorithms continue to grow in scale and reach, and in tandem with the technological advances of the digital age and the proliferation of "big data" (Kitchin, 2014b). Meanwhile, the process of using information from the past to predict the future so that populations labeled as "dangerous" risks can be controlled and managed has been described as central to "actuarial justice" (Feeley & Simon, 1992). But as the actuarial tools used for such classifications continue to evolve into advanced algorithmic systems, the process can be reconceptualized as algorithmic justice. An example of the commonly used theory-driven, predictive algorithms is the Correctional Offender Management Profiling for Alternative Sanctions (COMPAS) algorithm (Brennan et al., 2009). COMPAS is applied by prison and probation services in some parts of the United States. It shares features in common with the Level of Service (LS) family of predictive tools applied internationally (Bonta & Andrews, 2017) and the Offender Assessment System (OASys) used in the United Kingdom.

Together, the algorithms can be described as digital technologies since they are computerized tools with integrated algorithms trained on administrative and other datasets to compute risk of reconviction scores. In England and Wales, the technologies are applied to most people coming into contact with the justice system and they are used to predict recidivism (risk). Levels of predicted risk can inform key life-changing decisions such as sentencing and parole decisions. They are also used to identify rehabilitation targets and goals. As HMPPS and MOJ (2019) note, "much decision making in criminal justice needs to be informed by an assessment of whether someone poses a risk to the public. For example, is there a risk that they might break the law again and might that be for a serious offence?".

This consideration informs levels of penal intervention but as with other data-driven technologies, several data-related issues can cause theory-driven, predictive algorithms to produce outputs (risk predictions) which entrench the "knowledge" that specific groups are riskier than others. Despite these potential harms, the discourse and knowledge produced by the algorithms are depicted at policy level as useful for a form of penal governance that is primarily technocratic in its focus on several intersecting systemic goals: (1) cost-effective risk management; (2) ostensibly scientific criminal justice; and (3) efficient surveillance (HMPPS & MOJ, 2019; Home Office, 1999; National Offender Management Service [NPS], 2016). Thus, the epistemological power of the algorithms manifests in their ability to inform penal governance, reflecting Foucault's (1977) analysis of how power is exercised through discourse and knowledge production. But despite their role in penal governance, the remaining sections of this chapter demonstrate that several data-related problems undermine the quality of their outputs.

Predictive Algorithms as Mechanisms of Cost-Effective Risk Management

Algorithmic outputs (predictions) are portrayed as sources of knowledge for technocratic, systems-focused penal governance through cost-effective risk management. According to Feeley and Simon (1992), this form of penal governance emerged as a result of the diminished faith in the ability of the penal system to attain more ambitious social goals such as individualized, welfare-based rehabilitation. Feeley and Simon (1992) also note that the approach emerged in response to calls from penal institutions such as the courts, for rational and accountable penal approaches. The systems-focused approach has as such been conceptualized as the rationalization of justice (Garland, 2001) or bureaucratic rationalism (Pratt, 2002). It is an approach that forms part of a technocratic penal order that emphasizes the use of standardized risk prediction algorithm to categorize individuals into groups according to shared traits so that their risks can be collectively managed efficiently and cost effectively. But the depiction of such algorithms as appropriate sources of knowledge driving the approach masks the data-related problems that can influence algorithmic outputs. The problems stem mainly from the reliance on criminal justice datasets and are explained below.

Generalizations

One of the harms of relying on patterns in criminal justice datasets for algorithmic production of knowledge about risk stems from the underlying assumption that the attributes and circumstances of the criminal justice populations (people who have experienced criminal justice intervention such as arrests and recalls to prison for probation violation) from whom the datasets are derived, are generalizable to the individual risk subject. Therefore, the predictive algorithms arrive at their predictions through generalizations. Circumstances and characteristics gleaned from aggregated datasets are imputed to all risk subjects sharing those characteristics. Recognizing the harms of such generalizations, Hannah-Moffat (2016) notes in her critical analysis of risk technologies applied in justice systems that "variables shown to be correlated with recidivism on an aggregate level are erroneously ascribed to a decontextualized individual". A harmful implication of this is that it obscures personal and social factors that are unique to individuals, which may warrant intervention and support. Instead, it serves the technocratic function of placing people into categories of risk on the basis of attributes they appear to share with others, regardless of individual differences. As a penal approach, it represents the shift from more costly individualized assessment and penal responses, toward the risk management of populations according to categories of risk, partly to attain the systemic goal of cost-effective penal governance. Therefore, it reflects Feeley and Simon's (1992) contention that technocratic ideals have supplanted traditional penal ideals such as rehabilitative processes that emphasize broader social goals rooted in welfarism. The emergence of advanced Machine Learning models capable of mining large datasets to forecast risk (see, Brennan & Oliver, 2013) expands the pervasiveness of the approach beyond the scope depicted in Feeley and Simon's (1992) critique of actuarialism.

Obfuscations

Another data-related problem that can undermine the quality of algorithmic outputs and the knowledge that is realizable from them is the problem of risk inflation or overprediction. The emphasis on the tools' technocratic function also masks this problem which can emerge where the algorithms obfuscate the racial discrimination imbued in administrative datasets and automatically infer from patterns in the datasets, that higher rates of criminal justice interventions involving minorities, such as higher arrest rates, are predictors of recidivism (see, for example, Angwin & Larson, 2016; Hao & Stray, 2019). Where the systemic problem of racially biased decision making is ignored in this way, predictor and recidivism variables based on such interventions can operate as proxies for race. As official statistics consistently demonstrate, minorities, particularly black people, are over-represented at all stages of the criminal justice process, compared with their representation in the wider population across several jurisdictions where risk technologies are applied. Examples of these jurisdictions are Australia, Canada, the United Kingdom and the United States (Australian Bureau of Statistics, 2018; Bureau of Justice Statistics, 2018; Canadian Centre for Justice Statistics, 2018; MOJ, 2017). The possibility that their over-representation stems in part from racial discrimination cannot be ignored. Besides, racial differences in behavior cannot explain the substantial discrepancy (see also Phillips & Bowling, 2017).

The problem of risk inflation or overprediction also emerges where the tools automatically infer from patterns in criminal justice datasets that the structural problems that are known to particularly affect criminal justice populations are risk predictors. Examples include poor access to societal resources such as education and employment. Any predictor or recidivism variables based on problems such as these can operate as proxies for socioeconomic marginality (van Eijk, 2016), rendering affected populations more vulnerable to higher risk scores than others. Such overprediction can also entrench the belief that the affected groups are prone to criminality and deserve risk-focused, penal interventions. What these insights suggest is that the algorithms can be problematic for minorities and socially marginal groups.

Flawed Inferences

Another problem that is also de-emphasized in the focus on the knowledge-producing function of predictive algorithms is again, data-related and it concerns the tendency of the commonly used algorithms to infer that the link between the variables in data that are labeled by the creators as risk predictors and those labeled as indicators of recidivism is causal or etiological, rather than correlational (Hao & Stray, 2019; House of Commons Science and Technology Committee, 2018; Prins, 2016). Several problems arise from this conflation of correlation and causality. First, it moves the tools beyond the realm of predicting risks, to inferring crime causality from correlational statistics. It also erroneously presupposes that the etiology of initial involvement in crime is inherently similar to the etiology of recidivism, and that both are responsive to the same type of intervention. The conflation of correlation and causality is as such, another aspect of the data harms requiring criminological attention, and it has been conceptualized as "interpretational overreach" or "conceptual slippage" rooted in flawed inferences about the connection between prediction and explanation (Prins, 2016, p. 9). Furthermore, the conflation of correlation and causality presupposes that the variables labeled as risk predictors *cause*, rather than *correlate with*, those labeled as indicators of recidivism, and should as such inform degrees of penal intervention. The House of Commons Science and Technology Committee (2018) has also recognized this problem. Therefore, based on the advice it has received from experts and others, the Committee has noted that the tendency of algorithms to infer causation from detected correlations in data is a key source of racially biased predictions. The Committee cites the example of a generic algorithm the courts in Broward County, Florida, use for determining the severity of sentencing. This algorithm infers future criminality from a defendant's revelation that his or her parent has been to jail or prison. Commenting on this, the Committee (2018, p. 21) alludes to: the unfairness of the inference that "a defendant deserves a harsher sentence because his father went to prison". These data-related problems of generalizations, obfuscations, and flawed inferences are masked by depictions of predictive algorithms as reliable sources of knowledge that can enhance systemic efficiency.

Predictive Algorithms as Mechanisms Scientific Criminal Justice

Predictive algorithms are also depicted as capable of producing knowledge that can inform scientific, evidence-based criminal justice, thus contributing to the broader technocratic goal of systemic efficiency. Specially, the knowledge they produce about risk and whom to target for risk-focused intervention is portrayed as the objective output of robust scientific methods. As such, they are deemed key components of evidence-based practice (HMPPS & MOJ, 2019). But again, this image obscures several data-related issues that influence algorithmic outputs. In particular, the notion of scientific objectivity and neutrality overlooks the fact that all aspects of algorithmic design stem from the values, decisions, and choices of those who design or develop them (Eaglin, 2017; Hamilton, 2015). Data selection, predictor construction, and recidivism definitions are all products of theoretical, cultural, and personal choices that can influence algorithmic outputs and the knowledge they produce about risk.

The privatization of predictive algorithms means that non-state actors are now involved in the design of risk tools and would imbue the technologies with their personal choices. This poses further implications because it confers epistemic power over risk construction on non-state actors and it further exemplifies Foucauldian analysis of the epistemic power of discourse and his accounts of the ubiquity or decentralization of power in advanced liberal societies (Foucault, 1977). Central to the epistemic power of non-state creators of risk technologies is the ability to make data choices which produce the algorithmic risk classifications that inform discourses about risk. Given the depiction of the tools at policy level as useful mechanisms of risk identification and management, it is clear that the discourses evolve into accepted knowledge about riskiness and how best to regulate conformity. The emergence of privatized risk technologies influencing the socio-political contexts of knowledge production concerning risk and its management also exemplifies Foucauldian allusions to "governmentality" or new modes of governance involving the devolution of penal power traditionally reserved for the state to non-state actors. Of relevance here is the reality that non-state actors have been responsibilized and drafted into the crime control project of which risk management and control represent key examples (Rose & Miller, 2010).

Predictive Algorithms as Surveillance Mechanisms

So far, we have seen that the notion of algorithms as technocratic mechanisms of knowledge production for systemic efficiency and scientific criminal justice, overlooks the data-related issues that can undermine the quality of their outputs and the knowledge they produce about risk. The portrayal of the algorithms as producers of knowledge that can enhance the effective surveillance of groups designated as risky and, as such, further the technocratic goal of systemic efficiency represents yet another official discourse. It disregards the fact that the aforementioned data-related harms of generalizations, obfuscations, and flawed inferences can trigger overpredictions or risk inflation. This can, in turn, legitimize the unnecessarily extensive penal surveillance and control of affected populations (typically minorities and socially marginal groups) and contribute to the pervasiveness of mass supervision that is fueling penal expansionism (McNeill, 2018).

An additional problem arises when the algorithms are applied periodically to determine penal intensity or access to life-changing opportunities such as parole or other forms of early release, and this concerns the panopticon quality of the algorithms. When used for periodic assessments, they operate much like the invisible but ever-present panoptic observation measures to which Foucault (1977) alluded in his aforementioned analysis of the knowledge producing processes and powers of the human science disciplines. Thus, with panoptic surveillance through periodic risk assessments, knowledge about changes in risk levels is generated and documented. However, the processes of observation, such as the timing and mechanisms of risk prediction, are not clearly defined or readily amenable to scrutiny by risk subjects, undermining the visibility and transparency of the process. A key exacerbating factor is the opacity of data-driven computations of risk scores. This is particularly the case where complex Machine Learning models with opaque decision making or "black boxed" processes that are unamenable to reasonable scrutiny and rebuttal. In penal contexts, this poses implications for procedural fairness. The existence of trade secret laws which hold that creators do not have to reveal the contents of their algorithmic black box means that groups affected by the systems are unable to scrutinize or challenge their decisions.

Yet, despite the uncertainty and opacity surrounding applications of assessment tools and algorithmic predictions, risk subjects are required to self-regulate and reduce their risk. They are assessed over the duration of their prison or probation order to observe and document how well they are achieving this goal, and their performance (as indicated by their risk score and category) can have profound implications for their rights and freedoms. Therefore, much like the penal subjects in Foucault's account of the opaque panoptic surveillance, the objective seems to be to maintain a visage of constant surveillance in order to induce self-regulation through compliance with constructed norms of "non-risky" behavior and attitudes. Crewe (2011) conceptualizes the uncertainty provoked by coercive but unclear processes such as those initiated through risk technologies, as central to the "pain of self-regulation". Given the aforementioned data-related problems of overprediction and risk inflation, minorities and groups affected by socioeconomic disadvantage are more likely to experience this than other groups. This is particularly likely where generic tools that rely on criminal justice datasets are used for risk assessment and prediction.

Meanwhile, in a broader sense, the risk-focused panoptic approach to inducing self-regulation also reflects the tenets of neoliberal responsibilization whereby the causes of social problems such as crime and risk and their solutions are located within the individual while the state's role is minimized. In this scenario, responsibilization through criminal justice programs that are said to inculcate self-regulation is defined as an effective risk reduction strategy (Rose & Miller, 2010). This "individualization of risk" (Hannah-Moffat, 2018, p. 37) means that the need for structural transformations through social justice programs is ignored.

Conclusion

Using the example of generic, risk technologies now dominating key penal processes (from sentencing to the delivery of punishment), this chapter has shown that certain harms can emerge from applications of data-driven algorithms. Of particular relevance here is that their outputs evolve into dominat discourses and knowledge about risk, the groups that should be labeled as risky, and the levels of penal intervention required for achieving the twin aims of risk management and public protection. Yet, there are data-related problems that call into question their status as appropriate sources of knowledge for risk-focused criminal justice. One such problem is that the criminal justice data on which some of the tools rely contain higher rates of criminal justice intervention such as arrests for minorities and reflect racially biased patterns, particularly the over policing of this group (see, for example, Lum & Isaac, 2016; Vomfell & Stewart 2021). Overprediction occurs where such criminalization is conflated with criminality, without consideration of the impact of racial bias. Similarly, overprediction of risk along socioeconomic lines can occur where the higher incidence of socioeconomic disadvantage among the criminal justice populations from which the datasets are derived prompts the construction of socioeconomic problems as criminogenic/risk predictors (van Eijk, 2016).

Several harms also emerge from relying on data-driven predictors that operate as proxies for socioeconomic disadvantage and race. An example is that such practices reintroduce protected social categories into sentencing, contrary to anti-discrimination laws and constitutional due process protections. Reinforcing this in his legal-philosophical analysis of prediction technologies, Tonry (2014) notes that "including socioeconomic factors violates the ethical proposition that ascribed characteristics for which individuals bear no responsibility, such as race, ethnicity, gender and age, should not play a role in parole and sentencing decisions". Starr (2014), also makes it clear in a review of the constitutional and policy implications of predictive algorithms, that allowing socioeconomic variables such as education, employment, and income to influence sentencing decisions is constitutionally questionable and could undermine equality protections. Another penal harm that accrues from the reliance on data that operate as proxies for race and socioeconomic problems is the problem of disproportionality: affected groups are typically designated as high risk and deserving of severe punishment such as incapacitation for public protection. Added to these penal harms, a broader social problem that also arises is that through overpredictions, predictive algorithms can produce forms of knowledge which entrench the notion that risk is somewhat connected to race (for instance, being black) or socioeconomic status (being poor). This can legitimize the stereotyping and profiling of affected groups. Despite these harms, the knowledge produced by the technologies through their predictions are depicted at policy level as useful technocratic means of attaining intersecting policy goals: systemic efficiency through cost-effective targeting of penal resources; scientific, evidence-based criminal justice; as well as effective surveillance to induce self-regulation. This official depiction of the technocratic functions of predictive algorithms masks the data-related problems that impact on the quality their outputs and structure or configure any knowledge they produce about risk and its effective management.

References

Ajunwa, I., Friedler, S. A., Scheidegger, C., & Venkatasubramanian, S. (2016). *Hiring by algorithm: Predicting and preventing disparate impact.* Yale Law School Information Society Project Conference Unlocking the Black Box: The Promise and Limits of Algorithmic Accountability in the Professions http://sorelle.friedler.net/papers/SSRN-id2746078.pdf.

Amnesty International. (2017). *Artificial intelligence: The technology that threatens to overhaul our rights.* Available at https://www.amnesty.org/en/latest/research/2017/06/artificial-intelligence-the-technology-that-threatens-to-overhaul-our-rights/.

Andrejevic, M. (2018). Data collection without limits: Automated policing and the politics of framelessness. In A. Završnik (Ed.), *Big data, crime and social control.* Routledge.

Andrews, D. A., Bonta, J., & Hoge, R. D. (1990). Classification for effective rehabilitation: Rediscovering psychology. *Criminal Justice and Behaviour, 17,* 19–52.

Angwin, J., & Larson, J. (2016). *Bias in criminal risk scores is mathematically inevitable, researchers say.* Available at https://www.propublica.org/article/bias-in-criminal-risk-scores-is-mathematically-inevitable-researchers-say.

Australian Bureau of Statistics. (2018). *Persons in corrective services.* Available at www.abs.gov.au/AUSSTATS/abs@.nsf/Lookup/4512.0Main+Features1June%20quarter%202018?OpenDocument.

Benjamin, R. (2019). *Race after technology: Abolitionist tools for the New Jim Code.* Polity Press.

Bennet Moses, L., & Chan, J. (2016). Algorithmic prediction in policing: Assumptions, evaluation, and accountability. *Policing and Society, 28*(7), 806–822.

Berk, R. A., & Bleich, J. (2013). Statistical procedures for forecasting criminal behavior: A comparative assessment. *Criminology & Public Policy, 12,* 513–544.

Bonta, J., & Andrews, D. A. (2007). *Risk-need-responsivity model for offender assessment and rehabilitation.* Available at http://securitepubliquecanada.gc.ca/res/cor/rep/_fl/Risk_Need_2007-06_e.pdf.

Bonta, J., & Andrews, D. A. (2017). *The psychology of criminal conduct* (6th ed.). Routledge.

Bourdieu, P. (1994). *Language and symbolic power.* Harvard University Press.

Brennan, T., Dieterich, W., & Ehret, B. (2009). Evaluating the predictive validity of the COMPAS risk and needs assessment system. *Criminal Justice and Behaviour, 36*, 21–40.

Brennan, T., & Oliver, L. (2013). The emergence of machine learning techniques in criminology: Implications of complexity in our data and in research questions. *Criminology & Public Policy, 12*, 551–562.

Bureau of Justice Statistics. (2018). *Prisoners in 2016*. Available at www.bjs.gov/content/pub/pdf/p16_sum.pdf.

Canadian Centre for Justice Statistics. (2018). *Adult and youth correctional statistics in Canada, 2016/2017*. Available at https://www150.statcan.gc.ca/n1/en/pub/85-002-x/2018001/article/54972-eng.pdf?st=-60eEXbF.

Chan, J., & Bennett Moses, L. (2017). Making sense of big data for security. *British Journal of Criminology, 57*, 299–319.

Chapman, T., & Hough, M. (1998). *Evidence based practice: A guide to effective practice*. HM Inspectorate of Probation, Home Office.

Crawford, K. (2013). The hidden biases in big data. *Harvard Business Review*. Available at https://hbr.org/2013/04/the-hidden-biases-in-big-data.

Crewe, B. (2011). Depth, weight, tightness: Revisiting the pains of imprisonment. *Punishment & Society, 13*(5), 509–529.

Desmarais, S. L., Kiersten, L., Johnson, K. L., & Singh, J. P. (2016). Performance of recidivism risk assessment instruments in U.S. correctional settings. *Psychological Services, 13*, 206–222.

Desmarais, S. L., & Singh, J. P. (2013). *Risk assessment instruments validated and implemented in correctional settings in the United States*. Council of State Governments Justice Centre.

Eaglin, J. M. (2017). Constructing recidivism risk. *Emory Law Journal, 59*–122.

Eubanks, V. (2018). *Automating inequality: How high-tech tools profile, police, and punish the poor*. St. Martin's Press.

Feeley, M., & Simon, J. (1992). The new penology: Notes on the emerging strategy of corrections and its implications. *Criminology, 30*, 449–474.

Foucault, M. (1977). *Discipline and punish: The birth of the prison*. Pantheon Books.

Garland, D. (2001). *The culture of control: Crime and social order in contemporary society*. Oxford: Oxford University Press.

Goldblatt, P., & Lewis, C. (1998). *Reducing offending: An assessment of research evidence on ways of dealing with offending behaviour*. Home Office Research Study 187. Home Office.

Hamilton, M. (2015). Risk-needs assessment: Constitutional and ethical challenges. *American Criminal Law Review, 231,* 236–239.

Hannah-Moffat, K. (2016). Conceptual kaleidoscope: Dynamic risk, social conditions, and responsibilisation of individual agency. *Psychology, Crime and Law, 2*(1–2), 33–46.

Hannah-Moffat, K. (2018). Algorithmic risk governance: Big data analytics, race and information activism in criminal justice debates. *Theoretical Criminology, 23*(4), 453–470.

Hao, K., & Stray, J. (2019). Can you make AI fairer than a judge? Play our courtroom algorithm game. *MIT Technology Review.* Available at https://www.technologyreview.com/s/613508/ai-fairer-than-judge-criminal-risk-assessment-algorithm.

Harper, G., & Chitty, C. (Eds.). (2005). *The impact of corrections on reoffending: A review of "what works"* (3rd ed.). Home Office Research Study 291. Home Office.

HMPPS & MOJ. (2019). *Risk assessment of offenders: A summary of evidence relating to offender risk assessment, risk of reoffending and risk of serious harm.* Available at https://www.gov.uk/guidance/risk-assessment-of-offenders.

Home Office. (1999). *What works: Reducing re-offending: Evidence-based practice.* Home Office.

House of Commons Science and Technology Committee. (2018). *Algorithms in decision-making: Fourth report of a session 2017-9.* Available at https://publications.parliament.uk/pa/cm201719/cmselect/cmsctech/351/351.pdf.

Kaufmann, M., Egbert, S., & Leese, M. (2019). Predictive policing and the politics of patterns. *British Journal of Criminology, 59,* 674–692.

Kehl, D., Guo, P., & Kessler, S. (2017). *Algorithms in the criminal justice system: Assessing the use of risk assessments in sentencing. Responsive communities initiative.* Berkman Klein Centre for Internet & Society: Harvard Law School.

Kitchin, R. (2014a). Big data, new epistemologies and paradigm shifts. *Big Data & Society, 1*(1).

Kitchin, R. (2014b). *The data revolution: Big data, open data, data infrastructures and their consequences.* Sage.

Law Society. (2019). *Algorithm use in the criminal justice system report.* Available at https://www.lawsociety.org.uk/support-services/research-trends/algorithm-use-in-the-criminal-justice-system-report.

Ledford, H. (2019). Millions of black people affected by racial bias in healthcare algorithms. *Nature, 574*(7780), 608–609.

Lum, K., & Isaac, W. (2016). To predict and serve? *Significance, 13,* 14–19.

Lyon, D. (2014). Surveillance, Snowden, and big data: Capacities, consequences, critique. *Big Data and Society, 1*(2).

McGuire, J. (Ed.). (1995). *What works: Reducing re-offending.* Wiley.

McNeill, F. (2018). *Pervasive punishment: Making sense of mass supervision.* Bingley.

MOJ. (2017). *Statistics on race and the criminal justice system 2016: A Ministry of Justice publication under Section 95 of the Criminal Justice Act 1991.* Ministry of Justice.

National Offender Management Service. (2016). *Public protection manual 2016 edition.* Available at https://www.justice.gov.uk/downloads/offenders/psipso/psi-2016/psi-18-2016-pi-17-2016-public-protection-manual.pdf.

Noble, S. (2018). *Algorithms of oppression.* New York University Press.

O'Neil, C. (2016). *Weapons of math destruction.* Crown Publishers.

Oswald, M., Grace, J., Urwin, S., & Barnes, G. C. (2018). Algorithmic risk assessment policing models: Lessons from the Durham HART model and "experimental" proportionality. *Information & Communications Technology Law, 27*(2), 223–250.

Phillips, C., & Bowling, B. (2017). Ethnicities, racism, crime, and criminal justice. In A. Liebling, S. Maruna, & L. McAra (Eds.), *The Oxford handbook of criminology.* Oxford University Press.

Pratt, J. (2002). *Punishment and civilization: Penal tolerance and intolerance in modern society.* London: Sage.

Prins, S. J. (2016). *Is criminogenic risk assessment a prisoner of the proximate? Challenging the assumptions of an expanding paradigm.* Doctoral Thesis, Columbia University.

Raji, D. I., Gebru, T., Mitchell, M., Buolamwini, J., Lee, J., & Denton, E. (2020). Saving face: Investigating the ethical concerns of facial recognition auditing. In *Proceedings of the AAAI/ACM Conference on AI, Ethics, and Society (AIES '20).* Association for Computing Machinery, New York.

Rose, N., & Miller, P. (2010). Political power beyond the state: Problematics of government. *British Journal of Sociology, 61*(1), 271–303.

Rovastos, M., Mittelstadt, B., & Koene, A. (2020). *Landscape summary: Bias in algorithmic decision-making—What is bias in algorithmic decision-making, how can we identify it, and how can we mitigate it?* Available at https://assets.publishing.service.gov.uk/government/uploads/system/uploads/attachment_data/file/819055/Landscape_Summary_-_Bias_in_Algorithmic_Decision-Making.pdf.

Starr, S. B. (2014). Evidence-based sentencing and the scientific rationalization of discrimination. *Stanford Law Review, 66*, 803–872.

Tonry, M. (2014). Legal and ethical issues in the prediction of recidivism. *Federal Sentencing Reporter, 26*(3), 167–176.

Ugwudike, P. (2015). *An introduction to critical criminology*. Policy Press.

Ugwudike, P. (2020). Digital prediction technologies in the justice system: The implications of a 'race-neutral' agenda. *Theoretical Criminology* (online first).

Underdown, A. (1998). *Strategies for effective offender supervision*. HM Inspectorate of Probation, Home Office.

van Eijk, G. (2016). Socioeconomic marginality in sentencing: The built-in bias in risk assessment tools and the reproduction of social inequality. *Punishment and Society, 19*, 463–481.

Vomfell, L., & Stewart, N. (2021) Officer bias, over-patrolling and ethnic disparities in stop and search. *Nat Hum Behav 5*, 566–575. https://doi.org/10.1038/s41562-020-01029-w.

Wacquant, L. (2008). *Pierre Bourdieu*. In R. Stones (Ed.), *Key sociological thinkers* (2nd ed.). Palgrave.

Završnik, A. (2019). *Big data, crime and social control*. Routledge.

Part II

Methodologies and Strategies for Cybercrime Research

Anita Lavorgna and Thomas J. Holt

Introduction to Part II

Cybercrime is often discussed as a new or novel problem by the media and policymakers. The research community has explored these issues since the origins of the internet, whether in the social or technical sciences. Academics in the 1980s and 1990s often adapted data collection and analysis techniques applied in offline settings to understand the practices of actors in unique online environments. Typically, this involved the use of interviews with participants in online communities, though some also adjusted media analysis models to discussions in online communities, whether BBS in the 1980s or forums in the 1990s.

As online experiences were transformed by social media and more recently the rise of the Dark Web, research methods expanded to address the glut of user-generated data available for analysis. The use of so-called big data analytics to explore the behaviours of massive populations of users on Twitter, Facebook and other platforms became an important tool for research. Similarly, researchers in both the computer and social science communities began to utilise automated scripts to collect posts from online communities in lieu of prior hand collection techniques.

The evident tensions between these methodological strategies currently dominate the landscape of online research. This section of the book explores the benefits and shortcomings of various research strategies used in cybercrime research and provides direction for scholars seeking to navigate their way through online communities to better understand their practices.

In Chapter 6, Marleen Weulen Kranenbarg departs from her research experience in carrying out empirical comparisons of cybercriminals and traditional criminals to discuss the challenges of such an approach. She also discusses the importance in both comparative research and research specifically focused on cybercrime. The divide between the online and offline dimensions in cybercrime research is found again in Chapter 7, where E. Rutger Leukfeldt and Edward Kleemans focus their attention on the use of a traditional method of criminological research, police investigations, to shed light on critical aspects of cybercrimes that would otherwise be lost by looking only at digital data.

In Chapter 8, we enter the realm of digital data by exploring the potential of digital open source and crowdsourced data to investigate patterns of offending and victimisation through the contribution of Rajeev V. Gundur, Mark Berry and Dean Taodang. The potential of open source data collection is furthered by Emily Ann Greene-Colozzi, Joshua Freilich and Steven M. Chermak in Chapter 9. The authors focus on the best practices needed to create a good open source database, including issues of reliability and validity.

As noted throughout this book, one of the greatest challenges of cybercrime research lies in having to deal with "too much" data. Jack Hughes, Yi Ting Chua and Alice Hutchings in Chapter 10 and Stuart Middleton in Chapter 11 address this issue. Hughes and colleagues focus, respectively, on the opportunities and challenges of large datasets and the potential of automatised approaches in dealing with them. Middleton considers the merits of using Artificial Intelligence tools in this domain, especially when integrated with manual and qualitative analyses to mitigate the possibility algorithmic bias and error.

Some other innovative methodologies to investigate online data are explored in this section, starting with Robert Perkins and Jordan Howell who, in Chapter 12, provide a detailed overview of honeypots for cyber-crime research. The authors discuss their use in the context of both computer and social science to shed light on deviant human behaviour in cyberspace, and to test criminological theories. In Chapter 13, Elena Pavan offers an introduction to social and semantic network analysis, which are increasingly useful tools to deal with large amounts of online data.

In Chapters 14 and 15, written, respectively, by Nicholas Gibbs and Alexandra Hall, and Ashton Kingdon, we move from computational approaches to qualitative methodologies combining traditional elements of social science tradition with innovatory strategies. Their chapters focus on digital ethnography, or the use of traditional ethnographic methods modified to interact with online communities and environments, and the use of memes for visual research respectively.

These chapters emphasise that there is no single best approach for examining a problem like cybercrimes. Instead, researchers are encouraged to assess the core issue of interest to them and identify the method, or the methods, that will enable them to best answer their questions and provide direction for policy and practice.

6

The Challenges of Empirically Comparing Cybercriminals and Traditional Offenders

Marleen Weulen Kranenbarg

Introduction

Many criminological theories and explanations for offending have been tested extensively. In recent years, criminologists have applied these theories and explanations to a new type of crime: cybercrime. While many of these theories were developed before the rise of cybercrime, they seem to be quite useful in explaining crime in the digital age. Most empirical research on cybercrime has relied on established theories such as social learning (Holt et al., 2010; Morris & Blackburn, 2009), techniques of neutralization (Hutchings & Clayton, 2016; Turgeman-Goldschmidt, 2009), strain (Hutchings, 2016), and labeling (Turgeman-Goldschmidt, 2008; Van Der Wagen et al., 2016). Interestingly, the theoretical literature has discussed many unique features of cybercrime, which challenges

M. Weulen Kranenbarg (✉)
Department of Criminal Law and Criminology, Vrije Universiteit (VU) Amsterdam, Amsterdam, The Netherlands
e-mail: m.weulenkranenbarg@vu.nl

© The Author(s), under exclusive license to Springer Nature Switzerland AG 2021
A. Lavorgna and T. J. Holt (eds.), *Researching Cybercrimes*,
https://doi.org/10.1007/978-3-030-74837-1_6

these theories' applicability. Most notably, the discussion on the lack of convergence in time and space for routine activity theory (Grabosky, 2001; Yar, 2005). Additionally, some authors have suggested new theories or frameworks to explain cybercrime (Goldsmith & Brewer, 2015; Goldsmith & Wall, 2019; Jaishankar, 2009; Suler, 2004; Van Der Wagen, 2018). This gap between the empirical and theoretical literature asks for empirical studies that compare the applicability of traditional criminological theories and explanations between cybercrime and traditional crime.

This chapter will discuss the need for and challenges with such a comparison. The chapter is mostly based on the experiences with the first empirical comparison between cybercriminals and traditional criminals (Weulen Kranenbarg, 2018) and a recent follow-up study (Van der Toolen et al., 2020). First, some examples will be used to give some background on what the field can gain from these types of comparisons. Afterward, several important elements of this type of research, and its challenges will be discussed, including both steps at the beginning of the study, e.g., sample selection and different types of comparable data, and steps that are relevant in designing and conducting the study, such as interaction with respondents and designing a comparative survey in which traditional measures are adjusted to the digital context of the crimes. The chapter concludes by giving a short summary of the main challenges and lessons learned and outlining directions for future research. While the main goal of this chapter is to stimulate future empirical comparisons, many lessons learned will also be informative when designing a study that focuses on cybercrime specifically.

Background

Of all traditional criminological theories, social learning (Akers, 1998) is one of the most often applied theories for cybercriminal behavior. In short, this theory assumes that criminal behavior can be learned from criminal peers. When a person associates with criminal friends (differential association), this person can start to commit crimes. This process is stimulated by deviant definitions, imitation, and differential reinforcement. Friends who commit crimes can have criminal norms that justify criminal behavior (deviant definitions). These norms can be adopted from these friends. Furthermore, criminal behavior of friends can be imitated. Lastly, friends can stimulate each other to commit crimes (differential reinforcement).

These processes can be applied to cybercriminal behavior. With respect to differential association, cybercriminal friends can be found both online and offline. Social learning from offline friends may be different from traditional crimes, as online behavior of friends is less visible; social learning of offline friends may not impact a person's cybercriminal behavior as much a traditional criminal behavior would (Weulen Kranenbarg et al., 2021). However, studies have shown that many cybercriminals also have online criminal contacts. They meet and interact with these contacts on, for example, forums (Holt, 2007; Hutchings, 2016). It is difficult to say to what extent these contacts are seen as friends, as the anonymity of the Internet may limit the extent to which there is personal contact between online criminal friends. Deviant definitions may also be present on, for example, these forums. Studies have shown that techniques of neutralization and the justification of criminal behavior play a role in cybercriminal subcultures (Hutchings & Clayton, 2016; Turgeman-Goldschmidt, 2009). Additionally, apart from direct imitation of criminal behavior of friends, imitation may also include imitation of behavior based on online instructions or videos. Lastly, differential reinforcement in online communities can be very strong, as status and showing skills are important aspects of these subcultures (Steinmetz, 2015).

Empirical research in this area has shown that, for many different types of cybercrime (from low-tech to high-tech), the self-reported offending of an individual is correlated to the offending of his or her friends. However, while many studies support the effect of differential association and deviant definitions, imitation and reinforcement are less clearly linked to cybercriminal behavior (see, among others, Berenblum et al., 2019; Holt et al., 2010; Morris & Blackburn, 2009). While this body of research has shown that social learning should be included in research on cybercriminal behavior, it is unclear to what extent this social learning is just as strong for cybercrime as it is for traditional crimes. Additionally, there may be variation between different cybercrimes in the extent to which social learning plays a role (see discussion on cyber-dependent versus cyber-enabled crime in the next section in this chapter), which means that the question remains to what extent traditional interventions directed at social learning processes are expected to have the same effect on different types of cybercrime as they have on traditional crimes.

This gap in the literature has been addressed in 2021 (Weulen Kranenbarg et al., 2021). In this study, a high-risk sample of Dutch adult cybercriminals and traditional criminals answered self-report survey questions on their online and offline criminal behavior. In addition, they also indicated to what extent their strong social ties committed these offenses. Traditionally, strong social ties show the strongest correlation in criminal behavior. The results of this study first confirmed the results from previous cybercrime research by finding a significant correlation between the cybercriminal behavior of an individual and the cybercriminal behavior of his or her strong social ties. However, this study also clearly showed why the empirical comparison is very important. Compared to traditional crime, the correlation between the self-reported cybercriminal behavior of social ties was significantly less strong for cybercrime.

This result could indicate that social learning is less important for cybercrime as it is for traditional crimes. On the other hand, it may also be an indication that other types of social ties are more important for cybercrime (Van der Toolen et al., 2020; Weulen Kranenbarg et al., 2021). As suggested by qualitative studies on hacking, online social ties, for example, on forums, may be an important source of social learning (Holt, 2007; Hutchings, 2016). A follow-up study among Dutch youth at IT-schools showed that this might be the case (Van der Toolen et al., 2020). In this study, the criminal behavior of offline friends (both friends from school and other offline friends) was equally significantly correlated with both cybercrime and traditional crime. While this finding was not in line with the findings from Weulen Kranenbarg and colleagues (2021), the study also showed that the criminal behavior of online social ties (who a respondent did not know or see offline) was relatively more important for cybercriminal behavior of an individual than for traditional criminal behavior (Van der Toolen et al., 2020). In line with this finding, research in the United States on traditional crime (McCuddy, 2020) has shown that online peer groups are important for traditional criminal behavior but only secondary to offline peer groups. Together these studies indicate that other types of social contacts should be included in research on cybercrime and social learning. In addition, the differences in the results for the importance of offline friends for cybercrime ask for follow-up comparisons in different samples to see to what extent these results are replicated in other studies.

The examples in this paragraph have shown what we can gain from comparing cybercriminals and traditional criminals on a specific criminological theory. Apart from testing specific theories or explanations for cybercrime, many studies also try to include measures for several different explanations for offending simultaneously. A recent study in the Netherlands has shown that comparing these types of risk profiles between cybercriminals and traditional criminals can also be very useful (Rokven et al., 2017, 2018). This study showed that cybercriminals who do not commit traditional crimes have a less serious risk profile and report different risk factors such as frequent gaming. This outcome could mean that prevention should be directed at different individuals and different risk factors. While these studies provide first insights into empirical differences between cybercriminals and traditional criminals, many differences have not been tested yet or should be replicated in different samples or other countries. This chapter provides some lessons learned that could help in future empirical comparisons.

Challenges of Empirically Comparing Cybercriminals and Traditional Criminals

Finding Comparable Samples

Comparing cybercrime with traditional crimes means that the data on both groups should be comparable. While studies on cybercrime have used many unique datasets based on, for example, forums or criminal markets (Dupont et al., 2016; Holt et al., 2016), these data sources usually do not include comparable data on traditional crim, meaning that comparisons will generally be based on more traditional data sources, such as surveys or registration data on criminal cases or registered criminals.

Before selecting one of these sources, one first needs to decide which specific crimes will be compared. The umbrella term "cyber-crime" includes a large variety of offenses with potentially very different correlates. Cybercrime is generally divided into cyber-dependent and cyber-enabled crime (McGuire & Dowling, 2013a, 2013b). Cyber-dependent crimes are new offenses that cannot be committed without using IT-systems. The main target of these crimes is the IT-system itself. Examples are hacking, malware, and DDoS-attacks. Cyber-enabled crimes are traditional crimes that already existed but are now committed using digital means. For example, online harassment, online stalking, and online fraud. Based on the existing comparisons, cyber-dependent criminals seem to have more unique features (Rokven et al., 2017, 2018), which may to some extent be the result of the skills that are needed to commit some of these crimes and the mostly digital context in which these crimes are committed. The modus operandi for cyber-enabled offenses, on the other hand, can also have offline components as the target is not an IT-system but a human being. In addition, some offenses such as harassment may be committed both online and offline simultaneously, and may be the reason why these criminals seem to be more similar to traditional criminals.

Nevertheless, for cyber-enabled offenses, it is usually quite easy to determine which traditional offline crime it should be compared to. Studies have, for example, compared online and offline bullying (Navarro et al., 2015). For cyber-dependent crimes, there are no clear offline traditional counterparts. Therefore, determining the type of crime to compare to is more difficult. Consequently, the first empirical comparison included a random sample of traditional criminals, which means that this is a very broad category (Weulen Kranenbarg, 2018). While this is a good start for comparisons, future studies may choose a specific type of traditional crime depending on the theory that is being applied. For example, when studying the effect of employment, it may be worthwhile to compare white-collar crime and cybercrime as both crimes can be committed in the course of an occupation (Weulen Kranenbarg et al., 2018).

After deciding which types of crime will be compared, the data source should be selected based on the type of question that has to be answered. Depending on the country, there may or may not be registration data on criminal cases or registered criminals available. This data includes both cybercrime and traditional crime. In the Netherlands, this type of data on crime suspects can in some cases be linked to other registration data such as data on employment, income, marital status, etcetera (Weulen Kranenbarg et al., 2018). This data enables longitudinal analyses and comparing different criminals in the entire population of crime suspects. However, in-depth information, for example, about the strength of social bonds at work or in the family is not available. Therefore, many studies use self-report survey data to examine how these types of constructs are related to offending. The types of crime that are being compared may influence which respondents will be selected for these surveys. High volume crimes can be studied using a general population sample. For cybercrime, however, especially the more technically advanced types of crime may not be that common. Therefore, it may be worthwhile to select criminals based on their previous convictions for both cybercrime and traditional crime (Weulen Kranenbarg, 2018). For studies among youth, selecting schools that specifically focus on IT-education may be a way to find enough respondents who at least have the skills to commit the more sophisticated types of cybercrime (Van der Toolen et al., 2020).

Defining Comparative Groups and Testing Differences

In addition to choosing which types of crime will be compared, it is also necessary to consider some difficulties in defining and empirically comparing these groups. First of all, criminals may commit both online and offline crimes. For example, Dutch registration data showed that 26% of criminals had been a suspect of both cybercrime and traditional crime in a specific year (Weulen Kranenbarg et al., 2018). Similarly, cybercriminal networks in different countries usually commit a range of crimes that includes online and offline activities (Leukfeldt et al., 2016; Lusthaus, 2018). Additionally, self-report data shows that there is a group of criminals who commit both types of crimes (Rokven et al., 2017, 2018; Weulen Kranenbarg, 2021), although it should be mentioned that most cyber-dependent criminals seem to specialize in cybercrime (Weulen Kranenbarg, 2021). However, they may still commit a few offline crimes as well. This overlap in offending complicates the comparison. One should decide how criminals who commit both types of crimes should be classified. They can be a separate group in the comparison (Rokven et al., 2017, 2018), included in both groups (Weulen Kranenbarg et al., 2018), or classified based on their most recent or most frequently reported crime. In addition, survey studies may be able to ask specific questions about each individual self-reported crime (Weulen Kranenbarg, 2021), which means that analyses could compare crimes instead of criminals, which minimizes the problems of overlapping offending in one individual. Nevertheless, choosing one of these strategies will also impact the type of statistical analyses that can be used to compare the groups, as many tests require independent groups.

Apart from comparing between groups of cybercriminals and traditional criminals, it may also be worthwhile to compare different types of cybercriminals. Cybercriminals may differ in factors such as their IT-skills, routine activities, personal characteristics such as self-control, or motivation depending on the types of crime they commit. Some technically advanced cybercrimes, for example, may require much more IT-skills and self-control than other easy-to-commit cybercrimes (Holt et al., 2020). On the other hand, criminals may combine different types of crime in one criminal act. For example, by first hacking into a system, stealing its data, and selling that data on the Internet (Weulen Kranenbarg, 2021). Cybercrime is an umbrella term that includes a wide variety of offenses. Therefore, it is important to investigate to what extent different types of criminals commit different types of cybercrime and to what extent different offenses are committed by one individual. However, similar to comparing online and offline crime, as discussed in the previous paragraph, one should consider how to deal with criminals who commit a wide variety of cybercrime.

Each dataset that includes information on different types of criminals or offenses is different. A researcher should first decide which analyses are required for the research question under study. However, simply running, for example, two separate models for each group in the comparison is not enough. In order to conclude to what extent the groups differ in a specific aspect, the results on both groups should be statistically compared. For some analyses, one could compare both groups within one model (Weulen Kranenbarg et al., 2021). For other analyses, one should test differences in effect sizes between two separate models (Weulen Kranenbarg et al., 2018, 2021). These choices will largely depend on the type of data and research question under study. As discussed in the previous paragraphs, one should also consider to what extent both groups are independent.

Comparisons Based on Judicial Registration Data of Crime or Criminals

After deciding on a strategy for comparing between groups, the next steps will differ depending on the type of data that is available. With respect to judicial registration data of crimes or criminals (data from police, prosecutor's office, courts, etc.), a few factors should be considered. It may, first of all, be the case that not all types of cybercrime can be identified in this type of data. Some sources of registration data may include a categorization of the type of crime. Depending on the organization that created the data, this categorization may or may not include a specific category for cybercrime. In addition, it may not always be clear which crimes are included in this category and how accurately they are categorized by, for example, the police officer who registered the crime. One may, therefore, decide to make this categorization oneself. In other sources, this may be necessary as there is no categorization or cybercrime may only be registered as a separate category in the more recent years (Weulen Kranenbarg et al., 2018).

There are roughly two ways to determine which crimes should be categorized as cybercrimes in registration data. First, depending on the country, there may be specific criminal laws for cybercrimes. For example, in the Netherlands, cyber-dependent crimes are punishable under specific articles of law (Weulen Kranenbarg et al., 2018). In the United States, it may be possible to select crimes under the Computer Fraud and Abuse Act and in the UK under the Computer Misuse Act. If these laws include all crimes of interest, registration data could be categorized based on these laws. However, it may, for example, be difficult to determine how technically advanced a hacking offense was only based on the article of law. In addition, many cyber-enabled crimes such as harassment may be registered under a general article of law that includes both the online and offline variety of that crime. Therefore, the second way to find the cybercrimes in this type of data is by analyzing descriptions of the crime that might be included in the data or the underlying reports. Doing this by hand can be a very time-consuming process. A recent study in the Netherlands has, therefore, investigated how text-mining techniques can be used to facilitate this process (Van der Laan & Tollenaar, 2021).

When using registration data, one should always consider its' limitations with respect to selectivity and generalizability. As this data is influenced by the efforts of the judicial system, not every criminal has the same chance of being included in the dataset. When comparing cyber-crime to traditional crime with this type of data, one should consider to what extent this selectivity differs between both groups. Cybercrime has quite low apprehension rates, which means that data on cybercrime could be more selective. It could also mean that, for example, data on recidivism is less reliable for cybercrime. Furthermore, cybercriminals can use many techniques to prevent them from being caught and this may mean that the criminals who are being caught are the less skilled criminals (Weulen Kranenbarg et al., 2018).

Even though cybercrime rates are increasing, it is still a minority of all crimes registered by the police. As there are still many more traditional crimes, sample sizes of the two groups can be very different. In the Netherlands, a twelve-year period of registration data included 870 cyber-dependent criminals and approximately one million traditional criminals (Weulen Kranenbarg et al., 2018). Statistical tests that compare these groups should be suitable to compare groups with large differences in sample size.

Interaction with Respondents for Surveys Among High-Risk Samples

While registration data could enable longitudinal analyses and comparing different criminals in the entire population of crime suspects, in-depth information on factors related to offending is generally not available in this type of data, and many crimes go undetected. Therefore, many studies use self-report survey data. As discussed, there are different ways to find respondents for a comparative survey, such as general population studies or high-risk groups of convicted criminals or students from specific schools. This paragraph will specifically discuss these high-risk samples and how these could be approached.

The study by Weulen Kranenbarg (2018) is based on two high-risk samples of previously apprehended cybercriminals and traditional criminals. They were invited to participate in this survey by sending them a letter. Based on the responses to this invitation, a few elements should be considered when inviting participants from two different types of criminal groups. Response rates largely differed between both groups. For cybercriminals, the response rate was 29%, while for traditional criminals, the response rate was only 16%. This may have been the result of differences in personal characteristics such as self-control between both groups. In addition, the invitation letter put some more emphasis on online crimes, by stating that the study was interested in the respondents' knowledge on computers and the Internet and their experiences with unsafe online and offline situations and crime. Therefore, the cybercrime sample participants may have thought that the survey was more relevant for them. As showing one's skills is an important aspect of cybercriminal behavior (Steinmetz, 2015), they may have been more interested in the study because of its focus on their knowledge of computers. Lastly, some criminals who contacted the research team to ask questions about the survey indicated that they felt that the judicial system was not suitable for cybercriminals. Therefore, they were strongly motivated to participate in the study to help future criminals who come into contact with the judicial system. Overall, these experiences show how cybercriminals could be specifically stimulated to participate. Still, these also show that it is important to consider how to stimulate both groups to participate in order to have more equal sample sizes and response rates.

Apart from these experiences, the privacy awareness of the cybercriminal sample has been an important factor in the study. As cybercriminals were expected to be more aware of their privacy, this was already considered in designing the study. The survey was hosted on both a normal Web site and a Tor hidden service Web site. Participants could choose how they wanted to participate. In addition, the information on the first page of the survey clearly explained how participants were selected and how confidentiality was safeguarded. Nevertheless, many more cybercriminal sample participants contacted the research teams with questions about their privacy. Therefore, it is very important to think about the participants' privacy awareness before sending out the survey. Communication about these issues should be very clear, and there should always be a way to contact the research team directly. With this type of sample, researchers can expect more questions than usual.

How to Develop a Comparative Survey

In addition to sending invitation letters that appeal to both types of criminals, the survey should also be suitable for both groups in the comparison. While questions about traditional crime will usually be quite easy to understand, questions about cybercrime can be very complex. In the Weulen Kranenbarg (2018) study, self-report items on cybercrime were therefore quite broad. For example, there were two questions on hacking: "breaking in or logging on to a network, computer, or web account by guessing the password" and "gaining access to a network, computer, web account, or files that were saved on that in another way". While these two questions were probably understandable for all respondents, they could not completely distinguish between more or less sophisticated types of hacking. In the follow-up (Van der Toolen et al., 2020) with self-report questions at IT-schools, five different specific ways of hacking were included (guessing the password yourself, automatic tools for guessing passwords, exploits, SQL-injections, other). While these questions appeared to be difficult for some respondents, the offline way of conducting the study at the school enabled them to ask for clarification. In addition, respondents who did not understand these questions simply seemed to assume that they did not apply to them, which is probably correct most of the time. In offline settings, where researchers are directly available to answer questions, it may not be problematic to include questions that some participants may not understand. In online settings, however, these should be avoided. Many difficult questions could also demotivate non-technical participants.

In order to compare the level of technical expertise of participants and investigate the potential correlation between IT-skills and offending, it is interesting to include a measure for IT-skills in the survey and can be done subjectively by providing respondents with statements that represent different levels of expertise (Holt et al., 2012; Rogers, 2001), ranging from "I don't like using computers and don't use them unless I absolutely have to" to "I can use Linux, most software, and fix most computer problems I have". The range of these statements should be adjusted to the expected expertise of respondents in the comparison. On the one hand, it is important to include a statement for participants with no interest in computers. On the other hand, in, for example, Weulen Kranenbarg and colleagues (2021), some respondents in the cybercrime sample were expected to have very strong IT-skills which is why the following statement was added "I can use different programming languages and am capable of detecting programming errors".

In addition to subjective measures of IT-skills, objective measures such as an IT-test should be considered as well as these may be more accurate. In the Weulen Kranenbarg and colleagues (2021) study, ten test questions were added to the survey (see online supplementary materials of Weulen Kranenbarg et al., 2021). As this comparison also included traditional criminals, these questions needed to measure a broad range of expertise. Therefore the questions started very easy such as "Which of the following email addresses can be valid?: 1. www.infobedrijfx.nl; 2. info@bedrijfx.nl; 3. https://www.infobedrijfx.nl; 4. info@bedrijfx; 5. I do not know", correctly answered by 93% of all respondents. Followed by more advanced questions such as "In what order are webpages loaded? 1. URL ==> IP ==> DNS; 2. IP ==> DNS ==> URL; 3. URL ==> DNS = > IP; 4. IP ==> URL ==> DNS; 5. I do not know", correctly answered by

28%. Finally, the most difficult question included a piece of code with a bug, and respondents had to indicate which technique could be used to prevent the exploitation of this bug, correctly answered by only 4% of all respondents (all from the cybercriminal sample). Weulen Kranenbarg et al. (2021) showed that this objective IT-test was strongly correlated (Pearson's $r = 0.75$, $p < 0.001$) to the subjective statements discussed above. However, for the analyses, the objective test was included as it had more explanatory power, and this measure could be more accurate as respondents could not overestimate their expertise. Future research may benefit from including subjective and objective measures (including a wide range of expertise) to find out which are best suitable in predicting offending behavior.

In addition to testing correlations with IT-skills, survey studies will probably have many other constructs they want to measure. For comparisons, it is important to keep in mind that both traditional correlates of offending and new cyber-related correlates of offending should be included. Rokven et al. (2017) note, for example, that they may have missed important correlates of cybercrime as their biennial survey among a representative sample of youth is strongly based on constructs related to offline crime. In Weulen Kranenbarg (2018), on the other hand, the focus was more on cybercrime, which resulted in a better model fit for the cybercrime models compared to the traditional crime models. Therefore, the Van der Toolen and colleagues (2020) follow-up study included both potential online and offline correlates of certain constructs where possible. Examples are perceptions on both online and offline rules, online and offline parental control, and online and offline supervised and unsupervised activities. As both traditional and cyber aspects need to be included in comparative research and surveys should still be rather short, it is important to consider which constructs are most relevant for the specific comparison.

Applying Traditional Theories to Cybercrime in an Empirical Comparison

In the paragraph above, it has already been discussed that explanations of crime such as parental control and routine activities should be adjusted to the digital age in order to have explanatory power for cybercrime. However, for measures such as routine activities, it is sometimes more difficult to ask these questions about online activities, as most people are online almost 24/7, making it difficult to report how much time is spent on specific online activities. In addition to this example, there is a wide variety of other traditional theories that could explain both cybercrime and traditional crime. This chapter aims to stimulate empirical comparisons of these theories and shows which aspects should be considered when designing such a comparison. This paragraph will briefly discuss two examples, in order to spark ideas for future comparisons on other explanations of criminal behavior.

Life-course criminological research has shown that employment generally reduces offending (Kazemian, 2015; Lageson & Uggen, 2013). Some first results on cybercrime have shown that this also seems to be the case for cybercrime (Weulen Kranenbarg et al., 2018). However, this study also indicated that employment in IT might be a risk factor because of employment-related opportunities for cybercrime. Similar to research on white-collar criminals, research on cybercrime should separate the effect of employment in general and employment in which opportunities for cybercrime could arise.

As discussed in the background section, social learning is frequently studied for cybercrime. New types of social ties, most importantly, online social ties, may influence cybercriminal behavior (Van der Toolen et al., 2020; Weulen Kranenbarg et al., 2021). They should, therefore, be included in research on cybercrime. However, it is difficult to distinguish when a social tie is an online tie. Some respondents may have met someone once or twice, but otherwise only communicate online. Differentiating between online and offline friends may, therefore, not be as simple as it seems. In addition, it is more difficult to ask respondents questions about their online social ties, as they may not even know their gender or age. Furthermore, for both online and offline social ties, their online behavior is less visible and this means that traditional ways of measuring peer-influence may not be as accurate for cybercrime. Research has shown that it is particularly difficult for respondents to report on the online criminal behavior of their friends (Van der Toolen et al., 2020). Comparing the extent to which social ties are similar in their online and offline criminal behavior, therefore, has its limitations.

Conclusion

This chapter has discussed the challenges of empirically comparing cybercriminals and traditional criminals. Most information is based on personal experiences in the first comparisons in this area. Hopefully, this chapter will spark ideas for future comparisons and provide some guidance on how to design these studies. As the chapter has shown, many aspects of the research design are influenced by decisions on which specific groups will be compared. Subsequently, in contrast to studies that only focus on cybercrime or a specific traditional crime, comparative research should consider two potentially very different groups of respondents in their study design.

There are still many questions that could be answered in a comparative design. First of all, most studies discussed in this chapter are based on Dutch criminals. Future comparisons in other countries would be very valuable. In addition, the explanatory power of other criminological theories should be compared, such as attachment to school or parents, use of neutralization techniques, and strain-theory.

Lastly, this chapter has only discussed quantitative empirical comparisons. These comparisons can statistically test to what extent a specific estimate differs between two different outcome variables. However, qualitative research may also provide very beneficial insights. For example, criminals who commit both online and offline crimes may be able to provide in-depth information on the extent to which their behavior is driven by different factors online than offline. Secondly, qualitative research on cyber-enabled crime such as harassment may compare qualitative interviews of online and offline criminals to find nuanced differences in how and why these crimes are committed.

Research on cybercrime has provided many insights into cybercriminal behavior. It has introduced new theories and tested traditional theories for explaining this specific behavior. This chapter hopefully stimulates future empirical comparisons that could further put these results in perspective. These comparisons can show us to what extent cybercrime is different from traditional crimes.

References

Akers, R. L. (1998). *Social learning and social structure: A general theory of crime and deviance.* Northeastern University Press.

Berenblum, T., Weulen Kranenberg, M., & Maimon, D. (2019). Out of control online? A combined examination of peer-offending and perceived formal and informal social control in relation to system-trespassing. *Journal of Crime and Justice, 42*(5), 616–631.

Dupont, B., Côté, A. M., Savine, C., & Décary-Hétu, D. (2016). The ecology of trust among hackers. *Global Crime, 17*(2), 129–151.

Goldsmith, A., & Brewer, R. (2015). Digital drift and the criminal interaction order. *Theoretical Criminology, 19*(1), 112–130.

Goldsmith, A., & Wall, D. S. (2019). The seductions of cybercrime: Adolescence and the thrills of digital transgression. *European Journal of Criminology* (online first).

Grabosky, P. N. (2001). Virtual criminality: Old wine in new bottles? *Social & Legal Studies, 10*(2), 243–249.

Holt, T. J. (2007). Subcultural evolution? Examining the influence of on- and off-line experiences on deviant subcultures. *Deviant Behavior, 28*(2), 171–198.

Holt, T. J., Bossler, A. M., & May, D. C. (2012). Low self-control, deviant peer associations, and juvenile cyberdeviance. *American Journal of Criminal Justice, 37*(3), 378–395.

Holt, T. J., Burruss, G. W., & Bossler, A. M. (2010). Social learning and cyber-deviance: Examining the importance of a full social learning model in the virtual world. *Journal of Crime and Justice, 33*(2), 31–61.

Holt, T. J., Cale, J., Brewer, R., & Goldsmith, A. (2020). Assessing the role of opportunity and low self-control in Juvenile Hacking. *Crime & Delinquency* (online first).

Holt, T. J., Smirnova, O., & Hutchings, A. (2016). Examining signals of trust in criminal markets online. *Journal of Cybersecurity, 2*(2), 137–145.

Hutchings, A. (2016). Cybercrime trajectories: An integrated theory of initiation, maintenance, and desistance. In T. J. Holt (Ed.), *Crime online: Correlates, causes, and context*. Carolina Academic Press.

Hutchings, A., & Clayton, R. (2016). Exploring the provision of online booter services. *Deviant Behavior, 37*(10), 1163–1178.

Jaishankar, K. (2009). Space transition theory of cyber crimes. In F. Schmalleger & M. Pittaro (Eds.), *Crimes of the Internet*. Pearson Education.

Kazemian, L. (2015). Desistance from crime and antisocial behavior. In J. Morizot & L. Kazemian (Eds.), *The development of criminal and antisocial behavior*. Springer.

Lageson, S., & Uggen, C. (2013). How work affects crime—And crime affects work—Over the life course. In C. L. Gibson & M. D. Krohn (Eds.), *Handbook of life-course criminology*. Springer.

Leukfeldt, E. R., Kleemans, E. R., & Stol, W.Ph. (2016). Cybercriminal networks, social ties and online forums: Social ties versus digital ties within phishing and malware networks. *British Journal of Criminology, 57*(3), 704–722.

Lusthaus, J. (2018). *Industry of anonymity: Inside the business of cybercrime*. Harvard University Press.

McCuddy, T. (2020). Peer delinquency among digital natives: The cyber context as a source of peer influence. *Journal of Research in Crime and Delinquency* (online first).

McGuire, M., & Dowling, S. (2013a). *Chapter 1: Cyber-dependent crimes*. Home Office.

McGuire, M., & Dowling, S. (2013b). *Chapter 2: Cyber-enabled crimes*. Home Office.

Morris, R. G., & Blackburn, A. G. (2009). Cracking the code: An empirical exploration of social learning theory and computer crime. *Journal of Crime and Justice, 32*(1), 1–34.

Navarro, R., Yubero, S., & Larrañaga, E. (2015). Psychosocial risk factors for involvement in bullying behaviors: Empirical comparison between cyberbullying and social bullying victims and bullies. *School Mental Health, 7*(4), 235–248.

Rogers, M. K. (2001). *A social learning theory and moral disengagement analysis of criminal computer behavior: An exploratory study* (Doctoral dissertation). University of Manitoba. Available at https://www.cerias.purdue.edu/assets/pdf/bibtex_archive/rogers_01.pdf.

Rokven, J. J., Weijters, G., Beerthuizen, M. G. C. J., & van der Laan, A. M. (2018). Juvenile delinquency in the virtual world: Similarities and differences between cyber-enabled, cyber-dependent and offline delinquents in the Netherlands. *International Journal of Cyber Criminology, 12*(1), 27–46.

Rokven, J. J., Weijters, G., & Van Der Laan, A. M. (2017). *Jeugddelinquentie in de virtuele wereld: Een nieuw type daders of nieuwe mogelijkheden voor traditionele daders?* WODC.

Steinmetz, K. F. (2015). Craft(y)ness: An ethnographic study of hacking. *British Journal of Criminology, 55*(1), 125–145.

Suler, J. (2004). The online disinhibition effect. *Cyber Psychology & Behavior, 7*(3), 321–326.

Turgeman-Goldschmidt, O. (2008). Meanings that hackers assign to their being a hacker. *International Journal of Cyber Criminology, 2*(2), 382–396.

Turgeman-Goldschmidt, O. (2009). The rhetoric of hackers' neutralizations. In F. Schmalleger & M. Pittaro (Eds.), *Crimes of the Internet*. Pearson Education.

Van der Laan, A. M., & Tollenaar, N. (2021). Textmining for cybercrime in registrations of the Dutch police. In M. Weulen Kranenbarg & E. R. Leukfeldt (Eds.), *Cybercrime in context: The human factor in victimization, offending, and policing* (pp. 327–350). Cham: Springer International Publishing.

Van der Toolen, Y., Weulen Kranenbarg, M., & Weerman, F. M. (2020). Online jeugdcriminaliteit en "verkeerde vrienden": Wanneer is de samenhang het sterkst? *Tijdschrift Voor Criminologie, 62*(2–3), 153–180.

Van Der Wagen, W. (2018). *From cybercrime to cyborgcrime: An exploration of high-tech cybercrime, offenders and victims through the lens of actor-network theory* (Doctoral dissertation). Rijksuniversiteit Groningen & Erasmus Universiteit Rotterdam, The Netherlands. Available at https://www.rug.nl/research/portal/en/publications/from-cybercrime-to-cyborg-crime(f3a5c5e0-ff0f-4dad-ac6c-2bc91d96a1b4).html.

Van Der Wagen, W., Althoff, M., & Swaaningen, R. (2016). De andere "anderen." *Tijdschrift over Cultuur & Criminaliteit, 6*(1), 27–41.

Weulen Kranenbarg, M. (2018). *Cyber-offenders versus traditional offenders: An empirical comparison* (Doctoral dissertation). Vrije Universiteit (VU) Amsterdam, The Netherlands. Available at http://dare.ubvu.vu.nl/handle/1871/55530.

Weulen Kranenbarg, M. (2021). Cyber-dependent crime versus traditional crime: Empirical evidence for clusters of offenses and related motives. In M. Weulen Kranenbarg & E. R. Leukfeldt (Eds.), *Cybercrime in context:*

The human factor in victimization, offending, and policing (pp. 195–216). Cham: Springer International Publishing.

Weulen Kranenbarg, M., Holt, T. J., & Van Gelder, J. L. (2019). Offending and victimization in the digital age: Comparing correlates of cybercrime and traditional offending-only, victimization-only and the victimization-offending overlap. *Deviant Behavior, 40*(1), 40–55.

Weulen Kranenbarg, M., Ruiter, S., & Van Gelder, J. L. (2021). Do cyber-birds flock together? Comparing deviance among social network members of cyber-dependent offenders and traditional offenders. *European Journal of Criminology, 18*(3), 386–406.

Weulen Kranenbarg, M., Ruiter, S., Van Gelder, J.-L., & Bernasco, W. (2018). Cyber-offending and traditional offending over the life-course: An empirical comparison. *Journal of Developmental and Life-Course Criminology, 4*(3), 343–364.

Yar, M. (2005). The novelty of 'cybercrime': An assessment in light of routine activity theory. *European Journal of Criminology, 2*(4), 407–427.

7

Breaking the Walls of Silence: Analyzing Criminal Investigations to Improve Our Understanding of Cybercrime

E. Rutger Leukfeldt and Edward R. Kleemans

Introduction

Cybercrime researchers try to understand why cybercrime occurs. Researchers have a variety of research methods at their disposal to study offenders (see, for an overview, Gadd et al., 2012). Each method has its own pros and cons and, ideally, multiple methods are used to improve our understanding of cybercrime and cybercriminals. Cybercrime researchers have used both fairly traditional methods and relatively new research methods. Traditional methods include offender interviews, surveys, and ethnographic research (see, for instance, Holt, 2009;

E. R. Leukfeldt (✉)
Netherlands Institute for the Study of Crime and Law Enforcement (NSCR)
and The Hague University of Applied Sciences, Amsterdam, The Netherlands
e-mail: RLeukfeldt@nscr.nl

E. R. Kleemans
Vrije Universiteit Amsterdam, Amsterdam, The Netherlands
e-mail: e.r.kleemans@vu.nl

A. Lavorgna and T. J. Holt (eds.), *Researching Cybercrimes*,
https://doi.org/10.1007/978-3-030-74837-1_7

127

Weulen Kranenbarg, 2018), as covered more in details in Chapters 6, 14, and 24–26 of this book. The innovative methods used by cybercrime researchers are often linked to the unique opportunities the internet creates to gather data about criminals who use the very same internet to commit their crimes. Examples include scraping data from criminal forums and markets on both the clear web and the dark web (Dupont et al., 2017; Hutchings & Holt, 2015; see Chapters 10, 11, 13, and 22), using publicly available online data (see also Chapters 8 and 9), and using honey pots to study attacker behavior (see Chapter 12).

Currently, cybercrime research is still in its infancy. Although an increasing number scholars from various disciplines are involved in cybercrime studies, many of the "big" questions remain unanswered (see, e.g., Holt and Bossler, 2014; Leukfeldt, 2017; Maimon & Louderback, 2019). A major problem is that it is simply difficult to study the criminals committing cybercrimes. Indeed, criminals try to hide their illegal activities and are usually not disposed to talking openly to researchers, which limits the usefulness of the more traditional social sciences' research methods. Furthermore, the innovative methods come with their own limitations: Although they usually provide big datasets with sometimes hundreds of thousands of data points, they only provide superficial data or, in the case of scraped data, only contain information about one very small step in the crime scrips of cybercriminals. In-depth police investigations, therefore, can be very useful as an extra tool in the toolbox of cybercrime researchers. Indeed, these investigations provide a unique insight into cybercriminal networks and their members because of the wide use of intrusive investigation methods, such as wiretaps, IP taps, observations, undercover policing, and house searches. Together with more traditional methods (such as interviews and surveys) and innovative methods (such as analysis of scraped data or open source data), police files can be used to improve our understanding of cybercrime and offender behavior.

Getting access to police data can be difficult. Hence, scientific progress in cybercrime research is hindered by the general lack of cooperation between the police and academic researchers. For outside academic observers, only the tip of the iceberg of cybercrime is visible and much of the iceberg is only revealed if the police use special investigative powers such as undercover operations, wiretapping, intercepting internet communication, bugging, seizing and decrypting information on servers, house and computer searches, and interrogations. A prime example of this problem is that academic researchers are able to scrape data on the internet on a massive scale but this only provides rather superficial information about Darknet markets, since we remain unaware of structures and actions hidden behind transactions and fake identities. This underlying information only becomes available if the police target the marketplaces and academic researchers gain access to the data. Other cybercrime phenomena share similar problems for academic researchers: The incidents can be described but it often remains unclear which (cooperating) offenders and actions create the patterns that are observed. The offender perspective is often lacking and research projects to liaise with relevant cybercrime offenders are scarce. Furthermore, the efforts to persuade them to share concrete information about offender behavior and incidents have a very high cost–benefit-ratio. Lastly, this scarce information is dwarfed by the rich information that is collected by police in specific cybercrime operations. Of course, it is precisely the job of the police to break these walls of silence, but the rich information gathered in such operations often remains hidden behind other walls of silence and is not put to use for academic research. For academic research, therefore, strengthening cooperation with the police is an important endeavor that would greatly benefit theoretical and empirical progress in cybercrime research.

This chapter describes the pros and cons of using police investigations to shed light on cybercrimes. First, we describe the Dutch Organized Crime Monitor, an instrument that has been used to systematically analyze police files about organized crime (including cybercrime) for over two decades. Next, we focus on the use of police data to analyze cybercrimes. Since researchers in many countries do not have easy access to police investigations, we also discuss an alternative option: reconstructing cases based on interviewing case officers involved in criminal investigations. Lastly, based on recent publications, the chapter demonstrates how the analysis of criminal investigations can produce cybercrime knowledge which other research methods simply cannot provide: By breaking the walls of silence, police files provide a rich picture of the hidden world of cybercriminals.

The Dutch Organized Crime Monitor and Cybercrime

In the Netherlands, law enforcement institutions, such as the police and the Public Prosecution Office, are generally more willing than in other countries to cooperate in academic research, particularly in the area of organized crime and cybercrime research. This cooperative spirit may be ascribed to a rather progressive police force but also to the backlash of a huge political scandal which forcefully shattered the walls of silence of the police monopoly on information about organized crime. This scandal, the so-called IRT-affair, took place in 1994–1996 and concerned police undercover operations in organized crime, resulting in a Parliamentary Inquiry Committee into Criminal Investigation Methods. The Committee discredited existing police reports on organized crime and opened up the police for independent academic research. An external academic research group—the research group *Fijnaut*—was appointed and produced an extensive report on organized crime which was published as an appendix to the report of the committee in 1996 (Fijnaut et al., 1996, 1998; PEO, 1996). After the publication of this report, the Dutch Minister of Justice promised the Dutch Parliament to produce reports on a regular basis on the nature of organized crime in the Netherlands. From 1996 onwards, the Dutch Organized Crime Monitor, a collaboration of the Research and Documentation Centre (WODC), Vrije Universiteit Amsterdam, and Erasmus University Rotterdam, has conducted an ongoing systematic analysis of closed police investigations of criminal groups to provide insight into the nature of organized crime in the Netherlands (see for a more extensive discussion of the origins and methodology of the Dutch Organized Crime Monitor, see Kleemans, 2014).

The basic idea behind the Dutch Organized Crime Monitor is to collect solid empirical data on a wide cross section of organized crime cases in order to inform policy and practice. The main sources for the Dutch Organized Crime Monitor are the closed police files of criminal groups, often spanning a period of several years (for more information, see Kleemans, 2007, 2014). In five data sweeps, 180 large-scale investigations were systematically analyzed. Major reports to Parliament were published in 1998, 2002, 2007, 2012, 2018, and 2019 (Kleemans et al., 1998, 2002; Kruisbergen et al., 2012, 2019; Van de Bunt & Kleemans, 2007). A specific report was drafted on the topic of organized crime and IT (Kruisbergen et al., 2018) and the last data sweep also included cybercrime cases. Until the last data sweep, there were very few available large-scale investigations into cybercrime that would qualify as organized crime (see below).

Each case analysis started with structured interviews with police officers and/or public prosecutors. After these interviews, the police files (to which researchers had direct access) were analyzed and summarized, using an extensive checklist on the following topics: the police investigation and the investigation process; the criminal network; the criminal activities and modus operandi; contacts with the licit and illicit environment; criminal proceeds, investments, spending, money laundering, and seized assets; judicial procedure and verdict; and evaluation (lessons learned, new insights, prevention opportunities, new developments, effectiveness of policing strategies see Kruisbergen et al., 2019). The checklist was also used and adapted in specific research into cybercriminal networks by Leukfeldt and colleagues (e.g., Leukfeldt, 2016; Leukfeldt et al., 2017a).

Police Data and Cybercrime Research

When the Dutch Organized Crime Monitor was developed, several trade-offs had to be made. Below, we briefly review three topics and answer the question whether such trade-offs may also be germane to (certain types of) cybercrime.

Opting for Solid and "Older" Evidence

How solid should evidence be to be used in criminological research and who decides upon what amounts to being solid evidence? Tappan (1947) and Sutherland (1945) already fiercely debated this topic decades ago, as Tappan claimed that only the courts could rule whether someone was guilty or not. Conversely, Sutherland argued that criminal activities should be investigated as close to the sources as possible; otherwise, some criminal activities, such as white-collar crime, would remain largely unexplored as a subject of criminological research.

Two aspects are relevant in this mature but still topical debate. First, the process of investigation and prosecution also involves a selection process which is influenced by police priorities, successes, and failures in criminal investigations, and all kinds of decisions and trade-offs that are made during investigation and prosecution. Second, the last part of the judicial process provides a high level of solidity (confirmed by the court, in appeal, or even by the Supreme Court) regarding an extremely small part of—very old—cases. In reality, a criminal investigation may take two to five years (or even longer), whereas waiting for a final judgment may take another five to ten years. Furthermore, judicial considerations do not always regard the solidity of evidence but may also observe formal procedures in investigation (e.g., international exchange of information) and prosecution. Consequently, exclusion of evidence on the basis of admissibility by the court does not always mean that this information is unsuitable for scientific research.

The Dutch Organized Crime Monitor opts for solid and "older" evidence and focuses on recently closed police investigations into criminal groups that provide enough evidence for the public prosecutor to take the case to court. In brief, these are "strong cases" (according to the public prosecutor) but the analysis should not wait until a final verdict has been reached. The evidence is analyzed at an earlier point in time, as soon as the first independent check (by the public prosecutor) is completed. An advantage of this timing is that the police team has just finished the largest part of the investigation and can answer a lot of the questions. In follow-up research, court cases and the procedures allowing confiscation of assets can be followed and case descriptions accordingly extended and updated.

Extensive Analysis of Rich Information

The focus on "older" cases and the extensive analysis of rich information of a large-scale police investigation, however, also have drawbacks. Case descriptions may be solid yet not very "fresh" at the time of publication. Furthermore, soft intelligence revealing new phenomena and trends might be disregarded. For this reason, during the first data sweep of the Dutch Organized Crime Monitor (1996–1998) a lot of time and effort was spent collecting all the available intelligence and crime analysis reports on organized crime in the Netherlands and many interviews were conducted with key informers in criminal intelligence units. With the benefit of hindsight, it was concluded that the cost–benefit-ratio of all these efforts was possibly too high for an empirical research project.

For cybercrime, one might argue that despite rapidly developing malware technology and criminals constantly looking for new weaknesses in the security of systems, the general business models for crimes (such as phishing, ransomware, and other cybercrimes) are quite stable and changes in crime scripts may not actually be substantial. On the other hand, one cannot know that in advance and other types of research, based on case debriefs or interviews with investigators, might also be a feasible option to include information of more recent cases. These methods might be less solid and less extensive but they may also be less labor-intensive and an appropriate alternative for more recent cybercrime cases.

Criminal Groups as Prime Target of Police Operations

The quest of the Dutch Organized Crime Monitor team to find "large-scale" cybercrime cases fitting the definition of organized crime also revealed three important insights for cybercrime research. First, many cybercrime cases do not qualify as large consolidated cases of organized crime but often concern small cases or clusters of small cases (including small cases with large impact value). Second, the criminal group is not always the prime target of police operations; instead, police operations may target markets (with neither capacity nor priority to investigate all buyers and all vendors, all over the world); seize and decrypt information on servers; or just focus on prevention by finding the source of an incident (a hack, a virus, a DDoS-attack) and taking preventive action (e.g., by warning responsible parties and suggesting changes in software, systems, or procedures). Third, much more data can be seized during police operations into cybercrime than can be investigated by the police, given their limited capacity. Therefore, the population of cybercrime cases and cybercrime operations is rather diverse and only specific police operations can focus on a larger group of collaborating offenders carrying out activities with significant harm to society. For the last category, the extensive analysis on the Dutch Organized Crime Monitor might be the best option. For other investigations and operations, however, other types of analysis might be more appropriate and the "big data" that are seized may offer other opportunities for researchers as well.

An Alternative for Police Data: Reconstructing Case Files Based on Interviews

Reconstructing case files based on structured interviews was used as a method by Leukfeldt and colleagues in countries other than the Netherlands, where direct access to the original police files was not possible (Leukfeldt, 2016; Leukfeldt et al., 2017b). There may be several reasons why reconstructing case files based on interviews might be a good alternative for analyzing the original police data.

First, interviews provide insight into more recent cases. Police are often more willing to be interviewed on a recent case than to share all original data and all details, as the investigation may still be evolving and/or other procedures may hinder sharing data at that point in time. The interconnectedness of cases also has to be taken into account: Prosecuted cases are sometimes linked to other cases still under investigation and/or potential cases for new investigations, which gives rise to different opinions about the sensitivity of sharing information with researchers.

Second, cybercrime cases often have an international component, which means that not all data can easily be shared with researchers. For example, national investigations have spin-offs abroad in investigations on offenders operating or residing in other countries, or data have been seized from servers abroad and have been shared with national authorities. Sharing "national" information is sometimes already difficult but the international component may add more complexity, sensitivity, and caution about sharing the original data. Sharing more abstract information about a case in a structured interview, however, may be far less sensitive and thus a viable alternative option.

Third, specific offender information is often very sensitive, particularly for offenders who are not already subjected to actual investigation and prosecution. By contrast, interviews can already shed light on phenomena and criminal activities, without sharing specific information on offenders.

Fourth, cybercrime cases sometimes result in information overflow, for instance, when communication data have been seized on servers and decrypted or when the police are able to infiltrate criminal marketplaces on the dark web. Police capacity is limited and the police simply cannot and do not want to investigate all offenders and all criminal activities, all over the world. A structured interview can be a viable alternative in such cases. Furthermore, such interviews can also be combined with a more focused analysis of specific parts of the underlying information, for instance, on interactions between the organizers of the Darknet markets (instead of all buyers, sellers, and transactions on these markets).

Proof of the Pudding: Examples of Added Value of Cybercrime Studies Based on Police Investigations

This section, based on recent publications, shows how analyzing criminal investigations can produce cybercrime knowledge other research methods simply cannot provide: by breaking the walls of silence to get a rich picture of the hidden world of cybercriminals.

One Case Can Change the Landscape

One of the first articles about cybercriminal networks based on police files was the study of Leukfeldt (2014) on phishing. The author provided an in-depth description of the modus operandi and organizational structure of one network active in phishing. The article demonstrated that the literature about these types of networks prior to 2014 provides an incomplete picture of the landscape of such networks. In contrast to prior research, the study showed a well-organized group of criminals whose relationships are long-lasting and based on real-world social ties rather than ad-hoc relationships formed on online meeting places, and who mainly use social engineering rather than malware as a tool to acquire information from their victims. This analysis not only had implications for the way we have to view cooperating cybercriminals, it also offered an entire set of new possibilities for situational crime prevention: The focus can be much more on real-world social ties, subcultures, and establishing trust, in addition to the technological measures which are usually aimed at disturbing online meeting places. In later studies, the importance of social ties within cybercriminal networks shown by this singular case described in Leukfeldt (2014) has been corroborated (e.g., Kruisbergen et al., 2019; Leukfeldt et al., 2017a; Lusthaus, 2018; Lusthaus & Varese, 2017).

Changing the Concept of "Organized" in Organized Crime

Bulanova-Hristova and colleagues (2016) studied police investigations in Sweden, Germany, and the Netherlands to examine the intertwinement of organized crime and cybercrime. The researchers focused on the modus operandi, the organizational structures of the criminal groups, and the profiles of the offenders involved in these groups. First, the authors show that the Internet enables new types of organizational structures that do not necessary fall within the traditional definitions of organized crime. As traditional crime and cybercrime become increasingly intertwined (Kruisbergen et al., 2018; Leukfeldt, Lavorgna et al., 2017; Leukfeldt et al. 2019; Leukfeldt & Roks, 2020), this could mean a shift in the way we view organized crime groups. Furthermore, a remarkable finding of the study by Bulanova-Hristova and colleagues (2016) is that a "new type" of offender became visible in these cases: very young offenders; offenders with an IT background; and ill or disabled offenders who barely came out of their homes. In a subreport, Odinot and colleagues (2016) concluded that characteristics of offenders which are important in the offline world, such as age, physical health, and social behavior, seem to be less important for organized cybercrime.

Mapping Hidden Social Processes

Police files can be used to gain insight into social processes within cyber-criminal networks. These processes have always been very important for the origin and growth of criminal networks (see, for instance, Ianni & Reuss-Ianni, 1972; Kleemans & De Poot, 2008; Bouchard & Morselli, 2014). However, increasingly, studies based on data scraped from online forums have suggested that the importance of social relations is diminishing (Décary-Hétu & Dupont, 2012; Décary-Hétu et al., 2012; Yip et al., 2012; Holt & Smirnova, 2014) as trust can be gained faster by using rating and review systems and geographical limitations of social networks no longer exist. However, an important limitation is that the studies based on scraped data provide an incomplete picture of criminals or networks of criminals who actually use such forums.

Using police data, Leukfeldt and colleagues (2017a) zoomed in on the importance of these online forums and markets for cybercriminal networks: Important questions were how cybercriminals meet, how cybercriminal networks develop, and what this means for the criminal capabilities of these networks. It turned out that—although online meeting places certainly did play an important role in a number of networks, for example, to find suitable co-offenders or to get into contact with enablers with highly specific knowledge or skills—traditional offline social ties still played an important role in the processes of origin and growth of the majority of networks. Leukfeldt and colleagues (2017c) demonstrated in another article that from a crime script perspective, these forums even have a very modest role. When looking at the hidden social processes behind cybercriminal networks, cybercriminals turned out to me much more traditional than expected.

In another study, Leukfeldt and Holt (2019) examined the organizational structure of cybercriminals involved in financially motivated attacks. Although the common view of hackers is that they work alone, criminological research has shown that in general, most criminals in fact need others—with specific knowledge, contacts, or cash—to carry out their crimes (such as Andresen & Felson, 2010; Reiss & Farrington, 1991; Shaw & McKay, 1931; Sutherland, 1937). Police files provide a wealth of data about ties between criminals. Leukfeldt and Holt (2019) demonstrated, using the Best and Luckenbill (1994) sociological framework, that the majority of the networks they studied showed organizational sophistication based on their division of labor and extended duration over time. Indeed, most networks could be classified as "teams" or "formal organizations." In contrast to prior studies—based on either interviews with individual offenders or analysis of scraped data from online meeting places—no loners were present and only a few networks could be classified as "colleagues" or "peers." Consequently, prior studies provided an incomplete picture of criminal collaboration.

Using Interrogations to Focus on Subcultures

Police investigations usually contain the results of the use of various (special) investigative powers. Leukfeldt and Kleemans (2019) demonstrated that it is possible to use the results of police interrogations to gain unique insight into the subculture of money mules. Leukfeldt and Kleemans used fourteen Dutch criminal investigations containing interrogations of 211 money mules. As 69 suspects did not cooperate during the interrogation ("no comment") and 30 claimed to be innocent, interrogations of 112 money mules were used in the analysis. The statements of the money mules clearly showed that they were part of a subculture where it is considered normal to be asked to cooperate in fraudulent transactions on a daily basis (see Box 1). The analysis of these 112 interrogations can also be used to draft various situational crime prevention measures (see Leukfeldt & Kleemans, 2019).

Box 1: Subculture (Quotes from: Leukfeldt & Kleemans, 2019)
During an interrogation Suspect 38 states: "I get text messages on a regular basis from several guys. These guys ask me if I know anyone who wants to make money. They simply ask you if you have cash cards". Suspect 38 shows a text message that she got that morning from F: "Don't you know a girl who wants booty?"

"Since about 2 years rumor has it that you can earn easy money by providing your bank account. Also through the Internet messages are sent that you can earn money by offering your bank account. I didn't want to cooperate, I am not a money mule or errand-boy. Some months ago I changed my mind. I really could use the money. I ran into a Surinamese boy and he introduced me to S1".

Suspect 9 states: "This is general knowledge in Amsterdam. It's a big hit. They do it with everything. They earn a lot of money with fraud". About the person to whom she would have offered her cash card, she states: "They call him Prince. It's from the streets. Really, everybody knows him. He's from Ghana. Together with his uncle he commits fraud [...], I said already that everybody in the Netherlands is involved. Many people do it. Especially youngsters. You can earn easy money and many want to do that. Many youngsters or junkies who have nothing to lose".

Conclusion

Cybercrime is on the rise, and with the ongoing digitization of our society, it will probably keep rising in the near future. Insight into cybercrime and offender behavior, therefore, is necessary to develop measures to prevent criminals from successfully carrying out attacks. In this chapter, we demonstrated the added value of analyzing police investigations—or alternatively case reconstructions based on interviews—to improve our understanding of cybercriminals. We do not claim that only police files should be used to study cybercriminals. Both traditional and innovative research methods should be used to collect as much information as possible, ideally within the same study (ensuring triangulation). However, we would like to emphasize that analyzing police files yields unique and rich information about important processes within criminal networks that often remain hidden when using other research methods. Without the studies based on police files, we would not have had so much detailed information about the processes of origin and growth of cybercriminals networks; the hidden subcultures; and the intertwinement of traditional crime and cybercrime.

We acknowledge that in some countries it is difficult or even impossible to get access to police files. However, the examples in this chapter of cybercrime studies based on police investigations clearly show that in many countries this is a feasible option: researchers in the Netherlands, Germany, and Sweden got access to police files and, in countries such as the UK and the USA, case reconstructions based on interviews with case officers were carried out. Indeed, it might be hard to get access but not impossible, and once researchers get such access, this is extremely useful in breaking down the walls of silence.

References

Andresen, M. A., & Felson, M. (2010). Situational crime prevention and co-offending. *Crime Patterns and Analysis, 3*(1), 3–13.

Best, J., & Luckenbill, D. F. (1994). *Organizing deviance* (2nd ed.). Prentice Hall.

Bouchard, M., & Morselli, C. (2014). Opportunistic structures of organized crime. In L. Paoli (Ed.), *The Oxford handbook of organized crime*. Oxford University Press.

Bulanova-Hristova, G., Kasper, K., Odinot, G., Verhoeven, M., Pool, R., de Poot, C., Werner, W., & Korsell, L. (Eds.). (2016). *Cyber-OC—Scope and manifestations in selected EU member states*. Bundeskriminalamt.

Décary-Hétu, D., & Dupont, B. (2012). The social network of hackers. *Global Crime, 13*(3), 160–175.

Décary-Hétu, D., Morselli, C., & Leman-Langlois, S. (2012). Welcome to the scene: A study of social organization and recognition among Warez hackers. *Journal of Research in Crime and Delinquency, 49*(3), 359–382.

Dupont, B., Côté, A. M., Boutin, J. I., & Fernandez, J. (2017). Darkode: Recruitment patterns and transactional features of "the most dangerous cybercrime forum in the world." *American Behavioral Scientist, 61*(11), 1219–1243.

Fijnaut, C., Bovenkerk, F., Bruinsma, G., & van de Bunt, H. (1996). Bijlage VII: Eindrapport Onderzoeksgroep Fijnaut. In Parlementaire Enquêtecommissie Opsporingsmethoden (PEO), *Inzake opsporing: Enquête opsporingsmethoden.* Sdu Uitgevers.

Fijnaut, C., Bovenkerk, F., Bruinsma, G., & van de Bunt, H. (1998). *Organized crime in the Netherlands.* Kluwer Law International.

Gadd, D., Karstedt, S., & Messner, S. F. (Eds.). (2012). *The SAGE handbook of criminological research methods.* https://doi.org/10.4135/9781446268285.

Holt, T. J. (2009). Lone hacks or group cracks: Examining the social organization of computer hackers. *Crimes of the Internet, 336*–355.

Holt, T. J., & Bossler, A. M. (2014). An assessment of the current state of cybercrime scholarship. *Deviant Behavior, 35*(1), 20–40.

Holt, T. J., & Smirnova, O. (2014). *Examining the structure, organization, and processes of the international market for stolen data.* U.S. Department of Justice.

Hutchings, A., & Holt, T. J. (2015). A crime script analysis of the online stolen data market. *British Journal of Criminology, 55*(3), 596–614.

Ianni, F. A. J., & Reuss-Ianni, E. (1972). *A family business: Kinship and social control in organized crime.* Routledge and Kegan Paul.

Kleemans, E. R. (2007). Organized crime, transit crime, and racketeering. In M. Tonry & C. J. Bijleveld (Eds.), *Crime and justice: A review of research 35.* The University of Chicago Press.

Kleemans, E. R. (2014). Organized crime research: Challenging assumptions and informing policy. In J. Knutsson & E. Cockbain (Eds.), *Applied police research: Challenges and opportunities.* Crime Science Series. Willan.

Kleemans, E. R., Brienen, M. E. I., & Van de Bunt, H. G. (2002). *Georganiseerde criminaliteit in Nederland: Tweede rapportage op basis van de WODC-monitor.* WODC.

Kleemans, E. R., & De Poot, C. J. (2008). Criminal careers in organized crime and social opportunity structure. *European Journal of Criminology, 5*(1), 69–98.

Kleemans, E. R., van den Berg, E. I. A. M., & Van de Bunt, H. G. (1998). *Georganiseerde criminaliteit in Nederland: Rapportage op basis van de WODC-monitor*. WODC.

Kruisbergen, E. W., Leukfeldt, E. R., Kleemans, E. R., & Roks, R. (2018). *Georganiseerde criminaliteit en ICT. Rapportage in het kader van de vijfde ronde van de Monitor Georganiseerde Criminaliteit*. WODC.

Kruisbergen, E. W., Leukfeldt, E. R., Kleemans, E. R., & Roks, R. (2019a). Money talks: Money laundering choices of organized crime offenders in a digital age. *Journal of Crime and Justice, 42*(5), 569–581.

Kruisbergen, E. W., Roks, R. A., & Kleemans, E. R. (2019b). *Georganiseerde criminaliteit in Nederland: daders, verwevenheid en opsporing. Rapportage in het kader van de vijfde ronde van de Monitor Georganiseerde Criminaliteit*. Boom.

Kruisbergen, E. W., van de Bunt, H. G., & Kleemans, E. R. (2012). *Georganiseerde criminaliteit in Nederland. Vierde rapportage op basis van de Monitor Georganiseerde Criminaliteit*. Boom.

Leukfeldt, E. R. (2014). Phishing for suitable targets in the Netherlands: Routine activity theory and phishing victimization. *Cyberpsychology Behavior and Social Networking, 17*(8), 551–555.

Leukfeldt, E. R. (2016). *Cybercriminal networks: Origin, growth and criminal capabilities*. Eleven International Publishing.

Leukfeldt, E. R. (Ed.). (2017). *Research agenda: The human factor in cybercrime and cybersecurity*. Eleven International Publishers.

Leukfeldt, E. R., & Holt, T. J. (2019). Examining the social organization practices of cybercriminals in the Netherlands online and offline. *International Journal of Offender Therapy and Comparative Criminology, 64*(5), 522–538.

Leukfeldt, E. R., & Kleemans, E. R. (2019). Cybercrime, money mules and situational crime prevention. In S. Hufnagel & A. Moiseienko (Eds.), *Criminal networks and law enforcement: Global perspectives on illicit enterprise*. Routledge.

Leukfeldt, E. R., Kleemans, E. R., & Stol, W. P. (2017a). Cybercriminal networks, social ties and online forums: Social ties versus digital ties within phishing and malware networks. *British Journal of Criminology, 57*(3), 704–722.

Leukfeldt, E. R., Kleemans, E. R., & Stol, W. P. (2017b). Origin, growth and criminal capabilities of cybercriminal networks: An international empirical analysis. *Crime, Law and Social Change, 67*, 39–53.

Leukfeldt, E. R., Kleemans, E. R., & Stol, W. P. (2017c). The use of online crime markets by cybercriminal networks: A view from within. *American Behavioral Scientist, 61*(11), 1387–1402.

Leukfeldt, E. R., Lavorgna, A., & Kleemans, E. R. (2017). Organised cybercrime or cybercrime that is organised? An assessment of the conceptualisation of financial cybercrime as organised crime. *European Journal on Criminal Policy and Research, 23*(3), 287–300.

Leukfeldt, E. R., Kleemans, E. R., Kruisbergen, E. W., & Roks, R. (2019). Criminal networks in a digitized world: On the nexus of borderless opportunities and local embeddedness. *Trends in Organized Crime.* https://doi.org/10.1007/s12117-019-09366-7.

Leukfeldt, E. R., & Roks, R. (2020). Cybercrimes on the streets of the Netherlands? An exploration of the intersection of cybercrimes and street crimes. *Deviant Behavior* (online first).

Lusthaus, J. (2018). *Industry of anonymity: Inside the business of cybercrime.* Harvard University Press.

Lusthaus, J., & Varese, F. (2017). Offline and local: The hidden face of cybercrime. *Policing: A Journal of Policy and Practice* (online first).

Maimon, D., & Louderback, E. (2019). Cyber-dependent crimes: An interdisciplinary review. *Annual Review of Criminology, 2,* 191–216.

Odinot, G., Verhoeven, M. A., Pool, R. L. D., & De Poot, C. J. (2016). *Cybercrime, organised crime and organised cybercrime in the Netherlands: Empirical findings and implications for law enforcement.* WODC.

PEO. (1996). Parlementaire Enquêtecommissie Opsporingsmethoden. In *Inzake opsporing: Enquête opsporingsmethoden.* Sdu Uitgevers.

Reiss, A. J., & Farrington, D. P. (1991). Advancing knowledge about co-offending: Results from a prospective longitudinal survey of London males. *Journal of Criminal Law and Criminology, 82*(2), 360–395.

Shaw, C. R., & McKay, H. D. (1931). *Report on the causes of crime: Volume II.* Government Printing Office.

Sutherland, E. H. (1937). *The professional thief.* The University of Chicago Press.

Sutherland, E. H. (1945). Is "white collar crime" crime? *American Sociological Review, 10,* 132–139.

Tappan, P. (1947). Who is the criminal? *American Sociological Review, 12,* 96–102.

Van de Bunt, H. G., & Kleemans, E. R. (2007). *Georganiseerde criminaliteit in Nederland. Derde rapportage op basis van de Monitor Georganiseerde*

Criminaliteit. Reeks Onderzoek en Beleid 252. WODC/Boom Juridische Uitgevers.

Weulen, M. (2018). *Cyber-offenders versus traditional offenders: An empirical comparison*. VU University.

Yip, M., Shadbolt, N., & Webber, C. (2012). Structural analysis of online criminal social networks. In *IEEE International Conference on Intelligence and Security Informatics (ISI)* (pp. 60–65).

8

Using Digital Open Source and Crowdsourced Data in Studies of Deviance and Crime

Rajeev V. Gundur, Mark Berry, and Dean Taodang

Introduction

In the twenty-first century, people around the world, even in developing economies and rural communities, have become increasingly connected to the internet (James, 2021). Most human–computer transactions generate data points. Data are generated whenever someone logs onto the internet, clicks on an ad, posts on social media, takes digital photos, calls using voice over IP (VOIP), uses digitally connected services, or engages with internet-of-things (IOT). Consequently, human beings generate petabytes of data on a daily basis, and this rate of data generation means that more data are created in any given year than any previous year, a trend that is likely to continue (DOMO, 2020). All of these data

R. V. Gundur (✉) · D. Taodang
Flinders University, Adelaide, Australia
e-mail: r.gundur@oxon.org

M. Berry
Bournemouth University, Bournemouth, England

© The Author(s), under exclusive license to Springer Nature
Switzerland AG 2021
A. Lavorgna and T. J. Holt (eds.), *Researching Cybercrimes*,
https://doi.org/10.1007/978-3-030-74837-1_8

145

provide opportunities not only for entrepreneurs, who use data analytics to understand their clients' behavior and preferences, but also for social scientists and practitioners, who study patterns of behavior of people who might be otherwise difficult to reach, including cybercriminals and their victims (An & Kim, 2018).

For the better part of the twenty-first century, social scientists such as criminologists and sociologists have been using digital resources and methodologies to make their research more efficient and to explore new facets of deviant behavior (Powell et al., 2018; Smith et al., 2017). Digital strategies have allowed criminologists to assess deviance and crime in online and offline environments in terms of recruitment (Gundur, 2019; Wood et al., 2019), communication (Cheng, 2017), data collection (Dragiewicz et al., 2018; Giommoni & Gundur, 2018; Lavorgna & Sugiura, 2020; Lawson & Nesbit, 2013; Lynch, 2018; Poletti & Gray, 2019; Potter, 2017; Ramo & Prochaska, 2012), and criminal innovation with technology (Berry, 2018; Cross & Gillett, 2020; Décary-Hétu & Bérubé, 2018; Gillett, 2018; Moule et al., 2013). Overwhelmingly, these methodologies focus on collecting and analyzing open source data, that is, "information derived from sources and by means openly available to and legally accessible and employable by the public" (Schauerer & Störger, 2013, p. 53). Some of these methodologies employ crowdsourcing to engage the public via the internet for the public's input for a defined problem. By aggregating the collective efforts of many, researchers can collect data and/or solve problems efficiently (Brabham, 2013; Solymosi et al., 2018).

Accordingly, this chapter discusses the collection and application of open source and crowdsourced data for criminological research and how researchers can collect and use these data to expand research capacity (see Chapter 9 for the process of using open sources to develop databases). This chapter proceeds as follows. First, it discusses the historic value of open source and crowdsourced data. Then, it describes common open source data collection tools, techniques, and technologies. Next, it discusses the analysis of open source and crowdsourced data. Finally, this chapter explores the potential to marry open source research with crowdsourcing as a means to further expand research capacity.

Why Are Crowdsourced and Open Source Data Valuable?

At their core, crowdsourced and open source data are readily available to and efficiently accessed by anyone. Although these terms were coined in the twentieth century, the concepts predate their coinage. In 1879, James A.H. Murray, the first editor of the *Oxford English Dictionary*, crowdsourced information in his global appeal for help in chasing definitions and etymologies of specific words (Winchester, 2018). An early notable example of open source intelligence (OSINT) is also British. In 1939, the British government realized that secret knowledge was useful knowledge and, accordingly, asked the BBC to monitor the public media communications of foes, which could provide insight, regarding key actors, events, and strategies, without having a human resource embedded on site (Schaurer & Störger, 2013). OSINT continues to be a staple of intelligence, military, and policing communities who value the richness of information that adversaries and targets put into the public domain (Akhgar et al., 2016; Trottier, 2015). Likewise, open source data have long been of value to the academic community (Schaurer & Störger, 2013). Social scientists routinely draw on information from public records and datasets to inform the basis of their knowledge.

For OSINT practitioners and academics, open source data collection techniques are inexpensive compared to fieldwork and can provide access to spaces that would be impractical or difficult to access personally. Accordingly, intelligence, policing, and academic applications will continue to use open source data indefinitely and will expand its use to reach under-researched communities as members of those communities become more internet connected. Nonetheless, the increasing volume of data means how data can be collected and analyzed at scale will evolve. The digitization of communication has increased the volume of information that is publicly available, thereby requiring, in some cases, automated or technically advanced techniques of data collection and analysis to engage in efficient OSINT (Hribar et al., 2014).

Besides OSINT applications, there are purposeful compilations of information presented for the public good without the expectation of direct monetary gain. Several examples exist which can aid cybercriminological and cybersecurity research, such as the cataloging of malware and ransomware (Roth, 2020), the documentation of scams in scamwatching forums (e.g., ScamWarners, 2021), and the sharing of public datasets such as those provided by the Cambridge Cybercrime Centre (2020) or the CARE lab at Temple University (2020).

Before proceeding, a quick aside on the ethics of open source data collection and analysis is necessary. The systematic collection and analysis of open source data are now easier than ever. This fact has raised some ethical concerns among institutional review boards (ethics committees), especially those that view the collection and analysis of open source information without the express consent of the posters to be ethically problematic (Gearon & Parsons, 2019; Hribar et al., 2014). However, the de-privatized nature of posting to public or ungated spaces on the internet assumes that posters should be, at a minimum, aware that whatever they post is public information and can be surveilled by state agents (Higgs, 2001; Reidenberg, 2014). The imposition of hurdles, which researchers must overcome to collect and use open source data, is antithetical to the production of knowledge.

Open source information is valuable to researchers because it is, by its very nature, not stolen, not classified at its origin, and not proprietary (except for copyright); it is information that is public and can be legally accessed freely without clandestine tactics. These characteristics are important especially as individuals who are currently underrepresented both in academic and practitioner circles—often as a result of resource limitations—make notable contributions to the understanding of crime and deviance within their communities (Carrington et al., 2018). At the same time, certain skills, techniques, and technologies keep this process possible as the booming volumes of digital data require more efficient and accurate assessments.

Skills, Techniques, and Tools for Open Source Data Collection in a Digital Age

The digitalization of the social world sometimes causes students, teachers, and researchers to forget that basic, less-technical strategies are often the most effective and that knowledgeable analysts are necessary to make sense of the vast amounts of information that OSINT can potentially collect (Hribar et al., 2014). OSINT predates internet communication technologies both in terms of existence and wide-spread usefulness. Certainly, the digitization of resources has made what used to be manual, labor-intensive processes easier and faster to execute. Thus, much information can be extracted from traditional media sources, such as media broadcasts and periodicals, and from administrative records, which include sentencing comments, and the National Registry of Exonerations, all of which are often cataloged in databases (Bright et al., 2012; Hassan, 2019; Lynch, 2018). The use of focused search terms on databases and search engines for text- and image-based information deployed using Boolean operators (e.g., AND, OR, NOT) allows for large-scale searching of pertinent information and continues to be a cornerstone of threat assessments, government reports, and academic research (Neri & Geraci, 2009; Williams & Blum, 2018).

Nonetheless, the contemporary digital world (and, for that matter, the digital world of the future) offers new data collection and analysis opportunities. Although textual information offered online across various services is often chaotic, unstructured, and vast, it is readily accessible. Non-text data, such as images, videos, geospatial data, and digital forensic data, given the advances in consumer electronics, can be readily collected, shared, and analyzed without special equipment or access. However, advances in technology and data generation will always pose new questions which will present their own, sometimes unforeseeable, difficulties in answering them. Accordingly, the fundamental research strategies that underwrite open source techniques to collect data must be adapted and expanded to investigate the vast volume and diverse types of open source and crowdsourced data. Two notable techniques that help in the collection of this vast data are data scraping and crowdsourcing, both of which have open source applications and are capable of collecting various types of data.

Data Scraping

Data scraping, which involves using an automated program to harvest data that others have collected or posted to form a dataset, is a technique commonly deployed to collect text-based data in digital spaces, such as clear and dark web websites, forums, and social media accounts (Lynch, 2018; Mitchell, 2018; Turk et al., 2020); additionally, it can be used to collect any machine-readable data, such as geospatial or technical data (Ensari & Kobaş, 2018)—see also Chapters 10 and 11. Data scraping may be achieved via automated scraping programs, many of which are open source or can be coded from open source materials (Lynch, 2018). Data can also be mined using shell scripts, a computer program designed to run in the command-line interpreter (Copeland et al., 2020). Scraping can provide a snapshot of a website at a given point in time, can be used to systematically document a website over time, or can monitor data leaks from a website (Ball et al., 2019; Décary-Hétu & Aldridge, 2015; Turk et al., 2020). While some companies, such as Twitter, provide tools to facilitate the collection of data within them, via their application programming interfaces (APIs), others expressly ban the scraping of their content (Burnap & Williams, 2015). Collection from sites that bar data scraping, by definition, would not result in open source data and may fall afoul of institutional review boards (Martin & Christin, 2016); those considerations, however, may not deter intelligence and law enforcement officials who may not face such constraints (Sampson, 2016).

Data scraping, nonetheless, has been used to collect significant amounts of open source data for academic studies. Its ability to collect large swathes of data, efficiently and quickly, has made it useful in examining several criminogenic problems. Moreover, data scraping has many applications and, when done well, results in the structured collection of data (Décary-Hétu & Aldridge, 2015). For instance, scraped data have provided several insights into illicit markets, which may be otherwise difficult, risky, or time-consuming to obtain via fieldwork (de Souza Santos, 2018; Wong, 2015). Studies of illicit markets have used scraped open source law enforcement data and press releases to explore relationships between drug trafficking and serious organized crime (Hughes et al., 2020); job advertisements targeting women in Romania to identify possible human trafficking recruitment (McAlister, 2015); advertisements and listings on Darknet marketplaces to illuminate drug pricing (Červený & van Ours, 2019; Frank & Mikhaylov, 2020); advertisements and images on the dark web to illuminate the dark web firearms trade (Copeland et al., 2020), and user posts and comments on carding forums to identify customer dynamics in those forums (Kigerl, 2018).

In addition, scraped data have been used to identify scam and fraud patterns, providing insights beyond victimization surveys or officially collected data, which result in time-delays in terms of reporting new problems and how known problems evolve (Schoepfer & Piquero, 2009). For instance, scraped data from Twitter and Instagram posts have been used to understand the sale of false COVID-19 products (Mackey et al., 2020). Scraped data from geotagged Tweets have identified location spoofing and spoofing strategies undertaken by possible trolls and bots (Zhao & Sui, 2017). And scraped data from forum posts have determined scam posts from advance fee scammers and illuminated the scams' mechanics (Mba et al., 2017).

Researchers have also used scraped social media data to evaluate communication trends and to identify the existence of poorly reported events or phenomena, thereby allowing researchers to engage with settings to which they may not have physical access. Scraped blog data have identified hate groups and their members (Chau & Xu, 2007). Scraped data from Google Trends and Twitter have allowed researchers to explore how the public perceives serious crime (Kostakos, 2018). Scraped Tweets have shown how hate speech spreads and influences audiences on Twitter (Ball et al., 2019; Burnap & Williams, 2015; Ozalp et al., 2020). Scraped data from Twitter and Facebook reports have been used to detect terrorist events in the developing world where there may be less reliable journalistic reporting (Kolajo & Daramola, 2017; Oleji et al., 2008).

Moreover, there are numerous tools that facilitate the bulk collection of various types of machine-readable data. Some of these tools are open source while others are paid or government proprietary solutions that use open source data. Among these tools are Foca, which finds metadata and hidden information in documents; Spiderfoot, which amalgamates information relevant for cyberthreat intelligence assessments, such as suspicious IP and e-mail addresses and links to phishing campaigns; and

4NSEEK, an EU-funded tool, used by law enforcement practitioners, that scrapes and compares images of child sexual abuse to identify victims of child sexual exploitation (Al-Nabki et al., 2020; Pastor-Galindo et al., 2020). (Please note: Data, such as images, behind paywalls in illicit marketplaces do not constitute open source data. However, this application is useful for law enforcement, who will develop digital assets in order to get behind paywalls of such businesses.) Common scraping strategies have also yielded results. These strategies include the scraping of geospatial data, such as location reports of neighborhood disorder, to create maps of crime hotspots or to document the geography of a problem (Solymosi & Bowers, 2018), and the scraping of technical data from the clearweb (Cascavilla et al., 2018) and the dark web (see, e.g., Lewis, n.d.) to reveal flaws in operational security by identifying information leaks despite attempts to keep that information private and secure.

Evidently, data scraping is a versatile and powerful strategy that can be used to collect large quantities of data systematically. It has clear advantages: It offers free or inexpensive research resources to the research community; it shortens the time arcs required to collect and process data, and it provides insights into communities that might be time-consuming or difficult to access. Nonetheless, it has limitations, especially in academic contexts: researchers cannot ethically scrape online properties that explicitly bar the practice in their terms and conditions, and scraping cannot be used with data not freely offered online nor with proprietary datasets to which researchers lack access. Researchers have sometimes overcome these limitations with crowdsourcing strategies.

Crowdsourcing Data and Solutions

Not all information of criminological interest is accessible via publicly available data. Consequently, some researchers have used crowdsourcing to solicit private data or to solicit help in conducting analysis or solving problems from the public (Estellés-Arolas, 2020). Crowdsourcing data or solutions allow researchers and practitioners to have participants opt into contributing data or participating in solving a problem or investigation (Powell et al., 2018). Crowdsourcing initiatives typically have a clear crowdsourcer who initiates the project, which has a clear goal, with an open call to a crowd who must carry out the task (Estellés-Arolas, 2020; Estellés-Arolas & González-Ladrón-de-Guevara, 2012). While crowdsourcing can be open to whomever wants to participate, some crowdsourcing efforts, such as those conducted via online contract labor portals, resemble surveys as they are geared toward specific populations (Behrend et al., 2011; Litman et al., 2017).

Within a criminal justice context, there are crowdsourcing platforms deployed by researchers and practitioners designed to respond to specific initiatives, namely collecting data, analyzing data, or solving problems (Estellés-Arolas, 2020). Data collection applications include crime reporting mechanisms, like the Australian Competition & Consumer Commission's (n.d.) Scamwatch and the UK's ActionFraud's (n.d.) online scam reporting tool. These mechanisms seek to collect reports of scams in the immediate aftermath of victimization, rather than relying on recollection as traditional victimization surveys do.

In addition, there are platforms that allow users to submit data. For example, *FixMyStreet* (Society Works, n.d.) allows UK-based users to report the geospatial data of potholes, broken streetlights, and other blights in their area. Price of Weed (2019), a website not affiliated with researchers or government agencies, allows cannabis users in the USA, Canada, Europe, and Australia to submit the price of cannabis, in an effort to create a semi-global index of the street value of cannabis prices (Wang, 2016). Both *FixMyStreet* and *Price of Weed* register submissions on a regular basis, thereby providing data, apart from official estimates on these issues (local disorder and retail drug pricing), which are not always publicly available. The data collected by *FixMyStreet* have been used to assess locals' perceptions of disorder (Solymosi et al., 2018) and fear of crime (Solymosi et al., 2020). Likewise, researchers have used the data collected by the *Price of Weed* (often through scraping the website) to determine price responses to law enforcement and decriminalization (Larson et al., 2015; Lawson & Nesbit, 2013; Malivert & Hall, 2013), price shifts across a geographic market (Giommoni & Gundur, 2018), and demand and price elasticity (Halcoussis et al., 2017).

In addition to these open data collection mechanisms, there are online contract labor portals, such as Mechanical Turk, TurkPrime, or

Qualtrics, which have become commonly used participant pools for behavioral science researchers (Litman et al., 2017), including criminologists (Ozkan, 2019). These mechanisms have established pools of participants; through these pools, researchers can identify the participant attributes appropriate for completing the assigned task. Moreover, links to the collection tool can be independently distributed (Graham et al., 2020). These tools, however, are not necessarily accessed by relevant populations, particularly in underserved or underconnected communities. Thus, crowdsourced data may show only the direction of variables rather than their magnitude, thereby limiting the ability to generalize from the results (Thompson & Pickett, 2019).

Sometimes, researchers have established their own data collection tools, with variable success. To be successful, tools need to be known to a large crowd of willing participants. Connecting to that crowd, particularly in criminogenic settings, may be difficult, particularly if there is no immediate benefit for the participants. For instance, the now defunct drugsource.io was a platform set up in Europe to emulate the *Price of Weed*; in addition to cannabis, drugsource.io included several other controlled substances to report. The tool did not gain traction with potential contributors and failed to receive enough submissions to undertake any meaningful analysis. Likewise, one of the authors of this chapter set up an e-mail address to have victims of scams forward their scams. That effort was only moderately successful due to a lack of visibility and temporal duration. Accordingly, it must be noted that new crowdsourcing efforts likely need resources, such as advertisements, to target a potential crowd, and those resources need to be commensurate to the geographic scope of the project (Estellés-Arolas, 2020). In cases where the generation of information through collective reporting is the primary benefit, compensation of early contributors likely needs to occur until a critical mass is achieved. Nonetheless, crowdsourcing platforms show that systems can be built to collect nearly any kind of data.

Crowdsourcing can be used to analyze data and solve problems (Estellés-Arolas, 2020). Analysis includes identifying people, objects, or patterns in images. Social media has been used to identify specific people responsible for crimes whose likenesses were captured by CCTV. Social media allows potentially millions of users to view these images and then identify the subjects in them. In the case of searching for perpetrators of crimes, these efforts often identify assailants, such as the Boston Marathon bomber or members of hate groups (Douglas, 2020; Gray & Benning, 2019; Nhan et al., 2017). However, these efforts sometimes become an exercise in vigilantism and deviate from true crowdsourced efforts as they lack a clear crowdsourcer or a clear criminal justice purpose; moreover, if the target is misidentified, there is no clear response to remedy the error (Chang & Poon, 2017; Douglas, 2020; Loveluck, 2020).

There are, however, dedicated operational platforms set up to solicit crowdsourced analysis. For instance, the UK's *Crimestoppers* platform seeks crowdsourced help to identify suspects or missing people (Estellés-Arolas, 2020). Another example of an operational crowdsourced analysis platform is GlobalXplorer°, a platform that invites the public to search through satellite imagery to identify images with evidence of looting of cultural property. The platform trains volunteers by establishing the task as a game and then provides the over 66,000 volunteers with snippets from areas at risk of looting (Yates, 2018). These platforms show that large analytical jobs to answer unknown questions (e.g., to solve problems) can be crowdsourced in various digital and digitized criminological contexts.

Beyond the platforms in use, there are several platforms that have been conceptualized, particularly for security and safety applications, to make use of crowdsourced data. These platforms reflect the potential crowdsourcing offers to problem-solving. For instance, there is *Missing-Found*, a platform that would use various open source data points to track missing people (Liu et al., 2016). There are also conceptualized platforms to crowdsource surveillance, by making certain CCTV footage public to allow for the real-time monitoring of spaces (Trottier, 2014); to crowdsource investigation, by providing collected evidence related to child abuse available to the public to help with its examination (Açar, 2018), and to crowdsource digital vulnerability identification, by having kernel reports served to analysts who can determine malware execution patterns to better identify threat vectors (Burguera et al., 2011).

Analysis of Open Source and Crowdsourced Data

A lot of analysis, however, requires professional knowledge. Subject expertise and methodological training are critical to making sense of data collected from public sources. Subject expertise helps researchers to identify points of interest, anomalies, and misdirection within the data; to make informed assumptions when the data is incomplete; and to interpret the data vis-à-vis its context (Nichols, 2017). No tool or technology can completely replace a researcher's ability to understand the implications of settings and context. Likewise, methodological training, which teaches the fundamentals of research design and analysis, allows researchers to ensure that the established questions are worth answering and to confirm that the answers offered correspond with the questions posed.

To make sense of the data collected, various approaches have been used, depending on the type and the quality of the data. Qualitative methods have been used to analyze open source and crowdsourced data much in the same way that qualitative methods are used to analyze qualitative data collected via fieldwork. Qualitative methods have been used to conduct content analysis on text-based data to analyze posters' perceptions and behaviors (Holt, 2010; Lynch, 2018; Williams et al., 2017).

Additionally, quantitative methodologies have been employed to analyze open source and crowdsourced datasets (Tompson et al., 2015). One notable analytical technique is Social Network Analysis (SNA) (see also Chapter 13). Pioneered in criminology by the late Carlo Morselli (2009), SNA has been used to show how criminal actors are connected in a network using publicly available data such as sentencing comments (Bright et al., 2012, 2018) and archival material (Smith, 2019). SNA has also been used to show how drugs flow across and within borders (Berlusconi et al., 2017; Giommoni & Gundur, 2018). Another technique involves the mapping of geospatial data to predict accident and disorder hotspots (dos Santos et al., 2017; Solymosi et al., 2020). Geospatial data are used extensively in crime mapping software and military geographical intelligence (GEOINT) to provide "actionable knowledge" on specific events (US Geospatial Intelligence Foundation, 2015, p. 11). The data can be used to identify crime hotspots, understand crime distribution, assess the impact of crime reduction programs, and communicate crime statistics to a wide audience (Chainey & Ratcliffe, 2013).

Researchers have also recognized that big data sets, with sometimes millions of entries, and non-text-based data present their own challenges (Solymosi & Bowers, 2018; Williams et al., 2017). Accordingly, researchers have developed tools and methodologies to go beyond what traditional analytical processes have been able to illuminate using modest datasets, particularly when evaluating big data sets and non-text-based open source data. One notable example is with the analysis of malware or ransomware. Once malware is "released" to infect members of the public, its code becomes a piece of open source data which then can be subjected to digital forensics. Digital forensics involves the examination of digital devices and systems to assess the cause of a particular event, which may be criminal in nature. It uses a variety of scientific techniques on the "validation, identification, analysis, interpretation, documentation, and presentation of digital evidence" (Delp et al., 2009, p. 14). Various tools are available to help researchers collect data and conduct analysis of that data. Autopsy, for example, is a tool used to perform data analysis on imaged and live systems and to recover deleted data (Kävrestad, 2018). Other tools facilitate open source investigations into the actors behind cyberattacks. For instance, Maltego facilitates data mining and link analysis, using open source records, such as WhoIs, domain name system (DNS), and other digital records.

Open source data analysis—particularly when considering digital forensic data—often may be too complex for the computing power of one machine alone. As a result, data collection may require a networked computing system, like the Hadoop ecosystem, to aggregate computing power, and a distributed, networked approach, including machine learning, to aid in the analysis (Landset et al., 2015). Machine learning, which is a subset of artificial intelligence, enables computers to improve automatically through experience. Computers can detect complex patterns that are often unpredictable to humans (Chhabra et al., 2020; Pastor-Galindo et al., 2020). Machine learning has been used in the field of cybersecurity to resolve vulnerabilities from hacking and malware. From a technical viewpoint, machine learning has been also used to detect vulnerabilities in systems by analyzing code mined from open source projects (Bilgin et al., 2020). Moreover, machine learning algorithms can facilitate various types of cybercrime detection and prevention efforts, such as identifying hate speech (Burnap & Williams, 2015; Ozalp et al., 2020) and responding to cyberbullying and cyberstalking (Ghasem et al., 2015). The potential for machine learning to speed up analysis and trigger real-time responses makes it an important analytical strategy for big data.

Collaboration: The Future Direction in Digital Data Collection and Analysis

The collection and analysis of open source data will continue, and the production of available digital data will increase. This is also true in criminogenic settings as deviant behavior will increasingly leverage technology (Berry, 2018). This rich and diverse digital data will provide researchers, studying deviant and other social behaviors, with opportunities to ask questions that have been previously difficult or impossible to answer. Human–computer interactions will create an increasingly large part of the data generated. Accordingly, social and technical research questions must be combined, and, to answer these questions, academics of different disciplines, researchers, practitioners, and the public must work together to find agile, collaborative solutions to data collection and analysis.

Collaboration will allow researchers with distinct strengths to develop research programs with the potential to better pose questions in the social world and to examine them. The increase in digital data, and digital connectivity, means that researchers will need to continue to innovate in their data collection techniques, particularly if various terms and conditions of content providers bar them from using presently successful strategies. The increased penetration of internet-connected devices provides an increasing opportunity to ask members of the public to collect and contribute to crowdsourced efforts. Relevant efforts are already underway with the collection of geospatial data via smartphone apps (Moore et al., 2017).

Finally, researchers may find marrying various types of data helpful in painting nuanced and accurate pictures of social phenomena. By pushing past the limitations of using only one or two data types, which, when used singularly, can produce abstract, static, and simplified pictures of criminal activity, researchers will be able to present a more complex analysis which portrays the often chaotic nature of criminal activity (Hobbs, 2014). The evolution of data collection, however, will necessitate careful consideration of the ethical implications of data collection and use, particularly when the data collected are identifiable.

References

Açar, K. V. (2018). OSINT by crowdsourcing: A theoretical model for online child abuse investigations. *International Journal of Cyber Criminology, 12*(1), 206–229.

Action Fraud. (n.d.). *Reporting Fraud*. Action Fraud. Available at https://web. archive.org/web/20210104015305/https://reporting.actionfraud.police.uk/ login.

Akhgar, B., Bayerl, P. S., & Sampson, F. (2016). *Open source intelligence investigation: From strategy to implementation*. Springer.

Al-Nabki, M. W., Fidalgo, E., Vasco-Carofilis, R. A., Jañez-Martino, F., & Velasco-Mata, J. (2020). Evaluating performance of an adult pornography classifier for child sexual abuse detection. *arXiv preprint*. arXiv:2005.08766.

An, J., & Kim, H. W. (2018). A data analytics approach to the cybercrime underground economy. *IEEE Access, 6,* 26636–26652.

Australian Competition & Consumer Commission. (n.d.). *ScamWatch*. ACCC. Available at https://www.scamwatch.gov.au/report-a-scam.

Ball, M., Broadhurst, R., Niven, A., & Trivedi, H. (2019). Data capture and analysis of darknet markets. *SSRN 3344936*.

Behrend, T. S., Sharek, D. J., Meade, A. W., & Wiebe, E. N. (2011). The viability of crowdsourcing for survey research. *Behavior Research Methods, 43*(3), 800.

Berlusconi, G., Aziani, A., & Giommoni, L. (2017). The determinants of heroin flows in Europe: A latent space approach. *Social Networks, 51,* 104–117.

Berry, M. (2018). Technology and organised crime in the smart city: An ethnographic study of the illicit drug trade. *City, Territory and Architecture, 5*(1), 16.

Bilgin, Z., Ersoy, M. A., Soykan, E. U., Tomur, E., Çomak, P., & Karaçay, L. (2020). Vulnerability prediction from source code using machine learning. *IEEE Access, 8,* 150672–150684.

Brabham, D. C. (2013). *Crowdsourcing.* MIT Press.

Bright, D., Koskinen, J., & Malm, A. (2018). Illicit network dynamics: The formation and evolution of a drug trafficking network. *Journal of Quantitative Criminology,* 1–22.

Bright, D. A., Hughes, C. E., & Chalmers, J. (2012). Illuminating dark networks: A social network analysis of an Australian drug trafficking syndicate. *Crime, Law and Social Change, 57*(2), 151–176.

Burguera, I., Zurutuza, U., & Nadjm-Tehrani, S. (2011). Crowdroid: behavior-based malware detection system for android. In *Proceedings of the 1st ACM workshop on security and privacy in smartphones and mobile devices.*

Burnap, P., & Williams, M. L. (2015). Cyber hate speech on twitter: An application of machine classification and statistical modeling for policy and decision making. *Policy & Internet, 7*(2), 223–242.

Cambridge Cybercrime Centre. (2020). *Cambridge Cybercrime Centre: Description of available datasets.* Computer Laboratory, University of Cambridge. Available at https://www.cambridgecybercrime.uk/datasets.html.

Carrington, K., Hogg, R., Scott, J., & Sozzo, M. (2018). *The Palgrave handbook of criminology and the global south.* Springer.

Cascavilla, G., Beato, F., Burattin, A., Conti, M., & Mancini, L. V. (2018). OSSINT-open source social network intelligence: An efficient and effective way to uncover "private" information in OSN profiles. *Online Social Networks and Media, 6,* 58–68.

Červený, J., & van Ours, J. C. (2019). Cannabis prices on the dark web. *European Economic Review, 120,* 103306.

Chainey, S., & Ratcliffe, J. (2013). *GIS and crime mapping.* Wiley.

Chang, L. Y., & Poon, R. (2017). Internet vigilantism: Attitudes and experiences of university students toward cyber crowdsourcing in Hong Kong. *International Journal of Offender Therapy and Comparative Criminology, 61*(16), 1912–1932.

Chau, M., & Xu, J. (2007). Mining communities and their relationships in blogs: A study of online hate groups. *International Journal of Human-Computer Studies, 65*(1), 57–70.

Cheng, F. K. (2017). *Using email and Skype interviews with marginalized participants.* Sage.

Chhabra, G. S., Singh, V. P., & Singh, M. (2020). Cyber forensics framework for big data analytics in IoT environment using machine learning. *Multimedia Tools and Applications, 79*(23), 15881–15900.

Copeland, C., Wallin, M., & Holt, T. J. (2020). Assessing the practices and products of darkweb firearm vendors. *Deviant Behavior, 41*(8), 949–968.

Cross, C., & Gillett, R. (2020). Exploiting trust for financial gain: An overview of business email compromise (BEC) fraud. *Journal of Financial Crime* (online first).

Cybersecurity in Application Research and Education Lab. (2020). *Downloads.* CARE Lab. Available at https://web.archive.org/web/20210104012919/https://sites.temple.edu/care/downloads/.

de Souza Santos, A. A. (2018). Risky closeness and distance in two fieldwork sites in Brazil. *Contemporary Social Science, 13*(3–4), 429–443.

Décary-Hétu, D., & Aldridge, J. (2015). Sifting through the net: Monitoring of online offenders by researchers. *European Review of Organised Crime, 2*(2), 122–141.

Décary-Hétu, D., & Bérubé, M. (2018). *Délinquance et innovation.* Les Presses de l'Université de Montréal.

Delp, E., Memon, N., & Wu, M. (2009). Digital forensics. *IEEE Signal Processing Magazine, 26*(2), 14–15.

DOMO. (2020). *Data never sleeps 8.0.* DOMO, Inc.

dos Santos, S. R., Davis, C. A., Jr., & Smarzaro, R. (2017). Analyzing traffic accidents based on the integration of official and crowdsourced data. *Journal of Information and Data Management, 8*(1), 67.

Douglas, D. M. (2020). Doxing as audience vigilantism against hate speech. *Introducing Vigilant Audiences, 259.*

Dragicwicz, M., Burgess, J., Matamoros-Fernández, A., Salter, M., Suzor, N. P., Woodlock, D., & Harris, B. (2018). Technology facilitated coercive control: Domestic violence and the competing roles of digital media platforms. *Feminist Media Studies, 18*(4), 609–625.

Ensari, E., & Kobaş, B. (2018). Web scraping and mapping urban data to support urban design decisions. *A\Z ITU Journal of the Faculty of Architecture, 15*(1), 5–21.

Estellés-Arolas, E. (2020). Using crowdsourcing for a safer society: When the crowd rules. *European Journal of Criminology.* https://doi.org/10.1177/147 7370820916439.

Estellés-Arolas, E., & González-Ladrón-de-Guevara, F. (2012). Towards an integrated crowdsourcing definition. *Journal of Information Science, 38*(2), 189–200.

Frank, R., & Mikhaylov, A. (2020). Beyond the 'Silk Road': Assessing illicit drug marketplaces on the public web. In *Open source intelligence and cyber crime* (pp. 89–111). Springer.

Gearon, L. F., & Parsons, S. (2019). Research ethics in the securitised university. *Journal of Academic Ethics, 17*(1), 73–93.

Ghasem, Z., Frommholz, I., & Maple, C. (2015). Machine learning solutions for controlling cyberbullying and cyberstalking. *Journal of Information Security Research, 6*(2), 55–64.

Gillett, R. (2018). Intimate intrusions online: Studying the normalisation of abuse in dating apps. *Women's Studies International Forum.*

Giommoni, L., & Gundur, R. V. (2018). An analysis of the United Kingdom's cannabis market using crowdsourced data. *Global Crime, 19*(2).

Graham, A., Pickett, J. T., & Cullen, F. T. (2020). Advantages of matched over unmatched opt-in samples for studying criminal justice attitudes: A research note. *Crime & Delinquency.* https://doi.org/10.1177/0011128720977439.

Gray, G., & Benning, B. (2019). Crowdsourcing criminology: Social media and citizen policing in missing person cases. *SAGE Open, 9*(4), https://doi.org/10.1177/2158244019893700.

Gundur, R. V. (2019). Using the Internet to recruit respondents for offline interviews in criminological studies. *Urban Affairs Review, 55*(6), 1731–1756.

Halcoussis, D., Lowenberg, A. D., & Roof, Z. (2017). Estimating the Price elasticity of demand for Cannabis: A geographical and crowdsourced approach. *Revista De Métodos Cuantitativos Para La Economía y La Empresa, 23,* 119–136.

Hassan, N. A. (2019). Gathering evidence from OSINT sources. *Digital forensics basics* (pp. 311–322). Springer.

Higgs, E. (2001). The rise of the information state: The development of central state surveillance of the citizen in England, 1500–2000. *Journal of Historical Sociology, 14*(2), 175–197.

Hobbs, D. (2014). Organised crime as a community of practice. In C. Ellis (Ed.), *Disrupting organised crime: Developing the evidence base to understand effective action*. RUSI. Available at https://rusi.org/sites/default/files/201411_stfc_disrupting_organised_crime.pdf.

Holt, T. J. (2010). Exploring strategies for qualitative criminological and criminal justice inquiry using on-line data. *Journal of Criminal Justice Education, 21*(4), 466–487.

Hribar, G., Podbregar, I., & Ivanuša, T. (2014). OSINT: A "grey zone"? *International Journal of Intelligence and CounterIntelligence, 27*(3), 529–549.

Hughes, C. E., Chalmers, J., & Bright, D. A. (2020). Exploring interrelationships between high-level drug trafficking and other serious and organised crime: An Australian study. *Global Crime, 21*(1), 28–50.

James, J. (2021). Geographies of the Internet in rural areas in developing countries. In B. Warf (Ed.), *Geographies of the Internet* (pp. 93–114). Routledge.

Kävrestad, J. (2018). Open-source or freeware tools. In J. Kävrestad (Ed.), *Fundamentals of digital forensics: Theory, methods, and real-life applications*. Springer.

Kigerl, A. (2018). Profiling cybercriminals: Topic model clustering of carding forum member comment histories. *Social Science Computer Review, 36*(5), 591–609.

Kolajo, T., & Daramola, O. (2017, March 8–10). Leveraging big data to combat terrorism in developing countries. In *2017 Conference on Information Communication Technology and Society (ICTAS)*.

Kostakos, P. (2018). Public perceptions on organised crime, mafia, and terrorism: A big data analysis based on Twitter and Google Trends. *International Journal of Cyber Criminology, 12*(1), 282–299.

Landset, S., Khoshgoftaar, T. M., Richter, A. N., & Hasanin, T. (2015). A survey of open source tools for machine learning with big data in the Hadoop ecosystem. *Journal of Big Data, 2*(1), 24.

Larson, R. A., Rusko, C. J., & Secor, A. E. (2015). *A blunt analysis: Marijuana policy liberalization and market prices in Colorado and Washington* (Centre College Empirical Analysis Paper).

Lavorgna, A., & Sugiura, L. (2020). Direct contacts with potential interviewees when carrying out online ethnography on controversial and polarized topics: A loophole in ethics guidelines. *International Journal of Social Research Methodology*, 1–7.

Lawson, R. A., & Nesbit, T. M. (2013). Alchian and Allen revisited: Law enforcement and the price of weed. *Atlantic Economic Journal, 41*(4), 363–370.

Lewis, S. J. (n.d.). *Onion scan.* Available at https://web.archive.org/web/202012 22060839/https://onionscan.org/.

Litman, L., Robinson, J., & Abberbock, T. (2017). TurkPrime. com: A versatile crowdsourcing data acquisition platform for the behavioral sciences. *Behavior Research Methods, 49*(2), 433–442.

Liu, W., Li, J., Zhou, Z., & He, J. (2016). MissingFound: An assistant system for finding missing companions via mobile crowdsourcing. *KSII Transactions on Internet & Information Systems, 10*(10), 4766–4786.

Loveluck, B. (2020) The many shades of digital vigilantism. A typology of online self-justice. *Global Crime, 21,* 3–4, 213–241. https://doi.org/10. 1080/17440572.2019.1614444.

Lynch, J. (2018). Not even our own facts: Criminology in the era of big data. *Criminology, 56*(3), 437–454.

Mackey, T. K., Li, J., Purushothaman, V., Nali, M., Shah, N., Bardier, C., Cai, M., & Liang, B. (2020). Big data, natural language processing, and deep learning to detect and characterize illicit COVID-19 product sales: Infoveillance study on Twitter and Instagram. *JMIR Public Health and Surveillance, 6*(3), e20794–e20794.

Malivert, R., & Hall, J. C. (2013). The effect of medical marijuana laws on extralegal marijuana prices. *Atlantic Economic Journal, 41*(4), 455–456.

Martin, J., & Christin, N. (2016). Ethics in cryptomarket research. *International Journal of Drug Policy, 35,* 84–91.

Mba, G., Onaolapo, J., Stringhini, G., & Cavallaro, L. (2017). Flipping 419 cybercrime scams: Targeting the weak and the vulnerable. In *Proceedings of the 26th International Conference on World Wide Web Companion.*

McAlister, R. (2015). Webscraping as an investigation tool to identify potential human trafficking operations in Romania. In *Proceedings of the ACM Web Science Conference.*

Mitchell, R. (2018). *Web scraping with Python: Collecting more data from the modern web.* O'Reilly Media, Inc.

Moore, J., Baggili, I., & Breitinger, F. (2017). Find me if you can: Mobile GPS mapping applications forensic analysis & SNAVP the open source, modular, extensible parser. *The Journal of Digital Forensics, Security and Law, 12*(1), 15–29.

Morselli, C. (2009). *Inside criminal networks.* Springer.

Moule, R. K., Jr., Pyrooz, D. C., & Decker, S. H. (2013). From "what the F#@% is a Facebook?" to "who doesn't use Facebook?": The role of criminal lifestyles in the adoption and use of the Internet. *Social Science Research, 42*(6), 1411–1421.

Neri, F., & Geraci, P. (2009). Mining textual data to boost information access in OSINT. In *2009 13th International Conference Information Visualisation.*

Nhan, J., Huey, L., & Broll, R. (2017). Digilantism: An analysis of crowd-sourcing and the Boston marathon bombings. *The British Journal of Criminology, 57*(2), 341–361.

Nichols, T. (2017). *The death of expertise: The campaign against established knowledge and why it matters.* Oxford University Press.

Oleji, C., Nwokorie, E., & Chukwudebe, G. (2008). Big data analytics of Boko haram insurgency attacks menace in Nigeria using DynamicK-reference clustering algorithm. *International Research Journal of Engineering and Technology, 7*(1).

Ozalp, S., Williams, M. L., Burnap, P., Liu, H., & Mostafa, M. (2020). Antisemitism on Twitter: Collective efficacy and the role of community organisations in challenging online hate speech. *Social Media + Society, 6*(2), https://doi.org/10.1177/2056305120916850.

Ozkan, T. (2019). Criminology in the age of data explosion: New directions. *The Social Science Journal, 56*(2), 208–219.

Pastor-Galindo, J., Nespoli, P., Mármol, F. G., & Pérez, G. M. (2020). The not yet exploited goldmine of OSINT: Opportunities, open challenges and future trends. *IEEE Access, 8,* 10282–10304.

Poletti, C., & Gray, D. (2019). Good data is critical data: An appeal for critical digital studies. In A. Daly, S. K. Devitt, & M. Mann (Eds.), *Good data.* Institute of Network Cultures.

Potter, G. R. (2017). Real gates to virtual fields: Integrating online and offline ethnography in studying cannabis cultivation and reflections on the applicability of this approach in criminological ethnography more generally. *Methodological Innovations, 10*(1), 2059799117720609.

Powell, A., Stratton, G., & Cameron, R. (2018). *Digital criminology: Crime and justice in digital society.* Routledge.

Price of Weed. (2019). *Price of weed.* Available at https://web.archive.org/web/20201223133241/http://www.priceofweed.com/.

Ramo, D. E., & Prochaska, J. J. (2012). Broad reach and targeted recruitment using Facebook for an online survey of young adult substance use. *Journal of Medical Internet Research, 14*(1), e28.

Reidenberg, J. R. (2014). The data surveillance state in the United States and Europe. *Wake Forest Law Review, 49,* 583.

Roth, F. (2020). *Ransomware overview.* https://docs.google.com/spreadsheets/d/1TWS238xacAto-fLKh1n5uTsdijWdCEsGIM0Y0Hvmc5g/pubhtml.

Sampson, F. (2016). Intelligent evidence: Using open source intelligence (OSINT) in criminal proceedings. *The Police Journal, 90*(1), 55–69.

ScamWarners. (2021). Available at https://web.archive.org/web/2021010401145 5/https://www.scamwarners.com/forum/.

Schaurer, F., & Störger, J. (2013). The evolution of open source intelligence (OSINT). *Computers in Human Behavior, 19,* 53–56.

Schoepfer, A., & Piquero, N. L. (2009). Studying the correlates of fraud victimization and reporting. *Journal of Criminal Justice, 37*(2), 209–215.

Smith, C. M. (2019). *Syndicate women: Gender and networks in Chicago organized crime.* University of California Press.

Smith, G. J., Bennett Moses, L., & Chan, J. (2017). The challenges of doing criminology in the big data era: Towards a digital and data-driven approach. *British Journal of Criminology, 57*(2), 259–274.

Society Works. (n.d.). *Fix my street.* MySociety. Available at https://web.archive.org/web/20201202190436///www.fixmystreet.com/.

Solymosi, R., & Bowers, K. (2018). The role of innovative data collection methods in advancing criminological understanding. *The Oxford handbook of environmental criminology,* 210–237.

Solymosi, R., Bowers, K. J., & Fujiyama, T. (2018). Crowdsourcing subjective perceptions of neighbourhood disorder: Interpreting bias in open data. *The British Journal of Criminology, 58*(4), 944–967.

Solymosi, R., Buil-Gil, D., Vozmediano, L., & Guedes, I. S. (2020). Towards a place-based measure of fear of crime: A systematic review of app-based and crowdsourcing approaches. *Environment and Behavior.* https://doi.org/10.1177/0013916520947114.

Thompson, A. J., & Pickett, J. T. (2019). Are relational inferences from crowdsourced and opt-in samples generalizable? Comparing criminal justice attitudes in the GSS and five online samples. *Journal of Quantitative Criminology,* 1–26.

Tompson, L., Johnson, S., Ashby, M., Perkins, C., & Edwards, P. (2015). UK open source crime data: Accuracy and possibilities for research. *Cartography and Geographic Information Science, 42*(2), 97–111.

Trottier, D. (2014). Crowdsourcing CCTV surveillance on the Internet. *Information, Communication & Society, 17*(5), 609–626.

Trottier, D. (2015). Open source intelligence, social media and law enforcement: Visions, constraints and critiques. *European Journal of Cultural Studies, 18*(4–5), 530–547.

Turk, K., Pastrana, S., & Collier, B. (2020). A tight scrape: Methodological approaches to cybercrime research data collection in adversarial environments. In *2020 IEEE European Symposium on Security and Privacy Workshops (EuroS&PW)*.

US Geospatial Intelligence Foundation. (2015). *State of GEOINT 2015*. Available at http://usgif.org/system/uploads/3661/original/SOG_FINAL.pdf.

Wang, M. (2016). Crowdsourcing the landscape of cannabis (marijuana) of the contiguous United States. *Environment and Planning A, 48*(8), 1449–1451.

Williams, H. J., & Blum, I. (2018). *Defining second generation open source intelligence (OSINT) for the defense enterprise*.

Williams, M. L., Burnap, P., & Sloan, L. (2017). Crime sensing with big data: The affordances and limitations of using open-source communications to estimate crime patterns. *The British Journal of Criminology, 57*(2), 320–340.

Winchester, S. (2018). *The meaning of everything: The story of the Oxford English dictionary*. Oxford University Press.

Wong, R. W. (2015). A note on fieldwork in 'dangerous' circumstances: Interviewing illegal tiger skin suppliers and traders in Lhasa. *International Journal of Social Research Methodology, 18*(6), 695–702.

Wood, M., Richards, I., Iliadis, M., & McDermott, M. (2019). Digital public criminology in Australia and New Zealand: Results from a mixed methods study of criminologists' use of social media. *International Journal for Crime, Justice and Social Democracy, 8*(4), 1.

Yates, D. (2018). Crowdsourcing antiquities crime fighting: A review of GlobalXplorer. *Advances in Archaeological Practice, 6*(2), 173–178.

Zhao, B., & Sui, D. Z. (2017). True lies in geospatial big data: Detecting location spoofing in social media. *Annals of GIS, 23*(1), 1–14.

9

Developing Open-Source Databases from Online Sources to Study Online and Offline Phenomena

Emily Ann Greene-Colozzi, Joshua D. Freilich, and Steven M. Chermak

Introduction

This chapter discusses the process of using open sources to develop databases for researching online and offline phenomena, particularly within the criminal justice, extremism, cybercrime, and related fields. "Open source" refers to any data that are open and available to the public, and can include a diverse array of sources, such as news media coverage, court documents, police and government reports, and social media, among others. Use of open-source data has increased drastically in the Information Age (Ackerman & Pinson, 2016), especially for phenomena that are difficult to research via traditional firsthand data collection methods like surveys or interviews. Cybercrimes, for example,

E. A. Greene-Colozzi (✉) · J. D. Freilich
John Jay College of Criminal Justice, CUNY, New York, NY, USA
e-mail: egreene-colozzi@jjay.cuny.edu

S. M. Chermak
Michigan State University, East Lansing, MI, USA

© The Author(s), under exclusive license to Springer Nature Switzerland AG 2021
A. Lavorgna and T. J. Holt (eds.), *Researching Cybercrimes*,
https://doi.org/10.1007/978-3-030-74837-1_9

present an empirical challenge for researchers hoping to systematically document incidents. Many governments, including the United States (U.S.), do not maintain a national database of cyber-related incidents (Bossler & Berenblum, 2019; Holt & Bossler, 2016) that could lend itself to empirical study. Traditional methods to study crime, such as the U.S. National Incident-Based Reporting System (NIBRS), are not well suited to study cybercrimes because they currently lack cyber-specific crime categories (Bossler & Berenblum, 2019). Victimization surveys may similarly fail to capture the extent of the problem, since some cybercrime victims may not know or consider themselves to be victims (Holt & Bossler, 2014; Payne & Hadzhidimova, 2020). Thus, cyber-crime researchers, like many scholars who study other sensational crimes, frequently rely on open sources to gather data and develop empirical databases (see Chapter 8 for a discussion of the collection and application of open source and crowdsourced data for criminological research and to expand research capacity). Relatively little research has assessed the challenges of database development though. Below, we discuss the steps for developing open-source databases in general, review research evaluating reliability and validity issues in database development, and provide guidelines for best practices to maximize reliability and validity.

What Are Open Sources?

Although there is no universal definition of what constitutes an "open source", scholars agree that open-source data are (1) open to the public and (2) secondary data recorded by others (Ackerman & Pinson, 2016; Chermak et al., 2012). Open-source data are often collected for purposes other than research, and thus have different reporting and ethical standards from empirical research. The media, for example, is a common source for database development; however, the primary function of journalism is to report the news quickly, with accuracy sometimes taking a backseat to rapid reporting in the 24-hours news cycle. This certainly does not exclude media coverage as a critical open data source, but it requires consideration of any and all potential threats to validity or reliability, including biases and reporting errors.

Media coverage of violent or extremist events like terrorism, school violence, or certain types of cybercrimes tends to be extensive, as the media is eager to take advantage of the public's fascination with relatively rare but sensational crimes (Dugan & Distler, 2016). On the other hand, coverage is often dependent on certain characteristics of the event, which can lead to a severely skewed picture of the phenomenon. Chermak and Gruenewald (2006), for instance, found that the majority of terrorist incidents in the United States received very little news coverage, while a small number of cases involving casualties, domestic plots, airlines, and hijackings had significantly more articles and words devoted to them. Thus, to comprehensively capture an event like terrorism using the news media as a primary open source, researchers must acknowledge the tendency for media coverage to focus exclusively on a very particular type of terrorism and the fact that the ideological perspective of a media source could impact the content.

In addition to journalistic coverage, open-source data also include documents and reports associated with litigation and criminal investigation of events. Court records, such as indictments, appeals, and testimonial transcripts, offer highly accurate, factual evidence of an event that can be readily accessed through web searches or open-search court record Web sites. Similarly, local and federal police documentation, including arrest reports, critical incident/after action reports, autopsies, and other investigatory documents, are useful and accurate records. For person-based databases, Department of Corrections records, social media sites (e.g., Twitter, Facebook), people-searches (e.g., White Pages, Ancestry.com), obituaries and death records, and background check services may return a great deal of public information that can be compiled into an open-source database. During the searching process, the types of open sources used might evolve, sometimes in surprising ways. For example, a research assistant working to gather data on an incarcerated subject discovered the individual's profile on an inmate-specific dating Web site, which provided self-reported data relevant to several variables being studied. Though unexpected, this example demonstrates the flexibility and creativity of open-source data collection.

All database development requires a rigorous and empirical protocol, but because of the varied nature of open-source data, which can simultaneously encompass highly valid sources like court transcripts and questionable sources like social media accounts, achieving this rigor is particularly challenging. Currently, there are limited empirical guidelines for developing open-source databases. Below, we establish some necessary steps and discuss essential considerations at each step for open-source database development.

Developing Open-Source Databases

Identifying Cases

A first step to developing a database is clarifying precisely what phenomenon is being examined. For some phenomena, this is as simple as using a pre-existing definition that outlines the characteristics and features of interest. Other times, the process of determining how to define a phenomenon and setting up inclusion criteria is a critical starting point for establishing a valid study. Many forms of cybercrimes, school shootings, mass shootings, and terrorism are different types of events that are often studied using open-source databases, and yet none of these phenomena have an accepted definition among scholars and practitioners. A "typical" school shooting, for example, may bring to mind a specific type of incident, perpetrated by a violent teenager against his classmates. However, limiting the definitional criteria of a school shooting to only include student perpetrators would likely exclude many cases with adult or non-student perpetrators that nevertheless occur on school grounds. If the purpose of the open-source database is to investigate this very specific phenomenon—school shootings perpetrated by currently enrolled students—then this definition may suffice. However, comparative research often seeks to collect data pertaining to a broader conceptualization of the phenomenon of interest, thus requiring a precise set of inclusion and exclusion criteria that goes beyond the "typical" case, while still establishing constraints.

There are several questions a researcher can ask to help determine inclusion criteria. Some of the simpler inclusion criteria relate to temporal and geographical constraints. What are the dates of interest? What geographical areas will the database cover? Notably, these criteria can have significant effects on the big picture of the data. Terrorism in the United States, for example, looks very different from terrorism in other nations and regions. It is important both for the validity of the sample and the posterity of the data to clearly denote the when and where of database coverage, and it can further help researchers slim down an overwhelmingly large population into a more manageable pool of events.

Other criteria will likely be dependent on the phenomenon of interest. Many mass shooting databases include a victim criterion which designates a minimum number of casualties necessary for inclusion. Some mass shooting and terrorism databases institute a fatality criterion so that they only capture incidents that resulted in deaths. Still other databases examining violence or victimization implement restrictions related to motivation or ideology. The Extremist Cyber-Crime Database (ECCD), which examines cyber-terrorism in the United States, presents several main inclusion criteria, which adhere to crucial elements of the definition of cyber and extremist crime. First, the ECCD includes geographic and temporal prongs, to limit the case universe to those occurring in the United States (geographic criterion), and between 1990 and 2020 (temporal criterion). Additionally, the ECCD has an attitudinal or motivational prong: a non-state cyber-attack must be related to an ideology for a case to be included (Fig. 9.1a). Implicit in this second prong is the idea of sufficient and supportive evidence. The ECCD codebook includes extensive definitional criteria for each ideology that has to be established with evidence. Moreover, it must be determined that the ideology was part of the decision to commit the extremist act. Determining sufficient evidence for motivation can be a challenge. In the absence of a direct statement from the perpetrator, researchers must gather evidence—in essence, conducting preliminary searches—to weigh whether the case should be included, and it is important to identify what evidence establishes the motivational criteria. Often, if a case is borderline on motivational criteria, it is included with the understanding that subsequent rigorous searches might uncover evidence excluding it.

INCLUSION CRITERIA: To qualify as an incident to be coded the following criteria must be met:

1.) The attack must have occurred on or after January 1st, 1998.

2.) The attack must have targeted United States infrastructure or target(s).
   a. The server targeted must be registered on U.S. soil.

3.) If the perpetrator of the attack is a non-state actor, the attack must have been perpetrated for a specific ideological cause.

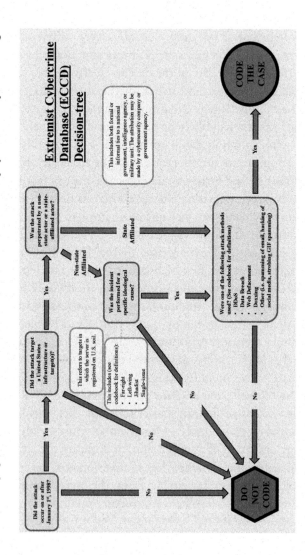

Fig. 9.1 (a) Inclusion criteria and (b) decision tree for case inclusion in the Extremist Cyber-crime Database (ECCD)

Cybercrimes and cyber-terrorism present a potentially unique challenge in terms of definitional scope and inclusion criteria. Geographical and temporal constraints, typically the easiest type of criteria to interpret, may become complicated when crimes occur in cyberspace. For example, targets and victims may be dispersed over large geographical areas, making it difficult to use space as an inclusion criterion. Likewise, targets and perpetrators may reside in different countries, or the target server may be located in a different country than the target's physical location. In situations with anonymous or unknown suspects, determining motivation and ideology becomes even more challenging, especially if a scheme involves multiple unknown suspects. These challenges should not be taken as evidence that several forms of cybercrime are ill suited for open-source data collection, however. Rather, they emphasize the importance of understanding, defining, and clearly articulating the rules for deciding whether a case meets the inclusion criteria for a particular database. And there are creative ways to overcome definitional issues. The Global Terrorism Database (GTD; National Consortium for the Study of Terrorism and Responses to Terrorism, 2014), for example, includes a case-specific variable related to the amount of doubt surrounding a terrorism incident. Researchers can therefore include cases that lack a clear terrorism denotation and record a higher level of doubt associated with this incident (Freilich & LaFree, 2016).

One way to simplify the decision-making process for determining case inclusion is to create a decision tree (see Fig. 9.1b). This can be an especially useful tool for databases that involve multiple institutions, researchers, and research assistants, since a decision tree helps ensure that all team members are aware of and adhering to the inclusion criteria. The definition and inclusion criteria also contribute to the next step in developing open-source databases, which is to designate a search protocol and search cases. Inclusion criteria will direct the type of key terms used to search cases, as well as the search engines used and how the search terms are entered (Chermak et al., 2012).

Once the inclusion criteria are established, researchers can begin exploring the universe of available sources to populate the database. For some phenomena, there may be pre-existing databases with similar definitions and timelines that can be reviewed and mined for relevant cases. In populating the Extremist Crime Database (ECDB; Freilich et al., 2014), for example, the developers referenced 10 types of open sources, including several online terrorism databases and watch-group agencies, such as the Global Terrorism Database (LaFree & Dugan, 2007), the Southern Poverty Law Center (splcenter.org) and Anti-Defamation League (adl.org), and the American Terrorism Study (Smith & Damphousse, 2007). Additionally, developers conducted systematic media searches using key words related to their definition of extremist crime. Since many sources and databases diverge on important inclusion criteria like time frame and motivation, not all cases included in one source will necessarily contribute to a new open-source database with its own unique definition. Furthermore, database developers should be aware of any biases inherent in pre-existing databases that might restrict the types of cases included in the database. Selection bias related to publicity and source effects is a common source of error that should be taken into consideration when reviewing a database for cases (Chermak & Gruenewald, 2006; Chermak et al., 2012; Snyder & Kelly, 1977), and it is critical that the universe of sources is exhausted to the best of researcher's ability.

Selection bias is a type of sampling error that arises when a database relies on a particular source (source effects) or only captures events that receive extensive media coverage (publicity effects). Empirical papers highlight the implications of these errors for database development. Chermak and Gruenewald (2006) examined media coverage of domestic terrorism in the United States, finding that major publications like *The New York Times* covered only 55% of the 412 incidents identified that met their inclusion criteria. Additionally, 15 domestic terrorism incidents accounted for 80% of all articles written in *The New York Times* about domestic terrorism, demonstrating the unequal distribution of coverage for high-profile incidents (Chermak & Gruenewald, 2006; Chermak et al., 2012). Because of the extensive coverage afforded to them, these incidents are more likely to be included in open-source databases, thus automatically biasing the database universe toward a particular type of incident with sensational and newsworthy characteristics like high fatality counts or dramatic plots (Chermak & Gruenewald,

2006). Hodowitz (2019) notes this issue as well, describing how geopolitical and plot aspects of an incident can impact its coverage: the 2015 Charlie Hebdo attack in Paris that resulted in 17 fatalities over the span of two days occurred at the same time as an attack by Boko Haram in Baga, Nigeria, which resulted in close to 2000 fatalities over the span of four days. Notably, the Paris attacks eclipsed the violence in Nigeria in terms of international news coverage (Hodowitz, 2019). When populating an open-source database with cases from news coverage, it is important for developers to consider how source and publicity effects may impact both their own open-source media searches for cases, and the cases included in pre-existing open-source databases being used as potential sources. Failing to account for selection biases can lead to Type I and Type II errors affecting the entire universe of the dataset (Reeves et al., 2006).

One method to empirically account for selection bias is to perform a "catchment-recatchment" analysis of all sources that are used to populate an open-source database. Chermak and colleagues (2012) describe "catchment-recatchment" as a process for confirming that the full universe of definitionally relevant cases are being consulted and added to the database. As stated by the authors, "once we take account of definitional and scope differences, all the sources we review should tap the same universe of events" (Chermak et al., 2012, p. 197). Two questions help guide the "catchment-recatchment" analysis: first, what did each individual source add to the database? And second, did each source provide a consistently increasing number of events previously identified in other data sources? If the sources are capturing the same universe of events, individual sources should tend to add fewer and fewer new events, while at the same time confirming an increasing number of previously identified events. For a comprehensive overview of the "catchment-recatchment" procedure, see Chermak and colleagues (2012).

Codebook Creation

An open-source database is potentially limitless in terms of the opportunity for discovery; in other words, a researcher creating a codebook can include any and all variables and constructs of interest as long as the coding values include a "missing" or "no evidence" option and clear instructions for what constitutes evidence of a positive or negative code. This allows researchers to conduct more comprehensive theory testing, as they can create variables that directly measure important constructs related to theory rather than relying on pre-composed datasets (Parkin & Freilich, 2015; Parkin & Gruenewald, 2017).

Other innovations in measurement have been suggested for complicated constructs like motivation or commitment to ideology. Kerodal et al. (2016), for instance, use factor-analysis to demonstrate that commitment to extremism can be reliably evaluated through a scalar measurement in place of conventional *yes/no* binary variables. Using scales instead of dichotomous values has many benefits for open-source data, which are not always clearly *yes* or *no*; more value categories between *yes* and *no* will immediately improve the reliability of the variable, and importantly, can later be aggregated to *yes/no* during analysis.

The issue of value categories and variable reliability merits substantial consideration when the codebook is first constructed. Ackerman and Pinson (2016) recommend including evaluation schema in the codebook that measures the reliability and inherent uncertainty of the case itself, as well as individual variables. This introduces a familiar issue in research overall: the balance between efficiency and effort. The larger the database, the more time and energy will have to be dedicated to its completion, which can mean that less attention is directed at evaluating the quality of sources and the quality of the codebook itself. At the start, developers must consider whether their data collection process has room for a full reliability evaluation to be included in the codebook itself, one that measures reliability of each source, reliability and uncertainty associated with each variable, and the reliability and uncertainty of the case. A stronger codebook will include each of these reliability considerations as well as instruct coders on the hierarchy of sources so that coders know which sources to prioritize when there is conflicting information (see Table 9.1). As with many other components of open-source data collection, it is usually best to proceed optimistically; that is, to assume that project constraints do allow for careful consideration of all aspects of reliability, and thus include them in the earliest iterations of the codebook.

Undoubtedly, the codebook will change throughout the database development process. Searches will uncover new information relevant to construct values and definitions, or perhaps demonstrate that certain variables are not particularly useful or are repetitive. Researchers should thus expect that the codebook will evolve during searching, and because of this we recommend compartmentalizing the process, and possibly the personnel, involved in searching and coding cases. While some open-source data collection proceeds with simultaneous searching and coding—that is, the same individual codes a case while searching the case—we find there is an advantage to the codebook reliability and the overall validity and reliability of the database if searching occurs before coding.

Table 9.1 Hierarchy of sources for coding

Reliability: Less < —————— > More	Appellate court proceedings Court proceedings subject to cross examination (e.g., trial transcripts) Court proceedings or documents not subject to cross examination (e.g., indictments) Corroborated information from people with direct access to information provided (e.g., law enforcement and other key informants) Uncorroborated statements from people with that access Media reports (local and major national [NYT, WSJ, WP, NPR] more reliable) Watch-group reports Personal views expressed in blogs, websites, editorials or Op-Ed, etc.

Adapted from The American School Shooting Study (TASSS)

Searching Cases

The process of searching via open-source engines is more of an art than a science, though it requires extensive training and data management. Identifying the best search engines and the appropriate key terms to search are crucial elements. If there are pre-existing open-source databases measuring the phenomenon of interest, then publications using those databases, or the database itself, may provide a listing of search engines. Otherwise, developers can incorporate a range of generalized and specialized search engines according to the needs of the database.

Generalized search engines (like Google) scour the surface web and return customized search results ordered by relevance. Metasearch engines (like Dogpile or Surfwax) can query multiple generalized search engines at once. Specialized search engines, as the name suggests, are dedicated to specific information types or themes; some examples are Lexis Nexis Academic (media and legal documents), Proquest (academic and scholarly works), and Inmate Locator (person-based corrections data). Researchers can add any number of search engines and Web sites to a protocol according to the topic. For example, a search protocol for a domestic U.S. terrorism database may require searchers to run key terms through the Homeland Security Digital Library or the Central Intelligence Agency's Center for the Study of Intelligence. These specialized search engines can help speed up the process of locating relevant search documents by narrowing down the search pool from the entire surface web to the individual Web site.

Some databases employ machine learning technology to aid with searches, such that the search process is a hybrid between computers and human searchers (Dugan & Distler, 2016). The Global Terrorism Database (GTD; National Consortium for the Study of Terrorism and Responses to Terrorism, 2014) uses machine learning to identify duplicate articles and assess the relevancy of articles for inclusion in the database (Jensen, 2013). This greatly reduces the number of articles under consideration for the GTD team, but machine learning and searching algorithms require a high degree of technical know-how and resources that might not be feasible for all database developers. At present, there is little scholarly work comparing human-produced versus machine-learning documents in terms of the quality of the results and the efficiency of each procedure (Hodowitz, 2019).

There are many ways to improve the reliability and replicability of a human search process. One is to create a search protocol using a simple spreadsheet which lists out search engines in rows and provides space in the columns for searchers to enter in the number of sources they identified using the engine, the quality of the sources, or the weblinks to the sources themselves (Fig. 9.2). Alternatively, developers might prefer a narrative document outlining each search engine and providing guidance for entering key terms and restricting results using filters or special characters.

Searching is another aspect of open-source database development that highlights the issue of time constraints versus comprehensive data collection. Even if a search protocol only involves a handful of search engines, searching a single case may take several hours or even days depending on the multitude (or lack thereof) of available open-source documents. It often falls to the searcher to decide when a case is satiated in terms of sources. The searcher must make important decisions, including whether to include duplicate articles from different sources (since some "seemingly" duplicative stories contain added material that include useful information) and when to stop searching the case (and thus insuring a "more manageable" search file). Some databases will cap the number of search results to include in an effort to reduce time spent searching; others endeavor to collect any and all available materials. While there are benefits to both strategies, it is worth noting that "uncapped' searches have the potential to fill in more variables since there is a greater amount of data.

There are several reliability issues that come up during searching. Since open-source data relies on the publicity afforded to the incident, researchers should bear in mind the effects of selection bias and publicity effect on data collection (Chermak & Gruenewald, 2006). Some cases may have very little news media coverage because they are eclipsed by other more sensational events, and these may benefit more from unconventional sources, such as social media, blogs, videos, or pictures. In such circumstances, noting the reliability of the source itself and the overall

Masterfile #:	Link:	# Sources	Comments
Hacker/Cyber News Sources:			
Hacker news	https://news.ycombinator.com/newest	2	Keywords used: cyber+attack+Sony
The Hacker News	https://thehackernews.com/	4	Keywords used: same as above
zdnet	https://www.zdnet.com	0	No sources found. Keywords used: cyber+attack; cyber+terrorism; hack
Threat Post	https://threatpost.com/		
Security Magazine	https://www.securitymagazine.com/		
Security News Magazine	https://www.scmagazine.com/home/security-news/		
Dark reading (Information IT network)	https://www.darkreading.com/		
Tech News World	https://www.technewsworld.com/		
Hack Read	https://www.hackread.com/		
The Register	https://www.theregister.co.uk/		
Security Week (cyber)	https://www.securityweek.com/cybercrime		
Wired	https://www.wired.com/		
Security Boulevard	https://securityboulevard.com/cybersecurity-news/		
Cnet	https://www.cnet.com/topics/security/		
Ciso Mag	https://www.cisomag.com/category/news/		
Cyber wire	https://thecyberwire.com/		
Info Security Group	https://www.infosecurity-magazine.com/news/		
Cyber Security Hub	https://www.cshub.com/news		
Information Week	https://www.informationweek.com/cyber-security.asp		
Cyber Crime Magazine	https://cybersecurityventures.com/		
Pastebin	Googledorking - inurl:pastebin.com		
Reddit pwned	https://www.reddit.com/r/pwned/		
Reddit hackers	https://www.reddit.com/r/hackers/new/		
Reddit cyber	https://www.reddit.com/r/cyber/		

Fig. 9.2 Search Protocol for the ECCD. Searchers record the number of sources per search engines in the #Sources column and the keywords and search terms they used in the Comments column

search document is key to maintaining the reliability and validity of the database. Ackerman and Pinson (2016) suggest conducting intrinsic and extrinsic evaluations of sources; looking at both the quality of the individual document (assessing things like inconsistent reporting, grammatical errors, biased advertisement, poor citations) and the quality of the larger source (noting signs of bias in the mission statement or the overall content of the source). These evaluations can be converted into a numerical search file reliability score. At its most basic, a search file reliability score may consider whether the file includes at least one court document, at least one police or other official document, and the quality and scope of the news media sources. Table 9.2 presents an example of such a reliability scale for assessing open-source search files documenting cyber-extremist incidents.

Often the magnitude of open-source databases requires multiple searchers and coders responsible for data collection. No doubt many researchers are familiar with the concept of interrater reliability to measure divergence among coders, but inter-searcher reliability should also be measured when there are several researchers collecting open-source data. As of now, documenting inter-searcher reliability is relatively uncommon among published open-source datasets, yet there is value in understanding the different ways that searchers might approach open-source data collection. Evaluating the quantity and quality of sources collected per searcher and per search engine can highlight potential

Table 9.2 Search File Reliability Scoring for the ECCD. Indicators are summed up to reveal a final reliability score depending on the sources in the document. The score will range from 0 (low reliability) to 8 (high reliability)

Indicator	Criterion
+ 1	Method of attack was clearly cyber-based
+ 1	Court record w/ factual description
+ 1	Government publication/document w/ factual description
+ 1	Perpetrator(s) clearly identified
+ 1	Perpetrator profile, background, DOC or related info
+ 1	Target(s) clearly identified
+ 1	Statement from target(s) about attack
+ 1	Target clearly based on U.S. soil

training gaps or inherent issues with search engines early in the process so that the search protocol can be made more efficient.

Once searching is underway, data management becomes important. Searchers are hopefully uncovering tens or hundreds (possibly thousands) of potential source documents. A search document, specific to each case, is helpful for managing copious amounts of data. The best search file will include live links to each source, as well as copied text or screen-grabs of the information; some researchers may also want to collect saved webpages. There is some added benefit of using an editable document, such as a Word document, to create a search file, as searchers and coders can review and annotate the document, highlighting information pertaining to key variables and/or inserting any necessary commentary. Clear and systematic organization of search files can speed up coding, more so when data are organized beneath headers differentiating types of data sources. For example, police reports and data could be one header; another could be news media; a third court documents; a fourth social media; a fifth Web sites, etc. Data may also be organized according to reliability, with the most reliable sources, like factual court documents or police reports at the top of the search file and subsequently less reliable sources in descending order.

Coding Cases

Coding an open-source database proceeds systematically and quickly if preceded by thorough and comprehensive searches, extensive coder training, and a validated, pretested codebook. Researchers may be tempted to search and code cases as a single step, with the same investigator coding a case he or she has searched, but there are some pitfalls to combining these steps. First is the potential for investigator burnout: A single individual responsible for searching and coding a case at the same time may be more likely to devote greater effort to only one of these responsibilities due to time and energy limitations. Breaking coding into a discrete step assigned to a different person can help ensure that coding receives an equivalent amount of human capital as searching. Further, the search procedure is likely to evolve and improve throughout the project, necessitating that some earlier cases are re-searched to incorporate new search procedures. This quickly becomes complicated and time-consuming if cases have already been coded in a database. However, if coders receive a thorough and organized search file that has undergone the full and updated search procedure, they can code the case with a higher degree of confidence in the information they are coding. Follow-up "targeted" searches should be considered a best practice for coding. This involves searching for individual variables during coding to confirm that missing values are truly missing. Freilich and colleagues (2014) found that coders on the ECDB successfully filled in 99–100% of certain missing variables using targeted searches.

Some developers may consider using computer algorithms rather than human coders to minimize interrater differences though, they should be aware of the potential limitations of machine learning for open-source database. Hodowitz (2019) cites the work of Wingenroth and colleagues (2016) as a compelling example of how algorithms can misfire for open-search research. In their comparison of human versus automated data collection and coding, Wingenroth and colleagues (2016) found that automated collection resulted in incorrect identification of over 5000 suicide attacks during the time period of interest and further erroneously reported the assassination of President Barack Obama several times. Coding inaccuracies in the automated process included incorrect locations, attack resolution, and outcomes—all of which are likely to be important dependent or independent variables in a database evaluating terrorism. Thus, although algorithms may save time and financial resources in place of human coders, they also may introduce significant error into a database (Hodowitz, 2019).

Coding has received much empirical attention over the years, most often in the context of terrorism database development (e.g., Freilich & LaFree, 2016; Freilich et al., 2014; Hodowitz, 2019). There are two key issues identified by scholars relating to reliability in coding: interrater reliability and coding missing values. Interrater reliability is perhaps the easier of the two issues to resolve. Many databases, especially those investigating dynamic phenomena like terrorism and extremism, are large-scale collaborations with multiple investigators coding cases. This is a simple reality of open-source efforts that attempt to collect quantitative data—they must rely on numerous and often changing personnel for completion. Measuring the degree of difference among these different coders is crucial for database reliability. Open-source codebooks may query multidimensional constructs, including motivation, ideology, emotional state, and commitment, and even in the presence of a clear and instructive codebook, there is likely to be some disagreement among coders when it comes to coding these constructs. The ECDB controls this potential for error through coder training, frequent review of coded cases, and a listserv for coders to share difficult issues or questions that arose. Additionally, ECDB developers conducted interrater reliability assessment for important independent and dependent variables and observed high coder agreement (Freilich et al., 2014). Of note, they also discovered that coding inconsistencies more often occurred when two coders disagreed on whether a variable was missing. Often, one coder had successfully identified information in a search document that another coder had not found, leading to the disagreement.

Missingness remains a critical issue in open-source database development (Dugan & Distler, 2016; Freilich & LaFree, 2016; Parkin & Freilich, 2015). Although targeted searches and comprehensive search files can somewhat mitigate missingness (Freilich et al., 2014), missing data should nevertheless be expected in any open-source database. A key component of this issue is distinguishing between "missing" and "no" codes. For instance, a comprehensive search file with no mention of a perpetrator having a criminal record may be interpreted as a "no" code for criminal history, especially if the search file contains other articles about the perpetrator's past and social history. Parkin and Freilich (2015) argue that this sort of inferential coding is necessary for an open-source database where a great deal of information is often left out of news coverage for lack of interest. Especially in sensational cases, the media are more likely to report positive evidence of an attribute (e.g., a terror suspect having prior arrests) than negative evidence (i.e., no prior arrests); instead, they may simply leave out any mention of an arrest record to save space for more relevant details. Systematic use of this protocol ensures that any Type I or Type II errors will be consistent across all comparison groups and therefore avoid biasing the results.

Evaluating the Database

Once an open-source database is successfully coded, researchers should take a figurative step back and think about any and all possible sources of error in the database (Ackerman & Pinson, 2016). This is also known as creating "error profiles" (Chermak et al., 2012). Error profiles document the various errors that could plague a database, including non-sampling errors such as misidentification of incidents or coding errors. The error profile presents these potential errors and describes the ways that they might influence analysis, while also noting what efforts were taken to avoid the errors. It is similar to writing up a limitations section in a peer-reviewed publication: it cautions the audience and provides future users with necessary information for drawing conclusions and implications. This improves the transparency of the database, as well as the defensibility of any empirical conclusions reached from the database (Ackerman & Pinson, 2016).

An open-source database that has successfully maintained empirical rigor throughout will have fewer errors to document, and also be easier to evaluate. Thus, adhering to the considerations outlined in the four previous sections can greatly facilitate evaluation. For instance, including individual event reliability ratings in the codebook will produce a quantitative representation of reliability for every single case that can be aggregated to show overall database reliability. Listing out cases that were initially included, but later excluded, similarly provides consumers and developers an opportunity to confirm that inclusion criteria were adequately followed. Likewise, recording source reliability in the search files or as part of a separate source codebook performs a similar function in providing a measurement of source reliability without requiring developers to go back and review sources after the fact (Ackerman & Pinson, 2016). For a dynamic database that continues to collect and code cases indefinitely, the error profile should also be continually updated for transparency.

Conclusion

The use of open-source databases has greatly benefited the study of certain types of crimes and behaviors that are difficult to investigate through traditional methods, including terrorism and school violence. Cybercrime falls into a similar category, in terms of empirical challenges to data collection. Surveys and national databases often fall short when it comes to capturing theoretically relevant variables related to cybercrimes, as well as documenting the incidence and nature of online crimes. Fortunately, scholarly interest in cybercrime is increasing (Bossler & Berenblum, 2019), paving the way for new and innovative methodologies to study cybercrime. Open-source database development is one such methodology that could prove to be enormously useful for cybercrime research. Constructing unique and standalone databases allows researchers to narrowly define the type of cyber-offense being studied, which can help with suggestions for specific prevention. Codebook creation can provide researchers a great deal of flexibility in terms of the theoretical constructs they aim to examine; rather than depend upon already established sources, which may have a limited number of relevant variables, researchers can start by identifying the constructs and variables most important to their particular study of cybercrime, and proceed inductively with data collection. Since cybercrime remains a relatively new topic in criminological research (Payne & Hadzhidimova, 2020), there is much still to explore, from gaining a basic understanding of the overall prevalence of cybercrime to developing a nuanced understanding of the different typologies of cybercrime, trends over time, and suspect and target characteristics. As cybercrime becomes more resonant for the public and media, the amount of open-source information will also increase, and further advantage open-source database development. The research and recommendations discussed in this chapter provide guidelines to advance open-source cybercrime research through rigorous database development. Importantly, these recommendations and insights need not be restricted to a single, or even a few, types of events. Open-source data is useful and available for any phenomena that comes to public and media attention and thus enters the information highway.

References

Ackerman, G. A., & Pinson, L. E. (2016). Speaking truth to sources: Introducing a method for the quantitative evaluation of open sources in event data. *Studies in Conflict and Terrorism, 39*(7–8), 617–740.

Bossler, A. M., & Berenblum, T. (2019). Introduction: New directions in cybercrime research. *Journal of Crime and Justice, 42*(5), 495–499.

Chermak, S. M., Freilich, J. D., Parkin, W. S., & Lynch, J. P. (2012). American terrorism and extremist crime data sources and selectivity bias: An investigation focusing on homicide events committed by Far-Right extremists. *Journal of Quantitative Criminology, 28*, 191–218.

Chermak, S. M., & Gruenewald, F. (2006). The media's coverage of domestic terrorism. *Justice Quarterly, 23*(4), 428–461.

Dugan, L., & Distler, M. (2016). Measuring terrorism. In G. LaFree & J. D. Freilich (Eds.), *The handbook of the criminology of terrorism.* Wiley.

Freilich, J. D., Chermak, S. M., Belli, R., Gruenewald, J., & Parkin, W. S. (2014). Introducing the United States Extremist Crime Database (ECDB). *Terrorism and Political Violence, 26*(2), 372–384.

Freilich, J. D., & LaFree, G. (2016). Measurement issues in the study of terrorism: Introducing the special issues. *Studies in Conflict and Terrorism, 39*(7–8), 569–579.

Hodowitz, O. (2019). *Recognizing and resolving issues in terrorism research, data collection, and analysis.* Resolve Network: Researching Violent Extremism Series. https://www.resolvenet.org/index.php/system/files/2019-10/RSVE_RVESeries_Hodwitz_October2019.pdf.

Holt, T. J., & Bossler, A. M. (2014). An assessment of the current state of cybercrime scholarship. *Deviant Behavior, 35*(1), 20–40.

Holt, T. J., & Bossler, A. M. (2016). *Cybercrime in progress: Theory and prevention of technology-enabled offenses.* Crime Science Series. Routledge.

Jensen, M. (2013). *The benefits and drawbacks of methodological advancements in data collection and coding: Insights from the Global Terrorism Database.* http://www.start.umd.edu/news/discussion-point-benefits-and-drawbacks 2010methodological-advancementsdata-collection-and-coding.

Kerodal, A. G., Freilich, J. D., & Chermak, S. M. (2016). Commitment to extremist ideology: Using factor analysis to move beyond binary measures of extremism. *Studies in Conflict and Terrorism, 39*(7–8), 569–579.

LaFree, G., & Dugan, L. (2007). Introducing the Global Terrorism Database. *Terrorism and Political Violence, 19*(2), 181–204.

National Consortium for the Study of Terrorism and Responses to Terrorism. (2014).

Parkin, W. S., & Freilich, J. D. (2015). Routine activities and Right-Wing extremists: An empirical comparison of the victims of ideologically-and non-ideologically-motivated homicides committed by American Far-Rightists. *Terrorism and Political Violence, 27*(1), 182–203.

Parkin, W. S., & Gruenewald, J. (2017). Open-source data and the study of homicide. *Journal of Interpersonal Violence, 32*(18), 2693–2723.

Payne, B. K., & Hadzhidimova, L. (2020). Disciplinary and interdisciplinary trends in cybercrime research: An examination. *International Journal of Cyber Criminology, 14*(1), 81–105.

Reeves, A., Shellman, S., & Stewart, B. (2006). *Fair and balanced or fit to print? Effects of media sources on statistical inferences.* Paper presented at the annual meeting for the International Studies Association, San Diego, CA.

Smith, B. L., & Damphousse, K. R. (2007). American terrorism study, 1980–2002. *Inter-University Consortium for Political and Social Research.* https://doi.org/10.3886/ICPSR04639.v1.

Snyder, D., & Kelly, W. R. (1977). Conflict intensity, media sensitivity and the validity of newspaper data. *American Sociological Review, 42*(1), 105–123.

Wingenroth, B., Miller, E., Jensen, M., Hodwitz, O., & Quinlan, K. (2016). Event data and the construction of reality. In *International Conference on Social Computing, Behavioral-Cultural Modeling, and Prediction and Behavior Representations in Modeling and Simulation* (SBP-BRiMS). Implications for Policy and Practice.

10

Too Much Data? Opportunities and Challenges of Large Datasets and Cybercrime

Jack Hughes, Yi Ting Chua, and Alice Hutchings

Introduction

The term "big data" is gaining popularity and attention among criminologists, ever since its introduction in a McKinsey report (Manyika, 2011). However, its definition and conceptualization varies across disciplines, with some computer scientists viewing it as a marketing term or buzzword. Some may view big data by unit of measurement, such as datasets that exceed a petabyte in size (Anderson, 2008), while others conceptualize big data in terms of the number of rows and columns in a dataset (Burrows & Savage, 2014; Lazer & Radford, 2017). In addition to volume, big data is characterized by other features such as exhaustivity

J. Hughes (✉) · Y. T. Chua · A. Hutchings
Department of Computer Science and Technology, University of Cambridge, Cambridge, UK
e-mail: jack.hughes@cl.cam.ac.uk

A. Hutchings
e-mail: alice.hutchings@cl.cam.ac.uk

© The Author(s), under exclusive license to Springer Nature
Switzerland AG 2021
A. Lavorgna and T. J. Holt (eds.), *Researching Cybercrimes*,
https://doi.org/10.1007/978-3-030-74837-1_10

191

(capturing an entire population), relationality (features allowing for integration with other datasets), and velocity (the speed of data collection and utilization) (Kitchin, 2014; Ozkan, 2019). Despite such variations, a shared notion of big data is that the size of the datasets creates challenges, with existing software and tools unable to manage the logistics of data collection, analysis, and management (Chan & Moses, 2016; Chen et al., 2014; Lynch, 2018; Manyika, 2011; Snijders et al., 2012). Given the complexities with "big data", the chapter will use the phrase "large datasets" in place of big data to minimize confusion.

As technology and digital devices become highly integrated into society, it creates tremendous amounts of digital data and information ranging from user-generated content to personal identifiable information (Burrows & Savage, 2014; Lazer & Radford, 2017; Ozkan, 2019). This data may not only become the target of cybercrime attacks (Porcedda & Wall, 2019; Yar, 2005), but also of academic research. Increasingly, social scientists are using these large datasets to understand human behavior. The shift toward digital data presents unique opportunities and challenges to criminologists and cybercrime scholars. The intersection of large datasets, data science, and social science has resulted in the birth of new fields such as computational social science (Lazer et al., 2009), digital criminology (Smith et al., 2017), and social computing (Wang et al., 2007). In addition, there are increasingly new tools and datasets previously inaccessible to scholars (Metzler et al., 2016; Moore et al., 2019). Such advancements require new developments in research, to process large datasets in a short span of time, and the use of new techniques such as natural language processing and machine learning (Benjamin et al., 2015; Chan & Moses, 2016; Chen et al., 2014; Lazer & Radford, 2017; Li et al., 2016) (see also Chapter 11). This creates new challenges in research methodology, such as sampling biases and missing data (Edwards et al., 2013). Current discussions on these impacts tend to revolve around criminology as a field, and do not account for unique issues faced by cybercrime scholars. The goal of this chapter is to provide an overview of the opportunities and challenges of large datasets in the context of cybercrime.

The chapter begins with a background on the emergence of large datasets in the field of criminology and recent trends of research in cybercrime using large datasets. The discussion is followed by detailed accounts of opportunities and challenges cybercrime scholars may encounter during the research process, ranging from data collection to data analysis. In addition, ethical issues unique to the use of large datasets in research are briefly considered.

Background

An early concern with the rise of large datasets is the decreased necessity for theoretical framework and discussions. Arguing that the era of large datasets is the "end of theory", Anderson (2008) states the sufficiency of correlation with large volume of data and cited Google as a demonstration of the power of algorithms and large datasets. Criminologists dismiss such notions, arguing that the expertise of scholars is necessary to make sense of data-driven findings. There has been a trend in criminology toward using large datasets as research data, as well as using data science tools (i.e., modeling and algorithms) to analyze them (Chan & Moses, 2016). These allow researchers to perform more complex and comprehensive modeling and analyses, and at faster pace due to automation (Chen et al., 2014; Lazer & Radford, 2017; Ozkan, 2019; Snaphaan & Hardyns, 2019). However, the necessity of theories is found in the ineffectiveness of data science methods to identify underlying causal mechanisms, or to distinguish between noises and true signals within large datasets (Chan & Moses, 2016; Ozkan, 2019) (see also Chapters 4, 5, and 11).

Some common types of large datasets used in criminology and criminal justice include administrative data, social media datasets (i.e., Facebook, Twitter, Reddit, etc.), and survey data (Burrows & Savage, 2014; Lynch, 2018; Metzler et al., 2016; Ozkan, 2019; Chapters 8 and 13), as well as leaked data of online communities (i.e., underground forums) (Holt & Dupont, 2019; Motoyama et al., 2011) and scraped data of online communities (Benjamin et al., 2015; Pastrana et al., 2018b; Westlake & Bouchard, 2016; Chapter 11). Recent research in criminology shows social scientists' keenness in incorporating such powerful items into their toolboxes. One example is the application of artificial intelligence and big data in the context of predictive policing and surveillance (Gerritsen, 2020; Hayward & Maas, 2020). Another example is in the advancement of environmental criminology, with a recent review by Snaphaan and Hardyns (2019) finding a shared recognition on the availability, scalability, and temporal and spatial granularity afforded by large datasets, allowing for greater insight on the time-place dynamics in crime. Lynch (2018) recognizes similar benefits with open-source data and administrative records in the advancement of criminology research in the Presidential Address to American Society of Criminology in 2017. As the awareness of the benefits of large datasets grows, there is undeniable evolution in criminology research.

The rise of large datasets, however, cannot be fully embraced without discussion on its unique limitations and challenges. Large datasets are a double-edged sword, especially in the context of cybercrime. In addition to being a data source and methodology, large datasets are potentially targets and means of cyber-attacks (Motoyama et al., 2011; Newman & Clarke, 2003). For cybercrime and cybersecurity scholars, this shift in attacks dictates changes in the nature and format of available datasets necessary for research. This shift raises a series of challenges at various stages of research, including data collection, data management, and data analyses. Three common challenges from the reported experiences of 9412 social scientists who work with large datasets include: (1) gaining access to commercial data; (2) finding collaborators with appropriate skills and knowledge; and (3) learning new software and analytical methods. Social scientists without large-dataset experience stated similar barriers, with the exception of accessibility (Metzler et al., 2016).

In addition, there are general issues and challenges due to the nature of large datasets (see also Chapters 4 and 5). First, there is the issue of generalizability (Edwards et al., 2013; Lazor & Radford, 2017). For example, social media platforms differ in regulations, format of organizations, and user demographics, with some platforms being more attractive to specific populations (Lazer & Radford, 2017). There is also the issue of authenticity of collected information, such as distinction between bot-generated content and real user information or the absence of demographic information from individual users on social media platforms (Edwards et al., 2013; Lazer & Radford, 2017). Second, there is the issue of data quality and biases in large datasets (González-Bailón, 2013; Lynch, 2018). With open-source data, there are no standards or quality assurance in place (Lee & Holt, 2020; Lynch, 2018). With large datasets provided by third parties or via application programming interfaces (APIs), there are sometimes limits and sampling filters imposed which researchers may not necessarily be aware of (González-Bailón, 2013; Lee & Holt, 2020). Both issues can affect the replicability of findings. This is further exacerbated when examined alongside with the accessibility of datasets (Lee & Holt, 2020). Although not exhaustive, these challenges and issues with large datasets merit further considerations for cybercrime scholars. In the following section, we will discuss in detail how some of these issues appear during cybercrime research.

Large Datasets and Cybercrime Research

Collecting Data

Cybercrime is a hidden activity, due to its illicit nature. One of the problems facing researchers is access to good quality data. Biases in datasets can sometimes tell us more about how the data were collected than about cybercrime itself. While some data may be available from industry sources through non-disclosure agreements, as researchers cannot disclose where it was obtained or share it with others, the data and research are non-reproducible. Research students, who are often time-limited, may find that a considerable duration is spent trying to access and collect data than actually analyzing it. The Cambridge Cybercrime Centre was established in 2015 in recognition of these issues. The Centre collects cybercrime-related datasets and makes them available to other academic researchers through data sharing agreements (Cambridge Cybercrime Centre, 2019). Some of these datasets are collected directly by the Centre, and others are provided by industry through incoming agreements.

The datasets being collected constantly evolves due to new criminal opportunities, as well as the methods available to us. As the datasets are continually being collected, they also tend to grow over time. One example is the various types of honeypots we operate (for an overview of the use of honeypots in cybercrime research, see also Chapter 12). Honeypots mimic vulnerable machines, and collect data about attacks. We operate honeypots that pretend to be vulnerable to certain types of malware (such as Mirai, which predominantly affects Internet of Things devices), devices that can be remotely accessed, as well as misconfigured servers that are used for amplifying denial-of-service attacks (Vetterl & Clayton, 2019).

In relation to the denial-of-service attack sensors, we operate around 100 sensors in various locations around the world (Thomas et al., 2017). These sensors pretend to participate in "reflected" or "amplified" denial-of-service attacks, in which the attacker sends the misconfigured server a small packet, but pretends the request is coming from the IP address they want to attack. The server replies to the request with a much bigger packet, but to the spoofed victim IP address. This means that the traffic being sent to the victim is considerably larger than the traffic initially sent by the attacker. Our sensors pretend to be a misconfigured server, but instead of sending on the response, captures data about the attack, including the victim IP address. In 2020, we had collected over 4 trillion packets, and this is likely to continue to increase. This dataset allows for research into attacks over time, such as measuring the impact of interventions (Collier et al., 2019).

The dataset requested most frequently by academic researchers is the CrimeBB dataset (Pastrana et al., 2018b). This includes posts scraped from publicly available underground forums that discuss cybercrime and related activities. Some of these forums have been operating for many years and we have now amassed a collection of over 90 million posts, some dating back more than 10 years. We have English, Russian, German, and Spanish-language forums, and are actively expanding to include other languages. We hold nearly complete collections of these forums, allowing for analysis across the whole dataset. We have also been collecting data from additional platforms, and currently hold over three million Telegram messages (from 50+ channels) and 2.5 million Discord messages (from over 3000 channels) that relate to cybercrime. Furthermore, we are expanding the scope beyond cybercrime, with the

ExtremeBB dataset including extremist forums related to hate groups, extremism and radicalization, as well as incel communities.

These datasets are collected by scraping the sites, using a custom script to crawl the forums for automatic collection (Pastrana et al., 2018b). There are also off-the-shelf tools for scraping, but all methods require continual monitoring and maintenance, as these can break when page layouts change. Additionally, some Web sites may be hostile to scraping methods, requiring the researcher to take steps to avoid detection (Turk et al., 2020). This can include limiting the rate of pages collecting and solving CAPTCHAs either manually or automatically.

Other data sources, such as Twitter, often have an API available, which provide a standard way to collect data, used by libraries in R and Python. This simplifies data collection. Furthermore, CrimeBB is not the only dataset available on cybercrime and underground forum data. Pushshift.io collects data from Twitter, Reddit, and Gab, and additionally provides a hosted Elasticsearch service for researchers to search, filter, and aggregate data without needing to download the entire dataset (Bevensee et al., 2020). This minimizes the need for researchers to transform and prepare the dataset.

Using the Data

In addition to the time-consuming data collection process of large datasets, there are additional challenges when it comes to their handling and analysis. Usability of these types of datasets is explored in an evaluation study by Pete and Chua (2019), who found that large datasets pose issues even for technology-savvy researchers.

Where the data has been self-collected, the researcher needs to convert the raw data into a format that is useful to them. CrimeBB is built upon PostgreSQL, which is useful for querying and aggregating data. Tools such as PgAdmin provide a visual interface for querying data and downloading CSV files, although this can also be carried out using the command line if preferred. Difficulties reported by Pete and Chua (2019) include challenges with downloading and setting up datasets due to version conflicts for PostgreSQL and compatibility of raw datasets with other tools such as mySQL, despite overall satisfaction with the data sharing and usage.

If the dataset is in the form of a database, some skill may be required in writing SQL queries, although there are off-the-shelf tools available for working with these either in R or Python, or in stand-alone programs. Scholars also face the decisions of sampling, if only using a subset of the larger datasets. In some cases, the researcher may wish to convert the database into a different format, such as CSV files or edgelists (e.g., for social network analysis). However, it may not be useful to transform the entire dataset immediately, as the analysis software used may not be able to handle files of that size. It may be useful to use scripts in R or Python to convert between different formats when working with large datasets, rather than by hand.

Before using the data for analysis, if the data are raw and unprocessed, data cleaning and preparation needs to be carried out. This may involve checking records contain data where required, checking that descriptors of variables make sense, noting limitations with the dataset (e.g., there may not be a full historical dataset of forum posts as some may have been deleted before collection), and removing unrelated data (e.g., removing link and image tags in posts). Dataset filtering can take place either before or after the cleaning step has taken place, depending on the method. Filtering includes selecting data required for analysis, such as by date range.

Toolkits

Toolkits are a set of analysis techniques, provided to either connect with your own dataset, or use a dataset provided with the toolkit. Examples of these toolkits include SMAT (Bevensee et al., 2020), which provides searching and visualization tools to explore the Pushshift database, and OSoMe (Davis et al., 2016) for analyzing the OSoMe Decahose dataset with tools for bot detection, trend tracking, and social network visualization. Toolkits vary in flexibility: Those which are linked with an existing dataset are useful in reducing the time taken in carrying out analysis, allowing for early exploration of the dataset.

Other types of toolkits, such as Gephi (Bastian et al., 2009), provide flexibility with the type of data used, with a trade-off in ease-of-use, and require the researcher to transform the data into a format suitable for the tool, and setup the software. While Gephi runs as a single program, some toolkits like SMAT use a collection of programs and can be accessed using a web browser. This adds some complexity, but the toolkit developers may implement newer techniques, such as using Docker to support reproducibility, by defining what programs need to run and how they connect, to automatically setup the software, isolated from the researcher's own computer programs.

Analyzing Large Datasets

There have been numerous studies working with large datasets relating to cybercrime. Some examples include the OSoMe project for Twitter data (Davis et al., 2016) and the IMPACT program with a wide range of data on the issues of cybercrime and cybersecurity (Moore et al., 2019). We specifically focus on our own work within this area, specifically on underground forums, working with CrimeBB.

Pastrana and colleagues (2018a) use the CrimeBB dataset to analyze key actors within HackForums, the largest and most popular underground hacking forum. The subset of CrimeBB containing HackForums data included more than 30 million posts created by 572k users. They analyzed key actors, defined as those of interest to law enforcement, using ground truth data obtained from various sources. For their analysis, they use different methods including natural language processing for text content, social network analysis to analyze the relations between users, machine learning for clustering (grouping) forum members based on their activity, and explore the evolving interests of key actors.

Some of the types of approaches we have used are covered in Chapter 17, in relation to machine learning and natural language processing (NLP). We provide a brief overview here, related to their use for analyzing large, unstructured, datasets. NLP is a field of computer science that focuses on analyzing and understanding text content. NLP techniques are therefore useful for analyzing large datasets of text, where qualitative coding is too time consuming. Caines and colleagues (2018) automatically classify posting intent and types using NLP and machine learning. They identify a set of words frequent in a small set of posts, but not frequent across all of CrimeBB ("TF-IDF"), as their dependent variables ("features" in machine learning terminology), to predict intent and type (dependent variable). They use a support vector machine (SVM) model for prediction. Given the large number of posts available on CrimeBB, this approach can scale a small set of manually curated annotations to automatically annotate all posts. However, care must be taken for validation to make sure that the automatic annotations are similar to the human annotations. In machine learning, the set of annotations is usually divided up into three sets: a training set, testing set, and validation set. The training set is used to create the model, and the testing set is used to evaluate the fit of the model and to tweak parameters. The validation set is used to create evaluation metrics, and should not be used to tweak parameters or re-fit the model.

Pastrana and colleagues (2018a) also use machine learning for clustering: grouping of similar members based on a set of variables. Specifically, they use k-means clustering. Clustering techniques can be found in statistical packages, as well as within Python and R libraries for machine learning. Other techniques used in these studies include social network analysis, with social networks based upon a user B replying directly to user A, or user C replying in a thread created by A. As the HackForums data includes positive and negative reputation voting, Pastrana and colleagues (2018a) were able to annotate the relations between users. Pastrana and colleagues (2018a) also explore the evolution of interest of members on the forum. They define a member's interest for a given time period based upon the number of posts created in a category added to three times the number of threads created in a category. This is used to explore the changing interests of key actors over time. For predicting key actors overall, the authors combine the predictions of different models, filtering out those selected by only one model. These predictions are validated by checking the similarity of hacking-related terms used by key actors to those predicted key actors. This metric-based approach supports validation of the predictions, although a qualitative sampling approach could be used instead.

Hughes and colleagues (2019) use a similar hybrid-model approach, outlined in Fig. 10.1, with a gaming-specific underground hacking forum. As ground truth data on actors of interest to law enforcement was not available relating to users of this forum, this research defined key actors as users who have a central role in overtly criminal activities, or activities which could lead to later offending, and hence might benefit most from interventions. This work explored creating a systematic data processing pipeline for the analysis of unstructured forum datasets. Predictive models used included logistic regression, random forest, and neural network models. Results were cross-validated using topic analysis. Furthermore, Hughes and colleagues (2019) extended the types of methods used for analyzing forum members to include group-based trajectory modeling, a statistical technique developed by Nagin (2005) that takes time-series data and groups these into different trends over time ("trajectories"). For validation, in addition to checking the similarity of terms used, Hughes et al. (2019) used methods to explore model predictions. For logistic regression, observing odds ratios is straightforward, but for some machine learning models, this is non-trivial. Partial dependency plots and permutation importance were used to identify important features (independent variables) used in prediction. These state-of-the-art techniques work by changing different input parameters to detect changes in the prediction, rather than inspecting the whole model directly.

The development of NLP tools to aid the analysis of cybercrime forums is ongoing. For example, to aid in the discovery of new topics that arise within underground forums, Hughes and colleagues (2020) developed a tool for detecting trending terms. Just like Twitter allows its users to view items being discussed at a particular time, the idea behind this tool is that researchers can uncover important topics within the noise of constant chatter (on the use of NLP is cybercrime research, see also Chapter 11).

Other studies have used CrimeBB to understand and quantify specific crime types, such as eWhoring, a type of online scam where offenders obtain money from customers in exchange for online sexual encounters

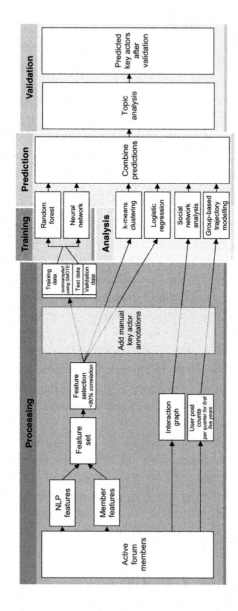

Fig. 10.1 Pipeline used to process data and analyze forum members (adapted from Hughes et al., 2019)

(Pastrana et al., 2019). As outlined in Fig. 10.2, eWhoring-related images shared on the forum were extracted and processed. There were significant ethical issues to address, as many of the images are pornographic, and there was a risk they may include child sexual abuse material. Therefore, the researchers worked with the Internet Watch Foundation, and were able to use their PhotoDNA service, which computes a hash of a given image and matches it against a database of known child abuse material. Indeed, some offending images were detected, which were subsequently reported for takedown and removed from the Cambridge Cybercrime Centre's servers.

The images were also processed to categorize them as "nude images" (e.g., pornographic photographs which are sold and shared on the forum), or "safe to view". This processing involved the use of a "NSFV" ("not safe for viewing") classifier, a machine learning model that provides a probability of an image containing indecent content, and an optical character recognition classifier, to identify images containing text. The nude images were then reverse image searched using the TinEye API, to identify where else on the Internet they could be found. This revealed most images were likely being obtained from adult and pornography sites, as well as social networking sites, blogs, photo sharing sites, and other online forums. Pastrana and colleagues (2019) also manually analyzed the images containing text, as these predominantly contained "proofs of earnings", namely screenshots of payment platform dashboards which were shared as a way of boasting and gaining kudos within the community. This allowed for the estimation of the amount of money being made per customer, popular payment platforms (PayPal and Amazon gift cards), and currency (predominantly USD).

We have also explored specific segments of forums, with Vu et al. (2020) focusing specifically on the evolution of HackForums' contract system, which was introduced to build trust on the marketplace by creating a partially public record of transactions between users. The use of the system was enforced for all members using the marketplace, and members could optionally make details of the transaction public. The researchers collected contracts across a two-year period, from the setup of the system to June 2020, which we examined using Tuckman's (1965) stages of group development, identifying three eras:

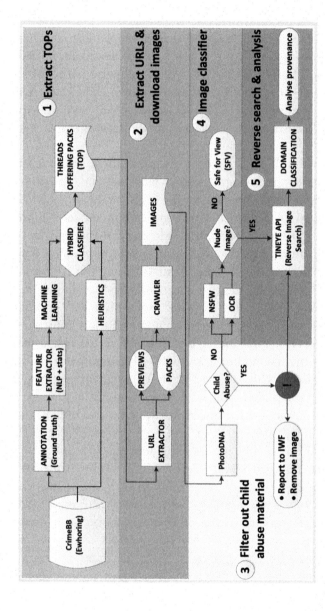

Fig. 10.2 Pipeline used to identify, download, and analyze packs of images used for eWhoring (adapted from Pastrana et al., 2019)

"setup" (forming and storming), "stable" (norming), and "COVID-19" (performing). The longitudinal dataset supported measurements of how the contract activity changed through different stages of the development of the system, and while the researchers were not able to identify the purpose of all contracts, they were able to measure the types of public contracts. They found most public contracts were linked to currency exchange and payments, indicating the marketplace was being used for cashing-out. Over time, the evolution of the types of products offered was stable, and Bitcoin remained the most preferred payment method, followed by PayPal.

The researchers also used Latent Transition Modeling to identify latent classes in the dataset, for modeling activity over time by different types of users, based upon making/accepting of contracts, power-users, and counts of contracts. This supported analysis of identifying flows between types of users, to find which were the most common types of makers and takers on the marketplace, for each of the three eras. Finally, the researchers investigated the cold start problem on the marketplace, in which new members starting in the second ("stable") era face the challenge of getting started on the market to build up reputation against members that have already built up reputation during the "setup" era. Using clustering and regression, followed by qualitative analysis, the researchers found groups of users of the contracts system would overcome the cold start problem by starting with low-level currency exchange. The results of clustering and regression were used to select a group of users who overcame the cold start problem, for further qualitative analysis to understand the types of products and services they were providing.

Comparative studies compare and contrast different forums. The research by Pete and colleagues (2020) takes this approach with six forums that are hosted as hidden services on anonymity networks. They use a social network approach to model interactions between members of forums, for identifying structural characteristics and patterns, and identifying a group of members of importance in communities. The six forums varied in size, from 1127 members to 40,763 members, and the researchers built an interaction network between users to observe these communities of members. Interactions on forums are not explicit, compared to Twitter mention data, and therefore some assumptions were needed including creating an interaction between members posting in the same thread. The researchers used scripts to automatically pre-process and run the network analysis given the size of the dataset, using social network analysis techniques including community detection, and network centrality. They used qualitative analysis to analyze and characterize the types of posts created by the central members of each community, who typically discussed general topics related to the content of each forum, and some members were administrators of forums.

Due to the size of the datasets we use, much of our work has focused on quantitative analysis methods, using social network analysis, natural language processing, and machine learning techniques. However, qualitative research methods come into their own when it comes to analyzing the richness of the available data. Our research using qualitative analysis relies on sampling techniques, such as stratified random sampling and snowball sampling, to obtain a dataset of suitable size. This uses an initial set of keyword searches, to find relevant posts and similar keywords, with the set of keywords increased until a suitable number of posts have been found. Limitations to be aware of include not collecting all relevant posts, particularly due to the use of informal language, variations of spelling, and the changing meaning of terms over time. Examples of research where we have used such qualitative research methods include a crime script analysis of eWhoring (Hutchings & Pastrana, 2019), and an exploration into masculinity and perceptions of gender (Bada et al., 2020).

Conclusion

Nils Christie (1997) differentiated between "near data", which includes information pertaining to a small number of participants while providing thousands of insights, and "distant data", such as large datasets from official records, which may contain thousands of cases but provides little in-depth understanding. With large datasets, particularly with the ability to match data and add value by combining with other data sources, we are perhaps entering a time of distant-yet-near data, with rich insights ascertainable from large numbers of cases. Criminologists have never before had access to the conversations of a large number of individuals who are starting to become involved in crime, covering their learning, interaction, benefits and rewards, concerns and fears, initiation, persistence, and desistance. We are just starting to collect such data, and the insights we can glean will be of benefit to a large body of criminological research, not just cybercrime, including critical criminology, policing studies, and crime prevention.

What will make this possible, however, is not just access to the data, but novel ways to interpret and analyze it. While the Cambridge Cybercrime Centre has spent many years collecting data, we are now also turning our efforts to develop better tools to enable use by researchers in the social sciences. Here, the techniques used by other disciplines, such as computer science, are valuable. Machine learning and natural language processing allow tasks previously undertaken manually (such as coding of large volumes of text data), to be automated.

Such progress will bring new challenges to the fore, not least ethical concerns. Much of cybercrime research involves processing data created by or of individuals. This opens up issues around informed consent, anonymity, and confidentiality, and whether the data was obtained as intentionally public data, or data which has been obtained from a leak and would otherwise be private. At the infrastructure-level, there needs to be consideration in protecting the anonymity and confidentiality of collected data across time and against evolving attack techniques (Moore et al., 2019). Another concern is anonymity where conventional de-anonymization techniques, such as removal of personal information, may no longer be sufficient. For example, Sweeney (1997) describes a case where the removal of identifiable information such as names and addresses from a hospital database does not guarantee anonymity since one's unique history of diagnosis remains and therefore identifiable through queries. Similarly, Narayanan and Shmatikov (2008) demonstrate the effectiveness of de-anonymization algorithm with the Netflix Prize dataset (containing movie ratings from users) by cross-referencing the anonymized data with publicly available information (e.g., the Internet Movie Database (IMDB)). Moving forward, discussion on ethical considerations with the use of large datasets requires an inter-disciplinary insight. For a more detailed discussion about ethical issues in cybercrime research, please see Part III of this book.

References

Anderson, C. (2008). The end of theory: The data deluge makes the scientific method obsolete. *Wired Magazine, 16*(7), 16–17.

Bada, M., Chua, Y. T., Collier, B., & Pete, I. (2020). Exploring masculinities and perceptions of gender in online cybercrime subcultures. In *Proceedings of the 2nd Annual Conference on the Human Factor in Cybercrime.*

Bastian, M., Heymann, S., & Jacomy, M. (2009). Gephi: An open source software for exploring and manipulating networks. In *Proceedings of the Third International ICWSM Conference* (pp. 361–362).

Benjamin, V., Li, W., Holt, T., & Chen, H. (2015). Exploring threats and vulnerabilities in hacker web: Forums, IRC and carding shops. In *2015 IEEE International Conference on Intelligence and Security Informatics (ISI)* (pp. 85–90).

Bevensee, E., Aliapoulios, M., Dougherty, Q., Baumgartner, J., McCoy, D., & Blackburn, J. (2020). SMAT: The social media analysis toolkit. In *Proceedings of the Fourteenth International AAAI Conference on Web and Social Media.*

Burrows, R., & Savage, M. (2014). After the crisis? Big Data and the methodological challenges of empirical sociology. *Big Data and Society, 1*(1), 1–6.

Caines, A., Pastrana, S., Hutchings, A., & Buttery, P. (2018). Automatically identifying the function and intent of posts in underground forums. *Crime Science, 7*(19), 1–14.

Cambridge Cybercrime Centre. (2019). *Process for working with our data.* Available at: https://www.cambridgecybercrime.uk/process.html.

Chan, J., & Moses, B. L. (2016). Is Big Data challenging criminology? *Theoretical Criminology, 20*(1), 21–39.

Chen, M., Mao, S., & Liu, Y. (2014). Big data: A survey. *Mobile Networks and Applications, 19*(2), 171–209.

Christie, N. (1997). Four blocks against insight: Notes on the oversocialization of criminologists. *Theoretical Criminology, 1*(1), 13–23.

Collier, B., Thomas, D. R., Clayton, R., & Hutchings, A. (2019). Booting the Booters: Evaluating the effects of police interventions in the market for denial-of-service attacks. In *Proceedings of the ACM Internet Measurement Conference*. Amsterdam.

Davis, C. A., Ciampaglia, G. L., Aiello, L. M., Chung, K., Conover, M. D., Ferrara, E., Flammini, A., Fox, G. C., Gao, X., Gonçalves, B., Grabowicz, P. A., Hong, K., Hui, P., McCaulay, S., McKelvey, K., Meiss, M. R., Patil, S., Peli, C., Pentchev, V., ... Menczer, F. (2016). OSoMe: The IUNI observatory on social media. *PeerJournal of Computer Science, 2,* e87.

Edwards, A., Housley, W., Williams, M., Sloan, L., & Williams, M. (2013). Digital social research, social media and the sociological imagination: Surrogacy, augmentation and re-orientation. *International Journal of Social Research Methodology, 16*(3), 245–260.

Gerritsen, C. (2020). Big data and criminology from an AI perspective. In B. Leclerc & J. Calle (Eds.), *Big Data*. Routledge.

González-Bailón, S. (2013). Social science in the era of big data. *Policy and Internet, 5*(2), 147–160.

Hayward, K. J., & Maas, M. M. (2020). Artificial intelligence and crime: A primer for criminologists. *Crime, Media, Culture,* 1741659020917434.

Holt, T. J., & Dupont, B. (2019). Exploring the factors associated with rejection from a closed cybercrime community. *International Journal of Offender Therapy and Comparative Criminology, 63*(8), 1127–1147.

Hughes, J., Aycock, S., Caines, A., Buttery, P., & Hutchings, A. (2020). Detecting trending terms in cybersecurity forum discussions. *Workshop on Noisy User-Generated Text (W-NUT)*.

Hughes, J., Collier, B., & Hutchings, A. (2019). From playing games to committing crimes: A multi-technique approach to predicting key actors on an online gaming forum. In *Proceedings of the APWG Symposium on Electronic Crime Research (eCrime)*. Pittsburgh.

Hutchings, A., & Pastrana, S. (2019). Understanding eWhoring. In *Proceedings of the 4th IEEE European Symposium on Security and Privacy*. Stockholm.

Kitchin, R. (2014). Big Data, new epistemologies and paradigm shifts. *Big Data and Society, 1*(1), 1–12.

Lazer, D., Pentland, A. S., Adamic, L., Aral, S., Barabasi, A. L., Brewer, D., Christakis, N., Contractor, N., Fowler, J., Gutmann, M., Jebara, T., King, G., Macy, M., Roy, D., & Van Alstyne, M. (2009). Computational social science. *Science (New York, NY), 323*(5915), 721.

Lazer, D., & Radford, J. (2017). Data ex machina: Introduction to big data. *Annual Review of Sociology, 43,* 19–39.

Lee, J. R., & Holt, T. J. (2020). The challenges and concerns of using big data to understand cybercrime. In B. Leclerc & J. Calle (Eds.), *Big Data*. Routledge.

Li, W., Chen, H., & Nunamaker, J. F., Jr. (2016). Identifying and profiling key sellers in cyber carding community: AZSecure text mining system. *Journal of Management Information Systems, 33*(4), 1059–1086.

Lynch, J. (2018). Not even our own facts: Criminology in the era of big data. *Criminology, 56*(3), 437–454.

Manyika, J. (2011). *Big data: The next frontier for innovation, competition, and productivity*. McKinsey Global Institute. Available at: http://www.mckinsey.com/Insights/MGI/Research/Technology_and_Innovation/Big_data_The_next_frontier_for_innovation.

Metzler, K., Kim, D. A., Allum, N., & Denman, A. (2016). Who is doing computational social science? In *Trends in big data research*.

Moore, T., Kenneally, E., Collett, M., & Thapa, P. (2019). Valuing cybersecurity research datasets. In *18th Workshop on the Economics of Information Security (WEIS)*.

Motoyama, M., McCoy, D., Levchenko, K., Savage, S., & Voelker, G. M. (2011). An analysis of underground forums. In *Proceedings of the 2011 ACM SIGCOMM Internet Measurement Conference* (pp. 71–80).

Nagin, D. S. (2005). *Group-based modeling of development*. Harvard University Press.

Narayanan, A., & Shmatikov, V. (2008). Robust de-anonymization of large sparse datasets. In *Proceedings of the IEEE Symposium on Security and Privacy (sp 2008)* (pp. 111–125).

Newman, G. R., & Clarke, R. V. (2003). *Superhighway robbery: Preventing E-commerce crime*. Willan.

Ozkan, T. (2019). Criminology in the age of data explosion: New directions. *The Social Science Journal, 56*(2), 208–219.

Pastrana, S., Hutchings, A., Caines, A., & Buttery, P. (2018a). Characterizing Eve: Analysing cybercrime actors in a large underground forum. In *Proceedings of the 21st International Symposium on Research in Attacks, Intrusions and Defenses (RAID)*. Heraklion.

Pastrana, S., Thomas, D. R., Hutchings, A., & Clayton, R. (2018b). CrimeBB: Enabling cybercrime research on underground forums at scale. In *Proceedings of the 2018 World Wide Web Conference* (pp. 1845–1854).

Pastrana, S., Hutchings, A., Thomas, D. R., & Tapiador, J. (2019). Measuring eWhoring. In *Proceedings of the ACM Internet Measurement Conference*. Amsterdam.

Pete, I., & Chua, Y. T. (2019). An assessment of the usability of cybercrime datasets. In *12th USENIX Workshop on Cyber Security Experimentation and Test (CSET 19)*.

Pete, I., Hughes, J., Bada, M., & Chua, Y. T. (2020). A social network analysis and comparison of six dark web forums. In *IEEE European Symposium on Security and Privacy (EuroS&PW) Workshop on Attackers and Cyber Crime Operations (WACCO)*.

Porcedda, M. G., & Wall, D. S. (2019). Cascade and chain effects in big data cybercrime: Lessons from the talktalk hack. In *IEEE European Symposium on Security and Privacy (EuroS&PW) Workshop on Attackers and Cyber Crime Operations (WACCO)* (pp. 443–452).

Smith, G. J., Bennett Moses, L., & Chan, J. (2017). The challenges of doing criminology in the big data era: Towards a digital and data-driven approach. *The British Journal of Criminology, 57*(2), 259–274.

Snaphaan, T., & Hardyns, W. (2019). Environmental criminology in the big data era. *European Journal of Criminology*, 1–22.

Snijders, C., Matzat, U., & Reips, U. D. (2012). "Big Data": Big gaps of knowledge in the field of internet science. *International Journal of Internet Science, 7*(1), 1–5.

Sweeney, L. (1997). Weaving technology and policy together to maintain confidentiality. *The Journal of Law, Medicine and Ethics, 25*(2–3), 98–110.

Thomas, D. R., Clayton, R., & Beresford, A. R. (2017). 1000 days of UDP amplification DDoS attacks. In *Proceedings of the 2017 APWG Symposium on Electronic Crime Research (eCrime)* (pp. 79–84). IEEE.

Tuckman, B. W. (1965). Developmental sequence in small groups. *Psychological Bulletin, 63*(6), 384.

Turk, K., Pastrana, S., & Collier, B. (2020) A tight scrape: Methodological approaches to cybercrime research data collection in adversarial environments. In *Proceedings of the IEEE European Symposium on Security and Privacy Workshop on Attackers and Cyber-Crime Operations (WACCO)*.

Vetterl, A., & Clayton, R. (2019). Honware: A virtual honeypot framework for capturing CPE and IoT zero days. In *Proceedings of the 2019 APWG Symposium on Electronic Crime Research (eCrime)* (pp. 1–13). IEEE.

Vu, A.V., Hughes, J., Pete, I., Collier, B., Chua, Y. T., Shumailov, I., & Hutchings, A. (2020). Turning up the dial: The evolution of a cybercrime market through set-up, stable, and COVID-19 eras. In *Proceedings of the ACM Internet Measurement Conference*. Pittsburgh.

Wang, F. Y., Carley, K. M., Zeng, D., & Mao, W. (2007). Social computing: From social informatics to social intelligence. *IEEE Intelligent Systems, 22*(2), 79–83.

Westlake, B. G., & Bouchard, M. (2016). Liking and hyperlinking: Community detection in online child sexual exploitation networks. *Social Science Research, 59,* 23–36.

Yar, M. (2005). The novelty of "Cybercrime": An assessment in light of routine activity theory. *European Journal of Criminology, 2*(4), 407–427.

11

Use of Artificial Intelligence to Support Cybercrime Research

Stuart E. Middleton

Introduction

Efficient processing of the ever-growing volume of cybercrime related posts, images, and videos appearing online is a significant challenge. In recent years, a multitude of artificial intelligence (AI) approaches relevant to cybercrime research has emerged, ranging from natural language processing for author attribution and information extraction to socio-technical AI approaches where the human is firmly in the loop. These AI approaches, and socio-technical AI approaches especially, can augment many of the existing manual cybercrime research methods outlined in some of the other chapters of this book. This chapter provides an overview of the major areas AI is helping with cybercrime research, some case studies where AI has been used for cybercrime research, and a

S. E. Middleton (✉)
School of Electronics and Computer Science, University of Southampton, Southampton, UK
e-mail: sem03@soton.ac.uk

© The Author(s), under exclusive license to Springer Nature Switzerland AG 2021
A. Lavorgna and T. J. Holt (eds.), *Researching Cybercrimes*,
https://doi.org/10.1007/978-3-030-74837-1_11

conclusion noting some of the main challenges that exist when using AI for cybercrime research.

When reading this chapter, it should be noted that in much of AI today training data is paramount, and many of the issues discussed in *Part 4* of this book (*Challenges and limitations of research datafication*) are amplified by the scale of processing that can be achieved with automated AI algorithms. The debate around AI training bias and misuse can often be seen in the news, such as mass surveillance and racial profiling concerns raised by companies like Amazon over use of facial recognition technology by law enforcement agencies. Recommendations such as formal AI reviews (Lavorgna et al., 2020) can help here, providing checklists prior to AI deployment so training data bias can be formally reviewed and understood, and the decision makers be made fully aware of the context in which AI evidence is produced.

Key Areas of Artificial Intelligence for Cybercrime Research

Facial Recognition Technology for Images and Video

Modern Facial Recognition Technology (FRT) can provide a sophisticated tool for identifying faces captured on images or videos from sources such as CCTV or social media. Typically, a face detection algorithm is trained using a large database of faces obtained from a variety of sources such as drivers' license databases, identity card records, criminal mug shot archives, or social media profile pages. The face detection algorithm is trained to recognize salient facial markers and can match markers in unknown faces to its database of known faces. Use of facial recognition technology by cybercrime researchers typically involves general surveillance, targeted photo comparisons, and active criminal case investigations (Hamann & Smith, 2019). The scientific reliability of facial recognition is not yet accepted for use as primary evidence in a court of law, so its application for cybercrime research has focused on investigation support leading to other evidence which is admissible in court.

Face detection algorithms have traditionally focused on techniques such as boosted decision trees which are fast to train but suffer from low accuracy. However, since 2015 deep learning approaches have significantly changed face detection research, with algorithms such as Faster Recurrent Convolutional Neural Networks (FRCNN) (Ren et al., 2017) and Single-Shot MultiBox Detector (SSD) (Liu et al., 2016) delivering significant advances in performance.

Known challenges for face detection (Zou et al., 2019) include *inter-class variation,* as human faces have a variety of skin tones, poses, expressions, and movement; *occlusion* of faces by objects such as clothing or other people; *multi-scale detection* of faces captured in images at different sizes; and *real-time detection* especially within video feeds. Figure 11.1 shows an example of a deep learning face detection algorithm delivering multi-scale face detection.

Object and Activity Detection from Images and Video

Automated object detection algorithms provide an effective means of automatically identifying objects from images and videos. Automation means that object detection can be deployed at scale, looking at potentially millions of images and endless hours of video content. Typical commercial applications (Zou et al., 2019) for object detection include pedestrian detection, face detection (as discussed previously), traffic sign and traffic light detection, handgun and knife detection and remote sensing target detection, such as military assets or surveillance targets in drone video feeds.

In cybercrime research, algorithms for human activity classification such as acts of violence are useful as well as techniques for object detection. Algorithms for handgun and knife detection have been applied to social media images and Closed-Circuit Television (CCTV) video footage (Warsi et al., 2020). Traditional non-neural algorithms include combinations of Harris Corner Detection (Derpanis, 2004) and Active Appearance Models (Cootes et al., 1998), which can achieve average detection precision of 84% for handguns (Tiwari & Verma, 2015) and 92% for knives (Glowacz et al., 2013). More recent deep

Fig. 11.1 Face detection of 800 faces out of the reportedly 1000 present. Deep learning-based detector confidence is indicated by box shade, with legend intensity bar on the right (Hu & Ramanan, 2017)

learning approaches do better still, with Recurrent Convolutional Neural Networks (FRCNN) (Verma & Dhillon, 2017) detecting handguns with up to 93% average precision. These approaches can handle about 7 frames per seconds (fps), but if faster detection is needed then the You Only Look Once (YOYO) algorithm (Redmon et al., 2016) can process images at 30 fps with an average precision of 70%. Deep learning approaches are also effective for human activity detection, such as deep multi-net Convolutional Neural Networks (Mumtaz et al., 2020) applied to violence recognition.

Known challenges for these applications include *dense and occluded images*, especially in real-world datasets where non-occluded rates are often around 29% (Dollar et al., 2009); *motion blur*, which occurs from on-board cameras which are in-motion; *weather and illumination effects*, such as sun glare, rain or snow; and *real-time detection*, especially for autonomous vehicles where decisions are made on sensor feeds in real time.

Audio Event Detection

Audio event detection, especially within noisy environments such as urban cities, is of interest for cybercrime research and law enforcement as it can identify audio events such as gunshots. Recent works have used datasets such as Urbansounds8k (Salamon et al., 2014) to train modes including Convolutional Neural Networks (Piczak, 2015) and Support Vector Machines (SVM) (Salamon et al., 2014) with recognition accuracies over 70%.

Challenges for environmental audio event detection (Chandrakala & Jayalakshmi, 2019) are *very small signal-to-noise ratios*, especially when the microphone is not located close to the acoustic source; *discriminative information existing in low frequency ranges*; and *environmental sounds with no specific structure*, such as is found with phonemes in human speech.

Author Attribution, Profiling and Information Extraction from Online Textual Posts

Being able to assign a true identity, or at least a demographic profile, of the author of an online document is important for any cybercrime research, and it is becoming more difficult with the now common-place use of technology such as the TOR onion router to avoid IP address tracing by law enforcement, and end-to-end encrypted direct messaging services such as WhatsApp. The problem of author attribution and profiling has been studied for a long time in the field of Natural Language Processing (NLP). Author attribution is usually split into either a closed-set attribution problem, where an unknown document is assigned an author from a set of known authors, or an open-set attribution where the author can be outside the known author set. Author profiling attempts to classify writing style according to demographics such as gender, age, or native country. Successful approaches (see, for instance, Kestemont et al., 2018) typically use an ensemble of Support Vector Machine (SVM) or Logistic Regression (LR) classifiers trained on character, word, and/or Parts of Speech (POS) n-gram features. Deep learning approaches tend not to be that successful due to the limited training data available per author. Challenges for author attribution and profiling are *cross-domain conditions*, when documents of known and unknown authorship come from different domains (e.g., thematic area or genre); *limited training examples for authors*, making it hard to assign authors to documents when they have only been seen a few times; and *attempts to obfuscate writing style*, such as deliberately using a different dialect.

Another useful area of NLP for cybercrime research is information extraction, including open event detection and entity/relation extraction. Open event detection is where relevant events are identified in a large corpus of documents, such as posts in an online forum. Closed-event detection is where examples of an event types are provided in advance. Early work in this area focused on feature engineering and statistical models (Hong et al., 2011), but more recent work has successfully explored deep learning approaches such as Convolutional Neural Networks (CNN) (Chen et al., 2015) and Graph Convolutional

Networks (GCN) (Pouran Ben Veyseh et al., 2019). More recent open event detection approaches include zero or few shot learning for event classification (Lai et al., 2020). Relation extraction aims to extract argument and predicate tuples from clausal grammatical structures within sentences, which can then be used to populate searchable knowledge bases. For example, the sentence "John is selling credit card dumps for $100, check out his latest offers" might generate a relation tuple (John; selling; credit card dumps for $100). Relation extraction is an active research area in NLP with approaches such as Piecewise CNN models (Smirnova & Cudré-Mauroux, 2018) and GCN's (Zhang et al., 2018) being explored, as well as approaches (Das et al., 2019) using word2vec and clustering of named entities within crime-related news posts. Open event and relation extraction challenges include *limited number of specific examples*, which can often lead to a need for few or zero-shot learning; *noisy training data*, especially if automatically annotated from a large corpus like Wikipedia using a distant supervision method; and *domain adaption*, where training and test data might be from different thematic areas.

Social Network Analysis, Data Mining, and Predictive Policing

Data mining techniques have been applied to historical crime data with the aim of discovering spatial and temporal patterns in criminal behavior, and predicting where future criminality is likely to occur to help focus law enforcement resources. Work on creating graphs of online criminal forum and social media posts has a long history (Xu & Chen, 2005), with recent approaches changing from manual visualization of criminal activity patterns toward crime data mining. Crime data mining includes entity extraction, clustering, association rule mining, classification, and social network analysis (SNA) (Chen et al., 2004). The CopLink project (Chen et al., 2004) is an example, where named entity extraction (of people, addresses, vehicles, and drug products) and a mix of hierarchical clustering and string matching-based identify disambiguation supports criminal network analysis for law enforcement applications. More recently the INSiGHT project (Hung et al., 2017) used nearest neighbor matching of person-focused subgraphs to compile suspicious activity reports around radicalization from government intelligence documents. Work involving social network analysis has usually utilized network centrality measures to identify key actors in a network. Examples include analysis of wiretapped contact data to explore the organizational structure of criminal groups (Natarajan, 2006), and analysis of drug trafficking networks focusing on the roles of key individuals (Bright & Delaney, 2013). Recent work has looked at the use of identifying codes to label graphs with specific topologies, such as binary cubes and trees, for analysis of drug trafficking network (Basu & Sen, 2019).

An interesting application of these approaches is predictive policing, which uses a mixture of methods including data mining and social network analysis alongside techniques such as audio event detection. A predictive policing experiment in Philadelphia 2015 looked at how the ShotSpotter (gunshot detection and localization commercial system) performed for "hot spot" policing (Ratcliffe et al., 2020). This work divided Philadelphia into city grid blocks, using Bayesian models and Markov Chain Monte Carlo simulations to predict the likelihood of both violent crime and property crime in an eight-hour time window. They found that the city block grids were too small to generate enough data for algorithms and defaulted to using larger city district block sizes. No statistically significant benefit was found from using the predictive policing models at this level of granularity.

The main challenges for crime data mining and predictive policing are focused on the *lack of fine-grained observation data* upon which to train models; and *efficient sub-graph classification* to reduce the number of nodes in complex networks that need to be analyzed.

Socio-technical Artificial Intelligence

Socio-technical AI systems offer the chance for "human in the loop" solutions, overcoming some of the problems associated with black box AI (Middleton et al., 2020a). When developing systems for combinations of AI and human researchers it is important to provide visualizations of results alongside underlying uncertainty, explainable results that enable human analysts or decision makers to understand them correctly, and repeatable results to allow confidence and trust to be developed when using AI algorithms over a period of time.

Often socio-technical AI solutions will be deployed in iterative workflows (Middleton et al. 2020b; Nouh et al., 2019), and the AI components will focus on learning and visualizing relevant but mundane patterns so cybercrime researchers can focus on subjective analysis which algorithms tend to struggle with. Efforts to develop explainable AI have seen approaches such as SHAP (Lundberg & Lee, 2017) and LIME (Ribeiro et al., 2016) used, training models to help explain black box AI algorithms. Alternatively, some algorithms such as decision trees or association mining offer a level of transparency in that underlying patterns and/or rules learnt can be understood by humans and directed inspected.

Known challenges in this area are *building inter-disciplinary teams* able to execute effectively socio-technical AI solutions; *representing the uncertainty associated with AI results*; and *trustworthiness in AI*, which often needs to be built over a period of time so decision makers are able to understand the strengths, weaknesses, and bias of AI systems in the field.

Case Studies

This section provides two concrete examples of research projects developing socio-technical AI methods for cybercrime research. The first case study is from the FloraGuard project (Lavorgna et al., 2020), and focuses on a socio-technical AI approach to help scale up the criminological analysis of the online illegal plant trade. The second case study is from the CYShadowWatch project (UK Defence and Security Accelerator funded contract ACC2005442) and focuses on cross-lingual information extraction to support intelligence analysis around online transnational crime.

Socio-technical Artificial Intelligence to Analyze the Online Illegal Plant Trade

The FloraGuard project (Lavorgna et al., 2020) ran a series of two experiments using a socio-technical AI approach (Middleton et al., 2020b) to develop intelligence packages centered around online vendors who were likely to be engaged in criminal behavior associated with the illegal trade of endangered plant species. The first focused on the species of *Ariocarpus* (cacti), and the second on species of *Euphorbia* (succulents) and *Saussurea costus* (thistle). The idea was to target Web sites with a lot of perfectly legal discussions and adverts for plant to trade, and try to identify people engaging in illegal activity "hiding in plain sight" in niche discussion threads that would otherwise be very hard to find. An inter-disciplinary team was setup for each experiment, consisting of a criminologist, a computer scientist, and a conservation scientist to provide domain expertise. Project partners Royal Botanic Gardens, Kew and UK Border Force helped evaluate the work.

Each experiment ran over a one-week period, with a criminologist using Bing searches to identify forums and marketplaces where posts contained mentions of species of interest. A preliminary criminology analysis was performed, manually browsing posts from 100's of authors to identify an initial set of suspect vendors per species. Next a series of iterations was executed, repeated until the final intelligence product was produced. The computer scientist would take target suspects identified by the criminologist and use AI tools to (a) crawl the HTML webpages of forums and marketplaces, (b) parse posts to extract text and metadata, and (c) extract from each post's text relevant named entities to build a directed intelligence graph for each target suspect. Extracted named entity types were focused on UK law enforcement and Home Office standard POLE entities (People, Object, Location, and Events). These target-focused intelligence graphs were then visualized and the criminologist was able to use them, in addition to extra manual browsing and checking of original posts containing visualized entities, to expand and/or filter the suspect target list ready for the next iteration.

The socio-technical AI workflow used is shown in Fig. 11.2. For crawling the open-source DARPA MEMEX undercrawler tool was used.

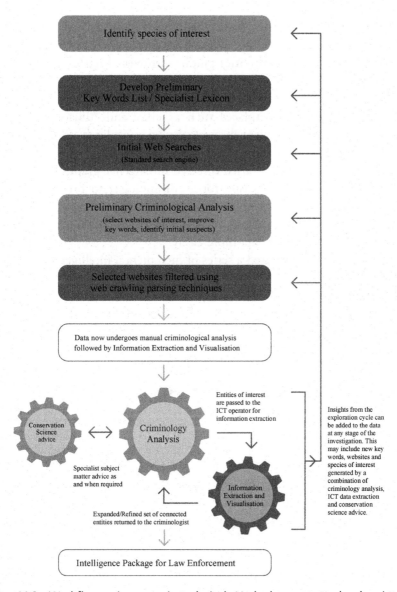

Fig. 11.2 Workflow using a socio-technical AI deployment to develop intelligence packages around the online illegal plant trade (Lavorgna et al., 2020)

Standard Python libraries were used for parsing HTML webpages, and the Stanford CoreNLP tool used for the named entity extraction task. The directed named entity graphs were visualized using a Python network-based open-source intel-viz tool (Middleton et al., 2020b). In total, nine Web sites were analyzed, providing 13,697 posts from 4009 authors including marketplaces such as eBay and Alibaba. For each species 4 or 5 vendors were discovered who were likely to be engaged in illegal trade activity.

An example of target-focused directed intelligence graphs can be seen in Fig. 11.3. To make it easier for a criminologist to process 100's of connected entities on a graph the nodes were color coded by entity type. The visualization was interactive, allowing it to be zoomed in and panned around to explore dense data more easily.

This case study generated a series of incremental intelligence packages relating to target suspects and their connected entities. In its raw form this type of intelligence package would not reach the evidential standard required to be presented in a court of law, but would be very useful for focusing law enforcement activity such as a full investigation or planning interventions aimed at disruption of illegal activity.

Cross-lingual Information Extraction from Online Cybercrime Forums

The CYShadowWatch project (UK Defence and Security Accelerator funded contract ACC2005442) explored how deep learning AI models for cross-lingual information extraction could be used to support analysis workflows around online transnational crime. The project included the UK's National Crime Agency (NCA) and Defence Science and Technology Laboratory (DSTL) who helped evaluate the work. Much modern online cybercrime activity exists in an online space that spans national borders and involves content written in many different languages. Law enforcement agencies have access to limited resources in terms of both human translators and intelligence analysis specialists. The large volume of online content that might be relevant to a specific case represents a real challenge, and AI technology is an obvious candidate

Fig. 11.3 Target-focused directed intelligence graph showing the target suspect (root node) and connected POLE entities such as locations, associated people, and traded plant species (Middleton et al., 2020b). Named of people have been hashed to pseudonymize the data

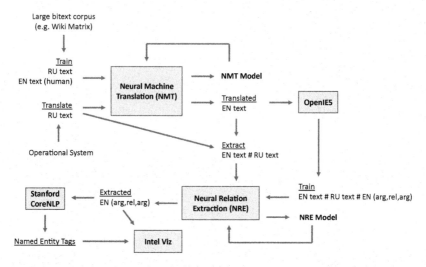

Fig. 11.4 Workflow for AI deployment targeting transnational online cybercrime forums and Web sites. Information pipeline includes Neural Machine Translation (NMT) and Neural Relational Extraction (NRE) which feeds sociotechnical AI intelligence tools to develop intelligence packages for law enforcement

to act as a "force multiplier" allowing individual cybercrime researchers to monitor orders of magnitude more cyberspace area that they would using manual analysis techniques alone.

The AI workflow developed is shown in Fig. 11.4. A combination of Neural Machine Translation (NMT) and Neural Relation Extraction (NRE) algorithms was used to provide an intelligence pipeline translating and then extracting English language intelligence from a stream of Russian language textual cybercrime posts. The intelligence visualization used the socio-technical AI tools developed in the FloraGuard project describes in the previous section and focused on summaries using extracted POLE entities.

The NMT model takes as input a corpus of Russian sentences and translates them into English. For training a Russian-English (RU-EN) bitext corpus sourced from WikiMatrix (Schwenk et al., 2019) and a professionally translated dataset of Russian cybercrime forum posts was used. The core NMT model was based on the architecture of Bhadanau and colleagues (2014) and Luong and colleagues (Luong et al., 2015a), which used a stacked Long Short-Term Memory (LSTM) encoder, attention layer, and a beam-search decoder. NMT systems have a limited vocabulary due to memory constraints on the Graphical Processing Unit (GPU) hardware they run on, and this NMT had a 50,000-word vocabulary. A rare word encoding scheme (Luong et al., 2015b) was used for words outside this vocabulary, based on a fallback translation dictionary computed automatically using the IBM *fast_align* statistical word alignment model (Dyer et al., 2013).

The NRE model takes as input a pair of sentences (English, Russian), consisting of the translated English sentence and the original Russian sentence, and transforms it into arguments and predicate tuples based on the clausal structures present in sentence grammar. For example, a Russian sentence translated into "I am releasing a new version of STUXNET" would be converted into tuple (I am; releasing; a new version of STUXNET). The model is a cross-lingual extension of the encoder-decoder framework from (Cui et al., 2018), trained using an annotated NMT bitext training corpus using the OpenIE5 relation extraction tool (which supports English sentences only). The NRE model consists of an encoder with stacked bidirectional LSTM layers, an attention layer, and decoder with stacked LSTM layers and used a source to target copy mechanism to handle out-of-vocabulary (OOV) words proposed by (See et al., 2017).

This case study produced a prototype information extraction pipeline that could be fed text by a real-time information stream from law enforcement sources. Its primary role was to help scale up transnational intelligence pre-filtering by law enforcement officers and/or cybercrime researchers, allowing human analysts to triage Open-Source Intelligence (OSINT) with much greater coverage than would normally be possible with manual methods.

Conclusion

There are many AI methods available to cybercrime researchers today. It is important to be mindful of the challenges that each method presents, many of which are highlighted in this chapter. Challenge areas are around *training data* (e.g., dense and occluded images, weather and illumination effects, very small signal-to-noise ratios, limited training examples for authors), the *deployment environment* (e.g., real-time detection, environmental sounds with no specific structure, cross-domain conditions, and domain adaption), handling *sources of uncertainty* (e.g., representing uncertainty and building trustworthiness), and the ways in which *AI results can be potentially subverted* (e.g., attempts to obfuscate writing style, use of bots to target AI algorithms with fake news/reviews).

Practical advice for those seeking to adopt AI in their research would include (a) review the amount of expertise required to deploy an algorithm if you are not buying it in via a commercial company, (b) perform an AI review before deployment to understand issues such as training data bias, and (c) consider how you might include the AI method in your existing analysis methodology and if a socio-technical AI approach is needed. Overall, there is a lot of benefit to be gained from using AI in cybercrime research and it is likely these benefits will only increase as the technology develops making this a growing area of interest in the years to come.

References

Bahdanau, D., Cho, K., & Bengio, Y. (2014). *Neural machine translation by jointly learning to align and translate.* arXiv.org. http://arxiv.org/abs/1409.0473.

Basu, K., & Sen, A. (2019). Monitoring individuals in drug trafficking organizations: A social network analysis. In *IEEE/ACM International Conference on Advances in Social Networks Analysis and Mining (ASONAM)*. https://doi.org/10.1145/3341161.3342938.

Bright, D. A., & Delaney, J. J. (2013). Evolution of a drug trafficking network: Mapping changes in network structure and function across time. *Global Crime, 14*(2–3), 238–260.

Chandrakala, S., & Jayalakshmi, S. L. (2019). Environmental audio scene and sound event recognition for autonomous surveillance: A survey and comparative studies. *ACM Computing Surveys, 52*(3), Article 63. https://doi.org/10. 1145/3322240.

Chen, H., Chung, W., Xu, J. J., Wang, G., Qin, Y., & Chau, M. (2004). Crime data mining: A general framework and some examples. *Computer, 37*(4), 50–56.

Chen, Y., Xu, L., Liu, K., Zeng, D., & Zhao, J. (2015). Event extraction via dynamic multipooling convolutional neural networks. In *ACL/IJCNLP-2015*.

Cootes, T. F., Edwards, G. J., & Taylor, C. J. (1998). Active appearance models. In *European Conference on Computer Vision*.

Cui, L., Wei, F., & Zhou, M. (2018). Neural open information extraction. *ACL-2018*, Association for Computational Linguistics. https://www.aclweb. org/anthology/P18-2065/.

Das, P., Das, A. K., Nayak, J., Pelusi, D., & Ding, W. (2019). A graph based clustering approach for relation extraction from crime data. *IEEE Access, 7*. https://doi.org/10.1109/ACCESS.2019.2929597.

Derpanis, K. G. (2004). *The Harris corner detector.* http://www.cse.yorku.ca/ ~kosta/CompVis_Notes/harris_detector.pdf.

Dollar, P., Wojek, C., Schiele, B., & Perona, P. (2009). Pedestrian detection: A benchmark. In *IEEE Conference on Computer Vision and Pattern Recognition*. https://doi.org/10.1109/CVPR.2009.5206631.

Dyer, C., Chahuneau, V., & Smith, N.A. (2013). A simple, fast, and effective reparameterization of IBM Model 2. *NAACL 2013*, Association for Computational Linguistics. https://www.aclweb.org/anthology/N13-1073.

Glowacz, A., Kmieć, M., & Dziech, A. (2013). Visual detection of knives in security applications using Active Appearance Models. *Multimedia Tools and Applications, 74*(12), 4253–4267.

Hamann, K., & Smith, R. (2019). Facial recognition technology: Where will it take us? *American Bar Association*. Available at: https://www.americanbar. org/groups/criminal_justice/publications/criminal-justice-magazine/2019/ spring/facial-recognition-technology.

Hong, Y., Zhang, J., Ma, B., Yao, J., Zhou, G., & Zhu, Q. (2011). Using cross-entity inference to improve event extraction. In *Proceedings of the 49th Annual Meeting of the Association for Computational Linguistics: Human Language Technologies*. ACL.

Hu, P., & Ramanan, D. (2017). Finding tiny faces. In *IEEE Conference on Computer Vision and Pattern Recognition (CVPR)*. https://doi.org/10.1109/CVPR.2017.166.

Hung, B. W. K., Jayasumana, A. P., & Bandara, V. W. (2017). INSiGHT: A system for detecting radicalization trajectories in large heterogeneous graphs. In *IEEE International Symposium on Technologies for Homeland Security (HST)* (pp. 1–7). Waltham, MA.

Kestemont, M., Tschuggnall, M., Stamatatos, E., Daelemans, W., Specht, G., Stein, B., & Potthast, M. (2018). Overview of the author identification task at PAN-2018: Cross-domain authorship attribution and style change detection. In L. Cappellato, N. Ferro, J. Y. Nie, & L. Soulier (Eds.), *Working Notes Papers of the CLEF 2018 Evaluation Labs Volume 2125 of CEUR Workshop Proceedings*. ISSN 1613–0073.

Lai, V. D., Nguyen, T. H., & Dernoncourt, F. (2020). Extensively matching for few-shot learning event detection. In *Proceedings of the First Joint Workshop on Narrative Understanding*. Storylines, and Events, ACL.

Lavorgna, A., Middleton, S. E., Whitehead, D., & Cowell, C. (2020). *FloraGuard, tackling the illegal trade in endangered plants: Project report*. Royal Botanic Gardens.

Liu, W., Anguelov, D., Erhan, D., Szegedy, C., Reed, S., Fu, C. Y., & Berg, A. C. (2016). *SSD: Single shot multibox detector*. Springer.

Lundberg, S. M., & Lee, S. (2017). A unified approach to interpreting model predictions. In *Proceedings of the 31st International Conference on Neural Information Processing Systems (NIPS'17)*. Curran Associates Inc.

Luong, T., Pham, H., & Manning, C. D. (2015a). Effective approaches to attention-based neural machine translation. *EMNLP 2015*, Association for Computational Linguistics. https://www.aclweb.org/anthology/D15-1166/.

Luong, T., Sutskever, I., Le, Q., Vinyals, O., & Zaremba, W. (2015b). Addressing the rare word problem in neural machine translation. *ACL-2015*, Association for Computational Linguistics. https://www.aclweb.org/anthology/P15-1002/.

Middleton, S. E., Lavorgna, A., & McAlister, R. (2020a). STAIDCC20: 1st international workshop on socio-technical AI systems for defence, cybercrime and cybersecurity. In *12th ACM Conference on Web Science (WebSci '20 Companion)*. ACM. https://doi.org/10.1145/3394332.3402897.

Middleton, S. E., Lavorgna, A., Neumann, G., & Whitehead, D. (2020b). Information extraction from the long tail: A socio-technical AI approach for criminology investigations into the online illegal plant trade. In *12th ACM Conference on Web Science Companion (WebSci '20)*. Association for Computing Machinery. https://doi.org/10.1145/3394332.3402838.

Mumtaz, A., Sargano, A. B., & Habib, Z. (2020). Fast learning through deep multi-net CNN model for violence recognition in video surveillance. *The Computer Journal*. https://doi.org/10.1093/comjnl/bxaa061.

Natarajan, M. (2006). Understanding the structure of a large heroin distribution network: A quantitative analysis of qualitative data. *Journal of Quantitative Criminology, 22*(2), 171–192.

Nouh, M., Nurse, J. R. C., Webb, H., & Goldsmith, M. (2019). Cybercrime investigators are users too! Understanding the sociotehnical challenges faced by law enforcement. In *Proceedings of the 2019 Workshop on Usable Security (USEC) at the Network and Distributed System Security Symposium (NDSS)*.

Piczak, K. J. (2015). Environmental sound classification with convolutional neural networks. In *Proceedings of the 25th IEEE International Workshop on Machine Learning for Signal Processing (MLSP'15)*.

Pouran Ben Veyseh, A., Nguyen, T. H., & Dou, D. (2019). Graph based neural networks for event factuality prediction using syntactic and semantic structures. In *Proceedings of the 57th Annual Meeting of the Association for Computational Linguistics*. ACL.

Ratcliffe, J. H., Taylor, R. B., Askey, A. P., Thomas, K., Grasso, J., Bethel, K. J., Fisher, R., & Koehnlein, J. (2020). The Philadelphia predictive policing experiment. *Journal of Experimental Criminology*. https://doi.org/10.1007/s11292-019-09400-2.

Redmon, J., Divvala, S., Girshick, R., & Farhadi, A. (2016). You only look once: Unified, real-time object detection. In *IEEE Conference on Computer Vision and Pattern Recognition (CVPR)*. https://doi.org/10.1109/CVPR.2016.91.

Ren, S., He, K., Girshick, R., & Sun, J. (2017). Faster r-cnn: Towards real-time object detection with region proposal networks. *IEEE Transactions on Pattern Analysis and Machine Intelligence, 6*, 1137–1149.

Ribeiro, M. T., Singh, S., & Guestrin, C. (2016) "Why Should I Trust You?": Explaining the predictions of any classifier. In *Proceedings of the 22nd ACM SIGKDD International Conference on Knowledge Discovery and Data Mining (KDD '16)*. Association for Computing Machinery. https://doi.org/10.1145/2939672.2939778.

Salamon, J., Jacoby, C., & Bello, J. P. (2014). A dataset and taxonomy for urban sound research. In *Proceedings of the 22nd ACM International Conference on Multimedia* (pp. 1041–1044). ACM.

Schwenk, H., Chaudhary, V., Sun, S., Gong, H., & Guzmán, F. (2019). *WikiMatrix: Mining 135M parallel sentences in 1620 language pairs from Wikipedia*. arXiv.org. https://arxiv.org/abs/1907.05791v2.

See, A., Liu, P. J., & Manning, C. D. (2017). Get to the point: Summarization with pointer generator networks. *ACL-2017*, Association for Computational Linguistics. http://aclweb.org/anthology/P17-1099.

Smirnova, A., & Cudré-Mauroux, P. (2018). Relation extraction using distant supervision: A survey. *ACM Computer Surveys, 51*(5), Article 106. https://doi.org/10.1145/3241741.

Tiwari, R. K., & Verma, G. K. (2015). A computer vision based framework for visual gun detection using Harris interest point detector. In *Eleventh International Multi-conference on Information Processing-2015 (IMCIP-2015)*.

Verma, G. K., & Dhillon, A. (2017). A handheld gun detection using faster R-CNN deep learning. In *7th International Conference on Computer and Communication Technology (ICCCT-2017)*. https://doi.org/10.1145/315 4979.3154988.

Warsi, A., Abdullah, M., Husen, M. N., & Yahya, M. (2020). Automatic handgun and knife detection algorithms: A review. In *14th International Conference on Ubiquitous Information Management and Communication (IMCOM)*. https://doi.org/10.1109/IMCOM48794.2020.9001725.

Xu, J., & Chen, H. (2005). Criminal network analysis and visualization. *Communications of the ACM, 48*(6), 100–107.

Zhang, Y., Qi, P., & Manning, C. D. (2018). Graph convolution over pruned dependency trees improves relation extraction. *EMNLP 2018*, Association for Computational Linguistics. https://www.aclweb.org/anthology/D18-1244.

Zou, Z., Shi, Z., Guo, Y., & Ye, J. (2019). *Object detection in 20 years: A survey.* arXiv:1905.05055.

12

Honeypots for Cybercrime Research

Robert C. Perkins and C. Jordan Howell

Introduction

The English proverb "You catch more flies with honey than with vinegar" exemplifies the foundational underpinning surrounding honeypots in the context of cybersecurity. In the same fashion, a fly can be lured into a trap with honey, it is believed that a cyber-offender can be baited into a honeypot system with proper allurement. Much like real-world sting operations, honeypots can be used to analyze the behavior of

R. C. Perkins (✉) · C. J. Howell
Department of Criminal Justice and Criminology, Georgia State University, Atlanta, Georgia, United States of America
e-mail: rperkins14@student.gsu.edu

C. J. Howell
e-mail: cjhowell@utep.edu

C. J. Howell
Department of Criminal Justice, The University of Texas at El Paso, El Paso, Texas, USA

A. Lavorgna and T. J. Holt (eds.), *Researching Cybercrimes*, https://doi.org/10.1007/978-3-030-74837-1_12

233

cyberthreats and hinder their activity. Sting operations are often utilized by law enforcement to not only assist criminal investigations, but to also deter criminal activity. The Center for Problem-Oriented Policing (Newman & Socia, 2007) outlines four underlying features that generally make up any sting operation: (1) The creation or exploitation of a criminogenic opportunity by police; (2) An identified criminal target and/or group; (3) Covert operations by law enforcement; and (4) A "Gotcha!" moment which culminates into an arrest. An example of a sting operation designed and deployed to apprehend auto thieves would work as follows: Law enforcement would first formulate and set up an opportunity to allure this type of criminal. Next, they may opt to simply leave a lavish vehicle unlocked in a predetermined location to monitor. Once a suspect is identified and begins to unlawfully interact with the vehicle, law enforcement spring from cover and apprehend the suspect. In this scenario, the lavish vehicle functioned as the bait. It was left alone for the sole purpose of deceiving and alluring an offender to engage with it. The offender showed up and interacted with the vehicle—clearly identifying their criminal intent. Next, police broke their observational cover and arrested the suspect in a "Gotcha!" climactic moment.

Despite being more technologically complex and sophisticated than real-world police sting operations, honeypots and sting operations are conceptually analogous. On the one hand, sting operations can be described as a deceptive operation which utilizes resources in a covert manner to investigate criminal behavior and mitigate crime. On the other hand, honeypots can be described as a deceptive security tool which utilizes computer resources in a covert manner to monitor malicious behavior online (Spitzner, 2002). Much like how a fly is lured by honey and how an auto thief is enticed by an abandoned and lavish vehicle, honeypots lure cyber-criminals by emulating cybersecurity flaws and known network vulnerabilities. Once a hacker is detected compromising a honeypot system, the honeypot engages and begins monitoring the intruder's activity. Although honeypots originated as a cybersecurity tool used to detect and mitigate intrusive cyberthreats, they have received a considerable amount of scholarly attention over the past two decades. For instance, computer scientists have developed many variations of honeypots with different capabilities and functionalities (e.g.,

Bringer et al., 2012; Fan et al., 2017; Nawrocki et al., 2016), whereas criminologists have weighed in on a honeypot's utility for conducting research and impacting policy (viz. Bossler, 2017; Holt, 2017; Howell & Burruss, 2020; Steinmetz, 2017). In the following section, the historical development of honeypots and how they emerged as a valuable tool in the cybersecurity community are discussed.

Background

In the early 1990s, honeypots were intellectually conceived through true events described in Clifford Stoll's (1990) *The Cuckoo's Egg* and Bill Cheswick's (1992) *An Evening with Berferd*. Each book, respectively, tells the author's efforts to monitor a hacker intruding within their computer networks. In *The Cuckoo's Egg*, Stoll discovered a discrepancy stemming from an unauthorized user who acquired access to their network by exploiting a vulnerability in their e-mail service. In lieu of blocking the user out of their system, Stoll opted to monitor their activities to learn more about their behavior and identity. This was accomplished by supplying their own comprised computer systems with fictitious information (i.e., financial and national security documents). By distracting the hacker with alluring, yet deceitful information, authorities were provided with enough time to identify and apprehend the individual (Stoll, 1990). In *An Evening with Berferd*, Chewick discusses his team's efforts in developing an intentionally comprisable computer network system to trick a hacker lurking in their system. They utilized a vulnerable computer system as a means to "Watch [the hacker] keystrokes, … trace [them], learn [their] techniques, and warn [their] victims" (Cheswick, 1992, p. 8). Although they were never able to fully identify the hacker (only known as "Berferd"), the team was able to learn considerable information about the perpetrator's behavior. By circumventing the hacker using technologically deceptive means, Stoll and Chewick were able to develop a much better understanding of the hackers' activities and behaviors. Although the subtle tactics used served as the conceptual foundation for present-day honeypot systems, it was not until several years later that this type of cybersecurity system would come to fruition.

In 1997, Fred Cohen developed "The Deception Toolkit" (DTK), the first honeypot-like system (Spitzner, 2002) advertised to "give defenders … [an] advantage over attackers" by using deception to "make it appear to [hackers] as if the system … has a large number of widely known vulnerabilities" (Cohen, 1998). The following year, the first publicly available honeypot system, CyberCop Sting (CCS), was released by Alfred Huger for commercial use (Spitzner, 2002). Although the CCS fell short in becoming a mainstream product at the time, the innovations it introduced have served as a stepping-stone for more advanced honeypot systems that were later developed. These include Marcus Ranum's Back-Officer Friendly (BOF) (Spitzner, 2002) and Martin Roesch's Snort (Roesch, 1999). By this point, honeypots demonstrated their utility and captivated the cybersecurity community. However, what remained absent was any form of systematic effort to begin researching what these network security tools can truly offer.

This changed in 1999 when a small body of researchers with a shared interest in studying honeypots and network security began collaborating. Since many different areas of expertise are involved with honeypots (i.e., computer scientists, forensic scientists, and social scientists) the group recognized the need for more robust and diverse body of people. Following successful recruitment efforts, they formally established themselves as a non-profit, security-research organization called the *Honeynet Project* (HP) (Spitzner, 2002). In fact, the term "Honeypot" made its first academic debut in the early 2000s (Even, 2000; Spitzner & Roesch, 2001) through the group's efforts. The HP's mission predominately focused on improving internet safety by studying the attacks perpetrated by the blackhat community (Honeynet Project, 2020). To facilitate their efforts, the group developed a honeypot system called the "Honeynet". Unlike this honeypot's predecessors, the Honeynet was unique in that it could emulate multiple honeypot systems in a manner that resembled its own computer network. Not only did this provide a way to "cover more ground" in terms of monitoring network activity, but it also served as a means to fabricate artificial networks (Spitzner, 2002). This was a major boon for the group, as they now had the ability to better understand the "tools, tactics, and motives of the blackhat community" (Spitzner, 2002, p. 243) in highly controlled environments designed at their full discretion.

Following the inaugural success of the HP, the group quickly became a prominent figure within the cybersecurity community in their efforts to advocate the "awareness, credibility, and value of honeypots" (Spitzner, 2002, p. 56). They began publicly releasing a series of white-page security reports entitled "Know Your Enemy". This helped HP attain a global presence, as group chapters became established in dozens of countries around the world including France, the United Arab Emirates, Mexico, and the UK (Honeynet Project, 2020). As a result, the HP was better equipped in their efforts toward advancing the capabilities of honeypots. By the end of the decade, the HP's efforts had left a significant impact on the future of honeypots and network security. With the help of the Honeynet, the group exemplified the highly configurable nature of honeypots as well as their potential to address and analyze online threats. Overtime, other groups became involved, including the Leurre Project (Leita et al., 2008), the European Network of Affined Honeypots (NOAH-Project) (Markatos & Anagnostakis, 2008), the mw-collect Alliance (Baecher et al., 2016), and Deutsche Telekom (Telekom, 2021). As honeypots continued to gain traction within the cybersecurity community, many different types of honeypots began to emerge. Resultingly, a number of classifications have been introduced to characterize the various types.

Characterizing Honeypots

Honeypots are versatile cybersecurity systems that can possess multiple capabilities. In and of itself, however, honeypots are not a catch all cybersecurity solution. Regardless, honeypots can be heavily tailored to address an array of cybersecurity roles (Spitzner, 2002). In fact, their multi-functionality has naturally resulted in a moderate number of classifications over the past twenty years (Fan et al., 2017; Nawrocki et al., 2016). Among the most straightforward of these is whether a honeypot is used for commercial (e.g., to deal with common forms of malware) or investigative (e.g., to analyze new forms of malware) purposes (Spitzner, 2001). However, most classifications among computer scientists have addressed the more idiosyncratic characteristics of honeypots, such as the nature of their deployment and how they respond to cyberthreats. For instance, honeypots have been categorized based on whether they are deployed alone or in groups called honeynets (Spitzner, 2003). Moreover, they have been described based on their degree of interaction (i.e., low, medium, or high) with detected cyberthreats (Spitzner, 2003). Despite varying classifications introduced within the literature, Fan et al. (2017, p. 3907) recognized a "lack of a distinct method" that could more intuitively "catch the key points" of these different honeypots to help facilitate "new insights … research and development". Their study addressed this problem by introducing a honeypot taxonomy that describes not only the deceitful components (decoy) of a honeypot, but also its security components (captor). Both the decoy and captor aspects of a honeypot are crucial to the honeypot's modus operandi.

Decoy Aspects of Honeypots

The decoy characteristics of a honeypot can be broadly described as the different resources utilized from computers and network systems in a honeypot's design and function (Fan et al., 2017). These characteristics vary in nature and address matters such as whether the honeypot is deployed using a virtual machine or whether it is operating on the client- or server-side of a computer network. In essence, there are various resources and known vulnerabilities that honeypots take advantage of as a means to lure and analyze cyberthreats. Currently, there are several defining characteristics that constitute the design of honeypot decoys. These include: (1) *fidelity*; (2) *scalability*; (3) *adaptability*; (4) *role*; (5) *physicality*; (6) *deployment strategy*; and (7) *resource type*.

The first decoy characteristic of a honeypot is its *fidelity* (Spitzner, 2002). This characteristic is described as a honeypot's level of interaction (or communication) between a given computer network system and a cyberthreat. The level of interactive honeypot needed is largely dependent on an organization's cybersecurity needs as the functional capacity for each honeypot level varies. The interactive levels of honeypot interaction include: (1) low-interaction; (2) medium-interaction; and (3) high-interaction. These levels directly reflect how much network privilege is granted to an invasive cyberthreat. For instance, on the one hand, a high-interaction honeypot (HIH) will grant a cyberthreat much greater network privilege, and in turn generate much more information about the intrusion. However, HIHs can be double-edged. The more network privilege granted to a cyberthreat, the more damage they are capable of causing. On the other hand, low-interaction honeypots (LIHs), as the name implies, operate with the lowest degree of interactive capabilities with cyberthreats (Fan et al., 2017). They are simple in both functionality and deployment. This type of honeypot emulates operating systems and other routine network services. Resultingly, their use is often limited to passive observations and the generation of statistical evaluations (Nawrocki et al., 2016).

The second decoy characteristic of a honeypot is its *scalability*. A honeypot's scalability directly reflects its capability to support additional decoys within a computer network. In particular, scalable honeypots are capable of deploying and monitoring multiple decoys whereas an unscalable honeypot can only carry out such activities using a fixed, predetermined number of decoys. For example, a honeypot can be described as unscalable when only capable of monitoring no more than one server at a time (Portokalidis et al., 2006). However, when the honeypot is capable of monitoring over several servers simultaneously, it can be described as scalable (Spitzner, 2005).

The third decoy characteristic of a honeypot is its *adaptability*. This refers to the honeypot's capability of being static or dynamic in its functionality. Specifically, a static honeypot will perform a fixed set of tasks as programmed (Poeplau & Gassen, 2012; Spitzner, 2003), whereas a dynamic honeypot is programmed to be much more flexible in its response to external stimuli (e.g., cyberthreats or researcher configuration) (Do Carmo et al., 2011; Rist, 2009). This concept can be more intuitively understood when comparing calculators to smartphones. Simply put, a calculator's use is fixed to computing mathematics, whereas a smartphone is much more flexible in its ability to perform other functions (e.g., mathematics, telecommunication, photography).

In the context of malicious activity being detected on a network, a static honeypot will respond in a preprogrammed manner. However, a dynamic honeypot's response is not fixed, but instead adaptable to configurable criteria. For example, a dynamic honeypot's response can be programmed to vary based upon different forms of malware detected.

The fourth decoy characteristic of a honeypot is its *role* (Seifert et al., 2007). This refers to a honeypot's operational location within a client–server system. In network computing, the client–server system can be described as a communicative digital network that exchange data. Specifically, clients send requests to servers, which in turn, respond to the request initiated by client systems (Oluwatosin, 2014). This can be illustrated by a student using his/her personal computer (the client system) to sign-in to their university's online library (the server system). In the context of honeypots, a honeypot can be deployed to actively monitor either the client- or server-side of such computer network systems. Server honeypots are typically passive, monitoring server-traffic until suspicious activity is detected. Client honeypots are typically more proactive, as they will pursue and engage with suspicious activity (Nawrocki et al., 2016).

The fifth decoy characteristic of a honeypot is its *physicality* (Provos, 2004). This term refers to the honeypot's state of being physical or virtual in nature. Simply put, honeypots can be placed across both physical and virtual environments. For instance, a honeypot can be recognized as being physical if situated onto a physical computer. In this context, the computer itself becomes the honeypot and functions accordingly. In contrast, a honeypot can be recognized as being virtual if situated onto a virtual machine (VM), which can be best described as a computer within a computer (Provos & Holz, 2007).

The sixth decoy characteristic of a honeypot is its *deployment strategy* (Fan et al., 2017). Much like how a multi-purpose tool offers different means to execute tasks, so too are there different methods that a honeypot can use in response to different security and investigative needs. Whereas the five aforementioned characteristics describe a honeypot's inherently programmed features, a honeypot's deployment strategy describes the manner in which the honeypot itself is utilized.

Throughout the past twenty years, several strategies have garnered recognition among computer scientists and security specialist. These include: (1) *sacrificial lamb*; (2) *deception ports*; (3) *proximity decoys*; (4) *minefield*; and (5) *redirection shield*. *Sacrificial lamb* is the deployment of a honeypot without any form of connection to the production (or protected) network. It waits until a computer network is compromised before conducting any form of in-depth analysis (Bailey et al., 2004; Poeplau & Gassen, 2012). *Deception port* is the camouflage of a honeypot within a production network (e.g., by disguising itself as a routine operating system service). This deployment strategy is utilized as a means to confuse and hinder cyberthreat activity (Pa et al., 2015; Podhradsky et al., 2012). *Proximity decoys* is the deployment of a honeypot on the same computer system as a production network. This deployment strategy may involve the duplication of the production network's structural composition. By doing so, this provides the honeypot a simpler means of rerouting or trapping intrusive cyberthreats (Leita & Dacier, 2008; Provos, 2004). The *Minefield* strategy refers to the deployment of a large number of honeypots within or around a computer network. Conceptually, these honeypots act much like real landmines. Upon contact (e.g., from an intruding cyberthreat), these honeypots "explode" and begin collecting information about whatever triggered them (Cui et al., 2006). *Redirection shield* functions much like a security checkpoint. Before any internet traffic enters a protected production network, the traffic is analyzed using intrusion detection software. Any suspicious traffic will be re-directed to the honeypot instead of the production network (Anagnostakis et al., 2005). In sum, each of these deployment strategies illustrates the different approaches in which honeypots can be utilized as a security tool on a given computer system or network.

The final decoy characteristic of a honeypot is its *resource type*. Comparable to the different resources people use to engage with internet-related technologies, this characteristic refers to the type of computer system utilized by the honeypot for a cyberthreat to attack and compromise. For instance, several computer system resource types are recognized among mainstream computer scientists. These include (but are not limited to): (1) *Web Application Honeypots* (Rist, 2009); (2) *Voice over Internet Protocol*

(VoIP) *Honeypots* (Do Carmo et al., 2011); (3) *Secure Shell* (SSH) *Honeypots* (Oosterhof, 2015); (4) *Bluetooth Honeypots* (Podhradsky et al., 2012); (5) *Universal Serial Bus* (USB) *Honeypots* (Poeplau & Gassen, 2012); (6) S*upervisory Control and Data Acquisition/Industrial Control System* (SCADA/ICS) *Honeypots* (Rist et al., 2013); (7) *Internet of Things* (IoT) *Honeypots* (Pa et al., 2015); and (8) *Internet Protocol version 6* (IPv6) *Network Honeypots* (Schindler et al., 2015).

Security-Related Aspects of Honeypots

The captor element of a honeypot constitutes the characteristics that execute security-related tasks. As with the decoy characteristics, these too vary in design and function (Fan et al., 2017; Nawrocki et al., 2016). Moreover, these components are generally clandestine in nature to mitigate the possibility of being detected by cyberthreats. Captor characteristics generally address matters that include (but are not limited to) the monitoring, analyzing, prevention, and detection of cyberattacks. Several defining characteristics make up this honeypot element. These include: (1) *attack monitoring*; (2) *attack prevention*; (3) *attack detection*; (4) *attack response*; and (5) *attack profiling*.

The first captor characteristic of a honeypot is *attack monitoring*. Attack monitoring involves the collecting and logging of cyberthreat activity. In the context of honeypots, this describes the location in which activity is being monitored. This generally occurs at either the computer network or computer system level. At the network level, activity is generally monitored in terms of network traffic (e.g., inbound or outbound connections) (Oosterhof, 2015; Spitzner, 2003). Suspicious traffic that is regularly detected on a given network may be scrutinized for further investigation. At the system level, activity is generally monitored in terms of system events (e.g., spyware, SQL injections, and rootkits) (Portokalidis et al., 2006). For example, the commands and other detectable keystrokes executed by an intruder can be scrutinized.

The second captor characteristic of a honeypot is *attack prevention*. As the name implies, attack prevention involves the obstruction or hindrance of cyberthreat activity. Currently, there are a handful of different tactics that honeypots employ as a means to prevent cyberthreat attacks. These tactics include: (1) *filtering*; (2) *tarpitting*; and (3) *containment*. *Filtering* involves the use of filtering technology to analyze and assess incoming traffic to a network. Much like a security checkpoint at an airport, if incoming traffic is identified as malicious, it can be blocked from entry (Lengyel et al., 2013). *Tarpitting* involves the throttling of computer network packet rates as a means to intentionally slow down intrusive cyberthreats (Jiang & Xu, 2004). *Containment* involves confining malicious network activity to only honeypot systems. In the event that a honeypot is compromised by a hacker, a separate honeypot can respond by circumventing the hacker's activity by redirecting any subsequent attacks to other honeypot systems (Alata et al., 2008; Bailey et al., 2004). Because this approach is not as apparent in its interaction with the hacker as compared to tarpitting, it is more effective in shrouding a honeypot's presence (Fan et al., 2017).

The third captor characteristic of a honeypot is *attack detection* (Spitzner, 2002). In essence, this describes how honeypots discriminate typical network activity (e.g., an employee carrying out daily tasks) from intrusive and suspicious network activity (e.g., an infiltrating hacker). This characteristic is particularly important because honeypots are not catch-all solutions for cybersecurity (Nawrocki et al., 2016; Spitzner, 2002). Indeed, a honeypot's ability to detect cyberthreats is only as effective as its programming allows it to be. Moreover, the ever-changing nature of cybercrime and other internet-related technologies also present a challenge in a honeypot's ability to detect newer forms of malicious activity. Because of this, a honeypot's attack detection is programmed in either one of two ways: *signature-based detection* and *anomaly-based detection*. A honeypot that uses *signature-based detection* identifies malicious activity by "recognizing malicious patterns", whereas anomaly-based detection identifies malicious activity based on "deviations from patterns of normal behavior" (Fan et al., 2017, p. 3912). This can be illustrated by a honeypot's ability to detect known (signature-based) or new forms of malware (anomaly-based). More often than not, honeypots that use signature-based detection are used for production (or commercial) purposes. This is because organizations are generally more interested in deterring cyberthreats rather than learning about them

(Spitzner, 2002). The purpose of a production honeypot is to heighten security within an organization's computer network by functioning as a form of guardianship against known cyberthreats. In contrast, honeypots that utilize anomaly-based detection are often used for research purposes as opposed to serving a security-oriented role. Where production honeypots seek to interact and obstruct cyberthreat activity (Poeplau & Gassen, 2012; Spitzner, 2003), research honeypots use anomaly-based detection as a means to study unknown forms of malware and cyberthreat behavior (i.e., by monitoring unknown behaviors or assessing new tools used by a hacker to infiltrate a network) (Leita & Dacier, 2008; Portokalidis et al., 2006). While research honeypots lack the defensive capabilities that production honeypots possess, the information obtained through research honeypots can be analyzed to develop a better understanding pertaining to new types of cyberthreats. By doing so, researchers can design and deploy much more effective production honeypots for commercial use (Fan et al., 2017; Nawrocki et al., 2016).

The fourth captor characteristic of a honeypot is its *attack response*. A honeypot's attack response can be best understood as the retaliatory action taken against, or in response to, a cyberthreat. This type of security function falls into one of two types: *traffic redirection* and *decoy reconfiguration*. *Traffic redirection* involves averting network traffic to a separate destination (Bailey et al., 2004; Lengyel et al., 2013). For example, a honeypot may redirect malicious traffic toward another honeypot designed to capture further information on said traffic. *Decoy reconfiguration* refers to a honeypot's ability to reconfigure its decoy characteristics in response to detecting certain events (i.e., malicious traffic entering the server or the unauthorized modification of data) (Cui et al., 2006). This concept can be illustrated by a honeypot that gradually becomes more interactive with a hacker in response to their degree of malicious activity.

The fifth and final captor characteristic of a honeypot is *attack profiling*. McGrew (2006) proposed that honeypots can analyze malicious activity in a manner that can profile attacks. The information that can be used to generate these profiles includes: (1) *motivation* (i.e., the purpose of the attack); (2) *breadth/depth* (i.e., the extent and scale of the attack); (3) *sophistication* (i.e., the technical finesse of an attack); (4)

concealment (i.e., the means used to obscure an attach); (5) *attacker*(s) (i.e., the source of the attack [e.g., solo actor, group, or program]); (6) *vulnerability* (i.e., the flaw exploited by the attack); and (7) *tools* (i.e., the utilized software behind the attack). This proposed framework opens the door for interdisciplinary efforts toward profiling online criminals in more complex and technical environments.

Honeypots in Academia

Due to the rapid advancements of both beneficial (e.g., wireless technologies) (Ryan, 2010) and malicious (e.g., malware) technologies (Yaqoob et al., 2017), interest in honeypots quickly spread beyond the HP. In fact, honeypots have drawn interest not only from other scholars within the computer sciences (Fan et al., 2017; Vetterl, 2020), but also from scholars within the social sciences as well (Holt, 2017; Maimon et al., 2014). However, while the computer sciences often focus on developing new and improved honeypots (Nawrocki et al., 2016; Vetterl, 2020), social scientists have mostly focused on using honeypots as a means to study the behavior of hackers (Maimon et al., 2014; Wilson et al., 2015). Although the approaches contrast more than they compare, they can together be understood as two sides of the same coin in their effort to strengthen online security and better understand online threats. Over the past two decades, this effort has generated a considerable number of advancements and findings across both disciplines as it relates to honeypots (Bringer et al., 2012; Maimon et al., 2014; Holt, 2017; Udhani et al., 2019; Vetterl, 2020).

Computer Sciences

Through the turn of the century, furthering the research and development of honeypots was essential as a means to keep up with the advancements of internet technologies (Vetterl, 2020). At the forefront of this effort, computer scientists have introduced dozens of new honeypots equipped with various functionalities and augmentations. However, as described earlier, honeypots are not an inclusive approach to network security. Any security operation, digital or real-world, can be conceptually broken down by its ability to prevent (e.g., hinder or stop), detect (e.g., identify and recognize), and react (e.g., retaliate and engage) to an intruder (Schneier, 2015). For any form of security to become its most effective, the three concepts should be managed so that they are complimentary to one another. Simply put, "reaction reinforces prevention and improves future detections" (Nawrocki et al., 2016, p. 2). However, this notion is easier said than done, as most forms of security typically specialize in only one of these three areas (Schneier, 2015). In the context of honeypots and network security, this issue is often the same (Nawrocki et al., 2016). Despite this, newly developed honeypots have still been successfully advantageous in the post-Honeynet era of network security. They have been improved in not only handling different forms of malicious activity online, but also in how they function and collect data (Bringer et al., 2012).

Regarding the matter of malicious online phenomena, different honeypots have been introduced to handle issues including (but not limited to) internet bots (Alberdi et al., 2007), denial of service attacks (Khattab et al., 2004), malware (Portokalidis et al., 2006), phishing (Li & Schmitz, 2009), and spam (Trivedi et al., 2007). Moreover, honeypots have also been developed to address new and unknown forms of online threats. One such example is Anagnostakis and colleagues' (2005) "shadow honeypot", a honeypot used to detect abnormalities in network activity. This honeypot was developed as a means to deal with balancing detection accuracy with detection coverage that previous honeypots faced. To improve detection coverage, the shadow honeypot utilizes an anomaly detection system that is calibrated to have a high false-positive detection rate. Any network traffic that is deemed malicious will be immediately directed to the shadow honeypot for further analysis. To improve detection accuracy, the shadow honeypot carefully monitors all network activity that made it through the initial detection system. If the shadow honeypot finds that a given network request is harmless, no further action will be taken. However, if any network activity is deemed malicious, all of the request's activity on the network will be ceased and rolled back (or undone) by the shadow honeypot (Anagnostakis et al.,

2005). Simply put, a shadow honeypot works as a second pair of eyes that helps discover unknown forms of malicious activity. Furthermore, it also exemplifies the concept of *anomaly-based detection* in its ability to detect abnormal network activity.

Honeypots have been utilized as a means to better understand network attacks through observable characteristics they can detect and measure (Nawrocki et al., 2016). These include the attack's frequency, the attack's target(s), and the attack's source. Attack frequency has been measured by means including (but not limited to) how long an intruder is on a network (Grégio et al., 2007; Kaaniche et al., 2007) and the time between network visits (McGrew, 2006). Moreover, an attacker's frequency has also been measured based on how often they visit (Grégio et al., 2007; Kaaniche et al., 2007) or exploit (Alata et al., 2006) a computer network over a period of time. As it relates to the attacker's target, this has been measured by assessing the network service that is attacked. Attack targets can range from a single computer's operating system (Leita et al., 2008) to entire networks (Kaaniche et al., 2007; Yegneswaran et al., 2005). To gather information on the origins of an attack, a honeypot can sometimes collect telling information on an attacker, such as their IP Address (Kaaniche et al., 2007; Yegneswaran et al., 2005), e-mail (Alata et al., 2006; Trivedi et al., 2007), or their operating system (Leita et al., 2008; Pouget & Dacier, 2004). Among other strides made within the computer sciences, researchers have developed honeypots that are more difficult for attackers to detect (Holz & Raynal, 2005), able to generate more manageable and robust data (Raynal et al., 2004) and more diverse in their deployment and configurational options (Hecker et al., 2006).

Social Sciences

Spitzner (2002) recognized that a "wide spectrum" of expertise is essential in the cybersecurity community's efforts to "analyze and research a variety of aspects of the blackhat community" (p. 235). Until recently, nearly all interests surrounding honeypots emanated from computer scientists.

In the past decade, however, a small number of scholars have intro-duced honeypots to the social scientific literature. This was not only instrumental in bridging the collaborative divide between technical (i.e., computer scientist) and non-technical (i.e., social scientists) scholars, but also in highlighting the feasibility of this type of interdisciplinary research. Indeed, social scientists have utilized data generated from honeypots to address a number of criminological inquiries. Researchers have used honeypot systems to investigate the effectiveness of warning banners (Howell et al., 2017; Maimon et al., 2014, 2019b; Testa et al., 2017; Wilson et al., 2015, system trespassing involving brute-force attacks (Maimon et al., 2015), self-protective behaviors among internet users (2020b; Maimon et al., 2017), and online fraudulence (Maimon et al., 2019a, 2020b). Moreover, many of these studies were guided by contemporary social scientific perspectives and theories including deter-rence theory (Howell et al., 2017; Maimon et al., 2014, 2019b; Testa et al., 2017; Wilson et al., 2015), routine activity theory (Maimon et al., 2015, 2017), situational crime prevention (Maimon et al., 2017), and interpersonal deception theory (Maimon et al., 2019a, 2020b).

The first study using honeypot data as a means to answer questions central to the social sciences was conducted by Maimon and colleagues (2014). In the first, of a series of studies, Maimon and colleagues (2014) developed and deployed a large number of honeypot computers and conducted two independent experiments to investigate the influence of a warning banner on the progression, frequency, and duration of system trespassing incidents. In both experiments, hackers who infil-trated the system were either randomly assigned to the treatment group and presented with a warning banner or randomly assigned to the control group and not presented with a warning banner. Findings revealed that although a warning banner did not lead to an immediate termination or a reduction in the frequency of trespassing incidents, it significantly reduced the duration of system trespassing incidents.

In a follow-up study, Wilson and colleagues (2015) found that a warning banner's presence (within a compromised computer system) reduced the probability of commands being typed in the system during longer incidents involving first-time trespassers. They further found the probability of commands being logged during subsequent system trespassing incidents (on the same honeypot computer) was conditioned by the presence of a warning banner and by whether commands were logged during previous trespassing incidents. Moreover, Testa and colleagues (2017) found the effect of warning banners in preventing hackers' command typing behaviors differed based on the amount of administrator privilege taken by the system trespasser in the attacked system. Furthermore, Howell and colleagues (2017) used data gathered by honeypots deployed in China and found hackers were more likely to log some intelligence gathering commands when presented with a threat of sanction. Simply put, when faced with the threat of legal sanction, hackers alter their behavior to reduce their probability of being detected and sanctioned. In a similar vein, Maimon and colleagues (Maimon et al., 2019b) configured their honeypot systems to display varying levels of ambiguity regarding the presence of surveillance and found hackers alter their behavior by entering clean tracks commands in the presence of unambiguous signs of surveillance. They also found hackers who believe they are being monitored were more likely to alter their behavior to avoid being caught.

In addition, scholars have also used honeypot data to examine the efficacy of routine activity theory (Cohen & Felson, 1979). Specifically, Maimon and colleagues (2015) deployed a large number of honeypot systems in China and Israel and gathered data on the brute-force attacks and system trespassing incidents launched against these systems. In support of the theory, the authors found system trespassers launch their first attack from IP addresses originating in geographical locations that are proximate to the target computers, and during the computer networks' most active times (i.e., 9:00 a.m.–5:00 p.m.). In other words, the hackers' geographical location and temporal trends are predictive of attack frequency. Overall, these studies demonstrate how honeypot data can be used to expand the scope of criminological theory by gathering data on live system trespassing incidents. Specifically, the authors argue the warning banners presented to hackers alter their behavior in a manner consistent with the principals of restrictive deterrence (Gibbs, 1975; Jacobs, 1993) and that hackers operate in a manner consistent with routine activity theory (Cohen & Felson, 1979).

Moving beyond the examination of system trespasser behavior and exploring the propositions of interpersonal deception theory (Buller &

Burgoon, 1996), Maimon and colleagues (Maimon et al., 2019a, 2020b) have also demonstrated how honeypots can be used to gain insight into the modus operandi of e-mail fraudsters. Specifically, Maimon and colleagues (2019a, 2020b) posted a large number of "For Sale" advertisements (i.e., honeypots) over classified-ad websites and interacted with online fraudsters and legitimate users who responded to their ads via e-mail. In their first study, they found that e-mail fraudsters' presentations of verbal cues of urgency during the early stages of a fraud attempt are followed by a consistent presentation of verbal and nonverbal urgency cues. In a follow-up investigation that focused on the two most common types of deceptive strategies employed by fraudsters (i.e., politeness and urgency), the authors examined which type of cue— politeness or urgency—is more likely to result in an e-mail fraud attempt and whether these cues are mutually exclusive and consistent throughout the progression of a fraud attempt. The authors found that e-mail fraud attempts are more likely to follow probe e-mails that include cues of urgency than cues of politeness. Additionally, they also found that the majority of fraudsters' probe e-mails include deceptive cues of either politeness or urgency, whereas the majority of fraudsters' subsequent e-mails include deceptive cues of both politeness and urgency (Maimon et al., 2020b). Together, these studies provided partial support for interpersonal deception theory and demonstrate how honeypots can be used to study less technical forms of cybercrime.

Lastly, although honeypots originated to gather intelligence on active offenders, honeypot data are also useful in observing the behavior of internet users more generally. Maimon and colleagues (2017) deployed a honeypot Wi-Fi network at 109 locations around the DC Metropolitan area and monitored the behavior of the internet users who connected with the rogue Wi-Fi network. The study found when internet users are logged onto a Wi-Fi network that had some degree of uncertainty surrounding its legitimacy and security practices; they were less likely to engage with websites that handled sensitive information. In other words, security cues in the virtual environment impact Wi-Fi users' self-protective behaviors. In a later study, Maimon and colleagues (2020a) found the implementation of security cues in the physical environment decreases the probability of a public Wi-Fi user accessing the rogue (honeypot) network. Taken together, these studies provide support for situational crime prevention (Clarke, 1980) by demonstrating that interactions with honeypots are altered by the security of both the network and the surrounding physical environment in which the network is deployed.

Criticism of Honeypot Research

While honeypots have been used in the study of cybercrime, their application as a means to collect and analyze data raises a number of concerns that warrant serious consideration. Among these concerns are the reliability and validity of honeypot data (Howell & Burruss, 2020). Honeypots allow researchers to gather data on active offenders or internet users more generally, which as noted above can be used to expand the scope of social scientific theories and guide evidence-based cybersecurity policies. However, honeypots were not designed with the intent to conduct practical research in the social sciences and by design are unable to gather variables of typical interest to social scientists (e.g., sociodemographic, perceptions, attitudes, etc.) (Bossler, 2017; Holt, 2017). With such measures absent within any theoretically driven study, it is argued that researchers may "[...] make incorrect assumptions about the actors" (Holt, 2017, p. 740). Although conventional honeypots are unable to test certain social scientific theories such as Akers' (2011) theory of social learning (which requires information concerning an offender's learned behaviors), behavioral patterns can be monitored and analyzed. Thus, researchers can use honeypots to observe offenders' behavioral response to certain stimuli (i.e., network configuration, physical location, warning banners) to test theories such as situational crime prevention, restrictive deterrence, and routine activity theory (see also Chapter 6). Of course, tests of these theories are limited in their ability to generalize to the entire hacker population.

The issue of generalizability is of noteworthy concern. It is argued that honeypots may be capturing data pertaining to the behavior of script kiddies (hackers with little or amateurish skill) (Bossler, 2017; Holt, 2017) as opposed to more sophisticated hackers. This should certainly be considered when implementing policy based on findings derived from honeypot research. However, it is worth noting the majority of hackers are not technologically adept (Holt, 2017; Maimon & Louderback, 2019; Testa et al., 2017) and that all hackers begin as novices. Thus, perhaps honeypots can be used to conduct research into how to nudge novice hackers into conventional cybersecurity careers (known as a white-hat hacker) before becoming sophisticated malicious hackers (known as a black hat hacker). Moreover, the issue of generalizability is not limited to honeypot research but is inherent within all research designs that are unable to capture the entire population of interest. Therefore, honeypot research should not be abandoned, but instead expanded using different types of honeypots in different environments to determine if the findings can be replicated.

Another problem emanating from the use of honeypots is their inability to differentiate attacks or intrusions between humans and scripted programs (otherwise known as bots). This has led critics to argue that even theories such as restrictive deterrence, which can be tested by observing offenders' behavioral response to warning messages, cannot be properly tested due to researchers' current inability to empirically differentiate human activity from bot activity (Bossler, 2017; Steinmetz, 2017; Udhani et al., 2019). Again, this limitation should be considered when discussing both theoretical and policy implications. However, it is unknown what proportion of attacks are scripted and the presence of bots would deflate rather than inflate the findings supportive of restrictive deterrence (Testa et al., 2017). Perhaps differentiating humans from bots in effort to examine behavioral patterns resulting from deterrent cues is yet another opportunity for cross-disciplinary collaboration.

Future of Honeypot Research

As society is becoming more and more entrenched with the use of internet-based technologies (otherwise known as the Internet of Things) the use of honeypots offers new and promising opportunities for future research. With everyday household items (i.e., refrigerators and door locks) becoming increasingly internet connected (or becoming IoT devices), consumers have, in turn, quickly adopted and become reliant on the modern conveniences of living in a smart home (Hsu & Lin, 2016). Smart homes are often equipped with home appliances such as thermostats, lighting fixtures, security systems, and cameras that can be controlled using a smartphone or smart speakers connected to the same network. Although convenient, these devices can often be unsecure and easily accessible by hackers (Vlajic & Zhou, 2018). For instance, it has been demonstrated across several accounts that hackers have exploited design vulnerabilities inherent within baby monitoring systems to view and record private household exchanges (Stanislav & Beardsley, 2015). What is more troubling is once a hacker gains access to these vulnerable devices, they can then freely execute attacks against other devices within the same network to further invade privacy and steal sensitive information (Heartfield et al., 2018). Likewise, such threats can extend to vehicles with IoT technology (Kennedy et al., 2019). Once hackers' gain access to their victims' vehicles, safety features can be compromised, and geographical coordinates can be monitored and used to track the vehicle.

While vulnerable IoT devices have become a common target for cyber-offenders (Patton et al., 2014), only few criminological studies have examined the causes and correlates of attacks against such emergent technologies (Rege, 2013). To date, no known study has conducted these examinations using data generated from honeypot systems. Much of the honeypot research has been limited to traditional targets such as personal computers (Howell et al., 2017), web servers (Maimon et al., 2019a), and network routers (Maimon et al., 2020b). Moving forward, researchers should design honeypots to emulate IoT devices to better understand attacks perpetrated against these types of devices. Such research could aid in the development of proactive policy by examining how situational cues in the physical and virtual environment impact both offender and target decision making (Maimon et al., 2020a). Similarly, as vehicles become increasingly internet connected (Kennedy et al., 2019), the development of honeypots for IoT-infused vehicles should be considered to increase safety and security of those operating such vehicles.

Conclusion

The use of honeypots in criminological research was unheard of nearly a decade ago, yet this is no longer the case. Scholars have demonstrated that honeypots can be utilized in the testing of criminological and sociological theory. While their use as a means to collect and analyze data endures both methodological and theoretical shortcomings, these shortcomings do not outweigh the potential contribution to social scientific discovery. It is our belief that honeypots are instrumental in further developing the cyber-criminological literature. This notion is fortified by the following considerations.

First, honeypot research provides a unique opportunity to foster interdisciplinary collaboration between technical (i.e., computer scientist) and non-technical (i.e., sociologist and criminologist) scholars. This type of joint effort radiates a number of notable benefits. Not only will it help guide the testing and advancement of criminological theory in more technologically complex environments, but it will also facilitate the development of more fruitful cybercrime policies and strategies. It is important to consider that the possible insights generated by this kind of collaboration could not be adequately achieved by either academic discipline alone (see also Chapters 1 and 3).

Next, interdisciplinary honeypot research permits the ability to concurrently examine both the technical and human components behind the perpetration of cyberattacks. With a computer scientist's understanding of internet-technologies coupled with a social scientist's understanding of human behavior, honeypots can be developed to permit the generation of data with greater levels of reliability and validity. This can open the doors to new possibilities and avenues for cybercrime research using honeypots. Technical scholars can calibrate how honeypots function in order to adequately permit the investigation of a number of research questions of interest to social scientists. For example, a honeypot's response to intrusive activity can be modified to a given researcher's methodological framework. Similarly, a honeypot can be tailored to generate attack profiles of intrusive activity that is detected. With the honeypot taxonomy provided by Fan et al. (2017), one can intuitively gauge all the dynamic possibilities offered by these security systems.

Although still in its infancy, honeypot research for the study of cybercrime has a promising future. In spite of existing criticisms over their use, honeypots can certainly help expand our understanding of hackers and network security. No methodological approach is without limitation— especially new and emerging designs. However, by virtue of the aforementioned trials and tribulations, it is our belief that honeypot research is central to the advancement of the cyber-criminological literature. As technology continually advances, we encourage scholars interested in the study of cybercrime to develop and deploy honeypots disguised as emergent technologies to garner insight into hackers' modus operandi to aid in the development of a safer cyberspace. Additionally, we hope future research recognizes the utility of honeypots for research into less technical forms of cybercrime and internet use more generally.

References

Akers, R. L. (2011). *Social learning and social structure: A general theory of crime and deviance.* Transaction Publishers.

Alata, É., Alberdi, I., Nicomette, V., Owezarski, P., & Kaâniche, M. (2008). Internet attacks monitoring with dynamic connection redirection mechanisms. *Journal in Computer Virology, 4*(2), 127–136.

Alata, E., Nicomette, V., Kaâniche, M., Dacier, M., & Herrb, M. (2006). Lessons learned from the deployment of a high-interaction honeypot. In *2006 Sixth European Dependable Computing Conference* (pp. 39–46). IEEE.

Alberdi, I., Philippe, É., Vincent, O., & Kaâniche, N. M. (2007). Shark: Spy honeypot with advanced redirection kit. In *Proceedings of the IEEE Workshop on Monitoring, Attack detEction and Mitigation* (pp. 47–52).

Anagnostakis, K. G., Sidiroglou, S., Akritidis, P., Xinidis, K., Markatos, E., & Keromytis, A. D. (2005). *Detecting targeted attacks using shadow honeypots.*

Baecher, P., Holz, T., Kötter, M., & Wicherski, G (2016). *The Malware Collection Tool (mwcollect).* Available at: http://www.mwcollect.org/.

Bailey, M., Cooke, E., Watson, D., Jahanian, F., & Provos, N. (2004). *A hybrid honeypot architecture for scalable network monitoring.* Univ. Michigan, Ann Arbor, MI, USA, Tech. Rep. CSE-TR-499–04.

Bossler, A. M. (2017). Need for debate on the implications of honeypot data for restrictive deterrence policies in cyberspace. *Criminology and Public Policy, 16,* 679.

Bringer, M. L., Chelmecki, C. A., & Fujinoki, H. (2012). A survey: Recent advances and future trends in honeypot research. *International Journal of Computer Network and Information Security, 4*(10), 63.

Buller, D. B., & Burgoon, J. K. (1996). Interpersonal deception theory. *Communication Theory, 6*(3), 203–242.

Cheswick, B. (1992). An evening with Berferd in which a cracker is lured, endured, and studied. In *Proceedings of Winter USENIX Conference* (pp. 20–24). San Francisco.

Clarke, R. V. (1980). Situational crime prevention: Theory and practice. *British Journal of Criminology, 20,* 136.

Cohen, F. (1998). *The RISKS Digest* (Vol. 19, Issue 62). Available at: http://catless.ncl.ac.uk/Risks/19.62.

Cohen, L. E., & Felson, M. (1979). Social change and crime rate trends: A routine activity approach. *American sociological review,* 588–608.

Cui, W., Paxson, V., & Weaver, N. (2006). *GQ: Realizing a system to catch worms in a quarter million places.* Technical Report TR-06–004, ICSI.

Deutsche Telekom. (2021). Available at: https://www.telekom.com/en.

Do Carmo, R., Nassar, M., & Festor, O. (2011). Artemisa: An open-source honeypot back-end to support security in VoIP domains. In *12th IFIP/IEEE International Symposium on Integrated Network Management (IM 2011) and Workshops* (pp. 361–368). IEEE.

Even, L. R. (2000). *Honey pot systems explained.* Available at: https://www.sans.org/security-resources/idfaq/honeypot3.php.

Fan, W., Du, Z., Fernández, D., & Villagrá, V. A. (2017). Enabling an anatomic view to investigate honeypot systems: A survey. *IEEE Systems Journal, 12*(4), 3906–3919.

Gibbs, J. P. (1975). *Crime, punishment, and deterrence.* Elsevier.

Grégio, A., Santos, R., & Montes, A. (2007). Evaluation of data mining techniques for suspicious network activity classification using honeypots data. In *Data Mining, Intrusion Detection, Information Assurance, and Data Networks Security 2007* (Vol. 6570, p. 657006). International Society for Optics and Photonics.

Heartfield, R., Loukas, G., Budimir, S., Bezemskij, A., Fontaine, J. R., Filippoupolitis, A., & Roesch, E. (2018). A taxonomy of cyber-physical threats and impact in the smart home. *Computers and Security, 78,* 398–428.

Hecker, C., Nance, K. L., & Hay, B. (2006). Dynamic honeypot construction. In *Proceedings of the 10th Colloquium for Information Systems Security Education* (Vol. 102). MD, USA.

Holt, T. J. (2017). On the value of honeypots to produce policy recommendations. *Criminology and Public Policy, 16,* 737.

Holz, T., & Raynal, F. (2005). Detecting honeypots and other suspicious environments. In *Proceedings from the Sixth Annual IEEE SMC Information Assurance Workshop* (pp. 29–36). IEEE.

Honeynet Project. (2020). Available at: https://www.honeynet.org.

Howell, C. J., & Burruss, G. W. (2020). Datasets for analysis of cybercrime. In *The Palgrave handbook of international cybercrime and cyberdeviance* (pp. 207–219).

Howell, C. J., Maimon, D., Cochran, J. K., Jones, H. M., & Powers, R. A. (2017). System trespasser behavior after exposure to warning messages at a Chinese computer network: An examination. *International Journal of Cyber Criminology, 11*(1), 63–77.

Hsu, C. L., & Lin, J. C. C. (2016). An empirical examination of consumer adoption of Internet of Things services: Network externalities and concern for information privacy perspectives. *Computers in Human Behavior, 62,* 516–527.

Jacobs, B. A. (1993). Undercover deception clues: A case of restrictive deterrence. *Criminology, 31*(2), 281–299.

Jiang, X., & Xu, D. (2004). Collapsar: A VM-based architecture for network attack detention center. In *USENIX Security Symposium* (pp. 15–28).

Kaaniche, M., Deswarte, Y., Alata, E., Dacier, M., & Nicomette, V. (2007). *Empirical analysis and statistical modeling of attack processes based on honeypots.* arXiv preprint. arXiv:0704.0861.

Kennedy, J., Holt, T., & Cheng, B. (2019). Automotive cybersecurity: Assessing a new platform for cybercrime and malicious hacking. *Journal of Crime and Justice, 42*(5), 632–645.

Khattab, S. M., Sangpachatanaruk, C., Mossé, D., Melhem, R., & Znati, T. (2004). Roaming honeypots for mitigating service-level denial-of-service attacks. In *24th International Conference on Distributed Computing Systems, 2004. Proceedings* (pp. 328–337). IEE.

Leita, C., & Dacier, M. (2008). SGNET: a worldwide deployable framework to support the analysis of malware threat models. In *2008 Seventh European Dependable Computing Conference* (pp. 99–109). IEEE.

Leita, C., Pham, V. H., Thonnard, O., Ramirez-Silva, E., Pouget, F., Kirda, E., & Dacier, M. (2008). The leurre.com project: Collecting Internet threats information using a worldwide distributed honeynet. In *2008 WOMBAT Workshop on Information Security Threats Data Collection and Sharing* (pp. 40–57). IEEE.

Lengyel, T. K., Neumann, J., Maresca, S., & Kiayias, A. (2013). Towards hybrid honeynets via virtual machine introspection and cloning. In *International Conference on Network and System Security* (pp. 164–177). Springer, Berlin, Heidelberg.

Li, S., & Schmitz, R. (2009). *A novel anti-phishing framework based on honeypots* (pp. 1–13). IEEE.

Maimon, D., Alper, M., Sobesto, B., & Cukier, M. (2014). Restrictive deterrent effects of a warning banner in an attacked computer system. *Criminology, 52*(1), 33–59.

Maimon, D., Becker, M., Patil, S., & Katz, J. (2017). Self-protective behaviors over public WiFi networks. In *The {LASER} Workshop: Learning from Authoritative Security Experiment Results ({LASER}* (pp. 69–76).

Maimon, D., Howell, C. J., Jacques, S., & Perkins, R. C. (2020a). Situational awareness and public Wi-Fi users' self-protective behaviors. *Security Journal* (online first).

Maimon, D., Howell, C. J., Moloney, M., & Park, Y. S. (2020b). An examination of email fraudsters' modus operandi. *Crime and Delinquency* (online first).

Maimon, D., & Louderback, E. R. (2019). Cyber-dependent crimes: an interdisciplinary review. *Annual Review of Criminology, 2*, 191–216.

Maimon, D., Santos, M., & Park, Y. (2019a). Online deception and situations conducive to the progression of non-payment fraud. *Journal of Crime and Justice, 42*(5), 516–535.

Maimon, D., Testa, A., Sobesto, B., Cukier, M., & Ren, W. (2019b). Predictably deterrable? The case of system trespassers. In *International Conference on Security, Privacy and Anonymity in Computation, Communication and Storage* (pp. 317–330). Springer.

Maimon, D., Wilson, T., Ren, W., & Berenblum, T. (2015). On the relevance of spatial and temporal dimensions in assessing computer susceptibility to system trespassing incidents. *British Journal of Criminology, 55*(3), 615–634.

Markatos, E., & Anagnostakis, K. (2008). Noah: A european network of affined honeypots for cyber-attack tracking and alerting. *The Parliament Magazine*, p. 262.

McGrew, R. (2006). Experiences with honeypot systems: Development, deployment, and analysis. In *Proceedings of the 39th Annual Hawaii International Conference on System Sciences (HICSS'06)* (Vol. 9, pp. 220a–220a). IEEE.

Nawrocki, M., Wählisch, M., Schmidt, T. C., Keil, C., & Schönfelder, J. (2016). A survey on honeypot software and data analysis. *arXiv preprint arXiv:1608.06249*.

Newman, G. R., & Socia, K. (2007). *Sting operations*. US Department of Justice, Office of Community Oriented Policing Services.

Oluwatosin, H. S. (2014). Client-server model. *IOSR Journal of Computer Engineering (IOSR-JCE)*, *16*(1), 67.

Oosterhof, M. (2015). *Cowrie—Active kippo fork*.

Pa, Y. M. P., Suzuki, S., Yoshioka, K., Matsumoto, T., Kasama, T., & Rossow, C. (2015). IoTPOT: Analysing the rise of IoT compromises. In *9th {USENIX} Workshop on Offensive Technologies ({WOOT} 15)*.

Patton, M., Gross, E., Chinn, R., Forbis, S., Walker, L., & Chen, H. (2014). Uninvited connections: A study of vulnerable devices on the Internet of Things (IoT). In *2014 IEEE Joint Intelligence and Security Informatics Conference* (pp. 232–235). IEEE.

Podhradsky, A., Casey, C., & Ceretti, P. (2012). The Bluetooth honeypot project: Measuring and managing bluetooth risks in the workplace. *International Journal of Interdisciplinary Telecommunications and Networking (IJITN)*, *4*(3), 1–22.

Poeplau, S., & Gassen, J. (2012). A honeypot for arbitrary malware on USB storage devices. In *2012 7th International Conference on Risks and Security of Internet and Systems (CRiSIS)* (pp. 1–8). IEEE.

Portokalidis, G., Slowinska, A., & Bos, H. (2006). Argos: An emulator for fingerprinting zero-day attacks for advertised honeypots with automatic signature generation. *ACM SIGOPS Operating Systems Review, 40*(4), 15–27.

Pouget, F., & Dacier, M. (2004). Honeypot-based forensics. In *AusCERT Asia Pacific Information Technology Security Conference*.

Provos, N. (2004). A virtual honeypot framework. In *USENIX Security Symposium* (Vol. 173, No. 2004, pp. 1–14).

Provos, N., & Holz, T. (2007). *Virtual honeypots: From botnet tracking to intrusion detection.* Pearson Education.

Raynal, F., Berthier, Y., Biondi, P., & Kaminsky, D. (2004). Honeypot forensics part 1: Analyzing the network. *IEEE Security and Privacy, 2*(4), 72–78.

Rege, A. (2013). Factors Impacting Attacker Decision-Making in Power Grid Cyber Attacks. In *International Conference on Critical Infrastructure Protection* (pp. 125–138). Springer, Berlin, Heidelberg.

Rist, L. (2009). Glastopf project. *The Honeynet Project.*

Rist, L., Vestergaard, J., Haslinger, D., Pasquale, A., & Smith, J. (2013). *Conpot ics/SCADA honeypot.* Honeynet Project (conpot.org).

Roesch, M. (1999). Snort: Lightweight intrusion detection for networks. In *Lisa* (Vol. 99, No. 1, pp. 229–238).

Ryan, J. (2010). *A history of the Internet and the digital future.* Reaktion Books.

Schindler, S., Schnor, B., & Scheffler, T. (2015). Hyhoneydv6: A hybrid honeypot architecture for IPV6 networks. *International Journal of Intelligent Computing Research, 6.*

Schneier, B. (2015). *Secrets and lies: Digital security in a networked world.* Wiley.

Seifert, C., Welch, I., & Komisarczuk, P. (2007). Honeyc-the low-interaction client honeypot. In *Proceedings of the 2007 NZCSRCS* (Vol. 6). Waikato University, Hamilton, New Zealand.

Spitzner, L. (2001). The value of honeypots, part one: Definitions and values of honeypots. *Security Focus.*

Spitzner, L. (2002). *Honeypots: Tracking hackers Addison Wesley Professional.*

Spitzner, L. (2003). Specter: A commercial honeypot solution for windows. *Acesso em, 26* (8).

Spitzner, L. (2005). Know your enemy: Honeynets. *Honeynet Project.*

Spitzner, L., & Roesch, M. (2001). *The value of honeypots, part one: Definitions and values of honeypots.*

Stanislav, M., & Beardsley, T. (2015). Hacking IoT: A case study on baby monitor exposures and vulnerabilities. *Rapid7 Report.*

Steinmetz, K. F. (2017). Ruminations on warning banners, deterrence, and system intrusion research. *Criminology & Pub. Pol'y, 16*, 725.

Stoll, C. (1990). *The cuckoo's egg: Tracking a spy through the maze of computer espionage.*

Testa, A., Maimon, D., Sobesto, B., & Cukier, M. (2017). Illegal roaming and file manipulation on target computers: Assessing the effect of sanction threats on system trespassers' online behaviors. *Criminology and Public Policy, 16*(3), 689–726.

Trivedi, A. J., Judge, P., & Krasser, S. (2007). Analyzing network and content characteristics of spim using honeypots. In *SRUTI*.

Udhani, S., Withers, A., & Bashir, M. (2019). Human vs bots: Detecting human attacks in a honeypot environment. In *2019 7th International Symposium on Digital Forensics and Security (ISDFS)* (pp. 1–6). IEEE.

Vetterl, A. (2020). *Honeypots in the age of universal attacks and the Internet of Things*. Doctoral dissertation, University of Cambridge.

Vlajic, N., & Zhou, D. (2018). IoT as a land of opportunity for DDoS hackers. *Computer, 51*(7), 26–34.

Wilson, T., Maimon, D., Sobesto, B., & Cukier, M. (2015). The effect of a surveillance banner in an attacked computer system: Additional evidence for the relevance of restrictive deterrence in cyberspace. *Journal of Research in Crime and Delinquency, 52*(6), 829–855.

Yaqoob, I., Ahmed, E., ur Rehman, M. H., Ahmed, A. I. A., Al-garadi, M. A., Imran, M., & Guizani, M. (2017). The rise of ransomware and emerging security challenges in the Internet of Things. *Computer Networks, 129*, 444–458.

Yegneswaran, V., Barford, P., & Paxson, V. (2005). Using honeynets for internet situational awareness. In *Proceedings of the Fourth Workshop on Hot Topics in Networks (HotNets IV)* (pp. 17–22).

13

Social and Semantic Online Networks

Elena Pavan

Introduction

Current investigations of cybercrime are proceeding at full speed pushed by the rapid development of computational analytical techniques such as Natural Language Processing, machine learning, and high-dimensional network analysis (see also Chapter 11). Consistently, complex social and semantic network modeling and forecasting methods are increasingly important for the emergent field of socio-technical analyses of crime and deviancy in cyberspace, also called "social cybersecurity" (Carley, 2020): a new domain merging scientific analysis and engineering, and wherein computational social science methods and techniques are applied to identify, measure, and counter-act malicious manipulations of unprecedented communication possibilities. While the application of network

E. Pavan (✉)
Department of Sociology and Social Research, University of
Trento, Trento, Italy
e-mail: elena.pavan@unitn.it

analysis within social cybersecurity studies is contributing to one of the most interdisciplinary and cutting-edge areas of socially relevant "big data research" (see, for instance, Chapters 10 and 11), its roots are to be found in a long-standing interest for personal and organizational relational structures as drivers and, at the same time, spaces for criminal and deviant dynamics.

This chapter aims at adding to the cross-fertilization of knowledges that sustains this interdisciplinary area of research by offering a handful of seeds to grow an aware and purposive attitude to the study of online networks. It begins by rooting our interest for online structures within existing attempts to conceptualize and analyze social phenomena and, more specifically, crime, harm, and deviance from a network point of view. Compared to existing studies, some specifications about the peculiar nature of online networks will be made, especially with respect to the type of data we use to trace them.

The chapter then illustrates a set of key passages and practical instruments to trace and analyze two different, yet tightly interrelated, types of online networks. On the one hand, *social networks* in which an enormous variety of individual and organizational actors are tied via multiple communicative interactions enabled by digital media features. On the other hand, *semantic networks* in which contents produced and circulated by digital media users are connected based on a variety of relationships— from semantic similarity to common sharing patterns passing through content-marking procedures such as tagging. While the basic notions offered throughout the chapter remain admittedly far from more sophisticated applications of network analysis in social cybersecurity studies, they nonetheless constitute some of the building blocks of these complex approaches and, more relevantly, provide a necessary entry point to an aware and sound study of networked dynamics of cybercrime at the macro, meso, and micro levels.

Background: Offline and Online Networks

Crime and deviance studies are not new to the application of network perspectives and tools. Typically centered on offline illicit, harmful, or deviant activities, extant studies that adopt a relational approach place social ties at the center of their inquiry albeit assigning them a different role—of *conduit*, according to differential association theories, or of *moderation*, according to social control theories (Carrington, 2011). In this tension, social network analysis has been nonetheless applied transversally to shed light on dynamics occurring at different levels: at the micro level, networks served to investigate the effects of individual ties, especially on adolescents' propensity to delinquency (e.g., Haynie, 2002); at the meso level, they allowed to explore the diffusion of criminality within different neighborhoods (e.g., Pattillo, 1998); and at the macro level, structures of ties have been traced and analyzed to grapple with broader organized criminal or terrorist initiatives (e.g., Krebs, 2002; Morselli, 2009). Notably, inquiries based on static representations of individual and organizational networks are increasingly accompanied by dynamic approaches able to describe and, in some cases, simulate and predict changes in the structure and the composition of criminal networks (McCulloh & Carley, 2008; Ouellet et al., 2017).

Such a variety of applications has leaned on data derived from field observation, police records, archived materials, and self-report surveyed data (Ouellet & Hashimi, 2019). In fact, none of these collection techniques lead to data that are at the same accurate, valid, reliable, and produced without excessive costs. For example, recent critical assessments of criminal justice records underline how intrinsic limitations that characterize police reporting activity (e.g., in terms of completeness, discrepancies, veracity) are incubated directly within secondary analyses that use them (Bright et al., 2021). Similar considerations have been done with respect to media or court reconstructions (Ouellet & Hashimi, 2019), while self-reported survey data have been found to be lacking in precision, especially when individuals are asked about their friends or acquaintances' behaviors (Carrington, 2011).

Against this background, the increasing production and availability of digital data particularly from social media platforms have been welcomed with enthusiasm, especially in light of the relative low cost of these data and because they afford to include within observations a wide variety of actors and elements that are hardly fetched through more traditional data collection procedures (Ouellet & Hashimi, 2019). In fact, recent reflections that address the use of Big Data within social sciences do outline how features of large-scale collections of digital data can be both advantageous and troublesome (Salganik, 2018). On the one hand, the unprecedented scale of observation enabled by extensive of digital data, the possibility to produce longitudinal accounts and even time-based simulations, as well as the (alleged) non-reactivity of data harvested from social media platforms do certainly mark unique advantages in comparison with past data sources. On the other hand, digital Big Data are also recognized to be highly incomplete as, irrespectively of their scale, much information that is necessary to respond to research questions or to operationalize challenging concepts such as that of "digital harm" is often lacking. Similarly, albeit digital data refer to unprecedented numbers of observations, they are hardly representative of entire populations (e.g., the citizens of a nation) that are central in crime and deviance studies. Thus, digital Big Data enhance the study of specific groups assembling or converging on social media platforms but can hardly substitute other data sources such as national crime statistics. Finally, digital Big Data tend to be instable, as the platforms through which they are produced change over time together with users' media practices. In this sense, even if they allow longitudinal analyses, these data also invite caution on how the element of time is incorporated and empirically modeled within research courses.

Leaning on digital data potentialities and finding creative solutions to their intrinsic limitations, a torrent of studies is rapidly mushrooming across disciplines that employ large-scale online network analysis to innovate traditional study lines like those on terrorist and extremist groups (e.g., Benigni et al., 2018; Klausen, 2015) but also to shed light specifically onto emergent forms of digital crime and deviancy, such as the malicious manipulation of online conversations for illicit purposes or to spread of fake news and conspiracy theories (Carley, 2020), the viral circulation of hateful contents (e.g., De Smedt et al., 2018; Mathew et al., 2019), or cyberbullying (e.g., Menini et al., 2019).

Tracing and Analyzing Online Social and Semantic Networks

As they are deeply embedded within our daily courses of action, digital media intervene in our social relations (Marres, 2017) and inevitably enrich our personal and collective relational milieus. In this context, courses of communications become courses of actions (Rainie & Wellman, 2012) that can be traced employing a twofold set of networks. On the one side, online social networks which, borrowing from widely adopted definitions in the field, can be defined as a "finite set or sets of actors and the relation or relations defined on them" (Wasserman & Faust, 1994, p. 20). On the other side, semantic networks, which are "structured representation of knowledge" (Diesner & Carley, 2011, p. 766). Each type of network offers an entry point to explore and understand cybercrime: the former more centered on interactions established between actors partaking in criminal or harmful courses of action; the latter more focused on the contents and, thus, on the systems of meanings and symbols that give cybercrime its substance.

Like any other network structure, online social and semantic criminal or harm networks are formed by two elements: *nodes* (also called vertices), which are the entities whose relations we aim at studying; and *ties* (also called edges), which are the relation(s) joining nodes within systems of interdependency. As they often generate from the structuration of data coming from social media platforms, online social and semantic networks will tend to be more heterogeneous in terms of node composition in comparison with offline structures. Indeed, online social networks will include not only offenders and targets (as it often happens when networks are derived from official sources) or personal ties (as in the case of self-reported individual networks), but also a myriad of bystanders which assemble around, for example, the usage of a shared harmful hashtag thus partaking in collective and distributed dynamics of abuse (Pavan & Lavorgna, 2021). Also, online social networks will not be composed exclusively by social actors, whether of individual or organizational nature, but also by a variety of nonhuman and semi-human agents such as bots, trolls, and cyborg whose contribution to criminal and harmful digital courses of action needs to be factored in (Carley,

2020). Similarly, online semantic networks will be shaped by a multiplicity of nodes depending on what entities are considered to be the more adequate semantic unit to respond to research questions—e.g., single words rather than noun phrases (Diesner & Carley, 2011)—and where these units are to be searched for—e.g., within social media or forum posts or along semantic processes taking place before content publication such as image or video tagging (for some example outside the field of cybercrime studies, see Gibbs et al., 2015; Mattoni & Pavan, 2020).

As much as in the offline space, online social and semantic network ties can be traced in manifold and creative ways depending on the type(s) of relation that are deemed theoretically relevant to answer research questions. Depending on platforms' specific materiality, that is, how they are designed and function (Leonardi, 2012), digital media allow individuals to interact in different ways: building (allegedly) stable friendship or following relationships, reacting immediately to contents via *likes* or little hearts, commenting on someone else's posts, or re-broadcasting existing contents via sharing, reposting, or retweeting procedures. Some of these interactions are mutual—that is, ties joining entities lack direction, like it happens with friendship relations on Facebook—while others are asymmetrical—that is, ties generate from a specific entity and are directed toward some other node, like in the case of retweets. From a semantic perspective, meanings associations can be the most diverse, as units of content can be tied, for example, looking at co-occurrence relationships (i.e., entities such as hashtags or words can be used in conjunction within texts) or at similarity patterns (i.e., entities concur to define broader topics of discussions within online conversations).

Relevantly, in spite of this richness, possibilities are not infinite particularly because social media platforms release only certain sets of information on online relations among their users and texts remain structured by language and platform vernacular constraints which cannot be disregarded (Diesner & Carley, 2011; Gibbs et al., 2015). When designing a network approach to analyze cybercrime instances, it is then crucial to factor in the different meanings and the directionalities that are associated by design as well as by usage patterns to specific interactional or associational features as these, in turn, ground different and, therefore, more or less meaningful digital relational structures (Pavan, 2017).

Setting Network Boundaries

Defining the boundaries of criminal or harmful networks (i.e., the identification of the set of entities among which links are to be traced) has always been a particularly challenging task. Traditionally, social network studies have specified network boundaries in two different ways (Laumann et al., 1989). On the one hand, the *realist approach* locks network membership to actors' perceptions so that boundary lines are traced by actors themselves (e.g., when members of a group identify other individuals as members). Conversely, the *nominalist approach* leaves up to the researcher to set boundaries following theoretical considerations (e.g., when all individuals whose names are registered within police records of a specific city are assumed to be part of a criminal network). Similar strategies can be adopted to define the set of texts or documents from which content units are to be extracted.

To be sure, setting network boundaries is a crucial research step for two interrelated reasons. On the one hand, network boundaries define substantively the contours of the criminal or harm dynamics under examination. Thus, a misleading or vague boundary definition results, as it has been claimed particularly with respect to terrorist networks (Van der Hulst, 2011), in analyses with scant social usefulness. On the other hand, boundary specification leads to identify a definite set of entities for which measurements of structural variables (i.e., variables concerning the types of relations that a network member has) and entities' attributes (such as individual gender, years of activity for an organization, etc.) need to be available. However, abovementioned difficulties to access accurate, valid, and reliable data yields to subordinate the identification of network boundaries to the availability of information collected by actors outside the research context (Bright et al., 2021).

When it comes to online social and semantic networks, the identification of network boundaries continues to remain a crucial task for substantive and practical reasons. At the same time, though, it is of paramount importance to factor in the features of the platforms that users decide to adopt as well as the presence of nonhuman agents—especially bots—within networked dynamics we wish to examine. On platforms like Twitter or Facebook, for example, boundaries of a social online network can be traced by combining a nominalist approach leading to the inclusion of a predefined set of users with a snowball sampling technique that would add any user that is followed or mentioned by the initial set (Klausen, 2015). On Twitter, network boundaries of a social network can be drawn following the nominalist approach also starting from a semantic criterion—most notably, the use of a specific hashtag to mark one's tweet—so to include in the analysis all users that have actively intervened within a specific conversation (whether these are individuals, organizations, or bots). As mentioned above, choices on how to set network boundaries should be driven by theoretically informed research questions but, in fact, are more often conditioned (when not limited) by practical considerations about the adequacy of available data.

Network Types

Choices on how to delimit the perimeter of networks go hand in hand with a further set of considerations that have to be made about the type(s) of structure that should be traced. Network types are defined at the crossroads between types of nodes and variety of content ties that we wish to examine (Contractor et al., 2011). As shown in Table 13.1, one or more types of node can be matched with one or more tie contents yielding to more simplified or increasingly complex representation of digital dynamics.

The simplest and yet more diffused type of representation is the unidimensional network where a single tie content is traced within a group

Table 13.1 Network types

		Ties content	
		Single	Multiple
Types of nodes	Single	Unidimensional networks	Unimodal multiplex networks
	Multiple	Multimodal Uniplex networks	(Fully) Multidimensional networks

Source Adapted from Contractor et al. (2011)

of nodes which are all of the same type. Thinking about a platform like Twitter, an example of a unidimensional social network is provided by the structure of direct mentions between users that participate in a specific conversation. In this case, there is a single type of nodes (users) and a single tie content (direct mentioning). On the same platform, an example of a unidimensional semantic network would be the structure defined between all hashtags jointly used within tweets. In such case, there is again just one type of nodes (hashtags) and a single tie content (co-occurrence within the same tweet). When more than one tie content is traced for the same group of nodes, networks are unimodal and multiplex—like when users participating in a Twitter conversation are tied together by both mentions and following relationships. Albeit unidimensional and unimodal multiplex networks are both traced considering just one type of nodes, differences can nonetheless be made between members of this single set based on composition variables, which in the online space may also refer to attributes such as actors' nature (often obtained by applying classification schemes, see, for example, Lotan et al., 2011) or the number of contacts they have within a specific platform.

When networks comprise more than one type of nodes, they achieve to render higher levels of complexity. A typical example of multi-mode uniplex networks is a two-mode network which contemplates one content tie traced between two groups of nodes, such as Facebook users and the posts they comment on. When more than one type of tie content is taken into consideration, networks are traced according to a multidimensional framework (Contractor et al., 2011) such as in the case of structures defined at the intersection of Facebook users and the post they like and/or comment on. Importantly, within multimode networks, ties are traced exclusively *between* sets of entities. Fully multidimensional networks, instead, include also ties between members of the same set—for example, when not only likes and comments are factored in but also friendship relations between users themselves.

Interestingly, multimodal networks allow to overcome the distinction between social and semantic networks allowing researchers to grapple with the increasing complexity of digital dynamics. For example, even a simple multimodal uniplex network mapping how users employ specific hashtags within Twitter conversations configures as a socio-semantic structure which allows to "analyze structurally not only social connections, and not only the content of texts, discourses, and meaning systems, but also and simultaneously the linkages between social and cultural relations" (Basov et al., 2020, p. 1).

Analyzing Social and Semantic Online Networks at the Macro Level

Looking at the macro features of online social and semantic networks provides a first necessary step to characterize the communication flows as well as the knowledge systems that result from the use of digital media within instances of cybercrime. One pivotal macro feature of online networks is its cohesiveness—that is, the extent to which the structure resembles a close-knit system in which all entities are connected and/or reachable from any other point of the network. Network cohesiveness is often found to be relevant with respect to the unfolding of criminal dynamics at all levels and, in fact, to be a marker of distinctiveness amon different sectors of organized crime (Bruinsma & Bernasco, 2004).

When it comes to the online space, high cohesiveness within social networks points to the existence of tightly connected structures often characterized by shared collective identities, which have in turn been seen as playing a key role within individual radicalization patterns (Lindekilde, 2016) but also for the formation of harmful when not directly violent online publics (Massanari, 2017). Similarly, high cohesion within semantic networks signals the existence of a "shared knowledge system" (Diesner & Carley, 2011) spurring from a variety of cultural artifacts— from social media posts to digital images—produced and circulated along network ties. While applications of semantic networks remain still rare within cybercrime and social cybersecurity studies, sociological accounts of hashtags, or meme usage within far-right groups invite to extend research endeavors in this direction (e.g., Froio & Ganesh, 2019).

As a consequence of their large-scale, especially online social networks tend to be rather sparse insofar as nodes tend to interact only with a limited number of other network members and, in fact, to catalyze their attention towards nodes that are already widely acknowledged according to a mechanism of preferential attachment (González-Bailón et al., 2013). Therefore, a typical measure of cohesion such as network density—that is, the proportion of existing ties on total possible ties (Wasserman & Faust, 1994, p. 101)—is poorly informative. Alternative ways of looking at network cohesiveness pass through the evaluation of its overall segmentation, which in the online space relates to the extent to which communication and exchanges among users flow more or less easily.

Along these lines, a cohesive network shows low levels of segmentation, which can be approximated by looking at two factors: the inclusiveness of the network main component and the percentage of isolated nodes (Pavan, 2017). More often than not, online networks are not completely connected and are thus partitioned into components, which are network subsets in which all nodes are either directly or indirectly connected (Wasserman & Faust, 1994, p. 109). The largest of these subsets is called the network "main component" and represents the main portion of a relational structure, whereas subsets formed by one single node are "isolates," that is, entities which for some reason are not connected to the rest of the network. Broadly speaking, the higher the number of components, the higher is network segmentation. Given a certain level of segmentation, though, the larger the percentage of nodes included in the main component, the higher the cohesiveness of the assembled collectivity we are tracing. Conversely, the higher the percentage of isolates, the more online structures show lines of exclusion that are active at the micro-level. A closer analysis of incumbents of different network components allows to begin reasoning on the type of communications or meanings systems that are supporting digital criminal or harmful courses of action.

The Meso Level: Clusters of Actors and Concepts

In addition to their sparseness, online networks tend to be structured around a core of high-degree nodes (see the section below), surrounded by many small clusters of low-degree nodes (Mislove et al., 2007,

p. 30). Such configuration invites to expand current concerns for the internal community structure of criminal networks (Calderoni et al., 2017) and to think about large-scale structures as networks-of-networks which can be explored more closely via clustering procedures. Broadly speaking, clusters can be thought of as network areas in which nodes tend to be more densely connected among themselves than with nodes of other clusters (Newman & Girvan, 2004). In general, clusters tend to be internally homogeneous as they are likely to be formed by nodes that share some characteristics or behaviors. For this reason, identifying these densely connected areas is a relevant analytical step which can be performed automatically via algorithms that lean on modularity—a measure of how clustered a structure is (Blondel et al., 2008; Newman & Girvan, 2004)—or try to maximize connectivity within communities (Traag et al., 2019). Clustering techniques are extensively used in the study of online social networks to different aims—from the identification of communities within the far-right transnational milieu in Europe to the automated spread of hate speech during the COVID-19 pandemic (Uyheng & Carley, 2019) and also to trace cross-platform, cross-language, and cross-country circulation of hateful messages (Johnson et al., 2019).

Nodes Prominence: The Micro Dynamics That Count

Online social structures are often shaped by severe structural asymmetries, as they are held together by few "disproportionally connected nodes [that] keep the network small in terms of path length or average distance between any two nodes" (González-Bailón et al., 2013, p. 954). One way of differentiating nodes from a structural point of view is to assess their prominence, that is, the extent to which they are "involved in relationships with others" (Wasserman & Faust, 1994, p. 173). Especially upon social media, social nodes' prominence acquires a multilayered nature as it is jointly platform-based—i.e., resulting from the overall position of an entity within the overall platform space, for example, in terms of followers and friends one user has—and contextual—that is, measured with respect to the role played within specific conversations developed around hashtags or specific posts and threads.

A good indicator of online prominence which can be measured both at the platform level and contextually remains node degree or "the number of nodes that are adjacent to it" in the network structure (Wasserman & Faust, 1994, p. 100). When network ties have a direction, a node degree can also be further detailed distinguishing between indegree (i.e., the number of ties that a node receives from others in the network) and outdegree (i.e., the number of ties a node sends to the rest of the network). Nodes that are extensively reached out by others tend to catalyze attention flows within the social interaction structure and, more often than not, hold some peculiar characteristics that explain their extensive centrality. Similarly, nodes that show eccentric levels of activity by sending many ties to the rest of the network can be considered as warning signs of potential malicious communication flows. As such, measuring incoming and outcoming centrality in combination with platform prominence remains a crucial entry point for the identification of bots and malwares (Carley, 2020).

Besides offering the possibility to complicate more traditional conceptualizations of prominence, online social networks maintain the possibility to uncover nodes that play a more strategic role as they mediate connections between other network members (Morselli, 2009). Node betweenness, which expresses the extent to which a network node mediates the shortest path between two other disconnected actors (Freeman, 2002 [1979]), remains also in this case the baseline measure to grasp this aspect. A particularly fruitful way of mastering the informative potential of betweenness consists of coupling its declination in terms of brokerage, that is, the extent to which mediation is exerted within or between different groups of nodes (Gould & Fernandez, 1989), with information coming from the identification of clusters so to identify the so-called "network *switchers*" (Padovani & Pavan, 2016): nodes that contribute to the organization of the overall online relational structure by acting more than others as bridges between different network sub-communities.

Within semantic structures, reasoning along centrality helps disentangling the role played by different content units in substantiating cybercrime dynamics. Semantic network analysis theories suggest treating nodes centrality in conjunction with edge weight (a property of network ties that expresses the frequency of an association) to identify prominent symbols within knowledge systems (Carley & Kaufer, 1993). More specifically, prominent symbols are defined as nodes of semantic networks that score high in terms of *density* (i.e., connected to a greater share of other nodes), *conductivity* (i.e., mediating a higher number of network paths between unconnected nodes), and *consensus* (i.e., involved in frequent associations with other nodes). While node density can be measured through degree and consensus via an evaluation of the weights of edges that are incident with a certain entity, node conductivity is better grasped by measuring node betweenness.

Conclusion

In a context in which cybercrime instances are multiplying rapidly along the continuous spread of digital media in our "deeply mediated lives" (Couldry & Hepp, 2017), including the investigation of online social and semantic structures within research endeavors is certainly of increasing importance. To be sure, crime and deviancy studies have already demonstrated a growing interest in tracing and analyzing social networks with respect to offline courses of action, whereas the employment of semantic networks has remained rather limited. This unbalance is mirrored online, with semantic dimensions of cybercrime more often approached through artificial intelligence and Natural Language Processes tools than from a network point of view. Relevantly, also applications of online social network analysis do rarely stand alone and are often coupled with different methods of content analysis—whether automated or of a more qualitative nature.

All in all, the investigation of online social and semantic networks appears to be a pivotal piece of an increasingly complex puzzle of techniques pushed forward to cope with the complexity of current cybercrime dynamics. Increased availability of digital data invites to develop our methodological capacities in this direction and yet, on its own, does not guarantee the production of a scientifically valid and, more relevantly, socially relevant knowledge. While social media data are increasingly adopted to investigate particularly some prominent instances, such as terrorism propaganda and recruitment or the spreading of hateful contents, they do hold only limited potential to study "darker" crime instances such as drug dealing or weapon selling.

Different instances of cybercrime, deviance, and harm are carried out often at the margins when not outside of the public space of social media, whereas in these spaces new and emerging forms of abuse are rapidly diffusing, such as technology facilitated gender violence (Henry & Powell, 2018). Persisting difficulties in recognizing some digital experiences as harmful, abusive, or even violent even by those who live them (Martellozzo & Jane, 2017) are limiting the potentialities of cross-fertilization between knowledges and methods developed across different disciplines, from crime studies to media and communication studies passing through gender, migration, and race studies. At the same time, instances of collection and analysis of data from the Dark Web that combine social and semantic networks with automated annotation techniques for example to "decode" criminal jargon do exist but seem to remain exceptional (Yuan et al., 2018). Thus, approaching in a purposive and aware way online semantic and social structures appears to be of paramount importance. Nonetheless, even if online networks are capable of shedding a much-needed light on specific courses of criminal and deviant action, they are hardly "all mighty" tools. Mastering their application entails therefore not only a continuous work of methodological training but, perhaps more relevantly, a thorough theoretical and conceptual job aimed at disclosing the manifold and, sometimes, not so evident ways in which digital interactions can not only infringe the law but, more radically, bite and hurt to the bone.

References

Basov, N., Breiger, R., & Hellsten, I. (2020). Socio-semantic and other dualities. *Poetics, 78*(2020), 1–12.

Benigni, M., Joseph, K., & Carley, K. M. (2018). Mining online communities to inform strategic messaging: Practical methods to identify community level insights. *Computational and Mathematical Organization Theory, 24*(2018), 224–242.

Blondel, V. D., Guillaume, J., Lambiotte, R., & Lefebvre, E. (2008). Fast unfolding of communities in large networks. *Journal of Statistical Mechanics, 2008*, 1–12.

Bright, D., Brewer, R., & Morselli, C. (2021). Using social network analysis to study crime: Navigating the challenges of criminal justice records. *Social Networks, 66*(2021), 50–64.

Bruinsma, G. J. N., & Bernasco, W. (2004). "Criminal groups and transnational illegal markets: a more detailed examination on the basis of social network theory." *Crime Law and Social Change, 41*(1), 79–94.

Calderoni, F., Brunetto, D., & Piccardi, C. (2017). Communities in criminal networks: A case study. *Social Networks, 48*, 116–125.

Carley, K. M. (2020). Social cybersecurity: AN emerging science. *Computational and Mathematical Organization Theory, 26*(2020), 365–381.

Carley, K. M., & Kaufer, D. S. (1993). Semantic connectivity: An approach for analyzing symbols in semantic networks. *Communication Theory, 3*(3), 183–213.

Carrington, P. J. (2011). Crime and social network analysis. In J. Scott & P. J. Carrington (Eds.), *The Sage handbook of social network analysis* (pp. 236–255). Sage.

Contractor, N., Monge, P., & Leonardi, P. (2011). Multidimensional networks and the dynamics of sociomateriality: Bringing technology inside the network. *International Journal of Communication, 5*, 682–720.

Couldry, N., & Hepp, A. (2017). *The mediated construction of reality*. Polity Press.

De Smedt, T., De Pauw, G., & Van Ostaeyen, P. (2018). Automatic detection of online jihadist hate speech.

Diesner, J., & Carley, K. M. (2011). Semantic Networks. In G. Barnett (Ed.), *Encyclopaedia of social networking* (pp. 766–769). Sage.

Freeman, L. C. (2002 [1979]). Centrality in social networks: Conceptual clarifications. In J. Scott (Ed.), *Social networks: Critical concepts in sociology* (Vol. I, pp. 238–263). Routledge.

Froio, C., & Ganesh, B. (2019). The transnationalisation of far right discourse on Twitter: Issues and actors that cross borders in Western European democracies. *European Societies, 21*(4), 513–539.

Gibbs, M., Meese, J., Arnold, M., Nansen, B., & Carter, M. (2015). #Funeral and Instagram: death, social media, and platform vernacular. *Information, Communication & Society, 18*(3), 255–268.

González-Bailón, S., Borge-Holthoefer, J., & Moreno, Y. (2013). Broadcasters and hidden influentials in online protest diffusion. *American Behavioral Scientist, 57*, 943–965.

Gould, R. V., & Fernandez, R. M. (1989). Structures of mediation: A formal approach to brokerage in transaction networks. *Sociological Methodology, 19*, 89–126.

Haynie, D. L. (2002). Friendship networks and delinquency: The relative nature of per delinquency. *Journal of Quantitative Criminology, 18*(2), 99–134.

Henry, N., & Powell, A. (2018). Technology-facilitated sexual violence: A literature review of empirical research. *Trauma, Violence, & Abuse, 19*(2), 195–208.

Johnson, N. F., Leahy, R., Restrepo, N. J., Velasquez, N., Zheng, M., Manrique, P., Devkota, P., & Wuchty, S. (2019). Hidden resilience and adaptive dynamics of the global online hate ecology. *Nature, 573*(7773), 261–265.

Klausen, Y. (2015). Tweeting the Jihad: Social media networks of western foreign fighters in Syria and Iraq. *Studies in Conflict & Terrorism, 38*(1), 1–22.

Krebs, V. (2002). Uncloaking terrorist networks. *First Monday, 7*(4).

Laumann, E. O., Marsden, P. V., & Prensky, D. (1989). The boundary specification problem. In R. S. Burt & M. J. Minor (Eds.), *Applied network analysis: A methodological introduction* (pp. 18–34). Sage.

Leonardi, P. M. (2012). Materiality, sociomateriality, and socio-technical systems: What do these terms mean? How are they different? Do we need them? In P. M. Leonardi, B. A. Nardi, & J. Kallinikos (Eds.), *Materiality and organizing: Social interaction in a technological world* (pp. 25–48). Oxford University Press.

Lindekilde, L. (2016). Radicalization, de-radicalization, and counter-radicalization. In R. Jackson (Ed.), *Routledge handbook of critical terrorism studies* (pp. 248–260). Routledge.

Lotan, G., Graeff, E., Ananny, M., Gaffney, D., Pearce, I., & d. boyd (2011). The revolutions were tweeted: Information flows during the 2011 Tunisian and Egyptian revolutions. *International Journal of Communication, 5*(2011), 1375–1405.

Marres, N. (2017). *Digital sociology*. Polity Press.

Martellozzo, E., & Jane, E. A. (2017). Introduction: Victims of cybercrime on the small 'I' internet. In E. Martellozzo & E. A. Jane (Eds.), *Cybercrime and its victims*. Routledge.

Massanari, A. (2017). #Gamergate and the fappening: How Reddit's algorithm, governance, and culture support toxic technocultures. *New Media and Society, 19*(3), 329–346.

Mathew, B., Saha, P., Tharad, H., Rajgaria, S., Singhania, P., Maity, S. K., Goyal, P., & Mukherje, A. (2019). Thou shalt not hate: Countering online hate speech. *Proceedings of the International AAAI Conference on Web and Social Media, 13*, 369–380.

Mattoni, A., & Pavan, E. (2020). Activist media practices, alternative media and online digital traces: The case of YouTube in the Italian Se non ora, quando? Movement. In H. Stephansen & E. Treré (Eds.), *Citizen media and practice currents, connections, challenges* (pp. 152–168). Routledge.

McCulloh, I. A., & Carley, K. M. (2008). *Social network change direction.* CASOS Technical Report CMU-ISR-08-116. Pittsburgh, PA: Carnagie Mellon University.

Menini, S., Moretti, G., Corazza, M., Cabrio, E., Tonelli, S., & Villata, S. (2019). A system to monitor cyberbullying based on message classification and social network analysis. In *Proceedings of the Third Workshop on Abusive Language Online* (pp. 105–110).

Mislove, A., Marcon, M., Gummadi, M. P., Druschel, P., & Bhattacharjee, B. (2007). Measurement and analysis of online social networks. *Proceedings of the 7th ACM SIGCOMM Conference on Internet measurement* (pp. 29–42).

Morselli, C. (2009). *Inside criminal networks.* Springer Publishing.

Newman, M. E. J., & Girvan, M. (2004). Finding and evaluating community structure in networks. *Physical Review, 69*(026113), 1–12.

Ouellet, M., & Hashimi, S. (2019). Criminal group dynamics and network methods. *Methods of criminology and criminal justice research—Sociology of crime, law and deviance* (Vol. 24, pp. 47–65).

Ouellet, M., Bouchard, M., & Charette, Y. (2017). One gang dies, another gains? The network dynamics of criminal group persistence. *Criminology, 57*(2017), 5–33.

Padovani, C., & Pavan, E. (2016). Global governance and ICTs: Exploring online governance networks around gender and media. *Global Networks, 16*(3), 350–371.

Pattillo, M. E. (1998). Sweet mothers and gangbangers: managing crime in a black middle-class neighborhood. *Social Forces, 76*(3), 747–774.

Pavan, E. (2017). The integrative power of online collective action networks beyond protest: Exploring social media use in the process of institutionalization. *Social Movement Studies, 16*(4): 433–446.

Pavan, E., & Lavorgna, A. (2021). Promises and pitfalls of legal responses to image-based sexual abuse: Critical insights from the Italian case. In A. Powell, A. Flynn, & L. Sugiura (Eds.), *The Palgrave handbook of gendered violence and technology.* Palgrave.

Rainie, L., & Wellman, B. (2012). *Networked: The new social operating system.* The MIT Press.

Salganik, M. (2018). Bit by bit: Social research in the digital age. Princeton University Press.

Traag, V. A., Waltman, L., & van Eck, L. J. (2019). "From Louvain to Leiden: guaranteeing well-connected communities." *Scientific reports, 9*(5233), 1–12.

Uyheng, J., & Carley, K. M. (2019). Bots and online hate during the COVID-19 pandemic: Case studies in the United States and the Philippines. *Journal of Computational Social Science, 3,* 445–468.

Van der Hulst, R. C. (2011). Terrorist networks: The threat of connectivity. In J. Scott & P. J. Carrington (Eds.), *The Sage handbook of social network analysis* (pp. 256–270). Sage.

Wasserman, S., & Faust, K. (1994). *Social network analysis: Methods and applications.* Cambridge University Press.

Yuan, K., Lu, H., Liao, X. and Wang, X. (2018). Reading Thieves' cant: Automatically identifying and understanding dark jargons from cyber-crime marketplaces. In *Proceedings of the 27th USENIX Security Symposium* (pp. 1027–1041).

14

Digital Ethnography in Cybercrime Research: Some Notes from the Virtual Field

Nicholas Gibbs and Alexandra Hall

Introduction

Ethnography has a long and vibrant history in criminology. While it may not be the most widespread methodology in the discipline, the immersive cultural lens offered by the ethnographic approach has produced some of the twentieth century's most illuminating and memorable in-depth accounts of crime and crime control. Ethnography was initially established by anthropologists to explore cultural groups by observing and engaging with them in their local environments over an extended

N. Gibbs
Department of Social Sciences, Northumbria University, Newcastle Upon Tyne, UK
e-mail: nicholas.gibbs@northumbria.ac.uk

A. Hall (✉)
Department of Social Sciences, Northumbria University, Newcastle upon Tyne, UK
e-mail: alex.hall@northumbria.ac.uk

© The Author(s), under exclusive license to Springer Nature Switzerland AG 2021
A. Lavorgna and T. J. Holt (eds.), *Researching Cybercrimes*,
https://doi.org/10.1007/978-3-030-74837-1_14

283

period of time. However, ethnography must now confront the multi-sited, digital and mobile nature of social, cultural and economic life. To come to terms with this shift, the ethnographer must now look beyond the traditional local research site to global, transnational and virtual spaces. As a result, the use of digital ethnography, basically traditional ethnographic methods modified to interact with online communities and environments, has steadily increased in anthropology and the social sciences.

Criminologists are also beginning to make use of this method in response to the increasing need to account for the complex digital features of contemporary forms of criminality, victimization, policing and punishment. In this chapter, we offer some initial reflections on the use of digital ethnography in criminology by outlining some of our experiences as ethnographers conducting research in virtual environments—specifically, Hall's research on the trade in illicit medicines and Gibbs' PhD research on the market in image and performance-enhancing drugs (IPEDs). We cover key issues that range from practical challenges and ethical quandaries through analytical capabilities to epistemological issues. As we outline the possibilities and pitfalls of this nascent methodological approach, we argue that criminological ethnographers must balance both online and offline research if we are to keep pace with the contemporary landscape of crime, harm and control.

The Ethnographic Tradition in Criminology

Although we do not intend to provide a thorough history of criminological ethnography in this chapter (for this, see Treadwell, 2020), it is worth highlighting some important aspects of the approach's rich heritage. Ethnography's entrance into the study of crime and deviance can be traced back to the Chicago School of the 1920s. Early ethnographers responded to Robert Park's now famous appeal to "go get the seats of your pants dirty in real research" (Park, quoted in McKinney, 1966) by getting out onto the city's streets to uncover the experiences and narratives of everyday life. Characterized by Maguire (2008) as a "minority tradition" in criminology, ethnography nevertheless flourished in the

1960s and 1970s as researchers sought to explore the highly nuanced and personal nature of deviance in order to generate valuable empirical and theoretical insights. Having weathered the "dark ages" of the 1980s and 1990s (Ferrell & Hamm, 1998; Hobbs, 1993), criminological ethnography has experienced something of a revival (Fleetwood & Potter, 2017; see also Hall & Winlow, 2015).

Ethnography is an inherently messy, hands-on research methodology (Liebling, 2001). Settling on a definition of ethnography is therefore quite difficult (Gobo, 2008). Traditionally, the principal aim of ethnographic research was to gain insights into the everyday meanings and practices that allow individuals to live together in specific local contexts. At the core of this method is participant observation. Sustained contact with the field and its inhabitants allows the researcher to produce rich and nuanced data. However, different approaches to this method have proliferated in recent years to reflect a diverse and changing research landscape. Digital ethnography, auto-ethnography (Jewkes, 2011) and visual ethnography (Van de Voorde, 2012) now underpin a diversifying ethnographic sensibility in the contemporary era and highlight criminology's versatility and relevance in a world characterized by accelerated cultural and technological change.

"Going Digital": Moving Criminological Ethnography Online

Today, engagement with the online world is a mundane daily occurrence for many people, particularly in the Global North (Powell et al., 2018). Criminology must now reach beyond the well-versed "cybercrimes" of the Web 1.0 era to explore the impact of digitization on criminal and harmful activities as diverse as child sexual exploitation, state crime, gang violence, drug markets and far-right extremism. Moving beyond the traditional understandings of computer integrity, computer-assisted crime and computer content crime (Wall, 2007), criminology has begun to explore the alteration in criminal subjectivities brought about by Web 2.0 (see Yar, 2012) and how the ubiquity of online platforms such as social networking sites (SNS) has affected traditionally offline offenses, including hate crime, organized crime and even murder (see Yardley & Wilson, 2014). In line with this shift, the long-held principles of ethnographic study have been reimagined to reflect increasing digitization.

Put simply, digital ethnography refers to any ethnographic study undertaken on platforms that use binary code (Horst & Miller, 2012). Though this seemingly straightforward methodology belies a rather fractious history (see Abidin & de Seta, 2020), its current iteration can be traced back to Hine's (2000) concept of "virtual ethnography," which, when first proposed, acted as something of a harbinger of our current view of the Internet as a site of interaction in itself, and thus a space in which the toolkit of traditional ethnography could be repurposed following the mass uptake of home computing. Following this first iteration, ethnographic research in the digital world has splintered to incorporate a vast array of specialized "buzzword" approaches, ranging from "social media ethnography" (Postill & Pink, 2012) and "trace ethnography" (Geiger & Ribes, 2011) through to "networked anthropology" (Collins & Durington, 2015) and "netnography" (Kozinets, 2010). While we accept the worthiness of these increasingly specialized approaches, we advocate for a more holistic and versatile definition of digital ethnography that can be adopted by researchers from varying backgrounds to explore every aspect of digital lifeworlds. For this reason, our understanding of digital ethnography is deliberately open-ended, and we encourage criminological ethnographers to be adaptive and flexible as they explore this approach in the context of their research.

Our own work offers two examples of digital ethnography in criminology. We will explain the practicalities in more detail below (see also Antonopoulos & Hall, 2016; Hall & Antonopoulos, 2016). Alongside our work, for those considering moving their ethnography at least partially online (more common during the COVID-19 global health crisis), several recent noteworthy examples highlight the strength and reach of digital qualitative and ethnographic research in criminology. These include Forrest Stuart's *Ballad of the Bullet* (2020), an excellent mix of online and offline ethnography exploring the lives of Chicago's urban youth, who, living precarious lives amidst poverty and gang violence, have begun to use social media profiles as a marketing strategy to capitalize on the public fascination with ghetto culture and DIY drill music. Similarly, Keir Irwin-Rogers (2019) provides a UK-based account of violence, drug markets, online performances and identities. Sarah Lageson's *Digital Punishment* (2020) offers a fascinating and much-needed analysis of the digital life of criminal records in the US, where criminal justice agencies have turned to private IT companies in the search for cost-effective criminal record-keeping. The result is a system of "digital punishment" with collateral damage impacting every facet of private and civic life in America. A budding sub-field is now emerging in drug studies, which includes innovative work on user and supplier communities on darknet markets (Martin et al., 2020) and social network sites (SNS) (Demant et al., 2020). Similarly, new work now focuses on aspects of "organized" crime and illicit markets operating online, for instance the role of technology in counterfeit markets in Brazil (Dent, 2020) and illegal moneylending in China (Wang et al., 2020). These are just some of the most recent examples of an ever-expanding body of literature in criminology. In the next section, we draw on our own experiences to provide some reflections and practical guidance for those planning to conduct ethnographic fieldwork in virtual environments.

Conducting a Digital Ethnography

The practice of conducting a digital ethnography can be broken down into two broad phases: non-reactive and reactive (Janetzko, 2008). The non-reactive phase, sometimes referred to as "lurking," simply requires the ethnographer to inhabit the online field-site, passively observing subjects' behaviors and the platforms' norms to learn the cultural language of the space. For Hall and Antonopoulos (2016), this entailed lurking on a range of platforms including online pharmacy (OP) surface websites, public drug-related forums and SNS, and building a dataset of screenshots tracing the interactions and transactions taking place, which were then coded and analyzed. To focus the research in a mass of online information, decisions were made after general searches, observations and discussions with experts to ascertain which online sites were most commonly used by users and suppliers of pharmaceutical drugs—for example, forums that related to specific topics with links to pharmaceutical consumption, such as bodybuilding, men's and women's health, drug forums and their prescription drug sections. Similarly, Gibbs (forthcoming) observed both the consumption and supply of gym-related IPEDs during the non-reactive stage, familiarizing himself with the community-specific norms and lexicon on various SNS. Crucially, this aspect of the digital ethnographic process uncovered what Enghoff and Aldridge (2019) term "unsolicited" data, which, given its organic, entirely user-generated nature, represent the most unmediated content online. Screenshots were then contextualized with researcher fieldnotes to paint a basic picture of the online field-site.

The reactive phase involves interacting with participants in online spaces and physically shaping the field-site to elicit data. Just like the traditional ethnographer builds relationships and negotiates access in the field, here the digital ethnographer follows the norms of the platform under study, interacting with forum users, creating social media accounts and generating content. In the reactive phase, Hall (Hall & Antonopoulos, 2016) established social media and forum profiles alongside email accounts through which she interacted with customers and sellers of pharmaceutical drugs. Similarly, in Gibbs' (forthcoming) reactive phase, he created two SNS profiles on Instagram and Facebook, through which he solicited interviews with users as well as generating posts and liking/sharing his sample's content. Both of these profiles used the researcher's real name as well as his institutional affiliation and a brief "bio" explaining his research interests. The reason for this was twofold. First, as many participants who were initially approached online went on to interact with Gibbs face-to-face, any attempt to obscure his identity would have been damaging to his relationships in the field. Second, as Gibbs' reactive phase involved him producing content that mirrored his sample's SNS use, using his own images to post updates of his lifestyle and gym progression worked to add a certain degree of authenticity to the accounts, and allowed him further insight into the community's norms and practices as a "researcher participant" (Gans, 1967). Notably, the initial wave of participants that Gibbs approached appeared reticent to engage with these accounts until they were sufficiently populated and appeared as legitimate. This illustrates the challenges in cultivating a credible online presence for digital ethnographers. Following the creation of the profiles, Gibbs sampled fifty users who had geotagged[1] their posts to two local gyms under study and followed them to populate the account. Alongside this sample, Gibbs used a hashtag to search for IPED supplier accounts and requested to join several open and closed IPED Facebook groups. From here, he sent initial messages to the sample, inviting them to take part in online and offline interviews. This helped triangulate the data and provide a more robust analysis.

Digital ethnographers understand that platforms like SNS, online forums and webpages constitute field-sites just as much as physical spaces (Dalsgaard, 2016). Data collection can take the form of online interviewing, screenshots of meaningful interactions, images and text from publicly-available webpages, audio or video recordings, documents of varying types and, of course, ethnographic fieldnotes. Reactive and non-reactive phases of the research may overlap during the research process and should not be treated as discreet, sequential stages. Instead, the reactive and non-reactive phases work alongside one another to facilitate a thorough immersion in the field.

Readers can find detailed discussions of the ethics of online research elsewhere in this collection (see also Hall & Antonopoulos, 2016), but one issue we thought worthy of mention in relation to digital ethnography is that of consent. This is perhaps the most divisive ethical issue for budding digital ethnographers to navigate, especially with regard to the technique of "lurking" without deceiving participants. This issue fundamentally rests upon the degree to which data on the Internet are considered public or private (Hall & Antonopoulos, 2016; Lingel, 2012; McKee, 2013; Woodfield & Iphofen, 2018)—see also Part III of this book. It begs the question of whether user-generated content on SNS is public (due to its universal accessibility) or private (given that the user has generated it). Scholars writing on issues of informed consent tend to either advocate for consent regardless of context or platform (see Bond et al., 2013; Michaelidou et al., 2016), or suggest that, due to

---

[1] This term refers to Instagram users tagging their posts to a certain location, for example a landmark or business premises.

the public nature of SNS, data constitute public property, particularly when anonymized (see Alim, 2014; Beninger et al., 2014). This division is, to some extent, premised on the extent to which an average user is understood to be aware of their platform's data usage policy, which often contains clauses about third-party data use (Townsend & Wallace, 2016). However, in the case of SNS, terms and conditions go unread by most users (Denecke, 2014) and, even if one wishes to access them, they are in a state of constant flux (Beninger et al., 2014). Further, boyd and Crawford (2012) contend that simply because data are publicly available, this does not necessarily make it acceptable to use.

The ethical quagmire of "public versus private" was played out in the first author's Facebook data collection as he took screenshots of members' and admins' posts on a number of closed groups. These technically *public* platforms are perhaps best described as *semi-public* (Irwin-Rogers, 2019), given that one needs to be accepted by administrators in order to join. As a result, ambiguity surrounds the availability of data on these pages, particularly as the users' intended audience was presumably those in the private group rather than the public at large (or indeed a criminological researcher). Although we offer no definitive solution to this dilemma, Gibbs operated in line with Helen Nissenbaum's (2010) notion of "contextual integrity," wherein the need to receive informed consent was calculated on a case-by-case basis, regardless of the publicly-available nature of the data being gathered. This was consistent with the AoIR's (2019) advice that researchers make an ethical judgment call rather than rigidly following guidelines. Thus, data that the researcher adjudged to be in the public realm (including posts in these semi-public groups) were included, on the condition that users were anonymized and the post did not include any indicators of their location or other personal information.

Epistemological Possibilities at the Crossroads Between Online and Offline Worlds

A crucial question for ethnographers and social researchers in general is how much data should be collected online or offline. Depending on the nature of the research aims, ethnographic methods can be conducted entirely online. However, the research we conducted had important online and offline dimensions. Throughout our respective projects, we were acutely aware of academia's tendency to dichotomize "online" and "offline" research (Wilson et al., 2012) and the subsequent label attached to "virtual" researchers. Such dichotomous thinking, which can be traced back to the initial academic forays into "cyberspace" (see Sunden, 2002; Taylor, 1999), is unhelpful but unfortunately common within criminology and, more broadly, cybercrime research. Instead, we wish to stress the utility of applying a digital ethnographic approach to myriad forms of criminological inquiry, beyond the traditional focus on cybercrimes. Through a combination of online and offline methods, we were better able to research beyond the narrow confines of mainstream criminology's focus on legal definitions of crime, to reveal nuanced and contextualized meanings in the research and to ensure the validity of our research findings. In other words, our research questions demanded both online and offline elements which often merged, and a certain degree of flexibility in our approach.

To overcome some of the potential challenges, Gibbs' work made explicit use of a connective approach, which is concerned with the interconnections between online and offline spaces. Despite being coined by Hine (2000), this approach has its roots in education studies, where Leander and McKim (2003) first mobilized dual online/offline observation of adolescent teens in a learning environment. The practitioners of connective ethnography, as originally conceived, tend to dispute the notion that space is "static" (Leander & McKim, 2003, p. 217) and instead view the Internet not as a separate realm but as part of one's journey through the world. Importantly, the concept of online and offline is not disregarded, and practices can still be said to be "online" (e.g., creating a social media post) or "offline" (e.g., speaking to a friend in person). However, Leander and McKim (2003) accept that these realms are "blended" and inevitably impact on one another. Prince (2019) employs the terms "influence" and "flow" in connective ethnography to describe the continuum of online and offline. He talks of a state of "oneness," whereby no divide exists between the two. Here, *influence* describes the impact that one realm has on another, for example offline behaviors being replicated online. *Flow*, on the other hand, describes "the continuous back and forth movement between realms, making the boundaries between one realm and another progressively indistinguishable" (Prince, 2019, p. 47). Put simply, the concept of flow acts as the crux of connective ethnography, acknowledging that subjects and everyday practices drift in and out of online and offline spaces, thus advocating that researchers must do the same to elicit accurate data.

Crucially, from its inception, and in a move that contradicts most previous research, connective ethnography has acknowledged that "experiences in cyberspace are often not seen as exceptional by participants" (Leander & McKim, 2003, p. 218). Therefore, scholars ought to integrate online or digital ethnography because the use of the Internet and online communication is an accepted and mundane reality for most people living in the Global North. As discussed by Abidin and de Seta (2020), linguistically, the specter of this virtual/real divide can be found in the multiple online ethnographic methods that fall within the label of connective ethnography. Indeed, Hine's (2000) coinage of the term connective ethnography follows her former commitment to "virtual ethnography." The term "virtual" here is restricted to the historic moment of its inception, when the virtual world was viewed in opposition to the offline experience and, therefore, even in its most recent iteration, a hangover from this dichotomous view remains. Following Abidin and de Seta (2020), fluidity and messiness are now central considerations of this method.

A Note on Leaving the Digital Field

While a number of ethnographers have addressed the challenges of leaving the field after gathering the required data (see Snow, 1980; Iversen, 2009; Tickle, 2017), relatively little has been written around the unique struggles of disengagement from *digital* ethnography. Here, we will reflect on the first authors' recent research to offer some insights.

The researcher's SNS accounts that successfully facilitated large swathes of the data collection brought up an unexpected issue when it became time to withdraw from the field. Indeed, as both profiles were deleted upon completion of Gibbs' fieldwork in the name of ethical propriety, the participant network and all of the associated data stored on the platforms inevitably had to be surrendered. For this reason, what Lofland and Lofland (1995) term the "etiquette of departures" was unable to be followed in the traditional sense. Instead, prior to deleting both accounts, a message of gratitude was posted for participants to see, alongside a short explanation of the researcher's withdrawal from the field. Inevitably however, not all of the digital sample would have been privy to this post had they not logged onto their SNS accounts during this time period. As a result, to some it would have appeared that the digital ethnographer simply vanished into thin air, with all publicly-available traces of his online presence erased from existence, besides a number of archived conversations and now-defunct notifications. Clearly, this poses some ethical concerns, particularly about the assurances that were given to participants around their right to withdraw and, more broadly, their ability to contact the researcher after the completion of data collection. Though admittedly never truly mitigated against, the researcher's email address and contact number were included in the consent form that was distributed to all *active* participants, and therefore, this means of communication was deliberately left open to ensure the interviewees' sustained informed consent.

However, despite Gibbs' resolute exit, the question of whether the digital ethnographer ever truly leaves the field-site does not have as clear-cut an answer as one would assume (see also Chapters 23 and 24). Hammersley and Atkinson (2019) note that ethnographers inevitably retain certain key relationships and friendships even after data collection is complete by virtue of their sustained involvement in the field and the numerous social bonds they build during data collection. This is particularly apt within the discipline of criminology, as insider ethnographers like Winlow (2001), Treadwell (2012) and Ancrum (2013) cannot be said to have truly exited the field due to their key contacts and locations being a mainstay in their lives long before the fieldwork itself. Similarly, Smith (2014) notes that, despite his formal disengagement from the field, his forays in the local night-time economy inevitably saw him interact with former participants in the bars and pubs of his research site. Therefore, given the authors' sustained involvement in their respective

research areas, we cannot be certain that our relationships with participants ceased, even after online profiles were dismantled and online data
were deleted.

Furthermore, it would have been both a personal loss and an act
of academic self-sabotage to erase all contact with the digital sample.
With this in mind, the first author exchanged additional contact details
with a number of key participants prior to formally withdrawing from
the online field-site. Ultimately, just as he was able to build a robust
sample through the tools of SNS, the people under study remain just
a simple search away to this day. Therefore, the digital ethnographer
cannot be said to have truly *left* the field as much as stepped away
from the screen. Given the relatively unchartered territory that digital
ethnographers currently traverse (Gatson, 2011), this is yet another
example of situational decision-making in the field. As such, rather than
providing a prescriptive "how to" guide within this chapter, we simply
wish prospective digital ethnographers to remain vigilant to the compli-
cations precipitated by withdrawing from the field, and therefore advise
others to bear the first author's experiences in mind in their own research.

Conclusion

Online research methods are expanding and changing just as new technologies continue to develop and enter our social worlds in new and
complex ways. This is a matter that impacts research not only in terms
of methodology but epistemology, of the conditions of the possibilities,
sources and limitations of knowledge. In this chapter, we have outlined
some selected details of our experiences as ethnographers conducting
research in virtual worlds in the hope our reflections go some way in
helping budding digital ethnographers in criminology.

For us, immersion in a field-site using the central technique of participant observation is still key to ethnography, whether the field-site is
virtual or not. However, staying flexible and opening up the possibilities
of the research to other field-sites and methods are also fundamental if
research is to adequately trace and interpret the complexity of everyday

life at a time when networked technologies continue to develop at a staggering pace. That is not to say an ethnographic study cannot be situated entirely within a virtual world, but that the research should be driven by the research questions, rather than a priori assumptions about social interactions and cultural activities (Boellstorf et al., 2012). If research is rigorous, there is no reason for ethnographers to feel they must be selective about real versus virtual or single versus fixed field-sites (O'Reilly, 2009). As Boellstorf and colleagues (2012, p. 4) suggest:

> while the specificities of [virtual] spaces prompt their own set of considerations, the ethnographic research paradigm does not undergo fundamental transformation or distortion in its journey to virtual arenas because ethnographic approaches are always modified for each fieldsite, and in real time as the research progresses.

How researchers keep pace with technological change beyond the Web 2.0 era is still an open-ended question. Ethnographic researchers in virtual worlds will increasingly find themselves compelled to balance their focus on people versus machine in an age when the Internet of Things (see Greengard, 2015) is set to outstrip human interpretation and interaction. If our focus is on digital technologies more broadly, we must expand our empirical and theoretical nets to capture not only social media platforms and darknet markets but also machine learning, automation and artificial intelligence. These new fields present their own challenges for ethnographers interested in extending their research online. We look forward to exploring these issues with established academics and the new generation of researchers, for whom networked technologies and online worlds form an important part of their scholarship.

References

Abidin, C., & de Seta, G. (2020). Private messages from the field: Confessions on digital ethnography and its discomforts. *Journal of Digital Social Research, 2*(1), 1–19.

Alim, S. (2014). An initial exploration of ethical research practices regarding automated data extraction from online social media user profiles. *First Monday, 19*(7), 105–127.

Ancrum, C. (2013). Stalking the margins of legality: Ethnography, participant observation and the post-modern underworld. In S. Winlow & R. Atkinson (Eds.), *New directions in crime and deviancy*. Routledge.

Antonopoulos, G. A., & Hall, A. (2016). "Gain with no pain": Anabolic-androgenic steroids trafficking in the UK. *European Journal of Criminology, 13*(6), 696–713.

AoIR. (2019). *Internet research: Ethical guidelines 3.0 Association of Internet Researchers.* Available at: https://aoir.org/reports/ethics3.pdf. Last accessed 4 Jan 2021.

Beninger, K., Fry, A., Jago, N., Lepps, H., Nass, L., & Silvester, H. (2014). *Research using social media; users' views.* Available at: http://www.natcen.ac.uk/media/282288/p0639-research-using-social-media-report-final-190214.pdf.

Boellstorf, T., Nardi, B., Pearce, C., & Taylor, T. L. (2012). *Ethnography and virtual worlds*. Princeton University Press.

Bond, C., Ahmed, O., Hind, M., Thomas, B., & Hewitt-Taylor, J. (2013). The conceptual and practical ethical dilemmas of using health discussion board posts as research data. *Journal of Medical Internet Research, 15*(6), E112.

boyd, D., & Crawford, K. (2012). Critical questions for big data. *Information, Communication and Society, 15*(5), 662–679.

Collins, S., & Durington, M. (2015). *Networked anthropology: A primer for ethnographers*. Routledge.

Dalsgaard, S. (2016). The ethnographic use of Facebook in everyday life. *Anthropological Forum, 26*(1), 96–114.

Demant, J., Bakken, S. A., & Hall, A. (2020). Social media markets for prescription drugs: Platforms as virtual mortars for drug types and dealers. *Drugs and Alcohol Today, 20*(1), 36–49.

Denecke, K. (2014). Ethical aspects of using medical social media in healthcare applications. *Studies in Health Technology and Informatics, 198,* 55–62.

Dent, A. S. (2020). *Digital pirates: Policing intellectual property in Brazil.* Stanford University Press.

Enghoff, O., & Aldridge, J. (2019). The value of unsolicited online data in drug policy research. *International Journal of Drug Policy, 73,* 210–218.

Ferrell, J., & Hamm, M. (1998). *Ethnography at the edge: Crime, deviance and field research*. Northeastern University Press.

Fleetwood, J., & Potter, G. R. (2017). Ethnographic research on crime and control: Editors' introduction. *Methodological Innovations, 10*(1), 1–4.

Forrest, S. (2020). *Ballad of the bullet: Gangs, drill music, and the power of online infamy*. Princeton University Press.

Gans, H. (1967). *The levittowners: Ways of life and politics in a new suburban community*. Columbia University Press.

Gatson, N. (2011). The methods, politics, and ethics of representation in online ethnography. In N. Denzin & Y. Lincoln (Eds.), *The Sage handbook of qualitative research* (4th ed., pp. 513–527). Sage.

Geiger, R., Ribes, D. (2011). Trace ethnography: Following coordination through documentary practices. In *2014 47th Hawaii International Conference on System Sciences* (pp. 1–10). IEEE.

Gibbs, N. (forthcoming). *Insta-muscle: Examining the performance enhancing substance trade and male gym culture*. PhD thesis, University of Northumbria, Newcastle Upon Tyne.

Gobo, G. (2008). *Doing ethnography*. Sage.

Greengard, S. (2015). *The internet of things*. MIT Press.

Hall, A., & Antonopoulos, G. A. (2016). *Fake meds online: The internet and the transnational market in illicit pharmaceuticals*. Palgrave Macmillan.

Hall, S., & Winlow, S. (2015). *Revitalizing criminological theory: Towards a new ultra-realism*. Routledge.

Hammersley, M., & Atkinson, P. (2019). *Ethnography: Principles in practice* (4th ed.). Routledge.

Hine, C. (2000). *Virtual ethnography*. Sage.

Hobbs, D. (1993). Peers, careers and academic fears. In D. Hobbs & T. May (Eds.), *Interpreting the field: Accounts of ethnography* (pp. 45–68). Clarendon Press.

Horst, A., & Miller, D. (2012). *Digital anthropology*. Berg Publishers.

Irwin-Rogers, K. (2019). Illicit drug markets, consumer capitalism and the rise of social media: A toxic trap for young people. *Critical Criminology, 27,* 591–610.

Iversen, R. (2009). "Getting out" in ethnography: A seldom-told story. *Qualitative Social Work, 8*(1), 9–26.

Janetzko, D. (2008). Nonreactive data collection on the internet. In N. Fielding, R. M. Lee, & G. Blank (Eds.), *Online research methods* (pp. 161–174). Sage.

Jewkes, Y. (2011). Autoethnography and emotion as intellectual resources: Doing prison research differently. *Qualitative Inquiry, 18*(1), 63–75.

Kozinets, R. (2010). *Netnography: Doing ethnographic research online*. Sage.

Lageson, S. E. (2020). *Digital punishment privacy, stigma, and the harms of data-driven criminal justice.* Oxford University Press.

Leander, K., & McKim, K. (2003). Tracing the everyday "sitings" of adolescents on the internet: A strategic adaptation of ethnography across online and offline spaces. *Education, Communication, Information, 3*(2), 211–240.

Liebling, A. (2001). Whose side are we on: Theory, practices and allegiances in prison research. *British Journal of Criminology, 41*(3), 472–484.

Lingel, J. (2012, May 5–10). Ethics and dilemmas of online ethnography. Presentation at *CHI 2012*, Austin, Texas, USA.

Lofland, J., & Lofland, L. (1995). *Analyzing social settings: A guide to qualitative observation and analysis.* Wadsworth Publishing Company.

Maguire, M. (2008). Researching street criminals: A neglected art? In R. King & E. Wincup (Eds.), *Doing research on crime and justice* (2nd ed.). Oxford University Press.

Martin, J., Munksgaard, R., Coomber, R., Demant, J., & Barratt, M. (2020). Selling drugs on darkweb cryptomarkets: Differentiated pathways, risks and rewards. *The British Journal of Criminology, 60*(3), 559–578.

McKee, R. (2013). Ethical issues in using social media for health and health care purposes. *Health Policy, 110,* 298–301.

Mckinney, J. (1966). *Constructive typology and social theory.* Meredith Publishing Company.

Michaelidou, N., Moraes, C., & Micevski, M. (2016). A scale for measuring consumers? Ethical perceptions of social media research. In M. Obal, N. Kray, & C. Bushardt (Eds.), *Let's get engaged! Crossing the threshold of marketing's engagement era* (pp. 97–100). Springer.

Nissenbaum, H. (2010). *Privacy in context: Technology, policy, and the integrity of social life.* Stanford Law Books.

O'Reilly, K. (2009). *Key concepts in ethnography.* Sage.

Postill, J., & Pink, S. (2012). Social media ethnography: The digital researcher in a messy web. *Media International Australia, 12*(145), 123–134.

Powell, A., Stratton, G., & Cameron, R. (2018). *Digital criminology: Crime and justice in digital society.* Routledge.

Prince, S. (2019). (Re)Tracing the Everyday 'Sitings': A Conceptual Review of Internet Research 15 Years Later. *Issues and Trends in Educational Technology, 7*(1), 45–60.

Smith, O. (2014). *Contemporary adulthood and the night-time economy.* Palgrave Macmillan.

Snow, D. (1980). The disengagement process: A neglected problem in participant observation research. *Qualitative Sociology, 3,* 100–122.

Sunden, J. (2002). Cyberbodies: Writing gender in digital self-presentations. In J. Fornas, K. Klein, M. Ladendorf, J. Sunden, & M. Sveningsson (Eds.), *Digital borderlands: Cultural studies of identity and interactivity on the internet*. Peter Lang.

Taylor, T. (1999). Life in virtual worlds: Plural existence, multimodalities, and other online research challenges. *American Behavioral Scientist, 43*(3), 436–449.

Tickle, S. (2017). Ethnographic research with young people: Methods and rapport. *Qualitative Research Journal, 17*(2), 66–76.

Townsend, L., & Wallace, C. (2016). *Social media research: A guide to ethics.* Available at: www.gla.ac.uk/media/media_487729_en.pdf. Last accessed 23 June 2020.

Treadwell, J. (2012). From the car boot to booting it up? eBay, online counterfeit crime and the transformation of the criminal marketplace. *Criminology & Criminal Justice, 12*(2), 175–191.

Treadwell, J. (2020). *Criminological ethnography.* Sage.

Van de Voorde, C. (2012). Ethnographic photography in criminological research. In D. Gadd, S. Karstedt & S. Messner (Eds.), *The SAGE Handbook of Criminological Research Methods* (pp. 203–217). Sage.

Wall, D. (2007). *Cybercrime: The transformation of crime in the information age.* Polity Press.

Wang, P., Su, M., & Wang, J. (2020). Organized crime in cyberspace: How traditional organized criminal groups exploit the online peer-to-peer lending market in China. *The British Journal of Criminology* (online first).

Wilson, R., Gosling, S., & Graham, L. (2012). A review of Facebook research in the social sciences. *Perspectives on Psychological Science, 7*(3), 203–220.

Winlow, S. (2001). *Badfellas: Crime, tradition and new masculinities.* Berg Publishers.

Woodfield, K., & Iphofen, R. (2018). Introduction to Volume 2: The ethics of online research. In K. Woodfield (Ed.), *The ethics of online research* (pp. 1–12). Emerald Group Publishing.

Yar, M. (2012). Crime, media and the will to representation: Reconsidering relationships in the new media age. *Crime, Media, Culture, 8*(3), 245–260.

Yardley, E., & Wilson, D. (2014). Making sense of "Facebook Murder"? Social networking sites and contemporary homicide. *The Howard Journal of Criminal Justice, 52*(2), 109–134.

15

The Meme Is the Method: Examining the Power of the Image Within Extremist Propaganda

Ashton Kingdon

Introduction

Late modernity has borne witness to a progressive expansion of visual culture, encompassing media, film, television, advertising, and, most significantly, the Web, which over the last two decades has become a major focus for criminology, becoming both the object of study and the method of research. Extremist groups increasingly flourish online, and the advent of Web 2.0 technology, in particular, created new avenues for radicalization, having a profound impact on both the speed and scale in which propaganda could be disseminated (O'Shaughnessy, 2004). Consequently, academic research has focused on the expanding use of the technology employed by extremists to gain support, raise capital, recruit members, and engage in psychological warfare (Berger & Morgan, 2015; Conway, 2017; Gisea, 2015; Holt et al., 2018; Klausen, 2015).

A. Kingdon (✉)
University of Southampton, Southampton, UK
e-mail: A.R.Kingdon@soton.ac.uk

© The Author(s), under exclusive license to Springer Nature Switzerland AG 2021
A. Lavorgna and T. J. Holt (eds.), *Researching Cybercrimes*,
https://doi.org/10.1007/978-3-030-74837-1_15

301

The aftermath of the "Great Meme War," the internet-based warfare campaigns waged by supporters of various political candidates in the 2016 American Presidential election, led to an increase in research focused on the securing of strategic goals through the use of memes as a form of disinformation (Mayer, 2018; McKew, 2018; Meyer, 2018; Moody-Ramirez & Church, 2019; Piata, 2016; Ross & Rivers, 2017). The term "meme" was coined by evolutionary biologist Richard Dawkins (1976) to refer to units of cultural information spread by imitation, replicating in a similar way to genes, with cultural ideas passing from parent to child in the same way as biological traits. It is important to note that when defining memes, Dawkins was alluding not specifically to images and videos, but to any unit of culture that had the potential to be replicated and transmitted between individuals, arguing that memes spread like viruses, but instead of carrying diseases that infect the body, they convey ideas that infiltrate the mind.

Despite an increase in research focusing on the use and impact of memes in influencing behavior, and the cognitive debate that has consequently ensued, far less attention has been given to the ways in which the researchers themselves utilize memes as a core methodological approach for investigating crime, extremism, and radicalization. Consequently, this chapter will discuss some of the primary methodological considerations for researchers using memes as the sole object of study. By way of example, to emphasize the contrasting narratives that can emerge from imagery, the chapter will employ one distinctive meme of the Waco siege as a template to guide the reader through three different manifestations of anti-government extremism, and provide a conceptual framework on which future research can build. The value of this approach lies in its ability to capture both the universality of an individual meme—its overarching message on which all viewers can agree—and its distinctiveness—the specific intrinsic meanings and contrasting narratives perceived by individual users, operating on different social media platforms, at particular moments in time.

Background

Fringe internet platforms and imageboards, such as 4chan, 8chan, and Reddit, are often considered the birthplace of internet memes (Ludemann, 2018). In particular, 4chan drew attention in 2003, when it gave rise to the sensationalist and hacktivist movement Anonymous that used hacking as a form of social disobedience (Sorell, 2015). Neiwert (2017) highlighted the importance of a particular sub-section in 4chan titled "/pol/" (Politically Incorrect) that, in effect, became the headquarters for the early alt-right, who used this channel as a way of disseminating propaganda to a wide audience. There has been much academic research analyzing the reactionary shift in Web culture occurring between 2014 and 2015, particularly regarding the ability for online subcultures to repurpose their traditional cultural base to be more appealing to potential extremists (Lagorio-Chafkin, 2018; Nissenbaum & Shifman, 2017; Phillips & Milner, 2017; Tuters & Hagen, 2019). Through their memetic content, fringe platforms and imageboards can have a profound impact on popular culture as well as on political and ideological discourses, and there is thus a need for research to focus on the potentially radicalizing effects that memes can have (Crawford, 2020; Lee, 2020; Methaven, 2014). While the investigation of online cultures is not a new field of research, the increased political gravity of recent years gives this particular type of study far greater urgency (Knobel & Lankshear, 2007; Shifman, 2013).

Underpinning research into memes is the field of semiotics (i.e., the study of signs and symbols), a particularly important component when examining the historical and subcultural symbolism contained within propaganda (Hall, 2012). Semiotics is primarily concerned with systems of "signification," the fundamental object of study being the "sign," composed of two elements, the "signifier" and the "signified." The signifier represents the image itself, while the signified characterizes the cerebral image that the signifier induces within the person who is viewing it, that is, their perception. It is this association, between the signifier and the signified that creates what the audience internalize as the "sign" or the "symbol" (Chandler, 2017). Consequently, analysis of semiotic content is one of the most important methods of examination when using memes as the core focus of research, as it enables the extraction of both the evident and concealed influences within visual material (Rose, 2012). Semiotic analysis combines both quantitative and qualitative approaches, encompassing not only the generation of descriptive statistics, but also the interpretation of the cultural symbolism contained in the images themselves (Gray & Densten, 1998; Krippendorff, 2013).

When selecting a theoretical foundation for the analysis of memes, cultural and visual criminology is particularly valuable as they facilitate examination beyond the surface of static images and aid the development of theoretical and methodological tools to understand the underlying dynamic force and power of visual culture (Ferrell et al., 2015). Hayward and Presdee (2010) emphasize that the power of imagery is something the state and its agencies can never fully control because the influence of the visual spectacle is too multidimensional. Images shape the impact of cultural messages in a multitude of ways, and just as they can be used to serve the state, they can equally be used to criticize and undermine it. Likewise, everyday life becomes the stage upon which the personal and emotional experiences of extremist recruiters are played out, and, increasingly, the sphere in which new forms of legal and social control are deployed. Hence, a focus for this chapter has been on developing a sophisticated understanding of the disputed principles that underpin extremism, and how such ideas can control and influence through their incorporation into cultural manifestations.

Equally important is highlighting the existing research that has focused on the use of memes as propaganda. Gisea (2015) refers to the power of memetic warfare—that is, propaganda conducted primarily through the propagation of memes on social media. Such use of memes is a form of information warfare, a psychological operation employed by propagandists who seek to wage or influence campaigns that can alter behavior through unconventional means. While information warfare and operations have been in use since the Cold War, rapid deployments of both computing and network technology have led to the creation of a new participatory information environment and, particularly in relation to memes, social media have become the battlefield. When researching this often-anonymized environment, it is important to consider who the combatants are: are they state or non-state actors? Domestic or Foreign? Significantly, social media are environments that offer a level playing field for all. Increasingly, research has focused on the use of memes as a form of disinformation used to secure strategic goals, with divisive and disruptive technologies, such as automation and artificial intelligence, ushering in an age of deception executed on a mass scale (Mayer, 2018; Mckew, 2018; Meyer, 2018). Far less attention has been given to the methods and processes used by researchers focusing on the contribution and possible impact of memes on radicalization. Consequently, the focus of the next section of this chapter will be on providing a conceptual framework for examining the potential impact of anti-government extremist propaganda as it is repurposed and appropriated through time.

A Picture Is Worth a Thousand Words: Using Memes to Decode Anti-government Extremist Narratives

Anti-government extremism rose to prominence in the mid-1990s, in response to the sieges at Ruby Ridge and Waco, and the increased gun control legislation being ushered in by the Democratic Clinton Administration (Pitcavage, 2001). Together, these events sparked increased support for the Militia Movement, part of the broader Patriot Movement, which also encompasses the Sovereign Citizen and Tax Protest movements (Levin, 1998). Radicalism hit a high point in 1995, when a bomb, planted by Timothy McVeigh, exploded in front of the Alfred P Murrah federal building in Oklahoma City, killing 168 people. Following this act of domestic terrorism, leaders in the anti-government movement made a conscious effort to distance themselves from white supremacy, in the belief any perceived connection would make their message less palatable. However, following the September 11 attacks and the U.S. government's response to them, nativist hate, barely concealed under a thin veil of national security rhetoric, became central to the Militia Movement's ideology (Southern Poverty Law Centre, 2020). Furthermore, following the 2008 presidential election of Barack Obama, a new era of anti-government extremism was born, with groups like the Oath Keepers and Three Percenters gaining traction, fueled in part by changing demographics, a struggling economy, and the reality of an African-American president (Jackson, 2019).

The purpose of this section is to guide the reader through three different manifestations of extremism, using as a template one meme of the Waco siege (Fig. 15.1), an image which inherently conveys anti-government meaning, even before further new interpretations are ascribed to it.

The conceptual framework is structured around three stages in the development of anti-government sentiment. First, it encompasses the initial rise of the Militia Movement from the ashes of the sieges at Ruby Ridge and Waco, and the Oklahoma City Bombing, in the 1990s. Second, it documents the movement's resurgence during the 2014 and 2016 standoffs between the Bundy family and the Bureau of Land Management over grazing rights. Finally, it incorporates the expansion of anti-government extremism following the widespread protests that broke out over coronavirus lockdown measures and police brutality following the murder of George Floyd in 2020. This single image serves to typify many memes by demonstrating both the prominent anti-government sentiment on which the majority of users sharing the meme will agree on, and the inherent crystallizations—that is, the individual narratives that specific audiences will draw from the image when it is disseminated at particular times, or on certain platforms. The purpose of this method is to provide a framework for future researchers to utilize and build on when examining the links between imagery and crime, radicalization, or extremism. As memes are constantly evolving, it is important to explore beyond the surface of the image, decode the narratives, "finish the sentence," and gain a deeper understanding of the ways in which extremist sentiment is resonating with contrasting audiences.

Fig. 15.1 The Waco siege (meme)

Tier One: This Is About Waco

Anti-government extremists often consider themselves to be in a constant battle with the federal government, and, in many ways, the events at Ruby Ridge can be considered the opening shot of that war. The 11-day standoff between federal agents and the white separatist Weaver family began following Randy Weaver's failure to appear in court after being charged with selling two illegally sawn-off shotguns to an undercover agent from the Bureau of Alcohol, Tobacco, Firearms, and Explosives (ATF). Violence erupted on August 21, 1992, when six heavily armed U.S. Marshals were discovered on the Ruby Ridge property; although it remains unclear who fired first, an exchange of gunfire led to the deaths of Randy Weaver's 14-year-old son Sammy and U.S. Marshal William Degan (Crothers, 2019). Following the initial shootout, the Federal Bureau of Investigation (FBI) revised its rules of engagement, and, consequently, any armed adult seen on the Ruby Ridge property was to be shot on sight (May & Headley, 2008). Subsequently, on 22 August, an FBI sniper, on seeing an armed Randy Weaver outside his cabin, opened fire, accidentally killing his wife Vicki in the process. The deaths of Randy Weaver's wife and son at the hands of federal agents became a rallying cry for the extreme right, many of whom were already harboring distrust of the government (Barkun, 2007). Furthermore, the fact that Randy Weaver was arraigned on weapon charges prompted concerns relating to gun confiscation given that the siege occurred on Weaver's private property, where they were legally entitled to carry firearms, confront intruders, and defend themselves. For these reasons, the case of Ruby Ridge became an extremist justification for ordinary Americans stockpiling arms to defend themselves against a "tyrannical" government.

Similar validation was made of the siege at Waco, when on February 28, 1993, ATF agents attempted a raid on Mount Carmel—the compound of the Branch Davidians (an offshoot of the Seventh Day Adventist Church)—in the belief that illegal explosives and firearms were being stockpiled there (Agne, 2007). The 51-day siege that followed ended on 19 April, when the FBI tear-gassed the compound and a fire broke out in which 76 Davidians, including their charismatic leader

David Koresh, were killed. Controversy has since existed over whether the actions of federal law enforcement were excessively aggressive, leading to Waco being considered a prime example of the government's ability to exercise unwarranted power over its citizens. Analysis of the Waco meme naturally reveals parallels with Ruby Ridge, as both incidents represent government misjudgments that ended in gunfire and death, and are each perceived as evidence reinforcing underlying conspiracy theories regarding attempts to limit firearms and impose government tyranny.

Significantly, the Waco meme not only represents the FBI standoff with the Branch Davidians, but also a watershed moment in American history that indelibly transformed the way that the general public came to view domestic terrorism and public safety. On April 19, 1995, Timothy McVeigh detonated a five-ton fertilizer bomb in a Ryder Truck parked in front of the Alfred P. Murrah building in Oklahoma City, killing 168 people (Kellner, 2016). The Murrah building was chosen as the target because the ATF, who conducted the raid on the Branch Davidians, had an office there, and, the date of the attack, exactly two years following the fire at Waco, was clearly symbolic (Linder, 2007). It is important to note that compounding the concerns of conspiracy theorists, who believed that the government was seeking to take guns away from law-abiding citizens, was the introduction of government legislation imposing restrictions on gun sales and ownership, most notably the 1994 Brady Handgun Prevention Act and the Federal Assault Weapons Ban (Kahane, 1999). While McVeigh did not actually belong to a Militia group, he shared the same opinions regarding what he considered government overreach. Thus, for McVeigh, the key events—Ruby Ridge, Waco, and Gun Control Legislation—were all connected, leading down a path that would end with federal agents coming to his home, and the homes of gun owners across America, and taking their guns away.

The events at Ruby Ridge and Waco that influenced Timothy McVeigh to commit the worst act of domestic terrorism in American history became a central calling card for the extreme right, and a pivotal moment in the rise of the Militia Movement, together laying the foundation for the anti-government sentiment that still resonates today. It is important to recognize that the Waco meme does not represent one key event, but rather, a plethora of perceived governmental failures and over-steps that together can fuel the flames of radicalization among widely varying audiences. Hence, the first tier of analysis is designed to illustrate that the meme in question represents much more than the portrayal of the federal government "murdering" its own citizens at Waco. It also symbolizes the perceived government assassination of the Weaver family, conspiracy theories surrounding government tyranny, and the consequences of the implantation of strict gun control legislation; scenarios that resonate powerfully with past and present anti-government groups and can act as persuasive recruitment narratives for anti-government propagandists.

Tier Two: The Bundys Are the Bellwether

In April 2014, Bureau of Land Management (BLM) agents engaged in a standoff with armed anti-government protestors, while attempting to impound the cattle of rancher Cliven Bundy for unlawfully grazing on public land near Bunkerville, Nevada (Nemerever, 2019). When government convoys arrived to seize the cattle, the situation escalated into violence, and video footage of Cliven's son Ammon being tasered by a BLM agent was posted online to Facebook and YouTube, consequently becoming a rallying cry for the Militia Movement (Childress, 2017). Bunkerville became a magnet for anti-government extremists, as Militia groups, including the Three Percenters and the Oath Keepers, arrived to support the Bundys in the belief that the federal government was abusing its power by targeting hardworking Americans (Jackson, 2019). The protests quickly escalated as Ammon Bundy led hundreds of supporters to surround the lockup where his family's cattle had been impounded. In the end, the government capitulated; not a single protestor was arrested, and the Bundys got their cattle back, thereby providing the message that they had beaten the federal government (Makley, 2017). Immediately, the Bundy family were thrust into the national spotlight, and imagery of the Waco siege was shared across social media in tribute to the protest (LeMenager & Weisiger, 2019). Thus, not only does the second tier of this analysis portray the Waco meme as being used to represent a local battle over land rights, it also demonstrates how the Bundy case was appropriated as an injustice that further supported the universal message of there being an "out-of-control" federal government.

Two years later, in January 2016, Cliven's sons, Ammon and Ryan, gathered a group of anti-government protestors and took over the Malheur National Wildlife Refuge in eastern Oregon, announcing they were occupying the federal facility in protest against the imprisonment of Harney County ranchers Dwight and Steven Hammond for arson (Wang, 2018). Following a 41-day standoff, Cliven, Ammon, and Ryan Bundy were arrested, and one of their closest allies, Arizona rancher Robert LaVoy Finicum was shot dead by police reaching for a loaded handgun at a roadblock set up to arrest the leaders of the occupation. Finicum's death at the hands of federal agents transformed him into a martyr for the Militia Movement, as it was considered proof of a tyrannical government murdering innocent American citizens (Morgan, 2019). Following the standoff, imagery of Waco was used to represent not only the death of rural America, but also the fight for freedom, with Finicum's death becoming a spur for future dissent. Furthermore, the acquittal of the Bundy family for their role in the occupation was perceived as a triumph for liberty that galvanized the Militia Movement and further legitimized their battle against the federal government.

The narrative created by Cliven Bundy regarding his vision for a radical libertarian utopia is reinforced through the Waco meme, and spurred on by his family's success in the standoffs. The Bundy name became a symbol of hope, recalling the heroism of David slaying Goliath, and, perhaps, most significantly, offered a fight to those who were seeking one (Sottile, 2018). In particular, Cliven promoted the illusion that he was the savior of the American West; his message was desperate, almost apocalyptic in nature, and this desperation both justified violence and resonated with other desperate people (Denton, 2019). The Bundy family saw themselves as saviors of the constitution and this belief was deeply woven into their cultural values. They were able to tap into an anti-government worldview that exists under the surface in the American West and create an image of a patriotic American cowboy around whom people could rally. Symbolically, cattle ranchers are representative of the "Old West," a testament of how America ought to be, and these traditional masculine values are part of what fuel the modern-day Militia Movement. It is about America being a frontier, emblematic of every man for themselves, about men owning guns and slowing the tide of the tyrannical government. In a way, the Waco meme relates to the Bundys as a window: too small to see the whole picture, but a window nonetheless into anti-government ideologies, and into how these beliefs could escalate into violence.

Tier Three: Civil War 2—Electric Boogaloo

The Militia Movement became notably active again in April 2020, when, in response to many states introducing stay-at-home orders to combat the coronavirus pandemic, a wave of anti-lockdown demonstrations was organized. While the Militia Movement had always been strongly anti-federal government, it was now becoming distinctly anti-state government, as restrictions and lockdowns were considered a clear example of government overreach (Coaston, 2020). Tensions were exacerbated in May 2020, when nationwide protests broke out against police brutality following the murder of George Floyd, resulting in citizens facing off against well-armed police officers and National Guard Troops (Stanley-Becker, 2020). While Militia groups had long championed the importance of individual constitutional rights, particularly the use of armed resistance when confronted with government overreach, many members who were supporters of President Trump found themselves in a quandary, as he was openly discussing the sort of far-reaching government intervention of which these groups were fearful. Specifically, Trump's threat to invoke the 1807 Insurrection Act to use federal military force against protestors coincided with what constitutionalists fear the most—the forceful expansion of governmental power against its own people (D'Amore, 2020).

One of the most prominent anti-government groups at the forefront of public attention during the anti-lockdown and George Floyd protests was the "Boogaloo Movement" (Evans & Wilson, 2020). The name "Boogaloo" is a reference to the 1984 movie *Breakin 2: Electric Boogaloo*, which was extensively criticized for being a near exact copy of the first *Breakin* movie. The term was subsequently adopted by anti-government extremists as a call to a second American Civil War, subsequently becoming a metaphor for a violent uprising against the state, political opponents, and law enforcement (IntelBrief, 2020). The term Boogaloo morphed through online meme culture into phrases such as "Big Igloo" and "Big Luau" the latter term celebrated for being a Hawaiian feast in which pigs, code for police, are roasted (Kingdon, 2020). The Boogaloo Movement gained traction in January 2020 amid rapidly spreading disinformation regarding gun control and threats to the Second Amendment; members began showing up at state capital protests wearing Hawaiian shirts as though they were on their way to a Luau. Significantly, the pro-Second Amendment messaging contained within Boogaloo inspired memes appealed to people by reinforcing the ideals of comradery that develop from bonding with likeminded people who were portrayed as standing up for what they believed was a noble and righteous cause.

Boogaloo groups proliferated rapidly on platforms such as *Facebook* and *Twitter* during the 2020 coronavirus lockdowns; many people were spending more time online consequently increasing their chances of being exposed to the widespread disinformation and misinformation campaigns circulating about the virus and shelter-in-place orders (Druzin, 2020; Kunzelman, 2020). It is important to note that while certain components of the Boogaloo Movement may be unique; the anti-government sentiment that provides the foundation for its ideology is more traditional. For example, many Boogaloo supporters operating on *Facebook* idolize David Koresh, often using his image in their profile pictures, or stating their geo-location as being at Mount Carmel—the former compound of the Branch Davidians (Argentino, 2020). It is clear that the same kind of mobilization that had previously occurred regarding the alleged state infringement on Second Amendment rights shifted to new perceived threats in which individuals felt their freedoms were being restricted, and they were consequently losing control of their country, a similar sentiment to that which fueled the Militia Movements of the mid-1990s.

Exploring Beyond the Frame

The visual aspects of memes can be considered a methodological template, and, in the case of this analysis, the Waco meme becomes the frame upon which new narratives can be set. It is beneficial to consider memes as reflections of particular moments in history, as well as representations of contemporary events. For example, the Waco meme being disseminated on the anniversary of the standoff, or in homage to the Oklahoma City Bombing, may be interpreted as representing the anti-government sentiment that fueled the Militia groups of the 1990s. The same meme may also be considered to signify support for the Bundy family's armed uprisings against the federal government, and the Mormon values that drove them, a case of wrapping a flag around a cross to make radical ideas more palatable. It may just as easily symbolize solidarity for anti-lockdown and Black Lives Matter protests, a way of harnessing frustrations and portraying government overreach to attract new recruits and gain support for anti-government sentiment. A major advantage of this approach is that, by capturing the frequency with which a single image is displayed across various platforms, it is possible to gain insight into the communication routes along which the meme has spread.

The benefit of employing memes as the primary method of research when seeking to understand pathways to extremism is that they offer both comprehensive and focused views of a group of individuals, representing both the bigger picture and an illusion of coherence within the social collective from which they originate. In particular, self-referential memes like Waco specifically influence the opinions of the larger target collective. Regardless of the period of time over which the image is disseminated, there is a sense of an "us" versus "them" contained within the meme. Consequently, any use of the meme in an in-group narrative will subliminally construct a boundary between those who will resonate with the anti-government message and those who will not. Memes are important objects of study because they act as metaphors that can bind groups together. In this chapter, we have seen that, while a meme has an overarching narrative, it also contains many subtle and ideological crystallizations that encompass user-specific meanings (which might be time-

or platform-dependent). The Waco meme represents much more than the fiery end of David Koresh and his Davidians; it also captures the complex and often contradictory ideological underpinnings of various Militia groups, at different moments in time. The example of the Waco meme emphasizes the increased need for researchers to view memes as units of communication that occur between factions, and to translate the impact of their narratives over time.

Practical Considerations of Using Memes in Research

A primary consideration when using memes in research centers upon copyright, and whether the content of the images contained within memes can be used by researchers in their studies. If, for example, someone created an image used within a meme, that image could be copyrighted, thus any memes consequently created would likely be deemed derivative or protectable works (Bonetto, 2018). However, if the creator did not have the rights to the original image, it would be unlikely that copyright protections could be obtained (Marciszewski, 2020). Therefore, while it depends on the details of each particular meme, a very large amount of them are not copyrightable, which is why they are often used so extensively in research.

A further key issue centers on the fact that the vast majority of memes used in research are sourced from social media fora. This raises concerns regarding the extent to which such images are considered "public" or "private" data, and whether or not it is ethically necessary to seek informed consent from the person who posted the content before including it within research (Fossheim & Ingreid, 2015). Hogan (2008) maintains that research conducted on social media should not be deemed ethical solely on the basis that any data accessed is in the public domain, a stance that also applies to the utilization of memes within analysis. However, it can be assumed that the proposed, albeit unwitting, participants of studies had agreed to a specified set of terms and conditions when they created their accounts (on the public vs private debate, see also Chapters 16–22). Therefore, it is important that, when using memes collected from social media fora, researchers carefully read the terms and conditions of the platform to ensure that any public data can be legally accessed and that there are clauses specifically stating that data can be retrieved by third-party researchers. However, it is also important to remember that it is probable that many, if not most, users off these platforms will not have read the terms and conditions before agreeing to them and, consequently, may not be aware that their data may be the subject of research (see also Part III of this book, and particularly Chapters 16 and 17). Therefore, it is debatable whether such an agreement should be taken as formal consent to memes being used in research (Fossheim & Ingreid, 2015). Taking this into account, it is incumbent for researchers using memes to exercise particular vigilance to protect the privacy of potential participants, by ensuring that all data used is strictly anonymized, so there is absolutely no identifiable link between the image and the person who disseminated it.

While anonymity in all research is a core ethical concern, even greater care must be taken when the data being accessed is extremist in nature. There are certain scenarios in which it would be ethically mandatory to seek unambiguous informed consent, such as accessing memes that are shared in private conversations, or disseminated from the accounts of minors. However, in sensitive research, such as that examining criminal or extremist subcultures, it is not always straightforward or responsible to seek informed consent, not least because it could be potentially dangerous to contact the contributors. To avoid such a dilemma, it is vital that researchers planning to use memes as the object of their study collect data solely from accounts in the public domain, and not from any private conversations or from profiles publicly stating they are minors (although user age may be almost impossible to ascertain).

Conclusion

In conclusion, it is evident that examination of the historical and subcultural elements contained within memes provides an important opportunity to analyze how ideologies of extremism can become intertwined with cultural representations, thereby establishing the importance of the contribution of visual criminology in making research more integrated and influential. With their penchant for humor and satirical interpretation, their irony, and recursivity, memes are an important object of study because they embody what is unique about contemporary digital culture. Taking this into account, future research should focus particularly on internet memes as a distinctive medium that has the capability to convey ideologies, easily and seamlessly, between groups. In contrast to other, more traditional media, it is difficult for the dominant or mainstream culture to exert power or control over the dissemination of memes. Therefore, this form of communication is increasingly likely to have significant real-world implications for, and impact on, potential extremists, and thus merits careful examination. Memes have become a favored means through which deviant content can be spread, and, as demonstrated in this chapter, in the case of anti-government extremist propaganda, the socio-political issues encapsulated by Waco imagery feed deep-rooted fears that galvanize the modern-day Militia Movement. The significance of the Waco meme is that it opens a door into the emerging fears and preoccupations of subcultural groups; hence, the image can no longer be considered a natural medium, but rather an ideological template that enables the audience to extract their own narratives.

Looking below the surface of the static image is fundamental to reveal the conceptual framework that takes account of the underlying dynamic force and power of visual culture. Repeatedly, propagandists borrow style and techniques from popular culture; moreover, the perception of anti-government extremism and contemporary events has become so complexly intertwined that individuals like the Bundys commit uprisings with an eye to how the events will play out across social media. Therefore, it is important for researchers to consider the complexity of the extremist/social media relationship to clarify the ways in which extremism and its representation in the media feed off one another and spiral toward ever more dramatic occurrences. In the contemporary world of the digital spectacle, narratives of extremism are promulgated as much through the image as through the word; consequently, researchers need to utilize the visual evidence provided by propagandists within memes to understand the power of the image in shaping popular understanding and the social construction of extremism and radicalization.

References

Agne, R. R. (2007). Reframing practices in moral conflict: Interaction problems in the negotiation standoff at Waco. *Discourse & Society, 18*(5), 549–578.

Argentino, M. A. (2020). *Digital platforms and extremism 2: Electric Boogaloo.* Available at: https://gnet-research.org/2020/06/08/digital-platforms-and-extremism-2-electric-boogaloo/.

Barkun, M. (2007). Appropriated martyrs: The Branch Davidians and the radical right. *Terrorism and Political Violence, 19*(1), 117–124.

Berger, J. M., & Morgan, J. (2015). The ISIS Twitter consensus. *The Brookings Project on US Relations with the Islamic World: Analysis Paper* 20(1). Available at: https://www.brookings.edu/wpcontent/uploads/2016/06/isis_twitter_census_berger_morgan.pdf.

Bonetto, G. (2018). Internet memes as derivative works: Copyright issues under EU law. *Journal of Intellectual Property Law & Practice, 13*(12), 989–997.

Chandler, D. (2017). *Semiotics: The basics* (3rd ed.). Routledge.

Childress, S. (2017). *The Battle over Bunkerville: The Bundys, the Federal Government, and the New Militia Movement.* Available at: https://www.pbs.org/wgbh/frontline/article/the-battle-over-bunkerville/.

Coaston, J. (2020). *The private militias providing "security" for anti-lockdown protests, explained.* Available at: https://www.vox.com/2020/5/11/21249166/militias-protests-coronavirus-michigan-security.

Conway, M. (2017). Determining the role of the internet in violent extremism and terrorism: Six suggestions for progressing research. *Studies in Conflict and Terrorism, 40*(1), 77–98.

Crawford, B. (2020). *The influence of memes on far-right radicalisation.* Available at: https://www.radicalrightanalysis.com/2020/06/09/the-influence-of-memes-on-far-right-radicalisation/.

Crothers, L. (2019). *Rage on the right: The American Militia Movement from Ruby Ridge to the Trump Presidency.* Rowman & Littlefield Publishers.

D'Amore, R. (2020). *George Floyd: What is the US Insurrection Act of 1807 and what can Trump do with it?* Available at: https://globalnews.ca/news/7015546/george-floyd-protests-trump-military/.

Dawkins, R. (1976). *The selfish gene.* Oxford University Press.

Denton, S. (2019). *Apocalyptic prophets: Reading the fine print of Ammon Bundy's divine mandate.* Available at: https://lithub.com/apocalyptic-prophets-reading-the-fine-print-of-ammon-bundys-divine-mandate/.

Druzin, H. (2020). *Armed militias see the pandemic as a recruiting opportunity.* Available at: https://wamu.org/story/20/06/11/armed-militias-see-the-pandemic-as-a-recruiting-opportunity-2/.

Evans, R & Wilson, J (2020). *The Boogaloo Movement is not what you think.* Available at: https://www.bellingcat.com/news/2020/05/27/the-boogaloo-movement-is-not-what-you-think/.

Ferrell, J., Hayward, K., & Young, J. (2015). *Cultural criminology: An invitation* (2nd ed.). Sage.

Fossheim, H., & Ingreid, H. (2015). *Internet research ethics.* Available at: https://press.nordicopenaccess.no/index.php/noasp/catalog/view/3/1/9-1.

Gisea, J. (2015). *It's time to embrace memetic warfare.* Available at: https://www.stratcomcoe.org/jeff-giesea-its-time-embrace-memetic-warfare.

Gray, J. H., & Densten, I. L. (1998). Integrating quantitative and qualitative analysis using latent and manifest variables. *Quality & Quantity, 32*(1), 419–431.

Hall, S. (2012). *This means this, this means that: A user's guide to semiotics.* Laurence King Publishing Ltd.

Hayward, K., & Presdee, M. (2010). *Framing crime: Cultural criminology and the image.* Routledge.

Hogan, B. (2008). Analysing social networks via the internet. In N. Fielding, R. Lee, & G. Blank (Eds.), *The Sage handbook of online research methods.* Sage.

Holt, T. J., Frelich, J. D., Chermack, S., & LaFree, G. (2018). Examining the utility of social control and social learning in the radicalisation of violent and non violent extremists. *Dynamics of Asymmetric Conflict, 1*(1), 1–19.

IntelBrief. 2020. *The Boogaloo Movement—From eccentric distraction to domestic terror* [Online]. Available at: https://thesoufancenter.org/intelbrief-the-boogaloo-movement-from-eccentric-distraction-to-domestic-terror/. 23 July 2020.

Jackson, S. (2019). Nullification through armed civil disobedience: A case study of strategic framing in the Patriot/Militia Movement. *Dynamics of Asymmetric Conflict, 12*(1), 90–109.

Kahane, L. H. (1999). Gun lobbies and gun control: Senate voting patterns on the Brady Bill and the Assault Weapons Ban. *Atlantic Economic Journal, 27*(4), 384–393.

Kellner, D. (2016). *Guys and guns amok: Domestic terrorism and school shootings from the Oklahoma City bombing to the Virginia Tech massacre.* Routledge.

Kingdon, A. (2020). *The gift of the gab: The utilisation of COVID-19 for neonazi recruitment.* Available at: https://gnet-research.org/2020/05/07/the-gift-of-the-gab-the-utilisation-of-covid-19-for-neo-nazi-recruitment/.

Klausen, J. (2015). Tweeting the Jihad: Social media networks of western foreign fighters in Syria and Iraq. *Studies in Conflict and Terrorism, 38*(1), 1–22.

Knobel, M., & Lankshear, C. (2007). Online memes, affinities and cultural production. In K. Michele & C. Lankshear (Eds.), *A new literacies sampler* (pp. 199–227). Peter Lang.

Krippendorff, K. (2013). *Content analysis: An introduction to its Methodology* (3rd ed.). Sage.

Kunzelman, M. (2020). *Coronavirus restrictions Fuel anti-government 'Boogaloo' Movement with roots in online meme culture steeped in irony and dark humour.* Available at: https://www.chicagotribune.com/coronavirus/ct-nw-anti-government-boogaloo-movement-20200513-ksbczwsahzhydb32wtttr m2a44-story.html.

Lagorio-Chafkin, C. (2018). *We are the nerds: The birth and tumultuous life of REDDIT the internet's culture laboratory.* Piatkus.

Lee, B. (2020). 'Neo-Nazis have Stolen our Memes': Making sense of extreme memes. In M. Littler & B. Lee (Eds.), *Digital extremisms: Readings in violence, radicalisation, and extremism in the online space.* Palgrave Macmillan.

Lemenager, S., & Weisiger, M. (2019). Revisiting the radical middle (What's left of it). *Western American Literature, 54*(1).

Levin, B. (1998). The Patriot Movement: Past, present, and future. In H. W. Kushner (Ed.), *The future of terrorism: Violence in the new millennium.* Sage.

Linder, D. (2007). *The Oklahoma City bombing and the trial of Timothy McVeigh.* Available at: https://papers.ssrn.com/sol3/papers.cfm?abstract_id= 1030565.

Ludemann, D. (2018). /pol/emics: Ambiguity, scales, and digital discourse on 4chan. *Discourse, Context & Media, 24*(1), 92–98.

Makley, M. J. (2017). *Open spaces, open rebellions: The war over America's public lands.* University of Massachusetts Press.

Marciszewski, M. (2020). The problem of modern monetization of memes: How copyright law can give protection to meme creators. *Pace Intellectual Property, Sports & Entertainment Law Forum, 9*(1), 1. Available at: https://digitalcommons.pace.edu/cgi/viewcontent.cgi?article=1076&con text=pipself.

May, D. A., & Headley, J. E. (2008). *Reasonable use of force by the police: Seizures, firearms, and high-speed chases.* Peter Lang.

Mayer, J. (2018). *How Russia helped swing the election for Trump.* Available at: https://www.newyorker.com/magazine/2018/10/01/how-russia-hel ped-to-swing-the-election-for-trump.

Mckew, M. (2018). *Brett Kavanaugh and the information terrorists trying to reshape America.* Available at: https://www.wired.com/story/information-ter rorists-trying-to-reshape-america/.

Metahaven. (2014). *Can jokes bring down governments? Memes, design and politics.* Strelka Press.

Meyer, R. (2018). *The grim conclusions of the largest-ever study of fake news.* Available at: https://www.theatlantic.com/technology/archive/2018/ 03/largest-study-ever-fake-news-mit-twitter/555104/.

Moody-Ramirez, M., & Church, A. B. (2019). Analysis of Facebook meme groups used during the 2016 US presidential election. *Social Media & Society, 1*(1), 1–11.

Morgan, L. (2019). "Trespassing in sovereign territory": Place, patriarchy, and the ideology of public lands in Longmire. *Western American Literature, 54*(1), 19–35.

Neiwert, D. (2017). *Alt-America: The rise of the radical right in the age of Trump.* London. Verso.

Nemerever, Z. (2019). Contentious federalism: Sheriffs, state legislatures, and Political Violence in the American West. *Political Behaviour.* Available at: https://link.springer.com/article/10.1007/s11109-019-09553-w.

Nissenbaum, A., & Shifman, L. (2017). Internet memes as contested cultural capital: The case of 4chan's /b/ board. *New Media & Society, 19*(4), 483–501.

O'Shaughnessy, N. J. (2004). *Politics and propaganda: Weapons of mass seduction.* Manchester University Press.

Phillips, W., & Milner, R. M. (2017). *The ambivalent internet: Mischief, oddity, and antagonism.* Polity Press.

Piata, A. (2016). When metaphor becomes a joke: Metaphor journeys from political ads to internet memes. *Journal of Pragmatics, 106*(1), 39–56.

Pitcavage, M. (2001). Camouflage and conspiracy: The Militia Movement from Ruby Ridge to Y2K. *American Behavioural Scientist, 44*(6), 957–981.

Rose, G. (2012). *Visual methodologies: An introduction to researching with visual methods.* Sage.

Ross, A., & Rivers, D. (2017). Digital cultures of political participation: Internet memes and the discursive delegitimization of the 2016 US presidential candidates. *Discourse, Context & Media, 16*(1), 1–11.

Shifman, L. (2013). *Memes in digital culture.* MIT Press.

Sorell, T. (2015). Human rights and hacktivism: The cases of wikileaks and anonymous. *Journal of Human Rights Practice, 7*(3), 391–410.

Sottile, L. (2018). *Bundyville chapter one: A war in the desert.* Available at: https://longreads.com/2018/05/15/bundyville-chapter-one-a-war-in-the-desert/.

Southern Poverty Law Centre. (2020). *Anti Government Movement.* Available at: https://www.splcenter.org/fighting-hate/extremist-files/ideology/antigovernment.

Stanley-Becker, I. (2020). *Militia groups threaten to attack US protestors as they enter small-town America.* Available at: https://www.independent.co.uk/news/world/americas/us-protests-omak-ohio-militia-groups-george-floyd-blm-a9573576.html.

Tuters, M., & Hagen, S. (2019). (((They))) rule: Memetic antagonism and nebulous othering on 4chan. *New Media & Society*, 1–20.

Wang, G. A. (2018). Who controls the land? Lessons from armed takeover of the Malheur National Wildlife Refuge. *Case Studies in the Environment, 2*(1), 1–6.

Part III

Geographies and Cultures of Ethics in Cybercrime Research

Anita Lavorgna and Thomas J. Holt

Introduction to Part III

Cybercrime and online experiences have been topics of interest to researchers for the last three decades, cutting across both the social and technical sciences. As noted, there has been little consensus developed over best practices for research methods to address common research questions. There has been even less recognition of the scope of ethical dilemmas presented by the use of online data. In fact, there appears to be a patchwork approach to the treatment of online data by researchers. Some institutions may define online data as an issue devoid of a need for human subjects protections, as information can be accessed by anyone through search engines and websites. Others argue that the use of online data presents a great risk to personal privacy and confidentiality, as individuals may be unable to consent to participate in a research study in any way.

The lack of consistency has led to *ad hoc* approaches to the best ethical practices to apply to online research, much of which may vary by place. This section of the book attempts to identify these issues and highlight the variations in the ways online data and methods are viewed by academic institutions. Overall, this section should be viewed as a snapshot of the field as it exists. Researchers must take great care when preparing to conduct a study, as well as when entering and exiting any space. Setting the right balance between doing ethical research while avoiding overly conservative attitudes remains a topical puzzle and a contested ground. We need to be careful in respecting and developing sound ethical practices without discouraging researchers from carrying out novel and interesting studies that are in the pursuit of public good and knowledge advancement.

We must also note that researchers from different parts of the world were identified to discuss issues related to the ethics of online research. Despite our best efforts, we recognise that there are whole regions of the world that are not represented which is a limitation of this work, especially when discussing geographically dependent ethical practices and guidelines. Nonetheless, these chapters provoke a dialogue that we hope engages researchers from around the world, especially from under-represented regions. Such efforts are necessary, as is further cross-country conversations on ethics in online research, to help move the field forward.

Chapter 16 by Francisco Castro-Toledo and Fernando Miró-Llinares considers the ways that the European Union has attempted to inject ethical protections into all aspects of online life, and the challenges they present for researchers. Chapter 17 by Brian Pickering, Silke Roth and Craig Webber presents a similar review of these issues in the UK and gives direction for cybercrime researchers attempting to engage in online data collection.

Moving west across the globe, Chapter 18 by Kacy Amory and George W. Burruss considers the ethical stance of institutions in the USA towards online data collection and analysis, and the ways in which institutions may reflexively limit researchers from being effective scholars in the field. Felipe Cardoso Moreira de Oliveira provides an assessment of the state of research ethics in Brazil in Chapter 19 and notes the inherent gaps in protections for both researchers and participants in academic studies.

Chapter 20 by James Martin emphasises the state of ethics review in Australia relating to online data collection, with an emphasis on the Dark Web. Lennon Yao-Chung Chang and Souvik Mukherjee present a discussion of the challenges of conducting research across Southeast Asia in Chapter 21, noting geographical variations across the region. This part of the book concludes with some specific ethical and research concerns that are often not well understood. Chapter 22 by Russell Brewer, Bryce Westlake, Tahlia Hart and Omar Arauza provides a discussion of the use of automated data collection tools and the ways in which this process can harm various entities. Ashley Mattheis and Ashton Kingdon discuss the importance of research safety strategies in online environments in Chapter 23. Similarly, Chapter 24 by Lisa Sugiura details her experiences with data collection in communities that are innately hostile to females and researchers seeking to understand the views of the "involuntarily celibate". In Chapter 25, Cassandra Cross presents the inherent difficulties of conducting research with victims of online crimes and the ways that this can be performed more effectively to the benefit of both researcher and participants. This section concludes with Chapter 26, by Tully O'Neil, which focuses on the challenges and the best practices in conducting ethical digital methodologies with marginalised population groups or participants who are deemed to be "vulnerable", such as victim-survivors of sexual violence using digital platforms to disclose their experiences of violence and abuse.

16

Researching Cybercrime in the European Union: Asking the Right Ethics Questions

Francisco J. Castro-Toledo and Fernando Miró-Llinares

Introduction

European Union (EU) research is based on the commitment to embed ethics from the first conceptual stage of the research through the implementation of the project. As a result, and just to mention the most relevant EU research and innovation framework executed at the moment, in Horizon 2020 all research activities must comply with the ethical principles and the relevant legislation at national, European, and international level. Article 14 of the *Horizon 2020 Rules for Participation* (REGULATION (EU) No. 1290/2013) states that "The Commission shall systematically carry out ethics reviews for proposals raising ethical issues. That review shall verify the respect of ethical principles and legislation and, in the case of research carried out outside the Union,

F. J. Castro-Toledo (✉) · F. Miró-Llinares
Centro CRÍMINA para el estudio y prevención de la delincuencia,
Universidad Miguel Hernández de Elche, Elche, Spain
e-mail: fj.castro@crimina.es

© The Author(s), under exclusive license to Springer Nature
Switzerland AG 2021
A. Lavorgna and T. J. Holt (eds.), *Researching Cybercrimes*,
https://doi.org/10.1007/978-3-030-74837-1_16

that the same research would have been allowed in a Member State." Accordingly, work programs focused on topics such as security and cybersecurity, health, Information and Communication Technologies, climate change or advanced manufacturing must allocate part of their respective budgets to properly address the issues directly connected with ethics. Likewise, programs such as *Science with and for Society* have funded more than 130 European projects on RRI (Responsible Research and Innovation) focused on ethics, gender equality, governance, open access, public engagement, and science education. Addressing ethics issues is an essential part of research today, and regarding our field, social research is surrounded by numerous ethics issues. In a more specific way, in cybercrime research, given the special sensitivity of its targets and the serious implications of its findings, it is even more important to emphasize the responsibility of researchers and provide some criteria and principles to guide their work correctly (Castro-Toledo, 2021). To date, existing specialized literature on ethics applied to criminological issues (Alexander & Ferzan, 2019; Arrigo, 2014; Banks, 2018; Kleinig, 2008; Miller & Gordon, 2014; Pollock, 2014; Roberson & Mire, 2019) has addressed ethical challenges such as the participation of offenders or victims in research without their consent, coercive participation in different areas of the criminal justice system (especially in highly hierarchical contexts), withholding information from participants or direct use of deception by researchers (typical of covert research), conduct control and mood change research, the exposure of participants to physical and mental stress, the breach of privacy and confidentiality, the stigmatization of groups or the unbalanced distribution of benefits and burdens in intervention models based on experimental or quasi-experimental designs, among others.

Given this context, and while the concern for ethics in criminological research has been widely addressed, very few contributions have yet shifted their interest on this issue with respect to the growing research on cybercrime. As a starting point, James Moor (2017) posed the question "what is so special about computers" in order to better understand whether computers had any features that made them special, including their impact on ethics. For instance, we might ask, as a preliminary matter, whether or not the collection of data in a school of cyberbullying victims (Beran & Li, 2007; Miró-Llinares et al., 2020) has the same ethical implications in comparison through a closed group in a social network (Van Hee et al., 2018; Yao et al., 2019); whether or not asking people about their hacking routines (Chua & Holt, 2016; Marcum et al., 2014) or evaluating posts on hacking forums has the same ethics challenges (Stockman et al., 2015); or whether or not observing radical groups in specific neighborhoods (O'Connor et al., 2018) has the same ethics scope as doing web scraping on radical websites (Burnap & Williams, 2016; Miró-Llinares et al., 2018). Thus, the exponential growth of scientific publications on cybercrime during the last decades has shown that cyberspace is not only as a different place (different from physical space) for the occurrence of phenomena of criminological interest, but also as a widely used tool for the scientific approach to them (D' Arcy et al., 2009; Holt & Bossler, 2014; Bossler, 2016; Maimon & Louderback, 2019; Miró-Llinares & Johnson, 2018). As a consequence, a reflection is needed on whether research strategies on cybercrime using the cyberspace as a methodological tool are ethically different.

Accordingly, in this chapter, we state that cybercrime researchers could improve their practical toolbox by firstly following the guidelines provided by the European Commission on ethical aspects of (cyber)crime research, and, secondly, by complementing these guides with new advances in Internet Research Ethics (IRE). Thus, the aim of this chapter is threefold: first, to identify the main European Commission research ethics guidelines and their applicability to crime research; second, to conceptually introduce IRE as a potential ethical framework that can serve as a complement to existing European reference documents; and third, to provide support on identifying some of its main challenges through practical key questions applied to cybercrime research.

Scope of Ethics on (Cyber)Crime Research in the European Union

(Cyber)crime research, its different dimensions, actors, and social implications are linked in EU to numerous ethical standards that should guide the daily practices of researchers. The European Commission's interest in an ethical approach to these issues has been reflected in the main two reference documents hereafter described, among others that have been partially or fully integrated such as *The European Code of Conduct for Research Integrity* (ALLEA, 2017); *General Data Protection Regulation* (Directive (EU) 2016/679); *Research, Risk–Benefit Analyses and Ethical Issues: A guidance document for researchers complying with requests from the European Commission Ethics Reviews* (European Commission, 2013a); and *Ethics for Researcher: facilitating research excellence for FP7* (European Commission, 2013b).

A first European reference document is entitled *Ethics in Social Science and Humanities* (European Commission, 2018a). The document invokes, in general, the *European Charter for Researchers*, and directly Article 13 of the *Charter of Fundamental Rights of the European Union*, to underline the idea that scientific freedom has its limits. Researchers have a considerable liability to safeguard rights, safety and security, welfare and interests of both the individuals and communities involved, as well as with society at large in terms of the contributions that research can make to socially useful and valuable development and change, but also in terms of avoiding possible misuse or unintended consequences of research results. While this report provides a general overview, allusions to crime research are varied. To be specific, the report explicitly mentions criminological research in relation to specific behaviors related to covert research (p. 7), identification of participants from vulnerable groups (p. 11), incidental or unexpected findings in the course of research (p. 14), discrimination or stigmatization (p. 15), location of research (p. 16), sensitive areas of research (p. 20), and finally, misuse of research (p. 21). Furthermore, while the absence of direct references to issues relating to cybercrime is noteworthy, we understand that it is mentioned under the "crime" umbrella, not appreciating its particularities.

In addition, the document includes a section focused on the practical issues arising from digital social science research from a general perspective. In the introduction, the report states that "Rapid technological development and political upheavals in recent years have raised new research ethics concerns, requiring sensitivity to identify ethically problematic areas in Social Science-Humanities research. Increasing use of the internet and social media data in research methodology is a case in point" (European Commission, 2018a, p. 3). A number of specific issues have been raised in research that is internet-mediated and/or uses social media data, such as whether all available data is also public and whether it is fair to use it in research, how the conditions for free and voluntary informed consent will be ensured in the context of social media research, measures to protect the anonymity of those involved, measures to mitigate the risk of harm through the tracking or exposure of the identity and profile of the social network user, or strategies to reduce uncertainty about whether some of the users studied are children or belong to other vulnerable groups (p. 9). Certainly, while all these aspects may affect cybercrime research, in this report other online research strategies (which popularity is currently increasing among criminologist) based on, for instance, metadata, sentiment analysis, or scraping techniques that would collect sensitive data related to criminal activities, are not examined under the same scrutiny.

There is a second European Commission reference document intended to establish the ethics parameters of research in general, and criminology in particular, namely "Ethics in Data protection" (European Commission, 2018b). Written by a group of experts under request of the European Commission (DG Research and Innovation), this document is designed to raise awareness among the scientific community that "data protection is both a central issue for research ethics in Europe and a fundamental human right. It is intimately linked to autonomy and human dignity, and the principle that everyone should be valued and respected. For this principle to guide the development of today's information society, data protection must be rigorously applied by the research community" (p. 3). Its utmost relevance lies in our regulatory background since the right to data protection is enshrined in the EU Charter of Fundamental Rights (see its chapter II) and in the Treaty on the Functioning of the European Union (art. 16) that enforce people's right to privacy by providing them with control over the way information about them is collected and used. Similarly, where research activities are concerned, data protection imposes an obligation on researchers to provide the subjects of the research with detailed information on what will happen to the personal data they collect. However, this also requires organizations that process the data to ensure that the data is properly protected, minimized, and destroyed when no longer needed (European Commission, 2018b, p. 3).

In general, the authors of this report suggest that there are certain cases of research involving specific processing methods of personal data that should be classified as high ethical risk and must incorporate measures to safeguard the privacy of those involved from the design stage. In particular, these include: (1) the processing of "special categories" of personal data (formerly known as "sensitive data," and which includes explicit information relating to criminal activity); (2) the processing of personal data relating to children, vulnerable persons or persons who have not given their consent to participate in the research; (3) complex processing operations and/or large-scale processing of personal data and/or systematic surveillance of a publicly accessible area on a large scale; (4) data processing techniques that are invasive and deemed to pose a risk to the rights and freedoms of research participants or techniques that are vulnerable to misuse (such as the use of data mining, scraping, AI, behavioral or psychological profiling of individuals or groups or other tracking techniques); or (5) the collection of data outside the EU or the transfer of personal data collected in the EU to entities in non-EU countries (p. 6). Furthermore, this report specifically refers to crime research concerning large-scale processing of "special categories" of personal data, or personal data relating to convictions and criminal offenses (p. 14) or the risk of discrimination or stigmatization of vulnerable groups (p.15).

Complementing the European Union's View with Internet Research Ethics' Insights

From a historical, as well as a conceptual perspective, internet research ethics is related to computer and information ethics, which we can trace back to the 1940s with Norbert Wiener's foundational on cybernetics, which identifies a new branch of applied science and some very specific social and ethical implications (Turner & Angius, 2017; Wiener, 2019). The interest in the interaction between human beings and technology, especially the emergence of the internet in the 1990s as a place and a tool for research, changed the scientific landscape completely. By the end of the 1990s, Frankel and Siang (1999) pointed out that the large amount of social and behavioral information potentially available on the internet has become a main objective for researchers who wish to study the dynamics of human interactions and their consequences in this virtual environment. Therefore, this led to an intense debate on whether new ethical dilemmas are emerging, or whether existing dilemmas are similar to dilemmas in other research areas (Elgesem, 2002; Walther, 2002). This field has been referred as "Internet Research Ethics" (IRE), defined by Buchanan and Ess (2008) as the analysis of ethical issues and application of research ethical principles as they pertain to research conducted on and in the internet. The authors also point out that "the specificity and characteristics of internet technologies and especially of interdisciplinary research online mean that IRE issues are usually intertwined and consequently more complex" (Buchanan & Ess, 2016). In other words, nowadays, with the internet becoming a more social and communicative space, the ethical issues of social research, including those related to cybercrime research, have moved from being exclusively data-based to include other dimensions related to the human factor and massive digital social interaction (Miró Llinares, 2012). We are facing numerous new ethical challenges in internet research, as well as the transformation of the traditional ones due to the current digital context (Buchanan & Zimmer, 2016; Turner & Angius, 2017). Over the remaining extent, however, we will address three of the main ethical challenges that arise in cybercrime research, and which are the potential questions that researchers might ask in order to properly identify them. At last, but not least, we would also like to point out that, as any reflection of a normative nature, such list is neither exhaustive nor complete and, of course, should be viewed critically.

Ethics Challenge I: Privacy and Other Legal Issues

With regard to the challenge of privacy, we know that cybercrime research requires large amounts of data of different natures, and that the current model is one of mass, automatic compilation that hardly requires any active behavior on the part of the person providing the information can be contrasted with the obligation to "protect individuals with regard to the processing of personal data" as a fundamental right (see Directive (EU) 2016/679). We have already discussed in previous sections that there are widespread concerns about the privacy of the person in terms of the level of linking of the data to individuals and the potential harm that disclosure or misuse of the data could represent. The fact is that internet has made this context more complex. An important issue in internet research ethics, however, is the distinction between public and private online spaces (Bromseth, 2002; Rosenberg, 2010; Zimmer, 2010) (see also Chapters 17–24). Such a distinction is often problematic because it is mediated by individual and cultural definitions and expectations (Buchanan, 2010; McKee & Porter, 2009). It is therefore essential to rely on instruments for privacy impact assessment against potential personal data breaches such as the PIA (Privacy Impact Assessment), which refers to the obligation of the data controller to carry out an impact assessment and to document it before starting the intended data processing (Clarke, 2009; Vemou & Karyda, 2019). In addition, the current normative scenario is defined by the existence of numerous blind spots around the exceptions reflected in the Directive 2016/680 on the protection of individuals with regard to the processing of personal data by the competent authorities for the purpose of the prevention, investigation, detection or prosecution of criminal offenses or the execution of criminal penalties and on the free movement of such data (Caruana, 2019; Jasserand, 2018). Furthermore, it is important to note that a relevant set of ethical challenges is the harmonization of research on the internet with current national and international regulations (Nolan, 2018). In this sense, serious ethical challenges may arise which is important to identify.

1. When conducting research in Europe, how do we guarantee compliance with the GDPR? What if the digital site studied is owned by an administrator of a third country?
2. Sometimes, various research activities might violate GDPR, should we continue it if it is supported by the terms and conditions of the concrete website?
3. Should we make changes to a data set already collected from an online social network to fit it to the new terms and conditions?
4. If we collect data published in online social network accounts, how do we guarantee the privacy expectation of its users? And what if the profile is public, but only accessible to the users of this social network?
5. What information belongs to the private and public domains in cyberspace?
6. Does the type and amount of (meta)data together potentially disclose identity, and if so, what measures have been taken in order to protect human subjects?
7. When is (meta)data enough for research purpose?
8. Finally, social media big data analysis relies on platforms to share data to some extent with the research community and/or to allow researchers to collect data through APIs. Even if not legally prohibited, what are the levels of impacts possible from sharing large datasets?

Ethics Challenge II: Informed Consent

The collection of data on crime and deviancy online data is one of the most sensitive and ethically challenging moments in the empirical research process (Alexander & Ferzan, 2019; Kleinig, 2008; Pollock, 2014; Roberson & Mire, 2019). Its importance stems by the fact that it is the first moment in which the researcher decides to get in touch with the social or factual reality, controlling and restricting it to the parameters of a series of instruments and tools in which he has codified his models and conceptual structures about how political-criminal phenomena work and are related (Hagan, 1997). In this sense, a long-standing ethical challenge involves informed consent, which the internet has significantly affected. Broadly speaking, the major codes of ethics for research in the criminal justice context reflect the standard that human participants are guaranteed the right to full disclosure of the purposes of research as soon as it is appropriate to the research process, and are also entitled to the opportunity to have their concerns about the purpose and use of research answered (Braswell et al., 2017). Thus, one of the most controversial issues from the perspective we are interested in is those practices of observing people's behavior in their natural context without their knowledge or consent (see, for instance, Chapters 14, 23, and 24).

While this challenge was traditionally associated with the covert research based on ethnomethodology (Garrett, 2013), to date is mostly identifiable in online research on social networks (Castro Toledo, 2019; Castro-Toledo et al., 2020; Miró-Llinares et al., 2018) or through the dark web (Moneva & Caneppele, 2019; Zeid et al., 2020). Of course, this approach has been adopted by researchers when they foresee the risk that those who are aware that they are being observed will decide to act differently to their usual environment, especially when dealing with criminal or simply antisocial behavior, and thus invalidate the results of the study (Banks, 2018). At the level of the criminal justice system, several studies have shown how the importance of discretion in the criminal justice process and the hidden nature of many of the day-to-day decisions seem to support the increased use of these covert and non-consensual observation techniques in an effort to understand how police, prosecutors, and prison staff carry out their duties (Djanali et al., 2014; Miller & Gordon, 2014; Warren et al., 2020). To these essentially pragmatic reasons, others have been added, such as the degree of involvement of researchers in the observation context. On this, We believe that Braswell and colleagues (2017) are right when introducing the nuance that if a behavior being studied could have happened without the intervention of the researcher, then the absence of consent seems less problematic than in those research designs where researchers introduce ad hoc elements to produce some kind of response in the persons observed. On the other hand, a separate, but closely related, issue is that social research often unintentionally yields findings outside the scope of the original research questions, forcing the researcher under certain circumstances to resolve the dilemma between preserving confidentiality or disclosing the information to the relevant authorities.

In line with the European Commission's (2018a) standards of integrity in social science and humanities research, there is a statement that criminal activities witnessed or discovered in the course of research should be reported to the responsible and appropriate authorities, even if this means compromising prior commitments to participants to maintain confidentiality and anonymity. It is therefore essential to inform participants about the limits of the confidentiality that can be offered (i.e., the information sheet should cover the policy on incidental findings). For that reason, we must ask these questions during the execution of our cybercrime research:

1. How can informed consent of subjects be authenticated online?
2. How should consent be obtained in a community that has variable members, who may be from different cultures and different expectations of informed consent?
3. How do you overcome the uncertainty about whether some of the users studied are children or belong to other vulnerable groups?
4. Is the use of deception strictly permissible or necessary in your online research?
5. In research applying Big Data techniques, this is using a range of large data collection techniques, including automated scraping for semi-public data and the use of API processes for accessing private data, which specific measures must be implemented to mitigate the risks related to the automatic processing or profiling of personal data?

Ethics Challenge III: Protecting the Participants and Researchers

It is increasingly obvious to us that when scientific research is able to have a direct impact on the daily lives of people and their environments, the least that ought to do is raise real challenges and moral dilemmas for both social researchers conducting the studies and those responsible for using the evidence collected in legislative decision-making at all levels (Castro-Toledo, 2021). Actually, when it has been suspected that the achievement of the objectives could bring great social benefits, it has not been strange to be tempted to consider the outcomes more important than the protection of individuals, and thereby incur intolerable misconduct: these range from the need to protect individuals against self-incrimination or the dynamics of victimization, to ensuring both that they know what they have accepted by being part of an investigation and that they will offer their views or other data on a completely voluntary basis (Díaz Fernández, 2019; Israel, 2015; Mertens & Ginsberg, 2009). As a result, some remarkable social studies (e.g., Stanford's prison experiment or Milgram's experiment, among others) progressively underpinned the intuition among researchers that not everything is valid in obtaining scientific evidence.

However, it is important to emphasize that today, and with no expectation that it will evolve in the short-term, dissent seems to be the norm in the establishment of concrete ethical boundaries that will adequately guide social research in general (Mertens & Ginsberg, 2009), which seems to be more acute in criminology due, among other reasons, to its later development (Cowburn et al., 2017; Winlow & Hall, 2012), and with no reflection on cybercrime research. At the moment, it is important to note that the British Society of Criminology became the first international platform of social, legal, and professional researchers to create an ethics committee responsible for defining and monitoring the fulfillment of the specific duties of criminology researchers toward the participants of their studies. One year later, this purpose was stated in the first code of ethics for researchers in the field of criminology, which was strongly criticized for its unfeasibility as a working guideline and was requested to be modified up to three times (Dingwall, 2012). Recently imitated by other countries such as the United States or Australia, among others, these codes, guidelines, or ethical statements defend, in a general and consequently soft way, that the protection of potentially vulnerable participants in a research project should be an issue that cannot be ignored by researchers, and unless information is available that points in a different direction, it should be assumed that all participants are potentially vulnerable, including the researchers themselves (Alexander & Ferzan, 2019; Banks, 2018; Kleinig, 2008; Lavorgna & Sugiura, 2020; Miller & Gordon, 2014; Pollock, 2014; Roberson & Mire, 2019).

The above implies that there are many stakeholders to be taken into consideration for the right development of the cybercrime research, and their claims should be carefully considered when examining all ethical issues related to data collection, analysis, and presentation of information. The internet, like the people studied, also functions as an emotional, psychological, economic, reputational, and legal risk trigger for researchers, all of whom require protection. Identifying, preventing, and mitigating these online risks become a need. In this regard, some of the key questions to ask are:

1. Have you considered the safety of your participants or staff, especially if you plan to address sensitive topics (e.g., political views, sexual orientation, religion, organization membership) or involve marginalized groups?
2. How can you assess the degree of risk of an online site (ex. Darknet, TOR, hacker's forum, private groups in social networks of radical groups...)? If so, do you have measures in place to keep researchers, informants, and their associates safe from possible retaliation (e.g., publishing private information, hate-speech, threats...)?
3. How do you aim to mitigate the consequences on psychological health and well-being after the viewing or treatment of extremely violent or sensitive content (e.g., child pornography, animal abuse)?

Conclusions

As said, this chapter only scratches the surface of a more complex field. But what has been said until now means that the internet ethics research is an extremely suggestive proposal to identify the main ethical challenges faced by any research on cybercrime. As the European Commission's working group indicates, the risks of research are varied (emotional, psychological, economic, reputational, and legal) and need to be systematically addressed according to the research and ethics issues associated with each project. The responsibilities incumbent on the research teams to identify and prevent potential harm can be significant (European Commission, 2018a, p. 19). Broadly speaking, we have learned how in cybercrime research the emergence of the social network presents new challenges around subject or participant recruitment procedures, informed consent models, and protection of various expectations and forms of privacy and other risks in a world of increasingly widespread and ubiquitous technologies, anonymity, and confidentiality of data in spaces where researchers and their subjects may not fully understand the terms and conditions of those online sites or tools (Buchanan & Zimmer, 2016; Turner & Angius, 2017); challenges to data integrity, stored and disseminated through cloud computing or remote server locations, presenting a myriad of legal complexities given jurisdictional differences in data regulations (Nolan, 2018). Just to summarize the above, in the introduction of Cohen's *101 Ethical Dilemmas*, the author describes how ethics addresses those decisions that are most important to us, and no major decision is without posing a dilemma. For Cohen, ethical dilemmas are resources that, if well used, can help us to improve our sense of direction when faced with real problems of enormous consequence. Cohen (2003) offers a suggestive starting point: the effective resolution of moral dilemmas does not arise from the strict application of ethical reasoning, but rather from an adequate deployment of practical ethics, of real ethics, which incorporates, in addition to specific principles, a series of prosocial skills by the people involved. Therefore, we can state that asking the right questions is certainly an appropriate way to begin addressing these cybercrime research challenges.

Acknowledgments This chapter has been elaborated within the framework of the project "Criminología, evidencias empíricas y Política criminal. Sobre la incorporación de datos científicos para la toma de decisiones en relación con la criminalización de conductas – Referencia: DER2017-86204-R," funded by the Spanish State Agency for Research (AEI)/Ministry of Science, Innovation and Universities and the European Union through the European Regional Development Fund "ERDF- A way to make Europe."

References

All European Academies. (2017). *The European code of conduct for research integrity.* Available at: https://www.allea.org/wp-content/uploads/2017/05/ALLEA-European-Code-of-Conduct-for-Research-Integrity-2017.pdf.

Alexander, L., & Ferzan, K. K. (Eds.). (2019). *The Palgrave handbook of applied ethics and the criminal law.* Palgrave Macmillan.

Arrigo, B. A. (Ed.). (2014). *Encyclopedia of criminal justice ethics.* Sage.

Banks, C. (2018). *Criminal justice ethics: Theory and practice.* Sage.

Beran, T., & Li, Q. (2007). The relationship between cyberbullying and school bullying. *The Journal of Student Wellbeing, 1*(2), 16–33.

Bossler, A. M. (2016). Cybercrime research at the crossroads: Where the field currently stands and innovative strategies to move forward. In T. J. Holt (Ed.), *Cybercrime through an interdisciplinary lens.* Routledge.

Braswell, M. C., McCarthy, B. R., & McCarthy, B. J. (2017). *Justice, crime, and ethics.* Taylor & Francis.

Bromseth, J. C. (2002). Public places–public activities: Methodological approaches and ethical dilemmas in research on computer-mediated communication contexts. *SKIKT'Researchers–Researching IT in context, 33*–61.

Buchanan, E., & Ess, C. (2008). Internet research ethics: The field and its critical issues. In H. Tavani & K. E. Himma (Eds.), *The handbook of information and computer ethics.* Wiley.

Buchanan, E., & Ess, C. (2016). Ethics in digital research. In M. Nolden., G. Rebane, & M. Schreiter (Eds.), *The handbook of social practices and digital everyday worlds.* Springer.

Buchanan, E. (2010). Internet research ethics: Past, present, future. In C. Ess & M. Consalvo (Eds.), *The Blackwell handbook of internet studies.* Oxford University Press.

Buchanan, E., & Zimmer, M. (2016). *Internet research ethics.* Retrieved from http://plato.stanford.edu/entries/ethics-internet-research/.

Burnap, P., & Williams, M. L. (2016). Us and them: Identifying cyber hate on Twitter across multiple protected characteristics. *EPJ Data Science, 5*(1), 11.

Caruana, M. M. (2019). The reform of the EU data protection framework in the context of the police and criminal justice sector: Harmonisation, scope, oversight and enforcement. *International Review of Law, Computers & Technology, 33*(3), 249–270.

Castro Toledo, F. J. (2019). *Miedo al crimen y sociedad tecnológica*. B de F editorial.

Castro-Toledo, F. J., Gretenkort, T., Esteve, M., & Miró-Llinares, F. (2020). "Fear in 280 characters": A new approach for evaluation of fear over time in cyberspace 1. In V. Cecatto & M. Nalla (Eds.), *Crime and fear in public places*. Routledge.

Castro-Toledo, F. J. (2021). Exploring some old and new ethical issues in criminological research and its implications for evidence-based policy. *Spanish Journal of Legislative Studies, 2*.

Chua, Y. T., & Holt, T. J. (2016). A cross-national examination of the techniques of neutralization to account for hacking behaviors. *Victims & Offenders, 11*(4), 534–555.

Clarke, R. (2009). Privacy impact assessment: Its origins and development. *Computer Law & Security Review, 25*(2), 123–135.

Cohen, M. (2003). *101 dilemas éticos*. Alianza.

Cowburn, M., Gelsthorpe, L., & Wahidin, A. (2017). *Research ethics in criminology: Dilemmas, issues and solutions*. Routledge.

D'Arcy, J., Hovav, A., & Galletta, D. (2009). User awareness of security countermeasures and its impact on information systems misuse: A deterrence approach. *Information Systems Research, 20*(1), 79–98.

Díaz Fernández, A. (2019). *La investigación de temas sensibles en criminología y seguridad*. Tecnos.

Dingwall, R. (2012). How did we ever get into this mess? The rise of ethical regulation in the social sciences. In *Ethics in social research*. Emerald Group Publishing Limited.

Djanali, S., Arunanto, F. X., Pratomo, B. A., Baihaqi, A., Studiawan, H., & Shiddiqi, A. M. (2014, November). Aggressive web application honeypot for exposing attacker's identity. In *2014 The 1st International Conference on Information Technology, Computer, and Electrical Engineering* (pp. 212–216). IEEE.

Elgesem, D. (2002). What is special about the ethical issues in online research? *Ethics and Information Technology, 4*(3), 195–203.

European Commission. (2013a). *Research, risk-benefit analyses and ethical issues: A guidance document for researchers complying with requests from the European Commission Ethics Reviews*. Available at : https://ec.europa.eu/research/swafs/pdf/pub_research_ethics/KI3213113ENC.pdf.

European Commission. (2013b). *Ethics for researcher: Facilitating research excellence for FP7*. Available at: https://ec.europa.eu/research/participants/data/ref/fp7/89888/ethics-for-researchers_en.pdf.

European Commission. (2018a). *Ethics in social science and humanities.* https://ec.europa.eu/info/sites/info/files/6._h2020_ethics-soc-science-humanities_en.pdf.

European Commission. (2018b). *Ethics and data protection.* Available at: https://ec.europa.eu/info/sites/info/files/5._h2020_ethics_and_data_prot ection_0.pdf.

Frankel, M. S., & Siang, S. (1999). *Ethical and legal aspects of human subjects research on the Internet.* Association for the Advancement of Science. Available at: https://www.aaas.org/sites/default/files/2020-02/report_internet_res earch.pdf.

Garrett, B. (2013). *Explore everything: Place-hacking the city.* Verso.

Hagan, F. E. (1997). *Research methods in criminal justice and criminology.* Allyn and Bacon.

Holt, T. J., & Bossler, A. M. (2014). An assessment of the current state of cybercrime scholarship. *Deviant Behavior, 35*(1), 20–40.

Israel, M. (2015). *Research ethics and integrity for social scientist: Beyond regulatory compliance.* Sage.

Jasserand, C. (2018). Law enforcement access to personal data originally collected by private parties: Missing data subjects' safeguards in directive 2016/680? *Computer Law & Security Review, 34*(1), 154–165.

Kleinig, J. (2008). *Ethics and criminal justice: An introduction.* Cambridge University Press.

Lavorgna, A., & Sugiura, L. (2020). Direct contacts with potential interviewees when carrying out online ethnography on controversial and polarized topics: A loophole in ethics guidelines. *International Journal of Social Research Methodology* (online first).

Maimon, D., & Louderback, E. R. (2019). Cyber-dependent crimes: An interdisciplinary review. *Annual Review of Criminology.*

Marcum, C. D., Higgins, G. E., Ricketts, M. L., & Wolfe, S. E. (2014). Hacking in high school: Cybercrime perpetration by juveniles. *Deviant Behavior, 35*(7), 581–591.

McKee, H. A., & Porter, J. (2009). *The ethics of internet research: A rhetorical, case-based process.* Peter Lang Publishing.

Mertens, D., & Ginsberg, P. (2009). *The handbook of social research ethics.* Sage.

Miller, S., & Gordon, I. A. (2014). *Investigative ethics: Ethics for police detectives and criminal investigators.* Wiley.

Miró Llinares, F. (2012). *El cibercrimen. Fenomenología y criminología de la delincuencia en el ciberespacio.* Marcial Pons.

Miró-Llinares, F., & Johnson, S. D. (2018). Cybercrime and place: Applying environmental criminology to crimes in cyberspace. *The Oxford handbook of environmental criminology* (pp. 883–906).

Miró-Llinares, F., Drew, J., & Townsley, M. (2020). Understanding target suitability in cyberspace: An international comparison of cyber victimization processes. *International Journal of Cyber Criminology, 14*(1), 139–155.

Miró-Llinares, F., Moneva, A., & Esteve, M. (2018). Hate is in the air! But where? Introducing an algorithm to detect hate speech in digital microenvironments. *Crime Science, 7*(1), 15.

Moneva, A., & Caneppele, S. (2019). 100% sure bets? Exploring the precipitation-control strategies of fixed-match informing websites and the environmental features of their networks. *Crime, Law and Social Change,* 1–19.

Moor, J. H. (2017). *What is computer ethics? In Computer Ethics,* Routledge. (pp. 31–40).

Nolan, K. (2018). GDPR: Harmonization or fragmentation? Applicable law problems in EU data protection law. *Berkeley Technology Law Journal Blog, 20.*

O'Connor, F., Malthaner, S., & Lindekilde, L. (2018). Killing in Pairs: Radicalisation patterns of violent dyads. *International Journal of Conflict and Violence (IJCV), 12,* a640–a640.

Pollock, J. M. (2014). *Ethical dilemmas and decisions in criminal justice.* Nelson Education.

Roberson, C., & Mire, S. (2019). *Ethics for criminal justice professionals.* CRC Press.

Rosenberg, A. (2010). Virtual world research ethics and the private/public distinction. *International Journal of Internet Research Ethics, 3*(1), 23–37.

Stockman, M., Heile, R., & Rein, A. (2015, September). An open-source honeynet system to study system banner message effects on hackers. In *Proceedings of the 4th Annual ACM Conference on Research in Information Technology* (pp. 19–22).

Turner, R., & Angius, N. (2017). The philosophy of computer science. *Stanford Encyclopedia of Philosophy.*

Van Hee, C., Jacobs, G., Emmery, C., Desmet, B., Lefever, E., Verhoeven, B., De Pauw, G., Daelemans, W., & Hoste, V. (2018). Automatic detection of cyberbullying in social media text. *PLoS ONE, 13*(10), e0203794.

Vemou, K., & Karyda, M. (2019). Evaluating privacy impact assessment methods: Guidelines and best practice. *Information & Computer Security.*

Walther, J. B. (2002). Research ethics in Internet-enabled research: Human subjects issues and methodological myopia. *Ethics and Information Technology, 4*(3), 205–216.

Warren, I., Mann, M., & Molnar, A. (2020). Lawful illegality: Authorizing extraterritorial police surveillance. *Surveillance & Society, 18*(3), 357–369.

Wiener, N. (2019). *Cybernetics or control and communication in the animal and the machine.* MIT Press.

Winlow, S., & Hall, S. (2012). What is an "ethics committee"? Academic governance in an epoch of belief and incredulity. *British Journal of Criminology, 52*, 400–416.

Yao, M., Chelmis, C., & Zois, D. S. (2019). Cyberbullying ends here: Towards robust detection of cyberbullying in social media. In *The World Wide Web Conference* (pp. 3427–3433).

Zeid, R. B., Moubarak, J., & Bassil, C. (2020, June). Investigating the darknet. In *2020 International Wireless Communications and Mobile Computing (IWCMC)* (pp. 727–732). IEEE.

Zimmer, M. (2010). "But the data is already public": On the ethics of research in Facebook. *Ethics and Information Technology, 12*(4), 313–325.

17

Ethical Approaches to Studying Cybercrime: Considerations, Practice and Experience in the United Kingdom

Brian Pickering, Silke Roth, and Craig Webber

Introduction

Over the last few decades, more and more life-spheres have been digitalized, from commercial interactions such as retail and banking, to civic life, leisure and social behaviors (Fussey & Roth, 2020). These developments offer opportunities for criminal activities in cyberspace. Some commentators see the emergence of cybercrime as nothing more than the internet-enabled equivalent of what we already know (Grabosky, 2001). Others have identified not only an online version of offline criminal activity, but developing new types (Wall, 2001, 2007). Furthermore,

B. Pickering (✉) · S. Roth · C. Webber
University of Southampton, Southampton, UK
e-mail: J.B.Pickering@soton.ac.uk

S. Roth
e-mail: Silke.Roth@soton.ac.uk

C. Webber
e-mail: C.Webber@soton.ac.uk

© The Author(s), under exclusive license to Springer Nature
Switzerland AG 2021
A. Lavorgna and T. J. Holt (eds.), *Researching Cybercrimes*,
https://doi.org/10.1007/978-3-030-74837-1_17

some have argued that cybercrime can only be understood as an activity that "drifts" on and off-line, making ethical considerations complicated by the shifting locus of action (Webber & Yip, 2012). Understanding if and how this cyber landscape differs from what is already known is essential if lawmakers and law enforcers are to be able to provide effective measures to protect society. It falls to the research community through its work to inform this process.

Researchers based at universities and research institutions in the United Kingdom who conduct research involving human participants, animals and sensitive research in general are required to seek ethics approval when they have drafted their research protocol. The ethics review process encompasses all stages of the research lifecycle, from the recruitment of participants and collection of data, to data analysis, data storage and the dissemination of research findings. Research Ethics Committees (RECs) or Institutional Review Boards (IRBs) are responsible for providing training and guidance and for reviewing submissions. Principles of ethical research concern preventing harm to research participants and researchers as well as the reputation of research institutes and disciplines. Potential harm must be carefully assessed, avoided, mitigated and—if deemed unavoidable—justified. The Belmont Report (Belmont, 1979) sets out common principles such as autonomy, respect, beneficence, non-maleficence and equanimity. In many ways, though, these are ideals. What is more, although broadly in line with these ideals, different committees may well vary in their practical interpretation and application. Reviewing how these ideals relate to cybercrime research and how different institutions apply them is one goal of this chapter.

Important aspects of ethical research include informed consent and confidentiality, therefore. For most studies, this means that research participants are told about the aims of the study and on this basis consider the risks of taking part. Hence the concept of *informed consent*. These general principles for ethical research are a good starting point, but changes in society's views, in the affordances of technology, and what constitutes ethical research in different domains require a more nuanced approach. The focus of this chapter is to review how these principles are applied and develop recommendations for what needs to be considered when dealing specifically with cybercrime research.

Ess (2002), Markham and Buchanan (2012) and most recently Franzke et al. (2020) see also AoIR, (2020) stress that ethical guidance must be contextualized to the different online environments. RECs/IRBs and Professional Associations may need new guidance on how to evaluate research protocols submitted for review. For the cybercrime environment, though, it is unclear who the human participants should be. On the one hand, collaborative networks of criminals (Yip et al., 2013) involve multiple actors. On the other, risk-taking researchers become part of the cybercrime network they study (Decary-Hetu & Aldridge, 2015; Latour, 2005). Further considerations concern informed consent and deception, which could be justified under specific circumstances.

In this chapter, we begin with a brief overview of the typology of cybercrimes to provide a context within which to gauge impact on the various actors. This is important for research ethics since this enables ethics reviewers to judge the potential research benefit *versus* the burden on researchers and participants. These ethical principles are then applied to assess the effects on the main actors involved with cybercrime in connection with the cybercrime components we have identified. This offers an opportunity to critically evaluate existing guidance and to identify additional recommendations for researchers in this area.

Researching Cybercrime

Advances in technology, especially the pervasive reach of the internet, have many benefits (Chopik, 2016; Hoser & Nitschke, 2010; Norman, 2010). However, this comes at a cost (O'Neil, 2016; Turkle, 2017), not least in terms of individual privacy rights (Michael et al., 2006). This duality surrounding the impact of technology has motivated an extension in research ethics thinking Floridi (2002). Ethical behavior is regarded as contributing to the overall well-being (or "entropy") of a complex network of agents and objects (the "infosphere"). Applying this to cybercrime, the contention between individual rights and public benefit has been understood for some time (Barratt et al., 2013; Decary-Hetu & Aldridge, 2015; Holt & Bossler, 2014; Holt & Lampke 2010). In this section, we provide an overview of cybercrime in the context of the ethical challenges it poses.

Typology of Cybercrimes

There have been several attempts to classify the types of online crimes in recent years (Holt, 2016; Koops, 2010; Sabillon et al., 2016; Wall, 2001), suggesting cyberspace has provided new opportunities for criminal activity to be sanctioned appropriately (Upadhyaya & Jain, 2016). Grabosky (2001, 2014) sees cybercrime as little more than an online version of existing types of crime, whereas Holt and Bossler (2014) and Crown Prosecution Service (n.d.) include both traditional crime moving online and exclusively online activities. By contrast, Wall (2004) and subsequently (Bossler & Berenblum, 2019) identify traditional crime with cyber elements as distinct from cybercrime that solely exists online. For the current discussion, Wall's original typology (2001) summarized in Table 17.1 provides a useful starting point.

Koops (2010) offers a slightly different classification, based on the Council of Europe's Cybercrime Convention which may easily be mapped to Wall's. The importance of such classification in terms of ethics is the implications for the researcher. Firstly, with multiple victims and/or perpetrators, which of the research participant rights take precedence? But in addition, where there is no direct, individual victim such as attacks against infrastructure (Martin et al., 2018), should the assessment of impact be scaled up since more people are affected, or differentiated along the lines of personal *versus* economic effects? Similarly, if there is no single perpetrator but rather a group or network, do we need to consider the dynamics of that network and how individuals respond to group membership (Vilanova et al., 2017)? What is more, whether individual or networked, is it appropriate for researchers to engage directly with cybercriminals? The answers to these sorts of questions will affect how we assess and review ethical research. One final observation: the pervasive nature of the internet allows cybercriminals to transcend jurisdictional boundaries. This alone introduces additional complexity for research in this area.

Table 17.1 Typology of cybercrime adapted from Wall (2001)

Type	Brief summary	Perpetrator(s)	Victim(s)	Impact
Cyber-trespass	Gaining access to property or assets without the owner's permission	Individual hackers; Organized groups (scammers)	• Individual targets • Institutions	Loss of privacy and integrity; potential breaches
Cyber-deception and theft	Related to the above, taking possession of information or assets	Hackers/Scammers	• Individual targets • Institutions	Individual financial loss; loss of trust; economic loss to institutions; possible fines for institutions
Cyber-porn and obscenity	Access and sharing of indecent content	Organized groups; individuals	• Those depicted • Those in receipt	Individual distress (for anyone shown in content); socially unacceptable
Cyber-violence	Computer-mediated violence (bullying) or incitement	Organized groups; individuals; 3rd party states	• Individual targets • Political integrity • Society	Individual distress; Social disruption; Political extremism

Network of Actors

Collaboration between criminal actors is well established in the offline world, including youth gangs, organized crime groups and cross-border organizations (Aas, 2013). Cyberspace, however, is a unique system for facilitating collaboration and provides the means for various different forms of task-delegation; for example, it offers opportunities such as "crime-as-a-service" (Decary-Hetu & Aldridge, 2015, p. 123), where *ad hoc* relationships can be formed for specific activities or transactions (Grabosky, 2014; Lusthaus, 2012, 2018a, 2018b; Lusthaus & Varese, 2017; Yip et al., 2013). Carding fora, for example, display the kinds of relationship mechanisms, such as trust and reputation, found in offline collaborative networks (Holt & Lampke, 2010; Hoser & Nitschke, 2010; Webber & Yip, 2020). Not all actors within the network may be committed criminals, but also private individuals looking to make difficult or illegal purchases (Barratt et al., 2013; Sugiura, 2018). For the researcher dealing with networked activity has implications not least in seeking consent from research participants (Beaulieu & Estalella, 2012; Lusthaus, 2018b; Sugiura et al., 2017), but also in their relationship with the network under study (Sugiura et al., 2017; Yip et al., 2013).

Where Does the Researcher Fit?

Awareness of potential interlopers among online criminals (Holt & Lampke, 2010; Yip et al., 2013) leaves the cybercrime researcher in an equivocal position. It has been well attested in various domains that making yourself known may not always be welcome (Beaulieu & Estalella, 2012; Holt & Lampke, 2010; Lusthaus, 2018b; Sugiura et al., 2017). Specifically for cybercrime, it may well be inadvisable for researchers to identify themselves and risk retribution (Decary-Hetu & Aldridge, 2015; Lavorgna et al., 2020). Some researchers as well as cybersecurity experts will deliberately target the practices of cybercriminals exploiting the very vulnerabilities that the criminals use themselves (Spitzner, 2003a, 2003b). How ethical such practices are is not easy to determine. On the one hand, there is the societal effort to prevent and protect against crime; on the other, controlling it online may prevent the offline consequences (Pastrana et al., 2018). Ultimately, the researcher has to understand and obey the rules of the networked group they observe (Flick, 2016; Hoser & Nitschke, 2010; Markham & Buchanan, 2012; Yip et al., 2013), including differences between the clear and dark web. Finally, there is evidence of trauma for those exposed to various offenses (Burruss et al., 2018), including a displaced feeling of obligation to help remote victims (Lee, 2017). Researchers need to consider their own emotional well-being, therefore, depending on the research they undertake.

Ethics Landscape

Despite individual differences in definition, normative approaches to ethics stress duty or morally acceptable action (Kagan, 1992). This may be in terms of an actor doing the right thing (deontological), of the desirability of the outcome (utilitarianism), or more specifically, the equitability of outcomes (Rawls' theory of justice) (Franzke et al., 2020; Parsons, 2019). When associated with cybercrime, however, many issues arise. Can Australian law enforcement taking over a pedophile site and not shutting it down immediately be justified on utilitarian grounds (Safi, 2016)? Similarly, can online drug markets be justified based on keeping drug-related violence off the streets (Pastrana et al., 2018)? In one of the few references to regional differences, Ess (2002) observes that ethics in the United States tends to be utilitarian by nature seeking the best for the common good. By contrast, he claims, Europe is broadly deontological, stressing the rights of the individual. In general, research ethics calls for respect for research participants, equanimity in outcomes, and optimizing beneficence and non-malificence (Belmont, 1979). Where there are multiple actors, including multiple private individual and institutional victims (see Table 17.1), it is not always clear how impact (benevolent or otherwise) should be balanced across actors. The ALL European Academies, of course, take Belmont's principles further and require context sensitivity and risk awareness (ALLEA, 2017, p. 6), respect extended to all actors involved (ALLEA, 2017, p. 4) and independence from the interests (in this case law enforcement) of funders

(ALLEA, 2017, p. 8). There is clearly a need to examine how normative as well as research ethical principles inform the study of cybercrime. Such evaluation will doubtless lead to more specific recommendations for researchers and reviewers.

Research in cyberspace poses different challenges, of course. Floridi (2002), for instance, suggests ethical judgment be based on the contribution of an action to the general ecosystem. Accordingly, the online environment may need a different approach to ethical evaluation. Interestingly, others have highlighted that online distinctions between, for instance, individuals and their data are blurred (Markham & Buchanan, 2012). Many researchers, however, call for a fine-grained approach highlighting a need to contextualize ethical assessment (Ess, 2002; Flick, 2016; Markham & Buchanan, 2012). The researcher must identify and respect the normative expectations of a specific forum or space online (Hoser & Nitschke, 2010), and continually assess what is appropriate across the different stages of the research process (Pastrana et al., 2018). Private and public cyberspaces are no longer distinct (Ess, 2002; Markham & Buchanan, 2012; Sugiura et al., 2017). Individual attitudes to privacy change depending on context (Acquisti, 2012; Acquisti et al., 2015), with concern mainly about information being directed and used appropriately than necessarily being kept confidential (Nissenbaum, 2011). So, judgments about a research participant's expectations of privacy become all the more problematic. Even where it's possible to request, informed consent under such conditions no longer makes sense. Pastrana and colleagues (2018) suggest instead focusing on research on collective rather than individual behaviors and encourage additional pseudonymization of data prior to publication.

The general research ethics landscape poses many and varied problems for the researcher and the reviewer, therefore. No one size fits all, of course, as many have pointed out (Ess, 2002; Flick, 2016; Franzke et al., 2020; Markham & Buchanan, 2012). What is clear, though, and particularly relevant for cybercrime is that the researcher must consider firstly that the more vulnerable any of the participants or the stakeholders in their research may be, the higher their responsibility to be sensitive to context and the rights of the individual (Markham & Buchanan, 2012). In the next section, we turn from the general principles as they relate to cyberspace and specifically cybercrime to guidance offered currently in the United Kingdom.

UK Guidelines for Researchers

Having reviewed the general research ethics landscape, in this section we turn specifically to the United Kingdom. At universities in Britain, research ethics committees or institutional review boards are responsible for providing training, guidance and the review of ethics submissions. Ethics applications are usually screened and categorized as low(er) or high(er) risk. High-risk applications—such as cybercrime research—require extra-careful scrutiny by reviewers, chairs of research ethics committees and data protection officers. What guidance is available for researchers carrying out cybercrime research at universities and research institutes in the United Kingdom? We reviewed websites of funders, professional organizations and universities in the United Kingdom and spoke with colleagues based in criminology departments, ethics boards and involved with data protection. In our review, we included universities with criminology departments known for research of cybercrime (Cambridge, Leeds, Portsmouth, Southampton and Surrey) as well as other leading criminology departments (for example at Essex, Manchester and Oxford). We also conducted a web-search (using the search terms "security-sensitive research") which led us to guidance provided by a range of other universities (e.g., City, University of London and Huddersfield). In addition, we reviewed ethics guidance from the professional organizations representing our disciplines (the British Psychological Society [BPS], the British Society of Criminology [BSC] and the British Sociological Association [BSA]) and the Association of Internet Researchers.

Our review found that while there is little explicit guidance concerning ethical aspects of cybercrime research available, the following four frameworks provide useful resources:

- General research ethics;
- Guidelines concerning internet research;

- General Data Protection Regulation (GDPR) which regulates the management of personal data;
- Guidance on research on terrorism and extremism and the Prevent Strategy.

In each of the following subsections, we provide a brief introduction to each of these four areas and then identify any specific guidance available.

General Research Ethics

At the time of writing, all universities and research institutions in the United Kingdom have adopted ethics policies which are usually displayed on publicly accessible websites while some universities (e.g., Leicester and Kings College London) make this information available only to members of the university. Universities in the United Kingdom have research ethics committees (REC) or institutional review boards (IRB) which ensure that all research which requires ethics approval is reviewed and documented. Cybercrime research—as well as research on crime in general—requires ethics review and approval. It might be hampered by the usual practice of gaining informed consent. Therefore, deception and data collection without gaining consent can—but must—be justified. Furthermore, like other criminologists, those conducting cybercrime research must avoid getting involved in criminal activities while collecting data and interacting with (cyber) criminals.

Available Guidance

Researchers based in the United Kingdom have access to guidance concerning research ethics from professional organizations (e.g., the BPS [2017, 2018], the BSC [2018] and the BSA [n.d.]) and funders (e.g., the Economic and Social Research Council [ESRC, 2020]). Research ethics are taught at undergraduate and post-graduate levels. Individual universities and research institutes provide information about the ethics application process on public and/or internal webpages. Ethics applications are reviewed by ethics committees within the institution.

Ethics Guidelines for Internet Research

General ethics principles also apply to internet research. However, over the last decades, internet research has raised important questions concerning the conceptualization of "the public sphere" and to what extent it is justified to collect data in the public sphere of the internet without informing data subjects and obtaining their consent. Even if it might be legal to analyze data that has been shared on social media platforms, social media users have the legitimate expectation that their data is not used without obtaining consent or that every effort is undertaken to prevent the identification of data subjects.

In the previous sections, we have outlined different types of cybercrime which might be an extension of traditional forms of crime which utilize information and communication technologies (ICT) or internet-based crimes which do not have an offline equivalent. This includes researching the dark web (Gehl, 2018). Access to the dark web requires one of the anonymizing browsers, such as Tor ("The Onion Router" [Tor, n.d.]). This effectively makes users untraceable, though using such a browser may raise suspicion with the authorities. Activity on the dark web is not in itself illegal, though it has been estimated that around 52% (2723 out of 5205) of sites deal with illicit activities (Moore & Rid, 2016). As with accessing any online sites whether the clear or dark web, if this might endanger the researcher and the institution at which she is based, it requires careful consideration and data management.

Available Guidance

Guidance for internet research is available from the Association for Internet Researchers. The BSA has provided internet specific guidance, including case studies (e.g., "Researching Online Forums" and "Researching Social Machines," accessible from BSA, n.d.). Of particular interest for researchers of cybercrime is the BSA case study "Using Twitter for Criminological Research." UK universities provide limited guidance on internet-based guidance and ethical considerations concerning cybercrime. Oxford University is an exception and provides "Best Practice

Guidance" for "internet-based research" which addresses deception, dark web studies and deep fakes (CUREC, 2019). Some universities (City, Huddersfield, Aberystwyth, De Montfort) mention criminal activities under security-sensitive research and, for example, human trafficking or child pornography.

GDPR, Protection of Sensitive Personal Data

The General Data Protection Regulation (GDPR) (European Commission, 2016) concerns the collection, handling and storage of identifiable personal data. Some personal data is regarded as particularly sensitive ("special category," Art. 9) which includes information about race, sexual orientation, political attitudes and activities, as well as criminal behavior (Art. 10). Collection of such data must be minimal and well justified. Data collection might be online or offline. Cybercrime research will fall under the GDPR regulations if the data on criminal behavior includes identifiable personal data. Any such research may require additional approval from the appropriate authority. If published results are completely anonymous after data collection and analysis, then it falls beyond the scope of the GDPR. It therefore requires careful data management at different stages of the research process.

Available Guidance

GDPR guidance is widely available from the ESRC, the UK Data Service (2012–2020) and on the websites of individual universities. The guidance includes detailed information about the legal aspects and what it means for data management and processing.

Prevent, Research on Terrorism and Extremism

The recruitment to and planning of terrorist and extremist acts represent one specific category of cybercrime and in the United Kingdom are regulated through the "Prevent duty guidance: For higher education institutions in England and Wales" (HM Government, 2019) which requires that institutions, including schools and universities, monitor the online and offline activities of staff and students. Researchers who are studying the recruitment and planning of terrorist and extremist acts are carrying out security-sensitive research which requires not only the highest level of scrutiny during the ethics review process, but also secure data storage and registration of the research project with the appropriate authorities in order to prevent harm to the university and its community and the accusation leveled at researchers that they are involved in terrorist and extremist activities (see also Chapter 23).

Available Guidance

Universities UK (UUK) has provided guidance for the "Oversight of Security Sensitive Research Material at UK Universities" which responds to the Prevent Strategy and provides support for researchers who are carrying out research on security and terrorism (Universities UK, 2019). It details the obligations of researchers to register their research projects and use dedicated computers to access and store data related to terrorism. Many universities refer to the UUK guidance on their websites, in some cases citing the UUK document verbatim. Some examples of universities referring to Prevent and the UUK guidance include Cambridge, Sheffield, UWE, Glasgow, Cardiff and Keele.

Recommendations: Toward Ethics Guidelines for Cybercrime Research

Our review indicates that the ethics approval process at British universities and research institutions is rigorous and provides extensive guidance on research ethics, internet research, GDPR regulations and security-sensitive research. The guidance seeks to balance the risk to researchers and the institutions with which they are affiliated and their ability to carry out cutting-edge research. This balancing act requires case-by-case decision making in order to avoid being neither too risk-averse or overly risk-taking. We found that with the exception of terrorism and extremism specific guidance on cybercrime is limited.

The existing guidance provides an excellent basis for the development of cybercrime-specific research ethics. Such research ethics guidance must draw on and combine guidance on internet research, GDPR regulations and security-sensitive research. Core issues of cybercrime-specific ethics include:

- Lack of informed consent
- Deception
- Secure access and storage of data
- Registering cybercrime with data protection officers or REC/IRB boards
- Specific training for researchers and reviewers of cybercrime ethics applications.

With that in mind, the pointers below include specific factors concerning research around cybercrime. This is not intended as a cookbook, as others have said, but to encourage ongoing reflection. The researcher must be sensitive, for instance, to how different cyberspace is in terms of risks to the researcher, the vulnerability of individual actors and the fine line between research and the requirements of law enforcement. At the same time, both research and reviewer should evaluate each case on its individual merits, and in consideration of the different stages of the research lifecycle.

Our first two considerations are not specifically covered in the guidance we have reviewed in the previous section. The first, whether it is research or not, is intended to make researchers and reviewers examine whether what is proposed is crime agency monitoring rather than independent research. The second relates to the care and support that the researcher may need in regard to the types of information and behaviors they observe.

Is It Research?

The complexity and sensitivity surrounding any cybercrime (see Table 17.1) suggest that it is important to consider from the start whether a proposed engagement with online activity should be unequivocally research. This may be defined, for instance, with reference to Frascati. https://doi.org/10.1787/9789264239012-en. There are clear social imperatives to reduce the suffering and protect victims of crime; in addition, there are socio-economic motivators to prevent crimes against institutions, both enterprise and broader structures such as democracy. Although research into such activities could doubtless inform policy and support law enforcement, it is clear that research into cybercrime should be motivated primarily for the search for knowledge. Researchers have a responsibility to the research community; social and legal obligations are beyond the scope of ethical research. Although REC/IRB reviewers should point out any non-research obligations, their primary responsibility is to review the ethical appropriateness of research.

Does the Researcher Need Support?

Security-sensitive research may well need to register with an external agency to protect both the researcher and the reputation of the institution (see below). A more pertinent issue for the researcher themselves and therefore which needs to be evaluated during ethics review is the potential effect that exposure to crime may cause long-term distress to the researcher (see, for instance, Chapter 23). This would be particularly relevant where the moral code of the researcher and their peers finds the criminal activity unacceptable. This would often be the case for crimes against children, but also other forms of human trafficking and hate crime. Reviewers should look for the measures that are in place to provide emotional and psychological support to the researcher.

Consent

There needs to be a careful consideration about whether consent is possible, feasible or desirable and whether it can be truly *informed*. Reviewers therefore need to consider the researcher's position *vis-à-vis* the rights of research participants, and the relevance of consent. Notwithstanding confusions between consent as a legal basis for processing personal data, consent is not specifically about privacy. The researcher must clearly assess the expectation of privacy for the specific context under investigation. Certainly, in terms of privacy, research subjects may knowingly share information for reasons of their own and very much dependent on the context. Researchers should therefore consider the normative expectations around information sharing on a context-by-context basis. Reviewers should in turn, we suggest, consider not in absolute terms whether research consent can be waived, but rather whether the proposed research shows that it has taken account of the specific online context.

Deception

Well-motivated deception can be an acceptable research method, if appropriately managed (see BPS above). However, the rationale is typically to observe spontaneous responses. Similarly, lurking can be justified to avoid intrusion or influencing normal behaviors. Deception or lurking should be justified in terms of the expectations of research participants in the particular context and virtual environment in relation to the potential benefit of the research. It is important to ensure that researcher safety is appropriately handled (see also Chapters 23 and 24). In the case of deception in particular, researchers and reviewers should be clear that the researcher's actions are not construed as entrapment.

Secure Access and Storage of Data

GDPR and Prevent regulations require the secure storage of data in order to prevent harm to research participants, researchers and the institutions in which they work. This means that researchers are only allowed to access the dark web or contact terrorist networks using computers which are separate from the university IT infrastructure in order to avoid making it vulnerable to hacking and other cyber-attacks. Reviewers should consider an appropriate data management plan across the lifecycle of the research study, including publication of results. This should clearly describe how data is secured, how access is managed and how the data will be disposed of.

Registering Cybercrime with Data Protection Officers, RECs/IRBs and/or External Agencies

Researchers need to register projects that involve criminal and terrorist activities with data protection officers or chairs of ethics committees. They should also check whether their research activities need to be registered or made known to any relevant agency. This is so as to minimize the risk of being accused of illegal activities in the case of criminal investigations. However, registering does not necessarily provide legal protection for researchers. Reviewers should check that researchers demonstrate awareness of the legal requirements they should consider (see also Chapter 23).

Specific Training for Researchers and Reviewers of Cybercrime Ethics Applications

We are only aware that Portsmouth University carries out training for PGT students in the context of their MSc in Cybercrime. Further research is needed to assess the extent of cybercrime ethics guidance that is available to researchers and reviewers in the United Kingdom. As a minimum, we would recommend that ethics reviewers should be supported in understanding the specifics of the context (i.e., the normative expectations of cybercriminals), relevant regulatory requirements (including Prevent and the GDPR if personal data is involved) and the role of the researcher in relation to the individual or group they study (see, for instance, Chapters 22–26).

Limitations and Future Research

In the preceding sections, we have considered general research ethics and how these relate to research in the virtual world in regard to cybercrime. On that basis, we have summarized the available guidance and practices of ethics reviews for cybercrime research in the United Kingdom. It is essential, we believe, that research ethics keeps pace with the changes afforded by the virtual world and not only in regard to cybercrime. If academia is to retain a significant role within research when faced with competition from technology giants, then it must demonstrate that it can manage transparent and accountable research even within security-sensitive environments.

There is a final consideration, however, which is relevant especially to the study of cybercrime. The nature of the internet and ease with which individuals can ostensibly achieve some level of anonymity even on the clear web may have promoted this type of crime. But the reach of the internet also provides an opportunity for criminal activities to span jurisdictional boundaries. In consequence, law enforcement as well as research activities must take into account this international aspect, not least in encouraging cross-border collaboration and data sharing. Similarly, cybercrime ethics also concern the approach to contemporary counter-movements on the left and the right, and to what extent they are classified as extremist, and how foreign influence can affect civic life. The current political landscape, in particular Brexit and the reshuffling of international research relations, raises important questions about data management and international collaboration (Rotenberg, 2020).

Our chapter is only a starting point, though. Our contribution is intended to highlight the need to contextualize ethics review in regard to all stages of the research lifecycle. We welcome ongoing surveys of these practices to assess the needs of cybercrime researchers and university research ethics committees in order to balance the need to carry out cutting-edge and high-risk research and the security of universities.

References

Aas, K. F. (2013). *Globalization & crime*. Sage.
Acquisti, A. (2012). Nudging privacy: The behavioral economics of personal information. In *Digital enlightenment Yearbook*.
Acquisti, A., Brandimarte, L., & Loewenstein, G. (2015). Privacy and human behavior in the age of information. *Science, 347*(6221), 509–514.
ALLEA. (2017). *The European code of conduct for research integrity*. Allea.org.
AOIR. (2020). *Ethics*. Available at: https://aoir.org/ethics/.
Barratt, M. J., Ferris, J. A., & Winstock, A. R. (2013). Use of Silk Road, the online drug marketplace, in the United Kingdom. *Australia and the United States. Addiction, 109*(5), 774–783.
Beaulieu, A., & Estalella, A. (2012). Rethinking research ethics for mediated settings. *Information, Communication & Society, 15*(1), 23–42.
Belmont. (1979). *The Belmont report: Ethical principles and guidelines for the protection of human subjects of research*. Available at: https://www.hhs. gov/ohrp/regulations-and-policy/belmont-report/read-the-belmont-report/ index.html.
Bossler, A. M., & Berenblum, T. (2019). Introduction: New directions in cybercrime research. *Journal of Crime and Justice, 42*(5), 495–499.
BPS. (2017). *Ethics guidelines for internet-mediated research*. Available at: https://www.bps.org.uk/news-and-policy/ethics-guidelines-internet-med iated-research-2017.
BPS. (2018). *Ethical guidelines for applied psychological practice in the field of extremism, violent extremism and terrorism*. Available at: https://www.bps. org.uk/news-and-policy/ethical-guidelines-applied-psychological-practice-field-extremism-violent-extremism.
BSA. (n.d.). *Guidelines on ethical research*. Available at: https://www.britsoc.co. uk/ethics.
BSC. (2018). *Statement of ethics*. Available at: https://www.britsoccrim.org/eth ics/.

Burruss, G. W., Holt, T. J., & Wall-Parker, A. (2018). The hazards of investigating internet crimes against children: Digital evidence handlers' experiences with vicarious trauma and coping behaviors. *American Journal of Criminal Justice, 43*(3), 433–447.

Chopik, W. J. (2016). The benefits of social technology use among older adults are mediated by reduced loneliness. *Cyberpsychology, Behavior and Social Networking, 19*(9), 551–556.

Crown Prosecution Service. (n.d.). *Cyber/online crime*. Available at: https://www.cps.gov.uk/cyber-online-crime.

CUREC. (2019). *Internet-Based Research (IBR)*. Available at: https://researchsupport.admin.ox.ac.uk/files/bpg06internet-basedresearchpdf.

Decary-Hetu, D., & Aldridge, J. (2015). Sifting through the net: Monitoring of online offenders by researchers. *European Review of Organised Crime, 2*(2), 122–141.

ESRC. (2020). *Research ethics*. Available at: https://esrc.ukri.org/funding/guidance-for-applicants/research-ethics/.

Ess, C. (2002). *Ethical decision-making and Internet research: Recommendations from the AoIR ethics working committee*. Available at: https://aoir.org/reports/ethics.pdf.

European Commission. (2016). *Regulation (EU) 2016/679 of the European Parliament and of the Council of 27 April 2016*.

Flick, C. (2016). Informed consent and the Facebook emotional manipulation study. *Research Ethics, 12*(1), 14–28. https://doi.org/10.1177/1747016115599568.

Floridi, L. (2002). On the intrinsic value of information objects and the infosphere. *Ethics and Information Technology, 4*(4), 287–304.

Franzke, A. S., Bechmann, A., Zimmer, M., Ess, C., & the Association of Internet Researchers. (2020). *Internet research: Ethical guidelines 3.0*. Available at: https://aoir.org/reports/ethics3.pdf.

Fussey, P. & Roth, S. (2020). Digitizing sociology: Continuity and change in the internet era. *Sociology, 54*(4), 659–674. https://journals.sagepub.com/doi/full/10.1177/0038038520918562.

Gehl, R. W. (2018). Archives for the dark web: A field guide for study. In T. Levenberg & D. Rheams (Eds.), *Research methods for the digital humanities*. Palgrave Macmillan.

Grabosky, P. N. (2001). Virtual criminality: Old wine in new bottles? *Social & Legal Studies, 10*(2), 243–249.

Grabosky, P. N. (2014). *The evolution of cybercrime, 2004–2014* (RegNet Working Papers, 58).

HM Government. (2019). *Prevent duty guidance*. Available at: https://www.gov. uk/government/publications/prevent-duty-guidance.

Holt, T. J. (2016). *Cybercrime through an interdisciplinary lens*. Routledge.

Holt, T. J., & Bossler, A. M. (2014). An assessment of the current state of cybercrime scholarship. *Deviant Behavior, 35*(1), 20–40.

Holt, T. J., & Lampke, E. (2010). Exploring stolen data markets online: Products and market forces. *Criminal Justice Studies, 23*(1), 33–50.

Hoser, B., & Nitschke, T. (2010). Questions on ethics for research in the virtually connected world. *Social Networks, 32*(3), 180–186.

Kagan, S. (1992). The structure of normative ethics. *Philosophical Perspectives, 6,* 223–242.

Koops, B. J. (2010). The internet and its opportunities for cybercrime. In M. Herzog-Evans (Ed.), *Transnational criminology manual*. WLP.

Latour, B. (2005). *Reassembling the social-an introduction to actor-network-theory*. Oxford University Press.

Lavorgna, A., Middleton, S. E., Pickering, B., & Neumann, G. (2020). FloraGuard: Tackling the online illegal trade in endangered plants through a cross-disciplinary ICT-enabled methodology. *Journal of Contemporary Criminal Justice, 36*(3), 428–450.

Lee, D. (2017). *Submission of evidence to the all party Parliamentary Group Drones: How are RAF Reaper (drone) operators affected by the conduct of recent and ongoing operations*. Available at: http://appgdrones.org.uk/wp-content/ uploads/2014/08/Dr-Peter-Lee-Submission-to-APPG-Inquiry.pdf.

Lusthaus, J. (2012). Trust in the world of cybercrime. *Global Crime, 13*(2), 71–94.

Lusthaus, J. (2018a). Honour among (cyber) thieves? *European Journal of Sociology/Archives Européennes de Sociologie, 59*(2), 191–223.

Lusthaus, J. (2018b). *Industry of anonymity: Inside the business of cybercrime*. Harvard University Press.

Lusthaus, J., & Varese, F. (2017). Offline and local: The hidden face of cybercrime. *Policing: A Journal of Policy and Practice* (online first).

Markham, A., & Buchanan, E. (2012). *Ethical decision-making and internet research: Recommendations from the AoIR ethics working committee (version 2.0)*. Available at: https://aoir.org/reports/ethics2.pdf.

Martin, G., Ghafur, S., Kinross, J., Hankin, C., & Darzi, A. (2018). WannaCry—A year on. *British Medical Journal, 361*.

Michael, K., McNamee, A., & Michael, M. G. (2006). *The emerging ethics of humancentric GPS tracking and monitoring*. Paper presented at the 2006 International Conference on Mobile Business.

Moore, D., & Rid, T. (2016). Cryptopolitik and the darknet. *Survival, 58*(1), 7–38.

Nissenbaum, H. (2011). A contextual approach to privacy online. *Daedalus, 140*(4), 32–48.

Norman, D. A. (2010). *Living with complexity*. MIT Press.

O'Neil, C. (2016). *Weapons of math destruction: How big data increases inequality and threatens democracy*. Crown.

Parsons, T. D. (2019). *Ethical challenges in digital psychology and cyberpsychology*. Cambridge University Press.

Pastrana, S., Thomas, D. R., Hutchings, A., & Clayton, R. (2018). *CrimeBB: Enabling Cybercrime Research on Underground Forums at Scale*. Paper presented at the Proceedings of the 2018 World Wide Web Conference, Lyon.

Rotenberg, M. (2020). Schrems II, from Snowden to China: Toward a new alignment on transatlantic data protection. *European Law Journal* (online first).

Sabillon, R., Cano, J., Cavaller Reyes, V., & Serra Ruiz, J. (2016). Cybercrime and cybercriminals: A comprehensive study. *International Journal of Computer Networks and Communications Security, 4*(6).

Safi, M. (2016, 13 July). The takeover: How police ended up running a paedophile site. *The Guardian*. Available at: https://www.theguardian.com/society/2016/jul/13/shining-a-light-on-the-dark-web-how-the-police-ended-up-running-a-paedophile-site.

Spitzner, L. (2003a). The honeynet project: Trapping the hackers. *IEEE Security and Privacy, 1*(2), 15–23.

Spitzner, L. (2003b). *Honeypots: Catching the insider threat*. Paper presented at the 19th Annual Computer Security Applications Conference.

Sugiura, L. (2018). *Respectable deviance and purchasing medicine online: Opportunities and risks for consumers*. Palgrave.

Sugiura, L., Wiles, R., & Pope, C. (2017). Ethical challenges in online research: Public/private perceptions. *Research Ethics, 13*(3–4), 184–199.

Tor. (n.d.). *The Tor Project, Inc*. Available at: https://www.torproject.org/.

Turkle, S. (2017). *Alone together: Why we expect more from technology and less from each other* (3rd ed.). Basic Books.

UK Data Service. (2012–2020). *Applying GDPR in research*. Available at: https://www.ukdataservice.ac.uk/manage-data/legal-ethical/gdpr-in-research.aspx.

Universities UK. (2019). *Oversight of security-sensitive research material in UK universities: Guidance*. Available at: https://www.universitiesuk.ac.uk/policy-

and-analysis/reports/Pages/security-sensitive-research-material-UK-universit
ies-guidance.aspx.

Upadhyaya, R., & Jain, A. (2016). *Cyber ethics and cyber crime: A deep
dwelved study into legality, ransomware, underground web and bitcoin wallet.*
Paper presented at the 2016 International Conference on Computing,
Communication and Automation (ICCCA).

Vilanova, F., Beria, F. M., Costa, Â. B., & Koller, S. H. (2017). Deindividuation: From Le Bon to the social identity model of deindividuation effects.
Cogent Psychology, 4(1), 1308104.

Wall, D. S. (2001). Cybercrimes and the Internet. *Crime and the Internet*, 1–
17.

Wall, D. S. (2004). What are cybercrimes? *Criminal Justice Matters, 58*(1),
20–21.

Wall, D. S. (2007). *Cybercrime: The transformation of crime in the information
age* (Vol. 4). Polity Press.

Webber, C., & Yip, M. (2012). Drifting on and off-line: Humanising the cyber
criminal. In S. Winlow & R. Atkinson (Eds.), *New directions in crime and
deviancy*. Routledge.

Webber, C., & Yip, M. (2020). Humanising the cybercriminal. In R. Leukfeldt
& T. J. Holt (Eds.), *The human factor of cybercrime*. Routledge.

Yip, M., Webber, C., & Shadbolt, N. (2013). Trust among cybercriminals?
Carding forums, uncertainty and implications for policing. *Policing and
Society, 23*(4), 516–539.

18

Conducting Ethical Research with Online Populations in the United States

Kacy Amory and George W. Burruss

Introduction

Networked computing devices and social media platforms provide opportunities to study hard-to-reach populations of interest to criminologists, such as hackers, radicalized subcultures, illegal dark-web markets, and deviant support groups. Furthermore, networked computing devices generate digital forms of data with the potential to study myriad behaviors previously unmeasurable through traditional methods. This access to novel data presents challenges to the ethical practice of social science for researchers and institutional review boards (IRBs) in the United States. Current policies are inconsistent across organizations and may become increasingly problematic as more and more human interactions are done

K. Amory (✉) · G. W. Burruss
Department of Criminology, University of South Florida, Tampa, FL, USA
e-mail: kacyamory@usf.edu

G. W. Burruss
e-mail: gburruss@usf.edu

© The Author(s), under exclusive license to Springer Nature
Switzerland AG 2021
A. Lavorgna and T. J. Holt (eds.), *Researching Cybercrimes*,
https://doi.org/10.1007/978-3-030-74837-1_18

electronically, especially by at-risk groups, such as children, offenders, and political dissidents. In this chapter, we examine the challenges and discuss the implications for the ethical study of online behavior.

To introduce and illustrate some of the ethical issues faced by researchers collecting online data, we begin with a hypothetical example. Imagine a criminologist is interested in how advocates for pedophilia engage in techniques of neutralization. The researcher becomes aware of a public Internet forum where supporters of pedophilia discuss their views about society's reaction to their unaccepted predilections. The forum requires all those posting on the forum to register with a pseudonym, though they may include an e-mail address for private conversations. The forum's administrator lists a rule that no one may post admissions of actual sex acts with children or solicit sex or pornography on the forum; the administer states that discussions should focus on how society views the forum's members and their beliefs.

The forum presents a trove of attitudinal and behavioral artifacts, the kind that has been used to study a variety of deviant behaviors from criminality to unusual but permissible fetishes. Like the discovery of personal documents about Polish immigrants by Thomas and Znaniecki (1996), written artifacts provide a deep understanding of subjects' behaviors and attitudes that have been a staple of sociology since its inception. In this case, the forum provides written statements about beliefs and discussions with others that challenge or reinforce a member's position. As a source of data to answer the investigator's research question, the forum presents an ideal data source. Prior to the Internet, a researcher studying a similar population would need to find and identify a local support group, negotiate entrée with gatekeepers, develop rapport, and spend a great deal of effort and time collecting data. The online forum allows access to this subculture by simply joining it, which is likely geographically diverse and asynchronous; that is, conversations occur over back-and-forth without the need for subjects to be in each other's presence. The online conversations are text-based making them readily available for qualitative analysis.

Once admitted to the forum, the researcher lurks by reading posts but not engaging with the subjects. She then decides to collect all the forum posts for six months using a technique called scraping. A computer application, called a scraper, accesses the forum and copies information into a searchable dataset. The scraper indexes the post narratives along with metadata. The metadata includes members' pseudonym, email address if provided, IP address of the computer from which the post was made, postings date and time stamp. This will allow the researcher to search the entire six months of postings for specific data, including keywords, specific members who posted, counts of posts by keywords, and so on. The researcher considers that each person posting has read the forum's rules about not admitting any criminal behavior; furthermore, the forum is public and open source—anyone, including law enforcement, can get access to the website. Because of the public nature of the forum and the use of pseudonyms, the researcher concludes there are no ethical issues to collecting the data.

While an assumption of subjects' anonymity in this study is reasonable, there still remain some thorny ethical issues to consider. First, the nature of the postings, even if they adhere to the rules and do not admit engaging in sex with children, would have potentially serious consequences if the identities of the forum members were made public or available to law enforcement. Someone who posted in support of pedophilia would likely face sanctions by friends, family, and coworkers possibly resulting in verbal or physical harassment. Such an outcome would certainly violate the fundamental ethical principle of causing no harm to subjects while conducting social science research. Thus, the researcher would need to take special care to ensure that no subjects could be identified in the data or in any published reports.

Why worry about harm if the subjects used pseudonyms and they know their word could be read by anyone? Because the scrapped data contains metadata, it would be possible to identify subjects from an e-mail address or their IP address (the series of numbers that can identify a specific computer). The researcher might nullify this ethical problem by simply not collecting metadata during the scrape. However, it might be the case that members have used their same pseudonym in other forums or online interactions that could identify them, perhaps on social media platforms such as Facebook or Twitter. Thus, it is important for researchers to understand what the subjects' conception of confidentiality and anonymity are for online forums rather than assuming they are fully informed. If the researcher were to ask each member for permission, then a consent form might explain how anonymity and confidentiality work in an online context, especially in this particular forum. By not informing subjects of their participation in a study, their understanding of the potential risk of being involved is impossible to assess.

Furthermore, by analyzing the data and drawing conclusions about illegal and deviant behaviors that might affect the subjects' self-conception, the subjects may feel harmed by the findings of the study for which they did not agree to participate and were not informed of the study's purpose. This was one of the ethical criticisms of Milgram's obedience to authority study—in which American subjects were asked to administer increasingly severe shocks to another person to test negative reinforcement on learning a list of word pairs. The shocks were not actually administered, but the subjects were deceived into thinking they did. The deception, though necessary to conduct the experiment, was certainly posed an ethical dilemma, but the issue with potential to harm subjects was their performance in the study.

In the published report of that study (1974), subjects faced the implication they were just as likely to take part in crimes against humanity during the Holocaust as did many Germans simply because someone in authority asked them to harm another. Though misled about the nature of the experiment, Milgram did later debrief the subjects and concluded there was no psychological harm done to participants. Given a lack of consent in the hypothesized study above we are suggesting, harm to subject and their understanding of consent is problematic at a minimum.

We certainly do not mean to suggest such a research question or design is unfeasible or unworthy of consideration. A number of such studies have been carried out with any indication of harm coming to subjects (Holt et al., 2012) as well as provide important insights into the sociology of online deviance. The point of our hypothetical study is to highlight ethical issues that face those doing online research.

Background

As people interact more online, considerations from IRBs in the United States have also changed (Vitak et al., 2017). Policies for more traditional face-to-face forms of research are unable to apply to the myriad of opportunities that the Internet now provides. The Belmont Report (see also Chapter 17) is perhaps one of the most well-known reports that set forth guidelines to ensure ethical principles are followed within face-to-face research, emphasizing principles of respect for persons, beneficence, and justice. The Belmont Report gave way to the "Common Rule," which provides guidelines to IRBs in the United States for human subjects research. More specifically, the Common Rule refers to protections of human rights subjects, indicating that these boards must be diverse, indicates types of research that must be reviewed, and identifies elements of proposed research that must be reviewed (45 C.F.R. § 46, 2018). While traditional ethical considerations of harm, risk, and privacy are still relevant to online research, the concepts of what may be considered public or private are more complicated as noted above.

Further, the nuanced categorization of many Internet spaces as "public" is something much previous research has taken for granted, though there is little consensus about what constitutes public spaces online (Hudson & Bruckman, 2005; Rosenberg, 2010). Thus, issues about informed consent may arise. Subjects may post content for access by friends and family; they may not consent for their communications to be collected and published for research (Eysenbach & Till, 2001). Current guidelines by the Association of Internet Researchers (AoIR) (Markham & Buchanan, 2012) suggest ethical considerations should be made on a case-by-case basis. Markham and Buchanan (2012) suggest that ethical principles are best understood "inductively," meaning that online research requires ethical considerations to be made individually, based on each research project's merits. Furthermore, the authors suggest that defining harm in an online context is often more complex than in traditional methods (Markham & Buchanan, 2012).

While the available guidelines suggest more stringent policies in research are needed, in terms of the need to consider each case of online research independently, other empirical findings have suggested that the need for all research participants to give consent in the online sphere is not realistic or necessary (Sugiura et al., 2017). Conversely, Vitak and colleagues (2016), for example, found disagreement among researchers on what ethical practices are typically used, while simultaneously acknowledging that certain approaches may be better for certain types of data. They note there is agreement on four main facets of ethical considerations, including: (1) collecting data only when benefits outweigh the potential harms, (2) transparency in terms of notifying participants, (3) deliberation with colleagues on ethical practices, and (4) care in sharing results that may include possible identifiers.

Researchers often disagree, however, about the use of informed consent, particularly in large-scale studies (Vitak et al., 2016). Vitak and colleagues (2016) suggest that in addition to informed consent, data sharing and efforts to minimize harm were common areas of contention among researchers, indicating that some researchers take a more conservative approach to online research than others. These conflicting viewpoints highlight the current difficulties social science researchers face when choosing to conduct online research, despite opportunities for research that the Internet provides. Thus, it is important that researchers consider how traditional ethical principles such as informed consent, weighing benefits and harms, and ensuring participant privacy may function in their online research. Further, these considerations emphasize the importance of developing clear ethical guidelines, as the Internet provides researchers an avenue to access difficult-to-reach groups including hackers, a particular population of interest to criminologists.

The development of appropriate ethical considerations that take into account more modern issues of privacy and consent that online research poses is important in furthering empirical literature on difficult-to-reach groups, such as cybercriminals. Prior research suggests cybercriminals are different from that of their offline counterparts. For example, fraudsters are more organized, having specialization of tasks (i.e., hackers, virus writers, etc.). Despite the differentiation between online and offline fraudsters, research suggests that fraud committed in an online context should not be differentiated from offline fraud, as the definition of fraud acknowledges the dual nature of the offense (Cross, 2019). Little is known about the prevalence of cybercrime; however, it is suggested to have a large "dark-figure" of crime (Tsakalidis & Vergidis, 2017).

Current Issues in Cybercrime Research Within the United States

Some academics suggest that traditional ethical principles are sufficient to inform online research; however, developments in online capabilities present new issues of consent, confidentiality, and anonymity (Vitak et al., 2016). One main issue arises in that there is a disjunction between what researchers feel is public compared to that of online users, based on terms and conditions of online sites (Smith et al., 2011). That is to say, while researchers may be aware of online sites' policies on accessibility of data, users of these sites may not be equally aware that what they share is accessible. Thus, additional research suggests that we, as researchers, should consider the public's understanding of privacy and confidentiality in comparison with that of our own (Nind et al., 2013; Sugiura et al., 2017). This reflexive approach highlights that there may be a number of approaches which can be taken to ensuring ethical practicality of online research, suggesting that online research ethics may have to be innovative and adaptive (Nind et al., 2013).

Online panels, using Mechanical Turk (MTurk) and Qualtrics, are becoming more commonly used in academic research, specifically for research about Internet use. Online panels are managed by private firms who provide access to a pool of paid respondents who opt into take various surveys via the Internet. These firms offer their services to researchers for a fee. The firms are able to provide representative samples by filling demographic and other quotas required by the researcher. For example, they could provide a sample with the same proportions as the United States Census of males, Whites and Blacks, college educated, and median income. Participants could also be matched to a survey by answering various questions about online behaviors, such as shopping, banking, or trolling, and by passing a series of qualifying questions, with those who match then being added to the pool. While the pool of respondents is not a random sample of the general population because they are self-selected to be in the pool, they can be used to test general theories (Thompson & Pickett, 2020).

Thus, crowdsourcing platforms such as MTurk provide demographically and geographically diverse samples that capture survey responses equivalent to face-to-face data collection methods (Casler et al., 2013). Such samples can be useful for studying cybercrime victimization because little data on Internet use, especially in terms of cybercrime and cyber-victimization, is provided from official sources due to the nature of the data being difficult for police agencies to investigate (Holt et al., 2016). Much survey research that measures this behavior has been limited to college student populations and, most recently, to juvenile and young adult populations. Despite online panels' potential for generalizability and targeted groups, however, some have raised potential ethical concerns of exploitation among research participants in using platforms (Irani & Silberman, 2009; Pittman & Sheehan, 2017). Possible exploitation of MTurk subjects include wages less than the US minimum wage, the inability to exit a study without losing compensation, and a lack of transparency about the study—researcher affiliations, funding sources, and research goals (Pittman & Sheehan, 2017).

Mason and Suri (2012) discuss potential options for ensuring basic ethical concerns are taken into consideration for online panels, such as including informed consent and debriefing pages within a survey. The authors highlight that the purpose of the study, as well as risks and benefits, and a point of contact for any problems they experience during the study should be included on the first few pages upon a participant beginning a survey (Mason & Suri, 2012). Similarly, nearing the end of the survey, a page should reiterate the purpose of the study and the point of contact's information, particularly if the study contains any points of deception. These efforts at ensuring protection of participants are far from being mandated, though provide working guidelines for online research to work toward.

While informed consent is a central tenet of ethical research providing relevant information so subjects can weigh their risks, its practice is often muddled by bureaucratic oversight. IRBs often require researchers to include a long list of elements in an informed consent document that begins to resemble an end-user license agreement that accompanies any use of electronic media, such as software or applications. The longer and more legalistic the document, the less likely it will be read and understood. Most informed consent documents run from many paragraphs to a full page or two. Such disregard for readability makes informed consent forms practically useless. Therefore, researchers and IRB committee members should consider how their informed consent form will be read and understood by the subjects in their study.

Additionally, while the development of the Internet has provided new opportunities for research, so has it for individuals and organizations to engage in other daily activities, including leveraging new opportunities for crime. Continued developments in technology lend themselves to the ability of cybercriminals to adapt their efforts and make the identification and investigation of cybercrimes more difficult. This suggests that efforts to address ethical considerations for online research will need to continue to adapt, as methods for examining cybercrime will have to change as crime does.

Ethical Guidelines Can Be Problematic Despite Best Intentions

IRBs have been accused of engaging in *mission creep* or *ethics creep*, whereby review boards expand their authority to a wider range of activities outside their purview, and intensify their regulation of researchers' activities (Haggerty, 2004). The role of IRBs is to protect research subjects, to guide researchers in the protection devising studies that are safe, and to develop standardized ethical guidelines for online research. While standardized ethical guidelines are crucial to the future of Internet research, the nature of IRBs in the United States is often cautious and conservative and could pose further issues in consistent application of ethical guidelines. More troubling, an IRB may improve its own bureaucratic values on research questions, potentially scuttling valuable research (see also Chapter 23).

While most IRB members are motivated to protect human subjects, an overriding objective is to protect their institution from potential legal action or negative public criticism. Like many organizations, IRBs are aware of high-profile ethical violations that have harmed the reputations of institutions and scholars. Indeed, the main ethics training in the United States required for researchers, the National Institutes of Health or The Collaborative Institutional Training Initiative (CITI Program), provide a detailed history of blatant unethical research from Nazi medical research to the Tuskegee syphilis experiments. While the vast majority of social science research conducted in the United States poses little risk to human subjects, IRB members are vigilant about uncovering hidden risks as they evaluate proposals. This view of all research as having endemic risk makes IRB committees risk averse, often elevating minor issues as problematic and holding up approvals for research for extended periods, which can delay time-sensitive projects.

Also problematic is the fact that IRB committees are often interdisciplinary, comprised of members from various disciplines including law, medicine, social sciences, and biology. It is common for committee members to comment on or require corrections to research designs based on a flawed understanding of their own methodology applied outside their own domain. For example, IRB committee members who come from sociology may consider small samples that are often used in psychology experiments as statically problematic and request that the sample be larger. It is also likely that researchers who are used to tightly control random control trials may not have an appreciation for research done at the macro-level, which is often done in social-psychology or economics. IRBs making recommendations about methodology is outside the purview of their authority yet often done. The friction between IRB committees and researchers often results in conflict rather than a consensus approach to protecting human subjects. Thus, some researchers, feeling the process lacks legitimacy, avoid seeking IRB approval or abandon a research project altogether. If IRB committees sought consensus and acted as a resource rather than a sanctioning body, there might be more buy-in from researchers.

Research in criminology and criminal justice has shown that people are more likely to obey rules and the law when the authorities are viewed as legitimate in their exercise of power (Tyler, 2006). More specifically, legitimacy is achieved through displays of procedural fairness.

For example, people who find that the police explain the reasons for being stopped for a traffic violation and treated with respect are more likely to accept sanctions as well as less likely to reoffend. Failure by the police to explain actions and the reasoning behind them will likely result in less adherence to rules and regulations by the public. IRBs in the United States certainly wield authority over researchers who must comply with the bureaucratic regulations in order to have their research plans approved. Implied by Tyler's thesis and the body of research that supports it, researchers who feel IRBs do not exercise their authority legitimately are less likely to comply with the rules by not following protocols, seeking approval through colleagues' less stringent IRBs, or even simply not applying for approval in the first place. As rules and regulations concerning research on human subjects become more Byzantine and Kafkaesque researches are less likely to comply or view the whole enterprise as legitimate. Thus, IRBs should examine their own procedures for evidence of mission creep as well as solicit feedback from their constituents to evaluate how their legitimacy is viewed.

Conclusion

Altogether, the points above suggest there is a need for more empirical research on the publics' perception of their engagement in online spaces being used for research, as well as a need to reconsider how online research is considered in the sphere of ethical review boards. The development of consistent ethical guidelines should be a cautious venture to ensure practical principles are developed. Further, the development of ethical guidelines should be sure to consider the role in which participants play in terms of consent and privacy, as well as the extent of regulation in which IRBs have in controlling research production. New avenues of online research, including the use of online panels and adaptive skills of cybercriminals, suggest that ethical guidelines for Internet research will be a continuously transforming endeavor. In addition, it is important to realize the various contexts and populations online and the potential need to apply policies accordingly.

As indicated by Vitak and colleagues (2016), future studies may aim to take into account ethical considerations that have received a consensus across academics who conduct online research, including the traditional consideration of ensuring benefits outweigh risks, in addition to transparency, collegial consensus, and removal of identifying information. Going back to our hypothetical example, we would suggest the following to ensure the research was conducted in an ethical manner:

1. Ensure that scraped data does not contain any identifying metadata information unless disclosed in the informed-consent document. This is particularly crucial for considerations in data sharing, as it would reduce the likelihood of re-identification of participants within a dataset made available privately or publicly.
2. Approach the forum administration about the possibility of using the data from the website. Forum administration represents a form of "gate-keeping" to online data, as well as an opportunity to inform additional considerations for participant protection, such as not using direct quotes or forum member names.
3. Contact some of the forum members and interview them about their knowledge of the public nature of their posts—evaluate what their expectations are for confidentiality and anonymity. Taking into consideration forum members' opinions may further inform inconsistencies between researcher's and the public's understandings of public and private content and inform best practices for informed consent and potential harms. Further, it provides an opportunity for researchers to develop practices that most accurately reflect the public's interest, such as associating community member's identities with their own quotes if they so choose.
4. Consider what informed consent might look like and if it is even feasible for certain forms of online research. Informed consent may change the likelihood of subjects speaking freely and may influence results of research conducted on online platforms.
5. Relatedly, care should be taken in crafting informed-consent documents so they are clear and concise. An informed consent that is not read is of no value.

6. Discuss the potential harm to subjects with colleagues not involved in the research. This provides an opportunity to consider implications of one's research outside of their own field, such as potential participant harms that may not be traditionally discussed or examined.
7. Compare the context of the data being used to that of the research context. This ensures that the data being captured is being accurately represented through the research at hand and is important for ensuring data integrity. Using data that arises through forums or websites outside of your topic of interest has the potential for misconstruing participant's content.
8. IRBs should work with researchers to ensure their rules and regulations are viewed as legitimate by their research community. While IRBs will always serve a bureaucratic function and pose a potential barrier to conducting research unfettered, they are an important safeguard for the ethical conduct of research. Nevertheless, a consensus model for protecting human subjects is likely to be more effective and adhered to than a conflict model where research is viewed as a potential legal liability by university administrators.

References

Casler, K., Bickel, L., & Hackett, E. (2013). Separate but equal? A comparison of participants and data gathered via Amazon's MTurk, social media, and face-to-face behavioral testing. *Computers in Human Behavior, 29*(6), 2156–2160.

Collaborative Institutional Training Initiative. (n.d.). *Research, ethics, and compliance training.* Available at: https://about.citiprogram.org/en/hom cpagc/.

Cross, C. (2019). Is online fraud just fraud? Examining the efficacy of the digital divide. *Journal of Criminological Research, Policy and Practice, 5*(2), 120–131.

Eysenbach, G., & Till, J. E. (2001). Ethical issues in qualitative research on Internet communities. *British Medical Journal, 323,* 1103–1105.

Haggerty, K. D. (2004). Ethics creep: Governing social science research in the name of ethics. *Qualitative Sociology, 27*(4), 391–414.

Holt, T. J., Burrus, G. W., & Bossler, A. (2016). Policing cybercrime and cyberterror. *Security Journal, 29*, e13–e15.

Holt, T. J., Strumsky, D., Smirnova, O., & Kilger, M. (2012). Examining the social networks of malware writers and hackers. *International Journal of Cyber Criminology, 6*(1), 891–903.

Hudson, J. M., & Bruckman, A. (2005). Using empirical data to reason about Internet research ethics. In *Proceedings of the 9th European Conference on Computer-Supported Cooperative Work* (pp. 287–306).

Irani, L., & Silberman, M. S. (2009). Agency and exploitation in Mechanical. In *Internet as Playground and Factory Conference.*

Markham, A., & Buchanan, E. (2012). *Ethical decision-making and Internet research: Version 2.0. Recommendations from the AoIR working committee.*

Mason, W., & Suri, S. (2012). Conducting behavioral research on Amazon's mechanical turk. *Behavior Research Methods, 44*, 1–23.

Milgram, S. (1974). *Obedience to authority: An experimental view.* Harper-Collins.

Nind, M., Wiles, R., Bengry-Howell, A., & Crow, G. (2013). Methodological innovation and research ethics: Forces in tension or forces in harmony? *Qualitative Research, 13*(6), 650–667.

Pittman, M., & Sheehan, K. (2017). Ethics of using online commercial crowdsourcing sites for academic research: The case of Amazon's mechanical turk. In M. Zimmer & K. Kinder-Kurlanda (Eds.), *Internet research ethics for the social age.* Peter Lang.

Rosenberg, A. (2010). Virtual world research ethics and private/public distribution. *International Journal of Research Ethics, 3*(12), 23–37.

Smith. H. J., Dinev, T., & Xu, H. (2011). Information privacy research: An interdisciplinary review. *Management Information Systems Quarterly, 35*(4), 989–1015.

Sugiura, L., Wiles, R., & Pope, C. (2017). Ethical challenges in online research: Public/private perceptions. *Research Ethics, 13*(3–4), 184–199.

The Federal Policy for the Protection of Human Subjects, 45 C.F.R. § 46. (2018).

Thomas, W. I., & Znaniecki, F. (1996). *The Polish peasant in Europe and America: A classic work in immigration history.* University of Illinois Press.

Thompson, A. J., & Pickett, J. T. (2020). Are relational inferences from crowdsourced and opt-in samples generalizable? Comparing criminal justice attitudes in the GSS and five online samples. *Journal of Quantitative Criminology, 36*, 907–932.

Tsakalidis, G., & Vergidis, K. (2017). A systematic approach toward description and classification of cybercrime incidents. *IEEE Transactions on Systems, Man, and Cybernetics: Systems, 49*(4), 710–729.

Tyler, T. R. (2006). *Why people obey the law*. Princeton University Press.

Vitak, J., Proferes, N., Shilton, K., & Ashktorab, Z. (2017). Ethics regulation in social computing research: Examining the role of institutional review boards. *Journal of Empirical Research on Human Research Ethics, 12*(5), 372–382.

Vitak, J., Shilton, K., & Ashktorab, Z. (2016). Beyond the Belmont principles: Ethical challenges, practices, and beliefs in the online data research community. In *Proceedings of the 19th ACM Conference on Computer-Supported Cooperative Work and Social Computing* (pp. 941–953).

19

Investigating the Ethical Boundaries for Online Research in Brazil

Felipe Cardoso Moreira de Oliveira

Introduction

Debates about the ethics of research involving humans in the northern hemisphere became more explicit after the Second World War. First, the abuses committed by the Nazis in the concentration camps gave rise to the Nuremberg Code in 1947. Later, in 1964, the World Medical Association published the Declaration of Helsinki, and in 1979, the National Commission for the Protection of Human Subjects of Biomedical and Behavioral Research (USA) published the Belmont Report. However, in Brazil, the first attempts to regulate such an important area were only made in 1988, and this delay has caused a lack of standardization in the regulation of research studies involving humans. Therefore, this chapter intends to discuss the emergence of the ethical committees in Brazil and

F. C. M. de Oliveira (✉)
Pontifícia Universidade Católica do Rio Grande do Sul (PUCRS), Porto Alegre, Brazil
e-mail: felipe@felipedeoliveira.adv.br

© The Author(s), under exclusive license to Springer Nature Switzerland AG 2021
A. Lavorgna and T. J. Holt (eds.), *Researching Cybercrimes*,
https://doi.org/10.1007/978-3-030-74837-1_19

387

their regulations, trying to explain why the biggest developing country of South America has a scientific community producing research without fully understanding the role of ethics in online studies, which hampers discussions of the new ethical dilemmas that have been arising from internet-related research. It is also important to clarify that Brazil is the only country in the American continent where the written and spoken language is Portuguese. In this chapter, although the denomination of organs, committees, and councils has been translated into English, the acronyms used follow the Brazilian denomination.

The chapter is divided into four parts. Initially, I will talk about when and how the discussion about ethics in research emerged in Brazil and its close relationship to biomedical studies. Then, I will show how those early discussions prompted specific rules applied to research studies in the social sciences and the humanities, followed by my argument as to why these existing ethical regulations are not suitable for online research. Finally, I will show how also the new data protection law has not addressed the ethics of research in a proper way. In the conclusion, I will highlight the dangers of not having a specific regulation for online research in Brazil.

Short History of the Regulation of Research in Brazil

The Brazilian National Health Council (*Conselho Nacional de Saúde*— CNS), a branch of the Health Ministry, edited its first Resolution, no. 01, in 1988. This was the first Brazilian regulation on ethics and research regarding experiments with human beings in the health area. A Resolution, in Brazil, is a set of rules drawn up by public authorities which regulate a certain theme of interest and competency for these authorities. According to these rules, health research in Brazil should advance our knowledge in the following subjects: biological and psychological processes in human beings; the understanding of the causes of the diseases; medical practice and social structures; prevention and control of health problems; knowledge and evaluation of the effects of the environment on health; new techniques or methods recommended or used in the health services; and production of health supplies. The Resolution also defended the idea of respect for human dignity, the core principles of the Brazilian Constitution, and the related protection of individual rights and well-being. However, analyzing the text of the Resolution more carefully, it is possible to identify some parts that are not fully aligned with the existing international guidelines, as individuals in this Resolution were regarded more as objects than as subjects, which conflicts with the idea advocated by the Belmont Report (1979) where "individuals should be treated as autonomous agents."

On December 12, 2012, the Brazilian National Health Council decided to approve new guidelines and standards regulating studies involving human beings. Resolution no. 466/2012 made explicit the alignment of these guidelines with the Nuremberg Code (1947), the Universal Declaration of Human Rights (1948), the original Helsinki Declaration and its later versions (1964, 1975, 1983, 1989, 1996 and 2000), the International Pact regarding Economic, Social, and Cultural Rights (1966), the Universal Declaration regarding Human Genome and Human Rights (1997), the International Declaration regarding Human Genes Data (2003), and the Universal Declaration regarding Bioethics and Human Rights (2004). Those international documents were used to ensure consistency with the objectives and foundations of the Brazilian Constitution.

According to this Resolution, ethics in research involves the following: (a) respect for the research participant's dignity and autonomy, recognizing his/her vulnerability, and ensuring his/her will to contribute and remain, or not, in the study, by means of express, free, and informed statement; (b) researchers should balance the risks and benefits, both known and potential, individual or collective, and they should also commit themselves to maximize the benefits and minimize the risks and damages; (c) the assurance that preventable damages will be avoided; and (d) the research should be socially relevant, bearing in mind its social humanitarian goals.

Besides the changes and alignments made by Resolution no. 466/2012, this regulation was still focusing on biomedical studies, leaving social and human sciences in a kind of vacuum regarding a proper methodological regulation. This "blindness" toward the peculiarities of the studies in social and human sciences was paradoxical and incomprehensible as such studies have always been deeply rooted in ethics, which should have created not only rules but also a series of discussions to regulate the methodologies and objectives of their activities (Ferreira, 2013).

Finally, in 2016, a specific regulation for the social and human sciences studies involving human beings was created when Resolution CNS no. 510/2016 was approved. According to Guerriero and Minayo (2019), Resolution no. 510/2016 was a great advance for the development of Brazilian scientific thinking as it established specific ethical guidelines for the social sciences and the humanities. This Resolution tried to correct the monochord tone of the ethical regulation of Brazilian research and it was celebrated as important news for the Brazilian scientific environment. Despite the official recognition of the specificities regarding research in the social and human sciences, a more accurate look at the Resolution reveals that, while it represents an improvement, it is still far from regulating important issues arising from online studies, including cybercrime research.

Ethics in Online Research in Brazil

The gap of almost thirty years with no specific regulation for studies in social and human sciences in Brazil resulted in a period where many studies were not allowed to proceed as they did not fit into the standard biomedical model. Despite worldwide efforts to regulate ethics in research, for example the *Statement of Ethics for Researchers in the Field of Criminology* developed by the British Society of Criminology, in Brazil, the resistance to a single regulatory model has represented, in a certain way, a dispute over scientific power. However positive for our scientific production in Brazil, Resolution no. 510/2016 is again not enough to deal with the vast number of studies being increasingly produced using online tools and methodologies. Over the years, there have been about 800 Councils of Ethics in Brazil applying the same rules as onsite studies, as defined by Resolution nos. 466/2012 and 510/2016, and ignoring all the specificities and issues arising from digital. This specific nature of digital poses some challenges when the subject is ethics on online research, and it is necessary to understand what kind of threats online tools can entail.

Nosek and colleagues (2002), almost twenty years ago, identified three differences between internet and standard laboratory research that would have implications for ethics: (1) absence of a researcher; (2) uncertainty regarding adequate informed consent and debriefing; and (3) potential loss of participant anonymity or confidentiality. The authors also called attention to the real possibility that data could undesirably be accessed or intercepted by a third party who could violate the security of the transmission, the system, or the servers. It is also important to note that there may be some conflicts created by the online environment that can affect the scientific community as a whole, and ethics in science cannot be assumed. The researcher's integrity is not enough to validate a study.

Within this framework, Buchanan and Zimmer (2012) established six ethical issues that should be addressed when thinking about online research: privacy; recruitment; informed consent; cloud computing and research ethics; big data research and internet research ethics; and industry-conducted research. Considering the scope of this chapter, I will focus on only two subjects that may have different impacts on online research: (1) informed consent and the privacy of research participants, including data transmission, and (2) data storage.

Informed Consent in Brazil

The regulation of ethics in research in Brazil, according to Resolution nos. 466/2012 and 510/2016, defines what should be present in valid informed consent. First, I will present the characteristics of this document, as defined by the Brazilian rules, and then, I intend to show which of the specific elements of informed consent are not taken into consideration in the field of online research.

Informed consent should be presented to the research participant early in the study. The researcher must identify the most appropriate moment and place for it to be done, taking into consideration the subject's particular characteristics and privacy. All information related to the study must be given in clear language, adjusting the communication strategy to the subject's culture, age group, and socioeconomic conditions. In addition, the individual must be able to analyze the convenience of the research and, if necessary, consult family members or other people who can help him/her to make a free and informed decision. Therefore, the document named "Free and Informed Consent Term" will be given to the research participant to be read and signed.

However, according to the Brazilian resolution on research in social and human sciences, the research participant can express his/her consent in different ways, such as by signing the document, consenting orally, recording the consent, or in other ways related to the specifics of the research. It is also possible to give consent by means of testimony from a third person not involved with the research. On the other hand, informed consent, as stated in Resolution no. 510/2016, may not be considered essential if the researcher proves that its existence may pose a risk to the privacy and confidentiality of the participant's data or to the bonds of trust between the research participant and the researcher. The dispensation of the consent's register must be evaluated by the Ethics in Research Committee.

As stated by Resolution 196/1996, every research regarding human beings must be submitted to an Ethics in Research Committee (CEP). The institutions (e.g., hospital, university) in which research is carried out involving human beings should create one or more Ethics in Research Committees accordingly to their needs. It should be composed by at least seven members from different areas of knowledge (health, hard sciences, social and human sciences professionals), and it should also have, at least, one person from the society representing the subjects. The National Commission on Ethics in Research (CONEP) is responsible for approving the creation of the Ethics in Research Committees. It may also review and discontinue researches, and in some specific areas (human genetics and pharmaceuticals), it should accompany the research protocols. There have been 844 Ethics in Research Committees (CEP) in Brazil so far.

Returning to the issue of informed consent, it is possible to anticipate some problems that will arise regarding the ethics of informed consent in online research. The first conflict would emerge if we understand that informed consent should be issued just after the participants of the research have fully understood its risks and benefits (Buchanan & Zimmer, 2012). Therefore, an interview is probably the best way to evaluate it (Eynon et al., 2008). The importance of a "face-to-face context" is greater when the research takes place in a country like Brazil where there are 11 million illiterate people and where at least 29% of the population is considered functionally illiterate (INAF, 2018). This term means that even if the subject can read, they cannot understand the meaning of the text.

Informed consent is conceived as a process where the verification of understanding demands that researcher and participants should understand each other along the process (Buchanan & Zimmer, 2012). The idea of informed consent given on a digital document as a process in an online environment is threatened by the lack of meaningful negotiation between the researcher and the participant. Such absence of a face-to-face relationship in a society where a huge number of people face problems with understanding their own language clearly poses a threat to the research and to the individuals. If we consider the number of people in Brazil who cannot really understand all the implications laid out in an informed consent document (at least 29%) and contrast this number to the huge number of Brazilians who are online (around 74%) (NIC.br, 2020), the possibilities of selecting somebody who cannot fully understand the risks involved are quite high.

Given the above, the current situation regarding informed consent in online research should be carefully addressed. Therefore, it is necessary that further discussions should take place to find alternative ways to inform the research participants. Some new models of informed consent could be developed in a more friendly way, giving information about the study (justification, objective, procedures, methods, potential damages, subjective rights) and, instead of using long texts, visual design solutions could be used along with checklists submitted to the research participant. Another way to achieve more interaction between the researchers and the participants is the use of online interviews, which have been used more frequently since the beginning of the physical distancing introduced following the COVID-19 pandemic.

Privacy of the Research Participant (Concerning Data Transmission and Data Storage)

The second subject I have chosen to talk about in relation to the specific challenges of ethics in online research is privacy. In this regard, I believe it is necessary to show how Resolution nos. 466/2012 and 510/2016 deal with the subject of privacy and to discuss whether these Resolutions are enough to handle such an issue.

Resolution no. 466/2012 states that research involving human beings should provide procedures that would ensure the confidentiality and privacy of the research participant, and this is the only part in the resolution where privacy has a main role. Further in the resolution, we will find the concept of privacy again in the Free and Informed Consent Term (FICT), which should guarantee that the research participants' secrecy and privacy are maintained during all the steps of the research. Finally, privacy is one of the causes for requesting a waiver of the FICT, to the *Ethics in Research Committee*, as mentioned before.

Resolution no. 510/2016 defines privacy as the participant's right to keep control over his/her choices, intimacy, image, and personal data. At the same time, confidentiality of information, privacy of the participants and protection of his/her identity, and the use of their image or voice are considered as an ethical principle of research in the social sciences and the humanities.

When studying both Resolutions more closely, we see that they do not require the research participants to be informed about the possibility of their data being lost and/or accessed by unwanted people due to breaches that may happen in cyberspace. This lack of knowledge may affect the subjects' freedom of choice to be part of the research, or not.

Furthermore, the same resolutions do not address the need for data cryptography, and, with amount of data cloud storage always growing, the situation has become deeply worrisome, leading to an enhanced risk of data breaches.

The increase in data cloud storage is irreversible because of its economic and performance advantages. As stated by Yaghmaei and Binesh (2015), with this technology, universities can save money, increase the performance of their staff, and, also, improve speed and the quality of transferring data with less consumption of energy. There is no doubt that doing research has become easier; however, it has not taken into consideration the risks for the research participants. The Cloud Security Alliance (2019) published a guide about the main threats from cloud computing, and they realized that both data and security breaches deserve special attention. Therefore, if data are sent to a cloud, the research participant should be aware of this danger in regard to the risks posed to his/her privacy and data confidentiality. Data transmission and data storage should receive considerable attention when we discuss confidentiality (Nosek et al., 2002). Transmitted data must be encrypted to reduce the effect of potential interception by a third party; however, Brazilian resolutions have not yet addressed this issue.

The Brazilian Data Protection Law Concerning Research

The Brazilian General Law of Data Protection, *Lei Geral de Proteção de Dados* (LGPD), came into effect on September 18, 2020, and while it took inspiration from the European General Data Protection Regulation (GDPR) (Bisso et al., 2020; Souza et al., 2019; Pinheiro, 2020), the Brazilian legislature acknowledges the need for data protection 23 years after Directive 95/46/EC of the European Parliament. The LGPD was created to protect individuals' data and to define the conditions under which this data should be processed. It is important to clarify that the law authorizes the use of personal and sensitive data in studies promoted by a research institution, understood as any institution regulated by public law or a non-profit legal entity governed by private law. The institutional mission of these entities must be basic research or applied research in history, science, technology, or statistics. According to this conceptualization, it is possible to conclude that any research sponsored by profitable institutions should be conducted within the limits of the Brazilian data protection law.

If we analyze the LGPD, Resolution no. 466/2012 and Resolution no. 510/2016 as a system of rules, it is possible to conclude that it has not substantially changed the scientific research regulation in Brazil. If the

LGPD does not apply to certain research institutions, Resolution no. 466/2012 is there to require informed consent in the case of biomedical research studies and Resolution no. 510/2016 in the case of social and human sciences research studies.

At the same time, although profitable organizations are not considered research institutions by law, the LGPD authorizes these organizations to process data if the individuals sign a free, informed, and unambiguous written (or otherwise) consent form. So, it means that the Brazilian data protection law recreated the same instrument from both Resolutions, a form of informed consent, by another name. It may be claimed that the Resolutions do not specify that the informed consent must be unambiguous as stated in the LGPD, but the law does not clarify what unambiguous consent means in any way.

Whereas the LGPD defines who is responsible for protecting personal data, it does not take into consideration the research participant's possible inability to understand neither its contents nor risks. The Brazilian law seems to be much more concerned about defining which documents or authorizations are needed than to assure that the research participants are able or not to understand what they are agreeing to.

Another concern related to personal data is the concept of ownership of content available on social media. The law in this case dismisses the authorization for processing personal data when they are publicized by his/her owner. If someone publishes any personal or sensitive data on any social media, the law understands that this data is not subject to protection.

Conclusion

Online research has specific characteristics that challenge the way we conduct field research. I have been especially concerned about the ethical issues, as Brazil has been having difficulties in addressing them and they have been affecting the quality of our research for a long time. There was a gap regarding ethics in research between the time it was a relevant subject addressed in the northern hemisphere and the time it was first regulated in Brazil, in 1988, with a regulation for the biomedical field of research. A set of rules for social and human sciences research emerged only in 2016, and despite the importance of the internet in our lives at that moment, Resolution no. 510/2016 was simply silent and turned its back on the complexity of that issue. Finally, Brazilian Data Protection Law, although similar to and contemporaneous with the European GDPR, was approved more than 20 years after European countries had started to regulate the issue with Directive 95/46/EC of the European Parliament.

Focusing the analysis on informed consent and research participants' privacy in relation to data transmission and data storage, it may be concluded that the Brazilian regulation on ethics in research has been unable to confront the dangers of online research and that there has been a lack of specific rules concerning ethics in online research. The lack of understanding of the research participant regarding the risks to his/her privacy is enlarged when the informed consent is given in a digital document. Bearing in mind the peculiarities of the Brazilian population and its culture, the use of a single written consent form would not be appropriate for ensuring secure free and conscious consent.

The absence of rules determining encryption and storage in data clouds also creates potential risks that should be necessarily communicated to and understood by the research participant. Not only did the Data Protection Law fail to change substantially the scientific research rules in Brazil, it also created a presumed authorization for social media research, using big data tools to transform and study people's data without even addressing, or discussing, issues of consent.

Brazil needs a specific regulation for ethics in online research, so that the researchers can be fully aware of the risks and digital threats, and consequently, they can communicate them to better guide potential research participants in their decision to participate in a study. This would certainly give a solid methodological underpinning for national science output and strengthen it over time.

References

Batista, K. T., de Andrade, R. R., & Bezerra, N. L. (2012). O papel dos comitês de ética em pesquisa. *Revista Brasileira de Cirurgia Plástica, 27*(1), 150–155.

Bisso, R., Kreutz, D., Rodrigues, G., & Paz, G. (2020). Vazamentos de Dados: Histórico, Impacto Socioeconômico e as Novas Leis de Proteção de Dados (versão estendida). *Revista eletrônica Argentina-Brasil de Tecnologias da Informação e da Comunicação, 3*(1). https://doi.org/10.5281/zenodo. 3833275.

British Society of Criminology. (2015) *Statement of ethics for researchers in the field of criminology.* Available at: https://www.britsoccrim.org/ethics/.

Buchanan, E. A., & Zimmer, M. (2012). *Internet research ethics.* Available at: https://plato.stanford.edu/archives/win2018/entries/ethics-internet-research/.

Conselho Nacional de Saúde - Comitês de Ética em Pesquisa. (n.d.). Available at: http://conselho.saude.gov.br/comites-de-etica-em-pesquisa-conep.

Conselho Nacional de Saúde (Brazil) (Org.). (2002). *Manual operacional para comitês de ética em pesquisa.* Editora MS.

de Alves, D. A., & Teixeira, W. M. (2020b). Ética em pesquisa em ciências sociais: Regulamentação, prática científica e controvérsias. *Educação e Pesquisa, 46.*

Directive 95/46/EC of the European Parliament and of the Council of 24 October 1995 on the protection of individuals with regard to the processing of personal data and on the free movement of such data, 31995L0046, EP, CONSIL, OJ L 281 (1995).

Eynon, R., Fry, J., & Schroeder, R. (2008). The ethics of internet research. In N. Fielding, R. Lee, & G. Blank (Eds.), *The SAGE handbook of online research methods* (pp. 22–41). SAGE Publications, Ltd. https://doi.org/10.4135/9780857020055.n2 .

Eynon, R., Schroeder, R., & Fry, J. (2009). New techniques in online research: Challenges for research ethics. *Twenty-First Century Society, 4*(2), 187–199.

Ferreira, M. F. (2013). A ética da investigação em ciências sociais. *Revista Brasileira de Ciência Política, 11,* 169–191.

Guerriero, I. C. Z., & Minayo, M. C. (2019). A aprovação da Resolução CNS nº 510/2016 é um avanço para a ciência brasileira. *Saúde e Sociedade, 28*(4), 299–310.

INAF - Indicador de Alfabetismo Funcional Brasil 2018 – *Ação Educativa*. (2018). Available at: https://acaoeducativa.org.br/publicacoes/indicador-de-alfabetismo-funcional-inaf-brasil-2018/.

Nacional, I. ([s.d.]). *Resolução nº 510, de 7 de abril de 2016—Imprensa Nacional*. Available at: https://www.in.gov.br/materia.

Nosek, B. A., Banaji, M. R., & Greenwald, A. G. (2002). E-Research: Ethics, security, design, and control in psychological research on the Internet. *Journal of Social Issues, 58*(1), 161–176.

Núcleo de Informação e Coordenação do Ponto BR – NIC.br. (2019a). Survey on the use of information and communication technologies in Brazilian households. - *Publicações—Pesquisas CETIC.br.* - Centro Regional para o Desenvolvimento da Sociedade da Informação. Available at: https://cetic.br/media/docs/publicacoes/2/20201123121817/tic_dom_2019_livro_eletronico.pdf.

Núcleo de Informação e Coordenação do Ponto BR - NIC.br. (2019b). *Três em cada quatro brasileiros já utilizam a Internet, aponta pesquisa TIC Domicílios 2019*. CGI.br - *Comitê Gestor da Internet no Brasil*. Available at: https://cgi.br/noticia/releases/tres-em-cada-quatro-brasileiros-ja-utilizam-a-internet-aponta-pesquisa-tic-domicilios-2019/.

Pinheiro, Patricia P. (2020). *Proteção de Dados Pessoais: Comentários à Lei n. 13.709/2018 -LGPD*. Saraiva Educação S.A.

Resolução nº 466, de 12 de dezembro de 2012. Conselho Nacional de Saúde. Ministério da Saúde. Brasil. (2012). Available at: https://bvsms.saude.gov.br/bvs/saudelegis/cns/2013/res0466_12_12_2012.html.

Resolução nº 196, de 10 de outubro de 1996. Conselho Nacional da Saúde. Ministério da Saúde. Brasil. (1996). Available at: https://bvsms.saude.gov.br/bvs/saudelegis/cns/1996/res0196_10_10_1996.html.

Shuster, E. (1997). Fifty years later: The significance of the Nuremberg Code. *New England Journal of Medicine, 337*(20), 1436–1440.

Souza, C. A. P. de, Viola, M., & Padrão, V. (2019). CONSIDERAÇÕES INICIAIS SOBRE OS INTERESSES LEGÍTIMOS DO CONTROLADOR NA LEI GERAL DE PROTEÇÃO DE DADOS PESSOAIS. *Direito Público, 16*(90), Article 90. https://portal.idp.emnuvens.com.br/direitopublico/article/view/3744.

The Belmont Report. (2010). HHS.Gov. Available at: https://www.hhs.gov/ohrp/regulations-and-policy/belmont-report/index.html.

Wachelke, J., Natividade, J., de Andrade, A., Wolter, R., & Camargo, B. ([s.d.]). *Caracterização e Avaliação de um Procedimento de Coleta de Dados Online (CORP)*. 5.

Yaghmaei, O., & Binesh, F. (2015). Impact of applying cloud computing on universities expenses. *IOSR-Journal of Business and Management, 17,* 42–47.

20

Ethics and Internet-Based Cybercrime Research in Australia

James Martin

Introduction

The *National Statement on Ethical Conduct in Human Research* is intended to inform ethical research design, practice, and governance for all Australian research involving human participants. Early chapters are devoted to general themes such as risk, benefit, and consent, and to outlining broad ethical principles—specifically, respect, research merit and integrity, justice, and beneficence. These principles are intended to empower researchers to develop their own ethical research practices; to inform decision-making by members of institutional review boards (IRBs); and to facilitate the development of researcher-participant relationships that are characterized by "trust, mutual responsibility and ethical equality" (NHMRC, 2018, p. 9). Subsequent chapters cover

J. Martin (✉)
School of Social Sciences, Swinburne University of Technology,
Melbourne, VIC, Australia
e-mail: jrmartin@swin.edu.au

© The Author(s), under exclusive license to Springer Nature
Switzerland AG 2021
A. Lavorgna and T. J. Holt (eds.), *Researching Cybercrimes*,
https://doi.org/10.1007/978-3-030-74837-1_20

401

broad ethical considerations in research design and review, and the complexities of working with specific groups of participants, such as children and young people, people with cognitive impairments and disabilities, as well as those in dependent or unequal relationships. While useful in setting the tone with which research involving human participants (rather than archaic and passive "subjects") should be conducted, in practice criminologists and other social scientists are likely to find that the *National Statement* often falls short in providing more practical guidance necessary in the crafting of ethical research. This is due in part to the emphasis that the *National Statement* places on biomedical research matters relative to those relevant to the social sciences. For example, there are more than half a dozen chapters devoted to various medical ethical issues, ranging from the management of human biospecimens to the intricacies of animal-to-human xenotransplantation, while only one and a half pages is devoted to the ethics of managing participants who may be involved in illegal activities. A further shortcoming relevant to this chapter is the absence of advice concerning ethical matters specific to the use of online research methods. Despite the rapid expansion of online research methods over the last two decades, the Internet is mentioned just four times in the *National Statement*, with only passing reference made to the myriad new and emerging forms in which data may be collected and stored using digital technologies.

The absence of more detailed advice in the *National Statement* for criminologists, especially those of us involved in Internet-based research, is significant in that as a result we are largely left to our own devices, and to the still-developing norms of our research sub-disciplines, to manage the various ethical complexities inherent to our work. The consequences of this lack of more formal guidance are potentially serious. By nature, criminological research is often both fraught with ethical complexity, as well as at the risky end of the spectrum in terms of negative consequences for participants and researchers. Participants may risk arrest or informal retribution when disclosing crimes, or they may be unusually vulnerable to power imbalances and psychological distress in other ways, particularly as victims of crime. Meanwhile, researchers may experience harm if they are mistaken for undercover law enforcement, or if it is believed that the identities of participants or their associates, and the illegal activities in which they are involved will inadvertently be disclosed to authorities. Some of these risks, particularly those related to de-anonymization, may be amplified when conducting research in online environments, or when using digital research techniques that are unfamiliar and used inappropriately. It is therefore incumbent upon those involved in Internet-based criminological research to familiarize themselves not only with the broad ethical principles and general requirements articulated in the *National Statement*, but also with emerging best practices in online research methods developed here in Australia, as well as overseas.

The purpose of this chapter is to build upon the principles and requirements articulated in the *National Statement*, and to provide some additional clarity regarding how research involving online methods may be undertaken ethically when studying crimes committed in online spaces. Given the unprecedented and growing embeddedness of digital technologies in daily life, researchers are increasingly eschewing the implicitly rigid dichotomy between our offline and online worlds (Powell et al., 2018). This perspective is particularly apt in the field of illicit drug market research given that drug suppliers often use digital technologies (e.g., encrypted messaging apps) to engage in trading practices that may otherwise be generally considered "offline", and that "online" suppliers who use cryptomarkets still rely on "real world" practices such as sending drugs via traditional mail services. While noting the usefulness of this approach in much academic work, the online/offline dichotomy remains relevant in discussions of research ethics where there remain considerable differences between methodologies that rely on physical interaction with participants (such as face-to-face interviews), and those that rely on "online" methods, such as interviews using messaging applications and observation of online discussion forums. The chapter will therefore employ the terms online/offline noting that these are not intended to be interpreted literally.

The chapter is informed by my own experiences as a predominantly qualitative researcher involved with the study of cryptomarkets, which are pseudonymous marketplaces located on the anonymous Tor network, also known as the "dark web" (Martin, 2014a). Following a brief overview of the existing literature in this area, the chapter analyzes some of the principal ethical issues facing cybercrime researchers seeking to use online research methods. Specifically, these are: participant consent, ensuring anonymity and protecting both research participants and researchers themselves from harm, and the use of secondary data. While the focus of this chapter concerns the study of cryptomarkets and associated forums, it will hopefully also be of use to those involved in other areas of Internet-based cybercrime research, and assist in the crafting of research that is consistent with disciplinary norms and best practices, and which conform to both the spirit and explicit requirements of the *National Statement*.

Developments in the Field and Contemporary Issues

The ethics of Internet-based cybercrime research is an area only recently subject to broad academic inquiry. While studies exploring the ethics of online criminological research can be found as far back as the late 1990s—for example, Coomber's (1997) analysis of the ethics of using Internet surveys to engage with (offline) drug dealers—it was not until well into the 2000s that researchers began analyzing the ethics of using online methodologies to investigate crimes committed in *online* environments. An early outlier in this regard is a Masters study by Ferguson (1998) involving a digital ethnography of an online child sexual abuse material (CSAM) distribution network. The ethics section of the thesis covers a range of issues still at the forefront of contemporary debates, including: informed consent, participant anonymity and potential harm, and expectations of privacy in arguably public digital spaces. Subsequent early steps into this space were undertaken by cybersecurity researchers such as Spitzner (2003) who explored the ethics and legality of monitoring network traffic and identifying digital traces left by hackers, and Oswell (2006) who assessed the potential harms to researchers resulting from the inadvertent collection of online CSAM.

These initial forays into the ethics of Internet-based cybercrime research indicate that it began as an area of niche interest, primarily to those in cybersecurity. This changed, however, with the advent of "Web

2.0"—a wave of mass technological adoption characterized by the spread of online social networking, and an ever-increasing penetration of digital communications technologies into the fabric of everyday life (Powell et al., 2018). For the purposes of my own shift into the realm of "digital criminology", the seminal moment was the launch of the infamous cryptomarket *Silk Road* in 2011. The advent of cryptomarkets heralded a new era, not only as a significant criminal event in its own right, but also for those interested in the study of online crime; for the first time, literally thousands of online offenders could be easily and consistently located and their activities monitored using a rapidly diversifying range of both manual and automated data collection tools. This event sparked a flurry of Internet-based cybercrime research, with some 120 papers by 230 authors written on this topic between 2013 and 2018 (Martin et al., 2019).

The initial excitement surrounding the emergence of cryptomarkets was tempered somewhat by a creeping sense of unease amongst some of us working in the field regarding the ethical dimensions of our research. Were the new tools we were developing being used appropriately and in a manner consistent with our ethical responsibilities and obligations? Would the rapidly increasing speed of techno-methodological innovation outpace the development of appropriate ethical safeguards that govern research in more developed fields? A certain degree of confusion seemed inevitable given the novelty of the research environment, and the inability to simply transplant the ethics governing offline research to the dark web. Further complicating matters were divergences in approaches to ethics resulting from different national research cultures, as well as those between research disciplines, particularly criminology and cybersecurity, but also anthropology, medicine, law, computer science, and other disciplines.

Despite these limitations, a degree of consensus concerning the ethics of cryptomarket research has emerged since Barratt (2012) published the first academic missive on this topic. The earliest ethical reflections on cryptomarket research were confined to small methodology sections of larger papers that make reference to ethical issues specifically encountered in those studies, including the use of big datasets and digital trace (Christin, 2013), and encrypted communications when conducting online interviews (Van Hout & Bingham, 2013, 2014), with the use of both of these methods since becoming increasingly commonplace. Martin and Christin (2016) provided the first standalone study of research ethics investigating cryptomarkets, aiming to combine insights and research practice norms from the realms of computer science and critical criminology; Martin (2016) subsequently explored the ethics associated with different forms of data collection to researchers studying cryptomarkets (and also makes the only other reference to the *National Statement* in existing cybercrime literature); and Barratt and Maddox (2016) provided an insightful analysis of the ethical dilemmas and risks to researchers involved with digital ethnography on the *Silk Road*, a topic also explored by Ferguson (2017). In more recent years, Martin et al. (2019) have provided an overview of cryptomarket research methods and ethics, including a particular emphasis on the problems posed by academic collaboration with law enforcement; and Turk et al. (2020) have analyzed the methodological and ethical challenges associated with automated data collection on cryptomarkets. These studies provide a limited but nonetheless important basis from which we can draw an understanding of how Internet-based cybercrime research ethics have developed and what norms have been established in this particular sub-field of the discipline. Insights from these and other relevant works are threaded throughout the subsequent analysis section of the chapter.

Participant Consent

Gaining the informed consent of participants is a foundational principle of academic research, and is also a useful starting point to begin exploring some of the ethical and methodological complexities associated with Internet-based cybercrime research. This is because whether or not informed consent is required necessitates an understanding of a range of other inter-related ethical issues that are also covered in the chapter. As the *National Statement* makes explicit, there are a range of circumstances in which the usual necessity to gain the informed consent of participants may be reasonably waived. For research aiming to expose illegal activity, an IRB may waive requirements for consent when each of the following conditions is met: The value of the research justifies any adverse effects; there is sufficient protection of the privacy of participants and the confidentiality of data; and the waiver is not in conflict with any applicable laws. Research that relies on secondary data (i.e., data that has already been generated but not for the specific purpose of the intended research) may also be exempt from the need for participant consent if it is "impractical" to gain, if the data is essentially "public" in nature, and if the privacy of participants is sufficiently "respected".

At first glance, these conditions appear reasonably straightforward and sufficiently detailed to usefully inform research design and practice. However, the complexities underlying each condition quickly reveal themselves upon closer inspection. How does one accurately identify, let alone balance, potential benefits, and adverse consequences, such as harm to participants and researchers? And out of the myriad online forums, Web sites, chatrooms, and social media sites, which can be reasonably assessed as public or private?

Harm Resulting from Research

In addressing the first of these conditions—that of research needing to justify adverse consequences—there are three primary groups to consider: researchers, participants, as well others not directly involved in the research, including non-humans and the environment. Harm to each of these groups should be defined in its broadest possible sense, with reference to both *magnitude*—from individual discomfort and inconvenience through to serious physical and emotional distress and injury—as well as *prevalence*, or how likely the manifestation of a harm may come to pass (Israel & Hay, 2011). Given the potential for anxiety and other forms of psychological distress in response to the potential of harm, Israel and Hay advise that "researchers should try to avoid imposing even the *risk* of harm on others" (Israel & Hay, 2011, p. 504), even in those circumstances where risks may in fact be negligible. In other words, even imagined risks carry the potential to translate into "real'" harm. Researchers therefore have a duty to minimize and ameliorate these wherever possible, and to reassure participants and others appropriately.

Ferguson (2017) claims that risks to participants in cryptomarket research "are largely similar to the risks faced by subjects in offline drug market research – they might face exposure, arrest, loss of social or professional status" (Ferguson, 2017, p. 691). While this is undoubtedly true, it is important to note that conducting research online also significantly changes the ways in which these harms may manifest and be perceived by participants. Offline research, for example through the use of surveys or interviews, often involves transitory interpersonal contact between researchers and participants. Let's consider the example of someone involved in illegal drug market activity sharing their experiences in a face-to-face interview, receiving a cash payment for their participation, then parting ways with the researcher. Provided that their anonymity has preserved at the point of data collection—for example, by meeting at a discreet location and not recording any identifiable information—then participants are likely to be convinced that their safety is assured, and that ongoing risks will be negligible.

Now let's take the same example, but replace the offline context with an online one involving an interview conducted via email or instant messaging followed by an electronic cash payment. Unlike the face-to-face interview, this online interaction leaves a trail of potentially identifiable information, such IP addresses, online banking details, phone numbers, email addresses, and so on, any of which provide law enforcement agencies with data that may be harvested and used to identify participants long after research data has been collected. The change to an online environment therefore raises the possibility of de-anonymization occurring as a result of digital traces that are left online in virtual perpetuity (see also Coomber, 1997). The potential for de-anonymization to occur not only poses risks to those who do agree to participate, but is also likely to disincentivize prospective participants from engaging with researchers at all.

To compensate for these risks, researchers using online methodologies must be—and must be perceived to be by participants and the communities in which they are embedded—sufficiently familiar with the current and emerging technologies necessary to ensure participant anonymity. When conducting interviews online, this can be achieved through the use of encryption tools that significantly complicate the work of law enforcement agencies in identifying people engaged with online lawbreaking. For example, in a recent study involving interviews with dark web drug suppliers, Martin and colleagues (2020) offered a range of up-to-date encrypted messaging platforms to prospective participants, who were then able to select whichever communication option they felt best protected their identity. The identity of interviewees was further protected by a commitment on the part of the research team to avoid recording any identifiable information inadvertently during interviews, and to offer reciprocity payments to participants using encrypted electronic currencies, rather than relying on conventional—and readily traceable—online payment systems. This approach, building upon similar interview methods employed by Van Hout and Bingham (2014) and Maddox and colleagues (2016), demonstrates how online researchers can use a range of complementary encryption tools and interview protocols to both attract research participants as well as safely engage with vulnerable and at-risk populations.

Managing and preventing risk of harm to participants and others carries the additional benefit of reducing risk to researchers. It should be stated from the outset that online research is typically much safer for researchers, at least in terms of threats to physical safety, compared with other methodologies which involve face-to-face interaction with offenders and other potentially "risky" groups. However, online spaces in which crime is committed are not typically welcoming of external scrutiny, well intended or otherwise, and prospective and potentially hostile participants may themselves constitute a source of risk to researchers, particularly in those instances where they feel that research poses a risk to their anonymity, profits, or safety. Reflecting on their digital ethnography conducted on the cryptomarket *Silk Road*, Barratt and Maddox (2016) relate their experiences of gendered harassment and threats to their physical safety from hostile community members. While the researchers noted that this hostility, which included "graphic death threats", could have been trolling behavior intended to provoke and upset, rather than constituting a genuine intent to (physically) harm, such threats cannot be entirely dismissed on this basis, and in themselves are potentially damaging in terms of psychological distress.

How online researchers may go about limiting risk of harm to themselves is an area subject to limited academic research, and is only mentioned in passing in the *National Statement*. Notwithstanding this lack of attention, there are a variety of ways that risks to researchers may be minimized. For example, in my own early research on cryptomarkets (see Martin, 2014a, 2014b) I relied on a pseudonym to protect my offline identity during the course of passive observation or "lurking", an approach also initially employed by Ferguson (2017) in her own digital ethnography of *Silk Road*. Employing a pseudonym when undertaking unobtrusive observational research is a common research method to facilitate covert, passive observation in online spaces, and has been used by various researchers on both the clear and dark web. Part of the appeal in using pseudonyms is that it offers a simple way to ensure that those who may be hostile to researchers are ignorant of their presence, thereby effectively neutralizing them as threat. A further benefit is that pseudonyms also conceal the presence of a researcher such that observed communications are not disrupted or altered by the perceived presence of an outsider. The use of pseudonyms is also routine practice among cryptomarket users, and may arguably be interpreted as conforming to the social norms around user anonymity that are prevalent in these digital spaces.

The use of pseudonyms in conducting passive online cybercrime research is widespread and certainly defensible (see also Gehl, 2016), however, there are arguments against this approach. Barratt and Maddox's (2016) decision to use their real identities, and to link them to their university profiles and email addresses, was designed with the explicit intention to establish legitimacy and facilitate trust among community members, and to facilitate recruitment for one-to-one interviews as part of a second stage of their research. There were both negative and positive consequences resulting from the decision to rely upon their offline identities; on the one hand, it exposed the researchers to additional risk which included explicit threats to their safety. It also clearly aroused suspicion and hostility on the part of some community members who either did not trust that the researchers were who they said they were, or were generally dubious about the benefits of the community communicating with outsiders. We therefore cannot dismiss the possibility that the overt presence of the research team resulted in discomfort or distress among sections of the research population who either resented their presence or mistakenly believed that they were a cover for infiltration by law enforcement, and that community members modified their natural online behaviors as a result.

On the other hand, in maintaining a position of transparency, Barratt and Maddox (2016) went to considerable lengths to put into practice the principle of respect for participants so regularly emphasized in the *National Statement*, and demonstrated an act of good faith to a vulnerable, stigmatized, and often suspicious community. This demonstration of good faith facilitated a dialogue among community members regarding the need to engage with well-intentioned community outsiders who could "present its [the community's] point of view to the wider public through the non-judgmental lens of research practice" (Barratt & Maddox, 2016, p. 707). Many community members, including forum moderators and other community gatekeepers, clearly reciprocated the respect offered to them by the research team. These respectful interactions are worthy and empowering in their own right, and assisted the research team's efforts at recruitment for in-depth one-on-one interviews. It is also possible that in engaging in a transparent and respectful manner that community members would be more positively predisposed to other researchers subsequently entering the research space. These benefits do not, however, provide a compelling case that researchers should use their offline identities in all instances, but rather suggest that this decision should be made after careful consideration of the potential harmful and positive effects on researchers, participants, and others potentially affected by the research.

Use of Secondary Data, Privacy, and the Public Domain

A key stream of research involving cryptomarkets and the dark web is that which relies on information posted on cryptomarkets and associated discussion forums. These are rich repositories of data, and include customer feedback ratings and associated text, advertising information, pricing data, and discussion posts. Studies relying on this data include various qualitative analyses (Bancroft & Scott Reid, 2017; Morselli et al., 2017; Van Hout & Hearne, 2017), as well as quantitative research that analyzes long-term pricing and sales trends (Cunliffe et al., 2017, 2019; Soska & Christin, 2015), and the impact of particular events, such as law enforcement interventions and exit scams (Décary-Hétu & Giommoni, 2017; Martin et al., 2018; Van Buskirk et al., 2017). Overwhelmingly, such studies have sought neither the consent of those responsible for hosting or administering these forums, nor that of individual posters. The rationale in favor of treating this information as essentially in the public domain, and therefore able to be used without the consent of those responsible for either its hosting or posting is increasingly accepted as normal and ethical research practice. It is, however, also not without some controversy given that it is unlikely that those responsible for this data would universally consent for it to be used for research purposes. Using this data and potentially overlooking the principle of respect for participants therefore requires some justification beyond it simply becoming increasingly common research practice.

The *National Statement* briefly acknowledges that the advent of the Internet has complicated previously clearer differences between public and private domains, and that there exists a spectrum ranging from fully public (such as books and newspapers), to fully private (such as closed discussion forums which are restricted to small numbers of authorized participants). According to the *National Statement*, the "guiding principle" for researchers seeking to use information posted on the Internet without participant consent is that "although data or information may be publicly available, this does not automatically mean that the individuals with whom this data or information is associated have necessarily granted permission for its use in research" (NHMRC, 2018, p. 36). This is not only an obvious statement—authors of newspaper articles, for example, do not typically express explicit consent for their use in research—but also an unhelpful one; presumably forums closer to the public end of the spectrum are suitable sites for the harvesting and use of secondary data and vice versa. However, there is no further guidance within the *National Statement* regarding how to differentiate between forums hosting data that may be used without the explicit consent of participants. Instead, we must turn to existing research within the field to determine whether or not use of secondary data can and should be used without the express consent of participants.

The question of how to distinguish between public and private forums in the digital world has fortunately been subject to extensive discussion (Eynon et al., 2008; Eysenbach & Till, 2001; Martin, 2016; Sugiura et al., 2017). While some researchers contend that informed consent must be sought when engaging in covert observation of *any* online forum, others, including myself, argue that such a position is unnecessarily restrictive (see also Langer & Beckman, 2005), and that a more important indicator is whether the participants themselves are likely to believe that their forum is either private or subject to external observation. For example, there is a strong argument that online forums which tightly control access and which have limited membership should be considered private and that researchers should not gather data from these sources without the express consent of participants (Eysenbach & Till, 2001; Martin, 2016). By contrast, when information has been posted in an easily accessible forum with the express intention of communicating to a wide range of people, there is a compelling case to be made that there is no reasonable expectation of privacy on the part of participants. Customer feedback posted on cryptomarkets, for example, is written with the implied intention that it will be seen by a wide range of people not known to the poster. Pricing and advertising information posted by a dark web drug supplier can similarly be assessed as essentially public in nature. With regard to cryptomarket discussion forums, there are no significant barriers to entry and participants widely acknowledge that they are subject to monitoring by those outside the community, particularly by law enforcement. This indicates that these forums may also be used by researchers without the explicit consent of participants, so long as no identifiable information is captured as a result of the research (Martin, 2016).

Conclusion

This chapter discusses some of the principle ethical issues facing Internet-based cybercrime researchers, with explicit reference to the *National Statement* and cryptomarket research. The key lesson for those involved in the study of cryptomarkets and other forms of cybercrime research is that there is significant scope to gather data ethically from a range of online spaces, provided that they are sufficiently public in nature, and that harms to participants, particularly that of de-anonymization, are managed appropriately. Unobtrusive observational research methods, including lurking and the gathering of data from secondary sources, have provided a valuable source of data from which important insights have been made with minimal negative impacts upon both members of the communities studied as well as those undertaking the research. While some researchers elect to disclose their identities when undertaking passive observation, this is usually as a prelude to other forms of more interactive research which do clearly require participant consent, such as online interviews and digital ethnographies. Researchers who are contemplating the use of these methods, and the members of IRBs who assess their ethics applications, should be mindful of these practices, the wider arguments that underpin them, as well as the successful precedents that have been set in this rewarding and ever-expanding area of cybercrime research.

References

Bancroft, A., & Scott Reid, P. (2017). Challenging the techno-politics of anonymity: The case of cryptomarket users. *Information, Communication & Society, 20*(4), 497–512.

Barratt, M. J. (2012). Silk road: eBay for drugs. *Addiction, 107*(3), 683–683.

Barratt, M. J., & Maddox, A. (2016). Active engagement with stigmatized communities through digital ethnography. *Qualitative Research, 16*(6), 701–719.

Christin, N. (2013, May). Traveling the Silk Road: A measurement analysis of a large anonymous online marketplace. In *Proceedings of the 22nd international conference on World Wide Web* (pp. 213–224).

Coomber, R. (1997). Using the Internet for survey research. *Sociological Research Online, 2*(2), 49–58.

Cunliffe, J., Décary-Hêtu, D., & Pollak, T. A. (2019). Nonmedical prescription psychiatric drug use and the darknet: A cryptomarket analysis. *International Journal of Drug Policy, 73,* 263–272.

Cunliffe, J., Martin, J., Décary-Hétu, D., & Aldridge, J. (2017). An island apart? Risks and prices in the Australian cryptomarket drug trade. *International Journal of Drug Policy, 50,* 64–73.

Décary-Hétu, D., & Giommoni, L. (2017). Do police crackdowns disrupt drug cryptomarkets? A longitudinal analysis of the effects of Operation Onymous. *Crime, Law and Social Change, 67*(1), 55–75.

Eynon, R., Fry, J., & Schroeder, R. (2008). The ethics of internet research. In *Sage internet research methods* (pp. 23–41).

Eysenbach, G., & Till, J. E. (2001). Ethical issues in qualitative research on internet communities. *British Medical Journal, 323*(7321), 1103–1105.

Ferguson, I. (1998). *Sacred realms and icons of the damned; the ethnography of an internet-based child pornography ring.* Doctoral dissertation, Carleton University.

Ferguson, R. H. (2017). Offline "stranger" and online lurker: Methods for an ethnography of illicit transactions on the darknet. *Qualitative Research, 17*(6), 683–698.

Gehl, R. W. (2016). Power/freedom on the dark web: A digital ethnography of the dark web social network. *New Media and Society, 18*(7), 1219–1235.

Israel, M., & Hay, I. (2011). Research ethics in criminology. In *Sage handbook of criminological research methods.* Sage.

Langer, R., & Beckman, S. C. (2005). Sensitive research topics: Netnography revisited. *Qualitative Market Research, 8*(2), 189–203.

Maddox, A., Barratt, M. J., Allen, M., & Lenton, S. (2016). Constructive activism in the dark web: Cryptomarkets and illicit drugs in the digital "demimonde". *Information, Communication & Society, 19*(1), 111–126.

Martin, J. (2014a). Lost on the Silk Road: Online drug distribution and the 'cryptomarket'. *Criminology & Criminal Justice, 14*(3), 351–367.

Martin, J. (2014b). *Drugs on the dark net: How cryptomarkets are transforming the global trade in illicit drugs.* Springer.

Martin, J. (2016). Illuminating the dark net: Methods and ethics in cryptomarket research. In M. Adorjan & R. Ricciardelli (Eds.), *Engaging with ethics in international criminological research*. Routledge.

Martin, J., & Christin, N. (2016). Ethics in cryptomarket research. *International Journal of Drug Policy, 35*, 84–91

Martin, J., Cunliffe, J., Décary-Hétu, D., & Aldridge, J. (2018). Effect of restricting the legal supply of prescription opioids on buying through online illicit marketplaces: Interrupted time series analysis. *BMJ, 361*.

Martin, J., Cunliffe, J., & Munksgaard, R. (2019). *Cryptomarkets: A research companion*. Emerald Group Publishing.

Martin, J., Munksgaard, R., Coomber, R., Demant, J., & Barratt, M. J. (2020). Selling drugs on darkweb cryptomarkets: Differentiated pathways, risks and rewards. *The British Journal of Criminology, 60*(3), 559–578.

Morselli, C., Décary-Hétu, D., Paquet-Clouston, M., & Aldridge, J. (2017). Conflict management in illicit drug cryptomarkets. *International Criminal Justice Review, 27*(4), 237–254.

National Health and Medical Research Council. (2018). *National statement on ethical conduct in human research*. Canberra: Australian Research Council.

Oswell, D. (2006). When images matter: Internet child pornography, forms of observation and an ethics of the virtual. *Information, Communication & Society, 9*(2), 244–265.

Powell, A., Stratton, G., & Cameron, R. (2018). *Digital criminology: Crime and justice in digital society*. Routledge.

Sugiura, L., Wiles, R., & Pope, C. (2017). Ethical challenges in online research: Public/private perceptions. *Research Ethics, 13*(3–4), 184–199.

Soska, K., & Christin, N. (2015). Measuring the longitudinal evolution of the online anonymous marketplace ecosystem. In *24th {USENIX} security symposium {USENIX} security 15* (pp. 33–48).

Spitzner, L. (2003). The honeynet project: Trapping the hackers. *IEEE Security and Privacy, 1*(2), 15–23.

Turk, K., Pastrana, S., & Collier, B. (2020). A tight scrape: Methodological approaches to cybercrime research data collection in adversarial environments. In *2nd Workshop on Attackers and Cyber-Crime Operations*.

Van Buskirk, J., Bruno, R., Dobbins, T., Breen, C., Burns, L., Naicker, S., & Roxburgh, A. (2017). The recovery of online drug markets following law enforcement and other disruptions. *Drug and Alcohol Dependence, 173*, 159–162.

Van Hout, M. C., & Bingham, T. (2013). "Silk Road", the virtual drug market-place: A single case study of user experiences. *International Journal of Drug Policy, 24*(5), 385–391.

Van Hout, M. C., & Bingham, T. (2014). Responsible vendors, intelligent consumers: Silk Road, the online revolution in drug trading. *International Journal of Drug Policy, 25*(2), 183–189.

Van Hout, M. C., & Hearne, E. (2017). New psychoactive substances (NPS) on cryptomarket fora: An exploratory study of characteristics of forum activity between NPS buyers and vendors. *International Journal of Drug Policy, 40*, 102–110.

21

Researching Crime and Deviance in Southeast Asia: Challenges and Ethics When Using Online Data

Lennon Yao-Chung Chang and Souvik Mukherjee

Introduction

With the development of digital technology and the Internet, more data and information is being digitalized and much of it can be easily found online. Digitalization of data and information has provided researchers with a convenient way to acquire data for research without having to physically visit the place where the data is retained. A substantial amount of research is now being conducted by accessing digitalized data and information, including reports, statistics, laws and policy documents produced by governments and private companies. This is especially beneficial to researchers in the field of crime and deviance. While collection

L. Y.-C. Chang (✉)
Monash University, Clayton, VIC, Australia
e-mail: Lennon.Chang@monash.edu

S. Mukherjee
West Bengal National University of Juridical Sciences,
Kolkata, West Bengal, India

© The Author(s), under exclusive license to Springer Nature
Switzerland AG 2021
A. Lavorgna and T. J. Holt (eds.), *Researching Cybercrimes*,
https://doi.org/10.1007/978-3-030-74837-1_21

of self-reported crime and victimization data is popular, most research still relies on official statistics to understand not only the crime rates but also the prosecution rates and imprisonment rates. Digitalized court verdicts are often used by researchers to understand the trend in certain types of crime, the modus operandi, as well as factors influencing judicial decisions (Cai et al., 2018). With its comparative nature, much criminology research has relied on statistics and reports published online. For example, in cybercrime research, we see academics mapping state-laws with the Council of Europe's Convention on Cybercrime (Broadhurst & Chang, 2013; Chang, 2012, 2017; Liu et al., 2017; Luong et al., 2019).

Apart from digitalized government data and reports, we see that technology has also enabled the creation of new data sets and/or data dumps, including data generated by social media such as Twitter and Facebook (see also Chapters 1 and 13). Digital platforms also provide academics a new way to collect data through online surveys and interviews (Chang & Zhu, 2020; Ke & Lee, 2020) (see also Chapters 6 and 24–26). Big data analysis (Cai et al., 2018; Završnik, 2018) and social networking analysis (Ke & Lee, 2020) has become a new trend in researching crime and deviance (see also Chapters 10–13).

With the increase in academic focus on the global south and southern criminology, we see more crime and criminal justice research on Asia, especially South and Southeast Asia. More of this research is based on digitalized data and online surveys. However, as most of the countries in this region have not had the same level of academic research and data collection as the countries in the global north, the issues and concerns relating to using digitalized data and new online research methodologies have not yet featured in the discourse. This chapter aims to explore the concerns and challenges of online data collection and use of existing online data to conduct crime and deviance research in the region. It will start by overviewing digitalization of official data and information by selected countries in the region before discussing challenges and concerns. It will also discuss whether existing basic ethical principles of research developed in the west are directly applicable in this region.

Digitalization of Crime and Deviant Behaviour in South Asian and Southeast Asian States

Most jurisdictions, including some of the major South Asian and Southeast Asian nations, have adopted systems to collect and publish data relating to criminal and deviant behaviour. However, due to the digital divide, the capacity of data digitalization varies. Countries such as Singapore and Thailand have a higher digitalization rate compared with countries that are less developed and/or newly democratized such as Myanmar which have just started to digitalize their crime data. Here, we aim to briefly outline the situation in relation to the recording and preservation of data relating to crime and deviant behaviour in a digitized form in selected Southeast Asian countries, especially countries that are comparatively less advanced in the digitalization of information published online in English.

India

India's National Crime Records Bureau (NCRB) was established in 1986 with a mission to establish a national database on crime and criminals sharable to law enforcement agencies for their use in public service delivery (NCRB, 2017). Methodology for data collection and publication is clearly outlined in publications. For example, *Crime in India*, a yearly crime statistics report published by NCRB, adopts the "Principal Offence Rule" for counting crime in accordance with international standards. That is, if the crime involved several Indian Penal Code (IPC) offences, only the most heinous crime is recorded. The NCRB admit there exists the possibility of under-reporting of certain crimes under this rule, for example, a crime involving both murder and rape will be recorded as murder. However, there are certain exceptions to the principal offence rule such as crimes against women, children, historically oppressed classes, senior citizens and juvenile delinquency. *Crime in India* also includes the crime rate which is assessed through the number of crimes reported and the population of the segment. The portal also provides separate additional tables with data on other crimes (NCRB, 2019). Publications such as *Crime in India* (since 1967), *Accidental Death and Suicide in India* (since 1998) and *Crime against Women* (since 2001) are all available online at the National portal (https://data.gov.in).

Bangladesh

Bangladesh has also kept pace in terms of digitalization and has regularly been publishing crime-related data over the past nine years on the Bangladesh Police website (2011–2019). The primary classification of data is under headings including robbery, murder, speedy trial, riot, woman and child repression, kidnapping, police assault, burglary, theft and other cases. The data also includes some crimes which are governed by specialized legislation such as arms, narcotics, smuggling and explosives. The portal presenting the crime data does not describe the methodology which would enable the user to understand how the data has been collected and recorded. By simply providing numbers without a contextual understanding, there is a possible overlapping of crime data, limited means to verify the data and no gender or age-based classification (Bangladesh Police, 2019).

Sri Lanka

The Department of Census and Statistics is Sri Lanka's main government agency that collect and publishes official statistics according to the Statistical Act and Census Act. Statistics relating to agriculture, computer literacy, education, health, industry, gender statistics, population and poverty can be found on their website. Crime and criminal justice-related statistics can be found under gender statistics, including Judges/Magistrates by Type of Court and Sex, Officers in Key Positions of Prison Department by Sex, Convicted Prisoners by Age Group and Sex, Convicted Prisoners by Type of Offence and Sex, Convicted Prisoners with Previous Proved Offences and Violence against Women. However, most of the statistics are not collected every year which makes it difficult to understand the trend of the type of crime (Department of Census and Statistics, 2020).

The Sri Lanka Police website is the designated portal for crime statistics and hosts data from 2010 (Sri Lanka Police, 2020). The data is categorized in the following manner: grave crimes; disposal of grave crime; distribution of grave crime; civil state and standard education level for suicides; reason for suicides; race and religion for suicides, and nature and occupation of the persons committing suicides. It is to be noted the abovementioned categories were developed in 2010 and were further expanded in 2011 with the inclusion of sudden deaths; excise offences; vice detections; minor offences against children and women; grave offences against children and women; petty complaints as new categories. For two years (2012 and 2013), the categorizations were significantly reduced to grave crimes-related data before reverting to the previous categorizations. The changes in the published categories of crime reduce the previous usefulness of data for the users. And so, notwithstanding the appearance of detailed data, the fluctuating categorization and absence of readily accessible documents explaining the changes in categorization and methodology limits the utility of the data. Without visibility of the methodology, the data representation becomes mere numbers which may not be verified or challenged and have to be taken on their face value (Sri Lanka Police, 2020).

Philippines

The Philippines Statistical Authority has taken significant steps towards establishing statistical standards, including for the classification of crime (Philippine Statistics Authority, 2020). The authority approved and adopted the 2018 Philippine Standard Classification of Crime for Statistical Purposes (PSCCS) which resolved that a standard classification needed to be developed to achieve uniformity and comparability of statistics generated at the national and international level. Furthermore, they reaffirmed their commitment towards the principle laid down by the United Nation's International Classification of Crime for Statistical Purposes (ICCS) and 2018–2023 Philippine Statistical Development

Program which included the 2018 PSCSS. The PSCSS provides for a hierarchical classification, wherein crimes of a similar nature are classified under a standard head or category. The characterizations of the classification closely resemble the ICCS and have 11 categories of acts amounting to crime which are as following: Acts leading to death or intending to cause death; harm or intending to cause harm; injurious acts of a sexual nature; acts against property involving violence; narcotics and psychotropic substances; fraud, deception and corruption; acts against public order and authority; acts against public safety and state security; acts against the natural environment; and others. The technical note provided on the portal acts as a window to the methodology used in the classification process. The technical note elaborates on the purpose, scope and principles of PSCCS which have a close resemblance to the ICCS methodology discussed earlier. The approach to crime classification taken by the Philippines will eventually make it a viable jurisdiction for academic research and analysis (Philippine Statistics Authority, 2020).

Myanmar

Myanmar's Central Statistical Organization (CSO) was formed early in 1952 under the Central Statistical Authority Act No. (34-A) of 1952 to publish various government statistics. However, most of the data published related to agriculture and fisheries and it was not until recently that the CSO started to publish statistics in Yearbooks and Quarterly Statistic Bulletins. Since 2016 these publications have been available online. However, there is still no official report published by the Myanmar government in relation to crime and deviance. Even the publication in response to the UN Sustainable Development Goals has very limited information under SDG 16 on promoting a peaceful and inclusive society (Central Statistical Organization, 2016).

Vietnam

The General Statistics Office (GSO), formerly the Bureau of Vietnam Statistics, was established in 1946 by then President Ho Chi Minh to manage statistics and conduct statistical activities (https://www.gso.gov.vn/en/about-gso/). The Vietnamese government has been accelerating the introduction of e-government and digitalization of the economy. For its part, the GSO has been renovating and strengthening the statistics system through the use of modern technologies. While general statistics are digitalized by the GSO and published on their website, statistics relating to crime and deviance are not included. These statistics are the responsibility of the Ministry of Public Security which publishes crime statistics on their website (http://bocongan.gov.vn). However, they are only available in Vietnamese.

Challenges Using Digitalized Data

From the discussion above, we can see that digitalization of crime and deviance data is emerging in Southeast Asian countries. Although much data is still not available online, it is becoming easier for academics to conduct research using digitalized data than before. However, issues and concerns need to be addressed when using the data.

Digital Divide

As Chang (2017) indicated, cyber maturity differs across Southeast Asian countries. The digital divide, defined by the OECD (2001, p. 5) as "the gap between individuals, households, businesses and geographic areas at different socio- economic levels with regard both to their opportunities to access information and communication technologies (ICTs) and to their use of the internet for a wide variety of activities", is still large. In Singapore, more than 80% of the population are Internet users and in 2020 it was ranked 11th in the use of e-government by the United Nations. On the other hand, countries such as Myanmar are still at the infant stage in adopting new technology and e-government policy. As mentioned earlier, some countries do not digitalize their crime data which makes it impossible to conduct research on these countries using digitalized data. Similarly, in countries with low Internet penetration it is difficult to collect data through online methods.

Concerns with Data Collection

Within South Asia and Southeast Asia there is inconsistency in the collection and recording of crime-related data. Different jurisdictions record different types of crimes and deviant behaviours with certain behaviours not criminalized uniformly across all jurisdictions. Before using the data for comparison purposes or to understand the crime situation in a country, it is critical to review the methodology on how the data was collected and recorded. Although each jurisdiction might have documented their methodology for data collection and recording, these documents are sometimes not readily accessible or accessible at all. Among the countries above, not all have documented their methodology and therefore the researcher needs to be cautious about using the data or drawing conclusion from it.

Data Inconsistency

In addition to our inability to compare and understand data collection methodology, the non-uniform classification and categorization of crimes and fluctuation in what is collected within those categories present problems for the researcher.

The non-uniform classification and categorization of crimes among jurisdiction can result from a crime in one jurisdiction not being regarded as a crime in another. This might be the product of different cultures as well as different laws. Different capacities to investigate and record crime also makes use of online data for comparative purposes problematic. For example, most Southeast Asia countries still do not record statistics on cybercrime as their cybercrime law is still being drafted (Chang, 2017). The Philippines is adopting the International

Classification of Crime for Statistical Purposes (ICCS) endorsed by the United Nations in 2015 which provides a framework for classification at the national, regional and international level (United Nations Economic and Social Council, 2015). This will improve the consistency of data collected and recorded, but it will not itself address issues of under-reporting which can be significant, especially for gender-based crime and domestic violence, and in parts of the country where police resources are limited.

Fluctuations in the presentation of data are another challenge in many jurisdictions. For example, in certain jurisdictions different methodologies have been adopted in different years and the justification for such alterations is not available to researchers. This questions the credibility of the data and renders it useless on several counts.

Language and Access Barriers

Language is another barrier to online data collection for academic research. For the nations which we studied, data was recorded in six languages: English, Hindi, Bengali, Sinhala, Burmese and Vietnamese. Although English can be seen in most jurisdictions, some countries only provide short summaries in English and countries like Vietnam only have their crime statistics in Vietnamese. Although some data can be accessed using online translation services, not all the information posted online is in a translatable format, such as Myanmar Zawgyi font. Although Unicode has been promoted in Myanmar, it will take time for the new font to be widely used (Eaint Thet Su, 2019).

The portals used by the jurisdictions play a significant role in establishing their efficacy. A complex portal and user interface automatically limits access by the user. A portal may have numerous sections, and it is essential that access to those sections is straightforward. For this study, attempts were made to access the relevant portals representing digitalized data from several other countries from South Asia and Southeast Asia such as Pakistan. However, access to some jurisdictions was restricted, thereby limiting our ability to access the crime statistics and digitalized data, as well as the methodologies, applied in those jurisdictions.

Ethical Concerns of Research Conducted Through Online Data

The Internet is slowly becoming the laboratory of social sciences. However, there remains a significant void in terms of guidance offered on how to conduct research online both on the compatibility perspective and ethical perspective. Issues of confidentiality, anonymity, disclosure, informed consent, handling of data and treatment of secondary data pose significant challenges for researchers. Often online research is assumed as an extension of offline research with minor changes in the methodology. Although several aspects are theoretically the same, using online data for the purposes of research introduces new considerations. Already some guidelines have been developed on the ethics of online research. The Association of Internet Research has been developing Internet research ethics. The AoIR guidelines 2019 (Internet Research Ethics 3.0) addressed the concern of getting inform consent in research when using big data. Other ethical concerns include such as the protection of researchers (both mental and physical), the power balance/imbalance, respect of privacy and legal compliance (Franzke et al., 2020). The institutional Research Board, Ethical Review Board or similar research ethics oversight board have been set up to make sure that research is aligned with ethical principles.

However, most Southeast Asian countries are yet to frame such exclusive guidelines regulating online research, except in medical and health research. The research ethics oversight boards and guidelines are yet to develop in most Southeast Asian countries. That is, most of the online and offline research does not need to go through ethical review and get approval. Researchers from outside Southeast Asian countries doing online research in the Southeast Asian countries might need to get the ethical approval from their host country, but concerns relating to different countries might not be considered due to a lack of local knowledge.

Cultural Differences

Being sensible and understanding cultural difference are important to research and both online and offline data collection. It is important for researchers to be aware of the social norms and customs before conducting research. For researchers collecting data in the field, it is easier to sense differences in culture and even taboos and attitudes of local respondents. However, for online data collection, there is usually less chance for researchers to understand this as they do not really immerse themselves in the society. Without the knowledge of the cultural differences, there is a risk that researchers will translate the data in a wrong direction and the result might not reflect the real meaning of the data.

Data Censoring and Manipulation

Sometimes there is a suspicion that a government or law enforcement agency might have manipulated the recorded data. This might be motivated by a desire to improve their image or to conceal incidents of political violence or a heavy-handed response to civil disobedience situations. Human rights organizations might produce their own statistics on the scale of alleged crimes but these may be exaggerated to gain attention or simply overstate the volume of crime by not checking the veracity of reports which might be of the same incident. By their very nature, NGO-generated statistics might not provide an overall picture of the state of crime and deviance in a jurisdiction. They focus only on the crimes and behaviours that are of interest to the NGO, such as human rights abuses, environmental crimes or gender-based crime. And they rarely provide a time series to enable research into trends. It is difficult for the researcher to collect data independently and sampling technology may not be effective as members of the public have different perceptions of what constitutes a crime. For example, many victims of domestic violence do not report against their partners. The verification of older data is even more difficult.

The risk of data censoring applies equally to online data and offline data. Censoring might involve tampering with the data or simply the non-release of certain data. This is more likely for crimes relating to human rights abuses or crimes committed by the state itself. For example, researchers have sought to establish the execution rate for the death penalty in China but there is no official data available. This situation might also apply to some Southeast Asian countries. The government control of social media and the Internet might also impact the accuracy of research using data and information sourced from social media. In Vietnam, for example, the Communist Party of Vietnam seeks to censor and control social media that may be used to spread information, particularly calls for the formation of illegal groups and political activities directed against the Party (Thayer, 2010, 2014; Trong, 2020).

Conclusion

The collection and digitalization of data related to crime and deviance are growing and providing an enriched environment for research within a country and between countries. Digitalization of data can overcome geographical boundaries and can contribute significantly towards uniformity in the categorization and classification of data relating to crime and deviant behaviours. However, digitalization is relatively new and is not without its shortcomings. The countries sampled in this study reflect the significant challenges which continue to impair the efficacy of the process and raise questions on the credibility of the data and its further usage. Aside from a lack of uniformity, which is not unexpected among independent nation states, there remain challenges which hamper the credibility of the data. Foremost among them is the absence of a published methodology that is accessible to the user. Thus, the representation of the data cannot be verified and needs to be accepted on its face value. There are ethical questions around using data for research purposes when there are grounds for believing that the data is incomplete (as a result of constraints) or has been manipulated to influence perceptions. In 2015, the UNODC endorsed the International Classification of Crime for Statistical Purposes (ICCS), which provides a framework for the classification of crime statistics at the national, regional and international levels (United Nations Economic and Social Council, 2015). It was noted that the jurisdictions which have affirmed their commitment to the ICCS principles are better positioned in terms of representation of digitalized data and methodology, namely India and the Philippines, while data representation by Sri Lanka, Bangladesh, Myanmar and Vietnam has limited context, from the methodological perspective.

Apart from research using digitalized government data, researchers also now have an opportunity to conduct research using online surveys and other online sources. Although there are ethical principles developed by academic organizations, these are not followed or practices in most Southeast Asian countries. While academic who conduct research in Southeast Asian countries might need to get ethical approval from their host organization, they might not be aware of cultural differences, data quality issues and data manipulation activities.

In conclusion, it can safely be stated that digitalization and publication of data is a step towards better transparency and justice. Nonetheless, the process is still in the nascent stage and in the coming years one can expect further clarity in data management and uniformity of data representation relating to crime and deviant behaviour in South Asian and Southeast Asian countries. And for research using online data, it is important for researchers to have a sound background understanding of the country they are looking into before they conduct online research.

References

Bangladesh Police. (2019). *Crime statistics 2019*. Available at: https://www.pol ice.gov.bd/en/crime_statistic/year/2019.

Broadhurst, R., & Chang, Y. (2013). Cybercrime in Asia: Trends and challenges. In J. Liu, B. Hebenton, & D. Jou (Eds.), *Handbook of Asian criminology*. Springer.

Cai, T., Du, L., Xin, Y., & Chang, L. Y. C. (2018). Characteristics of cybercrimes: Evidence from Chinese judgment documents. *Police Practice and Research: an International Journal, 19*(6), 582–595.

Central Statistical Organization. (2016). *National strategy for development of statistics*. Ministry of Planning and Finance.

Chang, L., & Zhu, J. (2020). Taking justice into their own hands: Predictors of netilantism among cyber citizens in Hong Kong. *Frontiers in Psychology, 11*, 1–8.

Chang, L. Y. C. (2012). *Cybercrime in the Greater China Region: Regulatory responses and crime prevention across the Taiwan Strait*. Edward Elgar Publishing.

Chang, L. Y. C. (2017). Cybercrime and cyber security in ASEAN. In J. Liu, M. Travers, & L. Y. C. Chang (Eds.), *Comparative criminology in Asia*. Springer.

Department of Census and Statistics. (2020). *Statistical website of Sri Lanka*. Available at: http://www.statistics.gov.lk.

Eaint Thet Su. (2019). Zawgyi to unicode: The big switch. *Frontier Myanmar*. Available at: https://www.frontiermyanmar.net/en/zawgyi-to-unicode-the-big-switch/.

Franzke, A. S., Bechmann, A., Zimmer, M., Ess, C., & the Association of Internet Researchers. (2020). *Internet research: Ethical guidelines 3.0*. Available at: https://aoir.org/reports/ethics3.pdf.

Ke, H., & Lee, L. (2020). *How China's infodemic spreads to Taiwan and Southeast Asia*. Doblethink Lab.

Liu, J., Trevers, M., & Chang, L. Y. C. (Eds.). (2017). *Comparative criminology in Asia*. Springer.

Luong, T. H., Phan, D. H., Chu, V. D., Nguyen, V. Q., Le, K. T., & Hoang, L. T. (2019). Understanding cybercrimes in Vietnam: From leading-point provisions to legislative system and law enforcement. *International Journal of Cyber Criminology, 13*(2), 290–308.

National Crime Records Bureau (NCRB). (2017). *National Crime Records Bureau Flyer 2017*. Available at: https://ncrb.gov.in/sites/default/files/ncrbFlyer2017.pdf.

National Crime Records Bureau (NCRB). (2019). *Crime in India 2019*. Ministry of Home Affairs.

OECD. (2001). *Understanding the digital divide*. OECD.

Philippine Statistics Authority. (2020). *Inventory of statistical standards in the Philippines*. Available at: https://psa.gov.ph/ISSiP/methodologies-and-procedures.

Sri Lanka Police. (2020). *Crime statistics*. Available at: https://www.police.lk/index.php/item/138.

Thayer, C. (2010). Political legitimacy in Vietnam: Challenge and response. *Politics & Policy, 38*(3), 423–444.

Thayer, C. (2014). The apparatus of authoritarian rule in Vietnam. In J. London (Ed.), *Politics in contemporary Vietnam: Party, state, and authority relations.* Springer.

Trong, V. N. (2020). Cybercrime in Vietnam: An analysis based on routine activity theory. *International Journal of Cyber Criminology, 14*(1), 156–173.

United Nations Economic and Social Council. (2015). *Statistical Commission—Report on the forty sixth session.* United Nations.

Završnik, A. (2018). *Big data, crime and social control.* Routledge.

22

The Ethics of Web Crawling and Web Scraping in Cybercrime Research: Navigating Issues of Consent, Privacy, and Other Potential Harms Associated with Automated Data Collection

Russell Brewer, Bryce Westlake, Tahlia Hart, and Omar Arauza

Introduction

Over the past three decades, the internet has become an increasingly attractive location for conducting social science research (Askitas & Zimmermann, 2015; Hooley et al., 2012). Two driving forces are the

R. Brewer
School of Social Sciences, University of Adelaide, Adelaide, SA, Australia
e-mail: russell.brewer@adelaide.edu.au

B. Westlake (✉) · O. Arauza
Department of Justice Studies, San Jose State University, San Jose, CA, USA
e-mail: bryce.westlake@sjsu.edu

O. Arauza
e-mail: omar.arauza@sjsu.edu

T. Hart
College of Business Government and Law, Flinders University, Adelaide, SA, Australia
e-mail: tahlia.hart@flinders.edu.au

© The Author(s), under exclusive license to Springer Nature Switzerland AG 2021
A. Lavorgna and T. J. Holt (eds.), *Researching Cybercrimes*,
https://doi.org/10.1007/978-3-030-74837-1_22

abundance of quality data available (personal information, communications, videos, images, and other data) and the ease at which such data can be accessed. As the volume of data available online increases, researchers have turned to automated data collection tools. These include web crawlers (a process also known as mirroring), which systematically browses (i.e., crawls) and indexes various web pages (Olston & Najork, 2010) and web scrapers, which access and download large volumes of data from websites based on user-defined criteria (Thomas & Mathur, 2019)—see, for instance, Chapters 3, 8, 10, and 11. In recent years, the number of studies that have used software integrating both web crawlers and web scrapers (automated collection software, hereafter) has increased, as is the degree of sophistication and creative means by which these technologies have been deployed (see Chapters 8 and 10 for an overview of these developments). The rapid rise in their use has meant that guidelines for their ethical operation have been slow to develop and adapt.

The deployment of automated software by researchers (in criminology and beyond) has given rise to debates over ethical concerns surrounding informed consent, privacy, and other risks and potential harms. These concerns arise because of the automated nature of the data collection process, including decisions made by programmers and researchers, as well as inconsistent approaches taken by institutional human research ethics committees. While some scholars have made progress toward identifying and addressing said ethical dilemmas in psychiatry (Sidhu & Srinivasraghavan, 2016; Silva et al., 2017), psychology (Harlow & Oswald, 2016; Landers et al., 2016), and social work (Bent-Goodley, 2007; McAuliffe, 2005; Millstein, 2000), criminology has been slow to identify, acknowledge, and respond to these issues, as well as tackle more discipline-specific concerns. Some early pioneering criminological work (e.g., Décary-Hétu & Aldridge, 2015; Martin & Christin, 2016; Pastrana et al., 2018) has identified and acknowledged some of the ethical dilemmas facing specific key online research environments (such as cryptomarkets and web forums), but have not fully considered other criminological contexts. While this work has been instrumental in setting the scene, we suggest that taking a holistic view of the criminological domains within which automated collection software operates can provide a fuller understanding of the suite of ethical challenges. Identifying and addressing said challenges can serve to guide future applied research endeavors.

In this chapter, we aim to raise awareness among criminological researchers about the ethical challenges associated with automated collection software, which will be accomplished in two parts. First, we detail the extent and contexts within which automated software have been deployed within the field of criminology, which are useful in drawing out the unique contexts and ethical challenges facing the discipline. Notably, we demonstrate that the data collected by researchers often do not involve human subjects, or when they do, tend to involve experiences of criminality and/or victimization that ultimately require specific and due consideration. Second, we chronicle and critically engage with the ethical challenges confronting criminological researchers utilizing said software. In doing so, we argue that such data collection practices need not be unethical, provided special care is taken by the researcher to acknowledge and explicitly address the complexities surrounding consent, privacy, and a myriad of other potential harms (to subjects, websites, and researchers). We conclude by drawing together the key points emerging from the discussion to offer practical recommendations that we anticipate will provide researchers a path forward when navigating this burgeoning, yet challenging, terrain.

The Use of Automated Collection Software in Criminology

Criminologists have used automated software to collect data from myriad sources, emanating from both the surface and deep/dark web. This has included personal websites and blogs, social media, video streaming platforms, web forums, chat rooms, online marketplaces (both licit and illicit), and peer-to-peer networks. The data collected can be broadly classified into four types—media files, goods and services bought and sold online, digital communications regarding the commission of crimes, and experiences of victimization—and have been used to study a vast array of criminological phenomena.

First, the internet has transformed the way that *media files* are distributed and consumed. In some instances, the media is being distributed illegally (e.g., copyright infringement) or contains graphic content (e.g., child sexual abuse material [CSAM]). This has led criminologists to use automated software to investigate topics such as the impact of piracy on book sales (Hardy et al., 2014), the distribution of pirated (copyrighted) content (Décary-Hétu et al., 2014), the validity of anti-piracy tools on YouTube (Jacques et al., 2018), the automated identification of fake news videos (García-Retuerta et al., 2019), and the analysis of CSAM (Fournier et al., 2014; Kusz & Bouchard, 2020; Shavitt & Zilberman, 2013; Westlake et al., 2012, 2017).

Second, the global reach of the internet has facilitated an explosion of digital marketplaces—which has yielded unprecedented information about *goods and services (licit and illicit) that are being bought and sold online*. Researchers have leveraged automated software to find and collect vendor and transaction-based data on the sale of legal and illegal items through Darknet cryptomarkets and on the surface web. This has, for example, included credit cards (Bulakh & Gupta, 2015), drugs and precursor chemicals (Broadhurst et al., 2020; Cunliffe et al., 2017; Demant, Munksgaard, & Houborg, 2018; Demant, Munksgaard, Décary-Hétu, et al., 2018; Frank & Mikhaylov, 2020; Hayes et al., 2018; Paquet-Clouston et al., 2018), protected wildlife (Hansen et al., 2012; Xu et al., 2020), malware (Broadhurst et al., 2018), and other forms of contraband (Barrera et al., 2019; Broadhurst et al., 2020; Décary-Hétu & Quessy-Doré, 2017).

Third, the internet is often used to discuss the *commission of crimes or to incite others to engage in crime*. Criminologists have collected user-based data, including communications between users, to better understand the role of cyberspace in facilitating crime. This has included examining web forums for illicit, radical, sentiment (Mei & Frank, 2015; Scrivens et al., 2019) and violent agendas (Bouchard et al., 2014), collecting social media posts to study religious bigotry (Gata & Bayhaqy, 2020; Ozalp et al., 2020) predict real-world threats and security requirements (Subramaniyaswamy et al., 2017), and better understand the social mores of offending (Lyu et al., 2020). Other social media for social mores of movie piracy (Lyu et al., 2020). Automated collection software has also been used to explore the sharing of information on how to commit cyberattacks (Crosignani et al., 2020; Décary-Hétu & Dupont, 2013; Macdonald et al., 2015; Pastrana et al., 2018). Finally, software has been used to monitor malicious websites on the dark web (Pannu et al., 2018) and gather intelligence on organized crime's human trafficking recruitment (McAlister, 2015).

Fourth, the internet provides an opportunity for people to discuss their witnessing, or opinion, of crime and share their *experiences of victimization*. This information is important for understanding previous crime (Keyvanpour et al., 2011), informing the public, and preventing future crime. To explore this, criminologists have used automated software to collect, primarily, text-based descriptions on social media. From this, they have explored the discourse around media from cellular phones, dash cams, and law enforcement body cams (Pitman et al., 2019), sharing of potential scams or threats (Gorro et al., 2017), and experiences of, and responses to, crime, to predict future online bullying, harassment, and scams (Abbass et al., 2020).

Considered together, the preceding discussion illustrates the diversity of criminological studies leveraging automated collection software, both in terms of the data sources used, and the social phenomena explored. Critical appraisal of these studies, according to data type, reveals myriad ethical challenges, for which researchers must consider before data collection should commence. These are explained in further detail below.

Navigating the Ethical Minefield of Automated Data Collection in Criminology

Researchers within criminology, and indeed across other disciplines, are prone to using automated software for data collection purposes without due consideration, given there appears to be no clear ethical guidelines or regulations governing their use (Capriello & Rossi, 2013; Martin & Christin, 2016; Thelwall & Stuart, 2006). As a result, scholars have continually called for the development of consistent ethical guidelines (see further, Alim, 2013; Chiauzzi & Wicks, 2019; Gold & Latonero, 2018; Thelwall & Stuart, 2006). Without such guidance, researchers are expected to apply pre-existing institutional ethical (and legal) frameworks, which often fail to consider both technological advancements (Gold & Latonero, 2018; Thelwall & Stuart, 2006) and unique criminological contexts (Décary-Hétu & Aldridge, 2015). Further, responses by ethics committees may be influenced by their individual members' expertise and training rather than uniformed adherence to guidelines, whether they are directly relevant or not (McCann, 2016). These issues may raise concerns when proposing to use specialized technological tools in unique or novel settings and can result in the imposition of unnecessary or inappropriate restrictions that make the research unfeasible (Martin & Christin, 2016). Criminological researchers should not be deterred from using automated collection software for research, but do need to be cautious when approaching this method of data collection and also be informed about, and mitigate against, any potential risks or harms. These can overlap, but also diverge, depending on the types of data being collected. The following discussion engages with the principal issues arising from the criminological literature canvassed above and navigates the researcher through the ethical process, with particular emphasis on such emergent issues as consent, privacy, and potential harms that may arise.

The issue of informed consent (see also Chapters 16–20) is debated among researchers leveraging these technologies and is an issue arising from the software eliminating the need for researcher-subject interaction (see further, Décary-Hétu & Aldridge, 2015; Martin & Christin, 2016; Tsatsou, 2014). In offline research contexts, researchers are typically expected to obtain consent from human subjects to collect and analyze their data. However, since automated collection software extracts data that have previously been published online, and at a large scale, this process becomes problematic—regardless of the types of criminological data sourced by researchers. Without the fundamental interaction, human subjects associated with scraped data would not be able to consent. This bears out in practice as Alim (2014) found only 47% (n = 64) of surveyed multi-disciplinary researchers acquired consent for scraped user profile data. A closer examination of criminological articles reviewed in this chapter revealed that very few researchers explicitly addressed the issue of informed consent, or even flagged other ethical considerations associated with the data collection process. This may be due to ambiguity around whether data being collected by the automated software has been derived from a human subject. For example, some scholars have debated whether data automatically extracted from online sources (e.g., prices, reputation data extracted from digital marketplaces) should meet accepted definitions of human subjects (see Alim, 2013; Gold & Latonero, 2018; Solberg, 2010 for further treatment of these arguments). Moreover, the issue of "ownership" over data appearing online is complex, with Martin and Christin (2016) arguing that obtaining informed consent from one group to participate in the research (e.g., webmasters), does not extend to other parties who may also be entitled (e.g., a user posting to a forum about their experiences being victimized). Accordingly, the apparent lack of engagement by criminological researchers observed here, which are consistent with trends reported by Pastrana et al. (2018), may point to tacit acknowledgment of arguments in the field that it is appropriate to waive informed consent under certain conditions (Martin & Christin, 2016). These circumstances are complex and interwoven and are elaborated upon below.

Informed consent can be waived in instances where the anticipated benefits of the research outweigh any potential risks associated with the research (these risks are canvassed in detail below). Criminological studies, in particular, can produce considerable public benefit by providing crucial information that enhances understandings of the motivations driving certain criminal behaviors, such as the commission of hacking (Décary-Hétu & Dupont, 2013) and the inciting of extremist sentiment (Scrivens et al., 2017). Elsewhere, such studies have been used to identify key trends in the distribution of illicit drugs in digital marketplaces (Martin et al., 2018a, 2018b; Moeller et al., 2020) and CSAM (Joffres et al., 2011; Westlake & Frank, 2016; Westlake et al., 2011). To investigate such areas, there is often a need for stealthy crawling to avoid interfering with the natural behavior of subjects (see further, Soska & Christin, 2015). Whist studies involving limited disclosure or deception are often discouraged by institutional ethics committees, criminology has a long history of covert research, which have produced measurable benefits to public policy (Calvey, 2013; Décary-Hétu & Aldridge, 2015). As such, a criminological researcher looking to embark down such a path should be able to clearly articulate these benefits, while also being able to mitigate potential risks, particularly as they might relate to different data types.

Researchers seeking to waive consent need to ensure that their research activities will present a negligible or low risk of harm. This includes risk to the research subject, if one can reasonably be determined (e.g., users of a web forum, sellers/buyers on an e-commerce platform, those depicted within media files), as well as others who might be adversely affected by the research, such as website administrators and the website itself. Accordingly, researchers are typically required to consider and protect subject privacy, particularly when it pertains to the collection and storage of data, as well as in the reporting of results. However, ascertaining precisely what information appearing online should reasonably be considered in the "private" versus "public" domain is not necessarily straightforward and has attracted considerable scholarly debate (see further, Alim, 2014; Décary-Hétu & Aldridge, 2015; Solberg, 2010; Wilson et al., 2012). That is, there are various "public" fora online where a user has posted information online that is freely available for broader public consumption and therefore does not necessarily attract an expectation of privacy (e.g., Twitter). There are also domains that involve clear and identifiable "private" exchanges between individuals (e.g., direct messages). When it comes to collecting data online however, the separation between these two domains can quickly become blurred. For example, some digital marketplaces and web forums are not entirely "public," insofar as they require a user to first register as a member before access is granted—although registration may otherwise be free and open to anyone, without need for the researcher to compromise the website (Christin, 2013). Elsewhere, scholars have also drawn distinctions between online communities that have large memberships versus those that are only visible to a few members, arguing that the latter may assert a higher expectation of privacy (Martin & Christin,

2016). Accordingly, a researcher looking to employ automated collection software must carefully consider these contexts in order to draw conclusions about privacy in the online setting they wish to research. In guiding such decisions, some scholars have argued that assumptions about privacy should reflect and coincide with the norms of the community under study (Décary-Hétu & Aldridge, 2015; Martin & Christin, 2016; Pastrana et al., 2018; Turk et al., 2020).

Taking such a considered approach to privacy—before, but also during and after data collection has occurred—is vital to minimize any potential harms to subjects. The consolidation of a significant quantum of personal data has the potential to uncover associations or reveal subjects through collection of various information across different platforms. This can include data obtained through forums or social media, such as a list of contacts (or friends), the correspondence between parties, photographs, videos, "tags" and other metadata (Alim, 2013; Gold & Latonero, 2018). In circumstances where criminological researchers collect data pertaining to individuals who are desirable to law enforcement (e.g., users discussing the commission of a crime on web forums, those selling illicit items on cryptomarkets, and people sharing illicit media files), pressure could be applied to the researcher to provide such data. This could facilitate the arrest or prosecution of individuals (Israel, 2004; Martin & Christin, 2016) as well as other harms through instances of internet vigilantism (Chang, 2018). Elsewhere, the collection of personal data also presents a risk for victimization of new crimes—where any such information made publicly available could be used for spamming, phishing, and/or identity theft purposes (Giles et al., 2010; Menczer, 2011; Thelwall & Stuart, 2006). Finally, where scraped data could be analyzed, published, and subsequently read by and cause trauma to the subject, there is potential for re-victimization (Gueta et al., 2020). For example, in the examination of commonly experienced crimes and victimization on social media(Gorro et al., 2017), reproduction of profiles, photos, posts, and stories may be easily encountered by the victim or other individuals known to the victim. While the likelihood of such activities occurring is low given the expansive and global nature of web-based activities, this risk is nevertheless real and requires that the researcher approach with caution.

Given the potentially sensitive nature of personal data being scraped (regardless of data type), criminological researchers seeking to employ such methods must take several steps to minimize the potential for harm against subjects (e.g., those buying/selling items on digital marketplaces, posting comments or other media online, and even those persons contained within media files). This should be accomplished through a process of anonymizing individual outputs, avoiding analysis of identifiable information (Magdy et al., 2017; Xu et al., 2020), and securing the storage and transmission of any sensitive data (Tsatsou, 2014). This includes not only a subject's "user name" (where applicable), but also any other personal data (e.g., verbatim quotes, extracted biometric data) that might infer information back to a particular subject or even the source website (Décary-Hétu & Aldridge, 2015; Fussell, 2019). Practically, when researchers may not be able to strip all personal identifiers from data without compromising its useability (Israel, 2004), data should be reported on an aggregated level (Alim, 2014; Bouwman et al., 2013). This may prove particularly problematic for data sharing among researchers and in many cases will prohibit such practices. Furthermore, researchers must exercise care beyond the data collection process, and be attentive to data security, particularly as it pertains to data storage and processing procedures (Chiauzzi & Wicks, 2019; Magdy et al., 2017; Xu et al. 2020). To mitigate any potential harm, researchers are advised to maximize confidentiality and implement robust security safeguards, which include both strict access controls and data encryption (Alim, 2014; Bouwman et al., 2013; Gold & Latonero, 2018; Tsatsou, 2014). Finally, researchers need also be aware of any reporting requirements (e.g., being a mandatory reporter in a particular jurisdiction) and be mindful of those requirements prior to, during, and after data collection.

In addition to the potential harm against subjects, researchers seeking to collect data through the use of automated collection software must also be aware of the potential financial and technological harms to website administrators and the platforms themselves, and incorporate measures to mitigate against them. For example, to avoid overloading a server and preventing legitimate traffic from accessing a website (i.e., mimicking a DDoS attack, see further, Thewal & Stuart, 2006), or abusing the TOR network (see further, Christin, 2013), automated collection software should distribute their requests to servers in a measured way (Menczer, 2011). This could be accomplished by mimicking a single human accessing a website one page at a time. This will also limit potential "spider traps" for researchers (i.e., the web scraper becomes trapped in an infinite loop), which duplicate data and waste bandwidth (Menczer, 2011; Thelwall & Stuart, 2006). To combat against such risks, some websites actively employ tactics to set limits on the ways that automated collection software can function on a website, such as using CAPTCHA services (Pastrana et al., 2018) or articulating unenforceable advisory protocols that specify parameters around what information contained can (and cannot) be collected via automated collection software, through "Robots Exclusion Protocols" (robots.txt). This necessitates that the researcher(s) develop and implement internal protocols which dictate such aspects relating to automated collection software downloading, downloading priorities, server request rates, re-visiting, CAPTCHA bypass, and scraper politeness (Capriello & Rossi, 2013; Menczer, 2011). However, we agree with other scholars (e.g., Hand, 2018; Pastrana et al., 2018) who suggest that there may be situations where, after review, it might be justifiable to ignore such protocols—particularly when the benefits of the research outweigh the potential harms. As such, carefully considering the context within which a researcher encounters such protocols is fundamentally important in determining a path forward.

Criminological researchers employing automated collection software also need to be aware of, and mitigate against, unique risks to themselves (see also Chapters 23 and 24). Given the domain of study, data being collected could be both illegal and cause the researcher trauma. For example, the collection and analysis of media files containing graphic content, such as child sexual abuse (Latapy et al., 2013; Westlake & Bouchard, 2016a, 2016b), could cause psychological harm and open researchers up to criminal charges for accessing and possession. Elsewhere, the collection and analysis of textual depictions of heinous crimes or serious victimization could be distressing to the researcher(s) (Pitman et al., 2019; Xin & Cai, 2018). Prior to engaging in research of this nature, researchers need to mitigate against potential psychological harm by developing a study protocol. This would likely include taking care to separate personal electronic devices from data collection and analysis devices, requiring counseling for research team members, and determining how and when data will be analyzed within the department (e.g., office) to minimize accidental exposure to colleagues and students. To mitigate against potential dismissal or arrest, researchers should consult with ethics committees, departmental supervisors, and law enforcement about their research plan. In addition, there are situations where researchers may want to be discreet in their deployment of web scrapers. For example, researchers would be advised to not announce their intention to scrape data to the cryptomarkets, as doing so may impact the integrity of the data (e.g., changing buying and selling habits and biasing results), but also potentially put the researcher at risk, through possible reprisal (personal abuse, threats, physical or cyberattacks from site users) (Décary-Hétu & Aldridge, 2015; Holt et al., 2014; Martin & Christin, 2016). Similar risks are also present for data collected from other sources—including from websites where subjects correspond about the commission of crimes or about their personal victimization. Accordingly, researchers should be mindful of the context and circumstances before implementing such practices that disclose their information. While such practices as publishing a user-agent HTTP header to inform website administrators of the scraper's nature (i.e., by providing the scraper's name, version, and links to further information about the research project) have merit in some circumstances (see further, Menczer, 2011), the disclosure of such information could potentially put the research at risk and should be carefully considered.

It is also important to flag that researchers who engage in automated collection may, in certain situations, be subject to potential litigation, particularly in cases where the robots.txt protocol is ignored/misinterpreted, or the website's terms of service (TOS) forbid the harvesting of data (Alim, 2014; Giles et al., 2010; Gold & Latonero, 2018; Sun et al., 2010). Some criminologists have weighed in on this debate and suggested that TOS, particularly those appearing on illicit websites (e.g., criminal marketplaces), are not legally enforceable (see further, Martin & Christin, 2016). Elsewhere, scholars have debated whether the automated extraction of data that may be subject to copyright could present further risk of litigation (O'Reilly, 2007; Stokes, 2019). Given the multijurisdictional nature of legal proceedings, it is outside the scope of this chapter to provide researchers with resolute guidelines. In addition, it is difficult to provide specific advice to follow as legal aspects of data automatically collected are unclear, inconsistent, and difficult to interpret (Gold & Latonero, 2018; Landers et al., 2016). As a result, researchers should seek legal advice specific to their jurisdiction, as well as the context surrounding the website(s) and research endeavor(s) prior to data collection. However, from an ethical standpoint, scholars have argued that it can be permissible to breach TOS for research purposes, providing that the benefits of the research outweigh any potential harms (Freelon, 2018; Martin & Christin, 2016).

Beyond acknowledging and addressing any risks inherent in the research enterprise, a waiver of consent typically requires that attempts to do so would be impractical. Indeed, scholars have noted that obtaining informed consent using automated collection software is not only impractical, but often impossible (Tsatsou, 2014). Automated collection software typically seeks to obtain data for a full population (e.g., capturing all available data on a digital marketplace or web forum) as opposed to a more targeted sampling process. As such, the software extracts data for all users—whose true identities may be masked by avatars and pseudonyms, and who may be active on the website or long inactive. As such, researchers will typically not be in a position to obtain or collect reliable contact information for subjects under study before (or even after) the research is undertaken (Décary-Hétu & Aldridge, 2015).

This section has demonstrated that the use of automated collection software in criminological contexts is potentially rife with ethical challenges. Researchers need to thoroughly explore the ramifications of informed consent, particularly as it pertains to the type of data being collected and analyzed. Doing so requires a robust understanding of how subject privacy could be impacted by the research, and what protections will need to be implemented. Likewise, the investigation of criminal activity means that researchers need to fully understand and mitigate against the risks and potential harms, even if done unwittingly, that the research could pose to subjects, websites, and themselves. If due consideration is afforded in the ways we have outlined above, we argue that it is possible to use automated collection software in ethical and conscientious manners for criminological study.

Conclusion

Criminologists have successfully deployed automated collection software to identify and extract various types of data across numerous sources, to better understand phenomena such as terrorism, CSAM, illicit drug distribution, and hacking. Such data collection strategies enable innovative studies that afford global recruitment possibilities (Tsatsou, 2014), and can cluster data at an efficient speed and low cost (Tavani, 1999). At the same time, they can overcome deficiencies commonly associated with more traditional research methods, including low survey responses (Gök et al., 2015) and the need for researcher involvement and training (Gök et al., 2015; Landers et al., 2016). This chapter has shown that despite a proliferation in the use of such technologies, criminology has been slow to identify, acknowledge and respond to the unique ethical challenges confronting their use, and tackle discipline-specific concerns. This chapter elucidated and critically engaged with these ethical challenges, and in doing so, argued that such data collection practices need not be unethical, providing that special care is taken to explicitly address and justify matters pertaining to consent, and mitigation against risks and potential harms (to subjects, websites, and researchers).

While the use of automated collection software presents numerous ethical challenges that the researcher must consider, we close by stressing that it is not our intention to discourage criminologists from employing such data collection techniques. Rather, our aim in this chapter is to encourage researchers to acknowledge and engage with these tools in an ethical way and thus open the door to novel and fruitful means of better understanding various crime problems. It is our hope that the discussion and recommendations presented offer a useful path forward and will enhance consistency in, and understanding of, ethical practices.

References

Abbass, Z., Ali, Z., Ali, M., Akbar, B., & Saleem, A. (2020). A framework to predict social crime through Twitter tweets by using machine learning. *2020 IEEE 14th International Conference on Semantic Computing (ICSC)*, 363–368.

Alim, S. (2013). Automated data extraction from online social network profiles: Unique ethical challenges for researchers. *International Journal of Virtual Communities and Social Networking (IJVCSN), 5*(4), 24–42.

Alim, S. (2014). An initial exploration of ethical research practices regarding automated data extraction from online social media user profiles. *First Monday, 19*(7).

Askitas, N., & Zimmermann, K. F. (2015). The Internet as a data source for advancement in social sciences. *International Journal of Manpower, 36*(1), 2–12.

Barrera, V., Malm, A., Décary-Hétu, D., & Munksgaard, R. (2019). Size and scope of the tobacco trade on the darkweb. *Global Crime, 20*(1), 26–44.

Bent-Goodley, T. B. (2007). Teaching social work students to resolve ethical dilemmas in domestic violence. *Journal of Teaching in Social Work, 27*(1–2), 73–88.

Bouchard, M., Joffres, K., & Frank, R. (2014). Preliminary analytical considerations in designing a terrorism and extremism online network extractor. In V. Mago & V. Dabbaghian (Eds.), *Computational models of complex systems* (pp. 171–184). Springer.

Bouwman, H., de Reuver, M., Heerschap, N., & Verkasalo, H. (2013). Opportunities and problems with automated data collection via smartphones. *Mobile Media & Communication, 1*(1), 63–68.

Bulakh, V., & Gupta, M. (2015). Characterizing credit card black markets on the web. *Proceedings of the 24th International Conference on World Wide Web*, 1435–1440.

Broadhurst, R., Ball, M., & Jiang, C. (2020). Availability of COVID-19 related products on Tor darknet markets. *Statistical Bulletin, no. 24*. Canberra: Australian Institute of Criminology.

Broadhurst, R., Ball, M., & Trivedi, H. (2020). Fentanyl availability on darknet markets. *Trends & issues in crime and criminal justice, no. 590*. Canberra: Australian Institute of Criminology.

Broadhurst, R., Lord, D., Maxim, D., Woodford-Smith, H., Johnston, C., Chung, H.W., et al. (2018). Malware trends on Darknet crypto-markets: Research review. *ANU Cybercrime Observatory*. Canberra.

Calvey, D. (2013). Covert ethnography in criminology: A submerged yet creative tradition. *Current Issues in Criminal Justice, 25*(1), 541–550.

Capriello, A., & Rossi, P. (2013). Spidering scripts for opinion monitoring. In H. Rahman & I. Ramos (Eds.), *Ethical data mining applications for socio-economic development*. IGI Global.

Chang, L. Y. C. (2018). Internet vigilantism co-production of security and compliance in the digital age. In Brewer R. (Ed.), *criminal justice and regulation revisited: Essays in honour of Peter Grabosky*. Routledge.

Chiauzzi, E., & Wicks, P. (2019). Digital trespass: Ethical and terms-of-use violations by researchers accessing data from an online patient community. *Journal of Medical Internet Research, 21*(2).

Christin, N. (2013). Traveling the Silk Road: A measurement analysis of a large anonymous online marketplace. *Proceedings of the 22nd International Conference on World Wide Web. International World Wide Web Conferences Steering Committee, 213–224.*

Crosignani, M., Macchiavelli, M., & Silva, A. F. (2020). Pirates without borders: The propagation of cyberattacks through firms' supply chains. *SSRN Electronic Journal*.

Cunliffe, J., Martin, J., Décary-Hétu, D., & Aldridge, J. (2017). An island apart? Risks and prices in the Australian cryptomarket drug trade. *The International Journal of Drug Policy, 50*, 64–73.

Décary-Hétu, D., & Aldridge, J. (2015). Sifting through the net: Monitoring of online offenders by researchers. *European Review of Organised Crime, 2*(2), 122–141.

Décary-Hétu, D., & Dupont, B. (2013). Reputation in a dark network of online criminals. *Global Crime, 14*(2–3), 175–196.

Décary-Hétu, D., & Quessy-Doré, O. (2017). Are repeat buyers in cryptomarkets loyal customers? Repeat business between dyads of cryptomarket vendors and users. *American Behavioral Scientist, 61*(11), 1341–1357.

Décary-Hétu, D., Dupont, B., & Fortin, F. (2014). Policing the hackers by hacking them: Studying online deviants in irc chat rooms. In A. J. Masys (Ed.), *Networks and network analysis for defence and security*. Springer.

Demant, J., Munksgaard, R., & Houborg, E. (2018). Personal use, social supply or redistribution? Cryptomarket demand on Silk Road 2 and Agora. *Trends in Organized Crime, 21*(1), 42–61.

Demant, J., Munksgaard, R., Décary-Hétu, D., & Aldridge, J. (2018). Going local on a global platform: A critical analysis of the transformative potential of cryptomarkets for organized illicit drug crime. *International Criminal Justice Review, 28*(3), 255–274.

Fournier, R., Cholez, T., Latapy, M., Chrisment, I., Magnien, C., Festor, O., & Daniloff, I. (2014). Comparing pedophile activity in different P2P systems. *Social Sciences, 3*(3), 314–325.

Frank, R., & Mikhaylov, A. (2020). Beyond the 'Silk Road': Assessing illicit drug marketplaces on the public web. In M. A. Tayebi., U. Glässer, & D. B. Skillicorn (Eds.), *Open source intelligence and cyber crime*. Springer.

Freelon, D. (2018). Computational research in the post-API Age. *Political Communication, 35*(4), 665–668.

Fussell, S. (2019). You no longer own your face. *The Atlantic*. Available at: https://www.theatlantic.com/technology/archive/2019/06/universit ies-record-students-campuses-research/592537/.

García-Retuerta, D., Bartolomé, Á., Chamoso, P., & Corchado, J. M. (2019). Counter-terrorism video analysis using hash-based algorithms. *Algorithms, 12*(5).

Gata, W., & Bayhaqy, A. (2020). Analysis sentiment about islamophobia when Christchurch attack on social media. *Telkomnika, 18*(4), 1819–1827.

Giles, C., Sun, Y., & Councill, I. (2010). Measuring the web crawler ethics. *Proceedings of the 19th International Conference on World Wide Web*, 1101–1102.

Gök, A., Waterworth, A., & Shapira, P. (2015). Use of web mining in studying innovation. *Scientometrics, 102*(1), 653–671.

Gold, Z., & Latonero, M. (2018). Robots welcome? Ethical and legal consideration for web crawling and scraping. *Washington Journal for Law, Technology & Arts, 13*(3), 275–312.

Gorro, K. D., Sabellano, M. J. G., Maderazo, C. V., Ceniza, A. M., & Gorro, K. (2017). Exploring Facebook for sharing crime experiences using selenium and support vector machine. *Proceedings of the 2017 International Conference on Information Technology*, 218–222.

Gueta, K., Eytan, S., & Yakimov, P. (2020). Between healing and revictimization: The experience of public self-disclosure of sexual assault and its perceived effect on recovery. *Psychology of Violence, 10*(6), 626–637.

Hand, D. J. (2018). Aspects of data ethics in a changing world: Where are we now? *Big Data, 6*(3), 176–190.

Hansen, A. L. S., Li, A., Joly, D., Mekaru, S., & Brownstein, J. S. (2012). Digital surveillance: A novel approach to monitoring the illegal wildlife trade. *PLoS ONE, 7*(12), e51156.

Hardy, W., Krawczyk, M., & Tyrowicz, J. (2014). Internet piracy and book sales: A field experiment. *Faculty of Economic Sciences, University of Warsaw Working Papers, 23*(140), 1–22.

Harlow, L. L., & Oswald, F. L. (2016). Big data in psychology: Introduction to the special issue. *Psychological Methods, 21*(4), 447–457.

Hayes, D. R., Cappa, F., & Cardon, J. (2018). A framework for more effective dark web marketplace investigations. *Information (basel), 9*(8), 186–204.

Holt T. J., Smirnova, O., Strumsky, D., & Kilger, M. (2014). Advancing research on hackers through social network data. In C. D. Marcum & G. E. Higgins (Eds.), *Social networking as a criminal enterprise.* Taylor Francis.

Hooley, T., Marriott, J., & Wellens, J. (2012). *What is online research? Using the Internet for social science research.* Bloomsbury Academic.

Israel, M. (2004). Strictly confidential? Integrity and the disclosure of criminological and socio-legal research. *British Journal of Criminology, 44*(5), 715–740.

Jacques, S., Garstka, K., Hviid, M., & Street, J. (2018). An empirical study of the use of automated anti-piracy systems and their consequences for cultural diversity. *SCRIPT-Ed, 15*(2), 277–312.

Joffres, K., Bouchard, M., Frank, R., & Westlake, B. G. (2011). Strategies to disrupt online child pornography networks. *2011 European Intelligence and Security Informatics Conference,* 163–170. IEEE.

Keyvanpour, M. R., Javideh, M., & Ebrahimi, M. R. (2011). Detecting and investigating crime by means of data mining: A general crime matching framework. *Procedia Computer Science, 3,* 872–880.

Kusz, J., & Bouchard, M. (2020). Nymphet or lolita? A gender analysis of online child pornography websites. *Deviant Behavior, 41*(6), 805–813.

Landers, R., Brusso, R., Cavanaugh, K., & Collmus, A. (2016). A primer on theory-driven web scraping: Automatic extraction of big data from the Internet for use in psychological research. *Psychological Methods, 21*(4), 475–492.

Latapy, M., Magnien, C., & Fournier, R. (2013). Quantifying paedophile activity in a large P2P system. *Information Processing & Management, 49*(1), 248–263.

Lyu, Y., Xie, J., & Xie, B. (2020). The attitudes of Chinese online users towards movie piracy: A content analysis. In A. Sundqvist, G. Berget, J. Nolin, & K. Skjerdingstad (Eds.), *Sustainable digital communities* (pp. 169–185). Springer.

Macdonald, M., Frank, R., Mei, J., & Monk, B. (2015). Identifying digital threats in a hacker web forum. *Proceedings of the 2015 IEEE/ACM International Conference on Advances in Social Networks Analysis and Mining 2015*, 926–933.

Magdy, W., Elkhatib, Y., Tyson, G., Joglekar, S., Sastry, N. (2017). Fake it till you make it: Fishing for catfishes. *Proceedings of the 2017 IEEE/ACM International Conference on Advances in Social Networks Analysis and Mining 2017*, 497–504.

Martin, J., & Christin, N. (2016). Ethics in cryptomarket research. *International Journal of Drug Policy, 35*, 84–91.

Martin, J., Cunliffe, J., Décary-Hétu, D., & Aldridge, J. (2018a). Effect of restricting the legal supply of prescription opioids on buying through online illicit marketplaces: Interrupted time series analysis. *British Medical Journal, 361*, 1–7.

Martin, J., Cunliffe, J. D., Décary-Hétu, D., & Aldridge, J. (2018b). The international darknet drugs trade-a regional analysis of cryptomarkets. *Australasian Policing, 10*(3), 25–29.

McAlister, R. (2015). Webscraping as an investigation tool to identify potential human trafficking operations in Romania. *Proceedings of the ACM Web Science Conference*, 1–2.

McAuliffe, D. (2005). I'm still standing: Impacts and consequences of ethical dilemmas for social workers in direct practice. *Journal of Social Work Values and Ethics, 2*(1), 1–10.

McCann, M. (2016). The smartphones study: An analysis of disciplinary differences in research ethics committee responses to phone app-based automated data collection. *European Journal of Public Health, 26*(suppl. 1).

Mei, J., & Frank, R. (2015). Sentiment crawling: Extremist content collection through a sentiment analysis guided web-crawler. *IEEE/ACM International Conference on Advances in Social Networks Analysis and Mining (ASONAM), 2015*, 1024–1027.

Menczer, F. (2011). Web crawling. In B. Liu (Ed.), *Web data mining: Exploring hyperlinks, contents, and usage data, 311 Data-Centric Systems and Applications* (pp. 311–362). Springer.

Millstein, K. (2000). Confidentiality in direct social-work practice: Inevitable challenges and ethical dilemmas. *Families in Society, 81*(3), 270–282.

Moeller, K., Munksgaard, R., & Demant, J. (2020). Illicit drug prices and quantity discounts: A comparison between a cryptomarket, social media, and police data. *The International Journal of Drug Policy* (online first).

Olston, C., & Najork, M. (2010). Web crawling. *Foundations and Trends in Information Retrieval, 4*(3), 175–246.

O'Reilly, S. (2007). Nominative fair use and Internet aggregators: Copyright and trademark challenges posed by bots, web crawlers and screen-scraping technologies. *Loyola Consumer Law Review, 19*(3), 273–288.

Ozalp, S., Williams, M. L., Burnap, P., Liu, H., & Mostafa, M. (2020). Antisemitism on Twitter: Collective efficacy and the role of community organisations in challenging online hate speech. *Social Media + Society, 6*(2), 1–20.

Pannu, M., Kay, I., & Harris, D. (2018). Using dark web crawler to uncover suspicious and malicious websites. *International Conference on Applied Human Factors and Ergonomics* (pp. 108–115). Springer.

Paquet-Clouston, M., Décary-Hétu, D., & Morselli, C. (2018). Assessing market competition and vendors' size and scope on AlphaBay. *International Journal of Drug Policy, 54*, 87–98.

Pastrana, S., Thomas, D. R., Hutchings, A., & Clayton, R. (2018). Crimebb: Enabling cybercrime research on underground forums at scale. *Proceedings of the 2018 World Wide Web Conference*, 1845–1854.

Pitman, B., Ralph, A. M., Camacho, J., & Monk-Turner, E. (2019). Social media users' interpretations of the Sandra Bland arrest video. *Race and Justice, 9*(4), 479–497.

Scrivens, R., Davies, G., & Frank, R. (2017). Searching for signs of extremism on the web: An introduction to Sentiment-based Identification of Radical Authors. *Behavioral Sciences of Terrorism and Political Aggression, 10*(1), 39–59.

Scrivens, R., Gaudette, T., Davies, G., & Frank, R. (2019). Searching for extremist content online using the dark crawler and sentiment analysis. In M. Deflem & D. M. D Silva (Eds.), *Methods of criminology and criminal justice research (Sociology of Crime, Law and Deviance)*. Emerald Publishing Limited.

Shavitt, Y., & Zilberman, N. (2013). On the presence of child sex abuse in BitTorrent networks. *IEEE Internet Computing, 17*(3), 60–66.

Sidhu, N., & Srinivasraghavan, J. (2016). Ethics and medical practice: Why psychiatry is unique. *Indian Journal of Psychiatry, 58*(6), 199–202.

Silva, E., Till, A., & Adshead, G. (2017). Ethical dilemmas in psychiatry: When teams disagree. *Bjpsych Advances, 23*(4), 231–239.

Solberg, L. B. (2010). Data mining on Facebook: A free space for researchers or an IRB nightmare? *University of Illinois Journal of Law, Technology & Policy, 2*, 311–343.

Soska, K., & Christin, N. (2015). Measuring the longitudinal evolution of the online anonymous marketplace ecosystem. *In USENIX Security Symposium (USENIX Security)*, 33–48.

Stokes, S. (2019). *Digital copyright: Law and practice.* Hart Publishing.

Sun, Y., Councill, I. G., & Giles, C. L. (2010). The ethicality of web crawlers. *2010 IEEE/WIC/ACM International Conference on Web Intelligence and Intelligent Agent Technology, 1*, 668–675.

Subramaniyaswamy, V., Logesh, R., Abejith, M., Umasankar, S., & Umamakeswari, A. (2017). Sentiment analysis of tweets for estimating criticality and security of events. *Journal of Organizational and End User Computing, 29*(4), 51–71.

Tavani, H. T. (1999). Informational privacy, data mining, and the Internet. *Ethics and Information Technology, 1*(2), 137–145.

Thelwall, M., & Stuart, D. (2006). Web crawling ethics revisited: Cost, privacy, and denial of service. *Journal of the American Society for Information Science and Technology, 57*(13), 1771–1779.

Thomas, D. M., & Mathur, S. (2019). Data analysis by web scraping using python. *2019 3rd International conference on Electronics, Communication and Aerospace Technology (ICECA)*, 450–454.

Tsatsou, P. (2014). Research and the Internet: Fast-growing Internet research. In P. Tsatsou (Ed.), *Internet studies: Past, present and future directions.* Ashgate Publishing Ltd.

Turk, K., Pastrana, S., & Collier, B. (2020). A tight scrape: Methodological approaches to cybercrime research data collection in adversarial environments. *Workshop on Actors in Cybercrime Operations*, 428–437.

Westlake, B. G., & Bouchard, M. (2016a). Criminal careers in cyberspace: Examining website failure within child exploitation networks. *Justice Quarterly, 33*(7), 1154–1181.

Westlake, B. G., & Bouchard, M. (2016b). Liking and hyperlinking: Examining reciprocity and diversity in online child exploitation network communities. *Social Science Research, 59*, 23–36.

Westlake, B. G., Bouchard, M., & Frank, R. (2011). Finding the key players in online child exploitation networks. *Policy and Internet, 3*(2), 1–32.

Westlake, B. G., Bouchard, M., & Frank, R. (2012). Comparing methods for detecting child exploitation content online. *European Intelligence and Security Informatics Conference*, 156–163.

Westlake, B. G., Bouchard, M., & Frank, R. (2017). Assessing the validity of automated webcrawlers as data collection tools to investigate online child sexual exploitation. *Sexual Abuse, 29*(7), 685–708.

Westlake, B. G., & Frank, R. (2016). Seeing the forest through the trees: Identifying key players in online child sexual exploitation distribution networks. In T. Holt (Ed.), *Cybercrime through an interdisciplinary lens*. New York: Routledge.

Wilson, R. E., Gosling, S. D., & Graham, L. T. (2012). A review of Facebook research in the social sciences. *Perspectives on Psychological Science, 7*(3), 203–220.

Xin, Y., & Cai, T. (2018). Child trafficking in China: Evidence from sentencing documents. *International Journal of Population Studies, 4*(2), 1–10.

Xu, Q., Cai, M., & Mackey, T. K. (2020). The illegal wildlife digital market: An analysis of Chinese wildlife marketing and sale on Facebook. *Environmental Conservation, 47*(3), 206–212.

23

Does the Institution Have a Plan for That? Researcher Safety and the Ethics of Institutional Responsibility

Ashley A. Mattheis and Ashton Kingdon

Introduction

Over the past few years, discussions about the ethics of researcher safety—inclusive of mental and emotional health, and privacy and security online—have been increasing among academic researchers. These ethical considerations are particularly pertinent for cybercrime researchers investigating sensitive topics such as online hate crimes, criminal subcultures and violent extremism. Progressively, academic research has focused on the mental and emotional well-being and self-care of researchers studying violent online phenomena and the potential harms

A. A. Mattheis (✉)
Department of Communication, University of North
Carolina at Chapel Hill, Chapel Hill, NC, USA
e-mail: mattheis@email.unc.edu

A. Kingdon
University of Southampton, Southampton, UK
e-mail: A.R.Kingdon@soton.ac.uk

457

for those who disseminate their findings publicly online, including doxing and networked harassment (Gill et al., 2020; Kumar & Cavallaro, 2018; Marwick et al., 2016; Winter, 2019). This approach often positions ethical responsibility for researcher safety as an individual issue. It is, however, also essential to examine the ethical responsibility of institutions, in both ensuring ethical conduct of research, and researcher safety online.

Institutional ethical responsibility for research currently focuses on researcher compliance with ethical practices as defined by laws and disciplinary norms. Regardless of the discipline, researchers need to consider ethics in all aspects of their studies, from project planning, data collection and analysis, and the dissemination and potential publishing of their results. It is the individual responsibility of the researcher to utilize ethical guidance in line with their institutions' Research Ethics Committee/Institutional Review Board and any relevant legislation applicable to their jurisdiction. Despite an increase in literature concerning researchers' ethics-related responsibility, far less attention has been given to the ways in which institutions are responsible for ensuring the safety and ethical conduct of their researchers, specifically in relation to investigations conducted online. Taking this into consideration, the purpose of this chapter is to outline institutional responsibility in relation to online research, with a specific focus on researcher safety including awareness, planning, and support, as fundamental aspects for conducting ethical research online. While the chapter utilizes the authors' own personal experiences of studying extremism online as case studies, the potential solutions and recommendations outlined are designed to be relevant to all researchers conducting online studies on sensitive areas.

Background

One of the key issues with current ethical practices for research is that the conventional guidance sometimes does not translate directly to those examining online environments. The various technologies that enable cybercrime research also pose layers of ethical intricacy, stemming from the rapid pace at which internet-based technology, practices and phenomenon can change. For example, de-platforming—the banning of individuals or shutting down of accounts that host extremist material—may cause researchers to migrate from platforms deemed "conventional" for data gathering, to more controversial and risky sites (Conway, 2020; Hutchinson et al., 2017; Rogers, 2020; Squire, 2019). Social media and online research often takes place in commercially orientated environments, governed by less than transparent corporate communication paradigms and variable forms of nation state regulation. Such factors essentially short-circuit standard institutional review protocols for the following reasons: The distinctions between "public" and "private" data are unclear; the processes for providing and obtaining informed consent may not be possible; and the platform migration of group participants may require revisions of ethical consideration (Fossheim & Ingreid, 2015; Hogan, 2008; Rambukkana, 2019). Hence, the ethical guidance that has traditionally focused on the duties of the individual to protect themselves, the institution and research participants from harm can become increasingly insufficient when research is being conducted online (Ess, 2013).

At the time of writing, there exists only one set of guidelines that addresses ethical internet research from a transnational and transdisciplinary perspective—*The Internet Research: Ethical Guidelines 3.0* (IRE 3.0). The IRE 3.0 was produced by the Association of Internet Researchers (AOIR)—an international, transdisciplinary group of researchers of the internet and online phenomena—and builds on previous versions (IRE 1.0, 2002; IRE 2.0, 2012). The guidelines are intended for use by researchers, students, review board members and technical developers who face ethical concerns during their research, or have an interest in internet research ethics. In addition to the IRE 3.0, Marwick et al. (2016) produced a report for Data and Society (an independent non-profit research organization) titled *Best Practices for Conducting Research Online*, which provides a set of suggested practices for institutions and institutional actors. Significantly, both sets of guidelines emphasize that institutions should view researchers as vulnerable populations. This emphasis draws attention to the fact that many institutions are not aware of the ethical implications and potential harms for researchers attendant in online research, partly because institutional ethical frameworks primarily focus on research subjects as the "vulnerable" populations.

In online contexts, a primary source of researcher vulnerability stems from the specific targeting of researchers—often because of their identity (ethnicity, religion, gender, sexual identity, political identity and so on)—by bad actors using tactics such as doxing (publishing an individual's private, personal information online), death and rape threats, and public harassment campaigns on social media (Douglas, 2016; Linabary & Corple, 2019; Lumsden & Morgan, 2017; Riley, 2020). These tactics are used as strategic forms of abuse and harassment in efforts to silence any researchers that attackers may disagree with, or who have been identified as "enemies". Literature has indicated that online harassment campaigns can cause psychological and emotional harm, with broad-ranging effects on researcher's personal mental health, and in relation to their careers (Gill et al., 2020; Olsen & LaPoe, 2018; Veletsianos, 2016). One of the consequences of such campaigns is that they often force researchers to stop using online platforms to publicly engage their research and disseminate findings. Although intended to be a solution to harm, the disengagement from online platforms can have negative effects on researchers' careers, given the increasingly important role social media play in connection to multiple audiences, developing collegial networks, building collaborations, as well as seeking funding and employment. Additionally, dealing with harassment campaigns may cause delays for researchers in meeting deadlines or progression milestones, which, in turn, can directly impact career progress and self-esteem.

A further key source of vulnerability for researchers studying online phenomena stems from the data collection that frequently takes place on encrypted social media platforms such as Telegram, and the Dark Web. When conducting research on these platforms, burner phones and laptops are often required to protect the researchers' privacy and security. Likewise, a system titled Onion Routing is often employed so that researchers can collect information anonymously by redirecting data through a circuit of encrypted connections by hiding their own IP address. The software used to access this system is called The Onion Router, but is better known by its abbreviation Tor. Researchers working in these contexts typically develop a set of false online identities to engage in dangerous spaces or communities where they might otherwise be prohibited from entering (Ebner, 2020). Researchers are also encouraged to employ Virtual Private Networks (VPN's) to improve their online security and mask their identities and IP addresses, thus bringing to light additional ethical concerns not found in traditional research (Coomber, 2002; Wall & Williams, 2013). Taking this into account, when undertaking research into encrypted and Dark Web platforms, it is essential for researchers to read and familiarize themselves with the rules and regulations for collecting and storing security-sensitive research material within their country.

A lack of institutional awareness regarding some of the ethical considerations that accompany online research, particularly in the realm of cybercrime and online extremism, can translate to a lack of institutional support for researchers. Consequently, institutional guidelines for ethical and responsible research often do not provide the much-needed support or guidance for researchers undertaking certain, more sensitive online studies. This is particularly apparent for researchers undertaking secondary data analysis of social media content, using Open Source Intelligence (OSINT) to derive new insights from public data or analysing ideological documents such as far right pre-attack manifestos, as they are often not required to be submitted for ethical board review (Denzin, 2018; Kopp et al., 2016). This poses a structural problem in addressing ethical quandaries posed for online research in projects that are not designed using traditional methods (such as ethnography or interviews) that always require institutional or review board approval.

Institutional Responsibility in Context: Researching Extremism Online

For researchers studying extremist and terrorist groups and organizations online, the ethical considerations and responsibilities are magnified. Researchers have to work to keep their institution, participants and themselves safe, work with potentially traumatizing material and within online communities subject to legal restrictions, as well as avoid potential attacks from bad actors in the communities that they research.

This section of the chapter provides an exploration of institutional ethical concerns stemming from the authors' experiences of lack of institutional awareness in the United States (see also Chapter 21) and the implications of legal compliance and Cybersecurity in the United Kingdom (see also Chapter 20) in relation to their research into Right-Wing Extremists online. While institutional awareness and legal implications are specific to local contexts, they do share common features with other researchers' experiences globally, particularly in relation to the broad issues of researcher well-being and operational safety.

Awareness of Researcher Risk and Well-being

Academic researchers of radicalization, extremism and terrorism online must be aware of the potential risks of their research, which include the potential for targeted attacks by bad actors such as networked harassment, doxing and violent personal threats (Marwick et al., 2016). It is also advisable that researchers develop strategies for working with high volumes of violent content, which is increasingly in video formats including live stream mass attacks and murders (Winter, 2019). Moreover, it is important for researchers to provide empirical academic support for their research while attempting not to amplify extreme messaging and propaganda (Franzke et al., 2020). Institutional awareness of these issues is limited, in large part because of the relatively recent advent of online research, and the quickly changing pace of online phenomena and practices (Marwick et al., 2016). Moreover, the study of radicalization, extremism and terrorism is a multi-disciplinary endeavour, rather than a structured discipline, which consequently limits the visibility of the project as a field of study from an institutional perspective (Berger, 2019).

A lack of institutional awareness of the ethical issues and unique problems faced by researchers in this field often leads to a lack of support that researchers need to conduct their work. This lack of support is two-pronged, encompassing both ethical review processes and institutional supports such as services and policies. As such, institutional unawareness transposes ethical and employer responsibility for safe and ethical research into a poorly defined obligation for individual researchers. This transposition is problematic from multiple perspectives, but most crucially in relation to research compliance and occupational health and safety.

Research compliance is often addressed institutionally through ethical review, what in the United States is called Institutional Review Board (IRB), approvals processes. Researchers studying radicalization, extremism and terrorism online may face difficulty with research ethics reviews and approvals if appropriately knowledgeable faculty and administrators cannot be found to review their projects. The US context for institutional ethical review provides a particularly useful example of such problems because institutional awareness of research risk is largely associated with structures and systems developed for offline studies and focuses on protecting research subjects, not researchers (Franzke et al., 2020). Online research generally, and the study of radicalization, extremism and terrorism specifically, confound these standard frameworks (Franzke et al., 2020). Moreover, the risks posed by these areas of study are also experienced by researchers performing online text-based research that typically does not require ethical/institutional review board approval because the studies do not engage who would traditionally be defined as participants. Thus, the study of radicalization, extremism and terrorism online emphasizes that the scope of research compliance concerns is changing in ways that need to be addressed by developing institutional policies and procedures specifically for online research.

Occupational health and safety in "traditional" research frames often encompass "safe handling" of chemical materials or proper handling of lab equipment and specimens. However, in the context of research on radicalization, extremism and terrorism, occupational health and safety encompasses a different set of potential harms including interlocutor threats or criminal activity (Blee, 2003). This set of potential harms broadens further in online research contexts and has only recently been publicly discussed in academic and scholarly milieus. Anecdotal evidence from researchers suggests a myriad of mental health and emotional effects including anxiety, Post Traumatic Stress Disorder (PTSD), loss of appetite and sleep, that can harm researchers (Winter, 2019). These effects are tied to regular exposure to hateful, violent and traumatizing materials.

Along with the effects of difficult and traumatic research materials, online harassment of researchers is a particular problem (Marwick et al., 2016). Women and minority researchers report regular harassment by and concerns about harassment from extremist actors (Massanari, 2018). Occupational supports (essentially workplace accommodations) needed to address the impacts of such research include institutionally provided access to specialized trauma counselling, specific hardware and software to support safe research online, and legal support in cases of networked harassment and online threats. Along with these supports, mechanisms to request extensions to research timeframes or career milestones because of trauma or harassment are essential to support researchers' work.

Crucially, institutional invisibility is foundational to a lack of accessible support services and related policies. Guidelines, best practices and policies related to conducting safe research online including how to protect personal data, how to maintain mental and emotional well-being when studying violent and abusive materials, and explicit steps researchers should take if they are subject to trolling, networked harassment campaigns, or online threats and abuse are rarely available directly from institutions. These types of information for researchers, where they exist, have largely been produced by external entities such as foundations or consortia engaged with the topic of online research and journalism. As such, they provide much-needed information, but that information is not clearly delineated in relation to specific institutional policies and compliance requirements. Furthermore, attempts to connect to existing structures and administrative supports at institutions can result in frustration and difficulty for researchers as institutional actors are unlikely to be aware of these problems or potential supports available to address them. Important research may be abandoned because of lack of institutional support. Furthermore, because networked harassment attacks are more often targeted towards women and minority researchers, a lacking framework for timeline extensions may further disproportionate impacts already experienced by minority populations in academia. Thus, problems of researcher safety online cannot be solely addressed by individual researchers. From the perspectives of research compliance and occupational health and safety, institutional supports are necessary to ensure sustainable and successful research online, particularly for studies of radicalization, extremism and terrorism.

Researcher Legal Compliance and Operational Security

Academic researchers conducting studies into terrorism, extremism or radicalization need to be aware of any potential legal issues that may result from their chosen methodological processes. The UK provides an exemplar of this topic given its stringent legislation and compliance requirements regarding extremist and terrorist content. The UK Terrorism Acts of 2000 and 2006 introduced offences relating directly to the collection, transmission and distribution of content deemed "likely" to be useful to an individual preparing or committing an act of terrorism. Likewise, the 2015 Counter-Terrorism and Security Act placed safeguards around material that is considered to aid radicalization (Durham University, 2020). Thus, existing legislation makes it profusely clear that the possession or downloading of terrorist or extremist material places researchers at risk of arrest, detention and potential prosecution (Reynolds, 2012). Such legislation also applies to data obtained from social media platforms, as it is presumed that extremist organizations seeking to radicalize and recruit will be including links to propaganda deemed to be in breach of the regulations. Thus, in theory, if researchers download or save content to their personal devices, they would then be considered in possession of terrorist or extremist material, and consequently in violation of UK counterterrorism regulations.

Despite stringent counterterrorism legislation, it is important to note that within the UK it is permissible to collect material associated with terrorism and extremism provided the person in question has a reasonable and justifiable reason for possession of such content, and academic research falls into this category. Nevertheless, researchers accessing such content should be conscious that some of the sites and platforms sensitive data is collected from could be subject to surveillance by the intelligence services and law enforcement, and that accessing these sites could lead to subsequent inquiries. Therefore, it is often recommended that before any research begins, all necessary channels within the researchers' institution are notified of said research, in written form, so there is a clear and transparent trail clearly stipulating that the researcher is not up to anything nefarious, but rather engaged in justifiable and worthy research; this is particularly important if the authorities were to become suspicious and contact the researcher or institution for questioning or clarification. It is also advisable that ethics review boards inform researchers that if they have any concerns that the proposed use of the material in their research may be breaching legislation, they contact legal services for advice.

Although the preceding challenges are rather subjective depending upon the individual and focus of research, a primary issue affecting all researchers engaging with any sort of toxic online community or phenomenon is that of cybersecurity. Researchers undertaking research into sensitive or ethically problematic areas should place particular attention to personal operational security, colloquially referred to as "opsec", and consider the use of the following cybersecurity tools. Firstly, any researchers that may be collecting data from Dark Web platforms will require the use of Tor, a system for anonymous information exchange via the easily downloadable onion browser which uses onion routing, a form of layered encryption where traffic is processed through at least three nodes, encrypted at each stage so that the sender and destination are unknown (Huang & Bashir, 2016). Essentially, Tor is used to browse the Web as well as its own dedicated sites which form the bulk of what is known as the Dark Web. While the functionality to do so is unique to Tor, the browser itself is a fork of the popular Firefox browser.

Research into extremism also frequently requires the creation of false identities, colloquially referred to as "sock puppets" which are often defined as an online identity used for purposes of deception (Yamak et al., 2018). However, it is important to note that sock puppets are not exclusively used in deceptive operations, but they are also important for privacy—protecting not only researchers, but also participants. When creating sock puppets there is a clear need to define your intent; you can choose to either create a fake persona, or an avatar that is obviously fake with the masked excuse of "opsec" as its origin. For both options, it is recommended to create content, add media, photos and videos, interact with others online in an authentic way, and create multiple social media profiles (Creps, 2018).

To protect anonymity, it is also advisable that researchers use VPN's which provide the user with an encrypted data link from the user's device to an off-site server from which access is gained to the internet at large. This protects and obscures the user's internet activity from third parties, including bad actors, who will only be able to see the VPN connection and not the broader internet access. Researchers may often choose to take further action to obscure their identity and whereabouts. Frequent measures include the utilization of dedicated hardware including burner laptops and phones which include no personal details and encrypted email. Despite the key ethical issues regarding cybersecurity being self-evident, they are currently not catered for by institutions, thus calling into question the need for support and guidance to be adopted. More stringent guidance on legal compliance and cybersecurity will help ensure researchers are more prepared before they undertake research into terrorism, extremism and radicalization, which, in turn, will help mitigate any potential risks resulting from exposure to extremist and terrorist content.

Conclusions and recommendations

As emerges from this chapter, institutional responsibility when it comes to online research is an important and topical issue. From an institutional perspective, the responsible conduct of research and research ethics ensure compliance with laws, rules for accreditation, funding guidelines, and generally agreed upon research norms (ACHRE, 1995; UNI, 2020). These drivers of institutional compliance do not incorporate online research problematics in clearly delineated ways. Research regarding online phenomena and the use of online data downloaded or scraped from websites and social media platforms is increasing at a rapid pace across a wide range of disciplines, and is being utilized in a variety of research methods (Hine, 2015). It is a question of when, rather than if, this area of study will become a compliance concern.

Researchers are increasingly using online mechanisms and social media platforms to publicly disseminate their research, including news interviews, podcasts and social media. This has become a practice of academic "branding" that in interdisciplinary fields such as extremism research can significantly impact researchers' career success. However, regular online participation increases the potential for networked harassment, a tactic particularly used against women and minority researchers (Marwick & Caplan, 2018; Massanari, 2018). In the light of this, institutions should consider ethical responsibility for researcher safety online through a lens of work equity, or as a civil rights issue, given that generalized advice to withdraw from online engagement may negatively impact the advancement and retention of marginalized researchers at higher rates.

We recommend that, at a minimum, institutions consider developing a better understanding of the problematics of online research in relation to responsible conduct, ethics and researcher safety. This includes taking a proactive stance addressing online research ethics and safety by developing and promoting briefs, guidelines and infographics that highlight institutional resources and contacts, ethical questions to pose in relation to online research, and researcher safety awareness inclusive of institutional guidelines and best practices. Additionally, institutions should hire or train Information Technology Support (ITS) personnel specifically to assist researchers with sourcing appropriate technology (hardware/software) and consider institutional purchasing programs for technology to assist in promoting safety and security practices that benefit both researchers and the institution. Developing and providing training for researchers about online security, how to handle networked harassment and ethical online research study design can provide substantial benefits for researchers, and the institution as a whole.

Guidelines relating to informed consent should include institutional responsibilities for ensuring researchers are informed of the risks specifically relating to online research (Marwick et al., 2016; Zimmer, 2010). Rather than suggesting researchers change topics, or avoid public exposure, focus should be placed on increasing access to training, support and equipment to offset potential harms. Given the potential dangers for researchers, if they are transparent about their identities or purpose in online communities, researchers may need to develop aliases, create sock puppet accounts and use burner devices and VPN's to mask any traceable information. Institutions should, therefore, develop specific guidelines for training researchers about how to safely conduct online research in line with their policies that incorporates a focus on the ethical use of identity and IP masking technologies, and the use of false identities online as a necessary and ethical component.

We also recommend that institutions leverage extant ethical research compliance processes to address these issues. This can be achieved by extending protocols and procedures to account for researcher safety, alongside planning for ethical approaches to proposed research projects that address the problems specific to online research. It would also be sensible for institutions to provide faculty and administrative reviewers with basic training in regard to online research, cybersecurity, Open Source Intelligence practices and a variety of web-data gathering methods (Kopp et al., 2016). In addition, reviewers and review boards should develop a generic understanding of the online tactics used by bad actors to attack and harass researchers.

Regularized compliance practices such as the Responsible Conduct of Research (RCR) training aimed at medical research could be adapted for online research and incorporate essential information about online research ethics and safety. Modules could encompass digital foot-print management, security practices, cybersecurity equipment including hardware and software, researcher health and well-being inclusive of trauma counselling and best practices, as well as institutional guidelines and ethical approaches to study design and methods. Materials developed for review processes and trainings should be widely distributed to researchers along with institution specific materials for researcher support including institutional contacts, programs, guidelines and services related to conduction ethical online research.

The discussion about researcher safety online has focused primarily on both the experience and responsibilities of individual researchers. Broadening the discussion to an institutional frame is necessary to address the roots as well as the symptoms of the issue. The proposed recommendations require institutional commitments and ongoing collaborative efforts engaging administrators and researchers to discuss, develop and adapt guidelines, practices and policies. The benefits to both researchers and institutions, we believe, are worth this long-term labour. This chapter, we hope, helps develop the discussion in this important direction.

References

Berger, J. M. (2019). *Researching violent extremism: The state of play.* Resolve Network.

Blee, K. (2003). *Inside organized racism: Women in the Hate Movement.* University of California Press.

Conway, M. (2020). Routing the extreme right: Challenges for social media platforms. *The RUSI Journal, 165*(1).

Coomber, R. (2002). Protecting our research subjects, our data and ourselves from respective prosecution, seizure, and summons/subpoena. *Addiction Research & Theory, 1*(1), 1–5.

Creps, J. (2018). *Creating an effective sock puppet for OSINT investigations.* Available at: https://jakecreps.com/2018/11/02/sock-puppets/.

Denzin, N. K. (2018). *The qualitative manifesto: A call to arms.* London: Routledge.

Douglas, D. M. (2016). Doxing: A conceptual analysis. *Ethics and Information Technology, 18*(1), 199–210.

Durham University. (2020). *Guidance on accessing sites relating to terrorism or violent extremism.* Available at: https://www.dur.ac.uk/research.innovation/governance/ethics/considerations/data/terroristmaterials/.

Ebner, J. (2020). *Going dark: The secret social lives of extremists.* Bloomsbury.

Ess, C. (2013). *Digital media ethics.* Cambridge: Polity.

Fossheim, H., & Ingreid. (2015). *Internet research ethics.* Available at: https://press.nordicopenaccess.no/index.php/noasp/catalog/view/3/1/9-1.

Franzke, A.S., Bechmann, A., Zimmer, M., Ess, C. & the Association of Internet Researchers (2020). *Internet research: Ethical Guidelines 3.0.* Available at: https://aoir.org/reports/ethics3.pdf.

Gill, P., Clemmow, C., Hetzel, F., Rottweiler, B., Salman, N., Van Der Vegt, I., Marchment, Z., Schumann, S., Zolghadriah, S., Schulten, N., Taylor, H, & Corner, E. (2020). Systematic review of mental health problems and violent extremism. *The Journal of Forensic Psychiatry & Psychology* (online first).

Huang, H. Y., & Bashir, M. (2016). The onion router: Understanding a privacy enhancing technology community. *Proceedings of the Association for Information Science and Technology, 53*(1), 1–10.

Hine, C. (2015). *Ethnography for the Internet: Embedded, embodied and everyday.* Bloomsbury.

Hogan, B. (2008). Analysing social networks via the Internet. In N. Fielding R. M. Lee, & G. Blank (Eds.), *The Sage handbook of online research methods.* Sage.

Hutchinson, J., Martin, F., & Sinpeng, A. (2017). Chasing ISIS: network power, distributed ethics and responsible social media research. In M. Zimmer & K. Kinder-Kurlanda (Eds.), *Internet research ethics for the social age.* Peter Lang.

Kopp, C., Layton, R., Gondal, I., & Sillitoe, J. (2016). Ethical considerations when using online datasets for research purposes. In R. Layton & P. A. Watters (Eds.), *Automating open source intelligence: Algorithms for OSINT.* Elsevier.

Kumar, S., & Cavallaro, L. (2018). Researcher self-care in emotionally demanding research: A proposed conceptual framework. *Qualitative Health Research, 28*(4), 648–658.

Linabary, J. R., & Corple, D. J. (2019). Privacy for whom? A feminist intervention in online research practice. *Information, Communication & Society, 22*(10), 1447–1463.

Lumsden, K., & Morgan, H. (2017). Media framing of trolling and online abuse: Silencing strategies, symbolic violence, and victim blaming. *Feminist Media Studies, 17*(6), 926–940.

Marwick, A., Blackwell, L., & Lo, K. (2016). *Best practices for conducting risky research and protecting yourself from online harassment.* Available at: https://datasociety.net/pubs/res/Best_Practices_for_Conducting_Risky_Research-Oct-2016.pdf.

Marwick, A., & Caplan, R. (2018). Drinking male tears: Language, the manosphere, and networked harassment. *Feminist Media Studies, 18*(4), 543–559.

Massanari, A. L. (2018). Rethinking research ethics, power, and the risk of visibility in the era of the "Alt-Right" gaze. *Social Media & Society, 1*(1), 1–9.

Olsen, C. C., & LaPoe, V. (2018). Combating the digital spiral of silence: academic activists versus social media trolls. In J. R. Vickery, & T. Everbach (Eds.), *Mediating misogyny: Gender, technology, and harassment.* Palgrave Macmillan.

Rambukkana, N. (2019). The politics of grey data: Digital methods, intimate proximity, and research ethics for work on the "Alt-Right." *Qualitative Inquiry, 25*(3), 312–323.

Reynolds, T. (2012). Ethical and legal issues surrounding academic research into online radicalisation: A UK experience. *Critical Studies on Terrorism, 5*(3), 499–513.

Riley, C.L. (2020). *Men, behaving badly.* Available at: https://members.tortoisemedia.com/2020/02/19/campus-justice-riley-day-two/content.html.

Rogers, R. (2020). Deplatforming: Following extreme internet celebrities to telegram and alternative social media. *European Journal of Communication, 1*(1), 1.

Squire, M. (2019). *Can Alt-Tech help the far right build an alternate internet?* Available at: https://www.fairobserver.com/business/technology/alt-tech-far-righ.

The Advisory Committee on Human Radiation Experiments (ACHRE). (1995). *Final report.* Available at: https://bioethicsarchive.georgetown.edu/achre/.

University of Northern Iowa. (2020). *IRB manual noncompliance.* Available at: https://rsp.uni.edu/irb-manual-noncompliance.

Veletsianos, G. (2016). *Social media in academia: Networked scholars.* Routledge.

Wall, D. S., & Williams, M. L. (2013). Policing cybercrime: Networked and social media technologies and the challenges for policing. *Policing and Society, 23*(4), 409–412.

Winter, C. (2019). *Researching jihadist propaganda: Access, interpretation, and trauma.* Resolve Network.

Yamak, Z., Saunier, J., & Vercouter, L. (2018). SocksCatch: Automatic detection and grouping of sockpuppets in social media. *Knowledge-Based Systems, 149*(1), 124–142.

Zimmer, M. (2010). *Is it ethical to harvest public Twitter accounts without consent?* Available at: https://www.michaelzimmer.org/2010/02/12/is-it-ethical-to-harvest-public-twitter-accounts-without-consent/.

24

Engaging with Incels: Reflexivity, Identity and the Female Cybercrime Ethnographic Researcher

Lisa Sugiura

Introduction

It is well established that cybercrime is a complex and diverse problem necessitating increased scholarly attention focused on technological offending and victimization (Holt & Bossler, 2015). While methodological and ethical limitations in undertaking empirical cybercrime research, such as the lack of generalizable population studies, reliance on data produced from official statistics, and potential bias and privacy connotations in data collected from virtual communities, have been acknowledged (Holt, 2007, 2010; Holt & Bossler, 2015; Holt et al., 2015), less attention has been afforded to personal challenges faced by the cybercrime researcher, which are intensified depending upon the context of the research and the degree of personal investment to the

L. Sugiura (✉)
Institute of Criminal Justice Studies,
University of Portsmouth, Portsmouth, UK
e-mail: lisa.sugiura@port.ac.uk

© The Author(s), under exclusive license to Springer Nature
Switzerland AG 2021
A. Lavorgna and T. J. Holt (eds.), *Researching Cybercrimes*,
https://doi.org/10.1007/978-3-030-74837-1_24

topic studied. There is also a paucity of authentic online ethnographical cybercrime research, whereby knowledge and understanding of a particular cybercrime or cyberdeviance has been achieved via in depth lived experiences of an online environment. Although the risks, ethical, and moral dilemmas, in particular the practical and personal safety limitations, presented to criminological ethnographic researchers have been considered at length (see Ferrell & Hamm, 1998; Maguire, 2000; Worley et al., 2016; Yates, 2006), there has been minimal application to cybercrime ethnographic research beyond cursory methodological discussion (Yar & Steinmetz, 2019), taking into account the specificities and new challenges arising from the online environment impacting upon the identity and safety of the cybercrime researcher. Drawing on my research within online incel (involuntary celibate) communities as a case study, this chapter employs a reflexive approach, considering some of these risks and dilemmas. The origin of incel goes back to 1993, when a Canadian female student—Alana—created a website to talk about their "Involuntary Celibacy Project." Here, incel was described as "anybody of any gender who was lonely, had never had sex or who hadn't had a relationship in a long time." However, the term has since been appropriated to exclude women, propagate misogyny, hate, and violence.

Reflexivity was crucial in order to reconcile the challenging situations I (as a female academic) often found myself in during the course of the research with self-identifying misogynists. Reflexivity, according to Davies (2008, p. 4), is defined as "a turning back on oneself, a process of self-reference." Roberts and Sanders (2005) assert that reflexivity is not a single phenomenon but embraces different forms impacting upon the research process during all its stages.

The chapter begins with a critical discussion about the reflexive literature and concepts of online identity, before moving on to my experiences and the safety measures I employed. Including managing my online presence and evaluating potential risks in the methods adopted prior to commencing the research, as well as the challenges navigating the misogynistic terrain during the study. These reflections are situated within the broader feminist literature addressing the risks of online harassment to female academics researching sensitive topics and women's precautionary methods to protect themselves offline. I also consider the challenges to my academic credibility that I experienced and envisaged as a result of divulging emotive sensibilities. The chapter concludes with some recommendations to support future research of this nature. Although there are risks and challenges to all researchers irrespective of gender, who engage with research subjects from abusive communities online, I nonetheless present tensions inherent to women undertaking such study. I further acknowledge the heightened risks and challenges associated with being transgender or from marginalized communities based on ethnicity or sexual orientation, however, these are outside the scope of this chapter and indeed my own experiences. The risks and challenges faced by female academics conducting online research are markedly different, as women are more acute to potential sexualized violence and harm due to routinely experiencing them in their everyday lives (Kelly, 1987).

Background

Reflexivity

With research there is an implicit assumption that researchers are investigating something outside of themselves, that the requisite knowledge is unattainable via introspective means (Davies, 2008). Yet there is a tension between a clear separation of the researcher and the research object, and the researcher inevitably having some connection with the research topic. Debates about reflexivity coincide with concerns regarding subjectivity and objectivity, and questions about what we as researchers bring to the studies we conduct and what do the participants and topics researched elicit within us, are well-versed in qualitative social research (Band-Winterstein et al., 2014). The qualitative researcher is not concerned with facts or truth, the focus is on the construction of interpretations and how such interpretations have arisen from participant's experiences (Ben-Ari & Enosh, 2011; Hertz, 1997; Mayan, 2009; see also Chapter 1). Research is co-constituted as meanings are explored within specific social contexts by both the participant and the researcher (Finlay, 2011; King & Horrocks, 2010). Reflexivity has been noted as a way to validate qualitative research and resolve the subjective tensions inherent within it, self-examination enables us as researchers to reconcile our understandings and life experiences with those of our participants who appear diametrically situated to ourselves (see also Chapters 25 and 26). Demographic differences between participants and researchers, such as gender, race or ethnicity, and age, have been highlighted as considerations impacting upon the need for reflexivity (Underwood et al., 2010). However, Band-Winterstein et al. (2014) suggest concentrating upon different world view perceptions, positions, and attitudes, particularly when researching sensitive topics. Engaging in sensitive research may evoke feelings of vulnerability in the participant by drawing to the surface repressed memories or traumatic events (Morse, 2010). Concurrently, researchers might be experiencing their own challenges relating to the sensitive topic, which reflexivity can assist with comprehending (Dickson-Swift et al., 2007). Both gender and opposing worldview perspectives played a role in my research and impacted upon the identity I constructed throughout the process.

Identity

In regard to identity, people might describe themselves in terms of their ethnicity, politics, sexuality, or religion, while others might defer to personality traits. According to Marwick (2013), identity can mean subjectivity, representation, or self-presentation and can relate to our individual personal identity or our social identity as a group member. The majority of research on online identity has focused on self-presentation (Baym, 2010; Boyd, 2010; Papacharissi, 2002; Wynn & Katz, 1997). In his influential work, *The Presentation of Self in Everyday Life*, Goffman (1959) considered how the presence of others—the audience—allows individuals to adjust and perfect their behavior, a technique he termed "impression management." Goffman was especially interested in how different types of setting shape this impression management or performances. Drawing on the analogy of the theater, Goffman delineated "front" and "back" stage regions for interaction performances. The "front" stage is a place where the performance is public and seen by many, and "backstage" where access is more controlled and limited

(1959, p. 113). A key proposition from this work is that people have both impressions that they give and those that they give off. The former entails impressions
the individual intended to divulge, while the latter are impressions that were not intended to be seen but were received by the audience, nonetheless. Online environments are acknowledged to provide users with the ability to present and perform multiple identities (Bullingham & Vasconcelos, 2013; Jenkins, 2010; Miller & Arnold, 2009). In their 2013 study applying Goffman's conceptual framework to blogger's presentation of selves, Bullingham and Vasconcelos (2013) found that individuals emphasized certain aspects about themselves while minimizing others, highlighting the opportunities for self-editing. Referred to as an "embellishment of self," Bullingham and Vasconcelos (2013) describe this process as a subtle type of persona adoption, particularly when people might not realize they are presenting different representations of themselves online. Due to limited identity cues available online as opposed to face-to-face interactions, the digital information we provide can be used by others to make inferences about us. For the online researcher, such interpretations have the capacity to affect how participants interact with us and our studies, and indeed, whether they will engage in the research at all.

Researching Misogynists

Incels

The process of reflexivity began when I first started considering researching incels. With my gender being the object of their vitriol, I recognized that aspect of myself directly fed into my motivations, assumptions, and interests into this community. It would be inaccurate to ignore the established ties I have with my research subjects and not appreciate the value lead reasons I had for engaging with incels. Along with the usual academic curiosity and drive in exploring a social phenomenon, I also had a morbid fascination in wanting to comprehend the hatred against part of my own identity.

The aim of the research was to study the development of misogynistic online incel movements and their impacts, with the primary objectives of ascertaining the individual aspects and group dynamics of incel communities and exploring how and why people join them. Incels' hatred is often directed at feminists, they believe that feminism is to blame for societal issues, that feminism is unnecessary because equality has been achieved, and that advances of women's equality are detrimental to men (Jhaver et al., 2018). Incels are not an isolated phenomenon; they are part of larger backlash against feminism propelled by what has been defined as the "manosphere" (Marwick & Caplan, 2018), which involves groups of men including Men's Rights Activists (MRAs), Pick up Artists (PUAs), and Men Going Their Own Way (MGTOW), who are connected by a belief that feminine values have corrupted society and men need to retaliate against misandrist culture to preserve their very survival. Although the main interests of each group differ, their common anti-woman philosophy creates a unified identity. Among these, incels are considered particularly dangerous since their association with a series of killings committed in Isla Vista (2014), Oregon (2015), Edmonton (2016), Aztec (2017), Parkland (2018), Toronto (2018), and Tallahassee (2018).

Incels ascribe to an ideology named "the blackpill," which (allegedly) has evolutionary biology influences. Essentially incels are heteronormatively situated and believe in hypergamy, that it is within women's inherent nature to seek high status [male]partners, and therefore, women are solely driven by looks and wealth. In becoming "blackpilled", incels embrace fatalism—that they are subhuman zeta males who will never attract the women they want, and so turn their backs upon women and societal values regarding relationships and equality, which often manifests as hatred. To be an incel is to embrace a lonely existence, there is little positive about this identity, which begs the question as to why anyone would want to identify as one.

The insight the blackpill supposedly provides seems key. Although the blackpill is formulated and spread via online incel communities, it crosses over with the red pill ideology permeating other groups within the manosphere and the alt right. The red pill draws on the film the Matrix, whereby the protagonist, Neo, is presented with a choice about taking the red pill or the blue pill. If he takes the blue pill, he can continue to live blissfully unaware of the façade he is currently living in, whereas if he takes the red pill, he will know the truth about the world. In the manosphere, the red pill is a rejection of the blue pill—whereby conventional media sources and banalities about romantic relationships are unquestionably accepted. Incels consider the vast majority of the population to be bluepilled and criticize bluepillers for their lack of original thought and adhering to comforting well-versed tropes supporting common worldview. Hence, the redpill represents a counterculture challenging prevailing social norms, focusing on physical attraction and sexual success. Not all redpillers are incels and not all incels are redpillers; however, all incels are blackpilled, which is essentially the nihilistic, version of the red pill.

Research Design

The methodology utilized in this research was two-fold. Firstly, in order to explore how incel cultures and networks are enabling misogynistic extremist and violent behaviors online, an online ethnographic approach—netnography (Kozinets, 2010, 2020)—was utilized. The methods involved non-participant observation and thematic analysis of publicly available forum discussions and videos, comments on social media platforms—Reddit (e.g., the incels withouthate and Braincels[1] subreddits) 4chan, Twitter, YouTube—frequented by incels and men's rights activists, and dedicated incel sites such as Incels.co and Incelistan.net (now Yourenotalone.co). For this part of the study, there was no direct interaction with users/posters, but rather time was spent on the sites and I did not need to become a member of any communities to access data. Relevant posts were collected via manual means—that is, copying and pasting, analyzing memes and videos on YouTube chosen by starting with search terms such as "blackpill" and then using the recommended feature to explore how the platform's algorithms promote

---

[1] This was the most popular subreddit for incels after r/incels was banned, gaining 169,000 followers by April 2018. This was banned in September 2019 after posts were made condoning murder.

such content, and the software NodeXL, which obtains tweets over the previous seven days.

Secondly the research involved qualitative semi-structured interviews with self-identified incels. Participants were identified from convenience sampling and were all men. There are some women who identify as incel, who are known as femcels, and although the research was focused on incels not specifically male incels, it was only men who were interviewed. It is worth noting that this might be due to the spaces in which I was targeting, being less inclusive of female incels, as well as the potential reluctance of female incels to be interviewed.

Participants were identified via incel Reddit threads and by searching Reddit for phrases like "I am/I used to be an incel" and were messaged via Reddit's messaging service to invite them to interview. As users have pseudonyms, it is often unclear as to what gender they are, and I chose potential interviewees based on their profiles and contributions to the forums, rather than aiming for men solely. Nevertheless, all the participants stated that they were men. Interviews were conducted online via e-mail or private messages on Reddit. Although interviewees were offered the option of telephone or Skype interviews, none took up these modes of interview, preferring instead to remain within the online spaces they usually inhabit. Highlighting the significance of interacting with participants in the places they usually frequent and are comfortable in, and of them being able to preserve their anonymity. For those who undertook email interviews, there is the suggestion they were less concerned about anonymity than those who wanted to remain on Reddit and talk there. Those interviewees on email were happy to divulge what seemed to be their actual first names, as opposed to those on Reddit who remained masked by their reddit usernames.

Despite increased identity issues and risks, in using a multi-method approach, I felt it was important to directly engage with incels and observe their online interactions, in order to obtain an informed understanding of the culture and their reasons for joining the community. Furthermore, previous scholarly work had not involved speaking with incels themselves. Ethical approval was obtained from the University Faculty Ethics Committee, with particular regard to the sensitivity of the topic, the usual ethical considerations of obtaining informed consent from the interview participants and protection of confidentiality and anonymity, and issues specific to online research regarding the use of publicly available data.

Online Identity: Pre-Empting the Risks as a Woman

Realizing that my researcher identity could impact upon my ability to access incel communities and prevent participants from speaking with me, and potentially put myself at risk of abuse, I reviewed what I present online, in order to pre-emptively protect myself and the integrity of the research. Interestingly, I realized that much of what I already permitted on public spaces online—the "front stage"—was already unconsciously influenced by my identity as a woman. This was more than a purely deliberate choice to project a given identity. Taking into consideration the community I would be engaging with I edited facets of myself to present a persona that I thought would be appropriate to them (Goffman, 1959), but previously unbeknownst to me I had also been unintentionally policing my behavior in what I divulged and engaged with, and restricted information about myself online. These actions were beyond usual online presentations of self or measures to prevent becoming a victim of a cybercrime such as fraud, rather my actions had been unwittingly influenced by my lived experience as a woman and internalizing established precautionary measures to avoid interpersonal victimization. While I appreciate my knowledge informed from researching cybercrime topics, and awareness of the myriad sexual harassment leveled at women on social media (Banet-Weiser & Miltner, 2016; Henry & Powell, 2015; Jane, 2017; Mantilla, 2013; Megarry, 2014) would also play a part in my behavior online, I was also subconsciously motivated by the threat of everyday violence that women have been conditioned with (Stanko, 1990). The digital safety measures that women employ which impact upon their online interactions both consciously and subconsciously are much like the security measures they undertake in their everyday offline activities and encounters (Sugiura & Smith, 2020), which include walking with keys between fingers when out alone at night, or not daring to walking alone at night in the first instance. The digital keys between the fingers I undertook include the careful curation of public social media posts so as to not be too provocative, deliberation over whether to like/retweet feminist related materials/stories, elevated privacy measures, and the careful in/exclusion of aspects of my identity in social media bios. Nonetheless, I did actively choose to retain my feminist identity in the public domain and on various social media accounts, which I realized would present me as the worst kind of woman in the eyes of the incel community. There were certain moral principles and aspects of my identity I was not willing to sacrifice or conceal for this research. I also realized that even if I had removed this information, it could probably be deduced from previous work not exempt from public access.

Given the misogynistic and abusive nature of the incel community, there were increased prospects of me experiencing online harassment. In engaging with these narratives my work aligns with other scholars who have voiced concerns about their experiences with harassment related to their work in this field (see Barlow & Awan, 2016; Chess & Shaw, 2015). As Chess and Shaw note, while research on online harassment increases awareness, it also exposes scholars to the very harassment they are studying. As a feminist academic, I am fortunate that I have yet to experience online harassment, mere "fuck you"s as received from incels not wanting to be interviewed, aside. However, the onus is on the word *yet*. As someone who undertakes research in the field of gender abuse, I anticipate it and pessimistically view it as inevitable. The normalization of women being harassed online is expressed by Amanda Hess (2014), who in referring to her own abuse, claimed there is nothing exceptional about her experience rather "it just makes me a woman with an internet connection." The suggestion is that women should expect to be on the receiving end of harassment online one day, particularly as there are groups who hate women based on homogenizing predetermined biological notions about gender. Furthermore, as evidenced through the tragic events in places such as Isla Vista, etc. this hate has real implications for physical acts of violence.

However, I am also aware of my privilege as someone who benefits from hegemonic assumptions about my race and class, and so I am less vulnerable to harassment than other women (Citron, 2014). The majority of conversations around online harassment, particularly in the #MeToo era, center on the experiences of middle-class white women (Fileborn & Loney-Howes, 2019), therefore I feel visible and supported in this regard, but acknowledge heightened risks and abuse for women who already experience greater marginalization due to ethnicity or class (as well as sexuality, ableism, religion).

As a woman speaking with misogynists, extra care and attention was taken with my questions and responses during the interviews. I was relieved that my offer to conduct the interviews via Skype was not taken up by any participants. However, one participant did ask to speak via Facebook, while another requested to follow my personal Instagram account, I felt uncomfortable with these requests as I view these platforms for personal rather than professional use. Conscious of upsetting the participants, and potentially having them withdraw from the research, I diverted the Facebook request via a subtle suggestion as to email being a more efficient way to conduct the interview, and ignored the Instagram follow rather than refuse it. These situations also necessitate the importance of considering the publicness of social media profiles in the first instance.

Having been careful about what information was publicly available about myself so as to mitigate any negative preconceptions about me that could impact upon the research, I was nevertheless open about my being a feminist, which could have been a "red-flag" to participants. Yet, this was not directly challenged or addressed by any of the interviewees. The majority of people who chose to engage with me and participate in the research were polite and respectful when doing so. Nevertheless, I would be surprised if I were not googled before participants agreed to be interviewed, and so my worldview would have been easily discoverable. In most of the discussions, there were no comments aimed personally at myself, although there were a dearth of anti-feminist and misogynistic statements made, such as "women get away with a pussy pass," "feminism is cancer," "women are selfish, shallow, vile creatures," and "I despise women, they are vermin." Whether or not it was the overt intention of participants, these comments had the effect of making me feel uncomfortable and reminding me that this is their opinion of me.

Direct insults are unnecessary, when I am automatically included within generalized abuse against women.

There were also some actions that suggested being attributed to having prior knowledge about me. One participant, in particular, was very keen to impress his knowledge of studies to evidence the validity of the black-pill ideology on me, to the point where he continued to ask whether these had changed my view, throughout and beyond the interview. Naturally, I had not entered into the interview expressing a specific viewpoint and so the assumption is that any inference as to my perspective had been obtained elsewhere. This also made me question the motives of why this participant had agreed to be interviewed. What would they be achieving in changing my opinion though this process? The notion of "turning" a feminist did gain notoriety in the case of Cassie Jaye, who later became a poster girl for men's rights.[2] Incels are keen to downplay any association with radicalization or ideological grooming, however, a tactic they employ is to draw on "scientific" studies and evidence, to try and validate and further their ideology. To diffuse the situation, I provided non-committal responses that did not require me to be inauthentic but would not encourage further provocations.

I also had to avoid the role of reluctant counselor on more than one occasion while speaking with incels, who in divulging the experiences which led them to identify as incel would seek sympathetic responses from me. In these situations, I grappled with various tensions, not only did I have to be careful not to cross the boundary, as in any research setting (Dickson-Swift et al., 2008) but I was acutely aware a suitable reaction acknowledging their personal revelations was expected from me. Many members of the incel community are vulnerable; most suffer from mental illnesses such as depression, anxiety, and suicidal ideation, and so require compassion and kindness. However, this does not justify their worldview, which is harmful not only to society but to incels themselves, as it promotes a culture of emotional self-flagellation and resentment. In some discussions I also felt like I was obliged to apologize on behalf of my

---

[2] In the 2016 US documentary the Red Pill, the director—Cassie Jaye, charts her journey from feminist, who considered Mens Rights Activist (MRA) groups to be hate movements, to anti-feminist MRA supporter. Jaye is frequently cited by both MRAs and Incels, to further their contention that feminism is flawed.

gender, as unsurprisingly women had caused distress (whether directly or indirectly) resulting in the assumption of the incel identity. On this latter point, this was not something I was prepared to do; instead, I would express appreciation at the honesty of the accounts without expressing emotion or opinion. Exiting the research environment was also challenging with some participants wanting to continue conversations, implying they found them cathartic. After expressing gratitude for their time, I had to be firm and state the end of the interview meant this was the end of our contact. Again, the significance of protecting personal social media accounts did not escape me.

Navigating the Misogynistic Terrain

Throughout the data collection process, I continually engaged in self-reflection to build my resilience when engaging with content on incel sites. Often presented as satire and cultural in-jokes (Zillman, 1983), incels converse via images, memes, and forum posts, which involve the severe denigration of women, men who are successful with women ("Chads", the alpha males), and "cucked" men (those who support women and feminism). To be offended by these materials is to be an outsider, a "normie" who does not appreciate the gag and does not belong in the community. After initially attempting to separate my personal and researcher identities, in a bid not to take the content personally, I realized this was erroneous. It was necessary to situate myself fully into the research, observing and absorbing incel culture, to fully appreciate the forms it takes, the group dynamics and the impacts, which may or may not be intended. The misogynistic words, images, and memes in themselves were not deeply hurtful to me. Encountering sexism in various forms, from the seemingly micro and banal such as "cat calling" to the serious acts of violence like rape, is common experience for women and girls, what scholar Liz Kelly pertinently refers to as the "continuum of sexual violence" (Kelly, 1987, p. 46) However, the continuous interaction and accumulation of the hateful materials did inevitably lead to me being emotionally affected on occasion, but recognizing and giving voice to this helped me to process it. Ironically, the same defense that incels employ to condone their hatred—humor—also provided me with an armor to the ridiculously misogynistic content I had to contend with. Materials concerning roasties (where women's labia are compared to a roast beef sandwich) and the dogpill (where women are described as engaging in bestiality rather than having sex with incels) ended up being so ludicrous, that any initial shock or revulsion was diffused and ended up having comedic effect, not at women's expense, but at the sheer absurdity of incel's imagination. This is not to be flippant about the sexualized harms propagated, further contributing to the normalization of violence against women; rather this was a coping mechanism to offset the personal impacts upon myself.

Ethnography usually requires the researcher to spend continuous and extensive amounts of time in the research environment (Atkinson & Hammersley, 2007). However, to preserve my mental health and sanity, I would take regular breaks away from the communities and the research. The problem is that due to my searches and accounts I follow on different social media platforms, I would still receive incel-related updates, and so switching off from the research often meant refraining from personal social media use too. This was necessary for me to do to escape the intense rape culture fostered within incel communities. The thread r/Incels was shut down in 2017 for promoting violence and advocating rape (Bell, 2017); despite this incels have been able to continue disseminating their pro-rape views, even on mainstream platforms such as Twitter, as this example posted on 07/02/20 demonstrates:

The solution to incels is, they should find the "courage" to rape. If the female species don't want incels to rape, then the female species should "learn" to help out just say twenty percent and do some chasing.[3] Described as "socio-cultural support rape" by Powell and Henry in their book *Sexual Violence in a Digital Age* (Powell & Henry, 2017, p. 94), forms of rape promoting and violence against women content are facilitated by digital technologies. Researchers working in this field have highlighted the reach and pervasiveness of these technologies in our everyday lives, which in turn increases the normalization and support

---

[3] This Tweet and indeed the incel account that tweeted it has since been removed by Twitter.

of sexual violence (Jane, 2017; Mantilla, 2013; Megarry, 2014; Powell & Henry, 2017).

Academic Credibility

There is a tension facing academics: On the one side, there is the expectation of a professional online persona while personal characteristics are kept private, yet the professional and the personal often overlap meaning that more information is exposed than we would like, and this requires us to cultivate the identity we do want to divulge. Although in this regard there are some presentations of our online academic identity that are beyond our control. Having been encouraged to advertise my research interests on my university profile, I have received unsolicited correspondence questioning my credibility as an academic from Men's Rights Activists (MRAs) in researching polarizing topics, with the presumption that I will be taking a biased perspective on them. As a woman it is inconceivable that I would be able to undertake rigorous research on male-dominated groups. As this information is out in the public sphere this gives others license to contact me under the justification of freedom of speech and, when I do not engage, am accused of being averse to rigorous debate.

In 1967 Howard Becker compelled researchers of deviance to interrogate "whose side are we on?" (Becker, 1967). Highlighting the inevitability that personal and political sensibilities will affect research and impact upon where our sympathies lie. Naturally this calls into question whether a balanced perspective of the research can be presented. Becker suggested how the scoping of the research can be used as a disclaimer, to justify why one perspective is used over another. Becker's paper centered on the sympathies of the researcher toward their research participants and how this could contaminate any objectivity, rather than vested sympathies and indeed personal interests, opposite to one's participants, and how this positioning could be subject to criticisms of bias. The potential for the credibility and impartiality of researchers studying groups with actions or beliefs that are the polar opposite of theirs to be questioned, requires more debate.

Conclusion

Throughout this chapter, I have sought to connect my own personal reflections and experiences while undertaking ethnographic cybercrime research into a sensitive topic, with the broader scholarship of reflexivity, identity, and feminism. While this chapter is not intended to deter anyone from engaging in sensitive research positioning researchers in challenging and morally compromising situations, it does present some cautionary insights necessary of consideration. These are further accentuated by the online research environment, which in being all pervasive within our everyday lives makes it difficult to withdraw from the topic, and the issues faced by researchers having to contend with their personal and professional identities being blurred via the digital information available about them to their research participants.

I have demonstrated through this chapter how I navigated the challenges and risks to myself, both internally and externally, while researching the incel community. In writing this chapter I hold the apprehension that divulging personal emotive reflections might undermine my scholarly reputation, as there is the potential for others to question my credibility as an impartial academic. Nevertheless, I argue that this approach has enabled me to have a broader understanding of my research and the internal and external structural forces that influence it. There are also implications for others undertaking research on groups online that might potentially pose risks to them. Although I have discussed how I limited my online identity, both intentionally and unintentionally, it is certainly not my aim to encourage any silencing or minimizing of behaviors of marginalized groups, which already occurs on far too frequent a basis both on and offline, rather I hope to encourage resilience and rigorousness in undertaking online research. Core recommendations involve the curation of one's online public identity (where possible), stepping back from the research environment when it becomes too toxic and emotionally exhausting, conducting one on one research on platforms suitable for both the participant and the researcher, protecting one's values but also not jeopardizing the research, and providing limited vague responses if questioned about personal opinion on contentious topics. For cybercrime and online deviance scholars, online ethnography provides many benefits to access our research populations. However, in the process, it is fundamental to reflect upon our own roles that are shaped and influenced by our experiences and identities.

References

Atkinson, P., & Hammersley, M. (2007). *Ethnography: Principles in practice.* Routledge.

Band-Winterstein, T., Doron, I., & Naim, S. (2014). "I take them with me"– Reflexivity in sensitive research. *Reflective Practice, 15*(4), 530–539.

Banet-Weiser, S., & Miltner, K. M. (2016). # MasculinitySoFragile: Culture, structure, and networked misogyny. *Feminist Media Studies, 16*(1), 171–174.

Barlow, C., & Awan, I. (2016). "You need to be sorted out with a knife": The attempted online silencing of women and people of Muslim faith within academia. *Social Media + Society, 2*(4), 2056305116678896.

Baym, N. K. (2010). *Personal connections in the digital age.* Polity.

Becker, H. S. (1967). Whose side are we on? *Social Problems, 14*(3), 239–247.

Bell, C. (2017). Reddit bans "Involuntarily Celibate" Community. *BBC News.* Available at: https://www.bbc.co.uk/news/blogs-trending-41926687.

Ben-Ari, A., & Enosh, G. (2011). Processes of reflectivity: Knowledge construction in qualitative research. *Qualitative Social Work, 10*(2), 152–171.

Boyd, D. (2010). Social network sites as networked publics: Affordances, dynamics, and implications. In Z. Papacharissi (Ed.), *A networked self: Identity, Community and culture on social network sites.* Routledge.

Bullingham, L., & Vasconcelos, A. C. (2013). The presentation of self in the online world: Goffman and the study of online identities. *Journal of Information Science, 39*(1), 101–112.

Chess, S., & Shaw, A. (2015). A conspiracy of fishes, or, how we learned to stop worrying about# GamerGate and embrace hegemonic masculinity. *Journal of Broadcasting & Electronic Media, 59*(1), 208–220.

Citron, D. K. (2014). *Hate Crimes in Cyberspace.* Harvard University Press.

Davies, C. A. (2008). *Reflexive ethnography: A guide to researching selves and others.* Routledge.

Dickson-Swift, V., James, E. L., Kippen, S., & Liamputtong, P. (2007). Doing sensitive research: What challenges do qualitative researchers face? *Qualitative Research, 7,* 327–353.

Dickson-Swift, V., James, E., & Liamputtong, P. (2008). *Undertaking sensitive research in the health and social sciences: Managing boundaries, emotions and risks.* Cambridge University Press.

Ferrell, J., & Hamm, M. S. (1998). *Ethnography at the edge: Crime, deviance and field research.* Upne.

Fileborn, B., & Loney-Howes, R. (Eds.). (2019). *#MeToo and the politics of social change.* Palgrave Macmillan.

Finlay, L. (2011). *Phenomenology for therapists: Researching the lived world.* Wiley-Blackwell.

Goffman, E. (1959). *The presentation of self in everyday life.* Garden City: NY.

Henry, N., & Powell, A. (2015). Embodied harms: Gender, shame, and technology-facilitated sexual violence. *Violence Against Women, 21*(6), 758–779.

Hertz, R. (1997). *Reflexivity and voice.* Sage.

Hess, A. (2014). Why women aren't welcome on the Internet. *Pacific Standard,* 6.

Holt, T. J. (2007). Subcultural evolution? Examining the influence of on-and off-line experiences on deviant subcultures. *Deviant Behavior, 28*(2), 171–198.

Holt, T. J. (2010). Exploring strategies for qualitative criminological and criminal justice inquiry using on-line data. *Journal of Criminal Justice Education, 21*(4), 466–487.

Holt, T. J., & Bossler, A. M. (2015). *Cybercrime in progress: Theory and prevention of technology-enabled offenses.* Routledge.

Holt, T. J., Burruss, G. W., & Bossler, A. (2015). *Policing cybercrime and cyberterror.* Carolina Academic Press.

Jane, E. J. (2017). *Misogyny online: A short (and Brutish) history.* Sage.

Jenkins, R. (2010). The 21st century interaction order. In H. M. Jacobsen (Ed.), *The contemporary Goffman.* Routledge.

Jhaver, S., Ghoshal, S., Bruckman, A., & Gilbert, E. (2018). Online harassment and content moderation: The case of blocklists. *ACM Transactions on Computer-Human Interaction (TOCHI), 25*(2), 1–33.

Kelly, L. (1987). The continuum of sexual violence. In J. Hanmer & M. Maynard (Eds.), *Women, violence and social control.* Palgrave Macmillan.

King, N., & Horrocks, C. (2010). An introduction to interview data analysis. *Interviews in Qualitative Research,* 142–174.

Kozinets, R. V. (2010). *Netnography: doing ethnographic research online.* Sage.
Kozinets, R. V. (2020). *Netnography: The essential guide to qualitative social media research.* Sage.
Maguire, M. (2000). Researching street criminals: A neglected art. In R. King & E. Wincup (Eds.), *Doing research on crime and justice.* Oxford University Press.
Mantilla, K. (2013). Gendertrolling: Misogyny adapts to new media. *Feminist Studies, 39*(2), 563–570.
Marwick, A. E. (2013). Online identity. In J. Hartley, J. Burgess, & A. Bruns (Eds.), *A companion to new media dynamics.* West Sussex.
Marwick, A. E., & Caplan, R. (2018). Drinking male tears: Language, the manosphere, and networked harassment. *Feminist Media Studies, 18*(4), 543–559.
Mayan, M. (2009). Introduction to the Essentials of Qualitative Inquiry: Thinking About, Designing, and Executing Rigorous Qualitative Inquiry. *Journal of Qualitative Research,* 3–73.
Megarry, J. (2014). Online incivility or sexual harassment? Conceptualising women's experiences in the digital age. *Women's Studies International Forum, 47,* 46–55.
Miller, H., & Arnold, J. (2009). Identity in cyberspace. In S. Wheeler (Ed.), *Connected minds, emerging cultures: Cybercultures in online learning.* IAP.
Morse, J. M. (2010). How different is qualitative health research from qualitative research? Do we have a subdiscipline? *Qualitative Health Research, 20,* 1459–1464.
Papacharissi, Z. (2002). The presentation of self in virtual life: Characteristics of personal home pages. *Journalism & Mass Communication Quarterly, 79*(3), 643–660.
Powell, A., & Henry, N. (2017). *Sexual violence in a digital age.* Palgrave Macmillan.
Roberts, J. M., & Sanders, T. (2005). Before, during and after: realism, reflexivity and ethnography. *The Sociological Review, 53*(2), 294–313.
Stanko, E. A. (1990). *Everyday violence: How women and men experience sexual and physical danger.* Pandora.
Sugiura, L., & Smith, A. (2020). Victim blaming, responsibilization and resilience in online sexual abuse and harassment. In J. Tapley & P. Davies (Eds.), *Victimology.* Palgrave Macmillan.
Underwood, M., Satterthwait, L. D., & Bartlett, H. P. (2010). Reflexivity and minimization of the impact of age-cohort differences between researcher and research participants. *Qualitative Health Research, 20*(11), 1585–1595.

Worley, R. M., Worley, V. B., & Wood, B. A. (2016). "There were ethical dilemmas all day long!": harrowing tales of ethnographic researchers in criminology and criminal justice. *Criminal Justice Studies, 29*(4), 289–308.

Wynn, E., & Katz, J. E. (1997). Hyperbole over cyberspace: self-presentation and social boundaries in internet home pages and discourse. *Information Society, 13*(4), 297–327.

Yar, M., & Steinmetz, K. F. (2019). *Cybercrime and society*. Sage.

Yates, J. W. (2006). *An ethnography of youth and crime in a working-class community*. Unpublished PhD thesis. Leicester: De Montfort University.

Zillman, D. (1983). Handbook of humor research. *Basic Issues, 1,* 85–107.

25

Personal Reflections on Researching Fraud: Challenges Surrounding the Ethics of "Doing"

Cassandra Cross

Introduction

There is no shortage of academic scholarship on qualitative research (Silverman, 2016). Qualitative research aims "to see the world through someone else's eyes" (Stahlke, 2018, p. 2). In doing this, the researcher is seeking to gain an "insider perspective" through engaging with participant accounts of a particular phenomenon (Bahn & Weatherill, 2012, p. 23). In particular, the use of interviews to achieve this uses the power of a conversation to "lay open the thoughts and feelings" on a particular topic (Brayda & Boyce, 2014, p. 321). As stated by Dickson-Swift and colleagues (2007, p. 330), "we go into people's lives, sometimes at a time of crisis and stress, and we ask them to talk in detail about their experiences". For me, I have sought to understand the experience of fraud victimization through directly talking to individuals in conversations that

C. Cross (✉)
School of Justice, Queensland University of Technology, Brisbane, Australia
e-mail: ca.cross@qut.edu.au

© The Author(s), under exclusive license to Springer Nature Switzerland AG 2021
A. Lavorgna and T. J. Holt (eds.), *Researching Cybercrimes*,
https://doi.org/10.1007/978-3-030-74837-1_25

expose the harsh reality and trauma of their victimization. It can be difficult to listen, let alone recount these intimate details to a perfect stranger. It attempts to capture the "human story" of the events which have taken place. In focusing on the "human story" of events (Dickson-Swift et al., 2007, p. 334), concepts related to ethics are central to aspects of my work. These can be complex, nuanced and dynamic, depending on the specifics of the circumstances.

This chapter argues that there are many ethical considerations which are often unexpected and challenging to researchers when conducting interviews with fraud victims. I highlight six themes taken from three projects in my own research journey. In some ways, I argue this to be a direct correlate to fraud victimization itself, in the methods used by offenders to perpetrate their offences (particularly in an online environment) and the level of deception involved in fraud offences. However, there are also other themes which are not unique to fraud victims and are likely to resonate with other researchers involved in fieldwork across other sensitive areas. In this way, it is important to note that I am focused on the Internet as a phenomenon and a place where victimization takes place, rather than Internet (and associated online/virtual) research methodologies.

A Background to Researching Fraud

For over ten years, I have been researching fraud. Fraud is characterized by deception, lying and cheating for a financial advantage (Fletcher, 2007). Fraud is not new and can be perpetrated through all communication mediums, although the evolution of technology and the Internet has seen a change in the ways that victims are exposed and an exponential increase in the ability to target victims globally (Grabosky, 2001; Yar & Steinmetz, 2019). As part of my own research journey, I have completed several projects where the main source of data involved face-to-face interviewing of individuals who had been victims of fraud. There are those who had lost money to investment schemes, those who had lost money through romantic relationships and those who may not have lost money directly, but who had their identities compromised. There are many who were defrauded in an online context, but there were still others who were deceived through telephone and/or face-to-face interactions.

Each year, there are millions of fraud victims globally. For example, in 2019, the Internet Crime Complaint Centre (United States of America) recorded over US$3.5 billion (IC3, 2020), UK Finance (United Kingdom) reported £1.2 billion lost to fraud and scams (UK Finance, 2019), and the Canadian Anti-Fraud Centre (CAFC) reported CAD$98 million lost (CAFC, 2020), while the Hong Kong police intercepted more than HK$3 billion (USD$384 million) from victims of fraud in Hong Kong and beyond (Lo, 2020). Here in Australia, victims reported losses of over AUD$634 million to a variety of agencies in 2019 (ACCC, 2020). While the above statistics are significant, they likely under-represent the reality of fraud losses. Fraud is well-known to have one of the lowest reporting rates across all crime types (Button et al., 2014; Copes et al., 2001; van Wyk & Mason, 2001), with most estimates stating less than one-third of fraud is formally reported (Mason & Benson, 1996; Schoepfer & Piquero, 2009; Titus et al., 1995), and a further difference with online fraud reported less than offline fraud (Smith, 2007, 2008). Additionally, these statistics do not account for the many non-financial harms incurred through fraud victimization (Cross, 2019a).

For this reason, considerations of research ethics are critical to any project that engages fraud victims with the explicit goal of asking questions about victimization. Failure to consider an ethical approach to this type of project can have potentially disastrous results, particularly on the part of the participant (Fujii, 2012). Globally, researchers are bound by various codes of practice and government regulations which oversee and approve all research activity involving humans. In Australia, this is captured in the National Statement on Ethical Conduct in Human Research (2007, updated 2018—see Chapter 21), though other countries have similar frameworks. As noted by Newman and Kaloupek (2004, p. 383), "both ethics codes and government regulations require researchers to identify all pertinent risks so that potential subjects are able to make informed judgements about research participation on the basis of knowledge of potential consequences, including harm that might result". This is especially the case where the focus of the research is on those who might be considered "vulnerable" (Hamberger et al., 2020, p. 43)—in this case, victims of fraud.

One of the foremost ethical concerns for researchers and ethics committees is to ensure the benefit derived from the research outweighs any potential harm to participants, and that this harm is eliminated to the greatest degree possible. This can present as a particular challenge in research where participants have experienced abuse or violence, as these participants are already in a vulnerable position (Valpied et al., 2014, p. 674—see also Chapter 23). There is little consensus as to what constitutes "vulnerability" for research participants. In the National Statement, there are dedicated chapters to prescribed groups of people who are deemed to be "vulnerable" in some way and require additional considerations. While "a precise definition of vulnerability remains elusive… in many respects, conceptually, vulnerability is context dependent" (Aldridge, 2014, p. 113) and this extends to fraud victims. Similar to the impacts of fraud victimization, there are varying degrees of preexisting vulnerability exhibited by victims of fraud, and the need to consider the complex and dynamic ways in which fraud has contributed to or exacerbated existing vulnerabilities. This is recognized by Aldridge (2014, p. 13) in that an important distinction needs to be made "between people who are individually, uniquely and innately vulnerable and those who are vulnerable because of their circumstances, because of the environment or as a result of the structural factors or influences".

While acknowledging existing and potential vulnerabilities of fraud victims, they must not be used as an excuse to exclude these voices and perspectives from research agendas. Further, there is an important distinction to be made between the formal process of gaining ethical approval and the considerations required at the bureaucratic level, and the process of "doing research" and navigating the ethical challenges that surround the undertaking of the project. They are not the same thing. There is much debate and discussion focused on the process of gaining ethics approval from formal ethics committees (also known as Institutional Review Boards) (Israel, 2016), but there is less academic scholarship which focuses on the process of doing research once ethics has been received, and the unexpected nature of circumstances experienced in doing fieldwork (though Bartels & Richards, 2011 and Wadds et al., 2020 are two important Australian contributions).

This chapter focuses solely on the latter of these, in outlining the "messiness" involved in navigating ethics through the process of interviewing fraud victims. In particular, it details the many challenges that I have experienced as a researcher across my years interviewing fraud victims on their experiences of victimization, of attempting to gain justice and of trying to find support in the aftermath an incident. To do this, I am reflecting on my experiences across three main projects that directly engaged with victims. The first was entitled the Seniors Online Fraud Project (see Cross, 2015), the second, Improving responses to online fraud victims (see Cross et al., 2016) and the third, The benefits of a face-to-face support group for fraud victims (see Cross, 2019b). Each of these projects presented situations where I was forced to think through the ethical considerations of both my actions and the actions of my participants (fraud victims) which were not covered in the formal ethical approval documents I had officially received.

The Challenges Associated with Interviewing Fraud Victims

Over the years, I have made many ethics applications. In Australia (as with other countries), there are different levels of ethical review, depending on the type of research being conducted, the nature of the research and the level of risk to participants. Given my work with fraud victims, asking directly about victimization, my applications are mandated to be considered at a meeting of the full university ethics committee, rather than being considered administratively in my faculty as a low risk application.

Regardless of the approval process used for an ethics application, on several occasions I have had to make decisions based on ethical dilemmas posed to me in the field. No formal ethics approval will ever capture the reality of navigating ethics in a research project, particularly when doing fieldwork. The following presents six separate aspects to this which I have encountered and my reflections on working through these situations.

Trust

It is widely acknowledged that trust is an essential element required to do successful fieldwork (Bahn & Weatherill, 2012). The ability of a researcher to build trust and rapport with participants is crucial to the participant feeling comfortable and confident in opening up and disclosing highly personal and intimate details of their lives. In my own experience, the need to build and engender trust with interviewees has taken on a higher level of meaning, due to that type of victimization that individuals have suffered.

At its essence, fraud is about deception (Fletcher, 2007). Fraud encapsulates lying, cheating and the creation of a false narrative for financial benefit. For all of the victims I have interviewed, their trust rested in a particular individual or group of individuals for a period of time, hoping to achieve a certain outcome (whether it be a relationship or a successful business or a financial payoff). In many of these circumstances, offenders were not only able to successfully deceive the victim, they were able to manipulate and persuade the victim into doing things they would not usually have done. This included the direct transfer of money to an offender, but also captures the sending of personal information, as well as the receipt and transfer of money through their account (money laundering).

When an individual realizes they have been defrauded, the impacts can be devastating. My own research indicates the vast array of consequences experienced by fraud victims, which extends beyond pure financial losses, to include the physical deterioration of health and well-being; a decline in emotional well-being; varying levels of depression; relationship breakdown; unemployment; homelessness; and in extreme cases, suicide ideation (Cross et al., 2016). For many victims, there is also an intense feeling of shame and embarrassment at having been deceived by another person and having lost (often large) amounts of money (Cross, 2015, 2018a). There are feelings of betrayal and violation, and the level of deception often rocks victims to the core. Their ability to trust is compromised and they may take this forward with future relationships and interactions of all kinds. The challenges and difficulties that fraud victims face in terms of trusting others again can vary. It is against this backdrop of mistrust that researchers enter the lives of fraud victims. They ask victims to place their trust in the researcher, who may ask probing questions about the specifics of their victimization experiences. It is in the researchers' best interests to ask questions in ways that empowers the victim and does not cause additional distress. This is a challenging request that should not be taken lightly by anyone working in this space.

During our fieldwork for the *Improving responses to online fraud* project, my colleague and I would often arrive at our participant's house and when we knocked on the door, individuals would express some sort of shock that we actually did exist. Despite having communicated with them over email and phone, many did not believe that we existed and were going to turn up. Our arrival often came as a welcome surprise. This also highlights the methods we use as researchers often mirror those of the offenders who have deceived my participants. In using email, social media and web pages for our academic purposes, we expect fraud victims to discern the false accounts of offenders, while expecting them to believe us. This continues to pose challenges in gaining the trust of participants in the first place and being able to maintain that throughout the research process.

Sensitive Nature of the Topic

It is obvious that asking individuals to disclose highly personal and intimate details of their fraud victimization can be considered as a sensitive topic. This is further heightened depending on the nature of the fraud. For example, concerning those who have been deceived through a romantic relationship, they often have experiences that include details of sexually explicit conversations, requests and actions to accompany their fraud. It can also be overwhelming to recount the role of technology in this and the type of requests they have been asked to perform.

Adding to the sensitive nature of fraud is the overwhelming negativity that is associated with victimization. My research explicitly documents the existence of victim-blaming attitudes towards those who are deceived (Cross, 2015) and how individuals are consistently denied "victim" status (Cross, 2018a). It highlights the negative stereotype that is perpetuated by society more broadly of victims being greedy, gullible, uneducated and somewhat deserving of their victimization (Cross, 2013). The perceived negative consequences levelled at victims who disclose the details of what has occurred can be a powerful barrier to reporting and to seeking support. Understandably, this also holds true in a research context, talking to a researcher.

In a deliberate effort to overcome the stigma associated with fraud, I am careful with my choice of language and the ways in which I frame victimization with participants. I will never use the word "victim" in any of my research materials and I attempt not to use it in my interview (unless the participant uses the word first and I take their lead). Further, I have started to be explicit in my framing of fraud victimization in my participant information sheet, as demonstrated in the following excerpt for a current project targeting romance fraud.

It is important to know that you are not alone and not to blame for what has happened. There are thousands of people across the world who have been in similar circumstances to you and have lost money through an online relationship. It is important to know that there is no judgement implied of those who have been in this situation.

There is much debate and discussion on the need for researchers to be objective and neutral in their approach research (Fohring, 2020). However, in my case, I am deliberate about taking a stance and framing my project in a particular way. I want to be transparent with participants about my understanding of fraud and those who are victims. I want to be clear that I will not judge them for what has happened, and that I am genuinely interested in hearing about, and valuing, their experiences. For me, this is one way that I attempt to overcome some of the barriers and potential anxiety associated with participation in my research.

The Emotional Nature of Interviewing

There is an increasing recognition of the emotional aspects associated with fieldwork, and with interviewing vulnerable persons about sensitive issues (Doyle & Buckley, 2017; Melville & Hincks, 2016; Stahlke, 2018). Hence it is important to highlight that while the formal ethics approval process concentrates on the well-being of participants, there is limited consideration in this process for the well-being of the researcher and/or research team (see also Chapters 23 and 24).

One of the overriding ethical considerations is whether the potential for distress in an interview is justified, and how it can best be managed. Researchers must be aware of the impact that our research and lines of questioning can have on victims (Cross, 2018b). As part of my approval process, I have established protocols in place across the different stages of my research, from initial screening to the interview itself and to any follow up with participants. However, no amount of preparation or protocols can prepare you as a researcher to hear firsthand accounts of the brutality of victimization. The emotional labour involved in interviewing can be immense, in addition to the well-established potential for emotions to play an active presence in the narratives of participants.

Whether a researcher should show emotion during an interview is a contested topic (Dickson-Swift et al., 2009; Melville & Hincks, 2016; Shaw et al., 2020). I have often been conflicted by the emotional nature of the interviews I am conducting. In some interviews I have been able to keep my own emotions in check, regardless of the content. At other times, the sheer nature of the interview content has been so overwhelming that I have found it impossible to distance myself from emotions and have cried at kitchen tables across the country in response to the pain and suffering exuding from the victim before me.

There was one interview I conducted as part of the *Improving responses to online fraud* project. My colleague and I were interviewing a woman who had been the victim of romance fraud, and she was outlining the aftermath of what had occurred. This is detailed in the following excerpt.

Participant: I had literally torn up any personal things – letters, diaries, photos - so there would be no trace left.

Interviewer: Of this [online fraud] incident?
Participant: Of me....You just feel so stupid....[I felt] pretty useless really, that is what I kept thinking, a bit of a waste of space, that is what I kept thinking about myself.
Interviewer: Did you ever think of suicide?
Participant: Yeah I did. I just shut down, but I would make sure my underwear was clean. It was just so bizarre, and there would be no trace of me left, I would just evaporate (interview 44).

The sheer magnitude of her pain was overwhelming, and we cried together during the interview. Another example relates to another woman who was also a victim of romance fraud. As my colleague and I knocked on her front door, she opened it already in tears. The anticipation of talking to us about her experience was initially somewhat overwhelming. Despite implementing our protocols and offering to return at a different time, she was adamant that she wanted to talk to us there and then. In many of these situations, the atmosphere is charged with a mixture of anticipation, anxiety, pain, betrayal and embarrassment. In managing my emotions as a researcher, I am focused on being authentic and not necessarily acting how I think a "good researcher" should act in these circumstances. This may include showing emotion or it may revolve around staying neutral. Overall, this demonstrates the messy nature of interviewing fraud victims and the difficulties associated with interacting in such an emotive and highly charged environment.

Powerlessness of Being a Researcher

One of the ongoing challenges of fraud research is the constant state of powerlessness I feel as a researcher and a human. I am constantly in awe of many of the fraud victims I have interviewed, and the strength and courage they have demonstrated in talking to me about their experiences. For a group of victims that is so often invisible to wider society, and usually silenced, I feel a great sense of responsibility in being the keeper of their narratives and feeling the need to do them justice in my analysis and dissemination. This is not unusual (Dickson-Swift et al., 2007, p. 340). While some participants have expressed explicit benefits and satisfaction to participation in research (including my own) (Richards & Cross, 2018), this does not always provide a sufficient counter balance to the distress of fraud victims and the devastation that many experience across all aspects of their lives.

In the context of fraud victimization, the powerlessness I feel as a researcher is exacerbated by the overall state of the current system and response to fraud victimization. The ability of fraud victims to gain a satisfactory response is limited at best (Morgan et al., 2016). Many will never be able to lodge a complaint, and if they do, are unlikely to ever receive a response or follow up to their report (Cross, 2018b). When asked by victims what they can do to gain action, my response is limited. I know that if I suggest they report to any of the official channels, they will not receive a reply. I know that there is almost no chance that they will be able to recover any of their funds. I also know that there are limited support services available to assist them with recovery and moving forward. While this is one of the driving factors behind my motivation to conduct this research, when asked in the moment by a victim for assistance, I am constrained in what I can realistically offer.

One of my first fraud victim interviews as part of the *Seniors Online Fraud* project was with a couple in their 80's who had lost several thousand dollars in a lottery scheme. When I spoke to the husband, it was clear the burden he was carrying as the one who had responded to the fraudulent approach and convinced his wife that they should send the requested money. It was emotional to hear the impact on their lives, as it was clear the incident had a detrimental effect on his physical health as well as other aspects of his life. Sometime later I found out he had died, and it was impossible for me to disconnect his physical deterioration from the fraud he had experienced. It was not hard to consider that the impact of his fraud victimization had arguably led to a quicker decline in his overall health. It was a confronting lesson in the real consequences of fraud victimization on individuals.

Understanding What Has Occurred

The ways that victims are defrauded can be complicated, particularly in an online environment. In recounting victimization narratives, it is clear that not all participants understand what happened, what is real or what is false. It is easy for me as an outsider to identify parts of their narratives that are not consistent with what is likely to have occurred. The challenge for me as a researcher is determining my role (if any) in discussing this with the victim. Given the high levels of re-victimization that exist for fraud, it is imperative that victims are made aware of the approaches that offenders used to target them in the current context, as well as into the future. There have been many victims I have spoken to across the years who clearly do not understand the ways they were targeted; the methods used by the offenders to gain their trust; the techniques used by offenders to persuade them and gain compliance with their requests; and the various ways in which they may have been directly victimized (sending of money) or indirectly exposed to victimization (identity theft stemming from the sending of personal information).

A prime example was found in my *Seniors Online Fraud* project. A gentleman responded to a phishing email that gave the offender access to his bank accounts. The offender quickly emptied the accounts of tens of thousands of dollars. When asked about how this impacted on him and his future behaviours, the man stated he is now wary of letting his credit card out of his sight at restaurants. While this is good practice per se, it demonstrates the disconnect between his understanding of what happened to him, and what enabled his victimization, compared to what he thinks he should focus on in the future. There are countless other examples where it is evident in discussions that the intricacies of online fraud victimization mean that individuals who have been successfully defrauded do not have a full understanding of what occurred, or how to potentially prevent it from happening again into the future.

Further, there have several instances where fraud victims have indicated they are still in communication with their offender, and in some cases, are continuing to send money. This is usually premised on the fact that no one can tell them 100% that their circumstance is fraud, so they are holding on to the slim (and often futile) hope that the fraud is a type of misunderstanding and everything will be ok (i.e. they will get their money back). It is difficult as a researcher to sit and listen to this without reacting in any way. When directly asked, I usually respond with my knowledge of fraud, drawn from the experiences of others, hoping they will be persuaded by my arguments.

There is only one instance where I directly told an interviewee he as being defrauded. During the *Improving responses to online fraud* project a gentleman had lost several hundreds of thousands of dollars, travelled overseas to meet with offenders and was continuing to send money to an investment scheme. He was once wealthy but was now living in a one-bedroom public housing flat. Despite losing everything, he was continuing to send his pension to the offenders. He had openly talked about the ongoing impact of his experience and his desire to end his life. At the end of the interview, he asked if I thought it was fraud. I firmly said yes and advised him to stop sending money and cease all communications. In that moment, it was difficult as a human to say anything but what I felt.

Related to this is the question of how I, as a researcher, fit into the narrative of my participant's victimization? It is clear that through the interview process and the questions that I ask (or the responses I give to my participant's questions), that they are often processing what has occurred in new and different ways. In some cases, this may be realizing the extent to which they were deceived is greater than they first thought. For example, there are many individuals who willingly acknowledge that they have been defrauded and lost money. However, this recognition does not always extend to the identity of the offender. I am acutely aware of the fact that in all likelihood, the person does not exist, and has been created by an offender, but many victims perceive their identity to be genuine. Bearing witness to this evolution in thinking and recognition of a deeper level of victimization can be difficult to manage in the moment.

Expectations of Participation

It is important to remember that our participants are not likely to be familiar with the process of academic research, and the system in which we operate in as part of our daily routines. As researchers, we are familiar with the long time frames, the many competing interests for our time, the peer review process and the final desired outcome of publication (usually as a journal article or book/book chapter). This context is foreign to most of our research participants and may create unrealistic expectations. It is critical therefore to manage the expectations of participants throughout the research process. In the context of fraud victims, there is a further burden in that victims have often already faced high levels of dissatisfaction at the hands of the criminal justice system and other agencies. Many appear to have transferred their expectations of a result onto me as a researcher. This can lead to some challenging and uncomfortable situations.

On more than one occasion it is clear that participants either directly or indirectly hope that talking to me will assist their case; that I will be able to advocate or intervene for them and achieve an outcome which they are unable to achieve themselves. This is despite me being very clear up front across my participation materials and preamble to each interview. This manifests itself in a variety of ways. There are those victims who want me to have copies of their communications, receipts and other relevant materials, in the hope that I can do something with them. There are those who explicitly ask me to act on their behalf. There are also those who think that I already have details of their case, particularly if I am working with an industry partner such as police or consumer protection (as was the case for the *Improving responses to online fraud* project).

In other ways, it can be more difficult to diffuse. Some months after my second round of interviews for the *Benefits of face-to-face support groups* project, I received a text message from one of my participants. She asked whether I had been able to recover her money yet, as it was nearing Christmas and she needed the money to buy her grandchildren Christmas presents. In these types of circumstances, it is clear that individuals only hear what they want to hear and are driven by a hope and desire to gain an outcome to their situation. It also demonstrates the need to have ongoing discussions about this with participants, rather than simply stating this on a participant information sheet up front and believing it to be satisfactory.

Conclusion

Fraud victimization is brutal. The ease in which offenders deceive victims and manipulate them into sending money for their own financial gain is hard to comprehend. I have seen firsthand the brutal aftermath of fraud and its ongoing consequences. Conducting interviews with individuals on this topic requires a high degree of consideration, not only of how the project will impact on them but also as to how the project will impact on me and my role of researcher.

There are several challenges that exist in conducting interviews with fraud victims. While many of these are consistent with the broader literature on vulnerable populations and sensitive topics, the above chapter has sought to draw out the specifics relevant to fraud victims. Fraud has some unique characteristics that impact on the various ethical considerations needed to be accounted for across any research project.

While the above chapter contains many examples that are encompass sensitive and challenging materials, it would be a mistake to think that this should deter anyone from engaging in this type of research. While it can be emotionally exhausting, I could not picture myself doing anything different. Despite having moments in the field of wishing that I had chosen a different research method (usually a desktop analysis which I could conduct from the comfort of my own study), there are great rewards in being able to do the work that I do. Similar to the benefits of research stated by participants (Richards & Cross, 2018), there are likewise benefits I experience. However, it would be naïve to assume that ethical considerations required to undertake this type of research project would be straightforward or would be captured solely in the process of *gaining approval* rather than *conducting* the research.

Fraud is messy. Being invited into the sphere of fraud victims describing in acute detail the circumstances in which they were defrauded can be chaotic. It is important to acknowledge this up front, and to be able to discuss the realities presented by these situations with those around us. Ethics is far more than a process to tick a box or gain a piece of paper approving a project. Rather, the ethics involved in undertaking interviews with fraud victims requires constant reassessment and evaluation, to ensure that the best outcomes can be achieved. The importance of giving voice to fraud victims is vital, regardless of the challenges experienced in attempting to achieve this.

Acknowledgements The author gratefully acknowledges Bridget Harris, Bridget Lewis and Fiona McDonald for their helpful comments in reviewing earlier versions of this chapter.

References

Aldridge, J. (2014). Working with vulnerable groups in social research: Dilemmas by default and design. *Qualitative Research, 14*(1), 112–130.

Australian Competition and Consumer Commission (ACCC). (2020). *Targeting scams 2019: A review of scam activity since 2009.* Available at: https://www.accc.gov.au/publications/targeting-scams-report-on-scam-act ivity/targeting-scams-2019-a-review-of-scam-activity-since-2009.

Bahn, S., & Weatherill, P. (2012). Qualitative social research: A risky business when it comes to collecting "sensitive" data. *Qualitative Research, 13*(1), 19–35.

Bartels, L., & Richards, K. (2011). *Qualitative criminology: Stories from the field.* Hawkins Press.

Brayda, W., & Boyce, T. (2014). So you really want to interview me? Navigating "sensitive" qualitative research interviewing. *International Journal of Qualitative Methods,* 318–334.

Button, M., McNaughton Nicolls, C., Kerr, J., & Owen, R. (2014). Online frauds: Learning from victims why they fall for these scams. *Australian and New Zealand Journal of Criminology, 47*(3), 391–408.

Canadian Anti-Fraud Centre (CAFC). (2020). *Recent scams and frauds.* Available at: https://www.antifraudcentre-centreantifraude.ca/index-eng. htm. Accessed 2 June 2021.

Copes, H., Kerley, K., Mason, K., & van Wyk, J. (2001). Reporting behaviour of fraud victims and Black's theory of law: An empirical assessment. *Justice Quarterly, 18*(2), 343–363.

Cross, C. (2013). "Nobody's holding a gun to your head…" examining current discourses surrounding victims of online fraud. In K. Richards & J. Tauri (Eds.), *Crime, justice and social democracy: Proceedings of the 2nd International Conference.* Crime and Justice Research Centre, QUT.

Cross, C. (2015). No laughing matter: Blaming the victim of online fraud. *International Review of Victimology, 21*(2), 187–204.

Cross, C. (2018a). Denying victim status to online fraud victims: The challenges of being a "non-ideal victim." In M. Duggan (Ed.), *Revisiting the ideal victim concept* (pp. 243–262). Policy Press.

Cross, C. (2018b). Expectations vs reality: Responding to online fraud across the fraud justice network. *International Journal of Law, Crime and Justice, 55*, 1–12.

Cross, C. (2019a). Online fraud. In *oxford research encyclopaedia of criminology and criminal justice.* Oxford University Press.

Cross, C. (2019b). "You're not alone": The use of peer support groups for fraud victims. *Journal of Human Behavior in the Social Environment, 29*(5), 672–691.

Cross, C. Richards, K., & Smith, R. (2016). *Improving the response to online fraud victims: An examination of reporting and support.* Australian Institute of Criminology.

Dickson-Swift, V., James, E., Kippen, S., & Liamputtong, P. (2007). Doing sensitive research: What challenges to qualitative researchers face? *Qualitative Research, 7*(3), 327–353.

Dickson-Swift, V., James, E., Kippen, S., & Liamputtong, P. (2009). Researching sensitive topics: Qualitative research as emotion work. *Qualitative Research, 9*(1), 61–79.

Doyle, E., & Buckley, P. (2017). Embracing qualitative research: A visual model for nuanced research ethics oversight. *Qualitative Research, 17*(1), 95–117.

Fletcher, N. (2007). Challenges for regulating financial fraud in cyberspace. *Journal of Financial Crime, 14*(2), 190–207.

Fohring, S. (2020). The risks and rewards of researching victims of crime. *Methodological Innovations*, May–August, 1–11.

Fujii, L. (2012). Research ethics 101: Dilemmas and responsibilities. *The Profession*, 717–723.

Grabosky, P. (2001). Virtual criminality: Old wine in new bottles? *Social & Legal Studies, 10*(2), 243–249.

Hamberger, L., Larsen, S., & Ambuel, B. (2020). "It helped a lot to go over it": Intimate partner violence research risks and benefits from participating in an 18-month longitudinal study. *Journal of Family Violence, 35*, 43–52.

Internet Crime Complaint Centre (IC3). (2020). *2019 Internet Crime Report.* Available at: https://pdf.ic3.gov/2019_IC3Report.pdf.

Israel, M. (2016). *Research ethics and integrity for social scientists: Beyond regulatory compliance* (2nd ed.). Sage.

Lo, C. (2020). *Hong Kong police intercept more than US$384 million swindled from victims of internet and phone scams around world.* Available at: https://www.scmp.com/news/hong-kong/law-and-crime/article/306 4633/hong-kong-police-intercept-more-us384-million-swindled. Accessed 2 June 2021.

Mason, K., & Benson, M. (1996). The effect of social support on fraud victims' reporting behaviour: A research note. *Justice Quarterly, 13*(3), 511–524.

Melville, A., & Hincks, D. (2016). Conducting sensitive interviews: A review of reflections. *Law and Method,* 1–25. https://doi.org/10.5553/REM/. 000015.

Morgan, A., Dowling, C., Browns, R., Mann, M., Vice, I., & Smith, M. (2016). *Evaluation of the Australian Cybercrime Online Reporting Network.* Available at: https://aic.gov.au/sites/default/files/2018/08/acorn_evaluation_report_.pdf.

Newman, E., & Kaloupek, D. (2004). The risks and benefits of participating in trauma-focused research studies. *Journal of Traumatic Stress, 17*(5), 383–394.

Richards, K., & Cross, C. (2018). Online fraud victims' experiences of participating in qualitative interviews. *Criminal Justice Studies, 31*(1), 95–111.

Schoepfer, A., & Piquero, N. (2009). Studying the correlates of fraud victimisation and reporting. *Journal of Criminal Justice, 37*, 209–215.

Shaw, R., Howe, J., Beazer, J., & Carr, T. (2020). Ethics and positionality in qualitative research with vulnerable and marginal groups. *Qualitative Research, 20*(3), 277–293.

Silverman, D. (2016). *Qualitative research* (4th ed.). . Sage.

Smith, R. G. (2007). Consumer scams in Australia: An overview. *Trends and Issues in Crime and Criminal Justice, 331*, 1–6.

Smith, R. G. (2008). Coordinating individual and organisational responses to fraud. *Crime Law and Social Change, 49*, 379–396.

Stahlke, S. (2018). Expanding on notions of ethical risks to qualitative researchers. *International Journal of Qualitative Methods, 17*, 1–9.

Titus, R., Heinzelmann, F., & Boyle, J. (1995). Victimisation of persons by fraud. *Crime and Delinquency, 41*(1), 54–72.

UK Finance. (2019). *Fraud the facts 2019*. Available at: https://www.ukf inance.org.uk/system/files/Fraud%20The%20Facts%202019%20-%20F INAL%20ONLINE.pdf.

Valpied, J., Cini, A., O'Doherty, L., Taket, A., & Hegarty, K. (2014). "Sometimes cathartic. Sometimes quite raw": Benefit and harm in an intimate partner violence trial. *Aggression and Violent Behavior, 19*, 673–685.

Van Wyk, J., & Mason, K. (2001). Investigating vulnerability and reporting behaviour for consumer fraud victimisation: opportunity as a social aspect for age. *Journal of Contemporary Criminal Justice, 17*(4), 328–345.

Wadds, P., Apoifis, N., Schmeidl, S., & Spurway, K. (Eds.). (2020). *Navigating fieldwork in the social sciences: Stories of danger, risk and reward*. Palgrave Macmillan.

Yar, M., & Steinmetz, K. (2019). *Cybercrime and society* (3rd ed.). Sage.

26

At the Intersection of Digital Research and Sexual Violence: Insights on Gaining Informed Consent from Vulnerable Participants

Tully O'Neill

Introduction

There is a need to bridge some of the gaps between feminist and digital methodologies when working with vulnerable participants who have experienced harm. For instance, in the context of feminist research, particularly that which examines sexual violence, researchers often undertake qualitative and standpoint methodologies that center the experiences and narratives of participants (Hesse-Biber, 2012; Reinharz & Davidman, 1992). In these kinds of research projects, Human Research Ethics boards generally classify victim-survivors as vulnerable research participants, and researchers must be mindful of and plan for the potential traumatic impacts and consequences that their research can have. By comparison, many digital methodologies see researchers more removed from the data they are analyzing, especially when some types of data

T. O'Neill (✉)
Victoria University, Melbourne, VIC, Australia
e-mail: tully.oneill@vu.edu.au

© The Author(s), under exclusive license to Springer Nature
Switzerland AG 2021
A. Lavorgna and T. J. Holt (eds.), *Researching Cybercrimes*,
https://doi.org/10.1007/978-3-030-74837-1_26

513

are considered to be "public" information on the Internet that is freely open to collection and analysis (Dennen, 2012). That is, most digital researchers would not be required to nor consider it necessary to put in a high-risk ethics application to analyze publicly accessible data. However, throughout this chapter I argue that the extent to which researchers consider their data as "human" or "text" is a significant tension for digital researchers conducting studies about sensitive or high-risk topics, like sexual violence.

Digital ethics is an important aspect of all Internet-based research. The Association of Internet Research have acknowledged this and have published guidelines since 2002 advising researchers about existing and emerging ethical issues (as discussed more in details, for instance, in Chapters 17 and 23). Further to this, other research bodies and academic associations have developed digital ethics guidelines (see the following guidelines for examples, Clark et al., 2015; Davies et al., 2016; Markham & Buchanan, 2012). These types of ethics guidelines examine a range of prominent conversations and practices in digital ethics, including the extent to which gaining informed consent is necessary. This chapter reflects on how this issue played out in my research on victims of sexual violence and abuse by reflecting on whether digital data is public or private, whether informed consent is necessary, and whether researchers need to announce their presence when observing digital space. I reflect on some of the tensions that I noticed in my own research designs and methodologies, drawing from a recent two-stage qualitative study that included the content analysis of posts to an online community on reddit, and semi-structured interviews with victim-survivors. Both stages of the research received ethical approval from RMIT University, Melbourne, Australia. In particular, the discussion examines the implications of not seeking informed consent to collect data posted to a public online community. Following feminist best-practice, the research took a standpoint approach and aimed to center the voices and experiences of victim-survivors as the basis for new and emerging knowledge about digital practices and informal justice. Upon reflection, the content analysis I conducted could have made better efforts to center victim-survivors needs and autonomy for their own stories. In making these reflections, this chapter aims to tease out the potential consequences that arise when we analyzing textual data created by "vulnerable" participants about sensitive research topics.

Situating the Private in the Public Internet

The public versus private divide is a longstanding topic within digital ethics (see also the other chapters of Part III of this book). Scholars have questioned the extent to which methodologies conducted in digital space surmount to research with human participants, or the analysis of textual representations (White, 2012). Perhaps due to this, early scholarly conversations around digital ethics often likened posting content publicly online to speaking in a town square, and that such speech can be covertly observed and analyzed (Hudson & Bruckman, 2012). This rhetoric has contributed to digital research practices whereby any public information or content on the Internet can be used as data. However, as conversations about digital ethics have developed over time, many guidelines acknowledge that the definitions of public and private information can be blurred, and it is difficult to define what constitutes public space or data in digital contexts (Davies et al., 2016; Markham & Buchanan, 2012). As such, there are complexities in how various spaces and the types of online data within them are used for analysis.

Private digital spaces are typically closed, "secret", or require users to have some form of membership (such as a user account with the platform) to participate in the space. By contrast, "public" spaces are accessible to read without a user account. Many digital and social media platforms provide spaces that operate between these conceptualizations of public and private, blurring the boundaries further about what constitutes public data. For example, a lot of content "publicly" posted to Twitter, YouTube, and reddit (and to a lesser extent, Facebook and Instagram) are accessible to read without a user account. Social media companies like Facebook have tightened the control over what information posted to its platforms are accessible to those without an account, limiting the types and amount of information that are accessible (Boyd & Hargittai, 2010). Research practices have been shaped by these blurred boundaries of what constitutes a public/private digital space, as well as

the lacking clarity in ethics guidelines and review committee requirements and the diverse methodologies of other digital researchers. For
example, a substantial body of research has utilized methodologies where
public Twitter, reddit or other "public" data is mined, (typically) de-
identified, but often used without the informed consent of the original
author of the content. Some scholars, notably Dennen (2012) have
pointed out that the normalization and justification for researchers to
use "public" data requires critical reflection and engagement, and that
digital researchers ought to seriously consider the importance of online
authorship particularly when examining sensitive topics. Proponents of
this view often argue that it is necessary to gain informed consent from
the author to analyze digital content written by people who would in
other methodologies be considered as "vulnerable" participants.

Gaining informed consent is therefore another prominent thread in
conversations about digital ethics and became a central consideration in
my research with online communities for victim-survivors. Obtaining
informed consent is an essential aspect of most terrestrial research
conducted with human participants and is monitored by stringent
ethics committee processes. By contrast, the requirements of obtaining
informed consent in digital contexts is often determined by the extent
to which a space or data is public, and whether the content is considered merely text or as human participants (White, 2012). It is worth
briefly noting some of the varying scholarly perspectives on the necessity of gaining informed consent in digital contexts. For instance, Willis
(2019) argued that in a context like the Facebook newsfeed, gaining
informed consent for the use of data is not always appropriate, possible,
or necessary. Willis suggests that procedures to gain informed consent in
these contexts would impact the ways that people interacted with Facebook, thereby impacting the integrity of the data being analyzed. On the
other hand, Flick (2016) notes the "ethical oversight" rife in Facebook
research, suggesting that the lack of a means to gain informed consent
en masse can lead to researchers undertaking unethical research practices. Furthermore, collaboration with social media companies results in
practices where researcher's acceptance of company policies around data
collection rather than pursuing a university standard of informed consent

(Flick, 2016). There is somewhat of a divide within digital research ethics about whether informed consent should be a priority.

It seems that scholars are increasingly acknowledging the ethical importance of individual autonomy over one's digital data, and as a result, direct avenues to eliciting informed consent for access to digital data ought to be prioritized. Dennen (2012) contends that "requesting consent to participate and direct interaction are the only reliable ways to assess a participant's desire for privacy". Indeed, when researchers have direct interactions about their research, they can determine whether potential participants perceive their disclosures to be private or sensitive in nature (Dennen, 2012, p. 30). When researchers make meaningful attempts to gain informed consent in digital research, participants are afforded rights to withdraw their participation and access to researchers so that they might have awareness of how their digital data were used (Quinton & Reynolds, 2018). McKee and Porter (2009) suggest that the necessity for informed consent should be considered on the basis of not only the extent to which information is public, but also whether information being gathered is non-sensitive. For example, they suggest that digital content pertaining to sexual abuse should mostly require the informed consent of people posting about it, regardless of the public nature of the platform being researched (McKee & Porter, 2009, p. 21). The importance of gaining informed consent for the use of publicly accessible forms of digital data is rightly becoming a prominent aspect of debates around online methodologies that examine sensitive topics.

As I will argue further below, the digital ethical concerns high-lighted in the literature reviewed here bear particular significance when considering research with vulnerable participants. If we acknowledge, as Dennen (2012) does, that the classification of so-called sensitive topics is subjective and dependent on the participant, then perhaps it is questionable whether any public content online is open to our analysis.

Addressing the Concerns of "Public" Data About Sexual Violence: Reflections and Advice for Researchers

In this section, I reflect upon a qualitative methodology which included a content analysis of disclosures made to a publicly accessible online community for victim-survivors, as well as qualitative interviews with digital recruitment methods.

One of the main ethical tensions that arose throughout my research was whether online content ought to be considered as textual data, or as data created by human participants, thus necessitating informed consent. In aims to mitigate risk around these concerns, I submitted a low-risk ethics application before conducting a content analysis of an online community for victim-survivors. At the time, seeking ethics approval for this kind of public content seemed to diverge from other studies that had examined disclosures of sexual violence posted online. For example, Andalibi and colleagues (2016) who analyzed the same online community did not indicate that they had sought ethical approval. Elsewhere, I have argued that due to the vulnerability of victim-survivors, it is necessary to put these types of content analyses through ethical review (O'Neill, 2018). Indeed, in similar studies since, such as Mendes et al. (2019) study into online disclosures of rape and feminism, and Noack-Lundberg and colleagues (2019) study into transwomen's use of online forums—ethical approval has been sought and granted, indicating a growing propensity to have these types of methodologies reviewed prior to beginning data collection.

My ethics application went through the review process without amendment, allowing me to collect and analyze 200 reddit posts about experiences of rape and sexual assault and its aftermath. These posts were anonymous (or pseudonymous), reddit users have the option of using their main username or a "throwaway" account created for one-off use, thereby increasing their anonymity (see Andalibi et al., 2016; Choi et al., 2015; O'Neill, 2018). Andalibi and colleagues (2016) noted that anonymity and throwaway accounts were common in these kinds of reddit communities. Through my analysis of posts made to the community, I aimed to understand the motivations behind victim-survivors' disclosures in these digital contexts. It is worth noting that posts were treated from an assumption of belief of their legitimacy: likewise, members of the online community had a culture of belief, so disclosures were heard and validated in that space. The community had broad guidelines around not tolerating trolling or victim-blaming behaviors, with moderators advising that such posts would be removed. Likewise, although the community did not have a specific rule against it, there were norms that meant victim-survivors did not typically name their perpetrators (unlike other digital practices of speaking out where naming and shaming perpetrators is more common). Indeed, in the entirety of posts analyzed in this research, victim-survivors did not identify themselves nor their perpetrators in their posts, and often would omit other identifying details such as their specific location.

The posts analyzed varied in length, from one word to thousands of words, and most provided detailed descriptions about the harms and impacts of sexual violence. Although the data collection received ethical approval from my university and the data was de-identified, anonymous, and publicly available (see O'Neill, 2018), upon reflection there were several ways I would conduct this research differently in the future. Although it was an important step to receive ethical approval for this kind of study, in future I would endeavor to ensure that it made greater efforts to determine and center the needs of members of the community. Keeping research participant needs central to research is a vital aspect of feminist research practice and sexual violence scholarship and is arguably overlooked in many digital methods.

As such, I argue that the importance of gaining informed consent when accessing digital spaces that victim-survivors are accessing should not be overlooked. If I were designing this research project now, I would plan to obtain informed consent from the community and include this in an ethics application for review by a committee. Indeed, a survey study by Fiesler and Proferes (2018) highlighted that a majority of Twitter users in their sample were not aware that their public tweets could be used in research and thought that they should only be used by researchers with informed consent. Although these findings are not generalizable to all Twitter users, let alone other platforms with different politics and norms,

I believe that researchers must exercise caution by attempting to be as transparent about their research as possible, particularly when examining sensitive topics like sexual violence. By contrast, when I sought ethical approval in 2016, I outlined a "covert" methodology where my data was taken from a public community where people were able to lurk and freely observe posts. Comparative to covert observation that sometimes occurs in terrestrial ethnographies, the public nature of the digital space justified the decision not to announce my presence in gathering content from the online community (see also, Willis, 2019). However, there are several ways that I might have engaged with the community in order to gain informed consent. Firstly, I might consider writing a post to the community informing members about the research project. This kind of post would alert members of the community that research was being conducted in the space and therefore provide an opportunity for them to "opt out" by not posting. Some digital researchers have noted this method but are concerned that this type announcement might have negative consequences by impacting the ecosystem of the community and who posts to it (Morey et al., 2011; Willis, 2019).

Indeed, there is a chance that by announcing researcher presence in this way, a victim-survivor might choose not to post or ask for support, making this consideration particularly important for digital researchers examining sexual violence. Making an announcement could inadvertently limit victim-survivors' access to a potentially vital, anonymous, and supportive space and inadvertently discourage disclosures. This could be particularly harmful or impactful if a person had never disclosed their experience of sexual violence before and were planning to disclose for the first time on reddit. Sexual violence research has consistently demonstrated the importance of first disclosure experiences, highlighting that victim-survivors who have negative reactions to their disclosures or negative perceptions of disclosure are less likely to seek support (Ullman, 2010). Of course, this was a key consideration for me when I chose not to announce my presence on reddit. I did not want to unduly stop a victim-survivor from making a disclosure by being there. Having thought about it considerably over the last few years and by remaining engaged in developing scholarship on digital ethics, I believe that a compromise or middle ground in this situation should be contacting the moderators of any online community before collecting any kind of data or engaging in any research at all. This should occur regardless of whether a community is public or private, and researchers should make efforts to directly engage with representatives of the community in order to determine whether content online is "private" despite being publicly accessible. Some communities might be open to research, but others could prefer relative privacy but remain publicly accessible for the purpose of having the greatest reach for a vulnerable group. Although the community I researched was open to researchers (it often had pinned posts calling for research participants), it is unclear whether the community, or its representatives, would have approved the use of the data that I collected (see also, Fiesler & Proferes, 2018; Williams et al., 2017).

After researchers have made efforts to gain informed consent or create a dialogue with participants about their research, there are a number of other ways that they could consider using digital content in a way that respects the privacy or autonomy of the victim-survivor who has posted their experience. For instance, researchers might consider utilizing different analytical methods that require a less deep analysis of content or use of highly personal narratives. Conducting a content analysis of rape and sexual assault disclosures required the close reading and analysis of very personal and traumatic experiences. As noted above, victim-survivors may not have intended their disclosures to be used for research, and although consultation with moderators is a great step, this does not guarantee the free agreement of any individual reddit user of their post. Further to this, it is worth considering the impacts that reading and deeply analyzing these types of data has on researchers themselves, who might also be susceptible to secondary traumas. Therefore, potential alternatives to content analyses could include the use of summary level information and data, which could serve to mitigate these risks. Posts could also be excluded from the sample on the basis of word length to avoid the deep analysis of lengthy traumatic narratives that may impact upon researchers. Researchers should be considering how to present their data in different ways that protect participant identities. Examples of how I did this in my research included altering the words contained within quotes to ensure that they will not come up in a search engine and de-identifying usernames attributed to posts to better protect the digital identities of reddit users. Indeed, these strategies have been commonly used by digital researchers and are typically advised in digital research guidelines (see, for example, Clark et al., 2015; Davies et al., 2016). Likewise, researchers could choose not to identify or name the communities (as I have chosen not to do in this chapter) they are studying in any publications to protect the community from voyeuristic readers. Of course, these types of decisions come with considerations of authenticity of subjects and participants, so perhaps it is most important that researchers find a middle ground where they can discuss their research sites without advocating their searchability.

Although I do not deny that there are significant potential impacts that my methodology could have on members of the community if they were made aware of my research, it is worth noting that many of the ethical considerations outlined in this chapter are relatively low risk. For instance, when researching spaces that are already highly anonymous and pseudonymous, like reddit, there is a very low risk that use of data will impact upon the individuals who have posted it because the researcher is never aware of the identities of participants. So, unlike other sexual violence research methods, in my methodology, victim-survivors have complete anonymity. Of course, this does not necessarily negate the need to announce presence or attempt to alert the community of researcher presence. But it could be said that the anonymous nature of reddit makes it a comparably better setting to conduct these types of analyses than other social media sites. On reddit, users are not identified to researchers in any way, unless they happen to disclose their identities in a post. Of course, these reflections become murkier when researchers are analyzing disclosures on public forums where users have an account that identifies them with their name or a profile picture. For example, researchers who are analyzing data from Facebook, Twitter, and Instagram might need to consider the compounding issues of having content as well as any identifying details of a participant's social media profile.

The murkiness of public and private space should not deter digital researchers who are hoping to examine sensitive topics, but researchers should be prepared to consider the nuance and intersections of the needs of their research participants and their perceptions of privacy.

Digital researchers are continuing to have dynamic and didactic conversations about covert observations across a wide array of digital space. For example, scholars such as Barbosa and Milan (2019) have suggested that highly private spaces like WhatsApp groups still could be open to covert observation, so long as researchers embrace transparency and duly consider the potential for research projects to cause harm.

Conclusion: Lessons and Future Directions

This chapter has explored the tensions that arise when undertaking digital research that did not adequately consider the importance of gaining informed consent. Throughout this piece I have demonstrated the importance of researchers engaging in reflexivity and self-critique, as well as provided suggestions around the importance of actively involving communities in research. There will always be much for digital researchers to consider when attempting to engage in an ethical practice, and the most significant thing that I have learned thus far is that my ethical compass is ever evolving and significantly shaped by the needs of the people I conduct research with.

I'd like to end by highlighting the significance that research can have in the lives of victim-survivors and the importance of research like mine being conducted in the future. When I was conducting interviews with victim-survivors in the second stage of this project, I asked participants why they had chosen to take the time to participate in an interview (see also, Campbell et al., 2010). One of my participants, Tara, had used a range of online forums and communities, including communities on reddit. She said:

I really liked the idea of talking to somebody about my experience of using the sites, because it's not something that anyone's really asked me about before ... I really appreciate having the opportunity to talk about it because it's not something that I generally talk about and although people post on the forum, it doesn't have that kind of meta thing of you know, people post more about the things they've come to discuss than why they use it if you see what I mean, so it felt, I thought I'd be quite interested to take a step back and talk about my experiences of using it. And I think it was just quite exciting to see something where I could actually volunteer to take part.

Speaking with Tara, I was reminded that many victim-survivors place substantial value in participating in research because it can provide them with opportunities to have their experiences heard, known, and validated. It offers a way to feel a sense of contribution, and it was a something that Tara felt excited by. So, although there are things about the first stage of my methodology that I would have done differently, I completed this project feeling satisfied and proud to be a digital researcher committed to sustained ethical growth and reflexivity, feminist values, and research practices that center the narratives and experiences of victim-survivors first and foremost.

References

Andalibi, N., Haimson, O. L., De Choudhury, M., & Forte, A. (2016). Understanding Social Media Disclosures of Sexual Abuse Through the Lenses of Support Seeking and Anonymity. In *Proceedings of the 2016 CHI Conference on Human Factors in Computing Systems*, (pp. 3906–3918).

Barbosa, S., & Milan, S. (2019). Do not harm in private chat apps: Ethical issues for research on and with WhatsApp. *Westminster Papers in Communication and Culture, 14*(1), 49–65.

Boyd, D., & Hargittai, E. (2010). Facebook privacy settings: Who cares? *First Monday, 15*(8). https://doi.org/10.5210/fm.v15i8.3086.

Campbell, R., Adams, A., Wasco, S., Ahrens, C., & Sefl, T. (2010). "What has it been like for you to talk with me today?": The impact of participating in interview research on rape survivors. *Violence Against Women, 16*(1), 60–83.

Choi, D., Han, J., Chung, T., Ahn, Y.-Y., Chun, B.-G., & Kwon, T. T. (2015). Characterizing Conversation Patterns in Reddit: From the Perspectives of Content Properties and User Participation Behaviors. In *Proceedings of COSN'15*, (pp. 233–243).

Clark, K., Duckham, M., Guillemin, M., Hunter, A., Mcvernon, J., O'Keefe, C., Pitkin, C., Prawar, S., Sinnott, R., Warr, D., & Waycott, J. (2015). *Guidelines for the ethical use of digital data in human research.* Melbourne:

The University of Melbourne. Available at: http://ethics.iit.edu/codes/Eth ical-Use-of-Digital-Data.pdf.

Davies, H., Halford, S., Hine, C., Hotz, C., Martin, W., & Sugiura, L. (2016). *BSA ethics guidelines and collated resources for digital research: Statement of ethical practice annexe.* Available at: https://www.britsoc.co.uk/media/24309/ bsa_statement_of_ethical_practice_annexe.pdf.

Dennen, V. P. (2012). When public words are not data: Online authorship, consent, and reasonable expectations of privacy. In D. Heider & A. L. Massanari (Eds.), *Digital ethics: Research and practice.* Peter Lang Publishing.

Fiesler, C., & Proferes, N. (2018). "Participant" perceptions of Twitter research ethics. *Social Media + Society, 4*(1), 205630511876336.

Flick, C. (2016). Informed consent and the Facebook emotional manipulation study. *Research Ethics, 12*(1), 14–28.

Hesse-Biber, S. (2012). Feminist research: Exploring, interrogating, and transforming the interconnections of epistemology, methodology and method. In S. N. Hesse-Biber (Ed.), *The handbook of feminist research: Theory and praxis.* Sage.

Hudson, J. M., & Bruckman, A. (2012). "Go Away": participant objections to being studied and the ethics of chatroom research. In B. Dicks (Ed.), *Digital qualitative research methods: Volume IV, ethics, archiving and representation in qualitative research.* Sage.

Markham, A., & Buchanan, E. (2012). *AOIR guidelines: Ethical decision making and Internet research, 19.* Available at: www.aoir.org.

McKee, H. A., & Porter, J. E. (2009). *The ethics of Internet research: A rhetorical, case-based process.* Peter Lang Publishing.

Mendes, K., Keller, J., & Ringrose, J. (2019). Digitized narratives of sexual violence: Making sexual violence felt and known through digital disclosures. *New Media & Society, 21*(6), 1290–1310.

Morey, Y., Bengry-Howell, A., & Griffin, C. (2011). Public profiles, private parties: Digital ethnography, ethics and research in the context of web 2.0. In *Innovations in youth research* (pp. 195–209). Palgrave.

Noack-Lundberg, K., Liamputtong, P., Marjadi, B., Ussher, J., Perz, J., Schmied, V., Dune, T., & Brook, E. (2019). Sexual violence and safety: The narratives of transwomen in online forums. *Culture, Health and Sexuality, 22,* 1–14.

O'Neill, T. (2018). "Today I speak": Exploring how victim-survivors use reddit. *International Journal for Crime, Justice and Social Democracy, 7*(1), 44–59.

Quinton, S., & Reynolds, N. (2018). *Understanding research in the digital age.* Sage.

Reinharz, S., & Davidman, L. (1992). *Feminist methods in social research.* Oxford University Press.

Ullman, S. E. (2010). *Talking about sexual assault: Society's response to survivors.* American Psychological Association.

White, M. (2012). Representations or people? In B. Dicks (Ed.), *Digital qualitative research methods: Volume IV, ethics, archiving and representation in qualitative research.* Sage.

Williams, M. L., Burnap, P., & Sloan, L. (2017). Towards an ethical framework for publishing Twitter data in social research: Taking into account users' views, online context and algorithmic estimation. *Sociology, 51*(6), 1149–1168.

Willis, R. (2019). Observations online: Finding the ethical boundaries of Facebook research. *Research Ethics, 15*(1), 1–17.

Concluding Thoughts

This volume has the ambition to serve as both a guide and a critical reflection upon cybercrime research methods—a field of investigation that moves fast, as any technological change opens the way to new opportunities to both researchers and research subjects, but that can be anchored to core ideas, frameworks, and ethical principles. The previous chapters of this work demonstrate the complexities of engaging in cybercrime research, whether working individually or collaboratively with colleagues in other disciplines. The current state of the art is diverse and multifaceted, with researchers capturing very different aspects of crime and deviance in cyberspace, using different conceptual frameworks and methodological tools in their investigations. In this context, cooperation is key: Considering the multidimensional nature of cyberspace, multi- and interdisciplinary expertise is needed to address the challenges of the present, and of the future. This final chapter of the book is intended to summarize the key challenges of online research, and note potential directions to improve academic practices.

This work as a whole demonstrated the inherent value in understanding not only the criminogenic features of the Internet from a social and technical perspective, as well as its utility as a resource for data collection (Holt & Bossler, 2015; Lavorgna, 2020). The intersection of these issues requires researchers to understand not only what is present in their data, but also what is missing by virtue of the structure of the online spaces in which it was generated. For instance, analyzing public posts from a web forum provides only one perspective on communications which may take place in private within the site, and in other online communities the participants engage.

As a consequence, researchers must never forget that being able to utilize massive amounts of data from any online source does not mean that they will be able to understand the experiences of participants. They will only be able to assess one facet of a broader online experience that will constantly evolve and change. The inherent limitations presented by online research create an important responsibility for researchers, regardless of discipline: to critically and accurately assess the validity and generalizability of their data (Halford & Savage, 2017; Holt & Bossler, 2015). Those who are either unwilling or unable to recognize these boundaries risk making poorly informed policy recommendations and harming the broader state of knowledge on any given concept. This combination of opportunity and responsibility also extends to research ethics, as the absence of consensus on best practices creates a fragmented research literature with increased potential for harm to both human subjects and researchers in the field.

The highly siloed nature of cybercrime research across the social and technical sciences must also be broken down if we are to ever improve our overall capacity for online research (Bossler, 2017; Holt & Bossler, 2015; Martin, 2016). For instance, many criminologists still engage in hand collection of data from various Web sites and the use of traditional, slowly implemented analysis models that reduce their capacity to inform policy and practice efficiently. In fact, many researchers are simply reluctant to approach cybercrimes in their research endeavors (Lavorgna, 2020).

A new model of collaboration between the social and computer sciences is needed, a model which integrates computational skills with theoretical, methodological, and empirical expertise to study the social world (Halford & Savage, 2017). The goal should be not to replace or trivialize each other's expertise, but rather to learn a common language to better cooperate (Lavorgna, 2020). As an example, computer scientists and engineers are often in the position to advance the application of highly technical methodologies to gather datasets of better quality with greater efficiency. The analysis of that data is, however, limited by the researchers' ability to correctly measure and interpret the concepts through the correct criminological, socioeconomic, political, or psychological lenses (Benjamin et al., 2017; Westlake & Frank, 2017). The use of natural language processing and pattern recognition to analyze data is only as effective as the extent to which the researchers train the algorithms to identify and interpret concepts. This creates an opportunity for subject matter expertise from the appropriate social scientific field to provide input to improve the measurement of the tools (Benjamin et al., 2017; Westlake & Frank, 2017). Such partnerships are inherently valuable to minimize the risk of methodologies guiding research questions, and ensure results with greater fidelity. They are also exceedingly rare in the literature at this time.

Such frameworks fit into the "symphonic approach" proposed by Halford and Savage (2017), such that pursuing key social questions across multiple data streams including, but not limited to, new forms of digital data. If we acknowledge the limitations of much existing research on the digital world, we can then become methodologically pluralist, able to combine old and new data sources by exploring their contradictions and complementarities (Halford & Savage 2017, p. 9). Only then can we chart a more empirically robust and viable path forward to obtain a holistic understanding of cybercrime and online deviance which is prepared to address not only academic questions of interest, but improve the safety and security of online environments for years to come.

References

Benjamin, V., Samtani, S., & Chen, H. (2017). Conducting large-scale analyses of underground hacker communities. In T. J. Holt (Ed.), *Cybercrime through an interdisciplinary lens* (pp. 56–75). Routledge.

Bossler, A. M. (2017). Cybercrime research at the crossroads: Where the field currently stands and innovative strategies to move forward. In T. J. Holt (Ed.), *Cybercrime through an interdisciplinary lens* (pp. 37–55). Routledge.

Halford, S., & Savage, M. (2017). Speaking sociologically with big data: Symphonic social science and the future for big data research. *Sociology, 51*(6), 1132–1148.

Holt, T. J., & Bossler, A. M. (2015). *Cybercrime in progress: Theory and prevention of technology-enabled offenses.* Routledge.

Lavorgna, A. (2020). *Cybercrimes: Critical issues in a global context.* Macmillan.

Martin, J. (2016). Illuminating the dark net: Methods and ethics in cryptomarket research. In M. Adorjan & R. Ricciardelli (Eds.), *Engaging with ethics in international criminological research.* Routledge.

Westlake, B. G., & Frank, R. (2017). Seeing the forest through the trees: Identifying key players in the online distribution of child sexual exploitation material. In T. J. Holt (Ed.), *Cybercrime through an interdisciplinary lens* (pp. 189–209). Routledge.

Index

© The Editor(s) (if applicable) and The Author(s), under exclusive
license to Springer Nature Switzerland AG 2021
A. Lavorgna and T. J. Holt (eds.), *Researching Cybercrimes*,
https://doi.org/10.1007/978-3-030-74837-1

Printed by Printforce, United Kingdom